UMI ANNUAL COMMENTARY

PRECEPTS
FOR
LIVING™

MISSION STATEMENT

We are called of God to create, produce, and distribute quality Christian education products; to deliver exemplary customer service; and to provide quality Christian educational services, which will empower God's people, especially within the Black community, to evangelize, disciple, and equip people for serving Christ, His kingdom, and Church.

Urban Ministries, Inc.
The African American Christian Publishing
& Communications Co.

MATT. 9:37,38   " 7-22-08 "

    Jesus said unto His disciples
" The harvest truly is plentiful,
but the labourers are few;
    Pray ye therefore the Lord
of the harvest, that he will send
forth labourers into the harvest

also,
Lk. 10:2;
John 4:35
II Thess. 3:1

UMI
ANNUAL COMMENTARY
PRECEPTS FOR LIVING™
2005–2006
INTERNATIONAL SUNDAY SCHOOL LESSONS
VOLUME 8
URBAN MINISTRIES, INC.

Melvin E. Banks Sr., Litt.D., Founder and Chairman
C. Jeffrey Wright, J. D., President and CEO

All art: Copyright©2005 by UMI (Urban Ministries, Inc.)
Bible art: Fred Carter

Unless otherwise indicated, all Scripture references are taken from the
authorized King James Version of the Bible.

CONTRIBUTORS

Editorial Staff
Carl Ellis Jr., Editor
Kathryn Hall, Managing Editor
Herb Jackson, Contributing Editor
Cheryl Wilson, Editorial Assistant
Evangeline Carey, Staff Writer
Megan Bell, Copy Editor
Denise Gates, Copy Editor

Production
Shawan Brand, Assoc. Dir. of Production & Planning
Tiphany Pugh, Product Manager

Cover Design
Jason Vance Stewart

Bible Illustrations
Fred Carter

Layout & Design
Larry Taylor Design, Ltd.
Trinidad D. Zavala

Contributing Writers
Essays
Evangeline Carey
Aja Carr
Barbara Carr-Philips
Rukeia Draw
Dena J. Dyer
Bianca Elliot
James King
Frances Morkeh
Katherine Steward
Virginia Stith
Connie Taylor
Terri Thompson
Michael Washington

Bible Study Guides
Lisa Crayton
Robert Dulin
George Flennoy
Richard Gray, Ph.D.
Eugenia Harris
Jennifer King
Vanessa Lovelace
LaTonya Mason
Keyonda McQuarters
Jerii Rodman
Philip Rodman
Amy Rognlie
Fred Thomas
Faith Waters

More Light On The Text
J. Ayodeji Adewuya, Ph.D.
Moussa Coulibaly, Ph.D.
Hurby Franks
Marcia Gillis
Eric Greaux, Ph.D.
Beverly Ann Hawkins
Kevin Hrebik
James Irby
James Leary
Dr. Richard McCreary
Ransome Merith
Samuel Olarewaju
James Rawdon
Fred D. Smith
Raedorah Stewart-Dodd

Urban Ministries, Inc.

Dear *Precepts* Customer,

We are excited to bring you this year's *Precepts For Living*™, filled with changes to help make this an even more valuable Bible study tool!

Our most exciting announcement is the introduction of an annual *Precepts For Living*™ *Personal Study Guide.* Many of you were using our quarterly *Precepts For Living*™ *Workbook.* Now we've made it easier for you to get all of your lessons at once. This study guide is meant to help you take your study of the Word to a deeper level. It will help make sure that you not only have read the material in *Precepts* but understand it and can communicate it clearly. The study guide contains thought-provoking questions, activities, and additional resources to make your *Precepts* study even more valuable.

Another new feature is our Topical Index at the end of this book. This index works like a concordance, allowing you to search for a specific topic and read the *Precepts* lesson that addresses that topic.

We've also given you more options with *Precepts For Living*™. You can now order your commentary with or without a CD-ROM. We realize that each customer studies this resource in a different way, and now you can select the resource that works best for your needs.

Precepts For Living™ will continue to evolve in an effort to meet our customers' needs. We appreciate your comments and feedback. Please e-mail your feedback to precepts@urbanministries.com or mail your comments to UMI, *Precepts For Living*™, P.O. Box 436987, Chicago, IL 60643-6987.

We hope that your spirit is edified and lifted by the contents of this book.

Yours in Christ,

Carl F. Ellis Jr.

Carl F. Ellis Jr.
Editor

CYCLE OF 2004–2007

Arrangement of Quarters according to the
Church School Year, September through August

	Fall	Winter	Spring	Summer
2004–2005	The God of Continuing Creation	Called to Be God's People	God's Project: Effective Christians	Jesus' Life, Teachings, and Ministry
	(Bible Survey)	(Bible Survey)	(Romans, Galatians)	(Matthew; Mark; Luke)
	Theme: Creation (13)	Theme: Call (13)	Theme: Covenant (13)	Theme: Christ (13)
2005–2006	You Will Be My Witnesses	God's Commitment—Our Response	Living in and as God's Creation	Called to Be a Christian Community
	(Acts)	(Isaiah; 1 & 2 Timothy)	(Psalms; Job; Ecclesiastes; Proverbs)	(1 & 2 Corinthians)
	Theme: Community (13)	Theme: Commitment (13)	Theme: Creation (13)	Theme: Call (13)
2006–2007	God's Living Covenant	Jesus Christ: A Portrait of God	Our Community Now and in God's Future	Committed to Doing Right
	(Old Testament Survey)	(John; Philippians; Colossians; Hebrews; 1 John)	(1 John; Revelation)	(Various prophets; 2 Kings; 2 Chronicles)
	Theme: Covenant (13)	Theme: Christ (13)	Theme: Community (13)	Theme: Commitment (13)

TABLE OF CONTENTS

Fall Quarter, 2005

Winter Quarter, 2005-2006

The Sparrow

by Evangeline Carey

Look at the sparrow on the front cover. Know that this small creature (approximately six inches long in reality) is considered to be the most common of all birds. However, God uses the sparrow to illustrate to believers how much He loves and cares for His own. Jesus asks the question in Matthew 10:29-31(NIV) "Are not two sparrows sold for a penny? Yet not one of them will fall to the ground apart from the will of your Father. And even the very hairs of your head are all numbered. So don't be afraid; you are worth more than many sparrows." This Scripture is pregnant with hope and promise, because it tells all believers that Jesus is indeed "Immanuel"—God with us in the flesh. He is the "rock of [our] salvation" (2 Samuel 22:47). It says that God is sovereign and is aware of everything that happens to and within His creation.

The sparrow reminds us that no one is inconsequential in God's sight. In fact, we are so valued by God that He sent His one and only Son to die a cruel death on the Cross in our behalf. Jesus was willing to give His own life to redeem us from the sin-penalty that we so richly deserve. His death and resurrection reconciled us to the Father, who is a Holy God (John 3:16). Now we do not have to worry about our future; we have eternal life! We can rejoice because He loves us with unconditional love—not based on our looks, nationality, or pedigree, but just because we are His. We can be thankful because "no good thing will he withhold from them that walk uprightly" (Psalm 84:11). No good thing will He withhold from us because we are His children, His "called-out ones," who are saved by His own blood.

To appreciate Matthew 10:29-31 and Jesus' use of the sparrow, we first need to know the backdrop of this dynamic Word. You see, Jesus is preparing His disciples for the many persecutions they will face as they carry out the "Great Commission" to go into all the world with His Good News of salvation (Matthew 28:19). He knows that the Pharisees' opposition will be paramount, a force for them to reckon with. As they carry the Word, they will experience resistance from governments, courts, and even family and friends. He and His disciples will be beaten, thrown in jail, and even killed on their God-given mission fields. Therefore, to accomplish His work, Jesus wants His disciples to go out with a mind-set steeped in faith. He wants them to persevere in their efforts to win souls for Christ until they prevail, knowing who their Power Source is.

The lessons of the next four quarters affirm that God is watching every believer's journey, or walk, with Him, and He will lead and guide us by His Holy Spirit. Indeed, we are the children of the God of "much-ness," and He is willing to share His treasures from His vast storehouse. Therefore, the sparrow should remind us that God wants to pour out His Spirit upon us, and fill us with His light. He wants us to have a passion for Him and a desire for Him to have an unhindered way in our lives, making us vessels He can use for His own purpose.

The tiny sparrow should also help us to focus on the presence of the Holy Spirit in our life. He should remind us that we do not have to engage our world for Jesus under our own steam, but the Third Person of the Trinity, His Holy Spirit, is here to fuel and refuel us for our assignments. Thus, God does not want us to be afraid to invest in His Kingdom. We don't have to be afraid of those who want to harm or kill us, because they can only kill the body—never our soul, which belongs to God.

The sparrow should remind us that to prepare for our calling, God desires to empower us with His love and wisdom. He desires to give us hands and hearts that bless the Lord as we take His healing touch to those who are in the mire of bitterness, defeat, despair, and self-pity. He wants to fortify us with His Spirit as we point seekers toward Almighty God who can break through their chaos and confusion.

As we explore some Scriptures in Job for the Spring Quarter on "Living in and as God's

Creation," the tiny sparrow should suggest that God is *always* caring, loving, helpful, merciful, sovereign, and watchful, regardless of what we as believers are going through. Immanuel is there through the stress, tear, and wear of our everyday living. If He is in the driver's seat of our life as our High Priest, He can and will steer us on a path that leads to His joy, peace, and victory. With Jesus, we can stand up for righteousness in the midst of our troubles.

The hope and promise found in Matthew 10:29-31, then, can also be quite beneficial to believers, who are daily negotiating the raging seas of trials and tribulation—battling the storms of life! This passage of Scripture, utilizing the tiny sparrow, reminds us that:

Jesus is a fear-terminator;

Jesus is a stress-buster;

Jesus is a pain-soother;

Jesus is a heart-stiller;

and Jesus is an anchor to the soul.

It should help all believers to trust in Almighty God and live by faith, in spite of what Satan may bring against us.

The sparrow should also help open our spiritual eyes to the fact that God is our "Manna" when we need spiritual food (Exodus 16:31). We can become discouraged and jaded by the carnality we see in so many of our churches, but if we seek Him with our all, God will feed us until we want no more. He can and will give us spiritual nourishment when we hear the Word preached. Psalm 3:3 tells us that He is "the lifter up of [our] head."

Civilla D. Martin, noted author of the famous gospel hymn, "His Eye Is On The Sparrow," captures this concept of God's love and care for His children with her prolific words:

Why should I feel discouraged, why should the shadows come, why should my heart be lonely and long for heav'n and home when Jesus is my portion? My constant Friend is He:

His eye is on the sparrow, and I know He watches me; His eye is on the sparrow, and I know He watches me.

Whenever I am tempted, whenever clouds arise, When songs give place to sighing, when hope within me dies, I draw the closer to Him, from care He sets me free; His eye is on the sparrow, and I know He cares for me; His eye is on the sparrow, and I know He watches me.

Consequently, the sparrow should remind us that no one can watch over us with such precision, tenacity, and tenderness as our Heavenly Father. No one can come to our rescue, when we falter or fail, like Almighty God. No one can pick us up, dust us off, and give us another, and another, and yet another chance to get things right, like Jesus our Lord. He values us so much that He even knows the number of strands of hair on our heads. This reality of God's love and power can lift us up to real victory over Satan and sin.

Meditating on God's love and care for us should cause the heart to resonate with praises and thanksgiving to our Lord and King because of the fact that God watches our every footstep. He does not do it to "beat us down" or "beat us up" if we "fail" or "fall," but to patiently and lovingly "help us up" and "keep us on track" as we daily walk with Him. Whenever you are feeling insignificant and unloved in this vast turbulent world, remember the little sparrow. Recall that the Creator of the universe made him and He made you. However, He chose to die and rise again for Y-O-U! He chose to prepare a place—an eternal home for Y-O-U!

Evangeline Carey is a staff writer for UMI and has been an Adult Sunday School teacher for more than 25 years.

SEPTEMBER 2005 QUARTER AT-A-GLANCE

You Will Be My Witnesses

This study facilitates understanding of how God created His church by empowering men and women to carry and live the Gospel message. This message began in Jerusalem, and the Holy Spirit propelled it to Judea, Samaria, and the ends of the earth.

UNIT 1. IN JERUSALEM

This unit focuses on how God sent His promised Holy Spirit and then birthed the first church in Jerusalem with the 120 who were present in the Upper Room. God knew that to boldly witness for Him, His disciples needed the Comforter, the Teacher, and His indwelling Holy Spirit.

LESSON 1: September 4
The Coming of the Spirit
Acts 2:1-8, 38-42

The 120 in the Upper Room on the day of Pentecost, which occurred seven weeks after Jesus' resurrection, waited on one accord for the promised Holy Spirit. He came, just as Jesus said He would. He also filled them with His power—making them a covenant community, the first church.

LESSON 2: September 11
Life Among the Followers
Acts 2:43-47; 4:32-35

The Holy Spirit's transforming power unified the 3,000 new believers, who had become saved under Peter's anointed preaching. They became one in a community of caring and sharing. Not only did they concern themselves with each other's physical necessities, but spiritual as well: helping each other mature in their newfound faith.

LESSON 3: September 18
Peter and John Heal a Lame Man
Acts 3:1-16

The Holy Spirit was at work in Peter and John as they ministered to the needy. When they went to the temple for the afternoon prayer service, God used them to heal a crippled beggar, who asked alms at the "Beautiful Gate." Most of all, God used this incident for His glory and to further His Kingdom.

LESSON 4: September 25
The Time for Boldness
Acts 4: 1-4, 23-31

The Holy Spirit empowers God's people to be witnesses in the midst of persecution. Here, Peter and John had to go before the 70-member Council that included: the rulers, elders, and teachers of religious law. In fact, they were arrested for proclaiming God's Good News of salvation, for trying to win others to Christ. Yet, the Holy Spirit prevailed. The witnessing for Jesus continued.

UNIT 2. IN ALL JUDEA AND SAMARIA

The empowering Holy Spirit helped the growing church to take the Gospel to outlying communities and to people who were considered outcasts. These Scriptures showed how God grew His own church, and taught those who carried the message and those who heard it, that there is "no respect of persons with God" (Romans 2:11).

LESSON 5: October 2
Stephen
Acts 6:8-15; 7:53-60

Even though God's people are saved and filled with His Spirit, they will still face persecution from those who do not want God's Word to go forth—those in Satan's camp. Stephen, one of the seven deacons in the early church, is our example. He was a man full of God's grace, power, and wisdom; he performed amazing miracles and signs, yet he died for the cause. He was faithful to God, even in death.

1

LESSON 6: October 9
The Samaritans and Philip
Acts 8:4-17

In this text, God uses persecution again to scatter the believers, to expand His church—to spread His Good News of salvation. In fact, this persecution forced the Christians out of Jerusalem and into Judea and Samaria.

LESSON 7: October 16
The Ethiopian Official
Acts 8:26-38

Here again, with Philip's ministry, we see the outcome of successful Christian witnessing. Philip met the eunuch because He went where the Holy Spirit sent him. Because Philip obeyed God wholeheartedly, the Ethiopian heard the Good News, was led to faith in Jesus Christ, and was baptized. The eunuch then took the Gospel to his country and became a witness for Jesus Christ Himself.

LESSON 8: October 23
Cornelius and the Gentiles
Acts 10:1-20

God showed believers that not even prejudice would hinder His mission. His church is open to whoever comes to Jesus. Cornelius was a Roman officer, a God-fearing soldier, one who respected the Almighty God and lived uprightly. Peter entered Cornelius's home, breaking a whole list of Jewish rules and traditions, and shared the Gospel of Jesus Christ. God saved and filled this entire Roman family with His Holy Spirit. Now both Jews and Gentiles make up God's family.

LESSON 9: October 30
Peter in Prison
Acts 12:1-16

As the infant church spread, so too did the persecution by those who wanted to preserve the status quo. Here, Peter was imprisoned, but God was not finished with Peter yet, so his life was spared. Peter still had witnessing work to do for God. This lesson tells of Peter's dramatic escape from prison as God rescues him, using an angel.

UNIT 3. TO THE ENDS OF THE EARTH

God's message of salvation has gone from Jerusalem to Judea to Samaria, and now to the ends of the earth. Another character is introduced in les-

son 10, who was once a persecutor of Christians. His name is "Paul." He was converted and the Gentiles had a Christian overseer, another man after God's own heart, sold out for Him.

LESSON 10: November 6
Paul Becomes a Follower
Acts 9:3-18

Saul, the *persecutor* of Christians, was converted and became Paul, the *persecuted*, because he was a Christian. After meeting the risen Saviour on the Damacus Road, Paul became a follower of Christ. His salvation showed all believers how a true encounter with the cleansing power of Jesus transforms.

LESSON 11: November 13
Lydia: A Committed Woman
Acts 16:6-15

Paul did not let gender bias stand in the way of his mission and, because of his obedience, God's Word traveled geographically, saving others. In Philippi, Paul made evangelistic contact with a small group of women. Lydia was a woman of means, an influential, wealthy merchant, who became a committed woman to Jesus Christ.

LESSON 12: November 20
Priscilla and Aquila: Team Ministry
Acts 18:1-4, 18-21, 24-28

This very important lesson emphasizes that the promise of God to build His church is fulfilled when Christians unite and work together. Priscilla and Aquila (a Christian husband and wife team) are drawn to work with Paul and learn much. Apollos, a gifted and persuasive preacher in the early church at Ephesus, profited from their time spent with Paul who taught them the excellency of the Gospel.

LESSON 13: November 27
Paul's Farewell
Acts 20:17-28, 36-38

Before his imprisonment in Jerusalem and his transfer as a prisoner to Rome, and while seeking to deliver the monetary gifts already collected to the impoverished Jerusalem church, Paul came to the end of his third missionary journey. It was time to say "good-bye" to one of the churches he helped to establish.

THE CHURCH AS A WITNESS FOR GOD

by Evangeline Carey

In the book of Acts, Luke, a physician, gives us an accurate account of the genesis of the New Testament church. He tells us that during the festival of Pentecost (Gk. *pentekoste,* **pen-tay-kos-tay,** meaning "fiftieth"), God sends His own Spirit, the Holy Spirit.

According to Leviticus 23:15-16, Pentecost was celebrated on the "[day] after the seventh Sabbath" following Passover or on the 50th day. Originally, it was the festival of the firstfruits of the grain harvest (Exodus 23:16; Leviticus 23:17-22; Numbers 28:26-31). Later, it was seen as the anniversary of the giving of the Law at Mount Sinai and as a time for a rededication to the Mosaic covenant. Along with Passover and the Feast of Tabernacles, Pentecost was one of the three great pilgrim festivals of the Jews.

After the Holy Spirit comes upon this assembly in Jerusalem, God brings forth an international harvest of new believers. They are among the initial converts (or firstfruits) in the church. They are the first *Christian community*. From this diverse group, the church grows from the 12 disciples, to 120, to 3,000 (Acts 2).

Luke tells us how nearly 2,000 years ago, God used these ordinary human beings to do extraordinary things, as they spread His Gospel beyond the borders of Jerusalem and Judea to the utmost parts of the world. They were sent out, propelled by God's own Spirit. Today these stalwarts are our examples in witnessing and building the Christian community.

God built and still builds His own church. He creates and oversees His redeemed people, His Christian community. He is a "hands-on parent." He calls Peter (Acts 2:14-40), Stephen (Acts 6:5, 8), Philip (Acts 6:5), Paul (Acts 9), and Timothy (Acts 16)—men He used to build the foundation of His church, men who can and will walk with Him in their charge to carry out the Great Commission.

They, like us, are to go and teach all nations, baptizing them in the name of the Father, the Son, and the Holy Spirit. We are to teach them to observe all things whatsoever He has commanded (Matthew 28:19-20). We are to lead in building a Christian community—the universal church—by following God's edicts to the letter. God uses this first New Testament church as a blueprint for us to follow in assembling and interacting with the Christian population.

Note that God does not establish this new church until His Holy Spirit comes. Our omniscient (all-knowing) God knows that those He created, redeemed, and set apart for His purpose can carry out His commission only by the power of His Spirit. He also knows we need each other, therefore, we are to abide in a Christian community. The mark of a true Christian is *living out* the Christian life daily, under the magnifying glass of this desperately lost world. Therefore, Luke wants us to know that neither the Gospel (God's plan of salvation) nor the church is of human origin. They both move and have their being in God, just as all Christians should.

In the book of Acts, Luke shows us how God established His church for His glory! Luke knows that God created humankind to be in covenant relationship with Himself and with each other. This is what the Christian community should demonstrate before the world.

God promises to put His Spirit in us (Ezekiel 37:14). With God, there is no respect of persons (Acts 10:34-36). With God's indwelling Holy Spirit, believers, as members of the body of Christ, can choose to live together in peace (Colossians 3:15-16). Since we no longer let our sinful natures rule us, we can choose to participate in a Christian community where we can authentically share with each other and help meet each other's needs. We can pick each other up whenever one of us fails, falls, or falters.

Luke shows us how God, by His Spirit, leads, guides, and equips the church to care for each other, to minister to the unsaved, and to thrive in the crucible of persecution. The church is to be a light in the darkness of a sinful and dying world. There cannot be that light if there is no unity in the body—if there is no peace or if there is no community. The only way we can have communal fellowship and closeness is by drawing from the well of God's keeping and delivering power.

The book of Acts reveals how the Holy Spirit empowers God's "called-out ones" to do what He has called us to do. This should be commonplace among Christians today. We have the Spirit of God in us if we are His. God's Word tells us, "But ye are not in the flesh, but in the Spirit, if so be that the Spirit of God dwell in you. Now if any man have not the Spirit of Christ, he is none of his" (Romans 8:9). It goes on to say, "For as many as are led by the Spirit of God, they are the sons of God" (v. 14). In other words, if we are truly saved, we have His Spirit in us!

In fact, in Paul's letter to the Ephesians (Ephesians 2:19 NIV, *emphasis added*) he says, "Ye are no more strangers and foreigners, but *fellow citizens with the saints,* and of the household of God." He expounds further (4:1-3, NIV *emphasis added*) when he urges all Christians to "live a life worthy of the calling you have received. Be completely humble and gentle; be patient, *bearing with one another in love.* Make every effort to keep the unity of the Spirit through the bond of peace." To bear with one another in love means that we come alongside, sympathize, and empathize *in a locale with other fellow believers.* We bear each other's burdens. We pray for one another, lift each other up, and rejoice with one another.

From these Scriptures, we can appreciate that God is adamant about Christians living together in harmony. The book of Acts (2:43-47) also gives details of how the members of the early church, *in community,* were of one heart and mind. Every day they continued to meet together in the temple courts, but their togetherness did not end there. They even ate together in their homes with glad and sincere hearts.

These early saints worked together and had all things in common. Their possessions were not even considered to be their own. Therefore, there were not any among them who lacked, because they freely and gladly gave to others, creating a loving and caring community. Those who had land or houses sold them and brought the proceeds to the apostles to be distributed among those in need. This is truly a witness to our materialistic society that refutes the deceptive doctrine of "looking out for number one."

As we examine the Scriptures in this unit, we will readily see that, because God knew that His church would be scattered by persecution, He gave His Holy Spirit to unite believers as one body. He also knew that the church, on its own, was no match for satanic attacks and furious opposition to the Gospel. So, there was no room for backbiting, confusion, and schisms in the early church. This is still true today; we should not tolerate such hindrances to spiritual growth.

God also knew the religious leaders would be grieved that the apostles and others were teaching the people about Jesus. These malcontents would take decisive action, even beating, arresting, and killing some of the early Christians. As the Christian community did then, even now we need to stand as one, undivided and undeterred from our God-given mission. The church accomplishes these goals by the power of the Holy Spirit. God has prepared His church to stand on His Word and to "walk" on stormy seas. Indeed, "The church of God *one body is, One Spirit dwells within;* And all her members are redeemed, And triumph over sin" (Naylor, Charles W. *Hymnal of the Church of God* Anderson, Ind. Warner Press, 1953, 413).

Evangeline Carey is a staff writer at UMI. She has been an Adult Sunday School teacher for over 25 years.

THE CONCEPT OF CHRISTIAN WITNESS IN THE BOOK OF ACTS:

IMPLICATIONS FOR OUR LIVES AND SERVICE

by Frances Morkeh

Horatio Hackett, in his *Commentary on Acts* (1992), writes that the book of Acts furnishes us with the origin, systematic growth, and extension of the church through the work of the apostles, especially Peter and Paul. Conversely, Michael Anthony in *Introducing Christian Education* (2001) says it would be "incomplete and reductionism" for one not to mention or emphasize the presence and power of the Holy Spirit to transform the lives of the disciples and guide them as they step out in obedience to the Great Commission (Acts 1:8; Matthew 28:16-20). It is the Holy Spirit who fills and empowers the believer for effective Christian witness.

Proper Understanding of Christian Witness

It is important to understand the root meaning of the word "witness" from a biblical perspective. Colin Brown (1971) states that the word "witness," as used in Acts 1:8, has the idea or takes up the conception from the Greek word *martus* (**mar'-toos**). It means someone legitimized and authorized to witness both the declaration of the story of Christ's deeds on earth and His resurrection. It is to follow a particular way, or path, of suffering in the process. It is a path that can lead to rejection, suffering, and possibly death for Christ's sake. The Christian community is called to be a faithful witness that obeys Christ in all circumstances.

Community and Sharing

Duane Elmer (1994) describes two major types of cultures in the world: *individualistic* cultures in the west and *collectivist* cultures dominantly found in third world countries. The former centers primarily on the individual's (or simple majority's) feelings, needs, and desires. Many times this emphasis has robbed the Lord's people of having compassion for others within the group. The latter, *collectivist cultures,* focuses on interpersonal relationships, harmony, and community solidarity of the whole society, or group. It is, however, important to state here that collectivism as described from the perspective of third world countries may not necessarily be built or founded on biblical worldview. It should not be confused with communism, which is practiced in communist societies of the world. However, there are some basic values and principles commonly found in collectivist cultures that intersect with basic biblical principles of a need to build and live in a community from a scriptural point of view.

According to the biblical accounts, the disciples were of one heart and mind, and shared all that they had as that given to them by the Lord for their common good. This unified and gracious environment they created helped to set the pace for the apostles to do effective witness (Acts 4:33). It means to care by sharing, love by empathizing, and lift up by supporting each other spiritually, materially, and psychologically in the Christian community.

Healing and Miracles

Throughout church history, some individuals or groups have had some reservations and doubts about God's healing power. This may be because some people have abused, misused, and manipulated either the spiritual gifts or the process in itself. Others too have closed themselves up to this topic of divine healing today because of their secularized worldview that dismisses anything that is supernatural. But Scripture declares: "Jesus Christ [is] the same yesterday, and to day, and for ever"(Hebrews 13:8). He is the ultimate source for all forms of healing that bring glory to the name of the Lord.

Boldness and Total Surrender

In the Bible, we read about faithful believers who boldly stood up and died for the sake of the Gospel as ultimate sacrifice for Christ's sake. One example is Stephen. He was rejected, persecuted, and stoned to death by those who opposed the Gospel because of his unwavering faith in Christ through the empowerment of the Holy Spirit (Acts 6:8). God has sometimes called people, for sake of His purpose, to stay the course of their faith and conviction, and even die in the process. Our Bible teaches us that the only way to be saved is through Christ (Acts 4:12). Stephen's example and lifestyle should make us ready to make an ultimate sacrifice for our faith.

Beyond Prejudice and Bias

God commands the believer to proclaim the Gospel to every creature wherever we find ourselves (Mark 16:15-18). However, in human society, there are all forms of social stratification that have the potential of hindering evangelistic outreach.

In biblical times, the Jews had looked down on the Samaritans as heathen, unclean, and "unequal beings." Yet Philip, like Jesus in His earthly ministry (John 4; Acts 8), and in the power of the Holy Spirit, went beyond the ugly lines of prejudice to reach out to them. He was opposed and rejected in the process but he was determined and courageous, and God confirmed His Word with signs and wonders. We should, therefore, not be deterred by social or cultural/religious systems that have the potential to hinder our witness. Let us go all out for the Lord. The promise of the outpouring of the Holy Spirit, and its fulfillment in Acts 2 on the Day of Pentecost, was for ALL flesh (Joel 2:28-29; Acts 2:38). There should therefore be no basis why believers should be discriminatory in their evangelistic efforts. There is always an opportunity, in our Christian witness, for people of all backgrounds and ages to witness for Christ and also receive God's gift of salvation.

God's Word and Effective Witness

Christian witness becomes effective when the believer studies and grows in God's Word. Studying, understanding, and applying God's Word in the believer's life to shape his/her actions and understanding of the will of God is a sure foundation, or basis, for Christian faith and practice. This does not imply that Christians should not read or study other Christian or non-Christian books apart from the Bible that can help them develop a broad and holistic understanding of life and Christian worldview. It is important that we be encouraged to do this. However, these books or materials are not a substitute for God's Word—the Bible. As believers, we are called to follow Christ, our model and example, and be like Him by the help of the Spirit (Colossians 3:16-17). The only way to effectively do that is by prayerfully studying the Word of God and living according to its teachings (Stott 1982). Philip was able to help the Ethiopian official understand and grow in the Word of God (Acts 8:26-38). We must be encouraged to participate in Bible studies in the church, at home, and in the workplace. Bible study helps us grow emotionally and spiritually, and equips us in our Christian witness. Let us dive deep into God's Word!

Bibliography

Anthony, Michael. *Introducing Christian Education: Foundations for the Twenty-first Century*. Grand Rapids, Mich.: Baker Academic, 2001.

Brown, Colin. *The International Dictionary of New Testament Theology Vol.3*. Grand Rapids, Mich.: Zondervan Publishing Company, 1986

Elmer, Duane. *Cross-Cultural Conflict: Building Relationships for Effective Ministry*. Downers Grove, Ill.: InterVarsity Press,1994.

Hackett, Horatio. *Commentary on Acts*. Grand Rapids, Mich.: Kregel Publications, 1992.

Stott, John. *Between Two Worlds The Challenge of Preaching Today*. Grand Rapids, Mich.: Eerdmans Publishing Company, 1994.

Frances Morkeh *holds a B.A. in Biblical and Theological Studies, a M.A. in Educational Ministries, and is currently a Ph.D. Candidate at Trinity International University.*

WITNESS OF POWER

by Terri Thompson

I was fed up with this small but growing cult of Jesus' followers. I had to do something to protect our laws and traditions. Their false beliefs should have been wiped out by now. Their leader was dead. Who were they following anyway?

I carefully selected some common spies to help me find out where His followers lived. I got official papers from the high priest giving me authority to arrest any who claimed to believe in Jesus. With these documents in hand, I burst into their homes with a band of men ready to grab them if they tried to run.

Still their numbers increased. Many of them fled Jerusalem, but they took their faith with them and wouldn't keep their mouths shut about it. Perhaps, I decided, if I followed them to other towns, they'd give up this nonsense.

Several of us headed to Damascus on a mission to keep the Jewish faith pure. Suddenly, a blinding light shone down on us. Falling to the ground, I heard a voice say, "Saul, Saul, why are you persecuting Me?" (Acts 9:4, NKJV).

"Who are you, Lord?" I dared not stand (v. 5, NKJV). "I am Jesus" (v. 5).

Jesus is alive! The Resurrection must be true! Surely He is going to kill me for the things I've done to His followers. But He didn't strike me. He said to go into Damascus and wait. I'd be told what to do.

I waited three days, unable to see and unwilling to eat or drink. In a vision I saw one of Jesus' disciples come and pray for me.

On the third day, a man came to the house where I stayed. He touched me and said, "Brother Saul, the Lord Jesus, who appeared to you in the road as you came, has sent me that you may receive your sight and be filled with the Holy Spirit" (Acts 9:17, NKJV).

Something fell off my eyes, and standing before me was the man I'd seen in my vision. Ananias baptized me in water and we ate a meal together.

Saul later became Paul, and a great witness for Jesus. He went from town to town preaching the truth about Jesus to Jews and Gentiles. He never forgot that first encounter with Jesus. He was filled with the power of the Holy Spirit when Ananias prayed for him. Out of love for Jesus, Paul sacrificed his life daily to declare God's message. He related God's love in ways people could understand. The Holy Spirit granted miracles through him, proving the truth of his words.

Being an effective, power-filled witness in our day is no different than it was for Paul. We must first encounter God, have a definite vision of who He is and what His purpose is. We must be filled with the Holy Spirit. Only then is our witness based in the truth of Christ's teaching and taken to the realm of the miraculous. Finally, we make our way into the hearts of people when we meet them where they are, from a motivation of love. The book of Acts relates this model again and again.

We must first see our Master, Jesus Christ. Peter, James, John, and the other disciples spent three years with Jesus. They listened to His teaching, watched His example, assisted in His ministry, and were sent out to do the ministry themselves. He appeared to them after His resurrection for a period of 40 days. Then they saw Him ascend into heaven. Motivated by their eyewitness account, the early church spread the Gospel in the face of hardship.

Paul's vision of Jesus compelled him. He writes, "After that, [Jesus] was seen of above five hundred brethren at once. . . . After that, he was seen of James; then of all the apostles. And last of all he was seen of me also" (1 Corinthians 15:6-8). Paul's vision on the road to Damascus (Acts 9) was his "ground zero," his "origin." Paul was changed. He had a new life, a new calling, and a new name. Paul never turned back, but he did look back to that day on the road when he came face to face with Jesus. It assured him of his place among the apostles: "Am I not an apostle? . . . have I not seen Jesus Christ our Lord?" (1 Corinthians 9:1).

The believers of the early church were marked by their vision of the Lord. Until we are consumed with our own vision of Jesus, we will not be effective witnesses. On many occasions, Jesus waited in the presence of His Father late into the night in order to see what the Father was doing. He said, "Verily, verily, I say unto you, The Son can do nothing of himself, but what he seeth the Father do:" (John 5:19). How much longer do we need to wait in God's presence to see Him and grasp an understanding of what He's doing? Being a witness assumes we have witnessed something. We must have a revelation, a vision, to share. Then we need the power of the Holy Spirit to share it.

The Holy Spirit was the driving force behind the witness and power of the early believers. Jesus told them to wait in Jerusalem for the promise of the Father. "But ye shall receive power, after that the Holy Ghost is come upon you: and ye shall be witnesses unto me...unto the uttermost part of the earth" (Acts 1:8).

One hundred-twenty waited and prayed together in the Upper Room of where they were staying. Suddenly they heard a noise sounding like a violent, rushing wind. "There appeared to them divided tongues, as of fire, and one sat upon each of them" (Acts 2:3, NKJV). People from many nations heard the message in their own language that day because they had gathered in Jerusalem for the feast of Pentecost. Coincidence? Hardly! It was God's purpose and timing, carried out by the Holy Spirit.

Today people from every part of the world are flooding into our cities. The Lord is again giving the opportunity—a divine coincidence—to proclaim the Good News to this diverse group.

The Holy Spirit has several jobs. He reminds believers of Jesus' teachings. He sometimes gives them power to perform miracles, and produces in their lives the fruit of the Spirit, the greatest of which is love. This kind of Spirit will attract attention.

"And Stephen, full of faith and power, did great wonders and miracles among the people" (Acts 6:8). Stephen lived in the power of the Spirit to the glory of God the Father and Jesus Christ, who stood to receive him into heaven when he was martyred. Filled with the Spirit, Ananias prayed for Saul's healing. Philip preached in Samaria and many believed, "hearing and seeing the miracles which he did" (Acts 8:6). Tabitha gave her time and skill to help the poor and widowed (Acts 9). She showed God's love in tangible ways and it was noticed. When she died, they cried out to God, and when He raised her from the dead, many believed.

After encountering Christ and being filled with the Holy Spirit, we begin to grasp God's incredible love for every person. We live with a sense of destiny accomplished through love.

This is God's appointed time for the nations of the world to witness His power throughout the world. When we, as believers, have seen Jesus, are filled with His Spirit, and give of ourselves from a heart of love, the vision of Jesus will be made known to every nation, tongue, and tribe.

May the 'Acts' of the Spirit of God continue!

Terri Thompson is a short story writer, pastor's wife, women's ministry advisor, and Sunday School teacher.

8

AMANDA BERRY SMITH

Evangelist and Missionary

"O, Lord, if You will help me I will believe You," Amanda Berry Smith cried out to God as she struggled with her faith. Though she grew up in a Christian family, she was never quite certain of her own salvation. She prayed, she went to the altar, and yet she still yearned. It wasn't until Amanda verbalized her belief one day in a cellar in 1856 that she felt the inner peace that comes with salvation. That day, Amanda made a promise not only to grow in faith and her knowledge of the Lord, but to share that knowledge with others. She did just that as an evangelist and a missionary.

Amanda was born a slave in Maryland in 1837. By the time she was 3 years old, her father, Samuel, was able to buy his family's freedom and move them to Pennsylvania. As the oldest child of 13, Amanda had to help out her family, so she took a job as a domestic worker. She married twice; her first husband was killed during the Civil War, and by 1869, her second husband, James Henry Smith, an AME deacon, had passed on as well. She had five children from these marriages; four passed away in their youth.

Although she had a minimal amount of formal education, Amanda had a gift for singing and speaking. She became a very active member of the AME church, speaking to congregations in several parts of the United States and spreading the Word of God. Amanda met with some criticism for spending so much time speaking to White congregations, but no one could deny the impact that Amanda had on her listeners, regardless of race.

At the urging of some friends who realized how truly gifted a speaker Amanda was, she traveled to Europe in 1878 to begin a year-long missionary trip to work with churches there to spread the Good News of Jesus. She then headed to India to spread the Gospel. After his encounter with Amanda, a Methodist bishop, also doing missionary work in India, commented, "I had learned more that had been of actual value to me as a preacher of Christian truth from Amanda Smith than from any other person I had ever met."

Amanda returned to England for a short period of time and then traveled to Liberia. She did mission work in Liberia for eight years, preaching and working with various churches and groups of people to share biblical truths. Amanda served as a missionary on four continents. She diligently shared the Word of God throughout the world.

By this time, one could argue that Amanda had been a wonderful servant for the Lord, but she was not finished yet. She returned to the United States in 1890 to minister to others. By 1893, she settled in Chicago, and embarked on a truly amazing undertaking: She set out to open an orphanage for Black children. She was aware of the needs of Black children in a segregated America, and she wanted to do her part to address those needs. She decided to solicit private contributions, use money from her various speaking engagements and lectures, and use royalties from her autobiography, *An Autobiography, The Story of the Lord's Dealings with Mrs. Amanda Smith, the Colored Evangelist,* to fund the orphanage. Amanda even published the *Helper,* a newspaper designed to promote and garner support for the orphanage. She wanted the orphanage to be debt free when it opened, and after much hard work and persistence, the first orphanage for Black children in the state of Illinois opened in 1899 with five orphans and no debt. Many people heard about Amanda's orphanage, and it received support from several clubs for Black women. The orphanage also received the attention of Ida B. Wells, who served on its board of directors. The Amanda Smith Home, as it was called, stayed open and served many Black children until it was destroyed in 1918 by a fire.

Getting along in age and in poor health, Amanda retired and moved to Florida. She died on February 24, 1915. Her body was returned to Illinois to be buried near the orphanage. Her funeral brought out many who wanted to celebrate the life of the woman who kept the promise she made in the cellar so many years ago.

Katherine Steward *is the Editor for Juniorway® at UMI. She holds a B.S. and a M.S. in psychology.*

TEACHING TIPS

September 4
Bible Study Guide 1

1. Words You Should Know

A. Language (Acts 2:6) *dialektos* (Gk.)—The Greek word literally means "dialect." Foreigners not only spoke different languages but different dialects of the same language.

B. Amazed and **marvelled** (v. 7) *elstasis kai thaumazo* (Gk.)—The first verb denotes overwhelming surprise, and the second verb means to regard with wonder, i.e., begin to speculate on a matter.

2. Teacher Preparation

A. Read the UNIT 1 Introduction on p. 1. Then read through all five lessons of this unit.

B. Try to recall an incident in your life when the power of the Holy Spirit was needed and evident in your situation. Be prepared to share your testimony with the class.

3. Starting the Lesson

A. Assign a student to lead the class in prayer, focusing on the LESSON AIM.

B. Have a few students share their experiences from the MAKE IT HAPPEN section.

C. Ask a student to read the IN FOCUS story aloud. Encourage discussion regarding why students think Karen said "Thank You, Holy Spirit" at the end of the story. Had she made a decision? What? Why?

4. Getting into the Lesson

A. Ask a student to read the BACKGROUND information. Explain to the students that faith, prayer, and unity are keys to the fulfillment of God's promises.

B. Discuss THE PEOPLE, PLACES, AND TIMES. This will help the students understand the significance of the Day of Pentecost.

C. Have the students silently read the FOCAL VERSES for today's lesson. After they have read the verses ask them to identify some of the key points.

D. Use the questions in SEARCH THE SCRIPTURES as a closed Bible quiz. After the students have completed the quiz, review the answers together.

5. Relating the Lesson to Life

A. Share your testimony of an incident in your life when the power of the Holy Spirit was needed and evident in your situation.

B. Break the class into four groups and assign a question from the DISCUSS THE MEANING section to each group. After the groups talk over the questions, have each group present their conclusions to the rest of the class.

C. The LESSON IN OUR SOCIETY section can help the students see the parallels between the actions of the infant church and present-day opportunities they have to share their faith. Using today's lesson, ask the students how they plan to utilize the power within them to bring others to Christ.

6. Arousing Action

A. Challenge the students to read the DAILY BIBLE READINGS for the week. This will help build their faith and biblical knowledge.

B. Close the class with prayer.

WORSHIP GUIDE

For the Superintendent or Teacher
Theme: The Coming of the Spirit
Theme Song: "Pour Out Your Spirit"
Scripture: John 7:11
Song: "Till the Whole World Knows"
Meditation: Lord, the world is weary and needful of words of hope. You have given us the mission of taking Your Word to the world. You have given us the power to share our testimony. Holy Spirit, convict us to carry out our mission. In Jesus' name. Amen.

THE COMING OF THE SPIRIT

Bible Background • ACTS 2:1–42
Printed Text • ACTS 2:1–8, 38–42
Devotional Reading • PSALM 16

LESSON AIM

By the end of the lesson, we will:

KNOW the events surrounding the initial outpouring of the Holy Spirit;

BE CONVINCED that the Holy Spirit is available to all believers; and

DECIDE to rely on Him in every area of our lives.

KEEP IN MIND

"Then Peter said unto them, Repent, and be baptized every one of you in the name of Jesus Christ for the remission of sins, and ye shall receive the gift of the Holy Ghost" (Acts 2:38).

FOCAL VERSES

Acts 2:1 And when the day of Pentecost was fully come, they were all with one accord in one place.

2 And suddenly there came a sound from heaven as of a rushing mighty wind, and it filled all the house where they were sitting.

3 And there appeared unto them cloven tongues like as of fire, and it sat upon each of them.

4 And they were all filled with the Holy Ghost, and began to speak with other tongues, as the Spirit gave them utterance.

5 And there were dwelling at Jerusalem Jews, devout men, out of every nation under heaven.

6 Now when this was noised abroad, the multitude came together, and were confounded, because that every man heard them speak in his own language.

7 And they were all amazed and marvelled, saying one to another, Behold, are not all these which speak Galilaeans?

8 And how hear we every man in our own

LESSON OVERVIEW

LESSON AIM
KEEP IN MIND
FOCAL VERSES
IN FOCUS
THE PEOPLE, PLACES,
AND TIMES
BACKGROUND
AT-A-GLANCE
IN DEPTH
SEARCH THE SCRIPTURES
DISCUSS THE MEANING
LESSON IN OUR SOCIETY
MAKE IT HAPPEN
FOLLOW THE SPIRIT
REMEMBER YOUR THOUGHTS
MORE LIGHT ON THE TEXT
DAILY BIBLE READINGS

tongue, wherein we were born?

2:38 Then Peter said unto them, Repent, and be baptized every one of you in the name of Jesus Christ for the remission of sins, and ye shall receive the gift of the Holy Ghost.

39 For the promise is unto you, and to your children, and to all that are afar off, even as many as the Lord our God shall call.

40 And with many other words did he testify and exhort, saying, Save yourselves from this untoward generation.

41 Then they that gladly received his word were baptized: and the same day there were added unto them about three thousand souls.

42 And they continued stedfastly in the apostles' doctrine and fellowship, and in breaking of bread, and in prayers.

IN FOCUS

Around midnight Jamal came home reeking of alcohol.

Karen asked, "Where were you, Jamal? I was worried."

Without warning, Jamal grabbed her and shook her fiercely, throwing a fist toward her face that missed. It wasn't the first time in their three-year marriage that Jamal had become physically violent, but it was the worst. Karen stood frozen; she didn't run, scream, cry, or fight back, but stood glaring at Jamal with a strange look on her face. Suddenly, something overcame Jamal and he stormed out of the house.

Karen felt light-headed and hollow trying to

remember why she stayed with Jamal. She had repeatedly asked him to go with her to marriage counseling, but Jamal refused to go with her and also forbade her to meet with counselors. However, desperate to make some sense of her situation, Karen had been secretly attending pastoral counseling sessions for months. As she sat on her living room couch, she reflected back on the session she had earlier that morning with Pastor Thornton.

"I love him," she told Pastor Thornton.

"Do you think that being in love gives Jamal the right to mistreat you?" asked Pastor Thornton.

Karen defended her marriage, saying, "The Bible teaches that marriage is until death do us part."

"You're right, Karen, but God does not want us to suffer," Pastor Thornton added.

"Are you telling me to leave him?" Karen sighed.

"No, I am advising you to pray and depend on the Holy Spirit to guide you in how you should proceed," said Pastor Thornton.

When she returned home from the counseling session, Karen kneeled beside the couch and began to pray, "Dear God, I pray that Your Holy Spirit will guide me in doing the right thing about my marriage." She prayed all night, until she heard Jamal entering the house late that evening.

Now as she stood looking at her reflection in the bathroom mirror, she noticed her eyes were dry. It was at that moment she realized that no tears had fallen from her eyes—she had not shed one tear during Jamal's rampage. She finally realized what made Jamal storm out of the house—the look in her eyes showed no fear and reflected a sense of calm. Karen began to smile; deep inside her she knew that relief from her situation was imminent. Just at that moment, a warm feeling touched her heart. Karen answered, "Thank You, Holy Spirit."

In our lesson today, we will focus on how the Holy Spirit is available to all believers in all situations.

THE PEOPLE, PLACES, AND TIMES

The Day of Pentecost. By the time of Christ, the Feast of Firstfruits had become merged with the celebration of Passover. According to Leviticus 23:10-14, the offering of firstfruits was to be made on the day after the Sabbath. The more political priests, called Sadducees, interpreted this to mean that firstfruits would be offered on the Sunday after the Passover. The Pharisees, on the other hand, interpreted the day to fall on the first day of Passover week.

These specific days are significant for two reasons. First, if the Sadducees are correct, then Jesus was offered up as our eternal sacrifice on Passover Friday and resurrected on Sunday, becoming the "firstfruits of those who have fallen asleep" (1 Corinthians 15:20, NIV). The second reason the day is important is because it begins the countdown to the Day of Pentecost.

Pentecost celebrates the birth of the New Testament church when thousands were filled with God's Spirit, the Gospel was proclaimed to every nation, and the first missionaries were anointed for service.

BACKGROUND

Sometime between 835 and 830 B.C., the prophet Joel prophesied of a day when God would pour out His Spirit on all types of people. This outpouring would result in charismatic and prophetic manifestations among God's people. Joel declared that at that time everyone who called on the name of the Lord would be saved (Joel 2:28-32). Almost 900 years later, Joel's prophecy would be proven accurate.

After Jesus' resurrection from the grave, He spent 40 days revealing Himself to His disciples, reinforcing their mission, and giving them final instructions. On the day of His ascension, Jesus led His followers outside Bethany to Mount Olivet. There He affirmed that they were His witnesses and promised to send the Holy Spirit as promised by the Father (Luke 24:48-49).

The Lord instructed His disciples to go back to Jerusalem and wait for the promise (Acts 1:4). With the promised outpouring, the disciples would receive power to be witnesses for Christ, beginning in Jerusalem and spreading to the most remote corners of the world. After Jesus ascended to heaven before their eyes, the apostles worshiped Him and then returned to Jerusalem with great joy (Luke 24:52-53).

After completing the half-mile walk (a Sabbath

day's journey) to Jerusalem, the 11 remaining apostles, Mary the mother of Jesus, and 107 other disciples met in the Upper Room for prayer (Acts 1:15). Every day with singleness of purpose they sought God in prayer, crying out for the promise to be fulfilled.

AT-A-GLANCE

1. The First Outpouring (Acts 2:1-4)
2. The First Seekers (vv. 5-8)
3. The First Converts (vv. 38-42)

IN DEPTH

1. The First Outpouring (Acts 2:1-4)

Ten days after Jesus' ascension and 50 days after His resurrection, God moved to fulfill His promise. The disciples were all together in the Upper Room praying and praising God, when suddenly the room was filled with a noise that sounded like a violent tornado. This wind-like noise was the audible sign of the Holy Spirit's power. Those devout Jews who experienced the sound would no doubt be reminded of God's speaking to Job out of the whirlwind (Job 38:1; 40:6). They would recall how the wind blew over the waters and parted the Red Sea so that the Israelites could cross on dry land (Exodus 14:21). The sound would be a reminder of how the wind brought new life to dry bones in Ezekiel's vision (Ezekiel 37:7-10). Finally they would remember the words of Christ concerning those who are born of the Spirit (John 3:8). The sound of the "rushing mighty wind" was an indication that God was about to manifest His Holy Spirit in a dramatic and awesome way.

The second sign of the Spirit's outpouring was visual. Out of nowhere something materialized that appeared to be a mass of fire. The fireball dispersed itself into single small tongues of flames that settled over the heads of each disciple. It was not actual fire as we know it since nothing and no one was burned, but the disciples were well aware of what the fire symbolized. They knew that God had initially revealed Himself to Moses as a burning bush that would not be consumed (Exodus 3:2). They knew that when God led the Israelites out of Egyptian bondage, He led them through the darkness as a pillar of fire to give them light (13:21). They also knew that the first burnt animal sacrifice offered by the temple priests was consumed by fire that "came out from the presence of the LORD" (Leviticus 9:24, NIV). This holy fire signified God's acceptance of the church as a whole and of each individual believer as a temple for His indwelling Spirit (Ephesians 2:21-22; 1 Corinthians 3:16).

Having manifested His power through the sound of wind and His presence through the appearance of fire, God was now ready to fulfill Joel's prophecy and honor Jesus' promise. He would pour out His Spirit and fill all the believers in His infant church. As the 120 disciples were filled, they began manifesting the third sign of the Spirit's outpouring. They "began to speak in other tongues as the Spirit enabled them" (Acts 2:4, NIV). This final sign of speaking in other tongues refers to Holy Spirit-inspired expression whereby believers speak in languages they have never learned (1 Corinthians 14:4-15), or in languages unknown on earth (1 Corinthians 13:1).

The New Covenant was ratified with the blood of Jesus, and God's new instrument, the church, was empowered on the Day of Pentecost to proclaim it. That same power that was poured out on Pentecost continues to fill believers in every succeeding generation.

2. The First Seekers (vv. 5-8)

By the time of Christ, Jerusalem had become a cosmopolitan center. Many of the descendants of the Jews who had been scattered during the forced deportations (2 Kings 17:5-6; 25:8-12) had returned to Jerusalem and settled there.

Along with the returnees who were now "dwelling" in the city were Jews from all over the Roman world who had come to the Holy City to celebrate the feast of Pentecost. Luke describes these people as "devout men, out of every nation under heaven" (Acts 2:5). The phrase "every nation under heaven" was a common idiom used to refer to those in the known world or within the Roman Empire. By "devout" Luke refers to God-fearing Jews who were sincere in their worship and cautious in the practice of their faith.

13

The joyful excitement that began in the Upper Room soon spilled out into the streets and the sound of inspired commotion naturally attracted a large and curious crowd. As the sound of 120 disciples all praising God rose, the listeners were "confounded" (v. 6) and "amazed" (v. 7) at what they heard. They were confounded because the people doing the speaking were all Galileans. These people would be expected to speak Hebrew and Greek, but even in these languages they had a pronounced accent that was easily recognized. This fact is evidenced by those who recognized Peter's accent after Jesus was captured (Mark 14:70). Rather than just hearing the 120 disciples praising God in Greek or their own accented language, the crowd heard them perfectly enunciating their native languages. What made this so amazing was that there were representatives from at least 15 different countries present at that time (Acts 2:9-11).

3. The First Converts (vv. 38-42)

The response to Peter's prophetic word was immediate. His precise and logical presentation of the Gospel intellectually convinced many of those present. However, intellectual assent is not enough to cause people to turn away from wickedness. True repentance is a heart issue. King Solomon was correct in his advice, "Above all else, guard your heart, for it is the wellspring of life" (Proverbs 4:23, NIV), because as Jeremiah observed, "The heart is deceitful above all things and beyond cure" (Jeremiah 17:9, NIV).

The sin of rejecting and crucifying Jesus was great, yet Peter's words held out hope; so the question, "What shall we do?" undoubtedly means, "What shall we do to be saved?" This is the first time that the most important question ever asked was expressed and the first time it was ever answered. Peter was ready with an answer and issued the first altar call, "Repent, and be baptized every one of you in the name of Jesus Christ for the remission of sins" (v. 38). Although salvation is free, it is also conditional on heartfelt repentance. True repentance is a change of heart whereby one becomes sorrowful for having offended and disobeyed God. It determines to turn away from unrighteousness and to turn to Christ and follow

His example of holy living by His grace.

By repenting and calling on the name of the Lord, the people would receive both the forgiveness of their sins and the gift of the Holy Spirit. However, this promise was not limited to Peter's immediate audience or even to those of his generation. It was also a promise to the next generation and to every generation thereafter. The forgiveness of sin and gift of the Holy Spirit is the birthright of every new believer in every generation who answers the call of the Lord.

Those in the crowd whose hearts had been "pricked" by Peter's words accepted his call to repentance and were baptized that same day. On the birthday of the New Testament church, 3,000 people were converted to Christ. In one day, the disciples had won more souls than Jesus did in three years of ministry. No wonder Jesus had prophesied, "He that believeth on me, the works that I do shall he do also; and greater works than these shall he do; because I go to the Father" (John 14:12).

The 3,000 new converts formed the first Christian community. They were dedicated to learning about the teachings and life of Christ. They were dedicated to each other, fellowshiping, and sharing meals—especially the Lord's Supper. Finally they were dedicated to spending time in God's presence in both their private and public prayer times, and sharing their resources with those in need. The early Christian community remains the model for our contemporary church. Under the anointing of the Holy Spirit, we are called to reach our faithless and perverse generation with the Gospel message and to demonstrate our Christianity by loving God, His Word, and each other.

SEARCH THE SCRIPTURES

1. What were the three manifestations of the initial outpouring of the Holy Spirit on the Day of Pentecost (Acts 2:2-4)?

2. What spiritual event occurred before the believers began speaking in tongues (v. 4)?

3. How did the phenomenon that started in the Upper Room affect the curious crowd who came to investigate the commotion (vv. 7-8)?

4. Upon hearing the questions of the crowd, who stood up and delivered the first sermon (v. 14)?

5. After Peter's powerful sermon, the people were deeply moved. What question did they ask that reflected their sorrow for sin (v. 37)?

DISCUSS THE MEANING

1. Believers are the instruments God uses to spread the Gospel message. Why is it necessary for believers to be able to give a precise and logical explanation of their faith? How does one learn to give logical explanations, and where do believers get the courage to share their faith?

2. Many modern-day Christians believe that Spirit-filled believers are still gifted with the ability to speak in tongues, while many others strongly disagree. What do you believe about modern-day speaking in tongues and why? Is your belief based on church tradition or sound biblical study? How can one be sure?

LESSON IN OUR SOCIETY

Peter's sermon on the Day of Pentecost convinced the Jewish community of their sin in the rejection and crucifixion of Christ. As a result, they were compelled to ask what they had to do to remedy the situation. Today there are many sins that affect the quality of life in the Black community, such as premarital sex, drugs, and the breakdown of the family. How can the church effectively bring attention to these sins in a way that compels people to ask, "What can we do to remedy the situation?" How is Christ the answer to this question?

MAKE IT HAPPEN

One of the greatest things the Holy Spirit does in the lives of believers is to empower us to share our faith with others. We need to remember the words that Paul used to encourage Timothy: "For God did not give us a sprit of timidity, but a spirit of power, of love and of self-discipline" (2 Timothy 1:7, NIV). Determine to share your faith with three people this week. Be prepared to share your experiences with the class next week.

FOLLOW THE SPIRIT

What God wants me to do:

_____

_____

REMEMBER YOUR THOUGHTS

Special insights I have learned:

_____

_____

MORE LIGHT ON THE TEXT

Acts 2:1-8, 38-42

1 And when the day of Pentecost was fully come, they were all with one accord in one place.

The narrative opens with a reference to the time and place of the coming of the Holy Spirit. The time is precise: "when the day of Pentecost was fully come." The word "Pentecost" (Gk. *pentekoste,* **pen-tay-kos-tay'**) literally means "fiftieth," because it was celebrated 50 days after Passover. It was the second of the three great Jewish annual festivals (Deuteronomy 16:16), falling between Passover and the Feast of Tabernacles, or Feast of Booths. Pentecost was also called the Feast of Weeks because it was held seven weeks after Passover (Exodus 34:22). It had a double meaning. Pentecost celebrated the end of the grain harvest and was also known as the Feast of Harvest (Exodus 23:16). In later Judaism (toward the end of the period between the Old and New Testaments), it was observed as the anniversary of the giving of the law to Moses at Sinai. It is possible to draw out from the two meanings of Pentecost— a double symbolism for Christians. The coming of the Holy Spirit occurred 50 days after the crucifixion and resurrection of Christ, marking the beginning of the new covenant and the harvesting of the firstfruits of the Christian missionary enterprise.

The Day of Pentecost "was fully come" (Gk. *sumpleroo,* **soom-play-ro'-o**), which means that it was in the process of fulfillment or coming to an end.

The location of the coming of the Holy Spirit is stated in the expression "all with one accord in one place." The expression "all with one accord" (Gk. *Hapas homothumadon,* **hap'-as hom-oth-oo-mad-on'**) means all with one passion, purpose, or mind. The phrase "all together" (NIV) refers to the whole company of the disciples. It stresses an absolute unanimity among the disciples (cf. 1:14; 4:24; 15:25). This togetherness goes beyond mere assembly and activity; it includes agreement about what they were praying for.

The expression "in one place" (Gk. *epi autos,* **ep-**

ee' ow-tos') means "in the same place" and probably refers to somewhere within the temple areas, such as one of the many rooms or halls of the temple (Acts 2:46; 3:11; 5:12).

2 And suddenly there came a sound from heaven as of a rushing mighty wind, and it filled all the house where they were sitting.

The place where the disciples were gathered was suddenly filled with what sounded like "a rushing mighty wind" from heaven. The word "wind" (Gk. *pnoe*, **pno-ay'**) is frequently used in the Bible as a symbol of the Spirit (1 Kings 19:11; Ezekiel 37:9-14; John 3:8). The Spirit came upon them with great power (cf. Luke 24:49; Acts 1:8). This was the power promised by Jesus for witnessing.

3 And there appeared unto them cloven tongues like as of fire, and it sat upon each of them.

The disciples not only heard "a sound from heaven as of a rushing mighty wind," but they saw "tongues like as of fire." The word "fire" (Gk. *pur,* **poor**) also denotes the Divine presence (Exodus 3:2ff) and the Spirit who purifies and sanctifies (cf. Matthew 3:11; Luke 3:16).

The expression "cloven tongues" (Gk. *diamerizo glossa,* **dee-am-er-id'-zo gloce-sah'**) literally refers to tongues dividing, distributing, or parting themselves. The verb "sat" (Gk. *kathizo,* **kath-id'-zo**) refers to the tongues of fire. It is singular, giving the understanding that one of the tongues of fire sat on each person.

4 And they were all filled with the Holy Ghost, and began to speak with other tongues, as the Spirit gave them utterance.

The disciples were all filled with the Holy Spirit (cf. Acts 4:8, 31; 13:9; Ephesians 5:18), and they "began to speak with other tongues." Speaking in tongues is called "glossolalia" from two Greek words: *laleo* (**lal-eh'-o**) and *glossa* (**gloce-sah'**). It was not an unparalleled manifestation (cf. Acts 10:46; 19:6). It was also a spiritual gift that was highly valued by the church of Corinth (1 Corinthians 12–14). Without denying that it was a manifestation of the Holy Spirit, Paul denounced the undue importance that some people of the Corinthian church attached to it. The *glossolalia* in Corinth was

uttered in speech that could not be understood until someone present received the corresponding spiritual gift of interpretation. Speaking in tongues is similar to the prophetic utterances of people possessed by the Spirit of God in the Old Testament (Numbers 11:25-29; 1 Samuel 10:5-6; 1 Kings 22:10, 12).

In Acts 2, however, the disciples were speaking in tongues that were completely different from their native languages, as prompted by the Holy Spirit. The words they were speaking were immediately recognized by immigrants and visitors from many parts of the world. The following verses (v. 5ff) show that the purpose of the spirit-inspired speech *glossolalia* was to symbolize the universality of the Gospel (Acts 1:8). It shows that people from all nations will be brought into a unity of understanding through the preaching of the Gospel in the power of the Holy Spirit.

5 And there were dwelling at Jerusalem Jews, devout men, out of every nation under heaven.

The verb translated as "were dwelling" or "were living" (Gk. *katoikeo,* **kat-oy-keh'**) is not used for temporary dwellers who came for Pentecost, but to refer to Jews by race or by profession of faith (proselyte). They had come from "every nation under heaven" to live in Jerusalem near the temple within the city walls as permanent residents. The expression "every nation under heaven" (Gk. *pas ethnos hupo ouranos,* **pas eth'-nos hoop-o' oo-ran-os'**) also stresses the international nature of the crowd. The crowd was composed of permanent residents of Jerusalem and visitors who had came to celebrate the feast.

6 Now when this was noised abroad, the multitude came together, and were confounded, because that every man heard them speak in his own language.

They "were confounded" (Gk. *sugcheo,* **soong-kheh'-o**) as they heard loud praises to God uttered by the disciples in the indigenous languages and dialects (Gk. *dialektos,* **dee-al'-ek-tos**) of their native lands. The word "language" (Gk. *dialektos,* **dee-al'-ek-tos**) means the language of a nation or region. It can be translated both as "language" and "dialect" (dialects of the same language). The diversity of language is stressed here and in the following verses (v. 7-12; cf. 1:8). The desire of God is that every tribe and nation will be reached with the Gospel (cf. 1 Timothy 2:4-7; Revelation 5:9).

7 And they were all amazed and marvelled, saying one to another, Behold, are not all these which speak Galilaeans?

They were "amazed" (Gk. *existemi,* **ex-is'-tay-mee**), which literally means to be beside oneself or out of place, denoting an overwhelming surprise; they "marvelled" (Gk. *thaumazo,* **thou-mad'-zo**), denoting a continuing wonder and speculation as they heard loud praises to God uttered in languages others than Galilaean. The Galilaeans used a peculiar dialect which distinguished them from Judeans (cf. Mark 14:70; Matthew 26:73).

8 And how hear we every man in our own tongue, wherein we were born?

The crowd was composed of Jews and proselytes living in or visiting Jerusalem. They were representatives of the lands from which they originally came, and they spoke in the local dialects (Gk. *dialektos,* **dee-al'-ek-tos**) of those lands.

2:38 Then Peter said unto them, Repent, and be baptized every one of you in the name of Jesus Christ for the remission of sins, and ye shall receive the gift of the Holy Ghost.

Peter told the audience that they must repent of their sins and turn to God. The verb "repent" (Gk. *metanoeo,* **met-an-o-eh'-o**) is a compound word in Greek. It consists of the preposition *meta* (**met-ah'**), which means "after" or "with," and the verb *noieo* (**noy-eh'-o**), which means to perceive, to understand, or to gain an insight into something. Thus, it means to change one's mental attitude. The call to repentance, which is Peter's basic and primary demand, requires a complete change of mind and attitude about Jesus. It is an essential element in the proclamation of the Gospel.

Peter called on them to visibly demonstrate their repentance by receiving baptism, the sign of the New Covenant (cf. 13:24; 18:25; 19:3ff; Mark 1:4). The expression "in the name" (Gk. *epi onoma,* **ep-ee' on'-om-ah**) means to be baptized upon the name or on the ground of Jesus' name. The meaning is based on the belief in and confession of Jesus as Lord and Saviour. They must be baptized in the name of the very person they had previously rejected. This would be a clear token of their repentance and of their faith in Him. Submitting to baptism was a humiliating experience since Jews regarded baptism as necessary for Gentile converts only.

Then they would receive two free gifts from God: the forgiveness of their sins and the gift of the Holy Spirit. The "gift" of the Holy Spirit must be distinguished from the "gifts" of the Holy Spirit. The gift of the Holy Spirit is the Spirit Himself given by the Father through the Son. The gifts of the Holy Spirit are the spiritual abilities that the Spirit distributes as He wills (1 Corinthians 12:11). The Holy Spirit is a gift from God who brings the church to life, furthers its growth, and links its members collectively and individually with Christ and with one another (cf. Acts 2:43-47).

39 For the promise is unto you, and to your children, and to all that are afar off, even as many as the Lord our God shall call.

God had placed no limitations on His offer. On the contrary, the promise of the Holy Spirit was for them and for their children and for all who were far off (Jews and Gentiles included). The promise was extended to those who were present on the Day of Pentecost, to their contemporaries, and to their descendants as well. It was to both the people of Jerusalem and to those of distant lands (cf. Acts 1:8; Isaiah 57:19; Joel 2:32). The Greek word translated as "far off" (Gk. *eis makran,* **ice mak-ran'**) literally means "unto a long way" (cf. Ephesians 2:13, 17). Everyone God calls to Himself through Christ receives both gifts. Those who call upon the name of the Lord are those whom He has called to Himself (cf. Joel 2:32).

40 And with many other words did he testify and exhort, saying, Save yourselves from this untoward generation.

The phrase "with many other words" indicates that this was not the end of Peter's sermon. Peter both warned and pleaded with his audience. The essence of his warnings and pleadings was, "Save yourselves from this untoward generation" (Gk. *skolios genea,* **skol-ee-os' ghen-eh-ah'**), a generation that was both literally and morally crooked (cf. Luke 9:41; 11:29; Deuteronomy 32:5; 1 Thessalonians 1:10). The audience would have to change from a corrupt generation to a new community. By repenting, they would belong to the remnant of the righteous and save themselves from the perverse generation. Peter's words reflect the conviction of the disciples that they formed the faithful remnant of Israel. The new believing community was the faithful remnant of the old Israel (Joel 2:32). God's wrath would fall upon the faithless people of Israel (1 Thessalonians 1:10).

41 Then they that gladly received his word were baptized: and the same day there were added unto them about three thousand souls.

Large numbers of people gladly received "his word" (Gk. *ho logos autos*, **logos ow-tos'**, literally "the word of him," meaning Peter's message), repented, and were baptized. Three thousand were added to their number that day (v. 41; see also 4:4; 5:14; 6:1-7; 9:31; 11:21-24; 16:5—the growth of the church is regularly noted). Many visitors were in Jerusalem for Pentecost. Some returned to their own countries as baptized Christians, thus furthering the spread of the Gospel.

42 And they continued stedfastly in the apostles' doctrine and fellowship, and in breaking of bread, and in prayers.

The four foundations on which the early church was built included the following:

1. "The apostles' doctrine" (Gk. *apostolos didache*, **ap-os'-tol-os did-akh-ay'**), or the apostles' teaching. The early disciples "remained constant" (Gk. *proskartereo*, **pros-kar-ter-eh'-o**) in the apostolic teachings. These teachings consisted of facts about the ministry of Jesus, His works, and His words as incorporated later in the Gospels. They also included constant exposition of Old Testament prophecies as they related to Jesus. The New Testament is the final form of the teaching of the apostles. We must study it and submit to its authority.

2. "Fellowship" (Gk. *koinonia*, **koy-nohn-ee'-ah**) comes from the word *koinos* (**koy-nos'**), which means "common." It indicates a relation between individuals that involves an active participation in a common interest. It also has the meaning of gener-

ous participation or giving of oneself to one another (cf. 2 Corinthians 8:4; 9:13). The early disciples remained constant in fellowship. Their fellowship was not only a sense of belonging to a new community; it was also the practical expression of the fellowship of the Spirit through the sharing of personal possessions. Their fellowship is expressed in what they shared in together—their common share in God (2 Corinthians 13:14)—and in what they shared with each other—what they gave as well as what they received (cf. Acts 2:44-45; 4:32-37).

3. Their fellowship was expressed not only in caring for one another, but in the "breaking of bread" (Gk. *Klasis artos*, **klas'-is ar'-tos**). Jews see a religious significance in all meals, marked by the saying of a prayer of thanksgiving and the ceremonial breaking of bread. The breaking of bread here denotes something more than the ordinary partaking of meals together. It is a reference to the regular observance of Jesus' breaking of bread at His last meal with the disciples (Luke 24:35; 1 Corinthians 11:23ff; Acts 20:7).

4. The definite article "the" used with the word "prayers" (Gk. *proseuche*, **pros-yoo-khay'**) suggests a reference to prayer meetings in homes as well as public prayer services in the temple court and synagogues (cf. Acts 2:46; 3:1; 12:5, 12).

DAILY BIBLE READINGS

M: God's Spirit Will Be Poured Out
Joel 2:23-29

T: God Is Always with Us
Psalm 16:5-11

W: The Holy Spirit Comes
Acts 2:1-13

T: Peter Speaks to the Crowd
Acts 2:14-21

F: Peter Speaks About the Crucified Jesus
Acts 2:22-28

S: Peter Speaks About the Risen Christ
Acts 2:29-36

S: Three Thousand Are Baptized
Acts 2:1-8, 37-42

TEACHING TIPS

September 11
Bible Study Guide 2

1. Words You Should Know

A. Wonders and signs (Acts 2:43) *terata kai semeia* (Gk.)—Miracles that point to God's direct activity in the earthly realm.

B. Singleness of heart (v. 46) *apheloteti kardias* (Gk.)—Gladness and sincerity of heart.

2. Teacher Preparation

A. Begin preparing for this lesson by reading through all the FOCAL VERSES. Then read the entire BIBLE STUDY GUIDE for this lesson.

B. Review the TEACHING TIPS, and adapt the lesson to fit the needs of your class.

3. Starting the Lesson

A. Begin the lesson by asking one of the students to lead the class in prayer using the LESSON AIM.

B. Ask the students to share their experiences from last week's MAKE IT HAPPEN assignment and tell what they learned from their DAILY BIBLE READINGS.

C. Ask one student to read today's IN FOCUS story aloud. Then explain its relevance to today's LESSON AIM.

4. Getting into the Lesson

A. Assign three students to read the FOCAL VERSES according to the AT-A-GLANCE outline.

B. The information in the BACKGROUND section will help set the stage for today's lesson. Have the students read the section silently and write down their thoughts in the REMEMBER YOUR THOUGHTS section.

C. Refer to the SEARCH THE SCRIPTURES questions as you begin the discussion of the lesson.

D. Discuss THE PEOPLE, PLACES, AND TIMES, which will help the students understand the importance of Wisdom Literature to Christian life and spiritual growth.

5. Relating the Lesson to Life

A. Use the DISCUSS THE MEANING questions to help the students see some relationships between the lesson and the personal applications that can help the students put the "meat on the bones."

B. The LESSON IN OUR SOCIETY section should also be used to help the students see how the lesson parallels their present-day situation. Using today's lesson, ask the students what are some of the things they can do to impact their churches and communities, and challenge them to put their suggestions into action.

6. Arousing Action

A. Sum up the lesson with the KEEP IN MIND verse. Have students read it in unison, and ask how they can apply the verse to their everyday lives.

B. Challenge the students to follow through on the MAKE IT HAPPEN assignment. This will help them incorporate the biblical truths into their lives and make a personal commitment to the Lord and to other people.

C. Encourage the students to read the DAILY BIBLE READINGS. Explain that it will help them put the truths they learned into action and keep them in the Scriptures during the week.

D. Close the class with prayer, thanking the Lord for the love and mercy that He has shown to the students this week.

LIFE AMONG THE FOLLOWERS

Bible Background • ACTS 2:43–47; 4:32–35
Printed Text • ACTS 2:43–47; 4:32–35
Devotional Reading • ROMANS 8:9–17

LESSON AIM

By the end of the lesson, we will:

KNOW the essential elements that make a church great;

DESIRE to share in a church that promotes biblical teaching, fellowship, worship, and service to others; and

DETERMINE to apply ourselves to make our church great.

KEEP IN MIND

"And all that believed were together, and had all things common" (Acts 2:44).

FOCAL VERSES

Acts 2:43 And fear came upon every soul: and many wonders and signs were done by the apostles.

44 And all that believed were together, and had all things common;

45 And sold their possessions and goods, and parted them to all men, as every man had need.

46 And they, continuing daily with one accord in the temple, and breaking bread from house to house, did eat their meat with gladness and singleness of heart,

47 Praising God, and having favour with all the people. And the Lord added to the church daily such as should be saved.

4:32 And the multitude of them that believed were of one heart and of one soul: neither said any of them that ought of the things which he possessed was his own; but they had all things common.

33 And with great power gave the apostles wit-

LESSON OVERVIEW

LESSON AIM
KEEP IN MIND
FOCAL VERSES
IN FOCUS
THE PEOPLE, PLACES, AND TIMES
BACKGROUND
AT-A-GLANCE
IN DEPTH
SEARCH THE SCRIPTURES
DISCUSS THE MEANING
LESSON IN OUR SOCIETY
MAKE IT HAPPEN
FOLLOW THE SPIRIT
REMEMBER YOUR THOUGHTS
MORE LIGHT ON THE TEXT
DAILY BIBLE READINGS

ness of the resurrection of the Lord Jesus: and great grace was upon them all.

34 Neither was there any among them that lacked: for as many as were possessors of lands or houses sold them, and brought the prices of the things that were sold,

35 And laid them down at the apostles' feet: and distribution was made unto every man according as he had need.

IN FOCUS

Jessica and several members of her local church were devastated when they learned of the pastor's plans to divert funds designated for a new church building toward missions work in India.

The church had prayed for a new building for years. The new building would house a soup kitchen and provide 75 beds for the homeless in the community. As head of the homeless ministry, Jessica was devastated by the pastor's decision. Paranoid about what might happen to her church, Jessica confronted the pastor.

"How could you use the building funds for foreigners? Some of them are not even Christians," she said.

"Jessica, why don't you come with us next month on the missions trip to India?" Pastor Whitaker urged.

"Pastor, we need a bigger building. This community deserves our help" Jessica stated.

"We are getting a bigger church every time we save a soul or feed a body. It doesn't matter if it's here at home or throughout the world. Come with us next month and see for yourself," said Pastor Whitaker. Jessica agreed.

One month later Jessica and the members of her church arrived in the city of Katmandu, India, during monsoon season. The river banks were overflowing and the city of Katmandu was dirty and desperate. As Jessica walked down a wooden sidewalk, she stumbled and fell knee-deep in mud, and the smell of open sewage made her gag. As several people helped her out of the mud, Jessica realized why the pastor had urged her to come. She realized that the community of faith is much larger than the four walls of her local church body. These people needed help too.

In Katmandu, Pastor Whitaker shared the Gospel message and held nightly prayer meetings. They passed out medication, prepared meals, bathed babies, and sterilized linens and clothing for people left homeless and devastated by the monsoons. When Jessica returned home, the size of the church building was insignificant. She realized that because of the sacrifices she and the rest of the missions team made, God's church was increased.

Are you willing to sacrifice and share for the betterment of the entire church body? In today's lesson we will explore the elements of what makes a great church.

THE PEOPLE, PLACES, AND TIMES

The Apostles' Doctrine. The doctrine taught by the apostles and codified in the Bible sets forth the fundamental teaching of the Christian faith. The early church not only learned what God said, but lived according to His teachings and preserved them for us today. We will focus our attention on two primary aspects of Christianity: teaching correct doctrine and living according to correct doctrine.

God brings Christians into fellowship with Himself through the death and resurrection of His Son, Jesus Christ. The apostle Paul wrote that God was in Christ reconciling the world to Himself (2 Corinthians 5:19). Jesus Christ, the eternal Son, took on human flesh and walked among God's creation, thereby revealing the Father to the world. Believers find new life in

Him and come into union with the Father through Him. This is the simple message that the early Christians proclaimed about Jesus.

The early Christians understood that both belief and behavior were vital to a growing relationship with God. They knew that "true worshipers will worship the Father in spirit and truth" (John 4:23, NIV). What a Christian believed in his mind and felt in his heart would be acted out in his life. This is essentially what we mean when we speak of Christianity. It is new life lived by new creatures in Christ, which brings genuine obedience to God and His Word.

The apostles' doctrine not only focuses on individual salvation, but also teaches the importance of the brotherhood of believers. God brings His people into a family of the redeemed called the kingdom of God. In this kingdom, God requires His children to live in brotherly love. They are to practice the same moral values Christ lived by, and they are to work for the redemption of all humanity. Thus, the early Christians had a burning desire to win lost souls for Jesus and bring them into the Christian family.

BACKGROUND

At the end of our last lesson, Luke described how 3,000 converts were added to the infant New Testament church on its first day. This was a great blessing, but it was also a great challenge. The 3,000 new converts had not actually walked with Jesus, so they needed to be instructed in His teachings and have Christ's character modeled for them by the older members, whose goal was much more than simply recruiting new converts, it was making new disciples.

Jesus' followers clearly understood that He never asked them to increase the church numerically—that was His job (Acts 2:47). Their mission was to follow the Great Commandment (Matthew 22:37-40) and the Great Commission (28:18-20) and to allow God to build a great church. To accomplish their mission, the church would be built on four essential tenets: the apostles' doctrine, fellowship, the breaking of bread, and prayer.

The apostles' doctrine was authoritative because it was the teaching of Christ's commandments through the apostles under the anointing of the Holy Spirit. Much later, this apostolic doctrine would take on written form and have its authority confirmed by the apostle Paul (Ephesians 2:5; 3:20). The new converts were taught and nourished in the Word.

Fellowship implied partnership in purpose (1 John 1:3). Their fellowship included both their vertical relationship with God and their horizontal relationships with each other. This involved corporate and personal relationships based on what each member could contribute to the good of the others and the good of the whole. Breaking of bread was the practice of Christian love and hospitality and the ordinance of communion. Finally, prayer involved the sincere seeking of intimate and true fellowship with God. Prayer included inquiring about God's will for public and personal matters, petitioning Him for the needs of others, thanking Him for His blessings, praising Him for His mighty deeds, and worshiping Him for His being. Any church that bases its existence on these four pillars should be a successful church.

AT-A-GLANCE

1. The Church Unified (Acts 2:44-46; 4:32, 34-37)
2. The Church Glorified (vv. 43; 4:33)
3. The Church Multiplied (v. 47)

IN DEPTH

1. The Church Unified (Acts 2:44-46; 4:32, 34-37)

For the 3,000 new believers, acceptance of Christ as Lord and Saviour and the filling of the Holy Spirit opened them up to a new understanding of God and His purposes. They hungered to learn more about Jesus, and how they could pattern their lives after His.

The 3,000 new converts joined together with the original 120 believers (Acts 1:15) to form a community of believers who "had all things [in] common" (2:44; 4:32). This meant that everyone in the community was ready and willing to sacrifice for the good of the whole. They "were of one heart and of one soul" (v. 32), which refers to the commonality of their participation, prayer, and purpose. They regarded their material blessings as a means of being a blessing to others.

Many of the new converts were from countries and cities other than Jerusalem, and they eventually ran out of money. Some of them were widows and the poor, who needed assistance in meeting their daily needs. The apostles had totally given themselves to seeking God on behalf of the new church and communicating God's will to the congregation (6:3-4). They, too, needed material support. However, no one in the congregation had to do without the basic necessities of life because God used the generosity of the wealthy as a means of blessing the poor. All their possessions, talents, and time were dedicated to furthering the mission of the church and meeting the needs of the brothers and sisters.

To help meet the need, many believers sold land or personal property "and laid them down at the apostles' feet" (4:35). That is, they brought the money to the apostles and gave them authority to distribute the funds to the people as the need arose. The phrase "according to their need" (2:45; 4:35) is key to understanding this passage. As the need arose, different members would sell property and donate the proceeds to meet the need. What the passages teach is the Christian attitude to "do nothing out of selfish ambition or vain conceit, but in humility consider others better than yourselves. Each of you should look not only to your own interests, but also to the interests of others" (Philippians 2:3-4, NIV). Later in the narrative, Peter would make it clear that no one was under any obligation to give (Acts 5:4).

The group continued to meet daily in the temple and to gather together at various homes after the services to share meals and companionship. The table of fellowship was an essential element of the infant church. It provided members with an opportunity to gather together in small groups and discuss the day's teachings. Intimate relationships began and bonds formed between individuals, which contributed to the cohesion of the whole. Christian homes became centers of fellowship where rich and poor, male and female, and

Jew and Gentile gathered together to share in praise, worship, and friendship.

Jealousy, criticisms, and factions were minimized in the church, as each member shared generously with others and praised God with hearts full of love and joy. They modeled what the apostle Paul would later teach, "Let the word of Christ dwell in you richly as you teach and admonish one another with all wisdom, and as you sing psalms, hymns and spiritual songs with gratitude in your hearts to God" (Colossians 3:16, NIV). A church is unified when all of its members are committed to God, to each other, and to the mission of the church.

2. The Church Glorified (vv. 43; 4:33)

A church is glorified when God exerts His power and demonstrates His unconditional love through the congregation. When God's power is at work in the church, its members are compassionate and caring and the presence of God is evident in their lives by their spiritual growth.

For these first Christians the experience of Pentecost was not a passing phenomenon. Their transformation into new creatures in Christ (2 Corinthians 5:17) continued to impress upon them a sense of awe. Those who may have been thieves quit stealing, drunkards quit drinking, and adulterers quit philandering. Even those who had joined the mob on that fateful day and cried out, "Crucify Him!" were now pleading with others to surrender to Him.

The apostles continued to boldly preach the Gospel message: "with great power gave the apostles witness of the resurrection of the Lord Jesus" (Acts 4:33). The apostles' preaching did not center on the people's sin or even the death of Christ. Instead they focused on the most important part of the Gospel message: He that was dead is now alive. The living Christ had demonstrated His power over death, and since we are united with Him, believers are now free from the power of death.

The church was dedicated to God and the proclamation of His Word and "great grace was upon them all" (Acts 4:33). The phrase "great grace" refers to the unmerited goodwill of God. God demonstrates His goodwill through the expressions of His loving kindness to His people and the manifestations of His power through His people.

One aspect of God's grace was His confirmation of the apostles' preaching with many "wonders and signs" (Acts 2:43). These were God's people, and He signaled to the world that His presence was among them. Luke writes, "fear came upon every soul" (v. 43). Not only did the believers look to God with reverent awe, but those who witnessed the wonders of their changed lives and the miraculous signs done through the apostles regarded the entire congregation with respectful admiration.

We know that the religious leaders hated the upstart church, but the common people respected what they saw happening in their midst and feared antagonizing them because the presence and power of God were evident. This fear and respect soon turned into favor, and the people responded to them with a gracious and friendly attitude.

When the power and presence of God are evident in the life of a church, the community around them is drawn to it. A healthy Christian church praises God both with its voice and its deeds. As we love God and love each other, our love should naturally flow out to our community. As we share our lives and our testimonies with nonchurch members of our community, we gain the favor of many; and once we've gained their favor, we can point them toward Jesus.

3. The Church Multiplied (v. 47)

As the church was faithful in its mission, God demonstrated His faithfulness to the church. Not only did God continuously provide for the needs of His people, He "added to the church daily such as should be saved" (Acts 2:47). The church did its job, and God did His.

God has never asked His people to go out and increase the number of members in the church. Our command is to make disciples and teach (Matthew 28:19-20). We teach about Jesus with our lives and proclaim His truth with our lips. God uses our words and character to draw people to Him.

God converts people from sinners to saints, and He adds them to the body of Christ. We teach them His truth and they become Christ's disciples. Church growth happens in the same manner as the individual growth and prosperity of believers. The apostle Matthew summarized the teaching like this: "But seek first his kingdom and his righteousness, and all these things will be given to you as well" (Matthew 6:33, NIV). The church seeks God's righteousness and God adds to the church.

SEARCH THE SCRIPTURES

1. The church took on the responsibility of meeting the material needs of some of its people. How did they finance this ministry and how did they determine what a person received (Acts 2:45)?

2. How often did the first Christians attend meetings and share their homes and hospitality (v. 46)?

3. The early church experienced phenomenal growth. Who was responsible for adding people to the church (v. 47)?

4. What words and/or phrases in Acts 2:47 and 4:32 demonstrate the love and unity among the new Christians?

DISCUSS THE MEANING

1. The church assumed the responsibility of meeting the needs of its less fortunate members. Should our modern-day churches assume this responsibility? If so, how should this ministry be funded? Should this ministry be more than just a "giveaway" program? If so, what programs would you suggest?

2. Lifestyle and active evangelism were key elements of the early church. Do you believe that every Christian is called to active evangelism, or are some people called on just to let the light of their lives shine?

LESSON IN OUR SOCIETY

During the reconstruction period and through the period of Jim Crow segregation, the church was the spiritual, social, and political center of the Black community. In modern times, the church has become far less influential. What are some of the social and political factors that may have contributed to this decline? What are some of the

implications of the church's decline in influence? What can the church do to improve its relevance to Black society?

MAKE IT HAPPEN

Spend some time this week contemplating the lives of the early Christians. Think about their devotion to the apostles' doctrine, their commitment to the church, and the willing sacrifices they made for each other. Ask God to point out areas where you and your church may need to improve. Then determine to work on those areas. Be prepared to share your experiences with the class next week.

FOLLOW THE SPIRIT

What God wants me to do:

_____

_____

REMEMBER YOUR THOUGHTS

Special insights I have learned:

_____

_____

MORE LIGHT ON THE TEXT
Acts 2:43-47; 4:32-35

43 And fear came upon every soul: and many wonders and signs were done by the apostles.

The verb "came" (Gk. *ginomai*, **ghin'-om-ahee**) is used here as a descriptive verb describing what was happening again and again (in a continuous and habitual way).

The word "fear" (Gk. *phobos*, **fob'-os**) denotes awe, not terror. The people were in awe of the visible power of God at work through the disciples. By the Holy Spirit in the name of Jesus, the disciples were now able to perform the same kinds of "wonders and signs" that Jesus had done (cf. Acts 2:19-22; 3:6; John 14:12-14). The "wonders and signs" (Gk. *teras kai semeion*, **ter'-as kahee say-mi'-on**) accredited the messianic office of Jesus and authenticated the apostolic preaching (cf. 2 Corinthians 12:12; Hebrews 2:1-4). Just as the miracles performed by Jesus were a sign of the kingdom of God, the miracles done by the disciples had the same purpose.

44 And all that believed were together, and had all things common;

In addition to the expressions of fellowship mentioned in verse 42, the disciples ("all that believed"; Gk. *pisteuo*, **pist-yoo'o**) were together with a deep sense of their unity in Christ. They gave up their private property and "had" (Gk. *echo*, **ekh'-o**, denoting something done habitually) "all things common."

The word "common" (Gk. *koinos*, **koy-nos'**) denotes sharing their possessions, which as we see in verse 45, was an expression of their fellowship.

45 And sold their possessions and goods, and parted them to all men, as every man had need.

Property was regarded, not as private, but as held in trust from God to be donated for the common good. Those with real estate (Gk. *ktenos*, **ktay'-nos**, meaning "land") as well as those who had more portable possessions (Gk. *huparxis*, **hoop'-arx-is**, literally meaning "wealth" or "movable" possessions) began to sell their belongings and divide the proceeds among the members of the community according to their individual needs (Gk. *chreia*, **khri'-ah,** followed by *echo*, **ekh'-o,** referring to the need that was habitually there among the community members). This voluntary sharing of possessions was based on the deep sense of fellowship and unity of the Spirit that was exceptionally active. The attempt to maintain communal life was plagued with serious difficulties as soon as the flame began to burn a little lower (Acts 4:32–5:11).

46 And they, continuing daily with one accord in the temple, and breaking bread from house to house, did eat their meat with gladness and singleness of heart,

The daily practice of the disciples involved meeting in the temple for public worship and witness. They also met in each other's homes for fellowship meals and the breaking of bread in accordance with Jesus' ordinance. They were doing these practices regularly, or "continuing" (Gk. *proskartereo*, **pros-kar-ter-eh'-o**) "daily" or by day (Gk. *kata hemera*, **kat-ah' hay-mer'-ah**). The expression "with one accord" (Gk. *homothumadon*, **hom-oth-oo-mad-on'**) means in "unanimity."

Within the fellowship, there was a spirit of joy and generosity of heart. The believers are described as having "gladness" (Gk. *agalliasis*, **ag-al-lee'-as-is,** which means "extreme joy") and "singleness of heart" (Gk. *aphelotes kardia*, **af-el-ot'-ace kar-dee'-ah**) literally meaning "in exultation and sincerity of heart" (cf. Galatians 5:22). Their Spirit-filled worship was a joyful celebration of the mighty acts of God through Jesus.

47 Praising God, and having favour with all the people. And the Lord added to the church daily such as should be saved.

The believers enjoyed great popularity and favor with all the people because of the quality of their fellowship, and they ascribed all glory to God.

The disciples were not so preoccupied with studying the Word of God and fellowshiping that they forgot about bringing the Gospel to others. The Gospel was spreading through the witness of the disciples by the power of the Holy Spirit. Their numbers were constantly increasing as more people were added by the Lord to the new community. The Lord added to the church, no doubt, through the preaching and the impressive life example of the disciples. The verb "add" (Gk. *prostithemi*, **pros-tith'-ay-mee**) here means "kept adding." The increase was not sporadic; it was continuous and daily. Their worship and proclamation were the natural overflow of hearts full of the Holy Spirit.

The Greek verb translated as "should be saved" (Gk. *sozo*, **sode'-zo**) means "those who were being saved."

4:32 And the multitude of them that believed were of one heart and of one soul: neither said any of them that ought of the things which he possessed was his own; but they had all things common.

The fullness of the Spirit was expressed in words and in deeds. The word "multitude" (Gk. *plethos*, **play'-thos**) has an ordinary meaning and an acquired sense of a civic or religious community. Its acquired meaning is more usually rendered as "assembly" (Gk. *ekklesia*, **ek-klay-see'-ah;** cf. Acts 5:11; 6:2; 15:12, 30). The assembly of believers formed a close-knit group. They were together in heart and mind. The sharing of possessions was but one expression of their unity.

The early believers showed a remarkable unanimity as expressed in their attitude toward private property. Each member of the new community regarded his private estate as being at the disposal of the community.

33 And with great power gave the apostles witness of the resurrection of the Lord Jesus: and great grace was upon them all.

Verse 33 should be linked to verse 31. In verse 31, we are told that the disciples were filled with the Holy Spirit in answer to their prayers. The immediate result was that they spoke the Word of God boldly and witnessed to the resurrection of the Lord Jesus with great power (Gk. *dunamis,* **doo'-nam-is,** which literally means "dynamite"). No one but the Holy Spirit could have enabled the disciples to give such a powerful testimony.

Their witness (Gk. *marturion,* **mar-too'-ree-on,** from which we get the English word "martyr") was characterized with boldness and great power. They were ready to lay down their lives (cf. Acts 7; 12). God's grace was sustaining them, and they were all held in high esteem (Gk. *charis,* **khar'-ece,** meaning "grace" or "favor").

34 Neither was there any among them that lacked: for as many as were possessors of lands or houses sold them, and brought the prices of the things that were sold,

Members of the new community who had "lands and houses" voluntarily sold them in order that provision might be more conveniently available to the community for needy members. No one had any room to complain of hunger or want for a time. The word "lack" (Gk. *endees,* **en-deh-ace'**) can be translated as in "need" or "needy." There were no needy people among the members of the new community.

35 And laid them down at the apostles' feet: and distribution was made unto every man according as he had need.

The expression "at the apostles' feet" (Gk. *para tous bosis ton apostolos*) is an indication of the authority of the apostles. The expression conveys the thought of submission to the care and authority of someone or the idea of reverence and thankfulness. The apostles, as respected community leaders, received the freewill offerings that were brought. Under their authority, the distribution was made according to each member's needs. By their actions, we have a good example of sacrificial giving and care of the needy in an assembly (cf. Deuteronomy 15:4; Luke 4:18; 6:20; 7:22).

DAILY BIBLE READINGS

M: Share with Those in Need
Deuteronomy 15:4-8
T: Come to an Abundant Life
Isaiah 55:1-7
W: The Parable of the Rich Fool
Luke 12:13-21
T: Do Not Worry About Possessions
Luke 12:22-24
F: The Believers Grow in Faith Together
Acts 2:43-47
S: The Believers Share Their Possessions
Acts 4:32-37
S: Many Sick People Are Cured
Acts 5:12-16

TEACHING TIPS

September 18
Bible Study Guide 3

1. Words You Should Know

A. Feet and ankle bones (Acts 3:7) *basis kai sphuron* (Gk.)—The lower part of the body lying beneath the leg, upon which the leg rests. This precise description reflects the medical knowledge of the author.

B. Received strength (v. 7) *stereoo* (Gk.)—To strengthen or make firm or solid. In medical language, the phrase usually refers to bones.

2. Teacher Preparation

A. Begin preparing by reading through all the FOCAL VERSES. Then read through the entire BIBLE STUDY GUIDE for this lesson.

B. Review the TEACHING TIPS, and adapt the lesson to fit the needs of your class.

3. Starting the Lesson

A. Have a student lead the class in prayer, using the LESSON AIM.

B. Ask the students to share their experiences from last week's MAKE IT HAPPEN assignment and tell what they learned from their DAILY BIBLE READINGS during the week.

C. Begin the class by assigning one of the students to read today's IN FOCUS story.

D. Assign two students to read the FOCAL VERSES according to the AT-A-GLANCE outline.

4. Getting into the Lesson

A. The BACKGROUND section will help set the stage for today's lesson. Have the students read the section silently and write down their thoughts in the REMEMBER YOUR THOUGHTS section.

B. Refer to the SEARCH THE SCRIPTURES questions as you begin the discussion of the lesson.

C. Discuss the information in THE PEOPLE, PLACES, AND TIMES to help the students understand the common diseases of the time and how God used healings as a means to draw people to Him.

5. Relating the Lesson to Life

A. Use the DISCUSS THE MEANING questions to help the students understand how the lesson applies to the situations they face today.

B. The LESSON IN OUR SOCIETY section will also help the students see the parallels with their present-day situation. After reading this section, discuss the practicality of modern medicine and divine healing.

6. Arousing Action

A. Sum up the lesson with the KEEP IN MIND verse. Have the students read it in unison, then encourage them to apply the verse to their everyday lives.

B. Challenge the students to follow through on the MAKE IT HAPPEN assignment. This will help them incorporate the biblical truths in their lives as they make a personal commitment to love the Lord and other people.

C. Ask the students to read the DAILY BIBLE READINGS for the week. Explain that it will help them put what they have learned into action and keep them in the Scriptures during the week.

D. Close the class with prayer, thanking the Lord for the love and mercy that He has shown to the students this week.

WORSHIP GUIDE

For the Superintendent or Teacher
Theme: Peter and John Heal a Lame Man
Theme Song: "Old Time Power"
Scripture: Acts 3:6
Song: "The Great Physician"
Meditation: Thank You, Lord, for Your
faithfulness and commitment to my life.
Use me, Lord, like you used the disciples
in the early church to glorify Your name
and build Your church. In Jesus' name.
Amen.

PETER AND JOHN HEAL A LAME MAN

Bible Background • ACTS 3:1–26
Printed Text • ACTS 3:1–16
Devotional Reading • LUKE 7:18–23

LESSON AIM

By the end of the lesson, we will:

KNOW the story of Peter healing the lame beggar;

BE CONVINCED of the Holy Spirit's power to assist all believers; and

DECIDE to rely on the Holy Spirit to help us bring spiritual, emotional, or physical healing to someone this week.

KEEP IN MIND

"Then Peter said, Silver and gold have I none; but such as I have give I thee: In the name of Jesus Christ of Nazareth rise up and walk" (Acts 3:6).

FOCAL VERSES

Acts 3:1 Now Peter and John went up together into the temple at the hour of prayer, being the ninth hour.

2 And a certain man lame from his mother's womb was carried, whom they laid daily at the gate of the temple which is called Beautiful, to ask alms of them that entered into the temple;

3 Who seeing Peter and John about to go into the temple asked an alms.

4 And Peter, fastening his eyes upon him with John, said, Look on us.

5 And he gave heed unto them, expecting to receive something of them.

6 Then Peter said, Silver and gold have I none; but such as I have give I thee: In the name of Jesus

LESSON OVERVIEW

LESSON AIM
KEEP IN MIND
FOCAL VERSES
IN FOCUS
THE PEOPLE, PLACES, AND TIMES
BACKGROUND
AT-A-GLANCE
IN DEPTH
SEARCH THE SCRIPTURES
DISCUSS THE MEANING
LESSON IN OUR SOCIETY
MAKE IT HAPPEN
FOLLOW THE SPIRIT
REMEMBER YOUR THOUGHTS
MORE LIGHT ON THE TEXT
DAILY BIBLE READINGS

Christ of Nazareth rise up and walk.

7 And he took him by the right hand, and lifted him up: and immediately his feet and ankle bones received strength.

8 And he leaping up stood, and walked, and entered with them into the temple, walking, and leaping, and praising God.

9 And all the people saw him walking and praising God:

10 And they knew that it was he which sat for alms at the Beautiful gate of the temple: and they were filled with wonder and amazement at that which had happened unto him.

11 And as the lame man which was healed held Peter and John, all the people ran together unto them in the porch that is called Solomon's, greatly wondering.

12 And when Peter saw it, he answered unto the people, Ye men of Israel, why marvel ye at this? or why look ye so earnestly on us, as though by our own power or holiness we had made this man to walk?

13 The God of Abraham, and of Isaac, and of Jacob, the God of our fathers, hath glorified his Son Jesus; whom ye delivered up, and denied him in the presence of Pilate, when he was determined to let him go.

14 But ye denied the Holy One and the Just,

and desired a murderer to be granted unto you;

15 And killed the Prince of life, whom God hath raised from the dead; whereof we are witnesses.

16 And his name through faith in his name hath made this man strong, whom ye see and know: yea, the faith which is by him hath given him this perfect soundness in the presence of you all.

IN FOCUS

Pastor Thornton and his wife, Paula, both in their 60's, barely escaped death when a jeep pursued by police smashed into their bedroom at 3 a.m. and showered them with plaster and bricks.

Firefighters on the scene were amazed the sleeping couple survived. Paula was lying underneath the vehicle, untouched. However, Pastor Thornton's back was crushed beneath a large section of the bedroom wall. In the hospital, doctors declared that he would never walk again because his spine had been severely damaged in the accident.

Upon hearing the news, Pastor Thornton began to pray aloud. His thunderous voice startled the doctors. "God, your Word says, 'Many are the afflictions of the righteous, but the Lord delivers him from ALL of them.' I ask you to heal my body in the name of Jesus!" said Pastor Thornton.

The couple and their church family continued to pray for many months as Pastor Thornton continued in therapy. On the anniversary of the accident, Paula told her wheelchair-bound husband that she had faith in God and believed that he would walk again. As they began to pray together, Pastor Thornton noticed a slight sensation in his legs—a feeling he hadn't had in over a year. Excited about the sensation in his legs, he began to lift his leg slightly from the chair using both his hands. He believed the sensation was a sign that God was moving his spine into proper alignment.

Day after day, at least once a day, he and his wife prayed. And day after day, during regular therapy sessions, Pastor Thornton lifted his legs. One year later, God had healed him—Pastor Thornton rose from his wheelchair and walked!

Certainly God has the power and often heals at the request of His children. He does not always heal, but we are always free to pray for healing and rejoice when it happens.

In our lesson this week, we will observe God's power to heal at work through Peter.

THE PEOPLE, PLACES, AND TIMES

Sickness and Disease. The first mention of disease in Scripture occurs when the king of Egypt takes Abraham's wife into his harem (Genesis 12:17), but disease has plagued humanity since the fall in Eden. Diseases often affected the history of Israel and the ministry of Jesus. The following list describes some of the diseases and physical abnormalities that affected the people of Israel and the world.

Blindness. God placed a curse on anyone who misdirected a blind person (Deuteronomy 27:18). The first recorded person to suffer gradual loss of sight was Isaac (Genesis 27:1). Jesus explained that a part of His ministry entailed restoring sight to the blind (Luke 4:18), and He healed many blind people (John 9:1-41; Mark 8:22-25; Matthew 20:30-34).

Female Disorders. Mosaic Law declared that any woman suffering from menstrual problems be considered unclean (Leviticus 15:25). Luke describes one such woman, who had suffered menstrual bleeding for 12 years. She touched the hem of Jesus' garment and was immediately healed.

Leprosy. This was one of the most feared diseases. Until modern times, the only treatment for leprosy was isolation and ostracism from the community at large. The ancient Jews were instructed to cast the leper out of the camp (Leviticus 13:46). By the time of Jesus, leprosy was thought to result from moral corruption. Rather than ostracize these poor souls, Jesus reached out to them. He demonstrated His compassion for the lowest members of society by touching and healing them (Matthew 8:1-4; Mark 1:40-45; Luke 5:12-14).

Palsy. A term refering to all forms of paralysis.

Jesus healed a paralyzed man in Capernaum (Mark 2:1-12) and the apostles also healed those who suffered from this condition (Acts 8:7; 9:33-34).

BACKGROUND

The experience at Pentecost gave the apostles a new confidence in the power of Christ. They had witnessed the death and resurrection of Christ. For 40 days after His resurrection, Jesus had given them final instructions and explained many things to them. However, they still did not understand the spiritual meaning of it all until they were filled with the Holy Spirit. The Holy Spirit not only empowered them, but gave them the gift of faith.

Suddenly many of the things Jesus had said to them became clear. Christ had told them they would receive power, and now that power was within them. Peter, whose fear had previously caused him to deny Christ, jumped up and preached an unrehearsed sermon that was so powerful that 3,000 people came to Christ in one day.

Not only was their preaching anointed, but "many wonders and signs were done by the apostles" (Acts 2:43). The apostles began to understand that they could accomplish miraculous wonders through Christ, who gave them strength (Philippians 4:13).

The Holy Spirit worked through Peter to perform several miraculous healings. In Jerusalem, large crowds brought their sick to the apostles for healing. Some laid their stricken friends and relatives on mats in the streets, hoping that Peter's shadow would fall on them as he passed by (Acts 5:15-16). At a city called Lydda, Peter healed a paralytic named Aeneas, who had been bedridden for eight years (9:32-35). In Joppa, he raised a woman named Dorcas from the dead (vv. 36-43).

The end result of these miraculous healings was that many people believed in Christ and turned to Him. Peter gave his all to Christ, and Christ used him mightily to build His church. The third chapter of Acts contains the first detailed account of the many miraculous healings performed by the infant church.

AT-A-GLANCE

1. The Healing (Acts 3:1-8)
2. The Explanation (vv. 9-16)

IN DEPTH

1. The Healing (Acts 3:1-8)

In chapter 2, Luke briefly mentions that the apostles performed "many wonders and signs" (Acts 2:43). Now he gives a detailed account of one of them. Peter and John are often mentioned together in Scripture (Luke 5:10; 22:8; John 20:3; Acts 8:14). Here, the two are going to the temple for prayer. Jews customarily reserved three times for prayer: in the morning at 9:00 a.m., in the afternoon at 3:00 p.m., and in the evening at sunset. Devout Jews often went to the temple at these times to pray.

Luke tells us that on this particular day, Peter and John were on their way to the temple "at the hour of prayer, being the ninth hour" for the afternoon prayer. They were making their way from the Upper Room to the temple through the gate called Beautiful. There were nine temple gates, and this gate was probably on the east side of the building leading from the Court of Gentiles into the women's court. The doors of this entrance were 60 feet high and were made from Corinthian bronze that was highly polished to look like gold. In the sunshine, the gate radiated with a spectacular beauty.

Because the gate called Beautiful was one of the most popular entrances to the temple, many people passed through it on their way to worship. The giving of alms or charity was considered praiseworthy, so many beggars would place themselves near the heavily traveled gate where pious Jews on their way to prayer would see them. As Peter and John approached the gate and joined thousands of other worshipers who walked past the scores of beggars calling out for alms, their attention was suddenly drawn to "a certain [lame] man" (3:2). This man was over 40 years old (4:22), and he had been crippled from birth.

Peter looked at the man intently. His mind may

have wandered back to the time when Jesus healed a lame man by the pool of Bethesda. That man had suffered an injury or disease that had left him lame for 38 years. He had no hope of ever walking again. Jesus had compassion on the man and commanded him, "'Rise, take up thy bed, and walk,' and immediately the man was made whole" (John 5:8-9).

Peter and John's compassion for the poor beggar provided an opportunity for them to imitate their Lord and Saviour. Born with misaligned bones in his feet and ankles, he had never been able to stand. Jesus promised that His disciples would do greater works than He did and that whatever they asked in His name, He would do it (John 14:13). He had taught them that with a very small amount of faith they were capable of moving mountains (Matthew 17:20).

Peter commanded, "Look on us" (Acts 3:4). He wanted the man's complete attention. The beggar did as he was told, expecting to be rewarded for his obedience. But Peter's next words deflated the man's hopes: "Silver and gold have I none..." (v. 6). Onlookers may have thought, "If the two men didn't have any money to give him, why are they wasting his time when he could be soliciting others? Is this some kind of cruel joke?" However, many times Christians ask God for the things they want, when God desires to give them the things they need! Peter probably noticed the expression on the man's face, but he continued, "but such as I have give I thee: In the name of Jesus Christ of Nazareth rise up and walk" (v. 6).

"In the name of Jesus" means by the authority of Jesus. Jesus had promised to do whatever was asked in His name. Now Peter was directing the power of the Holy Spirit into the unseen place of the man's limbs and mind. The bones would have to be realigned; socket and joint would have to be joined together. Peter reached out, took the man's hand, and helped him up. The beggar, who had felt the power of God mending his bones, grabbed Peter's hand, leaped to his feet, and miraculously began walking without ever learning how. In excitement, the newly healed man began walking and leaping and praising God.

2. The Explanation (vv. 9-16)

The beggar went along with Peter and John into the temple court, jumping and loudly praising God. His antics drew the attention of worshipers in the temple. "And all the people saw him walking and praising God" (v. 9). Many of them recognized the excited man as the beggar who always sat outside the Beautiful gate begging for alms. They knew he had been born lame. How could he possibly be walking and jumping? They were amazed; the impossible had happened, and they were witnesses to it.

After the prayer and sacrifice ended, Peter, John, and the healed man left the inner court and made their way to Solomon's Porch on the east side of the temple. This was the area where Jesus had ministered (John 10:23) and where the church worshiped (Acts 5:12). Eagerly anticipating an explanation of the man's healing, a huge crowd grew around the three men.

Just as he had done on the Day of Pentecost, Peter proclaimed the Gospel to them and began by directing all credit for the miracle to Jesus. Peter proclaimed, "Why look ye so earnestly on us, as though by our own power or holiness we had made this man to walk?" (3:12). He explained that what they were witnessing was the result of the God of their forefathers glorifying His Son.

He reiterated how the Jews had rejected Jesus and turned Him over to the Romans for trial. When they were offered another chance to redeem themselves, they demanded that a murderer be released instead of Jesus. Peter declared they had "killed the Prince of life" (Acts 3:15).

The names that Peter used to describe Jesus are testaments to His deity. Peter called Him the "Holy One." This term was used for the majesty, glory, and purity of God. The title "just" was used to affirm the perfect harmony between God's nature and His acts. The phrase "Prince of Life" is also translated as "author of life" (NIV) and alludes to divine creative power. "All things were made by him; and without him was not any thing made that was made" (John 1:3). Christ is the source of life and the Creator of all things.

Peter explained that the secret to the man's healing was "faith in his name" (Acts 3:16). A man's name represented his authority, power, and character. By using Jesus' name, Peter demonstrated to the world who it was that gave the authority and the power to accomplish miraculous works. It was never a question of what the apostles could do, but rather what God could do through them.

What was true of the apostles in the early church is still true for us today. It is not what we can do for God, but what God can do through us. Jesus said, "If you remain in me and my words remain in you, ask whatever you wish, and it will be given you" (John 15:7, NIV). When we compassionately reach out to people under the authority of Jesus, He will accomplish the impossible through us.

SEARCH THE SCRIPTURES

1. Why were Peter and John going to the temple (Acts 3:1)?

2. At which temple gate did the lame man sit, and what was his purpose (v. 2)?

3. Why was the lame man initially disappointed (v. 5)?

4. In whose authority did Peter command the man to rise and be healed (v. 6)?

5. Who received credit for the man's healing?

DISCUSS THE MEANING

1. Beggars and street people are common sights on our city streets. As Christians, do we have any obligation to help them or contribute our money to them? How do we determine when and when not to give? Is it better just to give to organizations that help them?

2. Many people believe that healing and other miracles were only for the beginning of the church age. What is your opinion? If healing is still relevant for today's church, should people flock to well-known healers or follow the Bible's teaching to take our needs to the elders of the local church?

LESSON IN OUR SOCIETY

We live in a crippled society. It has been reported that more than 60 percent of the American population suffers from stress-related diseases, such as hypertension. The lame man of Acts 3 is a picture of the world, lying at the door of God, seeking peace. These unfortunate people believe they can eliminate the longing in their souls with material things. However, what is truly needed is what Peter and John gave the lame man—not silver or gold, but the power to walk in new life under the authority of Jesus. Every soul that turns to Christ improves our community.

MAKE IT HAPPEN

There are many sick and lonely people in our communities and churches. This week, demonstrate your compassion by reaching out to an elderly or sick person. If your church has a nursing home ministry, volunteer to join them for a visit. Or maybe just invite an elderly friend or neighbor out to lunch. Remember to call the members of your congregation who have been ill and let them know you're thinking about them. Be prepared to share your experiences next week.

FOLLOW THE SPIRIT

What God wants me to do:

_____

_____

REMEMBER YOUR THOUGHTS

Special insights I have learned:

_____

_____

MORE LIGHT ON THE TEXT
Acts 3:1-16

1 Now Peter and John went up together into the temple at the hour of prayer, being the ninth hour.

John is most likely the disciple who, with Peter and James, formed an inner circle within the 12 disciples of Jesus (cf. Matthew 17:1; Mark 14:33). One afternoon, John was going with Peter to the temple for prayer service. Daniel 6:10 mentions the Jewish custom of three daily prayers.

The verb "went up" (Gk. *anabaino*, **an-ab-ah'-ee-no**) literally means "were going up," referring to an action during which something happened. Peter and John's arrival at the temple coincided with the arrival of the crippled man (Acts 3:2).

The temple had a very high status in the life of Jerusalem; hence, worshipers went "up" to it. The time was "the ninth hour" (Gk. *ennatos*, **en'-nat-os**, literally, "the ninth"), which is about 3 p.m.

2 And a certain man lame from his mother's womb was carried, whom they laid daily at the gate of the temple which is called Beautiful, to ask alms of them that entered into the temple;

A man born crippled was being brought daily to lie at the temple gate. He was carried to the temple gate presumably by relatives or friends so that he could beg from worshipers going into the temple.

The temple's gate called "Beautiful" (Gk. *horaios*, **ho-rah'-yos**) seemed to have been to the east of the temple, adjacent to Solomon's portico (cf. v. 11).

3 Who seeing Peter and John about to go into the temple asked an alms.

The crippled man, seeing Peter and John about to enter the temple, asked for an alm. The Greek uses two verbs to convey the crippled man's request, "asked to receive" (Gk. *erotao*, **er-o-tah'-o** and *lambano*, **lam-ban'-o**) an alm. The first verb, "ask," is the action of asking until what is asked for is granted by another. The second verb "receive" completes the action expressed in the first verb ("ask").

4 And Peter, fastening his eyes upon him with John, said, Look on us.

Peter and John stopped and looked straight at him (Gk. *atenizo*, **at-en-id'-zo,** meaning to fix one's eyes on or to look intently at). Peter gave him two commands. The first was "look on us" (Gk. *blepo heis hemas*, **blep'-o hice hay-mas'**). We do not know the exact reason for Peter's command. Was he trying to get the man's whole attention since the man evidently was only expecting an alm? Was he trying to see if the man was a worthless beggar? Was he checking to see if the man had faith to be healed (Acts 3:16; 14:9; Matthew 9:2, 28-29)? The narrative does not expressly mention that faith was required of the man.

5 And he gave heed unto them, expecting to receive something of them.

The crippled man looked at (Gk. *epecho*, **ep-ekh'-o**) or paid attention to Peter and John, expecting to get something from them.

6 Then Peter said, Silver and gold have I none; but such as I have give I thee: In the name of Jesus Christ of Nazareth rise up and walk.

Then Peter gave him a second command. He had something better to give him than money: "in the name of Jesus Christ of Nazareth rise up and walk." The expression "in the name" (Gk. *en onoma*, **en on'-om-ah**) means "in the power of" or "by the authority of." The power of Jesus was called for by this use of His name (cf. Acts 16:18). It is a major theme of this passage. "The name" is equivalent to the Person of the risen Lord, Jesus Christ, the true author of this miracle (4:10, 30).

7 And he took him by the right hand, and lifted him up: and immediately his feet and ankle bones received strength.

Peter did not stand back and watch the man struggle to his feet. He leaned forward and "he took him by the right hand and lifted him up." Instantly the man received something more wonderful and more valuable than the largest gift of alms that a charitable worshiper had ever given him. His feet and ankles were made strong. The verb translated as "received strength" (Gk. *stereoo*, **ster-eh-o'-o**, which means "was made firm") is in the passive voice, indicating that the strength the crippled man received was from a source outside himself. The power by which Jesus had healed those who were lame during His ministry was still present.

8 And he leaping up stood, and walked, and entered with them into the temple, walking, and leaping, and praising God.

The man's feet and ankles became so strong that he jumped up in joy and began to walk. Three verbs are used here to describe the progressive steps of the man's recovery: leaping up, stood, and walked. The first verb, "leaping" (Gk. *exallomai*, **ex-al'-lom-ahee**), or "jumping," is used to strengthen the second verb "stood" (Gk. *histemi*, **his'-tay-mee**). The third verb, "walked" (Gk. *peripateo*, **per-ee-pat-eh'-o**), expresses a continued action; the man began to walk and did not stop walking.

The cripple walking is part of the fulfillment of Isaiah's prophecy regarding the messianic age when the lame would leap like a hart (Isaiah 35:5-6; Matthew 11:4ff; Luke 7:22ff; Acts 2:22). The man accompanied the apostles into the temple walking, jumping, and praising God.

9 And all the people saw him walking and praising God:

Many people witnessed the miraculous healing of the man who was crippled from birth. They saw him "walking and praising God." For the third time, the man is described as walking, as if to emphasize the incredible fact that his poor crippled legs were fully operational for the first time.

10 And they knew that it was he which sat for alms at the Beautiful gate of the temple: and they were filled with wonder and amazement at that which had happened unto him.

The people recognized the man as the crippled beggar who used to lie at the Beautiful gate. They knew that there was nothing false about his lameness, for he had been born crippled. "They were filled with wonder and amazement" at the spectacle. The word "amazement" (Gk. *ekstasis*, **ek'-stas-is,** from which we get the English word "ecstasy") literally means to be out of one's senses.

11 And as the lame man which was healed held Peter and John, all the people ran together unto them in the porch that is called Solomon's, greatly wondering.

The lame man was holding on to Peter and John and unwilling to let them get away from him. While he was holding on to the two apostles, the crowd, astonished beyond measure, "ran together unto them in the porch that is called Solomon's." This porch seems to have been a place where the disciples usually gathered together (Acts 5:12; John 10:23).

12 And when Peter saw it, he answered unto the people, Ye men of Israel, why marvel ye at this? or why look ye so earnestly on us, as though by our own power or holiness we had made this man to walk?

Peter seized the opportunity to present the Gospel message. He addressed the crowd as "men

of Israel," or literally, "man, Israelites" (Gk. *aner Isra´lit´s,* **an'-ayr is-rah-ale-ee'-tace**). The expression was a title of honor and a sacred name. It gradually gave place to the term "Jew."

Peter told the crowd that the man was not healed by any power or piety that he and John possessed. It was not dependent on their claim of personal holiness (Gk. *eusebeia,* **yoo-seb'-i-ah**).

The verb "to walk" used with the genitive article "the" (Gk. *tou,* **too**) expresses a purpose or a result. The man did not walk as the result of the apostles' power or their piety. It is clearly emphasized that the apostles by themselves could not enable this man to walk.

13 The God of Abraham, and of Isaac, and of Jacob, the God of our fathers, hath glorified his Son Jesus; whom ye delivered up, and denied him in the presence of Pilate, when he was determined to let him go.

In addressing the crowd, Peter chose his words wisely. He wanted not only to gain their attention but also to show that he identified himself with the nation and the hope of Israel. He saw in Jesus a direct continuity with the Old Testament, the fulfillment of the promise to their forefathers. The expression "God of our fathers" (Gk. *ho theos ho pater hemon,* **h' theh'-os h' pat-ayr' hay-mone'**) literally means "the God of the fathers of us." It is a title of God (Exodus 3:6) designed to emphasize the seriousness of the crime of which the crowd had been guilty. It is used in contrast with the honor (Gk. *doxazo,* **dox-ad'-zo,** glorify or honor) that God had given to His Son (Gk. *pais,* **paheece;** which means either "child" or "servant") Jesus.

14 But ye denied the Holy One and the Just, and desired a murderer to be granted unto you;

Pilate, the Roman governor, was willing to release Jesus, but the men of Israel denied Him freedom (Luke 23:22-24). The expression "the Holy One and Just" (Gk. *hagios,* **hag'-ee-os,** and *dikaios,* **dik'-ah-yos**) is a messianic title for Jesus, which occurs again in Acts 7:52 and 22:14. It no doubt derived from Old Testament references such as 2 Kings 4:9 (cf. Mark 1:24; Luke 4:34; 1 John 2:20), 2 Samuel 23:3, and Isaiah 53:11 (cf.

Acts 7:52; 22:14; 1 John 2:1). It is in strong opposition to the word "murderer" (Gk. *phoneuos*, **fon-yoo-o**), used for the person who was released instead of Jesus. These men of Israel had refused to acknowledge Jesus as their divinely appointed King and Saviour; instead, they had asked that a condemned murderer, Barabbas, be released (Luke 23:18-19).

15 And killed the Prince of life, whom God hath raised from the dead; whereof we are witnesses.

In so doing, they put the very "Prince of life" to death (an amazing paradox!). The expression "the Prince of life" (Gk. *archegos zoe,* **ar-khay-gos' dzo-ay'**) denotes Christ as the source of life and salvation (cf. Hebrews 2:10; Acts 5:31). It is also a messianic title for Jesus, meaning that He is the giver of the new life that overcomes death.

Although they killed Him, God restored Him to life again (Gk. *egeiro*, **eg-i'-ro**). Peter, John, and the apostles had been witnesses to Jesus' resurrection.

Here, Peter emphasizes the contrast between men's treatment of Jesus and God's.

16 And his name through faith in his name hath made this man strong, whom ye see and know: yea, the faith which is by him hath given him this perfect soundness in the presence of you all.

In order to explain how the man had been healed, Peter referred to the death and resurrection of Christ. God had honored Jesus, shown the divine nature of His Son (or Servant), and raised Him from the dead. He also further confirmed Jesus' power by this sign—the healing of the man born crippled—which all had seen.

The man had been healed by faith in the power of the name of the exalted Messiah, Jesus (the faith of the man who was healed as well as the faith of the apostles may be implied; cf. v. 5; Luke 17:6; 1 Corinthians 12:9; 13:2). From His place of exaltation, Jesus had endowed His disciples with power to act in His name and to perform mighty works just like those He had performed in the days of His bodily presence among them.

Peter affirmed that the man born crippled had been cured by "the faith which is by him." The expression "faith which is by him" indicates that such faith comes from Jesus (Hebrews 12:2); through His Spirit, Jesus is the object and source of faith (1 Corinthians 12:9). It is the faith that comes through Him, aroused by Him in those who grasp the implication of His name. The disciples had been channels of the power of Christ. It is through His name, the name of the once humbled and now glorified Servant of God, that this man had been cured.

DAILY BIBLE READINGS

M: Jesus Tells of His Healing Power
Luke 7:18-23

T: The Twelve Receive Power to Heal
Luke 9:1-6

W: Jesus Rebukes a Demon
Luke 4:31-37

T: A Beggar Asks for Alms
Acts 3:1-5

F: A Man is Healed
Acts 3:6-10

S: Peter Speaks to the People
Acts 3:11-16

S: Peter Tells the People to Repent
Acts 3:17-26

TEACHING TIPS

September 25
Bible Study 4

1. Words You Should Know

A. Chief priests (Acts 4:23) *archiereus* (Gk.)—The Jewish chief priests offered gifts and sacrifices for the people's sins and entered the Holy of Holies, appearing before the presence of God to make intercession for the people. In like manner, Christ is the Chief Priest of believers.

B. [Sovereign] Lord (v. 24) *despotes* (Gk.)—Despot, master, or supreme authority. Denotes the supreme universal authority.

2. Teacher Preparation

A. Begin preparing for the lesson by reading the BIBLE BACKGROUND Scriptures. Then prayerfully meditate on the DEVOTIONAL READINGS.

B. Carefully study the MORE LIGHT ON THE TEXT section so that you will be prepared for the student's questions.

3. Starting the Lesson

A. Assign a student to lead the class in prayer by focusing on the LESSON AIM.

B. Review the highlights of last week's lesson, and ask a few students to share their experience from last week's MAKE IT HAPPEN suggestion.

C. Ask the students to read the IN FOCUS story and relate it to the LESSON AIM objectives.

4. Getting into the Lesson

A. Assign one of the students to read the BACKGROUND information aloud.

B. Discuss THE PEOPLE, PLACES, AND TIMES to help the students understand the ruling body of Israel and their impact on the infant church.

C. Have the students silently read the FOCAL VERSES for today's lesson. After they have read the verses, ask them to identify some of the key points in the verses.

D. Pass out sheets of paper and use the questions in the SEARCH THE SCRIPTURES section as a Bible quiz for those who studied the lesson in advance and as a means of introducing the lesson to those who did not.

5. Relating the Lesson to Life

A. Give your testimony of a time when you were rejected for sharing your faith in God.

B. Break the class into three groups and assign a question from the DISCUSS THE MEANING section to each group. After the group discussions, have them present their conclusions to the class. Or you may discuss the questions as one large group.

C. The LESSON IN OUR SOCIETY section can help the students see how the lesson can be applied to many present-day situations. Ask the students how today's study might give them more courage to share their faith.

6. Arousing Action

A. The MAKE IT HAPPEN section contains a suggestion of what may be done to implement the principles learned. Since it is only a suggestion, you will want to tailor the implementation to your students' specific needs.

B. Challenge the students to read the DAILY BIBLE READINGS for the week.

C. Close the class with prayer.

WORSHIP GUIDE

For the Superintendent or Teacher
Theme: The Time for Boldness
Theme Song: "Tell Me the Old, Old Story!"
Scripture: Acts 4:29
Song: "Rescue the Perishing"
Meditation: Lord, I thank You for Your Holy Spirit, who gives me the boldness to spread the Gospel message. In Jesus, Name. Amen.

THE TIME FOR BOLDNESS

Bible Background • ACTS 4:1–31
Printed Text • ACTS 4:1–4, 23–31
Devotional Reading • EPHESIANS 6:10–20

LESSON AIM

By the end of the lesson, we will:

KNOW true faith is often best revealed during times of adversity;

BE CONVINCED the Holy Spirit can give boldness to share the Gospel in the midst of adversity; and

COMMIT to sharing our faith, even when confronted by adversity and opposition.

KEEP IN MIND

"And now, Lord, behold their threatenings: and grant unto thy servants, that with all boldness they may speak thy word" (Acts 4:29).

FOCAL VERSES

Acts 4:1 And as they spake unto the people, the priests, and the captain of the temple, and the Sadducees, came upon them,

2 Being grieved that they taught the people, and preached through Jesus the resurrection from the dead.

3 And they laid hands on them, and put them in hold unto the next day: for it was now eventide.

4 Howbeit many of them which heard the word believed; and the number of the men was about five thousand.

4:23 And being let go, they went to their own company, and reported all that the chief priests and elders had said unto them.

24 And when they heard that, they lifted up their voice to God with one accord, and said, Lord, thou art God, which hast made heaven, and earth, and the sea, and all that in them is:

25 Who by the mouth of thy servant David hast said, Why did the heathen rage, and the people imagine vain things?

26 The kings of the earth stood up, and the rulers were gathered together against the Lord, and against his Christ.

27 For of a truth against thy holy child Jesus, whom thou hast anointed, both Herod, and Pontius Pilate, with the Gentiles, and the people of Israel, were gathered together,

28 For to do whatsoever thy hand and thy counsel determined before to be done.

29 And now, Lord, behold their threatenings: and grant unto thy servants, that with all boldness they may speak thy word,

30 By stretching forth thine hand to heal; and that signs and wonders may be done by the name of thy holy child Jesus.

31 And when they had prayed, the place was shaken where they were assembled together; and they were all filled with the Holy Ghost, and they spake the word of God with boldness.

LESSON OVERVIEW

LESSON AIM
KEEP IN MIND
FOCAL VERSES
IN FOCUS
THE PEOPLE, PLACES, AND TIMES
BACKGROUND
AT-A-GLANCE
IN DEPTH
SEARCH THE SCRIPTURES
DISCUSS THE MEANING
LESSON IN OUR SOCIETY
MAKE IT HAPPEN
FOLLOW THE SPIRIT
REMEMBER YOUR THOUGHTS
MORE LIGHT ON THE TEXT
DAILY BIBLE READINGS

IN FOCUS

There wasn't much exceptional about Malik and his wife Aisha. A few years earlier, they had been homeless wanderers. Malik had a life-changing encounter with Christ through the Holy Spirit, and now he operated one of the largest homeless shelters in Florida.

One stormy night, the couple sat and talked in their small apartment over the mission. Malik expressed his lack of confidence in speaking in front of a crowd. You see, like Moses, Malik stuttered so badly that he felt compelled to invite local ministers to give the dinnertime sermons.

"But you are empowered, Malik! Just look at the thousands of people who have passed through these doors. When you speak to me you barely stutter at all," Aisha argued.

"In front of strangers, my tongue is too weak. I realize my confidence to do God's will is not in my own ability, but in God's power. You know I— I can't stay focused enough for preaching" Malik stammered. "I will someday maybe, but not now, Aisha."

The next morning, a hurricane tore through Florida with such unpredictable force that every wall in the homeless shelter collapsed. Malik and Aisha stood on the street in the driving rain distributing food and setting up tents. Panicked men, women, and children were all around them.

Aisha handed Malik a megaphone. "Talk to them; they will listen to you," she said.

Malik stood in the driving rain, asking the Holy Spirit to give him the right words to say. Instead of just talking, he preached in the fullness of God's power and shared his faith and testimony.

Over 300 converts offered their lives to Christ. Malik never stuttered again.

The will of the Holy Spirit is often revealed in times of adversity. Today's lesson focuses on how the Holy Spirit gives us boldness to proclaim the Gospel without timidity.

THE PEOPLE, PLACES, AND TIMES

Sanhedrin. In the Gospels and the book of Acts, the Sanhedrin, or council, refers to the Jewish body made up of 71 men, including the high priest. In Jesus' time, the Sanhedrin in Jerusalem served as a court that had authority to maintain the purity of Jewish custom and practice. Because the Old Testament law dealt with every aspect of Jewish personal and social life, as well as religious rituals, the Sanhedrin had wide powers.

The Sanhedrin had the power to punish and even impose the death sentence. However, the death sentence had to be confirmed by the Roman authority that governed the province. It was this council who gave Saul the "authority" to travel to Damascus (in Syria) to bring Christians back to Jerusalem as prisoners (Acts 9:1-2). This was possible because Roman law considered a person to be a citizen of the land of his birth and subject to the laws of his native country regardless of the country in which the person now resided.

The Sanhedrin sentenced Jesus to death. As Jesus predicted, Peter and John were dragged before the council after the healing of the lame man (Acts 4). Later, all 12 apostles were thrown in jail, but during the night an angel unlocked the door and released them. The next day, the Sanhedrin had them rearrested. They were furious that the apostles refused to obey their order not to teach in the name of Jesus; thus, the council wanted to kill them (Acts 5).

Stephen suffered the brunt of their anger when the Sanhedrin falsely charged him with blasphemy and sentenced him to be stoned to death (Acts 6:5-7:59). Later, the apostle Paul was brought before them, but he deftly provoked them to fight among themselves over the subject of resurrection (Acts 23).

BACKGROUND

The Jewish Sanhedrin was made up of 70 members, plus the high priest, who served as the leader. The 70 were divided into three groups: the elders, who were the tribal or family heads of the nation; the scribes, who were experts in the law and oral tradition; and the priests or rulers.

They were further divided into two religious parties: the Pharisees and the Sadducees. The Pharisees were strict conservative, nationalistic leaders who were committed to the preservation of the law and its teachings. They hated Roman domination of their country and looked forward to the resurrection. The Sadducees were the wealthy landowners. The high priest was a Sadducee, as were many of the chief priests in Jerusalem. They claimed to be religious, but they did not accept the traditions of the Pharisees and believed that only the Pentateuch, the first five books of the Bible, was to be followed. The Sadducees denied the existence of angels and demons and preached that there was no resurrection of the dead. Politically, they cozied up to the Romans because their main concern was the preservation of their wealth.

The Sadducees would not be impressed with or excited by any miracle. It would somehow anger the Romans, threaten their own wealth, and validate the preaching of resurrection if it was accompanied by a miracle. Consequently Peter's message of a resurrected Jesus as the source of the lame man's healing would incite them to action.

AT-A-GLANCE

1. The Persecution (Acts 4:1-4)
2. The Prayer (vv. 23-31)

IN DEPTH

1. The Persecution (Acts 4:1-4)

When word of the miracle and the apostles' preaching reached the Sanhedrin, the Sadducees quietly gathered as a group to quell the disturbance. The captain of the guard commanded a small force of soldiers made up primarily of Levite soldiers called the temple guard.

The Sadducees controlled the temple hierarchy and most of the resident priests. They disagreed with the Pharisees on the subject of resurrection, but the Pharisees were less of a threat than the upstart Christians. The death of their leader was supposed to end their sect, but instead they had grown stronger.

On Pentecost, the Christians had caused a commotion and added thousands more to their number, which appeared to be growing daily. Since that time, many miracles had been attributed to them. Now they had healed a lame man outside the temple walls, and people were flocking to them once again. Something had to be done, and the Sadducees were about to take matters into their own hands.

The hostile delegation from the Sanhedrin angrily burst in on the crowd suddenly. The healing of the lame man and the subsequent preaching of the resurrected Christ had stoked their anger. The idea that one person had already been resurrected as a guarantee of future resurrection

for others was a threat to the Sadducees' position as leaders of the people.

Peter and John had come to the temple at "the ninth hour" (Acts 3:1), around 3 p.m. By the time evening had arrived, the men from the Sanhedrin had taken the apostles into custody. Since it would be nightfall before a trial could be convened, the Sadducees had the apostles thrown into jail overnight.

Luke tells us that as a result of the apostles' preaching, 5,000 men believed and were added to their number. This count takes into consideration only the adult male believers who were converted. There was probably an equal number of women believers and many children who believed, so the actual number may well have been in excess of 10,000 people.

2. The Prayer (vv. 23-31)

When Peter and John were released, they immediately went back to the congregation and testified of how the Holy Spirit had enabled them to be bold witnesses for Christ as they faced the idle threats of their accusers. When the believers heard this, they lifted up their voices in unison and launched into a spontaneous, Spirit-inspired praise to God.

First, they praised God for His sovereignty. "'Sovereign Lord,' they said, 'you made the heaven and the earth and the sea and everything in them'" (Acts 4:24, NIV). God is intimately involved in every human experience, and He has overruling control of human events.

Peter, John, and the company of believers realized that God had even predicted the very opposition they were facing. "Why do the nations conspire and the peoples plot in vain?. . . The kings of the earth take their stand and the rulers gather together against the LORD and against His Anointed One" (Psalm 2:1-2; Acts 4:26, NIV). The opposition they were facing had been predicted. The Gentiles, Romans, and the people of Israel had set themselves against the Lord Jesus. It was exactly what God said would happen. "They did what your power and will had decided beforehand should happen" (Acts 4:28, NIV). They had killed Jesus and were now oppressing His people. However, God was using their very opposition to accomplish His purpose! The people tried to thwart God's plan, but God used their opposition to accomplish His will. Through the cross and the resurrection of Jesus, God brought salvation and the growth of His church.

First, He shook the place in which they were praying. In the book of Acts, God frequently uses symbolic acts to manifest Himself. On the Day of Pentecost when the Holy Spirit was poured out, God used three symbols: the mighty rushing of

Peter and John witness with boldness.

Finding strength in the sovereign God, who is in charge of all human events, the disciples made their request: "Now, Lord, consider their threats and enable your servants to speak your word with great boldness" (v. 29, NIV). They were asking God to give them the same boldness He had given to Peter and John. They further petitioned Him to verify their words: "Stretch out your hand to heal and perform miraculous signs and wonders through the name of your holy servant Jesus" (v. 30, NIV). Miraculous healings and signs would confirm the existence of divine power in their ministry, and wonders would cause the observers to wonder about the power behind the miracles.

God answered their prayer in a threefold way.

wind, the appearance of tongues of fire, and the gift of tongues (2:1-4). In this passage, the shaking of the place (4:31) is God's symbolic answer to the disciples' prayer. He would shake Jerusalem and the world with the message they were proclaiming.

God is still at work in society through His church. He is still enabling His people to do what the disciples of the early church did to proclaim God's Word with boldness. It is a message that will bring new life to a dying world. Just as they were filled with the Holy Spirit and "spoke the word with all boldness," we, too, can proclaim a message that will shake the foundations of modern society and change our communities.

SEARCH THE SCRIPTURES

1. What three groups joined forces to arrest Peter and John while they were preaching (Acts 4:1)?

2. How many new converts joined the church as a result of the miracle and Peter's preaching (v. 3)?

3. What was the response of the believers to Peter and John's testimony after they were released (v. 24)?

4. What blessing did the believers request for themselves to cope with the persecution they were facing (v. 29)?

5. What three actions did they ask God to perform to verify their teaching (v. 30)?

6. How did God acknowledge that He had heard their prayer and would meet their need (v. 31)?

DISCUSS THE MEANING

1. Many believers profess to trust God and acknowledge His control over the circumstances of their lives. Yet when adverse situations develop, they worry and fret just like those who have no hope in God. What message does this send to unbelievers? How should believers deal with the adverse situations that are sure to happen in life?

2. Is it reasonable to expect God to verify the Gospel message today through supernatural healings, signs, and miracles? If not, why not? If so, why don't we see more evidence of it?

3. Do you see signs of intolerance toward people of faith by individuals or groups in our society? How should God's people react to such intolerances?

LESSON IN OUR SOCIETY

Modern-day Western society believes that a person's faith is personal and should not be voiced in public or even discussed with others. Unfortunately, many Christians share this belief. If believers keep their faith to themselves, how will the Gospel be spread? In view of the lesson today, is fear of rejection an adequate reason not to share your faith with others? How might our communities be affected if more Christians had the boldness to share the Gospel message in spite of the rejection or mockery they experience? How might your community be impacted if you boldly shared your faith?

MAKE IT HAPPEN

This week, ask God to bless you with the same boldness the early believers had and to provide opportunities for you to share your faith. Look for an opportunity to speak to someone you don't know about the goodness of Christ. Be prepared to share your experience with the class next week.

FOLLOW THE SPIRIT

What God wants me to do:

_____

_____

REMEMBER YOUR THOUGHTS

Special insights I have learned:

_____

_____

MORE LIGHT ON THE TEXT

Acts 4:1-4, 23-31

1 And as they spake unto the people, the priests, and the captain of the temple, and the Sadducees, came upon them,

The verb "spake" (Gk. *laleo,* **lal-eh'-o**) is a present participle indicating that the apostles' speech was interrupted. The pronoun "they" (Gk. *autos,* **ow-tos'**) suggests that John had also addressed the crowd.

The expression "came upon them" (Gk *ephistemi,* **ef-is'-tay-mee**) is used of the notion of sudden appearance (cf. Acts 12:7; 23:2; Luke 2:9; 24:4), sometimes implying a hostile purpose (Acts 6:12; 17:5; Luke 20:1).

As Peter and John were speaking to the crowd in Solomon's colonnade, the authorities intervened. These authorities were formed of "the priests, and the captain of the temple, and the Sadducees." The "priests" (Gk. *hiereus,* **hee-er-yooce'**) were the particular priests on duty in the temple at the time—who, no doubt, took exception to this mass meeting in the precincts—or were some of the members of the high-priestly family. The "captain" (Gk. *strategos,* **strat-ay-gos'**) of the temple was perhaps the superintendent of the temple police (responsible for maintaining order and ranking next to the high priest himself) or one of his subordinates in charge of the temple guard. The "Sadducees" (Gk. *Saddoukaios,* **sad-doo-kah'-yos**) were an aristocratic religious party to which most high-priestly families belonged and from which a succession of high priests came. Unlike the Pharisees, the other religious party featured in Acts 5:34, the Sadducees occupied influential civil positions. They were the dominant party in the Sanhedrin. Theologically, they objected in principle to the doctrine of resurrection. They were not looking for a messiah because they believed that the Messianic age had begun in the Maccabean period.

2 Being grieved that they taught the people, and preached through Jesus the resurrection from the dead.

The verb translated as "being grieved" (Gk. *diaponeo,* **dee-ap-on-eh'-o**) indicates the grounds for the intervention of the authorities. They were greatly exasperated because of the teaching of the apostles about the resurrection (Gk. *anastasis,* **an-as'-tas-is**) of Jesus. In spite of the Sadducees' fierce opposition, the apostles were publicly insisting on the fact of Jesus' resurrection.

3 And they laid hands on them, and put them in hold unto the next day: for it was now eventide.

The Sadducees seized the apostles. It was evening (at least an hour or two must have gone by since the time of the afternoon prayers when Peter and John had gone up to the temple), and it was too late to convene the council and hold an inquiry into the apostles' conduct. They were, therefore, locked up for the night.

4 Howbeit many of them which heard the word believed; and the number of the men was about five thousand.

The authorities could arrest the apostles, but they could not stop the Gospel. The healing of the man born crippled and the preaching of the Word that followed it had the effect of adding a large number to the church.

The Greek word *aner* (**an'-ayr**) means "human beings," whether male or female; in contrast, the Greek word used here is *anthropos* (**anth'-ro-pos**),

which refers to men as distinct from women and children. Thus, the phrase indicates that the number of men alone now totaled some 5,000, not counting the women and children.

4:23 And being let go, they went to their own company, and reported all that the chief priests and elders had said unto them.

The expression "their own company" (Gk. *idios,* **id'-ee-os**), or "their own circle," denotes the Christian community. It suggests that after their release, Peter and John returned to "headquarters" (cf. Acts14:26-27), perhaps the Upper Room of Acts 1:13, where the new community had no doubt been engaged in intercessory prayer for them. They reported their experience before the council.

24 And when they heard that, they lifted up their voice to God with one accord, and said, Lord, thou art God, which hast made heaven, and earth, and the sea, and all that in them is:

With "one accord," they turned to God in prayer. The Greek word for "one accord" or "in unison" is *homothumadon* (**hom-oth-oo-mad-on'**), which indicates that they were like one person in prayer. It does not mean they all simultaneously gave utterance to the same words. One of the leaders may have uttered the words accompanied by the responsive "amen" of the rest. There is power in a gathering of believers when they are in "one accord" (see vv. 24-31).

They addressed God as "Lord" or "Master" (Gk. *despotes,* **des-pot'-ace**), a term denoting the sovereignty of God and His absolute control over all creation. The term is also used of a slave owner or of a ruler who holds unchallengeable power. In the disciples' prayer, the term certainly points to the fact that the authority of the council was subject to a higher authority still, and that the law of men cannot overturn the decrees of God (cf.vv. 19-20; cf. Isaiah 37:16-20).

The disciples filled their minds with thoughts of the sovereignty of God before stating their petition. The sovereign God is the God of creation. He made the heaven, the earth, the sea, and everything in them (cf. 14:15; 17:24, 26; see also Exodus 20:11; Nehemiah 9:6; Psalm 146:6; Isaiah 42:5).

25 Who by the mouth of thy servant David hast said, Why did the heathen rage, and the people imagine vain things?

The sovereign Lord is the God of revelation. He had revealed to His servant David the opposition Christ would face from various groups of people. "Why did the heaven rage" is quoted from Psalm 2:1-2. Psalm 2 probably originally referred to the accession of a Davidic king, the Lord's Anointed, and the revolt of His vassals. It was interpreted by the Jews as well as by the early Christians as a Messianic psalm (cf. Acts 13:33; Luke 3:22; Hebrews 1:5; 5:5).

The "heathen" (Gk. *ethnos,* **eth'-nos**), people other than the Israelites, raged against Jesus when the Romans sentenced Him to the Cross and executed Him (cf. Psalm 57:9; Zechariah 1:15; Romans 3:29; 15:27). The "people" (Gk. *laos,* **lah-os'**), referring here to the people of God who imagined vain things, were His Jewish adversaries (cf. 26:17, 23; Luke 2:32; Romans 15:10).

26 The kings of the earth stood up, and the rulers were gathered together against the Lord, and against his Christ.

"The kings of the earth" (Gk. *basileus'ge,* **bas-il-yooce' ghay**), who stood up against the Lord and his Christ, were represented by Herod Antipas, Tetrarch of Galilee and Peraea (Luke 23:7ff), while "the rulers" (Gk. *archon,* **ar'-khone**) were represented by Pontius Pilate.

The sovereign Lord is the God of history. The Greek particle *gar,* which means "for" proves the truth of the preceding prophecy by pointing to its historical fulfillment. Herod, Pontius Pilate, the Gentiles, and the people of Israel are clearly identified with the kings, the rulers, the nations, and the people of Psalm 2:1-2 as quoted in Acts 4:25-26.

27 For of a truth against thy holy child Jesus, whom thou hast anointed, both Herod, and Pontius Pilate, with the Gentiles, and the people of Israel, were gathered together,

The expression "thy holy child Jesus" explicitly identifies Jesus with the royal Son of God addressed in Psalm 2:7. Jesus is both the obedient Son and the One whom God anointed or made Messiah. There are some ambiguities in the Greek word *pais* (**paheece;** cf. v. 30; 3:13, 26; Mark

10:45; Isaiah 52:13-53:12). It may mean either "Servant" or "Son," and therefore makes the changeability in thought between the Messianic "servant" and the Davidic "son" more natural in Greek than in other languages.

Jesus, "whom thou hast anointed," refers to the Holy Spirit's identification of Jesus as Messiah at His baptism (cf. 10:38; Luke 3:21-22; 4:18-21; Isaiah 61:1). The word "anointed" (Gk. *ecrisas*) comes from the Greek word *chrio* (**khree'-o**); the verbal adjective *cristos* provides the title "Christ." Similarly, the word "messiah" comes from the Hebrew word *mashiah* (*mashiyach,* **maw-shee'-akh**), which means "to anoint."

28 For to do whatsoever thy hand and thy counsel determined before to be done.

The God of history causes even His enemies to do what He has determined beforehand.

The verb "to do" (Gk. *poieo,* **poy-eh'-o**) means "to cause." The purposes of the rulers and the people were overruled by the sovereign Lord for the accomplishment of His will. They were simply carrying out the foreordained counsel of God that His Messiah must suffer (cf. Acts 2:23a; 3:18).

The word "hand" (*cheir,* **khire**) refers to God's action, his controlling power (cf. 11:21; 13:11; Luke 1:66).

29 And now, Lord, behold their threatenings: and grant unto thy servants, that with all boldness they may speak thy word,

The threats (Gk. *apeile,* **ap-i-lay'**) of the council were not a cause for fear and silence but for increased boldness of speech. The apostles therefore prayed that they themselves might have courage to proclaim the Word of God "with all boldness."

The word "servants" comes from the Greek word doulos (**doo'-los**), which means "slave" and is distinct from the Greek word *pais* (servant or child) used for servant and applied to Jesus. David is also called a servant in this prayer (v. 25) in the same sense as Abraham (Genesis 26:24) and Moses (Exodus 14:31) were servants of God. The use of the word *doulos* (servant or slave) contrasts with the majesty of the term translated as "Lord" or "Master" (Gk. *despotes,* **des-pot'-ace**) in verse 24.

30 By stretching forth thine hand to heal; and that signs and wonders may be done by the name of thy holy child Jesus.

The next request of the disciples is that God would place the seal of His public approval on their witness by granting further mighty works of healing and similar signs and wonders through the same name that had cured the lame man, the name of Jesus. Instead of asking for punishment to come on their enemies, they asked for blessing. They did not ask to be delivered from danger but from fear, not to be protected but to have courage, and not for security but for boldness.

The term "hand" (Gk. *cheir*, **khire**), most frequently used to refer to God's act of punishment (cf. Exodus 3:20; Jeremiah 15:6; Ezekiel 6:14), here denotes God's action in bringing blessing (cf. Luke 5:13; 6:10). It was of course the apostles' hands that were stretched out to heal, but, as in Acts 3:12-16, they attributed their power to God working through them as they restored men to wholeness in the name of Jesus.

31 And when they had prayed, the place was shaken where they were assembled together; and they were all filled with the Holy Ghost, and they spake the word of God with boldness.

The account here is reminiscent of the description of what happened on the Day of Pentecost, both in the external signs of the Spirit's coming and in the prayerful attitude of the disciples when He comes. In answer to the united and earnest prayers of the disciples, the place was shaken, they were all filled with the Holy Spirit, and they proclaimed the Word of God boldly. They were encouraged to continue to proclaim the faith despite the threats of the council.

The shaking (Gk. *saleuo*, **sal-yoo'-o**) of the place where the disciples were symbolizes the presence of God (cf. Exodus 19:18; 1 Kings 19:11-12; Isaiah 6:4). The assurance of divine favor and help came even as they prayed. An earthquake might be a cause for fear to some, but to those who see it as an answer to prayer, it is an encouragement.

The verb "filled" (Gk. *pletho*, **play'-tho**) followed by the verb "spake" (Gk. *laleo*, **lal-eh'-o**) indicates the immediate and continuous action of the disciples. They were continuously proclaiming the Word of God with boldness.

DAILY BIBLE READINGS

M: Be Strong in the Lord
Ephesians 6:10-20
T: Paul Preaches the Gospel
Courageously
1 Thessalonians 2:1-8
W: Peter and John are Arrested
Acts 4:1-7
T: Peter Speaks About Jesus Christ
Acts 4:8-12
F: Peter and John Are Warned
Acts 4:13-17
S: Peter and John Refuse to Stop
Acts 4:18-22
The Believers Pray for Boldness
Acts 4:23-31

TEACHING TIPS

October 2
Bible Study Guide 5

1. Words You Should Know

A. Miraculous Signs (Acts 6:8) *semeion* (Gk.)—
In the plural, miracles that lead to something
beyond themselves. They are valuable not so much
for what they are as for what they point to—the
grace and power of God.

B. Witnesses (7:58) *martureo* (Gk.)—To be a witness or bear witness.

2. Teacher Preparation

A. Begin preparing for this lesson by reading all
the FOCAL VERSES. Then read through the
entire BIBLE STUDY GUIDE for this lesson.

B. Review the TEACHING TIPS, and adapt the
lesson to fit the needs of your class.

3. Starting the Lesson

A. Have a student lead the class in prayer using
the LESSON AIM.

B. Ask the students to share their experiences
from last week's MAKE IT HAPPEN assignment
and tell what they learned from their DAILY
BIBLE READINGS.

C. Begin the class by asking one of the students
to read today's IN FOCUS story. Discuss the question at the end.

D. Assign two students to read the FOCAL
VERSES according to the AT-A-GLANCE outline.

4. Getting into the Lesson

A. The BACKGROUND section contains information that will help set the stage for today's lesson. Have the students silently read the section
and write their thoughts in the REMEMBER
YOUR THOUGHTS section.

B. Refer to the SEARCH THE SCRIPTURES
questions as you begin the discussion of the lesson.

C. Discuss THE PEOPLE, PLACES, AND
TIMES. This information will help the students
understand the false charge that was brought
against Stephen.

5. Relating the Lesson to Life

A. Use the DISCUSS THE MEANING questions
to help the students discuss how today's lesson
applies to the practical situations they face today.

B. The LESSON IN OUR SOCIETY section will
also help the students see parallels with their present-day situations.

6. Arousing Action

A. Sum up the lesson with the KEEP IN MIND
verse. Have the students read it in unison, and ask
how they can apply the verse to their everyday
lives.

B. Challenge the students to follow through on
the MAKE IT HAPPEN assignment. This will help
them incorporate the biblical truths into their
lives and make a personal commitment to the
Lord and to other people.

C. Encourage the students to read the DAILY
BIBLE READINGS for the week to help turn the
learning into action and keep them in the
Scriptures during the week.

D. Close the class with prayer, thanking the
Lord for the love and mercy that He has shown to
the students this week.

WORSHIP GUIDE

For the Superintendent or Teacher
Theme: Stephen
Theme Song: "Jesus Hold My Hand"
Scripture: Acts 6:8
Song: "Jesus I Come"
Meditation: Thank You, Lord, for Your
faithfulness and commitment to my life.
Give me the courage to stand up for Your
Word without fear. In Jesus' name.
Amen.

STEPHEN

Bible Background • ACTS 6:8–7:60
Printed Text • ACTS 6:8–15; 7:53–60
Devotional Reading • ISAIAH 6:1–8

LESSON AIM

By the end of the lesson we will:

KNOW the events surrounding Stephen's ministry, trial, and martyrdom;

FEEL the boldness and contentment he felt despite persecution; and

DETERMINE to remain loyal to Christ despite opposition and persecution that we may face because of our faith.

KEEP IN MIND

"And Stephen, full of faith and power, did great wonders and miracles among the people" (Acts 6:8).

FOCAL VERSES

Acts 6:8 And Stephen, full of faith and power, did great wonders and miracles among the people.

9 Then there arose certain of the synagogue, which is called the synagogue of the Libertines, and Cyrenians, and Alexandrians, and of them of Cilicia and of Asia, disputing with Stephen.

10 And they were not able to resist the wisdom and the spirit by which he spake.

11 Then they suborned men, which said, We have heard him speak blasphemous words against Moses, and against God.

12 And they stirred up the people, and the elders, and the scribes, and came upon him, and caught him, and brought him to the council,

13 And set up false witnesses, which said, This man ceaseth not to speak blasphemous words against this holy place, and the law:

14 For we have heard him say, that this Jesus of Nazareth shall destroy this place, and shall change

LESSON OVERVIEW

LESSON AIM
KEEP IN MIND
FOCAL VERSES
IN FOCUS
THE PEOPLE, PLACES, AND TIMES
BACKGROUND
AT-A-GLANCE
IN DEPTH
SEARCH THE SCRIPTURES
DISCUSS THE MEANING
LESSON IN OUR SOCIETY
MAKE IT HAPPEN
FOLLOW THE SPIRIT
REMEMBER YOUR THOUGHTS
MORE LIGHT ON THE TEXT
DAILY BIBLE READINGS

the customs which Moses delivered us.

15 And all that sat in the council, looking stedfastly on him, saw his face as it had been the face of an angel.

7:53 Who have received the law by the disposition of angels, and have not kept it.

54 When they heard these things, they were cut to the heart, and they gnashed on him with their teeth.

55 But he, being full of the Holy Ghost, looked up stedfastly into heaven, and saw the glory of God, and Jesus standing on the right hand of God,

56 And said, Behold, I see the heavens opened, and the Son of man standing on the right hand of God.

57 Then they cried out with a loud voice, and stopped their ears, and ran upon him with one accord,

58 And cast him out of the city, and stoned him: and the witnesses laid down their clothes at a young man's feet, whose name was Saul.

59 And they stoned Stephen, calling upon God, and saying, Lord Jesus, receive my spirit.

60 And he kneeled down, and cried with a loud voice, Lord, lay not this sin to their charge. And when he had said this, he fell asleep.

IN FOCUS

In the Bible, we read about Christian persecution in the early church and see people thrown into prison, murdered, and cast out for witnessing about Jesus as the Messiah.

Often we forget persecution of Christians still

occurs today—in countries where a loincloth is a luxury, where an aspirin is as hard to obtain as a kidney donor, where flushing toilets are a miracle, and pencils are as rare as diamonds. Yet by the grace of God, Scripture is quoted like rain in a rain forest.

A case in point, recently I read a story of a 17-year-old girl in Africa who was abducted twice in two months. Her family had gone to the local police after the first abduction, but they refused to protect her.

The police and the government were even suspected of helping to kidnap and abuse the young Christian girl because of her bold efforts to convert others. The harassment became so great that her family sought out an American minister to adopt her, so she could travel to America. Once in America she still had nightmares, but she wore a brilliant smile and continued to minister the Word of God and stand boldly for Christ.

Christians in countries like Egypt, Nigeria, Sudan, and Ethiopia face persecution and similar circumstances on a daily basis. Nevertheless, you might be surprised to learn that nearly 50% of all Africans declare their belief in Christ even with the kind of threats the young African girl had to endure.

The story of Stephen reminds us that all around the world, the Gospel is nourished with martyrs. Stephen's life serves as a continual challenge to Christians. Would you be willing to die for your belief?

THE PEOPLE, PLACES, AND TIMES

Blasphemy. The Greek word for blasphemy means "to slander" or "to speak lightly of the divine." In the New Testament, blasphemy indicated a hostile attitude toward God. In the epistle to the Romans, Paul quotes Isaiah, who stated that God's name was blasphemed among the Gentiles because of the Jews (Romans 2:24; cf. Isaiah 52:5). This confirms the importance of believers living lives that bring praise to God rather than contempt for Him.

It is curious that both Jesus and Stephen were condemned to death under the false charge of blasphemy. This occurred because Jesus claimed the prerogatives that belong to God alone and Stephen accused the unbelieving Jews of murdering the long-awaited Messiah.

BACKGROUND

Two groups of people made up the early church. Grecians were Greek-speaking Jews who had come to Israel and were not fluent in the Aramaic language of the natives. The other dominant people were the natives, who spoke both Aramaic and Greek. As the church continued to grow, it became increasingly difficult for the apostles to minister to everyone. The Grecian widows were being neglected in the daily food distribution. This could have caused the first split in church history, but the apostles handled the situation with wisdom.

The apostles realized that they had become so bogged down in serving the people that they were neglecting the prayer and ministry of God's Word. To solve this problem, the apostles called the believers together and told them that it was not realistic to expect them to take time away from their ministry to wait on tables. They proposed that the people select seven men from among them to act as business managers over the fledgling church. The main requirements for the job were that the men must be full of faith and the Holy Spirit (Acts 6:3). Pleased with this decision, the believers set about selecting the men. The seven men they selected were all Grecians—Stephen, Philip, Prochorus, Nicanor, Timon, Parmenas, and Nicolas, a Greek convert from the city of Antioch. These seven men were brought before the apostles, who laid hands on them and anointed them into service. Philip and Stephen were two of these seven men who would receive prominent mention in Scripture.

Philip would become a great evangelist, who would be the first to preach the Gospel in Samaria (8:4-12). He would also meet an Ethiopian eunuch in the desert of Gaza and explain the Gospel to him. The Ethiopian would believe and be converted and precipitate the Gospel message being taken into Africa (vv. 26-40). Toward the end of his life, Philip would open his home to the apostle Paul during the apostle's last visit to Jerusalem (21:8-14). Stephen's life would be much shorter than Philip's, but his impact on the eternal Christian community would be just as great.

IN DEPTH

1. The Preaching of Stephen (Acts 6:8-15)

Stephen was one of the Greek-speaking Jews called the Hellenists. He had been born in another country and did not speak Hebrew or Aramaic. He was one of the 3,000 people who had heard the witness of the apostles on the Day of Pentecost and had become a Christian.

There were a number of synagogues in Jerusalem that had been formed by Greek-speaking Jews from various parts of the world. Luke records five of them (v. 9). One was the synagogue of the freedmen—Jews who were formerly slaves of Rome. There were two groups from Africa: the synagogues of the Cyrenians and of the Alexandrians. The other two were from the Roman provinces of Cilicia and Asia, which we refer to today as Asia Minor.

Stephen apparently went to these synagogues and preached the Gospel of Jesus and the resurrection in Greek. The capital of Cilicia was Tarsus. Therefore, it was probably in the synagogue of Cilicia where a young man named Saul of Tarsus joined other Greek-speaking Jews to argue with Stephen, "but they could not stand up against his wisdom or the Spirit by whom he spoke" (Acts 6:10, NIV).

When these men could not answer Stephen, they resorted to dishonest tactics to discredit him.

Stephen preaches to the people.

They secretly found false witnesses to testify against Stephen and claim that he had blasphemed Moses and God. After stirring up the people, the elders, and the scribes, they seized Stephen and brought him before the council.

Stephen was brought before the same Sanhedrin that had condemned Jesus to death and threatened Peter and John. The official charges against Stephen were narrowed to two very specific offenses: "This fellow never stops speaking against this holy place and against the law" (v. 13, NIV). They claimed that Stephen taught that Jesus would destroy the temple and change the Law of Moses. While they stared at Stephen, waiting for a reply, his face took on an angelic glow like Moses' face after he had been in the presence of God (Exodus 34:29-30).

Psalm 34:5 (NIV) says, "Those who look to him are radiant; their faces ...."

Stephen's statements were probably in response to the false witnesses' charges. So when the high priest asked, "Are these charges true?" (Acts 7:1, NIV), Stephen did not simply answer yes, or no; instead, he explained the truth and launched into the longest sermon in the book of Acts.

2. The Death of Stephen (7:53-60)

Stephen's accusers and the religious leaders were so outraged by this truth that they could not stand it. "When they heard this, they were furious and gnashed their teeth at him" (Acts 7:54, NIV). In contrast to his accusers, who were driven wild by their passions, Stephen continued to look to God: "But Stephen, full of the Holy Spirit, looked up to heaven and saw the glory of God, and Jesus standing at the right hand of God" (v. 55, NIV). These words are almost identical to the words Jesus had spoken to these men just a few weeks earlier: "But I say to all of you: In the future you will see the Son of Man sitting at the right hand of the Mighty One and coming on the clouds of heaven" (Matthew 26:64, NIV). When they heard this, they knew the issue was not Stephen, but Jesus.

They had brought Stephen to trial and he condemned them with the very Scriptures they professed to believe in. Like the men of the synagogue, they could not argue with his testimony. Consequently, these enraged Jews cried out at the top of their voices and put their hands up to their ears in a vain attempt to drown out Stephen. When confronted with the truth of Christ, one must either submit or resist. The Jewish leaders and Stephen's accusers decided to resist. Like their forefathers, instead of heeding God's prophet, they would kill him. The respectable Sanhedrin turned into an unruly mob, rushed at Stephen, and dragged him outside the city gates. They threw him down into a pit and stoned him.

The reference to the "witnesses" (v. 58) suggests that the stoning was carried out as a legal execution. The penalty for blasphemy was stoning (Leviticus 24:16). According to Jewish law, the witnesses would have to throw the first stones (Deuteronomy 17:7). These men took off their outer cloaks and laid them at the feet of a young Jewish Pharisee named Saul.

After the witnesses had thrown the first stones, the rest of the congregation picked up stones and began to hurl them at Stephen. If someone had a good aim and managed to hit Stephen in the head early on, he would lose consciousness and would not have to endure the prolonged agony. If not, his death would be long, slow, and very painful.

As the malicious and unforgiving crowd hurled their stones down on the defenseless Stephen, he first cried out in prayer for God to receive his spirit. Then, as he weakened from blood loss, he dropped to his knees and uttered his final words, "Lord, do not hold this sin against them" (Acts 7:60, NIV). Stephen, the first Christian martyr died at the hands of the same people who had delivered Jesus to be crucified, and he died with a similar prayer on his lips.

Scripture says that Stephen "fell asleep" (Acts 7:60; also see John 11:11; 1 Thessalonians 4:13). Because physical death is temporary for the believer, death is referred to as 'sleep.' The body sleeps but the spirit goes to be with the Lord (1 Corinthians 5:6-9).

God never wastes the blood of His saints. The persecution of the church that began with Stephen's murder forced the church to flee Jerusalem and take the Gospel to the uttermost parts of the world. And a young man named Saul, who gave his approval to the stoning of Stephen (Acts 8:1), was so moved by Stephen's death that he never forgot it. Although Saul would become the greatest persecutor of the early church, Stephen's death would always pick at the back of his conscience. There is little doubt that the Holy Spirit used Stephen's message and glorious death to prepare Saul for his meeting with the risen Lord on the Damascus Road (Acts 9). Saul, later called Paul, would become the single greatest evangelist the world has ever known.

Finally, the book of Acts is an unfinished book. Its pages are still being written today. There will be others who are called to lay down their lives for Jesus' sake. Stephen provides us with a godly example.

SEARCH THE SCRIPTURES

1. How did Luke describe Stephen, and what is Stephen credited with doing (Acts 6:8)?

2. Why were the Greek-speaking Jews so upset with Stephen (v. 10)?

3. What were the two charges that the false witnesses brought against Stephen (v. 13)?

4. What physical response did the Jews make that demonstrated their passionate anger with Stephen (Acts 7:54)?

5. How does Luke describe Stephen's death at the hands of his accusers (v. 60)?

DISCUSS THE MEANING

1. After studying the stories of Philip and Stephen, do you believe that the responsibilities of a deacon begin and end with the business of the local church? Do deacons have any responsibilities to the community they serve and to unbelievers?

2. Do you believe that many American Christians would be willing to sacrifice their lives for their faith? Some believe that a little persecution would actually strengthen the American church. Do you agree? How much are you personally willing to sacrifice to see the message of the Gospel spread?

LESSON IN OUR SOCIETY

Stephen is recognized as the first person to give his life to spread the Gospel. He was known as an outspoken leader and a man of great faith. He refused to compromise his beliefs and virtually spoke his own death sentence. In today's society, every day we are faced with issues that may compromise our Christian beliefs. The challenge for many Christians becomes: are we willing to suffer persecution despite what others may think? Are we willing to stand on God's Word when it is not popular? Like Stephen, we as Christians must have a mind-set that, regardless of what Satan

brings against us, we are going to tenaciously stand on the Word of God.

MAKE IT HAPPEN

Stephen was willing to make the ultimate sacrifice for the cause of Christ. Maybe God has not called you to make this kind of sacrifice, but Christianity does require some sacrifice from all of us. This week, look for ways to make sacrifices to God for the sake of the Gospel. These sacrifices can be time, money, or whatever you choose. Be prepared to share your experiences with the class next week.

FOLLOW THE SPIRIT

What God wants me to do:

_____

_____

REMEMBER YOUR THOUGHTS

Special insights I have learned:

_____

_____

MORE LIGHT ON THE TEXT

Acts 6:8-15; 7:53-60

8 And Stephen, full of faith and power, did great wonders and miracles among the people.

Stephen is described as a man "full of faith and power" (some New Testament Greek manuscripts have "full of grace and power"). The expression "full of faith" (Gk. *pistis*, **pis'-tis**) denotes an undivided conviction and confidence regarding Jesus as the Messiah (cf. 7:52). The term "power" (Gk. *dunamis*, **doo'-nam-is**) is the ability to work miracles (8:13; Luke 5:17). Stephen was doing great wonders and miracles. The verb "did" (Gk. *poieo*, **poy-eh'-o**) is in the imperfect tense, meaning "was doing."

9 Then there arose certain of the synagogue, which is called the synagogue of the Libertines, and Cyrenians, and Alexandrians, and of them of Cilicia and of Asia, disputing with Stephen.

Stephen's ministry provoked fierce antagonism in spite of all his outstanding qualities. The opposition "arose" (Gk. *anistemi*, **an-is'-tay-mee**, meaning "to rise up against") from "certain of the synagogue." It is not clear whether only one synagogue is being referred to, or more than one. There were many synagogues in Jerusalem (traditionally 480), and each of the groups mentioned in this verse may have met in a separate place. It is also possible to see here an integrated assembly of people from various origins.

The term "Libertines" (Gk. *Libertinos*, **lib-er-tee'-nos**) is a Greek transliteration of a Latin word meaning "freedmen." Some have suggested that instead of "Libertines" we should read "Libyans" (Gk. *libustinon*). However, the Libertines here were probably descendants of Jewish captives who had been taken to Rome by Pompeii in 63 B.C. and subsequently liberated by their Roman masters.

In the synagogue, there were also people originally from Cyrene and Alexandria in Africa as well as people from Cilicia and Asia. Cilicia lay in southeastern Asia Minor, with Paul's native city of Tarsus as its capital. Asia was the name given to the Roman province at the western end of Asia Minor.

They began "disputing" (Gk. *suzeteo*, **sood-zay-teh'-o**) with Stephen.

10 And they were not able to resist the wisdom and the spirit by which he spake.

They could not "resist" (Gk. *anthistemi*, **anth-is'-tay-mee**), or stand up against "the wisdom and the spirit by which" Stephen spoke (cf. Luke 12:1; 21:15; 1 Corinthians 2:6-16). The expression "wisdom and the spirit" (Gk. *sophia kai pneuma*, **sof-ee'-ah ka-hee pnyoo'-mah**) refers to the inspired words coming out of Stephen's mouth by the power of the Holy Spirit (cf. Matthew 10:20; Luke 12:11; Acts 4:8; 1 Corinthians 2:6-16). Stephen was both practical and powerful in his presentation of the Gospel message to the people who were disputing with him.

11 Then they suborned men, which said, We have heard him speak blasphemous words against Moses, and against God.

Pushed into a corner in open debate, Stephen's opponents used another strategy to get him. When arguments fail, mud has often been an excellent substitute. They "suborned" (Gk. *hupoballo*, **hoop-ob-al'-lo,** literally, "to put under," "substitute," or "secretly persuade") men to bring

false testimony against Stephen. They accused him of blasphemy against Moses and against God. False witnesses and the charge of blasphemy were also featured in the trial of Jesus (Matthew 26:60ff; Mark 14:56ff).

12 And they stirred up the people, and the elders, and the scribes, and came upon him, and caught him, and brought him to the council,

They stirred up the people, the elders, and the scribes against him. The verb "stirred up" (Gk. *sugkineo*, **soong-kin-eh'-o**) literally means "to move together." Despite Stephen's power of healing, which should have commended him to the ordinary citizens of Jerusalem, his opponents were able to move them against Stephen. They "caught" (Gk. *sunarpazo*, **soon-ar-pad'-zo**) him, or seized him by force and brought him before the Sanhedrin.

13 And set up false witnesses, which said, This man ceaseth not to speak blasphemous words against this holy place, and the law:

They produced false witnesses who accused Stephen of blasphemy against "this holy place and the law." The expression "holy place" (Gk. *hagios topos*, **hag-ee-os top'-os**) refers to the temple, to which the council chamber of the Sanhedrin was adjacent. The charges against Stephen were extremely serious. To Jews, nothing was more sacred and precious than the temple and the law. The "temple" was God's house, and "the law" was God's Word.

14 For we have heard him say, that this Jesus of Nazareth shall destroy this place, and shall change the customs which Moses delivered us.

The false witnesses explained their accusations by saying "we have heard him say." The verb "heard" (Gk. *akouo*, **ak-oo'-o**) refers to an action already accomplished with its results still present at the time of speaking. The meaning is thus, "Stephen said and he is presently still saying and continues to say this." Whatever Stephen had said was deliberately twisted, as at the trial of Jesus (Mark 14:58; 15:29; Matthew 26:61; 12:6; Mark 13:2; John 2:19-21).

Failing in a theological debate, Stephen's

opponents started a campaign of lies, and then took him to court with charges of false witness in order to get rid of him. They negatively portrayed everything Stephen said. They saw his views on the relationship between the Old Testament teachings and Jesus of Nazareth as a threat to their Jewish heritage.

15 And all that sat in the council, looking stedfastly on him, saw his face as it had been the face of an angel.

At this point, everyone sitting (Gk. *kathezomai*, **kath-ed'-zom-ahee**) in the council was looking intently (Gk. *atenizo*, **at-en-id'-zo**) at Stephen and saw that his face was "like the face of an angel," or in this way, God was showing that both Moses' law and Stephen's interpretation of it had His approval.

7:53 Who have received the law by the disposition of angels, and have not kept it.

They had not obeyed or kept the law they had been specially privileged to receive (Gk. *lambano*, **lam-ban'-o**). They had received the law "by the disposition of angels." The term "disposition" or (Gk. *diatage*, **dee-at-ag-ay'**) means an arrangement of angels (cf. Galatians 3:19; Hebrews 2:2).

Therefore, they were the real law breakers, not Stephen. Thus, the accused had become the accuser, using the same language as Moses and the prophets (Exodus 33:5; Deuteronomy 10:16; Isaiah 48:4; Jeremiah 4:4).

54 When they heard these things, they were cut to the heart, and they gnashed on him with their teeth.

Stephen's speech made them furious, particularly his accusation about them not being true observers of the Law of Moses. They "were cut to the heart" (Gk. *diaprio*, **dee-ap-ree'-o**), which literally means "to saw through" and denotes being infuriated and fiercely annoyed (cf. 5:33). They "gnashed" (Gk. *brucho*, **broo'-kho**) their teeth at Stephen in a hostile sense, as wild beasts leaping with rage on their prey (cf. Job 16:9-10; Psalm 35:16-17). They were full of hatred toward Stephen.

55 But he, being full of the Holy Ghost, looked up stedfastly into heaven, and saw the glory of God, and Jesus standing on the right hand of God.

Stephen, "being full of the Holy Ghost," had a vision of the glory of God. He saw Jesus standing at the right hand of God. Why was Jesus "standing" (Gk. *histemi*, **his'-tay-mee**) instead of sitting at God's right hand (cf. 2:34-35; Psalm 110:1; Luke 22:69; Ephesians 1:20; Colossians 3:1; Hebrews 1:3; 1 Peter 3:21-22)? It must be observed first that both expressions are symbolic of the authority given to Christ. The vision of Jesus standing evokes many possible interpretations. One is that Stephen testified that Jesus had arrived in the presence of God and had received all authority, thus fulfilling the vision of Daniel 7:13 (Matthew 28:18; Acts 13:33). Another is that Christ was standing either as Stephen's advocate or to welcome him into His presence. The "right hand" means the place of honor (cf. Matthew 20:21; 1 Kings 2:19).

56 And said, Behold, I see the heavens opened, and the Son of man standing on the right hand of God.

Stephen told them what he was seeing. He saw the heavens opened and the Son of man standing at the right hand of God (Mark 14:62; Daniel 7:13). The expression "Son of man" (Gk. *ho huios tou anthropou*, **ho hwee-os' tu anth'-ro-poo**) is a title for Christ (cf. Luke 6:22).

57 Then they cried out with a loud voice, and stopped their ears, and ran upon him with one accord,

They cried out (Gk. *krazo*, **krad'-zo**) loudly, determined to silence him. They "stopped" or "held together" (Gk. *sunecho*, **soon-ekh'-o**) their ears so that Stephen's words, which they regarded as blasphemous, could not be heard (cf. Matthew 26:65). They "rushed" (Gk. *hormao*, **hor-mah'-o**) at him "with one accord." The use of the aorist tense here shows how fast things went out of control as soon as Stephen identified the figure of the Son of man in glory as Jesus.

58 And cast him out of the city, and stoned him: and the witnesses laid down their clothes at a young man's feet, whose name was Saul.

They seized him and "cast him out" or "threw him out" (Gk. *ekballo,* **ek-bal'-lo**) of the city and began to stone (Gk. *lithoboleo,* **lith-ob-ol-eh'-o**) him to death. Death by stoning was the punishment for blasphemy (cf. Leviticus 24:14; Luke 4:29). It is not clear, however, whether Stephen's death was the result of judicial action by the council or mob lynching (similarly, in Jesus' trial and death, the Romans had taken away the Jews' right of capital punishment, John 18:31).

The actions all happened fast: "cried aloud," "stopped," "rushed," "cast out," and "stoned" indicating a repeated and continued action.

Yet, these events had some semblance of legality if the "witnesses" (Gk. *martus,* **mar'-toos**) here were the first to start the stoning as specified by law (cf. Deuteronomy 17:1; John 8:7).

They laid their clothes at the feet of a young man named Saul (cf. Acts 22:20; 26:10). This is the first mention of Saul in Acts. The term "a young man" (Gk. *neanias,* **neh-an-ee'-as**) gives no indication of his age. It can be applied to a person up to 40 years old (cf. Matthew 19:20, 22).

59 And they stoned Stephen, calling upon God, and saying, Lord Jesus, receive my spirit.

As they were stoning (Gk. *lithoboleo,* **lith-ob-ol-eh'-o**) him, Stephen called upon (Gk. *epikaleomai,* **ep-ee-kal-eh'-om-ahee**) God. His prayer was very similar to Jesus' prayer on the Cross (cf. Luke 23:46). While Jesus committed His spirit to the Father, Stephen committed His to Jesus. This is certainly a testimony to the divinity of Jesus.

60 And he kneeled down, and cried with a loud voice, Lord, lay not this sin to their charge. And when he had said this, he fell asleep.

Stephen fell on his knees (Gk. *tithemi,* **tith'-ay-mee**) and cried out "Lord, do not remember (or "hold against"; Gk. *histemi,* **his'-tay-mee**) this sin against them" (literally, "fix not this sin upon them'" cf. Luke 23:34). Stephen did not pray for his own vindication (2 Chronicles 24:22). He prayed for mercy (cf. Matthew 5:38-48; 6:12, 14-15; James 2:13).

The phrase "he fell asleep" (Gk. *koimao,* **koy-mah'-o**) is characteristic of the New Testament expression for death (Acts 13:36; Matthew 27:52; John 11:11; 1 Corinthians 7:39; 11:30; 15:6, 18, 20, 51; 1 Thessalonians 4:14; 2 Peter 3:4). The same Greek word is also used to refer to sleep, rest, lying, or death (Gk. *koimesis,* **koy'-may-sis**).

DAILY BIBLE READINGS

M: Stephen Is Arrested
Acts 6:8-15

T: Stephen Speaks to the Council
Acts 7:1-8

W: Stephen Tells the Joseph Story
Acts 7:9-16

T: Stephen Tells of Moses' Early Story
Acts 7:17-29

F: Stephen Tells of Moses, the Liberator
Acts 7:30-43

S: Stephen Challenges His Hearers
Acts 7:44-53

S: Stephen Is Stoned to Death
Acts 7:54-60

TEACHING TIPS

October 9
Bible Study Guide 6

1. Words You Should Know

A. Scattered abroad (Acts 8:4) *diaspeiro* (Gk.)—Denotes movement into foreign territories.

B. Palsies (v. 7) *paraluo* (Gk.)—Being feeble, infirm, or sick.

C. Used sorcery, and bewitched (v. 9) *mageuo kai existemi* (Gk.)—Practiced magic.

2. Teacher Preparation

A. Read Acts 7 to familiarize yourself with the content of the lesson.

B. Read the BIBLE BACKGROUND, Acts 8:4-25.

C. Research the previous persecutions of the Christians in Jerusalem to place this particular event in context.

3. Starting the Lesson

A. Ask a student to open the class with a prayer, using the KEEP IN MIND verse as a guide.

B. Ask a volunteer to read the BACKGROUND section aloud.

C. Have the class read the KEEP IN MIND verse in unison.

D. Have the students read the LESSON AIM in unison.

E. Read the IN FOCUS story aloud. Be prepared to relate the question at the end of the story to the action objective as stated in today's LESSON AIM.

4. Getting into the Lesson

A. Ask several students to take turns reading the FOCAL VERSES.

B. Use the AT-A-GLANCE outline to explore the IN DEPTH section.

5. Relating the Lesson to Life

A. Allow the students to work in groups of two or three to answer the questions and discuss the points in the SEARCH THE SCRIPTURES and DISCUSS THE MEANING sections. Have them report back to the class when they finish.

B. Have the students read the LESSON IN OUR SOCIETY section.

C. Ask the students to silently read the MAKE IT HAPPEN section and complete the FOLLOW THE SPIRIT and REMEMBER YOUR THOUGHTS sections.

6. Arousing Action

A. Have the students discuss their weekly activities, other than work and classroom settings, where they have an opportunity to interact with people of different races and ethnicities. Give them time to talk about the challenges that arise in these situations and the opportunities for learning that they encounter.

B. Remind the students to complete the DAILY BIBLE READINGS. Reading God's Word will strengthen their commitment to make evangelism a regular part of their lives.

C. Close the class in prayer.

THE SAMARITANS AND PHILIP

Bible Background • ACTS 8:4–25
Printed Text • ACTS 8:4–17
Devotional Reading • ACTS 19:1–10

LESSON AIM

By the end of the lesson, we will:

KNOW the events surrounding Philip's sharing the Gospel with Samaritans;

BE CONVINCED believers today are commissioned by Christ to be witnesses for Him regardless of race, ethnicity, class, or culture; and

COMMIT to witness to someone during the coming week.

KEEP IN MIND

"Now when the apostles which were at Jerusalem heard that Samaria had received the word of God, they sent unto them Peter and John" (Acts 8:14).

FOCAL VERSES

Acts 8:4 Therefore they that were scattered abroad went every where preaching the word.

5 Then Philip went down to the city of Samaria, and preached Christ unto them.

6 And the people with one accord gave heed unto those things which Philip spake, hearing and seeing the miracles which he did.

7 For unclean spirits, crying with loud voice, came out of many that were possessed with them: and many taken with palsies, and that were lame, were healed.

8 And there was great joy in that city.

9 But there was a certain man, called Simon, which beforetime in the same city used sorcery, and bewitched the people of Samaria, giving out that himself was some great one:

10 To whom they all gave heed, from the least to the greatest, saying, This man is the great power of God.

11 And to him they had regard, because that of long time he had bewitched them with sorceries.

12 But when they believed Philip preaching the things concerning the kingdom of God, and the name of Jesus Christ, they were baptized, both men and women.

13 Then Simon himself believed also: and when he was baptized, he continued with Philip, and wondered, beholding the miracles and signs which were done.

14 Now when the apostles which were at Jerusalem heard that Samaria had received the word of God, they sent unto them Peter and John:

15 Who, when they were come down, prayed for them, that they might receive the Holy Ghost:

16 (For as yet he was fallen upon none of them: only they were baptized in the name of the Lord Jesus.)

17 Then laid they their hands on them, and they received the Holy Ghost.

IN FOCUS

One evening Aisha and Malik (who were African American) invited their close friends Stephanie and Terry (who were White) over one

---

LESSON OVERVIEW

LESSON AIM
KEEP IN MIND
FOCAL VERSES
IN FOCUS
THE PEOPLE, PLACES, AND TIMES
BACKGROUND
AT-A-GLANCE
IN DEPTH
SEARCH THE SCRIPTURES
DISCUSS THE MEANING
LESSON IN OUR SOCIETY
MAKE IT HAPPEN
FOLLOW THE SPIRIT
REMEMBER YOUR THOUGHTS
MORE LIGHT ON THE TEXT
DAILY BIBLE READINGS

evening to watch Mel Gibson's movie *The Passion of the Christ.* Afterward the friends went out to dinner and discussed the movie's emotional impact.

Suddenly, Malik noticed Sonny, one of his long lost basketball teammates, entering the restaurant. Aisha suggested Malik go over and invite Sonny and his date, Angela, to join them. During dinner, Malik told Sonny they had just finished watching *The Passion of the Christ* at his home. Sonny grinned and dropped a mood-changing bomb. "Terry," he said slicing his steak, "when Angela and I saw the movie, we were debating if it would have been as successful if Mel Gibson had portrayed Jesus as a dark-skinned Hebrew Israelite instead of a European White man. What do you think?"

The table got quiet. Terry swallowed hard and carefully chose his words as he answered Sonny's question. "No doubt it may have made a difference for Mel Gibson's bank account. But personally, I have a problem with any portrayal of deity. Scripture states that we are not to create a graven image of God because images can divide and cause confusion."

Malik cleared his throat and said, "God is no respecter of persons. He knows the differences in gender and race and utilizes those differences to His glory, but He limits no one because of it! If we dwell on things like the skin color of Jesus, it limits the message of Christ."

Are you constrained by culture or can you witness to someone regardless of race or ethnicity? Today's lesson shows us how Philip extended the Gospel by sharing the Good News with everyone.

THE PEOPLE, PLACES, AND TIMES

Samaritans. This term is generally used to refer to the Israelite descendants of the northern kingdom who were not removed during the Assyrian conquest, and who married foreigners brought into the land by the Assyrians (2 Chronicles 34:6-9; 2 Kings 23:19-20). In spite of God's prohibition, mixed marriages between the Jews and the Assyrian settlers took place. While there were some similarities, the religious tenets of the Samaritans were distinctly different from those of the Jews. The Samaritans built their own temple,

worshiped on Mount Gerizim, and participated in idolatry. The Samaritans had a truncated version of the Scriptures that omitted the Psalms and the books of the Prophets. The Jews who returned from the Exile despised the Samaritans, calling them the foolish people that dwell in Shechem.

This disdain for the Samaritans by the Jews continued through Jesus' ministry. At one point in Jesus' ministry, He told His disciples to avoid the Gentiles and the cities of Samaria (Matthew 10:5-7). Nevertheless, Jesus willingly entered a Samaritan village and ministered to the woman at the well (John 4:7-42). In another instance, after Jesus received an unfriendly reception as He passed through a Samaritan village, the disciples asked Jesus' permission to "command fire to come down from heaven" on the village (Luke 9:51-55). Yet in the parable of the Good Samaritan (Luke 10:25-37), Jesus appears to teach that the Samaritan was more faithful to the law than the Jews. In spreading the Gospel, Jesus said, do not forget the Samaritans (Acts 1:8).

Adapted from: Packer, J.I., and M.C. Tenney, eds. Illustrated Manners and Customs of the Bible. Nashville, Tenn.: Thomas Nelson Publishers, 1980. 509-510.

BACKGROUND

The book of Acts is a book of history and faith. In addition to providing a transition between the Gospels and the Epistles, Luke, the writer of the book of Acts, provides us with the vital historical facts of how Christianity begins and spreads. In Acts selected events in church history are recorded that demonstrate both Christian doctrine and practice. It is clearly through the power of the Holy Spirit that the men and women of God are able to testify that Jesus is the Christ. There is great emphasis on the connection between the Old Testament, the Jews, and Christianity. There is even greater emphasis that salvation is not bound by a believer's race or ethnicity, rather it is extended to all mankind. In Acts it is clear that it is only Jesus, the Christ, who is able to fulfill the needs of the Gentiles and the Jews.

IN DEPTH

1. The Missionary's Method (Acts 8:4-5)

It is ironic that it took personal hardships to fulfill the commission to take the Gospel abroad. Being uprooted and having to flee their homes was certainly difficult for these Christians, but Christ had changed their lives. Rather than falling into despair, these believers began sharing the Good News of salvation with others.

The narrative moves quickly to the ministry of the deacon Philip. Along with six other men, Philip had been certified as one of "honest report, full of the Holy Ghost and wisdom" (Acts 6:3), and was entrusted to assist the apostles by handling the distribution of food among the widows in Jerusalem.

Following the onset of the persecution, Philip moved from the security of the Jerusalem congregation and into the hostile region of Samaria. There, under the unction of the Holy Spirit, he declared Christ to the Samaritans. This was no easy task as the Jews and Samaritans had no dealings with one another (John 4:9).

2. The Missionary's Effect (vv. 6-8)

On the surface, it appears that Philip had jumped from the frying pan into the fire. The Jews considered the mixed-race Samaritans beneath contempt. The Samaritans mixed pagan practices and teachings with a form of the Jewish religion and were considered "dogs" by the Jews. But Philip's preaching was well-received among the Samaritans. There may be a number of reasons for this.

First and foremost, we know that Philip's preaching was by the power of the Spirit. Second, we must remember that many of the Samaritans were already believers. They had met Jesus when He ministered to them and to the woman at the well. They may have needed to understand Jesus' sacrifice in order to be saved. In any case, it is clear that God called them into His Kingdom.

Through the Holy Spirit, Philip's ministry was empowered. The Samaritans witnessed Philip casting out demons and curing the crippled and lame. God's Word, accompanied by these signs, had a profound effect on the Samaritans. We must note that the people "gave heed" to Philip's preaching. True conversion comes as a result of preaching and not miracles. The miracles serve as "signs." The Samaritans were converted and baptized in great numbers, "and there was great joy in that city" (v. 8).

Great joy often accompanies a commitment to Christ. These new converts were experiencing forgiveness and were being filled with God's mercy and love. A converted, or changed, life often expresses itself in joy. We can only assume that Philip felt this joy too. He had entered a hostile area, running for his life, only to encounter people experiencing the love of God because of his evangelistic efforts.

3. The Missionary's Challenge (vv. 9-11)

Among the Samaritans who heard Philip's preaching and witnessed the accompanying signs and wonders was a sorcerer named Simon. Simon enjoyed tremendous popularity among the Samaritans. Scripture tells us that Simon had been practicing the magical arts and had deceived many with his false claims of greatness. Simon's abilities as a magician had "bewitched the people" (Acts 8:9).

Even today, people mistakenly believe that the only difference between magic and miracles is that the latter is more impressive and is practiced by Christians. The truth is far more important. Miracles clearly point to God, while magic manipulates and points away from God. Faith comes through hearing the Word and not through just seeing miracles.

4. The Missionary's Victory (vv. 12-13)

The Samaritans had previously believed in

Peter and John on their way to Samaria.

The sending of Peter and John is better understood in light of who the Samaritans were. They were a mixed-race people with some Jewish lineage having a rival worship system. They shared some of the same beliefs as the Jews: They claimed an Abrahamic lineage, and they were also awaiting a Messiah. By sending Peter and John, the church in Jerusalem was affirming their unity with the emerging church in Samaria.

The fact that the apostles "laid hands" on the Samaritan converts is no evidence that this was the only way for the Samaritans to receive the Holy Spirit. On the Day of Pentecost, there was no mention of laying on of hands, yet the Holy Spirit was imparted to all of the disciples who were present and believing. Additionally, when Peter preached to Cornelius's household, there is no mention of laying on of hands to receive the spirit (Acts 10:44).

There is also little scriptural evidence that the 12 apostles were the only men empowered to impart the Holy Spirit through the laying on of hands. When Paul, formerly Saul of Tarsus, was converted, it was Ananias who laid hands on him so that Paul might be healed and receive the Holy Spirit (Acts 9:17-18). Ananias was neither an apostle nor a deacon. Instead, the laying on of hands and the receipt of the Holy Spirit by the Samaritans at the hands of the apostles marked a critical breakdown of religious and racial barriers. Philip had already baptized the believing Samaritans; thus, they were already saved. The apostles now witnessed the inclusiveness of the church. They saw that God was giving these Samaritans the exact same gift of the Holy Spirit that He had given to the apostles and disciples in Jerusalem. There was no barrier between the believing Jew and the believing Samaritan. There was one faith, one baptism, and one spirit (cf. Ephesians 4:4-6).

When they arrived in Samaria, Peter and John did not preach. Instead, they prayed and laid hands on the Samaritan converts. As a result, the

Simon because of his magic. They had no faith in Simon; rather, their belief was predicated on his magical abilities. Through the preaching of Philip, the faith of the Samaritans was based on the Good News of Jesus, the Christ, and the kingdom of God. The Samaritans saw Philip's miracles as confirmation of the truth of the resurrection of Christ. The miracles aided—not caused—their faith. Now that faith in Jesus was the basis of their belief, they turned away from Simon. Even Simon himself believed and was baptized.

5. The Missionary's Validation (vv. 14-17)

When news of Philip's successful ministry in Samaria reached Jerusalem, the apostles immediately dispatched Peter and John to Samaria. That these two elder statesmen were sent to Samaria should not be misread. There was no lack of faith on the part of the church in Philip's ability to preach to salvation. This fact was proven when we see that Peter and John apparently did not preach in Samaria.

gift of the Holy Spirit was given to the Samaritans. The Holy Spirit ensured the unity of the church with the impartation of the Holy Spirit. The Holy Spirit also provided a witness in the form of the apostles Peter and John. The apostles were credible and authoritative witnesses to the Jews that the acceptance of Samaritans into the church was equal to that of the Jews.

SEARCH THE SCRIPTURES

1. Why did Philip go to Samaria (Acts 8:5)?
2. How did Philip garner the attention of the Samaritans (vv. 6-7)?
3. What did the Samaritans think of Simon (vv. 10-11)?
4. What was the Samaritans' response to Philip's teaching and preaching (v. 12)?

DISCUSS THE MEANING

1. Discuss the types of obstacles that Philip may have encountered when witnessing to the Samaritans. Then compare those obstacles with the types of obstacles Christians face today when witnessing to people of other races and ethnicities. What are the similarities? What are the differences?

2. Compare and contrast the Samaritans' response to Philip and their response to Simon. Where is the focus in each case? How do you think it affected their final response to each of these men? Are there similar circumstances in our lives today?

3. Why do you think it was necessary for Peter and John to go to Samaria given Philip's apparent evangelistic success there? How did the role of the two apostles differ from Philip's role?

LESSON IN OUR SOCIETY

The responsibility of evangelism is unclear to many Christians today. In some churches, "missions" activity appears to be the sole responsibility of a small group of ladies who meet in the monthly "Mission Circles." In other churches, members view missionaries as those brave souls who are willing to undergo the hardships of living in Third World countries. While we are familiar with the Scripture that tells us "and ye shall be wit-

nesses unto me both in Jerusalem, and in all Judaea, and in Samaria, and unto the uttermost part of the earth" (Acts 1:8), we often mistakenly believe that this mandate no longer applies to us.

The truth that each of us has been commissioned into missionary service eludes many Christians. The source of these misconceptions is irrelevant; what matters is that we begin to "get busy" and do what Jesus commanded each of us to do—witness. We are obligated to share the Good News regardless of the race, creed, or color of the listener. Salvation is open to anyone who believes, and it is our job to tell them.

MAKE IT HAPPEN

It is always easier to strike up conversations with people who look like us or who share our background or culture. This week, ask God to provide an opportunity for you to witness to someone with whom you may have little in common. Spend time in prayer and Bible study so that you are prepared when this opportunity presents itself.

FOLLOW THE SPIRIT

What God wants me to do:

_____

_____

REMEMBER YOUR THOUGHTS

Special insights I have learned:

_____

_____

MORE LIGHT ON THE TEXT

Acts 8:4-17

4 Therefore they that were scattered abroad went every where preaching the word.

Stephen's death led to persecution, and the persecution led to the scattering of the believers (Acts 8:1). Consequently, those who were "scattered abroad" (Gk. *diaspeiro*, **dee-as-pi'-ro**) preached the Word wherever they went. The verb "preaching" (Gk. *euaggelizo*, **yoo-ang-ghel-id'-zo**) means to bring or announce good news or to evangelize (cf. 10:36; 15:35; 17:18; Luke 8:1). The dispersion of the believers resulted in widespread evangelism. They were all involved in the task of spreading the Good

News even though not all were preachers in full-time vocation.

5 Then Philip went down to the city of Samaria, and preached Christ unto them.

Philip, one of the seven appointed in Acts 6:5, "went down" (Gk. *katerchomai*, **kat-er'-khom-ahee**) to the city of Samaria (or to a city of Samaria). We know from John 4:9 that Jews had nothing to do with Samaritans (cf. Luke 9:51-55). Samaria had a population of mixed ancestry dating back to the fall of the northern kingdom of Israel (2 Kings 17:24-41). We learn from 2 Kings 17:41 (NIV) "while [the Samaritans] were worshiping the LORD, they were serving their idols." They were opposed to the rebuilding of Jerusalem during the time of Nehemiah (Nehemiah 4).

It was a courageous act on Philip's part to go among Samaritans. However, he did not let racial barriers stop the spread of the Gospel. They were waiting for the coming of the Messiah, whom they called the *Taheb* ("the restorer"), and whom they identified with prophets like Moses (John 4:25, 29).

6 And the people with one accord gave heed unto those things which Philip spake, hearing and seeing the miracles which he did.

The people "with one accord" (Gk. *homothumadon*, **hom-oth-oo-mad-on'**) were listening eagerly to what Philip was saying. They heard and saw "the miracles" (Gk. *semeion*, **say-mi-on**) that he kept doing.

7 For unclean spirits, crying with loud voice, came out of many that were possessed with them: and many taken with palsies, and that were lame, were healed.

Philip's ministry among the Samaritans was marked by signs and wonders confirming the Gospel (cf. 2:43; 5:12). Evil spirits "came out" (Gk. *exerchomai*, **ex-er'-khom-ahee**) of many people calling out loudly. Many paralyzed and lame people "were healed" (Gk. *therapeuo*, **ther-ap-yoo'-o**).

8 And there was great joy in that city.

A "great joy" (Gk. *chara*, **khar-ah'**) came into the city because of Philip's preaching and healing ministry (cf. 13:48, 52; Luke 2:10).

9 But there was a certain man, called Simon, which beforetime in the same city used sorcery, and bewitched the people of Samaria, giving out that himself was some great one:

For some time before Philip arrived in Samaria, the town had been "bewitched" (Gk. *existemi*, **ex-is'-tay-mee**) by a man named Simon. He practiced witchcraft or "sorcery" (Gk. *mageuo*, **mag-yoo'-o**; literally "practice magic"). Simon used his magical skills to persuade the people of Samaria that he was somebody great (cf. 5:36).

10 To whom they all gave heed, from the least to the greatest, saying, This man is the great power of God.

Everyone, "the least" (Gk. *mikros*, **mik-ros'**) and "the greatest" (Gk. *megas*, **meg'-as**) crowded around him saying that Simon was in some way the special channel of the power of God or the supreme emanation of God Himself.

11 And to him they had regard, because that of long time he had bewitched them with sorceries.

For a long time the people "had regard" (Gk. *prosecho*, **pros-ekh'-o**) or were devoted to Simon because he had used witchcraft to bewitch them.

12 But when they believed Philip preaching the things concerning the kingdom of God, and the name of Jesus Christ, they were baptized, both men and women.

Philip did not preach about himself. Philip was preaching (Gk. *euaggelizo*, **yoo-ang-ghel-id'-zo**) "the things concerning the kingdom of God, and the name of Jesus Christ." The Samaritans "believed" (Gk. *pisteuo*, **pist-yoo'-o**) and "were baptized" (Gk. *baptizo*, **bap-tid'-zo**).

13 Then Simon himself believed also: and when he was baptized, he continued with Philip, and wondered, beholding the miracles and signs which were done.

Simon believed and was baptized. He followed Philip everywhere, amazed by the great signs and miracles he saw. After having amazed others with his magic practice, he himself was amazed.

In view of what is said later in verse 21, we do not know whether or not Simon really believed. The

Bible language does not always make a distinction between believing and professing to believe (cf. James 2:19). He may have been more amazed by the healing power of Philip than by his message.

14 Now when the apostles which were at Jerusalem heard that Samaria had received the word of God, they sent unto them Peter and John:

When the "apostles" (Gk. *apostolos*, **ap-os'-tol-os**) "heard" (Gk. *akouo*, **ak-oo'-o**) that Samaria "had received" (Gk. *dechomai*, dekh'-om-ahee) the Word of God, they "sent" (Gk. *apostello*, ap-os-tel'-lo; the Greek words for "sent" and "apostle" have the same root meaning, literally "the delegated delegated") two, Peter and John, to investigate. On one occasion, James and John had wanted to call fire down from heaven to consume a Samaritan city (cf. Luke 9:51-56). It was fitting that one of them should be part of the delegation that now went to welcome the people of Samaria into the church.

15 Who, when they were come down, prayed for them, that they might receive the Holy Ghost:

When they arrived, they discovered that although the people of Samaria had believed and had been baptized into the name of Jesus, they had not yet received the Holy Ghost. So they prayed for them that they might "receive" (Gk. *lambano*, lamban'-o) the Holy Ghost.

16 (For as yet he was fallen upon none of them: only they were baptized in the name of the Lord Jesus.)

The Holy Ghost had not yet come upon (Gk. *epi*, ep-ee; literally "to fall on") any of them. They had simply been baptized into the name of the Lord Jesus. This statement raises some questions that have caused much perplexity and division: How did the apostles know that the Samaritans had not received the Holy Ghost? In the light of Acts 2:38, how could the Samaritans have believed and been baptized and not received the Spirit? There are two general approaches to these questions. One is that here, as in Acts 2:41 and Acts 10:44-48, Peter was using the keys of the kingdom to open it successively to Jews, Samaritans, and Gentiles. It was a new departure in line with what Jesus said in Acts 1:8.

Thus, we should see it as an abnormal rather than a normal experience of Christian life. Another view is that the Samaritan Christians' experience is a typical experience of Christian life. Becoming a Christian is a two-stage process consisting first of conversion and water baptism, and second of the gift or baptism of the Spirit. The apostle Paul argues against the latter view in Romans 8:9. He states, "If anyone does not have the Spirit of Christ, he is not His." In other words, to be saved a person must have the Holy Spirit.

17 Then laid they their hands on them, and they received the Holy Ghost.

In addition to praying for them, the apostles "laid" (Gk. *epitithemi*, ep-ee-tith'-ay-mee) their hands, thus identifying the people for whom they prayed with the rest of the church, particularly the mother church in Jerusalem. In answer to their prayers, the believers received the Holy Ghost.

DAILY BIBLE READINGS

M: Jesus Teaches in Judea
Matthew 19:1-12

T: Healing in Jericho
Matthew 20:29-34

W: A Visit in Jericho
Luke 19:1-10

T: Jesus Meets a Samaritan Woman
John 4:1-10

F: Water Gushing Up to Eternal Life
John 4:11-15

S: Philip Preaches in Samaria
Acts 8:4-13

S: Peter and John Preach in Samaria
Acts 8:14-25

TEACHING TIPS

October 16
Bible Study Guide 7

1. Words You Should Know
A. Eunuch (Acts 8:27) *eunouchos* (Gk.)—A state officer.

B. Esaias the Prophet (v. 28) *Hesaias prophets* (Gk.)—Isaiah, an Old Testament prophet.

C. Declare his generation (v. 33) *diegeomai autos genea* (Gk.)—To be descendants of someone.

2. Teacher Preparation
A. Read the BIBLE BACKGROUND, using a modern translation of the Bible to gain a thorough understanding of the text.

B. Read THE PEOPLE, PLACES, AND TIMES.

3. Starting the Lesson
A. Read the LESSON AIM.

B. Ask a student to pray, focusing on the LESSON AIM.

C. Have the students read the KEEP IN MIND verse in unison. Ask a volunteer to read the IN FOCUS story.

D. Have another student volunteer to read the BACKGROUND section.

4. Getting into the Lesson
A. Allow your students five to ten minutes to share with one another any opportunities they had to witness in the past week.

B. Use a Bible map of the time of the New Testament to show the students Philip's missionary route.

C. Have the students take turns reading the FOCAL VERSES.

D. Ask volunteers to explain what they think each verse means. Be prepared to assist them with their explanations.

5. Relating the Lesson to Life
A. Ask the students to discuss particular Scriptures that they thought were confusing the first time they read them. List these Scriptures on a chalkboard or dry erase board.

B. Have the students discuss how they came to gain an understanding of those particular Scriptures. Be prepared to answer their questions or clarify the meaning of the FOCAL VERSES.

6. Arousing Action
A. Give the students a few minutes to silently reflect on today's lesson.

B. Ask them to jot down their thoughts in the REMEMBER YOUR THOUGHTS section.

WORSHIP GUIDE

For the Superintendent or Teacher
Theme: The Ethiopian Official
Theme Song: "Where He Leads Me, I Will Follow"
Scripture: Acts 8:35
Song: "Jesus Saves"
Meditation: Lord, I thank You for Your Word. I pray that I will obey Your will and live my life Your way by studying Your Word. Thank You that You have a plan for my life. Amen.

THE ETHIOPIAN OFFICIAL

Bible Background • ACTS 8:26–40
Printed Text • ACTS 8:26–38
Devotional Reading • ACTS 11:19–26

LESSON AIM

By the end of the lesson, we will:

KNOW the events surrounding Philip's use of God's Word to explain salvation to the Ethiopian Eunuch;

BE CONVINCED that studying God's Word is key in understanding God's will and shaping our behavior; and

COMMIT to making Bible study a regular part of our day.

KEEP IN MIND

"Then Philip opened his mouth, and began at the same scripture, and preached unto him Jesus" (Acts 8:35).

FOCAL VERSES

Acts 8:26 And the angel of the Lord spake unto Philip, saying, Arise, and go toward the south unto the way that goeth down from Jerusalem unto Gaza, which is desert.

27 And he arose and went: and behold, a man of Ethiopia, an eunuch of great authority under Candace queen of the Ethiopians, who had the charge of all her treasure, and had come to Jerusalem for to worship,

28 Was returning, and sitting in his chariot read Esaias the prophet.

29 Then the Spirit said unto Philip, Go near, and join thyself to this chariot.

30 And Philip ran thither to him, and heard him read the prophet Esaias, and said, Understandest thou what thou readest?

31 And he said, How can I, except some man should guide me? And he desired Philip that he would come up and sit with him.

LESSON OVERVIEW

LESSON AIM
KEEP IN MIND
FOCAL VERSES
IN FOCUS
THE PEOPLE, PLACES, AND TIMES
BACKGROUND
AT-A-GLANCE
IN DEPTH
SEARCH THE SCRIPTURES
DISCUSS THE MEANING
LESSON IN OUR SOCIETY
MAKE IT HAPPEN
FOLLOW THE SPIRIT
REMEMBER YOUR THOUGHTS
MORE LIGHT ON THE TEXT
DAILY BIBLE READINGS

32 The place of the scripture which he read was this, He was led as a sheep to the slaughter; and like a lamb dumb before his shearer, so opened he not his mouth:

33 In his humiliation his judgment was taken away: and who shall declare his generation? for his life was taken from the earth.

34 And the eunuch answered Philip, and said, I pray thee, of whom speaketh the prophet this? of himself, or of some other man?

35 Then Philip opened his mouth, and began at the same scripture, and preached unto him Jesus.

36 And as they went on their way, they came unto a certain water: and the eunuch said, See, here is water; what doth hinder me to be baptized?

37 And Philip said, If thou believest with all thine heart, thou mayest. And he answered and said, I believe that Jesus Christ is the Son of God.

38 And he commanded the chariot to stand still: and they went down both into the water, both Philip and the eunuch; and he baptized him.

IN FOCUS

Late Saturday evening, Jessica sat at her kitchen table working on her Bible study homework. The assignment was to list seven biblical verses that supported why studying Scriptures should be a daily routine. It was a good exercise for her because she had never been able to quote Scripture accurately.

She wanted to make good use of this exercise,

so she searched verses for hours and then she wrote the following:

1. "This book of the law shall not depart out of thy mouth; but thou shalt meditate therein day and night, that thou mayest observe to do according to all that is written therein: for then thou shalt make thy way prosperous, and then thou shalt have good success" (Joshua 1:8).

2. "But his delight is in the law of the LORD; and in his law doth he meditate day and night. And he shall be like a tree planted by the rivers of water, that bringeth forth his fruit in his season; his leaf also shall not wither; and whatsoever he doeth shall prosper" (Psalm 1:2-3).

3. "Thy word is a lamp unto my feet, and a light unto my path" (Psalm 119:105).

4. "But he answered and said, It is written, Man shall not live by bread alone, but by every word that proceedeth out of the mouth of God" (Matthew 4:4).

5. "And ye shall know the truth, and the truth shall make you free" (John 8:32).

6. "If ye abide in me, and my words abide in you, ye shall ask what ye will, and it shall be done unto you" (John 15:7).

7. "Study to shew thyself approved unto God, a workman that needeth not to be ashamed, rightly dividing the word of truth" (2 Timothy 2:15).

Did you realize that to know God's will, we need to know God's Word? In our lesson this week we will explore how Philip used the Scriptures to explain salvation to the Ethiopian Eunuch.

THE PEOPLE, PLACES, AND TIMES

Eunuchs. Throughout the Bible, there are references to royal attendants appointed by kings as official caretakers of queens, harems, and women (Esther 2:3, 12-15). Those eunuchs who served with distinction were able to rise in rank within the royal households. The Assyrians and the pharaohs of Egypt were known to have minor officials in their court who often served as trustees of the royal assets. While the term is often literal, referring to men who have been physically castrated, this was not always the case. The term "eunuchs" was also used to denote officials who were assigned to duties in the courts of kings. Since the Ethiopian man referred to in today's

lesson was a proselyte to the Jewish religion, we may deduce he was not castrated because the Mosaic Law would not have allowed him to become a part of the congregation of God's people (Deuteronomy 23:1).

Packer, J.I., and M.C. Tenney, eds. Illustrated Manners and Customs of the Bible. Nashville, Tenn.: Thomas Nelson Publishers, 1980. 324, 327.

BACKGROUND

In the book of Acts, the story of Philip's evangelistic effort serves as a transition between the ministries of Peter and Paul. It is Peter's confession of faith that provides the foundation, the very rock upon which Jesus built the church. The account of Paul describes how God adds to the church through Paul's bold and relentless preaching. Philip is right there in the middle of the record of these two great statesmen; Philip's efforts add to the church soul by soul.

We see Philip first serving as an elected deacon in the Jerusalem church (Acts 6:5). His effective witnessing efforts are described in Acts 8:4-25. Philip's witnessing fulfills Jesus' Great Commission to spread the Gospel from Jerusalem into Judea and Samaria and to the uttermost parts of the earth (Ethiopia).

AT-A-GLANCE

1. Philip Obeys the Spirit (Acts 8:26-28)
2. Philip Witnesses in the Spirit (vv. 29-35)
3. The Ethiopian Confesses Christ (vv. 36-38)

IN DEPTH

1. Philip Obeys the Spirit (Acts 8:26-28)

Acts 8 focuses on two great missionary efforts by Philip. In the first, Philip, under the direction of the Holy Spirit, has preached Christ, which led to the conversion of the Samaritans. His success with the Samaritans was verified by the receipt of the Holy Spirit by the Samaritans. This great outpouring of the Spirit was witnessed by Peter and John. Philip had helped to spread the Gospel from Jerusalem and Judea to Samaria and had thereby been instrumental in the fulfillment of Jesus' Great Commission.

The Spirit then directed Philip on another mission. We are told that "an angel of the Lord" directed Philip to go down from Jerusalem to Gaza. In Acts, the writer (Luke) presupposes that Jerusalem is ground zero for church activities. Here he implies that Philip had returned to Jerusalem from Samaria. Philip was now directed southwest into the desert. Initially, Philip was not told what to do at Gaza. However, this lack of information did not stop Philip. He was obedient to the Spirit of the Lord and immediately obeyed. We should note that while Peter and Paul are noted for their great preaching ability, Philip was outstanding in the area of obedience. Whenever the Spirit directed him, Philip heeded. It is clear that prayer and the study of God's Word must have been integral parts of Philip's life because

he was so sensitive to the direction of the Holy Spirit. How much more effective would Christians be today if we were more sensitive and obedient to the Holy Spirit?

On the road, Philip encountered a fellow traveler. Scripture tells us four important things about this man. First, we are told that he was a man from Ethiopia. Native Ethiopians were Black people. The man was from a distant country located along the upper Nile. At this time in history, Ethiopia was located in the area we now know as Sudan.

The next piece of information we have about the traveler is that he was a eunuch. This information is interpreted differently by biblical scholars. See THE PEOPLE, PLACES AND TIMES section.

The third piece of information we are given about the traveler is that he held a high position

The Ethiopian Eunuch learns the Good News.

in the court of Candace, queen of the Ethiopians, and was in "charge of all her treasure." The fourth and final piece of information we are given is that the Ethiopian had been in Jerusalem to worship.

2. Philip Witnesses in the Spirit (vv. 29-35)

The Gaza road was well traveled; certainly other chariots had passed Philip. The Spirit directed Philip to "Go near, and join thyself to this chariot" (v. 29). This was no chance meeting. Philip was being purposefully led by the Holy Spirit to be with this man at this time. In this way, Philip was like Jesus. He did not mind leaving the crowds behind to deal with one lost soul. Notice Philip's zealousness—he ran to the Ethiopian's chariot. Philip recognized the seriousness of his missionary work. Do we hasten to assist in the salvation of the lost?

Because the Ethiopian was reading from the book of Isaiah, we can safely assume that this man took the religion of Judaism seriously. Ethiopia was one of the areas among which the Jews were scattered after the Babylonian conquest (Isaiah 11:11). The eunuch may have had contact with Jews in Ethiopia or in nearby Egypt, where a great many Jews settled. Similarly, the fact that the Ethiopian could read Greek could be explained by the fact that from the time of Ptolemy II (306-246 B.C.), the Ethiopian kingdom had become partially Hellenized.

The custom of the time was to read Scripture aloud. Upon hearing the Ethiopian reading, Philip asked the Ethiopian if he understood what he was reading. The Ethiopian's response was candid. Literally he said, "How can I unless someone shows me the way?" The Ethiopian was confused by what he was reading and needed someone to explain the Scripture to him. The Ethiopian's sincerity and willingness to learn were demonstrated by his invitation to Philip to come into the chariot and sit with him. Like many people today, the Ethiopian was religious and was earnestly looking for the truth, but he lacked saving faith in Jesus Christ and needed someone to show him the way. We must recognize that God could have allowed an angel to explain the Scripture to the Ethiopian, but He commissioned Philip to witness to him. Similarly, Jesus has com-

missioned, ordered, and instructed each and every Christian to share the Gospel with others.

The Holy Spirit had been preparing Philip for this very moment. Philip opened his mouth and "preached unto him Jesus" (v. 35). Philip explained that the prophet Isaiah was describing Jesus, the Christ. The eunuch had no doubt heard a great deal about this Jesus while in Jerusalem.

3. The Ethiopian Confesses Christ (vv. 36-38)

During his preaching, Philip had probably talked about baptism. As soon as they came to a body of water, the eunuch asked if there was any hindrance to his being baptized right on the spot. Notice that Philip did not drill the Ethiopian on his knowledge and understanding of the Scripture. Philip simply asked him if he believed that Jesus was the Son of God. Did he, in other words, have faith? Obviously, at least to Philip, there were no impediments to this man's baptism. Upon the Ethiopian's simple confession of faith, "I believe," Philip recognized that the man was prepared to be placed under the Lordship of Jesus and incorporated into the church [some early manuscripts do not have v. 37]. Philip and the Ethiopian entered the water, and the Ethiopian was baptized.

SEARCH THE SCRIPTURES

1. Why was Philip on the road to Gaza (Acts 8:26)?

2. From where was the Ethiopian official returning when Stephen encountered him (v. 27)?

3. What was the Ethiopian doing in his chariot (v. 28)?

4. Why did Philip approach the Ethiopian (v. 29)?

5. When they reached the water, what did the Ethiopian ask Philip (v. 36)?

DISCUSS THE MEANING

1. Read Acts 1:8. What is the role of the Holy Spirit in Philip's evangelistic efforts?

2. Why do you think Philip was able to be so sensitive to the Holy Spirit's directives?

3. The lesson is clear that the Ethiopian official's faith was sincere. He read the Scripture and was seeking the truth, yet he was lost. Why do you think that was?

4. Are there any signs in today's society that people are seeking the truth? How can they be helped? What can we do to help them?

LESSON IN OUR SOCIETY

When Philip was finalizing his successful missionary work in Samaria, the Spirit ordered him to go to Gaza. Instead of dragging his feet, Philip heeded the unction of the Holy Spirit and performed a life-saving evangelistic appeal to the Ethiopian official. Today's Christians would do well to follow Philip's example and get up and go! If we are to be witnesses for the kingdom, we will have to "obey" the Spirit rather than follow our own course of action. We will be more effective witnesses when we allow God to order our steps in every area of our lives.

MAKE IT HAPPEN

Commit to a daily personal time of devotion, prayer, and Bible study. Select a quiet time and place to do uninterrupted reading of and meditation on the Word of God. You may find that early in the morning or in the evening just before you go to bed is best. Start with five minutes of reading the first week and add three to five minutes each week. A great place to start is with the DAILY BIBLE READINGS.

FOLLOW THE SPIRIT

What God wants me to do:

_____

_____

REMEMBER YOUR THOUGHTS

Special insights I have learned:

_____

_____

MORE LIGHT ON THE TEXT

Acts 8:26-38

26 And the angel of the Lord spake unto Philip, saying, Arise, and go toward the south unto the way that goeth down from Jerusalem unto Gaza, which is desert.

Angels play a critical role in the narrative of Luke and Acts (cf. Luke 2; 11; Acts 5;10; 12; 23; 27). Since Jerusalem was built on a hill, any

departure was considered "going down" from the city. Gaza was one of the five cities occupied by the Philistines in southwest Palestine. At the time Luke writes, it was on a caravan route leading to Egypt that someone traveling from Jerusalem to Ethiopia would naturally take.

27 And he arose and went: and, behold, a man of Ethiopia, an eunuch of great authority under Candace queen of the Ethiopians, who had the charge of all her treasure, and had come to Jerusalem for to worship,

Ethiopia bordered Egypt to the south of Israel and was known in the Bible as the ancient land of Cush (Genesis 2:13; 10:6; 1 Chronicles 1:8; Isaiah 11:11; Ezekiel 38:5). The Ethiopia referred to in antiquity was not modern Ethiopia, but what is now called Sudan.

Ethiopia was considered one of the most wicked nations of the world (Isaiah 20:3-5; 43:3; Ezekiel 30:1-9; Nahum 3:9; Zephaniah 2:11-12), and its people were among those foreigners who would be converted and acknowledge the true God of Israel. For example, Ethiopia figures prominently in a text of Isaiah concerning the restoration of the people (Isaiah 11:11-12; Zephaniah 3:10).

It was not uncommon for eunuchs (i.e., castrated males) to hold positions of importance in royal courts in the region. However, according to Deuteronomy 23:2, this condition meant a rejection of full participation in the Jewish assembly, and according to Leviticus 21:20; 22:24, an emasculated male is physically blemished and in a permanent state of ritual impurity. But Isaiah prophesied that a time would come when "eunuchs [would] keep my sabbaths," "take hold of [his] covenant," and would be given a place in God's house (Isaiah 56:4-5).

The Ethiopian eunuch held a high position in the Ethiopian government. He was in charge of the entire treasury of the Candace. According to ancient writers (Pliny the Elder, *Natural History and Pseudo-Callisthenes*, The Life of Alexander of Macedon), Candace, queen of the Ethiopians, was a dynastic rather than a personal name. That is, it was used to refer to a royal line of queens over various generations (e.g., "the Candace").

The Ethiopian eunuch had come to Jerusalem to worship. The narrative does not indicate whether he was a Jew or a proselyte (i.e., a Gentile who has converted to Judaism). He may have been a God-fearing person (i.e., a non-Jew who, although sympathetic to Judaism, did not submit to circumcision or observe the Torah in its entirety but did agree with the ethical monotheism of the Jews...sometimes attended their synagogue services). However, it would not have been possible for him to participate in the worship in the temple because of his physical blemish. In this regard, his status was like that of other foreigners who came to the temple in spite of being excluded from it.

28 Was returning, and sitting in his chariot read Esaias the prophet. 29 Then the Spirit said unto Philip, Go near, and join thyself to this chariot. 30 And Philip ran thither to him, and heard him read the prophet Esaias, and said, Understandest thou what thou readest?

The angel of the Lord delivered the original message. Here the Spirit of the Lord further instructs Philip. The point is the same: Philip was being directly guided by God.

When the Spirit told Philip to go and join up with the "chariot" (Gk. *harma*, **har'-mah**), he obeyed. As he came near, he heard the eunuch reading Isaiah. It was customary in the ancient world to read aloud, even when alone. This was especially the case with lengthy scrolls where there was no separation between words; it had to be read syllable by syllable to detect the word divisions. The eunuch follows the common practice.

Philip asks the eunuch, "Do you understand what you are reading?" Philip's question derives from the conviction that the prophetic writings contained deeper meaning for the future.

31 And he said, How can I, except some man should guide me? And he desired Philip that he would come up and sit with him.

The eunuch replies, "How can I understand, unless someone instructs me?" "Guide" (Gk. *hode-geo*, **hod-ayg-eh'-o**) literally means to lead along a road (see Jesus' use of the term "blind leaders" and "blind leading the blind" in Matthew 15:14). Here

"guide" gains the transferred sense of "leading" in righteousness or wisdom similar to its use in passages such as Psalm 5:8; 73:24; John 16:13.

Thus, the eunuch invited Philip to get in and sit with him under the assumption that he would be able to explain the passage Isaiah. Traditionally the Jews applied the concepts of suffering and humiliation in Isaiah 52:13–53:12 to the nation Israel or to the unrighteous Gentile nations. Thus the idea of a suffering Messiah was not thought of by the Jewish rabbis of the day. This passage, then, must have been unclear to the eunuch.

32 The place of the scripture which he read was this, He was led as a sheep to the slaughter; and like a lamb dumb before his shearer, so opened he not his mouth: 33 In his humiliation his judgment was taken away: and who shall declare his generation? for his life is taken from the earth.

The passage the eunuch is reading is from Isaiah 53:7–8. The Greek word for "humiliation" (Gk. *tapeinos*, **tap-i-no'-os**) provides a possible allusion both to Luke's theme of "humbling the haughty and exalting the humble" (Luke 1:52; 3:5; 14:11; 18:14), and to the humiliation of Jesus as described by the apostle Paul as "making himself of no reputation" (Gk. *kenosis*, **lem-os'-es**) (Philippians 2:5-11).

34 And the eunuch answered Philip, and said, I pray thee, of whom speaketh the prophet this? of himself, or of some other man?

The eunuch's question is the pertinent one. The traditional understanding of this passage did not address his deep spiritual hunger.

35 Then Philip opened his mouth, and began at the same scripture, and preached unto him Jesus.

After having been invited into the Ethiopian's chariot, Philip explained the Isaiah passage by beginning with the same text, and showed him that Jesus was the focus of the Scriptures. In Luke 24:13-35, the risen Jesus teaches the two on the road to Emmaus how to understand the Scriptures: "O fools, and slow of heart to believe all that the prophets have spoken: Ought not Christ to have suffered these things, and to enter into his glory? And beginning at Moses and all the prophets, he expounded unto them in all the scriptures the things concerning himself" (vv. 25-27).

The Scripture passage in Isaiah that the eunuch was reading focused on the humiliation and exaltation of the Messiah. Similarly, Acts 8:32-33 refers to Jesus generally and to His humiliation (vv. 32-33) and exaltation ("his judgment was taken away," v. 33) in particular.

This type of interpretation of the prophecy of Isaiah is also seen in other New Testament Scriptures. In Romans 10:16, Paul quotes Isaiah 53:1 and applies it to his own ministry. In John 12:38, Jesus quotes Isaiah 53:1 and applies it to His own ministry.

36 And as they went on their way, they came unto a certain water: and the eunuch said, See, here is water; what doth hinder me to be baptized?

After hearing the Scripture explained and being shown how it pointed to Jesus, the eunuch asked, "What hinders me from being baptized?" "Hinder" (Gk. *koluo*, **ko-loo'-o**) is also used in Luke 11:52, where Jesus accuses the lawyers of preventing ("hindering") others from entering the kingdom. Similar circumstances are seen later in Luke's account.

37 And Philip said, If thou believest with all thine heart, thou mayest. And he answered and said, I believe that Jesus Christ is the Son of God. 38 And he commanded the chariot to stand still: and they went down both into the water, both Philip and the eunuch; and he baptized him.

Since there was no reason for his exclusion from full inclusion in the followers of Jesus, the Ethiopian eunuch ordered the chariot to stop, Philip and the eunuch both went down to the water, and Philip baptized him.

DAILY BIBLE READINGS

M: Jesus Teaches About Responding to Others
Matthew 5:38-42
T: Jesus Teaches About Signs
Matthew 12:36-42
W: Jesus Teaches Nicodemus About Rebirth
John 3:1-15
T: Jesus Rebukes the Pharisees and Scribes
Matthew 15:1-9
F: Jesus Asks the Pharisees a Question
Matthew 22:41-46
S: Philip Meets the Ethiopian Official
Acts 8:26-31
S: Philip Proclaims the Good News
Acts 8:32-40

TEACHING TIPS

October 23
Bible Study Guide 8

1. Words You Should Know

A. Alms (Acts 10:2) *eleemosune* (Gk.)—Usually refers to money, but could also refer to compassionate deeds.

B. The ninth hour (v. 3) *ennatos hora* (Gk.)—Three o'clock in the afternoon.

C. Memorial (v. 4) *mnemosunon* (Gk.)—A reminder.

D. The sixth hour (v. 9) *hektos hora* (Gk.)—Noontime.

E. Creeping things (v. 12) *herpeton* (Gk.)—Reptiles or serpents.

2. Teacher Preparation

A. Read the BIBLE BACKGROUND.

B. Read the MORE LIGHT ON THE TEXT section to gain greater insight into the lesson's significance.

C. Read the FOCAL VERSES from several different translations (i.e., the *New International Version* and *Living Bible*) to increase your understanding of and familiarity with these Scriptures.

3. Starting the Lesson

A. Lead the class in prayer, using the LESSON AIM as a focus.

B. Read the IN FOCUS story and relate it to the action objective in the LESSON AIM.

C. Ask the class to read the KEEP IN MIND verse in unison.

D. Read the BACKGROUND section.

4. Getting into the Lesson

A. Read THE PEOPLE, PLACES, AND TIMES section to give the students more insight into Peter's dilemma.

B. Ask volunteers to read the IN DEPTH commentary aloud. Allow the students to discuss each section.

C. Ask the students to answer the questions in the DISCUSS THE MEANING section. Be prepared to assist them.

5. Relating the Lesson to Life

Have the students read the LESSON IN OUR SOCIETY section. Ask them to brainstorm ideas about how to implement the principles of evangelism they have studied today.

6. Arousing Action

A. Challenge the students to read the DAILY BIBLE READINGS for the week.

B. Close the class with prayer. Be sure to pray for the efforts of missionaries in our country and around the world.

OC
23F

CORNELIUS AND THE GENTILES

Bible Background • ACTS 10:1-48
Printed Text • ACTS 10:1-20
Devotional Reading • ACTS 13:44-49

LESSON AIM

By the end of the lesson, we will:

KNOW how God prepared Peter to share the Gospel with Cornelius, a Gentile;

FEEL Peter's transformed attitude about sharing the Gospel with someone different from him; and

DECIDE to adopt Peter's transformed attitude when it comes to sharing the Gospel with others.

KEEP IN MIND

"While Peter thought on the vision, the Spirit said unto him, Behold, three men seek thee. Arise therefore, and get thee down, and go with them, doubting nothing: for I have sent them" (Acts 10:19-20).

FOCAL VERSES

Acts 10:1 There was a certain man in Caesarea called Cornelius, a centurion of the band called the Italian band,

2 A devout man, and one that feared God with all his house, which gave much alms to the people, and prayed to God alway.

3 He saw in a vision evidently about the ninth hour of the day an angel of God coming in to him, and saying unto him, Cornelius.

4 And when he looked on him, he was afraid, and said, What is it, Lord? And he said unto him, Thy prayers and thine alms are come up for a memorial before God.

5 And now send men to Joppa, and call one Simon, whose surname is Peter:

6 He lodgeth with one Simon a tanner, whose

LESSON OVERVIEW

LESSON AIM
KEEP IN MIND
FOCAL VERSES
IN FOCUS
THE PEOPLE, PLACES, AND TIMES
BACKGROUND
AT-A-GLANCE
IN DEPTH
SEARCH THE SCRIPTURES
DISCUSS THE MEANING
LESSON IN OUR SOCIETY
MAKE IT HAPPEN
FOLLOW THE SPIRIT
REMEMBER YOUR THOUGHTS
MORE LIGHT ON THE TEXT
DAILY BIBLE READINGS

house is by the sea side: he shall tell thee what thou oughtest to do.

7 And when the angel which spake unto Cornelius was departed, he called two of his household servants, and a devout soldier of them that waited on him continually;

8 And when he had declared all these things unto them, he sent them to Joppa.

9 On the morrow, as they went on their journey, and drew nigh unto the city, Peter went up upon the housetop to pray about the sixth hour:

10 And he became very hungry, and would have eaten: but while they made ready, he fell into a trance,

11 And saw heaven opened, and a certain vessel descending unto him, as it had been a great sheet knit at the four corners, and let down to the earth:

12 Wherein were all manner of fourfooted beasts of the earth, and wild beasts, and creeping things, and fowls of the air.

13 And there came a voice to him, Rise, Peter; kill, and eat.

14 But Peter said, Not so, Lord; for I have never eaten any thing that is common or unclean.

15 And the voice spake unto him again the second time, What God hath cleansed, that call not thou common.

16 This was done thrice: and the vessel was received up again into heaven.

17 Now while Peter doubted in himself what this vision which he had seen should mean, behold, the men which were sent from Cornelius had made inquiry for Simon's house, and stood before the gate,

18 And called, and asked whether Simon, which was surnamed Peter, were lodged there.

19 While Peter thought on the vision, the Spirit said unto him, Behold, three men seek thee.

20 Arise therefore, and get thee down, and go with them, doubting nothing: for I have sent them.

IN FOCUS

Juan was a six-foot-four, 300-pound-man known as the meanest police officer in his district. One night as Juan was in the hospital emergency room waiting to interview a gunshot victim, he ran into a retired sergeant from his district. Juan looked in disbelief when he saw Curtis lying on an ambulatory cot waiting to be transported to a hospital room. Curtis was a legend in the police station. He once had the distinction of being the biggest, meanest police officer that ever walked the district. Juan discovered that Curtis had terminal cancer and was waiting for admission to a hospice care facility. In a weakened voice, Curtis asked Juan to come to his room later so the two could talk.

Upon entering the hospital room, Juan struggled for the right words to console Curtis: "Curtis, this is terrible. . . . I know . . . I didn't realize you were so sick."

Curtis pulled on Juan's shirt sleeve and motioned for him to bend down closer so he could hear Curtis speak. In a hushed voice Curtis said, "Juan, I'm fine. Do you know Christ?"

Startled, Juan replied, "What do you mean, man? No, nobody ever told me anything about Christ. Hey, you just lie back and relax; don't get yourself all worked up."

But Curtis insisted that Juan listen to what he had to say. With his family around him, Curtis began to witness to Juan about Christ. He told Juan the story of Jesus and how He died for our sins. In labored breaths Curtis told him, "All have sinned and come short of the glory of God. There's only one way to Christ—that's by being born again. Juan, every mean thing you and I

have ever done was placed on the body of Jesus when He died on that Cross."

On the ride home, Juan cried out loud. He realized that could be him lying in the hospital near death. The next week Juan accepted Christ as his Saviour and began attending church services. After several visits, he joined the church choir and the prison ministry.

Are you sharing the Gospel with all those willing to hear and receive it? In our lesson today, we will observe how Peter became convinced he must share the Gospel with people different from him.

THE PEOPLE, PLACES, AND TIMES

Clean and Unclean Animals and the Jewish Diet. The distinction between clean and unclean animals appears to have originated before the Flood. We read that Noah was instructed to take both clean (seven pairs) and unclean (one pair) animals into the ark. Animals were not eaten during this time, but the prohibition against eating the animals was lifted once Noah left the ark. Then God told Noah that he and his family could eat all "moving" and "live" animals (Genesis 9:3).

The dietary restrictions Peter refers to in Acts 10:14 were handed down to the Children of Israel by Moses. Only clean food was acceptable for eating. Four-legged animals with parted or split hoofs and those that chewed the cud were declared edible. These animals included cattle, sheep, goats, deer, and antelope. Animals lacking one or both of these features were unclean and not to be eaten. These forbidden animals would have included pigs, camels, hares, badgers, and the like. The law also forbade the eating of animals that moved about on their "paws." This included lions, bears, and wolves (Leviticus 11:4-8, 26-27).

The factors determining which birds were considered unclean are not expressly stated in the Bible, but it is clear that scavengers and birds of prey were considered unclean. Only water animals that had fins and scales were considered clean and could be eaten. Catfish, sharks, eels, and crustacea (shellfish), many of which live on sewage and decaying matter, were declared unclean (Leviticus 11:9-12); thus, Jews were forbidden to eat them.

Packer J.I. and M.C. Tenney, eds. Illustrated Manners and Customs of the Bible. Nashville, Tenn.: Thomas Nelson Publishers, 1980. 244-245.

BACKGROUND

In the past two lessons, the evangelist Philip has been the principal character. In today's lesson, the focus changes to the apostle Peter, one of the principal characters in the book of Acts. We must remember that both Philip and Peter are being guided and empowered by the Holy Spirit. It is through the workings of the Spirit that lives are touched and transformed.

As you may recall, two of the central themes of the book of Acts are the spreading of the Gospel outside of Jerusalem and Judea, and the incorporation of the Gentiles into the church. This cross-cultural theme is a very important theme in the book of Acts. The story of the conversion of Cornelius is one of the longest conversion passages in the book of Acts. More space is given to this telling than to the conversion of Paul.

Again we see the working of the Spirit to build and unify the church. The Spirit works through Peter and reaches beyond cultural, racial, and religious barriers to create one body of baptized believers. The baptism of the Ethiopian gives witness to an individual transformation. The conversion of Cornelius's household gives witness to the legitimization of the Gentile mission.

AT-A-GLANCE

1. God's Response to a Seeking Heart (Acts 10:1-8)

2. God's Revelation to a Praying Heart (vv. 9-16)

3. God's Reassurance to a Perplexed Heart (vv. 17-20)

IN DEPTH

1. God's Response to a Seeking Heart (Acts 10:1-8)

The first part of Acts 10 begins in Caesarea, an important seaport city located on the Mediterranean about 54 miles northwest of Jerusalem. During the New Testament era, Caesarea was also a seat of government and an official residence of the Roman procurators who governed Judea. While the population of Caesarea was primarily Gentile, it did have a large minority of Jews.

A garrison of Roman soldiers protected the city and the harbor. Cornelius is introduced as a Roman officer, a centurion. A centurion was a noncommissioned officer who commanded 100 men. This was the highest rank that could be achieved by a non-common soldier. Centurions served a vital role in the function of the Roman legions and were considered the most experienced and valuable men in the Roman army. The "Italian band" mentioned in verse 1 probably refers to an Italian regiment.

Luke describes Cornelius as being "devout" and "one that feared God." This devotion to God was a reality for all his household, not only for his immediate family but also for his personal servants. Cornelius was a Gentile who apparently recognized the emptiness of idol worship and sought to worship the one true God. Though he was not associated with Judaism, he was devoted to prayer and led a moral life. He also gave generously to those in need. Indeed, this spiritually sensitive Roman army officer had a heart that longed to be right with God.

The sincerity of Cornelius's prayer life is indicated by the fact that we find him praying at "about the ninth hour," or around 3:00 p.m. This would have been the hour of prayer in Jerusalem's temple. Cornelius was visited by an "angel of God." The angel called Cornelius and told him that both his prayers and alms have "come up as a memorial before God" (v. 4). Cornelius's devotion to God did not go unnoticed and was remembered by God himself.

The angel spoke in the language of Old Testament sacrifice. The "memorial offering" alludes to the offerings made from grain that were burned as "a memorial portion" (Leviticus 2:2, NIV). The angel went on to instruct Cornelius to "send men to Joppa" and have them find and bring back the apostle "Simon, whose surname is Peter" (Acts 10:5). The angel informed Cornelius that Peter was staying with a tanner, one who converted animal hides into leather, named Simon.

Cornelius immediately sent for two of his servants and a "devout" soldier who was one of his attendants and told everything the angel had said. The next morning, they left for Joppa, with instructions to bring Peter back to Caesarea.

The angel did not tell Cornelius why he needed to send men 30 miles to Joppa. Nor was Cornelius told why Peter needed to be brought back to Caesarea. Cornelius was simply ordered to blindly obey the command of the Lord. This is similar to the account of Philip being sent to the Gaza road. Neither Philip nor Cornelius knew the reason for the divine command; yet through their obedience, they were being guided by God to do His will.

2. God's Revelation to a Praying Heart (vv. 9-16)

The next day as the men from Caesarea approached Joppa (at about noon, or "the sixth hour"), Peter went to the rooftop of Simon's house to pray. Noon was not one of the official times for prayer among the Jews, yet devout Jews (based on Psalm 55:17; Daniel 6:10) regularly prayed at noon.

Peter grew hungry, and while a meal was being prepared, he fell into a trance. In the trance, Peter saw what looked like a sheet lowered from heaven. The sheet contained three categories of living creatures: animals, creatures that moved along the ground, and birds. These categories mirror the three divisions of animal life given in Genesis 6:20. Peter was offended by the presence of unclean animals among the clean ones. His offense was aggravated when he was commanded to "kill, and eat" with no distinction made between clean and unclean animals. Even though the command came from the Lord, Peter was determined not to defile himself by violating basic dietary restrictions of Leviticus 11.

The voice told Peter, "Do not call anything impure that God has made clean" (v. 15, NIV). Peter would soon learn that the vision had a much wider application regarding Jewish-Gentile unity in the body of Christ. Because this message was repeated three times, it made a deep impression on Peter.

Food was one of the factors that adversely affected relationships between the Jews and the Gentiles. Eating was the center of social life, but Jews felt they risked defilement by eating at the home of a Gentile. A Jew could not be certain that the food being served in a Gentile home was clean and that it had been prepared according to the requirements of the Law. Therefore, Jews avoided this type of fellowship and dealings with Gentiles. Three times Peter was told to eat, and three times he refused, even though he had been assured that God had cleansed the animals.

3. God's Reassurance to a Perplexed Heart (vv. 17-20)

Even though the voice admonished Peter not to call "common" or unclean what God had cleansed, Peter "doubted in himself," or wondered what this vision meant. Peter's dilemma is understandable. He was, for the most part, a faithful, law-abiding Jew, yet he was commanded by a heavenly voice to do something that was forbidden by the Law.

While Peter was puzzling over this vision, the emissaries from Cornelius arrived and stopped at the gate to Simon the tanner's house. Cornelius, a devout non-Jew, was aware of the tensions between Jews and Gentiles and had probably instructed his men to wait at the gate rather than appearing rude by coming directly to the door.

While the men stood at the gate and called out for him, "Peter thought on the vision, [and] the Spirit said unto him, Behold, three men seek thee" (v. 19). Their calling out to Simon from the gate is symbolic of the separation between Jews and Gentiles, which the Holy Spirit is working (through Peter and Cornelius) to correct. We may read the Holy Spirit's admonition to Peter — "Arise therefore, and get thee down, and go with them, doubting nothing: for I have sent them" (v. 20)—as more proof of Peter's reluctance to have direct association with Gentiles.

There can be no doubt in Peter's mind that God was dealing with him and directing him to fulfill some unknown mission. Peter needed this kind of reassurance from God because he was being led into uncharted territory. God was preparing to use Peter and Cornelius to usher in a new era in the church. Just as God declared all animals clean, so God declared the Gentiles clean and worthy of admittance into the kingdom as full citizens. There would be no more separation.

SEARCH THE SCRIPTURES

Fill in the blanks below.

1. "There was a certain man in Caesarea called _____, a centurion of the band called the Italian band" (Acts 10:1).

2. "A devout man, and one that feared God with all his house, which gave much _____to the people, and prayed to God alway" (v. 2).

3. "And now send men to Joppa, and call for one _____, whose surname is Peter" (v. 5).

4. "Wherein were all manner of fourfooted _____ of the earth, and wild beasts, and creeping things, and fowls of the air" (v. 12).

5. "And there came a voice to him, Rise, Peter; ____, and ____" (v. 13).

DISCUSS THE MEANING

1. Peter was told three times to eat, yet he refused. Why do you think Peter repeatedly refused?

2. Clearly, God uses clean and unclean food to make Peter aware of His plan for the inclusion of the Gentiles into the body of Christ. What do you think are some of the barriers to inclusion that exist in today's world? Are dietary restrictions still an issue? Are there others?

LESSON IN OUR SOCIETY

Most Christians would agree that Acts 10 marks the outreach of the Gospel to the Gentiles and the start of the modern missionary movement. While we would agree, most of us still view evangelism and missions as the work of the preacher and the missionary. We are content to attend church services, fellowship with other Christians, and go about our business. None of us, knowing that an elevator was broken, would stand idly by and allow a stranger to enter it. Yet we are often silent in the face of the unsaved. Our refusal to witness is a refusal to heed the call of the Great Commission. Christ instructed us to go and preach to every creature because whoever believes will be saved (Mark 16:15-16).

Refusal to heed the Great Commission is a

dangerous position for any Christian to take. The Great Commission is not a suggestion; it is a direct order. God loved us enough to send Jesus to save us. The Christian is obligated to love God enough to obey and to assist in the salvation of others.

MAKE IT HAPPEN

Today, make a decision to share the Gospel of Jesus Christ with someone, no matter who they are or how different they may be from you. A good place to start is by making a list of all the people you know who are unsaved. Pray and ask God to provide an opportunity to witness to at least one of these people on your list.

FOLLOW THE SPIRIT

What God wants me to do:

_____

_____

REMEMBER YOUR THOUGHTS

Special insights I have learned:

_____

_____

MORE LIGHT ON THE TEXT

Acts 10:1-20

1 There was a certain man in Caesarea called Cornelius, a centurion of the band called the Italian band,

Cornelius was a Roman citizen who served in the military as a "centurion" (Gk. *hekaton-tarches*, **hek-at-on-tar'-khace**) of the Italian band. A centurion was an officer in the Roman army. The reader may be reminded of the centurion who sent messengers to Jesus with a request for help (Luke 7:1-10).

2 A devout man, and one that feared God with all his house, which gave much alms to the people, and prayed to God alway.

Cornelius is further described as a "devout" (Gk. *eusebes*, **yoo-seb-ace'**) and God-fearing man. "Devout" here and in Acts 10:7 has much the same force as "devout" used in Luke 2:25 about Simeon. In Acts 2:5 about the visitors to Jerusalem on the Day of Pentecost, in 8:2 about the men who buried Stephen after his execution, and in 22:12 about Ananias, they specifically denote religious reverence. Cornelius is also said to have "feared God," a term that appears again in Acts 10:22, 35; 13:16, 26 (see also the use of the equivalent term "God worshiper" in Acts 16:14; 18:3). "God fearers" were non-Jews sympathetic to Judaism who did not submit to circumcision or observe the Torah in its entirety but did agree with the ethical monotheism of the Jews and sometimes attended their synagogue services.

This piety of Cornelius is expressed in traditional terms: "gave much alms to the people," meaning the Jews (like the centurion of Luke 7:5) and "prayed to God alway."

3 He saw in a vision evidently about the ninth hour of the day an angel of God coming in to him, and saying unto him, Cornelius.

"The ninth hour" (i.e., three in the afternoon) was a set time for sacrifice and prayer. The evening temple service goes back to the instructions of Exodus 29:38-42; Numbers 28:1-8; Daniel 6:10. This suggests it was a traditional time for prayer.

In contrast to the visions of Saul (Acts 9:3-6) and Ananias (Acts 9:10-16), Luke again reports that an angel delivered the message (Luke 1:11, 26; 2:9; Acts 7:30; 8:26). Visions are reported often in the Scriptures (Genesis 15:1-6; Exodus 3:1-6; Judges 6:11-16; 13:3-7). In Luke and Acts, appearances of angels signal events of great importance (Luke 1:5-23; 26-38; 2:8-20; 24:1-11; Acts 1:6-11). Compare Acts 10:30, where the "angel" is said to be "a man in bright clothing."

4 And when he looked on him, he was afraid, and said, What is it, Lord? And he said unto him, Thy prayers and thine alms are come up for a memorial before God.

Like Saul (Acts 9:5), Cornelius did not understand who was appearing to him and addressed the angel respectfully. Luke extended Cornelius's reaction to the apparition by reporting that he "looked (Gk. *atenizo*, **at-en-id'-zo**) on him and he was "afraid" (Gk. *emphobos*, **em'-tob os**). Afraid is also used in Luke 24:5 to describe the reaction of the women, who had prepared spices to anoint the body of Jesus, upon seeing the two men in dazzling apparel at the tomb, and in Luke 24:37 to describe the reaction of the disciples upon seeing Jesus after His resurrection. Fear is a normal reaction to a manifestation of the supernatural world (see, for example, Abraham in Genesis 15:12, David in 2 Samuel 6:9, Mary in Luke 1:30, and John in Revelation 1:17).

The angel told Cornelius that his prayers and almsgiving had ascended as "a memorial before God." Luke's language combines two notions. In using "memorial" (Gk. *mnemosunon*, **may-mos'-oo-non**), he uses the Septuagint word used to translate the Hebrew terms *zikrown* and *azkarah*, which was used for the cereal offerings made to God (Leviticus 2:2, 9, 16; 5:12) whose odor rises to the presence of the Lord, so that He "remembers" the person making the sacrifice (Leviticus 6:15).

The second notion, which develops in Judaism during this period, is that prayer and charity or even the study of Torah are in effect "spiritual sacrifices" that are roughly equivalent to those offered in the temple. In the New Testament, similar references are given in Philippians 4:18; Romans 12:1; Hebrews 13:15-16; 1 Peter 2:5.

5 And now send men to Joppa, and call for one Simon, whose surname is Peter:

In response to Cornelius's acts of piety, God was now acting to answer his prayers and to assist him. Luke used the verb "call for" (Gk. *metapempo*, **met-ap-emp'-o,** meaning send for, or summon) for the first time; it reappears in Acts 10:22, 29; 11:13; 24:24, 26; 25:3.

The apostle Peter's Greek name was Simon. The double naming will appear again in Acts 10:18, 32; 11:13. Luke 6:14 explains that Jesus named Simon "Peter." Though "Simon Peter" occurred earlier, in Luke 5:8, Peter (Gk. *Petros*, **pet'-ros**) is the only name used after Luke 6:14 and in Acts up to this point.

6 He lodgeth with one Simon a tanner, whose house is by the sea side: he shall tell thee what thou oughtest to do.

In Acts 9:43, Peter is identified as staying in Joppa with Simon, a tanner, a trade that was often scorned by ancient Pharisees because of the odors associated with it. The added detail that the house is by the seaside serves to further describe Joppa as a town on the coast of the Mediterranean Sea. Peter will tell Cornelius what he ought to do next.

7 And when the angel which spake unto Cornelius was departed, he called two of his household servants, and a devout soldier of them that waited on him continually;

After the angel finished speaking with Cornelius and left him, Cornelius called three men: two household servants and a devout soldier. Luke's use of "devout" tells us that this soldier shared Cornelius's faith (10:2) and would represent him well.

8 And when he had declared all these things unto them, he sent them to Joppa.

Cornelius told his underlings all that he had been told by the angel. "Declared" (Gk. *exegeomai*, **ex-ayg-eh'-om-ahee**) could be translated as "narrated." The recital here played the same role as in Acts 9:27 (using the Greek word *diegeomai*, **dee-ayg-eh-om-ahee**), namely to bring a private experience into the public realm (Acts 15:12, 14).

9 On the morrow, as they went on their journey, and drew nigh unto the city, Peter went up upon the housetop to pray about the sixth hour:

The sixth hour is noon and explains Peter's hunger (Acts 10:10). In contrast to using the roof as a place to worship false gods (Jeremiah 19:13; 32:29; Zephaniah 1:5), Peter used the roof terrace as a place of isolation for communing with God privately.

10 And he became very hungry, and would have eaten: but while they made ready, he fell into a trance,

While waiting for others to prepare the noon meal, Peter fell into a trance. Luke will use "trance" (Gk. *ekstasis*, **ek'stas-is**) to refer to a visionary state in Acts 11:5 and 22:17. *Ekstasis* is translated from the Hebrew word *tardemah* (**tar-day maw'**), which falls on Adam in Genesis 2:21 and on Abraham in Genesis 15:12.

11 And saw heaven opened, and a certain vessel descending unto him, as it had been a great sheet knit at the four corners, and let down to the earth:

Peter sees a sheet-like object descending from heaven. The opening of heaven is a standard feature of visions (John 1:51; Revelation 4:1; 19:11). The Greek literally has a "certain vessel" (Gk. *tisskeuos*, **tis-skyoo-os**) descending with the next clause functioning as a description: "like a great sheet." "Let down" (Gk. *kathiemi*, **kath-ee'-ay-mee**) describes the mode of descent: It is being "let down" by, or at, its four "corners" (Gk. *arche*, **arkhay'**).

12 Wherein were all manner of fourfooted beasts of the earth, and wild beasts, and creeping things, and fowls of the air.

The list is meant to be inclusive of all creatures (compare Genesis 1:24; 6:20; Leviticus 11:46-47; Romans 1:23) given to human beings as food (Genesis 9:3) without making any distinctions between them. The distinctions were legislated by Leviticus 11:1-47, which concludes, "To make a difference between the unclean and the clean, and between the beast that may be eaten and the beast that may not be eaten" (Leviticus 11:47).

13 And there came a voice to him, Rise, Peter; kill, and eat.

The instruction to "rise, kill, and eat" came from the same realm from which the sheet-like object descended, namely from heaven.

14 But Peter said, Not so, Lord; for I have never eaten any thing that is common or unclean.

Peter responds strongly. The term "not so" (Gk. *medamos*, **may-dam-ice**) expresses a strongly felt negative, found in the New Testament only here and in Peter's repetition of the story in Acts 11:8. The Septuagint uses it for similar sorts of responses (Genesis 18:25; Jonah 1:14). The most striking antecedent is Ezekiel 4:14: The Lord tells the prophet that the people will eat the bread unclean, and the prophet replies, "Lord God!...my soul hath not been polluted: for from my youth up even till now have I not eaten of that which dieth of itself."

In Leviticus 11:1-47 and Deuteronomy 14:3-20, one finds lists of animals that a Jew was not supposed to eat, and the distinction between ritually "clean" and "unclean" foods. Forbidden or defiling foods are called "unclean" (Gk. *akathartos*, **ak-ath'-ar-tos**).

15 And the voice spake unto him again the second time, What God hath cleansed, that call not thou common.

"Cleansed" (Gk. *katharizo*, **kath-ar-id'-zo**) is the word used by the Septuagint for the pronouncements of the priests on matters of ritual impurity (Leviticus 13:6, 13, 17; Luke 11:39); see also the use in Mark 7:19, "Jesus declared all foods clean" and its application to the healing of lepers in Luke 4:27; 5:12-13; 7:22; 17:14, 17. In his disregard for laws of purity in the interests of making disciples, Peter acts in a way that is in continuity with what the earthly Jesus had foreshadowed (Luke 5:29-32; 7:36-50; 10:29-37; 11:37-41; 15:1-2; 19:1-10). The implication is that all things God created are declared to be clean by Him, and are not affected by human discriminations (Romans 14:14; 1 Timothy 4:1-4).

16 This was done thrice: and the vessel was received up again into heaven.

The threefold repetition shows the divine initiative overcoming human resistance and the importance of the instruction that was given to Peter.

17 Now while Peter doubted in himself what this vision which he had seen should mean, behold, the men which were sent from Cornelius had made inquiry for Simon's house, and stood before the gate,

The meaning of the vision was not obvious to Peter. So he was perplexed.

18 And called, and asked whether Simon, which was surnamed Peter, were lodged there. 19 While Peter thought on the vision, the Spirit said unto him, Behold, three men seek thee. 20 Arise therefore, and get thee down, and go with them, doubting nothing: for I have sent them.

The vision was followed by a clear, divine command. Peter was not only addressed by the Spirit, but was told that God was at work in the disposition of this affair. The reader understands with Peter that it was not only the human Cornelius who sent the messengers, but that "I have sent them."

Peter was commanded to go with the three men who would take him to the home of Cornelius. "Doubting nothing" (Gk. *diakrinomenos*, **dee-ak-ree'no-me-nos'**) has a double nuance that is important for the development of the story. The Greek verb *diakrino* can mean to doubt or hesitate (James 1:6) with the result that one is "double minded" (James 4:8). It can also mean to make a discrimination or choose between (James 2:4). Peter, in effect, is told not to be filled with doubts about the course of events that will eventually lead him to understand how he is not to discriminate between people (see Acts 11:2, 12; 15:9).

DAILY BIBLE READINGS

M: Cornelius Has a Vision
Acts 10:1-8
T: Peter Has a Vision
Acts 10:9-16
W: Cornelius's Men Call on Peter
Acts 10:17-22
T: Peter Visits Cornelius
Acts 10:23-33
F: Peter Shares the Good News
Acts 10:34-43
S: Gentiles Receive the Holy Spirit
Acts 10:44-48
S: Peter Explains How Gentiles Also Believed
Acts 11:1-15

TEACHING TIPS

October 30
Bible Study Guide 9

1. Words You Should Know

A. Vex (Acts 12:1) *kakoo* (Gk.)—Denotes an intention to harm or hurt.

B. Quaternions (12:4) *tetradion* (Gk.)—Peter was heavily guarded by a squadron of four groups of four soldiers each, with each group taking a six-hour guard duty.

2. Teacher Preparation

A. Read the BIBLE BACKGROUND to familiarize yourself with the lesson content.

B. Reread the FOCAL VERSES using a modern translation of the Bible.

C. Read THE PEOPLE, PLACES, AND TIMES to familiarize yourself with the persecution that Peter and the other Christians were facing.

3. Starting the Lesson

A. Read the LESSON AIM.

B. Have the students read the KEEP IN MIND verse in unison.

C. Have the students read the IN FOCUS story and ask them to list some of the ways they have seen the power of prayer demonstrated in their lives. List their responses on a chalkboard or dry erase board.

4. Getting into the Lesson

A. Ask for volunteers to read the FOCAL VERSES.

B. Have the students take turns explaining what they think the verses mean. Be prepared to assist them with their explanations.

C. Allow 10 minutes for the students to discuss how the IN FOCUS story applies to today's lesson.

5. Relating the Lesson to Life

Have a student read the LESSON IN OUR SOCIETY section. Encourage the students to discuss this section and how it applies to their lives.

6. Arousing Action

A. Challenge the students to complete this week's MAKE IT HAPPEN exercise.

B. Have the class form a circle and hold hands. Ask if anyone would like to make a prayer request. Ask for volunteers to pray for the specific requests. You might begin the prayer session by praying for one of the stated requests.

WORSHIP GUIDE

For the Superintendent or Teacher
Theme: Peter in Prison
Theme Song: "In Times Like These"
Scripture: Acts 12:7
Song: "I Need Thee Every Hour"
Meditation: Lord, thank You for allowing me direct and immediate access to Your throne of grace through prayer. Amen.

PETER IN PRISON

Bible Background • ACTS 12:1–17
Printed Text • ACTS 12:1–16
Devotional Reading • PSALM 46

LESSON AIM

By the end of the lesson, we will:

KNOW the events surrounding Peter's imprisonment and deliverance;

BE CONVINCED that prevailing prayer can have wonderful results; and

COMMIT to praying for a particular situation, expecting God to answer according to His will.

KEEP IN MIND

"And, behold, the angel of the Lord came upon him, and a light shined in the prison: and he smote Peter on the side, and raised him up, saying, Arise up quickly. And his chains fell off from his hands" (Acts 12:7).

LESSON OVERVIEW

LESSON AIM
KEEP IN MIND
FOCAL VERSES
IN FOCUS
THE PEOPLE, PLACES, AND TIMES
BACKGROUND
AT-A-GLANCE
IN DEPTH
SEARCH THE SCRIPTURES
DISCUSS THE MEANING
LESSON IN OUR SOCIETY
MAKE IT HAPPEN
FOLLOW THE SPIRIT
REMEMBER YOUR THOUGHTS
MORE LIGHT ON THE TEXT
DAILY BIBLE READINGS

FOCAL VERSES

Acts 12:1 Now about that time Herod the king stretched forth his hands to vex certain of the church.

2 And he killed James the brother of John with the sword.

3 And because he saw it pleased the Jews, he proceeded further to take Peter also. (Then were the days of unleavened bread.)

4 And when he apprehended him, he put him in prison, and delivered him to four quaternions of soldiers to keep him; intending after Easter to bring him forth to the people.

5 Peter therefore was kept in prison: but prayer was made without ceasing of the church unto God for him.

6 And when Herod would have brought him forth, the same night Peter was sleeping between two soldiers, bound with two chains: and the keepers before the door kept the prison.

7 And, behold, the angel of the Lord came upon him, and a light shined in the prison: and he smote Peter on the side, and raised him up, saying, Arise up quickly. And his chains fell off from his hands.

8 And the angel said unto him. Gird thyself, and bind on thy sandals. And so he did. And he saith unto him, Cast thy garment about thee, and follow me.

9 And he went out, and followed him; and wist not that it was true which was done by the angel; but thought he saw a vision.

10 When they were past the first and the second ward, they came unto the iron gate that leadeth unto the city; which opened to them of his own accord: and they went out, and passed on through one street; and forthwith the angel departed from him.

11 And when Peter was come to himself, he said, Now I know of a surety, that the Lord hath sent his angel, and hath delivered me out of the hand of Herod, and from all the expectation of the people of the Jews.

12 And when he had considered the thing, he came to the house of Mary the mother of John, whose surname was Mark; where many were gathered together praying.

13 And as Peter knocked at the door of the gate,

a damsel came to hearken, named Rhoda.

14 And when she knew Peter's voice, she opened not the gate for gladness, but ran in, and told how Peter stood before the gate.

15 And they said unto her, Thou art mad. But she constantly affirmed that it was even so. Then said they, It is his angel.

16 But Peter continued knocking: and when they had opened the door, and saw him, they were astonished.

IN FOCUS

Jamal was a handsome 30-year-old man who grew up in a family that didn't attend church or practice Christianity. Jamal's dad died when Jamal was 8, and beginning that day a wall of hate and bitterness began to build around his heart. He didn't know about God's love or why God loved him. Not many people could see the bitterness behind his beautiful smile.

When he met his wife, Karen, Jamal felt peace for the first time. She was a praying young woman who talked to him often about God's love. Eventually the two were married and Karen became pregnant. Unfortunately, Karen underwent a difficult pregnancy and their child was stillborn. Soon after that, the bitterness crept back into Jamal's heart. Once again, he felt alone and abandoned. Nothing could soothe his pain; he and Karen began to argue constantly. Through the whole ordeal, Karen prayed earnestly for her husband to release the anger and bitterness she saw building inside of him. She attended church regularly and asked Jamal to come with her, but he refused. He resented Karen's going to church. Jamal felt that God had abandoned him—so he had turned his back on God.

Soon Jamal stopped coming straight home after work; he began to drink, and to smoke marijuana. After their worst fight, Jamal stormed out of the apartment drunk and ashamed he had actually tried to hit his wife in the face. Drunk, he drove aimlessly for hours before he was pulled over by the police and charged with a DUI and taken to jail.

In jail Jamal had a terrible nightmare that he was walking into the blazing flames of hell. He awakened trembling with a revelation that he had been a prisoner for the past 22 years not in a man-made jail, but in a jail bound by the chains of Satan's lies and deceit. Jamal realized that the hatred and resentment he had felt inside since he was a child were strongholds that the devil used to keep him bound. At that moment, he knew that an unforgiving spirit had taken hold of his life. The next morning, Jamal asked the guards for a Bible and began to pray and ask God to change his heart.

In this week's lesson, we will explore how prayer delivered Peter from certain death.

THE PEOPLE, PLACES, AND TIMES

The Persecution of the Early Christians. Prior to His death, Jesus warned His disciples that because of His name they would be the objects of great hatred (Matthew 10:23; John 15:20). The initial wave of persecutions took the form of threats, arrests, and beatings that began shortly after Pentecost (Acts 4:1-3) and accelerated with the martyrdom of Stephen (Acts 8:1). As a result of the persecutions, the Christian congregation in Jerusalem was scattered. This scattering led to the Gospel being preached to far-reaching areas and thousands of converts being added to the church. This continued to make the Christians objects of hatred by a number of sources, including the Jewish authorities, misinformed political leaders, and the Roman government (Acts 16:20; 17:6).

The second, and more violent, persecution of the Christians was led by Saul of Tarsus. Saul obtained letters of authorization from the Jewish leaders to pursue the Christians to Damascus and to have them imprisoned and executed. It was on the road to Damascus that Saul was converted.

Thousands of Christians were executed under the reign of Emperor Nero. Popular church history reckons that Peter was crucified upside down in Rome during Nero's reign. Persecution of Christians continued until Christianity was recognized under the Emperor Constantine (A.D. 305-337).

Packer J.I., and M.C. Tenney, eds. Illustrated Manners and Customs of the Bible. Nashville, Tenn.: Thomas Nelson Publishers, 1980. 40, 41, 111, 18, 532.

BACKGROUND

Peter's role as one of the apostles in Jesus' inner circle is undisputed. He also occupied a prominent part in the activity of the disciples following Jesus' ascension. It was Peter who presented the other apostles with scriptural evidence to replace Judas (Acts 1:15-26). On the Day of Pentecost, when the Holy Spirit filled the believers, Peter was clearly the spokesman for the apostles. Under the unction of the Holy Spirit, Peter proclaimed the resurrection of Jesus. His preaching was so powerful that some 3,000 Jewish converts were baptized that very day! What a change from the man who three times had denied even knowing Jesus.

In the book of Acts, Peter and John are the only original apostles mentioned, except for a brief mention of John's brother James, who was executed. While the book of Acts gives us an exhaustive account of Paul's travels, we must remember that Peter also traveled extensively. Following the onset of Saul's persecution of the church, Peter is active in Antioch, Syria, and possibly Rome.

It was Peter, along with John, who was sent by the church in Jerusalem to follow Philip to Samaria. There, he and John laid hands on the newly baptized Samaritans, who then received the gift of the Holy Spirit under his apostolic witness.

When Jewish Christians at Jerusalem convened to consider the question of circumcision for Gentile converts, it was Peter who testified so powerfully about God's dealings with the Gentiles that the entire assembly became "silent" (Acts 15:1-29). At that time it appeared that Jesus' brother, James, was also exercising a high level of leadership (Acts 15:13, ff).

AT-A-GLANCE

1. Peter's Imprisonment (Acts 12:1-4)
2. The Saints Pray for Peter (v. 5)
3. The Spirit Provides for Peter (vv. 6-11)
4. Peter Witnesses to the Saints
(vv. 12-16)

IN DEPTH

1. Peter's Imprisonment (Acts 12:1-4)

It had been 12 years since the death and resurrection of Jesus. The church had spread out from Jerusalem and Judea into Samaria and had finally reached the Gentiles. Just when things appeared to be going well with Peter and his colaborers in the Gospel, troubles began brewing in Jerusalem. The fifth persecution of the Christians began under Herod Agrippa I (the brother of the Herod before whom Jesus appeared, and the father of the Herod before whom Paul would have to appear).

Herod Agrippa's primary interest was in the preservation of the status quo. Therefore he sided with the majority and ruthlessly oppressed minorities when they did not go along with his policies. For him, Jewish Christians were divisive. He was afraid that they would cause controversy and inflame ill will among his subjects, so he had several Christians arrested and had James beheaded by the sword. This James was the brother of the apostle John, the two of whom Jesus affectionately named the "sons of thunder" (Mark 3:17). Many biblical scholars believe that John and James may have only been in their late teens when Jesus called them to be His disciples. This would have made them the youngest of the original 12 apostles. Ironically, while James would be the first of the apostles to die, his brother John would be the last, although the Bible does not tell us how John died.

It is interesting to note that the apostles did not appear to be targets of the persecution that was instigated by the stoning of Stephen. We can conclude this because while other believers fled from Jerusalem, there is no scriptural evidence that the apostles left the city. Conversely, it was the Christian church leaders who were the express targets of this persecution. Acts 12:1 tells us that Herod directed his attention to "certain of the church." The direct persecution of the apostles is first mentioned in Acts 5, when the apostles were imprisoned and miraculously freed by an angel. There is no reason to believe that the apostles were ever able to live without the threat of imprisonment, beating, and even death looming over their heads. Even so, news of the execution of James must have dealt a terrible blow to the Christians in Jerusalem.

Verse 7 tells us that Herod's intuition was correct; the killing of James "pleased the Jews" (v. 3). Thus emboldened, Herod continued his persecution and had Peter arrested and thrown into prison.

2. The Saints Pray for Peter (v. 5)

While there is no mention of how the Christians reacted when James was initially imprisoned, the church immediately reacts to Peter's imprisonment. The church's deep concern was expressed in their earnest prayers for Peter. These were not token prayers being offered for Peter's release; they were "fervent." We are told that the church prayed unceasingly to God on Peter's behalf.

3. The Spirit Provides for Peter (vv. 6-11)

Like Jesus before him, Peter had been arrested during the Passover. Herod Agrippa planned to try Peter as a divisive minority leader and then execute him to warn others not to follow Jesus or to continue their controversial activities. Herod did not wish to offend the Jewish officials; therefore, he could not immediately execute Peter. Peter's public trial and execution would have to be delayed until after the Passover. Perhaps because he recalled the previous miraculous escape of the apostles, Herod was taking no chances with Peter. He had a total of 16 men guarding this one man. Peter was under the watch of four soldiers at all times. Two of them were chained to his wrist while the other two stood guard at his cell door.

On the night before Peter's scheduled execution, Herod was fearful of the possibility that Peter might escape, and the Christians were fearful that Peter would not escape. Yet Peter was surprisingly calm during these tumultuous events. On what appears to be his last night on earth, Peter was sleeping (v. 6)! Only an unshakeable trust in the Lord could have allowed Peter to sleep peacefully at a time like this. Herod's judgment had been passed, the death warrant was ordered, and two armed guards were chained to his wrists, yet Peter slept. Peter could not know

how God would resolve this situation. Would God's glory be made manifest in Peter's death or his deliverance? Peter had no idea, yet he was obviously confident that God would and could resolve his present situation.

Peter's steadfast and unmovable confidence in God was well placed. The miraculous deliverance took Peter by surprise. While he was sleeping, the angel appeared in the cell and shined a bright light. In spite of the light, Peter continued to sleep and the four soldiers on guard were either supernaturally incapacitated or sound asleep. The angel had to strike the sleeping Peter on the side (v. 7) to get him up. Peter's sleep was so peaceful that he was bewildered and the angel had to order him to get dressed and tie on his sandals. The chains that bound Peter to the soldiers miraculously fell from his hands. The angel led Peter out of the prison, past the guards, and onto the street.

Peter followed the angel, unsure whether his release was actually happening or if he was having a "vision" (v. 9). Finally, "when Peter was come to himself" (v. 11) and was certain that he was fully awake and not dreaming, he declared that he knew "of a surety" (v. 11) that God had intervened on his behalf.

4. Peter Witnesses to the Saints (vv. 12-16)

Peter went to the home of Mary. Mary is the mother of John-Mark, the apostle, missionary, and writer of the gospel of Mark. He also went there to avoid the danger of being seen by one of Herod's soldiers. Bible scholars believe this is the same house that hosted the Last Supper and also the first meeting place after Jesus' resurrection. Luke informs us that "many were gathered together praying" (v. 12). Here we see the closeness of this Christian community.

A young servant girl named Rhoda heard Peter knocking at the door, recognized his voice, and ran back into the house to tell the others that Peter was at the door. The response by the group is somewhat surprising. They told the girl that she must be crazy. When Rhoda insisted that Peter was at the door, the group switched tactics and told her that it must be Peter's "angel" (v. 15).

The praying group had difficulty believing that

the very miracle they had prayed for had occurred. When Rhoda finally persuaded them to come to the door and they saw Peter for themselves, "they were astonished" (v. 16). Their initial response of disbelief and later amazement should not be judged too critically. The Christians were, no doubt, praying in faith and believed that God could deliver Peter. They were, perhaps, shocked at the sudden and supernatural way He did it.

SEARCH THE SCRIPTURES

Fill in the blanks below.

1. "Now about that time _____ the king stretched forth his hands to vex certain of the church" (Acts 12:1).

2. "And he killed _____ the brother of John with the sword" (v. 2).

3. "Peter therefore was kept in prison; but prayer was made without _____of the church unto God for him" (v. 5).

DISCUSS THE MEANING

1. In the lesson, the Jerusalem church is fervently praying during Peter's imprisonment. What are the occasions that cause today's church to rally together in corporate prayer? Does it happen frequently enough? What are the results?

2. Discuss some other biblical occasions when the prayers of the righteous moved the hand of God. How are these instances similar to Peter's situation? How do they differ? What is the common denominator?

LESSON IN OUR SOCIETY

In today's lesson, we find Peter was in prison and surrounded by chains, walls, and soldiers. But more importantly, Peter was also surrounded by the prayers of the saints! These saints were not just paying lip service but were earnestly and fervently praying on their brother's behalf. They were praying as Jesus had taught them to pray: "without ceasing." Our faith cannot exist without prayer. Yes, we may ask God for anything, but we must not fail to pray. As Christians, we are not exempt from hardships and suffering, but we are not powerless either! We have the mighty provision of prayer at our disposal.

The Christian who does not pray is like the

homeowner who stumbles around in a dark room, crashing into tables and chairs, because he does not turn on the light switch.

MAKE IT HAPPEN

During the week, make a list of all the people in your life who need prayer. Now research the Scriptures on prayer and the power of prayer. Set aside time in the day, either early morning or late evening, during which you earnestly pray for the needs of the people on your list. Pray that God's will would be done in their lives.

FOLLOW THE SPIRIT

What God wants me to do:

_____

_____

REMEMBER YOUR THOUGHTS

Special insights I have learned:

_____

_____

MORE LIGHT ON THE TEXT

Acts 12:1-16

1 Now about that time Herod the king stretched forth his hands to vex certain of the church.

The "time" referred to is during the famine in Judea (Acts 11:29). This is now the third Herod to (briefly) enter the narrative. The first was Herod the Great, who reigned during the priesthood of Zacharias, the father of John the Baptist (Luke 1:5). The second was Herod the Tetrarch, who shadowed Jesus' ministry, death, and resurrection (Luke 3:1, 19; 8:3; 9:7-9; 13:31; 23:7-15; Acts 4:27). This "Herod the king" in Acts 12:1 is Herod Agrippa I, the son of Aristolobus IV and Bernice I, the grandson of Herod the Great, and the father of Herod Agrippa II (Acts 25:13-26), Drusilla (Acts 24:24), and Bernice (Acts 25:13).

Agrippa had been brought up in Rome where he made many influential friends—among whom were Gaius Caligula and Claudius. When Caligula became emperor (A.D. 37-41), he granted Herod Agrippa I the tetrarchy of Philip and the tetrarchy of Lysanius (Luke 3:1). Later he added the tetrarchy of Herod Antipas (Luke 3:1; 9:7-9; 13:31;

Peter arrested and in chains.

1:13). He was also not to be confused with James, the half brother of Jesus (Galatians 1:19). The death of James signaled the end of the short period of tranquility enjoyed by the Jerusalem leadership after the persecution of Stephen (Acts 8:1).

3 And because he saw it pleased the Jews, he proceeded further to take Peter also. (Then were the days of unleavened bread.)

Upon seeing that his action pleased the Jews, Herod Agrippa I had Peter arrested. The reason "it pleased the Jews" may also lie in the means of James's execution. The rabbis considered beheading the most shameful of all deaths, reserved for those who had no share in the world to come. The execution of James was therefore a gesture of solidarity on Herod's part with the Jewish majority, a statement that he regarded the followers of Jesus as apostates and agitators.

Luke parenthetically told his readers that these "were the days of unleavened bread." Although the celebration of the feast began with the Passover meal on 14 Nisan (the first month of the Babylonian/Jewish calendar) and then the "days of unleavened bread" continued for seven days more (Exodus 12:3-20; 23:15; 34:18), Luke collapsed any distinction between them. The reader is expected to make the connection between this arrest and that of Jesus, which also occurred at Passover.

13:6-12) to Agrippa's possessions. After Caligula's assassination, Agrippa helped Claudius receive confirmation from the Roman senate as emperor. The new emperor added Judea and Samaria to Agrippa's kingdom. So from A.D. 41-44 when he died, Herod Agrippa I ruled over a reassembled kingdom of the same size as his grandfather, Herod the Great. He was as loved by the Jewish establishment as his grandfather was hated.

2 And he killed James the brother of John with the sword.

Herod Agrippa was committed to imposing on the Jews a peace favorable to Rome by preserving the status quo—a policy called "Pax Romana." Therefore, he supported the religious establishment and was hostile toward all who saw things differently. Because he saw Jewish Christians as disruptive, he sought to suppress them. To this end, he arrested some of Jesus' followers and had James executed. This James was one of the first followers of Jesus (Luke 5:10) and was one of the twelve (Luke 6:14-16; Acts 1:13). He, along with his brother John (sons of Zebedee) and Peter, enjoyed special intimacy with Jesus (Luke 8:51; 9:28, 54). He was often called James the Great to distinguish him from James the Less (Mark 5:40), and from James, son of Alphaeus (Acts

4 And when he had apprehended him, he put him in prison, and delivered him to four quaternions of soldiers to keep him; intending after Easter to bring him forth to the people.

The delay functions in the narrative to build tension and allows the reader to see the activity of the church working against that of the tyrant Herod. He probably planned for a public trial like that of Jesus' (Luke 23:1-5). Overall, the action stands in contrast to the summary execution of James by "the sword" in verse 2.

5 Peter therefore was kept in prison; but prayer was made without ceasing of the church unto God for him.

While Peter was in prison, the believers were continually praying to God for him. Throughout Acts, the church is portrayed as a praying community (Acts 1:14, 24; 2:42; 3:1; 4:24-30; 6:6; 8:15; 9:11, 40-41; 10:4, 9; 13:3; 16:25; 20:36; 21:5; 22:17; 28:8). The adverbial phrase "without ceasing" (Gk. *ektenos,* **ek-ten-ace'**) denotes eagerness and earnestness. The comparative form is used for the prayer of Jesus before His arrest (Luke 22:14). The community's prayer compensated for Peter's powerlessness and prepared for his miraculous escape.

6 And when Herod would have brought him forth, the same night Peter was sleeping between two soldiers, bound with two chains: and the keepers before the door kept the prison.

The custom with such squads was to have four men on duty at a time, in four revolving watches. Here two slept next to Peter and one was at each of the two guard posts (v. 10). These elaborate security measures heightened the wonder of the escape.

7 And, behold, the angel of the Lord came upon him, and a light shined in the prison: and he smote Peter on the side, and raised him up, saying, Arise up quickly. And his chains fell off from his hands.

The angel appeared to Peter and instructed him to get up. These messengers from God played an important role through substantial portions of the books of Luke and Acts (Luke 1:11, 26; 2:9, 13; 22:43; 24:23; Acts 8:26; 10:3, 7, 22; 11:13; 12:7-15, 23; 27:23). Together, the use of the words "behold" (Gk. *idou,* **id-oo**) and "came upon" (Gk. *ephistemi,* **ef-is-tay-me**) give the sense of a sudden and startling appearance (compare Luke 2:9; Acts 23:11). As in the appearance to Saul, "light" (Gk. *phos,* **foce**) was a sign of heavenly presence (Acts 9:3; 22:6, 9-11; 26:13).

8 And the angel said unto him, Gird thyself, and bind on thy sandals. And so he did. And he saith unto him, Cast thy garment about thee, and follow me. 9 And he went out, and followed him; and wist not that it was true which was done by the angel; but thought he saw a vision. 10 When they were past the first and the second ward, they came unto the iron gate that leadeth unto the city; which opened to them of his own accord: and they went out, and passed on through one street; and forthwith the angel departed from him.

Finally, the angel "departed from him" (Gk. *aphistemi,* **af-is-'-tay-mee**, literally "stood away from" as in Luke 4:13; 13:27; Acts 5:38; 15:38; 19:9).

11 And when Peter was come to himself, he said, Now I know of a surety, that the Lord hath sent his angel, and hath delivered me out of the hand of Herod, and from all the expectation of the people of the Jews.

The withdrawal of the angel of the Lord corresponds to Peter's "coming to himself," which is similar to Luke 15:17. The phrase "now I know of a surety, that the Lord hath sent his angel" is similar to the naming and context of Eliezer in Exodus 18:4. As in Acts 12:3, Luke joins the power of Herod (literally, the "hand" of Herod) to the hostile expectation of the Jews. For the first time in the narrative of Luke and Acts, he connects the distancing designation "Jews" to the term that previously had been used in a religious sense—"people" (Gk. *laos,* **lah-os'**).

Here the use of the term "expectation" (Gk. *prosdokia,* **pros-dok-ee'-ah**) is somewhat ironic in light of Luke's earlier usage for positive expectation (Luke 1:21; 3:15; 7:19-20; 8:4; Acts 3:5; 10:24).

12 And when he had considered the thing, he came to the house of Mary the mother of John whose surname was Mark; where many were gathered together praying.

The identification of the head of a household as a woman is striking but not unparalleled (cf. Luke 10:38-42; Acts 16:14-15; 1 Timothy 5:16). John-Mark (mentioned also in Colossians 4:10, the cousin of Barnabas; 2 Timothy 4:11; Philemon 24; 1 Peter 5:13) becomes an important, if contentious, figure in the next section of narrative. He joined Barnabas and Saul after they completed their mission to Jerusalem (Acts 12:25), and went with them on their first missionary journey (13:5), but left them in Perga to return to Jerusalem (13:13). His departure became the reason for the split between Barnabas and Saul in Acts 15:37-39.

The portrayal of the church was entirely consistent with Luke's understanding of the Christian community as defined by prayer—a theme that spans both volumes (Luke 3:21; 5:16; 6:12; 9:28-29; 11:1-4; 18:1; 22:41-44, 46; Acts 1:24-25; 4:24-30; 6:6; 8:15; 9:11, 40; 10:9, 30; 12:12; 13:3; 14:23; 16:25; 20:36; 21:5; 28:8). By bracketing the description of the marvelous escape by these notices of the church's prayer, Luke suggests the origin of the power at work.

13 And as Peter knocked at the door of the gate, a damsel came to hearken, named Rhoda.

The "damsel" (Gk. *paidiske*, **pahee-dis'-kay**) recalled Peter's earlier unhappy experience with a woman servant in Luke 22:56 when Peter was confronted in the courtyard. We are to picture here such a courtyard before the house proper, with a wall and a "door of the gate" (Gk. *thura*, **thoo'-rah**) separating the street from the inner courtyard on which Peter can pound.

14 And when she knew Peter's voice, she opened not the gate for gladness, but ran in, and told how Peter stood before the gate.

Luke said that although Rhoda did not see Peter, she recognized his voice and ran to tell those praying in the house. The phrase "for gladness" recalls the passage in Luke 24:41, when in joy and amazement, the disciples did not believe that they were seeing the resurrected Jesus.

15 And they said unto her, Thou art mad. But she constantly affirmed that it was even so. Then said they, It is his angel. 16 But Peter continued knocking: and when they had opened the door, and saw him, they were astonished.

The situation is narrated with a sense of irony and humor. Peter was left banging on the door, Rhoda forgot to open the door as she ran back and forth in joy, and the Christians believed that Rhoda's report of Peter's freedom from prison was insane, even though they had just been praying for him. In years to come, this story would be a source of great fun every time it was told.

The verb "mad" (Gk. *mainomai*, **mah'-ee-nom-ahee**) often communicates the sense of "raving," but it is used by Luke in Acts 26:24-25 in the sense of "being irrational." Note how similar this response is to that of the 11 upon hearing the women's message concerning the empty tomb in Luke 24:11(NIV): "But they did not believe the women, because their words seemed to them like nonsense."

DAILY BIBLE READINGS

M: Peter Heals One and Revives Another
Acts 9:32-42

T: Jesus Is Tempted
Luke 4:1-13

W: Jesus Prays in Gethsemane
Matthew 26:36-46

T: Jesus Dies on the Cross
Mark 15:33-37

F: James Is Killed and Peter Imprisoned
Acts 12:1-5

S: An Angel Frees Peter from Prison
Acts 12:6-11

S: Peter Tells the Others What Happened
Acts 12:12-17

TEACHING TIPS

November 6
Bible Study Guide 10

1. Words You Should Know
A. Damascus (Acts 9:3) *Damaskos* (Gk.)—One of the most ancient and important cities of Syria.

B. Journeyed (v. 7) *sunodevo* (Gk.)—To travel with someone.

2. Teacher Preparation
A. Pray for the students in your class, asking God to open their hearts to today's lesson.

B. Read and study the FOCAL VERSES, paying attention to the Lord's approach to Saul.

C. Carefully review the BIBLE STUDY GUIDE, making notes for clarification.

D. Share your personal conversion story with the class. How did it make you feel? How does it make you feel today?

3. Starting the Lesson
A. Before the class arrives, write the words "Damascus" and "Journeyed" on the board.

B. After the students arrive and are settled, lead the class in prayer. Pray specifically for godly insights on the lesson and blessings on the lives of the students.

C. Ask a volunteer to read the IN FOCUS story, and spend time discussing what the story means.

4. Getting into the Lesson
A. Ask volunteers to read THE PEOPLE, PLACES, AND TIMES and the BACKGROUND section.

B. Ask the students to read the FOCAL VERSES together, and then have a student read the corresponding IN DEPTH section. Allow time for discussion between each section.

5. Relating the Lesson to Life
A. Spend time answering the questions in the DISCUSS THE MEANING section.

B. Ask if any student has an insight that he/she would like to share regarding today's lesson.

6. Arousing Action
A. Read the LESSON IN OUR SOCIETY section to the class. Ask the class to share personal encounters with God they have had. Direct the students to the MAKE IT HAPPEN section and discuss it in class.

B. As a review, tell the students to complete the FOLLOW THE SPIRIT section during the week.

C. End the class with prayer.

WORSHIP GUIDE

For the Superintendent or Teacher
Theme: Paul Becomes a Follower
Theme Song: "Heaven Came Down and Glory Filled My Soul"
Scripture: Ephesians 4:18
Song: "Thank You, Lord"
Meditation: God our Heavenly Father, You created us in love and gave us insight that we might see Your handiwork. Open our eyes that we might truly see Your glory and understand our place in Your grand design.
Amen.

PAUL BECOMES A FOLLOWER

Bible Background • ACTS 9:1–31
Printed Text • ACTS 9:3–18
Devotional Reading • ACTS 9:23–31

LESSON AIM

By the end of the lesson, we will:

KNOW the events surrounding Paul's spiritual transformation;

BE CONVINCED no one is beyond the reach of God's love and transformation; and

DECIDE to repent of any known sin and become a faithful follower and servant of Jesus Christ.

KEEP IN MIND

"And immediately there fell from his eyes as it had been scales: and he received sight forthwith, and arose, and was baptized" (Acts 9:18).

LESSON OVERVIEW

LESSON AIM
KEEP IN MIND
FOCAL VERSES
IN FOCUS
THE PEOPLE, PLACES, AND TIMES
BACKGROUND
AT-A-GLANCE
IN DEPTH
SEARCH THE SCRIPTURES
DISCUSS THE MEANING
LESSON IN OUR SOCIETY
MAKE IT HAPPEN
FOLLOW THE SPIRIT
REMEMBER YOUR THOUGHTS
MORE LIGHT ON THE TEXT
DAILY BIBLE READINGS

FOCAL VERSES

Acts 9:3 And as he journeyed, he came near Damascus: and suddenly there shined round about him a light from heaven:

4 And he fell to the earth, and heard a voice saying unto him, Saul, Saul, why persecutest thou me?

5 And he said, Who art thou, Lord? And the Lord said, I am Jesus whom thou persecutest: it is hard for thee to kick against the pricks.

6 And he trembling and astonished said, Lord, what wilt thou have me to do? And the Lord said unto him, Arise, and go into the city, and it shall be told thee what thou must do.

7 And the men which journeyed with him stood speechless, hearing a voice, but seeing no man.

8 And Saul arose from the earth; and when his eyes were opened, he saw no man: but they led him by the hand, and brought him into Damascus.

9 And he was three days without sight, and neither did eat nor drink.

10 And there was a certain disciple at Damascus, named Ananias; and to him said the Lord in a vision, Ananias. And he said, Behold, I am here, Lord.

11 And the Lord said unto him, Arise, and go into the street which is called Straight, and inquire in the house of Judas for one called Saul, of Tarsus: for, behold, he prayeth,

12 And hath seen in a vision a man named Ananias coming in, and putting his hand on him, that he might receive his sight.

13 Then Ananias answered, Lord, I have heard by many of this man, how much evil he hath done to thy saints at Jerusalem:

14 And here he hath authority from the chief priests to bind all that call on thy name.

15 But the Lord said unto him, Go thy way: for he is a chosen vessel unto me, to bear my name before the Gentiles, and kings, and the children of Israel:

16 For I will shew him how great things he must suffer for my name's sake.

17 And Ananias went his way, and entered into the house; and putting his hands on him said, Brother Saul, the Lord, even Jesus, that appeared unto thee in the way as thou camest, hath sent me, that thou mightest receive thy sight, and be filled with the Holy Ghost.

18 And immediately there fell from his eyes as it had been scales: and he received sight forthwith, and arose, and was baptized.

IN FOCUS

As a young man, Sonny fell from being a top-ranked college basketball player on his way to the pros, to a convicted felon with a seven-year prison term for assault and battery. Although he was raised in a Christian home, while in prison he converted to Islam. Upon his release from prison, Sonny had a rough time finding a job. No one wanted to hire an ex-con.

A year out of prison, Sonny ran across an old girlfriend named Angela. Angela told Sonny her church had just expanded and needed someone to serve as head of the maintenance crew. Excited, Sonny went to interview with the pastor and was offered the position.

What touched Sonny deeply was the pastor's trust in him. He put the building completely into Sonny's care without hesitation. He even let Sonny temporarily move into a small room in the church basement to help reduce his living expenses. The pastor volunteered to mentor Sonny if he dedicated himself to the study of the Bible. Sonny accepted the pastor's help with gladness. But Sonny had a secret agenda: He thought that if he could learn the Bible well enough, it would be easier for him to lead other Christians to Islam. His goal was to get others to renounce Christ and follow Muhammad.

Sonny and the pastor met many nights. One night they got into a deep discussion about the deity of Jesus.

The Pastor asked, "Do you believe that God is all-powerful and that nothing is impossible for Him?"

"Yes," Sonny replied, "the Koran teaches that."

The pastor responded, "Then would it be possible for Him to come to earth in human form?"

Before Sonny could answer, the pastor was called away, which left Sonny alone to ponder the question. In the pastor's absence, Sonny searched hard in the Koran to find an answer to disprove the pastor, but he couldn't. It was the first time he conceded that what the pastor was saying about Jesus could possibly be true. The pastor's words represented the first seeds sown toward his conversion to Christ.

No one is beyond the reach of God's love. Are you serving as a living testimony of His graciousness? In our study this week, we will see how Saul, a notorious enemy of Christ, was converted, and became a preacher of the Gospel he once hated.

THE PEOPLE, PLACES, AND TIMES

The High Priest. The religious and political head of the Jewish nation. The high priest, as the religious and political head of the Jewish state, enjoyed the right of extradition. This privilege was confirmed by the Roman emperor, Julius Caesar, and was honored by all neighboring states. Letters of extradition from the high priest gave Saul legal authority to arrest any individual he suspected of being a Christian. This made him both very powerful and very feared.

Damascus. A Roman city about 150 miles from Jerusalem. It lies at the foot of Mt. Qasyam in a fertile plane called Ghutah. The city is mentioned in the Old Testament as the hometown of Eliezer, Abraham's servant. During the later Old Testament period, Damascus was part of the Assyrian Empire. By the time of Paul's conversion, it was a free city.

BACKGROUND

Following Jesus' resurrection, the followers of Jesus set Jerusalem ablaze with the good news that the Messiah (Jesus Christ) had come. The Jewish authorities reacted very strongly against this and began a campaign to arrest and punish anyone embracing this new teaching. Ultimately, this campaign resulted in the slaying of Stephen, a leader in this new Christian movement, and forced other believers to flee Jerusalem and settle as refugees in other parts of the Middle East.

Saul (called Paul after his conversion) expressed his agreement with the death of Stephen by guarding the coats of those who stoned him. After Stephen's death, Saul became a leader of the persecution of Christians and helped drive many of them from the city of Jerusalem. Then he sought permission to track down the ones who had fled to Damascus so they could be bound and returned to Jerusalem for trial.

IN DEPTH

1. A Dramatic Arrest (Acts 9:3-9)

This passage opens with Saul taking the lead in persecuting believers in this new sect, which has come to be called the Way. Not content just to drive members of the Way from Jerusalem, Saul approached the high priest and asked for official permission to pursue the refugees to Damascus, arrest any that he could find, and return them in chains to Jerusalem to stand trial.

With letters granting him the authority to arrest any members of the new sect he could find, Saul traveled with a small band of men toward Damascus. In his zeal to continue the persecution of the Christians who had escaped Jerusalem, Saul went ahead of the pack. Suddenly a light brighter than the sun surrounded him, and he fell to the ground. While lying on the ground, Saul heard a voice speaking in his ears and inquiring as to why the zealous persecutor was persecuting Him. No doubt Saul's training in Jewish Scripture had prepared him for heavenly visitations, and he calmly asked the visitor to identify himself. Saul was not prepared for the response; "I am Jesus, whom you are persecuting." Even though He is risen, Jesus remains so close to His church that when its members are being persecuted, He is being persecuted with them.

Saul, in his zeal to protect the traditional Jewish religion, had discovered that he was guilty of ignoring the Scriptures. Jesus truly is the Messiah, and Saul was looking at Him in His glory. Saul was instructed to get up and continue his journey into Damascus. However, when he rose to his feet, he discovered that he was blind. The men who were traveling with Saul had seen the brilliant flash of light and even observed him as he fell to the ground. Then together they watched as he spoke, but all they could hear was a sound, perhaps like thunder. Now they rushed to his aid and learned that he could not see, so they took him by the hand and led him the rest of the way to Damascus.

Paul's encounter with Jesus.

91

To say that Saul was shaken by this experience would be an understatement. He refers to the "Damascus Road" experience several times in his later writings as the pivotal point in his life when God personally intervened to correct and save him.

Saul was a classic fulfillment of what Jesus had told the disciples during the Last Supper: "A time is coming when anyone who kills you will think he is offering a service to God" (John 16:2, NIV). No doubt Saul was present during the trial of Stephen and heard every word of Stephen's defense, condemning Israel's history of stubborn rebellion against God and His prophets (Acts 7:1-59). This partly explains why Saul was breathing out murderous threats against the Lord's disciples (Acts 9:1). The brutal murder of Stephen did not quench his anger. Thinking he was serving God, Saul sought to eradicate this upstart group he saw as blasphemers. Saul's heart was sincere, but he was sincerely wrong. God Himself arrested the attention of this rampaging man on the Damascus Road. How often do we do harm to our fellow Christians in ignorance, thinking we are doing God's will? Does God have to arrest our attention in such a dramatic way?

2. An Available Disciple (vv. 10-14)

Saul was taken to the home of Judas, who lived on Straight Street in Damascus. There he began to fast and pray. Saul's spiritual world had been turned upside down. He believed that Stephen was a religious threat in Jerusalem and agreed with those who killed him. But Stephen had been right. Jesus is the Messiah. Now Saul began a process of applying all that he had learned in the Scriptures to Jesus of Nazareth. He was not learning a new religion; rather, he was learning the correct way to follow the religion he had always embraced. He also began to pray that God would restore his sight.

As wrong as Saul was about the church, he had the integrity to recognize the error of his ways when confronted by Jesus, identifying Himself as the Lord—the real object of his persecution. He simply obeyed Jesus' command to "go into the city" [Damascus] and wait to "be told what he must do." When confronted by the error of our ways, are we open to that kind of correction? Are we willing to simply obey God's commands telling us what we must do? Because Saul, an ordinary man, totally yielded himself to God, he became one of the greatest apostles.

3. A Divine Commission (vv. 15-18)

The Damascus Road experience had sent Saul into shock, and as he sat in the darkness at the home of Judas, he did not feel like eating or drinking. His blindness had caused him to focus on God. As he prayed, God gave him a vision of a man laying his hands on him so that he could see. At the same time, God spoke to Ananias, one of His disciples residing in Damascus, and instructed him to find Saul at the home of Judas and restore his sight by the laying on of hands.

Initially Ananias questioned God because he had heard of Saul and his reason for venturing to Damascus. Ananias rightly feared for his life. However, God assured him that He had intervened in Saul's life and intended to use him for the benefit of His kingdom. God also assured Ananias that Saul would suffer much in the role that he was about to be given. Ananias was obedient to the Lord and traveled to Straight Street and found Saul. Ananias greeted Saul as "brother" as an indication that he had received Saul into the family of the Way. Saul did not protest. If Jesus hadn't intervened and disrupted Saul's journey, Ananias would have been one of the individuals whom Saul was seeking to bring back to Jerusalem in chains, but now a change had taken place in Saul and he became obedient to the instructions that Ananias had given him.

As soon as Ananias laid his hands on Saul, Saul's vision was restored as something resembling scales fell from his eyes. Saul then left with Ananias and was baptized. This baptism indicates that Saul's transformation was complete. He was no longer Saul, who sought to persecute the church of Jesus Christ. He was now Paul, who would be used by God to carry the Gospel message to the Gentile world.

SEARCH THE SCRIPTURES

1. Why was Saul breathing out threats and slaughter against the disciples of the Lord (Acts 9:1)?

2. Why did the Lord instruct Ananias to go and heal Paul of his blindness (v. 15)?

DISCUSS THE MEANING

1. In what ways were the persecutions that the early Christians suffered good for the growth of the church?

2. How did the Damascus Road experience positively or negatively affect Paul?

3. What lessons can we learn from Ananias and his relationship with the Lord?

4. What can we learn from Paul's experience with religion? Is religious zeal a good thing or a bad thing? Should we ever be tough on people who don't believe the way we do?

5. Why was it necessary for the risen Christ to personally appear to Paul on the Damascus Road?

LESSON IN OUR SOCIETY

Paul was totally sold out for his beliefs. There was no gray area for him. Because he held to his beliefs so firmly, he was intolerant to those who didn't believe the way he did. The Lord Jesus had to personally visit Paul on the Damascus Road in order to convince him that he was wrong.

One of the founding principles of our nation is religious freedom. The Founding Fathers wanted to ensure that one person's beliefs would be respected by another person. Was this a good idea? Write a brief essay to share with the class next week.

MAKE IT HAPPEN

Make a list of your strongly held beliefs. Now make the same list of what your family believes and then of what your church believes. Compare the three lists and circle only the things that are common to all three lists. Are there any surprises? Make this a matter of personal reflection and prayer for the next week.

FOLLOW THE SPIRIT

What God wants me to do:

_____

_____

REMEMBER YOUR THOUGHTS

Special insights I have learned:

_____

_____

MORE LIGHT ON THE TEXT

Acts 9:3-18

3 And as he journeyed, he came near Damascus: and suddenly there shined round about him a light from heaven:

To get to Damascus, Saul would have had to travel from Jerusalem along the Great North Road. The adverb "suddenly" (Gk. *exaiphnes,* **ex-ah'-eef-nace**) is also used to describe the appearance of the heavenly choir in Luke 2:13 and the seizing of the youth by a spirit in Luke 9:39. The appearance of light (Gk. *phos,* **foce'**) is especially associated with the presence of God (Psalm 4:6; 36:9; 56:13; 78:14; 89:15; 97:11; 104:2).

The flash of lightning is a feature of theophanies in Exodus 19:16; 2 Samuel 22:15; Psalm 18:14; 77:18; 97:4; Ezekiel 1:4, 7, 13; and Daniel 10:6. In Paul's defense speech (Acts 22:6), he calls this a "great light." In Acts 26:13, he calls it "above the brigtness of the sun," as it surrounded both his companions and himself.

4 And he fell to the earth, and heard a voice saying unto him, Saul, Saul, why persecutest thou me?

The voice from the light not only recalls the voice from the bush (Exodus 3:3) and from Mount Sinai (Exodus 19:16-20), it also shows the reader that the risen Lord remains active. The voice repeats Saul's name. This addressing could be compared to the call of Jacob (Genesis 46:2) and especially of Samuel (1 Samuel 3:4, 10). See also similar references in Luke 8:24; 10:41; 22:31. By persecuting believers, it was as if Saul was persecuting Jesus Himself.

5 And he said, Who art thou, Lord? And the Lord said, I am Jesus whom thou persecutest: it is hard for thee to kick against the pricks. 6 And he trembling and astonished said, Lord, what wilt thou have me to do? And the Lord said unto him, Arise, and go into the city, and it shall be told thee what thou must do.

The use of the word "Lord" (Gk. *kurios,* **koo'-ree-os**) should be taken at full value. Saul does not yet know it is Jesus who is Lord, but he recognizes that he is involved in a theophany (e.g. divine manifestation). Such dialogue within a revelatory experience clearly serves the literary function of making the import of the experience clear to the reader (Genesis 15:1-6; Exodus 3:4-15; Judges 6:11-18; 13:8-20).

The use of the phrase "I am Jesus whom thou persecutest" identifies the risen Christ with His disciples (Acts 22:8; 26:15). To persecute Christians is to persecute Him who founded the movement (Luke 10:16; Matthew 25:35-40, 42-45).

In verse 6, the burden of this revelation is not information about Jesus, but a commission for Saul.

7 And the men which journeyed with him stood speechless, hearing a voice, but seeing no man.

The two other accounts of the event give additional detail. In Acts 22:9, the companions saw the light but did not hear (understand) the voice. In Acts 26:14-16, all the travelers fell to the ground.

8 And Saul arose from the earth; and when his eyes were opened, he saw no man: but they led him by the hand, and brought him into Damascus.

In this case, the blinding is not a punishment, but an indication of the helplessness of the one who was formerly a powerful opponent (Acts 22:11). However, Saul would later bring a similar blindness on his opponent, the magician Elymas, as a punishment (Acts 13:11).

9 And he was three days without sight, and neither did eat nor drink.

The fasting shows that Saul was going through a holy period of transition that ended by his resuming the consumption of food in Acts 9:19. Fasting can be associated with a period of preparation for receiving a revelation (Exodus 34:28; Deuteronomy 9:9; Daniel 9:3; 10:2-3) and also with repentance (Jeremiah 14:12; Nehemiah 1:4; Joel 1:14). In the account in Acts 13:1-3, Saul places himself in a position to receive further guidance from the Lord. The early practice of fasting before baptism may have found some of its foundation in this passage.

10 And there was a certain disciple at Damascus, named Ananias; and to him said the Lord in a vision, Ananias. And he said, Behold, I am here, Lord.

Ananias is identified as a "disciple" (Gk. *math-etes,* **math-ay-tees'**), and in Saul's speech in Acts 22:12 he is described as "a devout man according to the law." The pattern of call and response is similar to that in 1 Samuel 3:4, 10. His eager response is a sign of his obedience.

11 And the Lord said unto him, Arise, and go into the street which is called Straight, and inquire in the house of Judas for one called Saul, of Tarsus: for, behold, he prayeth,

The vivid details in the message—the name of the street, the owner of the house, and the place of Saul's origin—are compatible with reliable historical traditions and good story-telling.

12 And hath seen in a vision a man named Ananias coming in, and putting his hand on him, that he might receive his sight.

The narrator does not tell us of the vision directly, but only through the means of another vision.

13 Then Ananias answered, Lord, I have heard by many of this man, how much evil he hath done to thy saints at Jerusalem:

Ananias is allowed not only to voice his (understandable) reluctance to encounter such a dangerous person, but to help the reader deal with the obvious objections. Human hesitancy is legitimate, but it can be overturned by the command of the Lord. Ananias's version of the events gives us a slightly different perspective. Here Luke uses the term saints or holy ones with reference to God's people (Acts 9:41; 26:10). Later Saul frequently used this term for the same purpose (Romans 1:7; 8:27; 12:13; 15:25, 26, 31; 1 Corinthians 1:2; 6:1; 2 Corinthians 1:1; 8:4; Ephesians 1:1; Philippians 1:1).

14 And here he hath authority from the chief priests to bind all that call on thy name.

Here, Saul is explicitly said to have "authority" (Gk. *exousia,* **ex-oo-see'-ah**) from the chief priests. And the phrase, "all that call on thy name" echoes the statement in Acts 2:21: "whosoever shall call on the name of the Lord shall be saved."

15 But the Lord said unto him, Go thy way: for he is a chosen vessel unto me, to bear my name before the Gentiles, and kings, and the children of Israel:

Literally, "a chosen vessel unto me," can mean any sort of instrument (1 Thessalonians 4:4; Hebrews 9:21). Although it sometimes is used in context of divine instrumentality (Romans 9:21-23; 2 Timothy 2:20-21), in this case it "bears" the Lord's name; therefore, the translation "vessel" is appropriate. The image is remarkably like that used by Saul himself in 2 Corinthians 4:7: "we have this treasure in earthen vessels." The designation of Saul as "chosen," in turn, associates him with the description of Jesus as the "elect one."

16 For I will shew him how great things he must suffer for my name's sake.

The use of the phrase "must suffer" places Paul directly and deliberately in the line of suffering prophets like Moses and Jesus (Luke 9:22; 17:25; 24:26). To suffer for Jesus' name, in turn, means that he does so as Jesus' representative (Luke 6:22; 21:12, 17; Acts 5:41).

17 And Ananias went his way, and entered into the house; and putting his hands on him said, Brother Saul, the Lord, even Jesus, that appeared unto thee in the way as thou camest, hath sent me, that thou mightest receive thy sight, and be filled with the Holy Ghost.

The gesture of laying on of hands symbolizes the transfer of power. It appears in sacrificial rites (Exodus 29:10, 19; Leviticus 1:4, 11; 4:15; 16:21), and as part of the ordination of priests (Numbers 8:10). Even more impressive is the formal transfer of authority from Moses to Joshua through this gesture (Numbers 27:18-23; Deuteronomy 34:9). These passages make clear that the gesture signified that the people should now obey Joshua just as they had Moses (Numbers 27:20; Deuteronomy 34:9). In Luke, the laying on of hands appears as part of Jesus' healings (which Luke clearly understands as a communication of power) in Luke 4:40; 13:13. In Acts, the gesture accompanies the bestowal of the Spirit in baptism (8:17, 19; 19:6), healings (9:12, 17; 28:8), and commissioning for ministry (13:3). In the present case, the laying on of hands both works a healing and bestows the Holy Spirit.

The use of Saul's name with the title "brother" and the physical gesture of touching register as recognitions of Saul's acceptance as a member of God's covenant people.

18 And immediately there fell from his eyes as it had been scales: and he received sight forthwith, and arose, and was baptized.

The composition of what covered Saul's eyes is not clear. The text describes it as something like "scales" that fell from his eyes. Scales falling from one's eyes is often used figuratively to describe enlightened understanding or illumination. Saul "was blind but now can see;" the Light that blinded him paradoxically relieved him of his spiritual blindness. In Saul's case, his sight was associated with revelation.

DAILY BIBLE READINGS

M: Jesus Calls Disciples and Changes Lives
Luke 5:4-11

T: Peter Responds to Criticism from Believers
Acts 11:1-10

W: The Believers in Jerusalem Praise God
Acts 11:11-18

T: Saul Sees a Vision of Jesus
Acts 9:1-9

F: Ananias Receives Instructions in a Vision
Acts 9:10-16

S: Saul Begins to Proclaim Jesus
Acts 9:17-22

S: Saul and the Disciples Proclaim Jesus
Acts 9:23-31

TEACHING TIPS

November 13
Bible Study Guide 11

1. Words You Should Know
A. Besought (Acts 16:15) *parakaleo* (Gk.)—To beg, entreat, or beseech.

B. Constrained (v. 15) *parabiazomai* (Gk.)—To compel by employing force, intervention, or negotiation.

2. Teacher Preparation
A. Pray for the students in your class, asking God to open their hearts to today's lesson.

B. Read and study the FOCAL VERSES, paying attention to Lydia's response to the strangers.

C. Carefully review the BIBLE STUDY GUIDE, making notes for clarification.

D. Share a personal thought with the class about being in need and having someone come to your aid. How did it make you feel?

3. Starting the Lesson
A. Before the class arrives, write the words "Besought" and "Constrained" on the board.

B. After the students arrive and are settled, lead the class in prayer. Pray specifically for godly insights on the lesson and blessings on the lives of the students.

C. Ask a volunteer to read the IN FOCUS story and then spend time in discussion about how the story relates to the action objective found in the LESSON AIM.

4. Getting into the Lesson
A. Ask for volunteers to read THE PEOPLE, PLACES, AND TIMES and BACKGROUND sections.

B. Ask the students to read the FOCAL VERSES together, and then have a student read the corresponding IN DEPTH section. Allow time for discussion between each section.

5. Relating the Lesson to Life
A. Spend time answering the questions in DISCUSS THE MEANING.

B. Ask if any student has an insight that he or she would like to share regarding today's lesson.

6. Arousing Action
A. Read the LESSON IN OUR SOCIETY section to the class. Ask the students to share a personal experience of either helping someone or of being helped by someone. Direct the students to the MAKE IT HAPPEN section, and discuss it in class.

B. As a review, tell the students to complete the FOLLOW THE SPIRIT section during the week.

C. End the class with prayer.

LYDIA: A COMMITTED WOMAN

Bible Background • ACTS 16
Printed Text • ACTS 16:6–15
Devotional Reading • ACTS 16:25–34

LESSON AIM

By the end of the lesson, we will:

KNOW the events surrounding Lydia's conversion and hospitality;

FEEL the joy and satisfaction Lydia felt as she opened her home to Paul and his companions; and

DECIDE to open our hearts to someone during the coming week.

KEEP IN MIND

"And when she was baptized, and her household, she besought us, saying, If ye have judged me to be faithful to the Lord, come into my house, and abide there. And she constrained us" (Acts 16:15).

LESSON OVERVIEW

LESSON AIM
KEEP IN MIND
FOCAL VERSES
IN FOCUS
THE PEOPLE, PLACES, AND TIMES
BACKGROUND
AT-A-GLANCE
IN DEPTH
SEARCH THE SCRIPTURES
DISCUSS THE MEANING
LESSON IN OUR SOCIETY
MAKE IT HAPPEN
FOLLOW THE SPIRIT
REMEMBER YOUR THOUGHTS
MORE LIGHT ON THE TEXT
DAILY BIBLE READINGS

FOCAL VERSES

Acts 16:6 Now when they had gone throughout Phrygia and the region of Galatia, and were forbidden of the Holy Ghost to preach the word in Asia,

7 After they were come to Mysia, they assayed to go into Bithynia: but the Spirit suffered them not.

8 And they passing by Mysia came down to Troas.

9 And a vision appeared to Paul in the night; There stood a man of Macedonia, and prayed him, saying, Come over into Macedonia, and help us.

10 And after he had seen the vision, immediately we endeavored to go into Macedonia, assuredly gathering that the Lord had called us for to preach the gospel unto them.

11 Therefore loosing from Troas, we came with a straight course to Samothracia, and the next day to Neapolis;

12 And from thence to Philippi, which is the chief city of that part of Macedonia, and a colony: and we were in that city abiding certain days.

13 And on the sabbath we went out of the city by a river side, where prayer was wont to be made; and we sat down, and spake unto the women which resorted thither.

14 And a certain woman named Lydia, a seller of purple, of the city of Thyatira, which worshipped God, heard us: whose heart the Lord opened, that she attended unto the things which were spoken of Paul.

15 And when she was baptized, and her household, she besought us, saying, If ye have judged me to be faithful to the Lord, come into my house, and abide there. And she constrained us.

IN FOCUS

The first day of school was always difficult for Jennessa, a kindergarten teacher and devout Christian. It was on the first day of school 25 years ago when her then 5-year-old daughter, Tamika, was pulled into a car never to be seen again. From that day forward, Jennessa spent many nights praying about the conversation that would eventually reunite her with her long lost daughter:

"Tamika, baby, is that you?"
The voice on the other end would say, "Yes, Mama, it's me. I remember you, Mama, and I remember being snatched from in front of the school."

As another first day of school ended, Jennessa gathered her things and prepared to leave the building. As she approached the front entrance, her principal held the hand of a little kindergarten girl drenched in tears. The little girl's mother had been in a minor automobile accident and wasn't able to send anyone to pick her up.

"I need someone to take her to the hospital," said the principal. "We can't reach anyone in her family. Can you do it?" he asked.

"Please, could you take me to Mommy?" The teary youngster tugged her skirt.

Although Jennessa was late for a dinner date with her husband, she agreed.

In the car, Jennessa was talking softly to soothe the crying child when she noticed the girl was squeezing something in her fist.

"What's that you have?" Jennessa asked in hopes of calming her.

Her words had the opposite effect. "Please, please don't tell mommy! She never lets me take it out of the house. It's Mommy's special present!"

When the girl unclenched her fist, what she saw stole Jennessa's breath away.

It was a tiny custom-made bracelet with five ruby stones—an exact replica of the last gift she gave her daughter Tamika prior to her kidnaping. Jennessa struggled to hold back her tears so she wouldn't upset the child any further. But at the same time her mind was racing. Could this bracelet be the same one she had given her daughter 25 years ago? She could not stop her tears as she realized that she was about to see her daughter for the first time in 25 years. Just think, if she had not extended herself and agreed to take the little girl to the hospital, she may have never been reunited with her long lost daughter.

Has an act of Christian hospitality ever given you a miraculous blessing beyond belief? Today's lesson will explore how Lydia was blessed as a result of opening her home to Paul and his companions.

THE PEOPLE, PLACES, AND TIMES

Troas. A Roman port of mixed Gentile and Jewish population where two major routes between Rome, Asia, and Greece converged. This port was visited several times by Paul. It was here that he had a dream of the man from Macedonia

(Acts 16) and restored Eutychus to life (20:5-12; 2 Corinthians 2:12).

Macedonia. A Roman province across the Aeagen Sea from Troas.

Neapolis. A seaport 150 miles across the Aegean Sea from Troas in the province of Macedonia.

Philippi. A predominantly Gentile city 10 miles inland from Neapolis.

Lydia. A wealthy businesswoman from Thyatira. She became the sponsor of the apostles while in Philippi.

BACKGROUND

Paul teamed with Barnabas and after being commissioned by the believers in Antioch, the two men were sent throughout Syria to plant new churches. With this task now successfully completed, the two returned to the believers in Antioch and reported that God had opened the way for Gentiles to become Christian believers as well. A new journey to plant churches was planned—this time throughout Asia. Paul, Silas, and Timothy were teamed to make this journey (a short time later, Luke the physician joined the team). However, once en route, the Holy Spirit deflected the group's plans to go into Asia and guided the men to the Roman province of Macedonia.

AT-A-GLANCE

1. The Call from Macedonia (Acts 16:6-11)
2. The Ministry at Philippi (vv. 12-13)
3. The Conversion of Lydia (vv. 14-15)

IN DEPTH

1. The Call from Macedonia (Acts 16:6-11)

Paul and Barnabas desired to minister the Word of Christ in Asia, but found they were prevented from doing so. Instead, the Spirit directed them in a northwesterly direction around Asia and on to the city of Troas. One evening while in

Troas, Paul had a vision of a man (apparently Grecian from his dress) beckoning him to come to Macedonia (Greece) and help them.

Paul now knew that this was the direction the Lord wanted him to go in order to continue the ministry. Immediately the group set out by ship across the Aegean Sea for Neapolis, a seaport on the Macedonian coast.

2. The Ministry at Philippi (vv. 12-13)

It was apparent that Philippi was the direction that the Holy Spirit intended for Paul's ministry to go. The group had traveled 150 miles in less than two days. The final 10 miles between Neapolis and Philippi was an easy journey along the paved road Rome had provided. On the Sabbath, Paul and the others traveling with him made their way through the city gate and to the water's edge. They had discovered that since there was no synagogue in Philippi, those who sought to worship God did so down by the riverside. This gathering of Jewish celebrants consisted mainly of women, indicating that there were not 10 Jewish men in the community, as this number of men was all that was required to build a synagogue.

Paul and his friends began to preach Christ to these women. Paul had learned that God did not show favoritism and the women who had converted to Christ had become a major source for the spread of Christianity in other places where he had preached.

3. The Conversion of Lydia (vv. 14-15)

Lydia was a businesswoman from Thyatira who had grown wealthy by making purple dye and selling it for use in the production of clothing and carpets. Thyatira was well known throughout the region for its dyer's guilds and textiles. Also, Roman law did not prevent women, whether free-born or former slaves, from engaging in business enterprises.

Lydia's heart was already open to receive God's Word, so when Paul began to speak, she listened and accepted the truth of the things he had to say. Then after accepting Christ for herself and being baptized, she was blessed to see her entire household baptized into the Christian community of believers. The joy she experienced in Christ must have been tremendous, for after her conversion she invited Paul and his companions to stay in her home as her guests and refused to let them say no. Paul and the other missionaries traveling with him stayed with Lydia until their ministry in the city had concluded.

SEARCH THE SCRIPTURES

1. Who forbade the men to preach the word in Asia (Acts 16:6)?

2. How did the men know that they were to go to Macedonia (v. 9)?

3. Who was baptized with Lydia (v. 15)?

Lydia demonstrates godly hospitality.

DISCUSS THE MEANING

1. How did the Holy Spirit respond to the men's desires to plant a church in Asia? Why?

2. Why is it significant that Lydia already worshiped God?

3. When Lydia invited the strangers to stay at her home, why did she refuse to allow them to say no?

LESSON IN OUR SOCIETY

Missionaries who travel to Africa report that the nature of hospitality is such within the country that whenever anyone has a need for food and/or shelter, the members of the church rise up and take them into their own homes until they are able to correct whatever problem might have caused their circumstance.

Such hospitality is not uncommon across the world. What do you think would happen in America if Christians practiced that type of hospitality? Why do you suppose that we as Americans do not?

MAKE IT HAPPEN

In many societies of the world, women still occupy a subordinate position to men and yet God continually uses them to teach His people lessons of love and service. Can you write a poem about the type of heart one must possess to be used by God for His service? Share it with the class.

FOLLOW THE SPIRIT

What God wants me to do:

_____

_____

REMEMBER YOUR THOUGHTS

Special insights I have learned:

_____

_____

MORE LIGHT ON THE TEXT
Acts 16:6-15

Before arriving at the welcome mat of Lydia's hospitality in the principal point of this passage, we are compelled to pause and empathize with these spiritually frustrated disciples. As Paul and his companions zealously set out to fulfill the Great Commission (Matthew 28:18-20), they were held back by the Spirit from following a logical path to the next place to preach and to baptize. They were restrained by the Holy Spirit from going to places that were conveniently along the way. Before celebrating Lydia's conversion and commitment, it is important that we feel the frustration of releasing our desire to simply do good works in the church. We should want instead to mature in the Spirit—to grow up from being generally obedient to becoming strictly obedient to God's will. When we listen to and are led by the Holy Spirit, we can be assured that our fervent efforts will bring God glory.

6 Now when they had gone throughout Phrygia and the region of Galatia, and were forbidden of the Holy Ghost to preach the word in Asia,

Paul and his companions were making their way, on foot and by animal, through these regions and past these towns, along a winding, rugged road that was seldom traveled and certainly unpaved. Ministry is sometimes the same way—a hard walk through foreign lands. Still, the apostles submitted themselves to the leading of the Holy Spirit.

The Greek constructs the name of the Holy Ghost by compounding two words: *hagios* (**hag'-ee-os**) and *pneuma* (**pnyoo'-mah**). The former is an adjective meaning "a most holy thing," and the latter is a noun meaning "the spiritual nature of Christ." To expand the understanding of the Holy Spirit, one must regard the Holy Spirit, not as a disembodied "thing," but as the third person of the Trinity or Godhead.

Here we find that the apostles "were forbidden (Gk. *koluo*, **ko-loo'-o**) of the Holy Ghost to preach the word in Asia." The text does not tell us exactly just how the Holy Spirit revealed His will. God could have revealed His will through Silas. Acts 15:32 refers to him as a prophet. Or the Roman soldiers could have blocked the road.

As we witness in Jerusalem, Judea, Samaria, and to the ends of the earth, who are our traveling companions in the life of faith and ministry? How effectively do we rely on one another's spiritual gifts? How generous are we in sharing our spiritual gifts with one another?

7 After they were come to Mysia, they assayed to go into Bithynia: but the Spirit suffered them not.

The Greek verb *peirazo* (**pi-rad'-zo**), or "assayed," is in the imperfect form denoting an incomplete action. This is the image of an intense brainstorming session in which a company of leaders were engaging to solve a problem or to set forth a strategic plan. While brainstorming where to go next, looking for a way into the next place of ministry from all angles, attesting the possibilities for effective ministry, and determining their next steps, the apostles got another message from the Lord: "Do not go." Again, and even with calculated foresight and preparation, the disciples were prevented from going to that place that might have been a good place for ministry; instead, they waited to be led into the best place for ministry according to God's time and in God's will.

The Spirit referred to as the Holy Ghost is named in verse 6. The Greek phrase used here is *pneuma Iesou,* meaning the "Spirit of Jesus."

Have you desired to go minister conveniently, logically, and prayerfully, and then had the Holy Spirit prevent, delay, detour, deny, hinder, or forbid your going? Be encouraged to remain faithful to your work and your walk. Continue to seek the voice of God to guide. Trust the Spirit evermore and even more than your best laid plans.

8 And they passing by Mysia came down to Troas.

Still traveling over rugged terrain and past unevangelized regions, the apostles passed by another city devoid of ministry and hospitality on the way to their appointed destination. God, through the Holy Spirit, was their travel agent, and the apostles relied solely on God's timing to fulfill God's will. Arriving at Mysia, they attempted to enter, but the Holy Ghost prevented them from doing so. Now twice denied access to a people in need of the Gospel message, the apostles no doubt questioned whether or not they were going in the right direction. Even while waiting for God to open doors, these disciples did not assume a passive posture. Instead, they participated with active pursuit of God's will—ever going until God said, "Stop!"

A wide door stood open for them when they came to Troas. The city of *Troas* (Gk. **Tro-as**) was located near Hellesport, an economically vibrant intersection of race, class, culture, and language. Imagine the cacophony of sounds and smells, philosophies and theologies, and dress and demeanor on display at Troas. It was here in this place of diversity that the Holy Spirit released the disciples to minister.

How willing are you to be led to the right place and away from the wrong place for ministry? Are you as open to hearing God's "No!" as you are to hoping for God's "Yes!"? How diverse is your ministry? If it were not for the occasional "different" visitor, how intentional are you to spread the Gospel to people beyond your familiar comfort zones of race, class, culture, and language?

9 And a vision appeared to Paul in the night; There stood a man of Macedonia, and prayed him, saying, Come over into Macedonia, and help us.

The Greek noun *horama* (**hor'-am-ah**), or "vision," is a sight divinely granted, sometimes while sleeping (Acts 9:10, 12; 18:9; 22:17). It is likely that Paul was asleep when this vision appeared; yet he was fully aware of God's purpose and presence in this vision. The Holy Ghost forbade (v. 6) and prevented (Acts 16:7) the disciple's movement previously, here the Spirit manifests Himself in a form and function that is believable to the apostles.

The Greek verb *parakaleo* (**par-ak-al-eh'-o**), or "prayed," connotes the image of one begging for consolation, instruction, or teaching. This man from Macedonia showed up in Paul's dream pleading with passion and urgency for the apostles to come to this Roman province to help with some urgent cause that had not been met by all of Rome's prestige, privilege, or military prowess. There are times and circumstances where only the Word of God, proclaimed, taught, and lived, meets the needs of people who appear to have much.

10 And after he had seen the vision, immediately we endeavoured to go into Macedonia, assuredly gathering that the Lord had called us for to preach the gospel unto them.

After awakening from the dream and communicating the vision to his companions, they immediately responded to this word from the Lord. Here, companionship in ministry is illuminated as Luke records this first person plural account that "we endeavoured" (Gk. *zeteo*, **dzay-teh'-o**), or made a concerted effort, to get to Macedonia. Included in this group were at least Paul, Silas, Timothy, and Luke. This inclusive reference establishes a paradigm of Christian companionship and community that becomes a predominant theme in the rest of Paul's letters to the church.

This time, unlike the holy hindrances in verses 6 and 7, their collaborative effort to carry the Gospel to the next place of ministry was allowed. Note also that consensus was taken to test whether or not this vision was from the Lord. Although God spoke through visions, not every vision was unquestionably believed. Upon determining that this was the Holy Spirit's leading, the apostles acted in agreement ("assuredly") and with urgency to respond to the vision.

The prepositional phrase "to preach the gospel" (Gk. *euaggelizo*, **yoo-ang-ghel-id'-zo**) means to bring the Good News or joyful tidings, of God's kindness—in particular, the message of Messianic blessing and salvation through the Christ. A contemporary understanding of preaching the Gospel is to instruct others regarding the things that pertain to Christian salvation. A good sermon becomes just a speech when the preacher fails to teach Jesus so that others will seek the Christ and be saved.

11 Therefore loosing from Troas, we came with a straight course to Samothracia, and the next day to Neapolis; 12 And from thence to Philippi, which is the chief city of that part of Macedonia, and a colony: and we were in that city abiding certain days.

As the disciples set sail from Troas, even the wind was in their favor providing a straight course or smooth sailing in two days through two ports to their stated destination—the great city of Philippi.

At Philippi, the apostles found that preaching was easy. The Philippians (refer to Paul's letters to them) were eager to hear the Word and a large number of them received this Good News unto salvation! The disciples lingered at Philippi, preaching indeed, but also enjoying Christian fellowship and hospitality.

This region of Macedonia is identified as a Roman colony. Although located away from the center of Rome, this region was a military conquest and was regarded as a part of Rome nonetheless. The inhabitants of such colonies were protected and privileged as full-fledged Roman citizens. Some of the privileges of being a Roman colony were citizenship, voting rights, preferential legislation, and immunity from taxation.

13 And on the sabbath we went out of the city by a river side, where prayer was wont to be made; and we sat down, and spake unto the women which resorted thither.

"Sabbath" (Gk. *sabbaton*, **sab'-tat-on**) is the seventh day of each week, which was a sacred day when the Israelites were required to abstain from all work. On the Sabbath, it was customary to gather for worship, prayer, and read the Scriptures. Although the apostles could have taken a day off from the work of preaching the Gospel, they were compelled to leave the accommodations and accolades found in the great city of Philippi and journey a mile or two west of the city to a prayer meeting down by the Gangites River.

The Greek noun *proseuche*, (**pros-yoo-khay'**), or "prayer" possesses a triple-layered meaning. It describes (1) prayer addressed to God, (2) a place in the open air outside the cities and the synagogue where the Jews were known to pray, and (3) the specific place near a flowing river, stream, or seashore where there was a supply of water for washing the hands before prayer. At this intersection of *proseuche*, the disciples find women praying to God in a place outside the city where there was no synagogue, and at the specific place of prayer where ceremonial cleansing served to symbolize the purity of their prayers and prayer meeting.

The disciples were drawn to join this woman's

prayer meeting. No doubt following the leading of the Holy Spirit, the apostles did not bypass or dismiss this gathering of women worshiping God outside the synagogue on the Sabbath. Ever modeling Jesus' radical paradigm of teaching to the outcasts, the disciples were not constrained by gender (Galatians 3:28) nor limited by their surroundings when teaching and preaching God's Word. All they required was that hearts were open to hear what the Spirit was saying to the church!

For a synagogue to be established in a city, 10 Jewish men had to convene and lead it. With no synagogue in Philippi at this time, the apostles sought out a prayer gathering whose reputation trumped Jewish ritual. This prayer meeting was more than a highly emotive, hand-wringing, loudly lamenting, stereotypical prayer meeting led by well-meaning women. This prayer meeting had the structure and leadership of a worship service replete with the reading of Jewish prayers and praying to the God of Abraham, Isaac, and Jacob. In the absence of 10 male heads of household to found a synagogue, the women were found faithful worshiping God in spirit and in truth (John 4:23-24). The prayer that God's kingdom would come and God's will would be done on earth as it is in heaven, requires us to be open minded about how God works through His people.

Through the apostles the Holy Spirit of God brought forth the first evangelistic converts under Roman rule. He did this in this holy place, set up and sanctified by women. It is while attending to the divine act of worship that a certain woman and a gathering of women became the first European converts to our Christian faith. May women's work and women's worship ever be heralded in the annals of biblical and local church history as integral, not incidental, to the Good News—to the Gospel preached, taught, and believed!

14 And a certain woman named Lydia, a seller of purple, of the city of Thyatira, which worshipped God, heard us: whose heart the Lord opened, that she attended unto the things which were spoken of Paul.

Lydia was a woman of Thyatira, the city of commerce, and a seller of the purple cloth used for the official Roman garments. She was the first European convert of Paul and his hostess during his first stay at Philippi. Lydia was a businesswoman, a wealthy woman, a well-respected woman, and a woman who "worshipped" (Gk. *sebomai,* **seb'-om-ahee**) God. While leading this prayer gathering, Lydia (whose name befittingly means "to travail in prayer") welcomed the opportunity to hear the apostles preach, to hear the disciples teach, and to learn more about the God she worshiped and Christ, God's Son.

Lydia's enthusiastic and attentive listening was fertile ground for God to open her heart to understand and accept the Gospel. The "heart" (Gk. *kardia,* **kar-dee'-ah**) represents the soul or mind as the resident place of one's thoughts, passions, desires, appetites, affections, purposes, understanding, intelligence, will, character, and intentions. Lydia's "open heart surgery" was appreciably more than an emotional response to a well-crafted sermon and loquacious rhetoric. As she listened, Lydia engaged her thoughts, affections, and understanding about God to believe in Christ Jesus! While Lydia had been seeking God, God was in the background working His way into her heart and into this nation.

15 And when she was baptized, and her household, she besought us, saying, If ye have judged me to be faithful to the Lord, come into my house, and abide there. And she constrained us.

Lydia's response to accepting the Gospel of Christ Jesus was to be baptized. "Baptized" (Gk. *baptizo,* **bap-tid'-zo**) means to wash with water. Since they were already gathered praying at the riverside, it was convenient to baptize Lydia and her household immediately following conversion. (Study also the conversion and baptism stories of Cornelius in Acts 10, of the Roman jailer in Acts 16, and of Crispus in Acts 18 for similarities and differences).

Lydia was not the only person present at the prayer meeting listening to the disciples preach and teach. Her whole household (made up of family members and servants alike) heard the Good News, believed, and were baptized. Baptism into the Christian family is cause for celebration! After becoming a baptized member of the family of God, Lydia extended hospitality to her new-found family—the apostles.

Although her quantifiable wealth is not recorded, evidently Lydia had the means to comfortably accommodate her household as well as Paul and his companions. She was so emphatic to extend hospitality to these brothers in Christ that she "constrained" (Gk. *parabiazomai*, **par-ab-ee-ad'-zom-ahee**), or made a persuasive appeal, for them to stay at her home while in Philippi. Central to this plea for them to accept her hospitality was Lydia's assertion that the apostles found her "faithful" (Gk. *pistos*, **pis-tos'**), meaning trustworthy and reliable.

Lydia extended a hospitality paradigm that is simple to follow: Show kindness to one another, especially to those in the household of faith (Galatians 6:10). When the disciples accepted Lydia's hospitality, she and her household, as well as her Philippian neighbors, had the opportunity to receive more teaching and preaching of the Good News; share in discipleship, fellowship, and good company; and help birth and bless this new Christian community.

For further information on Paul's missionary journeys use the *Precepts For Living*™ CD-ROM; go to Dictionaries and Encyclopedias or visit Maps & Atlases to see how the Gospel spread from the persecution of Christians.

DAILY BIBLE READINGS

M: Show Hospitality to Strangers
Hebrews 13:1-6
T: Mary and Martha Welcome Jesus
Luke 10:38-42
W: Serve One Another Using Your Gifts
1 Peter 4:7-11
T: Lydia Becomes a Faithful Follower
Acts 16:11-15
F: Paul and Silas Are Imprisoned
Acts 16:16-24
S: Converted, the Jailer Shows Hospitality
Acts 16:25-34
S: Paul and Silas Are Freed
Acts 16:35-40

TEACHING TIPS

November 20
Bible Study Guide 12

1. Words You Should Know

A. Tentmakers (Acts 18:3) *skenopoios* (Gk.)—More accurately understood as a leather worker.

B. Vow (v. 18) *euche* (Gk.)—A prayer to God. Probably not a Nazarite vow, which could properly be made only in the Holy Land, but a personal pledge to God.

2. Teacher Preparation

A. Pray for the students in your class, asking God to open their hearts to today's lesson.

B. Read and study the FOCAL VERSES, paying attention to the relationship shared between Paul, Priscilla, and Aquila.

C. Carefully review the BIBLE STUDY GUIDE, making notes for clarification.

D. Share a personal thought with the class about an encounter with loneliness. How did it make you feel?

3. Starting the Lesson

A. Before the class arrives, write the words "Tentmakers" and "Vow" on the board.

B. After the students arrive and are settled, lead the class in prayer. Pray specifically for godly insights from the lesson and blessings on the lives of the students.

C. Ask a volunteer to read the IN FOCUS story and spend time discussing how it relates to the concept of teamwork expressed in the LESSON AIM.

4. Getting into the Lesson

A. Ask volunteers to read THE PEOPLE, PLACES, AND TIMES and the BACKGROUND sections.

B. Ask the students to read the FOCAL VERSES together; then have a student read the corresponding IN DEPTH section. Allow time for discussion between each section.

5. Relating the Lesson to Life

A. Spend time answering the questions in the DISCUSS THE MEANING section.

B. Ask if any student has an insight that he/she would like to share regarding today's lesson.

6. Arousing Action

A. Read LESSON IN OUR SOCIETY to the class. Ask the class to share personal encounters they have had with racism. Direct the students to the MAKE IT HAPPEN section and discuss it in class.

B. As a review, tell the students to complete the FOLLOW THE SPIRIT section during the week.

C. End the class with prayer.

WORSHIP GUIDE

For the Superintendent or Teacher
Theme: Priscilla and Aquila:
Team Ministry
Theme Song: "He Went About
Doing Good"
Scripture: Acts 18:3
Song: "Give of Your Best to the Master"
Meditation: Holy Father, You created us
in Your image that we might one day
shine brighter than the sun. Thank You
for bringing us all together through the
blood of Your Son, Jesus Christ. Amen.

PRISCILLA AND AQUILA: TEAM MINISTRY

Bible Background • ACTS 18:1–19:10
Printed Text • ACTS 18:1–4, 18–21, 24–28
Devotional Background • LUKE 10:1–11

LESSON AIM

By the end of the lesson, we will:

KNOW how Priscilla and Aquila demonstrated teamwork in serving the Christian community;

BECOME CONVINCED of the value of teamwork for accomplishing God's work in the church and community; and

DEVELOP a plan to engage in a team ministry project.

KEEP IN MIND

"And because he was of the same craft, he abode with them, and wrought: for by their occupation they were tentmakers" (Acts 18:3).

FOCAL VERSES

Acts 18:1 After these things Paul departed from Athens, and came to Corinth;

2 And found a certain Jew named Aquila, born in Pontus, lately come from Italy, with his wife Priscilla; (because that Claudius had commanded all Jews to depart from Rome:) and came unto them.

3 And because he was of the same craft, he abode with them, and wrought: for by their occupation they were tentmakers.

4 And he reasoned in the synagogue every sabbath, and persuaded the Jews and the Greeks.

18:18 And Paul after this tarried there yet a good while, and then took his leave of the brethren, and sailed thence into Syria, and with him Priscilla and Aquila; having shorn his head in

LESSON OVERVIEW

LESSON AIM
KEEP IN MIND
FOCAL VERSES
IN FOCUS
THE PEOPLE, PLACES,
AND TIMES
BACKGROUND
AT-A-GLANCE
IN DEPTH
SEARCH THE SCRIPTURES
DISCUSS THE MEANING
LESSON IN OUR SOCIETY
MAKE IT HAPPEN
FOLLOW THE SPIRIT
REMEMBER YOUR THOUGHTS
MORE LIGHT ON THE TEXT
DAILY BIBLE READINGS

Cenchrea: for he had a vow.

19 And he came to Ephesus, and left them there: but he himself entered into the synagogue, and reasoned with the Jews.

20 When they desired him to tarry longer time with them, he consented not;

21 But bade them farewell, saying, I must by all means keep this feast that cometh in Jerusalem: but I will return again unto you, if God will. And he sailed from Ephesus.

18:24 And a certain Jew named Apollos, born at Alexandria, an eloquent man, and mighty in the scriptures, came to Ephesus.

25 This man was instructed in the way of the Lord; and being fervent in the spirit, he spake and taught diligently the things of the Lord, knowing only the baptism of John.

26 And he began to speak boldly in the synagogue: whom when Aquila and Priscilla had heard, they took him unto them, and expounded unto him the way of God more perfectly.

27 And when he was disposed to pass into Achaia, the brethren wrote, exhorting the disciples to receive him: who, when he was come, helped them much which had believed through grace:

28 For he mightily convinced the Jews, and that publickly, shewing by the scriptures that Jesus was Christ.

IN FOCUS

Mrs. Felder, an 80-year-old committed Christian, always volunteered to help deliver food during the Thanksgiving holiday. Usually she drove her minivan herself, but lately her arthritis wouldn't let her get in and out of the van comfortably. This Thanksgiving, Mrs. Felder decided to ask Jamie and her friend Kisha, two teenagers from her congregation, to assist her in making deliveries and evangelizing throughout the community.

Jamie and Kisha loaded the van with frozen turkeys, fresh collard greens, yams, and all the fixin's for a complete Thanksgiving Day meal. As they started out, the girls were excited at the opportunity to give their testimonies and pass out food to those in need, even if they were a little uncomfortable when confronted with the elderly woman's game plan for the journey.

"I don't have any specific addresses," said Mrs. Felder. "We'll just stop as the Holy Spirit directs. Then you and Kisha can go to the door, deliver the care package, and give your testimony."

Jamie and Kisha discovered that the families were grateful for the food but declined to talk with them. After a few stops, Jamie and Kisha climbed into the van and reported to Mrs. Felder that they had failed once again. Mrs. Felder stuck to her guns, insisting that Jamie and Kisha attempt to witness at every home that received food.

"Mrs. Felder, we're wasting our time," Kisha complained. "We should just leave the food! They gave us all kinds of excuses for not wanting to talk with us; plus all the neighborhood teenagers are laughing at us."

The elderly woman peered sternly over her bifocals, "You young ladies need to understand, that we don't have to save souls. Just offer the Word. The glory isn't in your testimony, but in the spiritual seed that is planted when people see that someone cares. So you haven't failed in your work for God's Kingdom—your service alone has been a beautiful gift from God. Some of these families may not have had a meal today if we had not dropped by."

As you go about doing God's work, realize that the promise of God to build the church can only take place as Christians work together to support, encourage, and minister to one another.

THE PEOPLE, PLACES, AND TIMES

Paul. Initially known as Saul of Tarsus, he was born into the tribe of Benjamin and was a Roman citizen (Acts 16:37; 21:39; 22:25). He emerges in the Bible as a zealous member of the Pharisee party (Romans 11:1; Philippian 3:5; Acts 23:6). According to Acts 22:3; 26:4, he was born in Tarsus, brought up in Jerusalem, and educated at the feet of Gamaliel, a renowned Jewish scholar and rabbi. As a 'young man' Saul was given official authority to direct the persecution of Christians (Acts 26:10). On his way to Damascus to carry out one of his missions of persecution, Saul of Tarsus encountered the risen Jesus and converted to Christ (Acts 9:1-18). He became known as Paul the apostle and became one of the greatest champions of the Christian faith.

Priscilla and Aquila. Aquila was a Jewish tentmaker (Acts 18:3). Along with Priscilla his wife, they were both close friends of Paul. Aquila was a native of Pontus, but the couple were in Rome when Emperor Claudius forced all Jews from the city in A.D 49. The expulsion apparently came after disorder among Roman Jews regarding Christianity. By the time they met Paul in Corinth, they were probably Christians already. They partnered with Paul in ministry and business.

Apollos. An Alexandrian Jew who came to Ephesus in A.D. 52 (Acts 18:24). He had an accurate understanding of the story of Jesus and a profound understanding of the Old Testament. He was eloquent, articulate and enthusiastic as he preached truth as he knew it (Acts 18:24-25). However, he lacked knowledge about the outpouring of the Holy Spirit and Christian baptism. Priscilla and Aquila patiently instructed Apollos, filling in the gaps in his knowledge (Acts 18:26). As a result, Apollos went on to become a powerful proclaimer and defender of the Christian faith (Acts 18:27-28).

Corinth. A city in Greece that controlled the trade routes between northern and southern Greece as well as across the isthmus. The city was the temple site of Aphrodite, the goddess of love. The influence of this religion gave rise to the city's reputation for immorality.

BACKGROUND

After ministering for an extended period in Philippi following the conversion of Lydia, Paul and Silas left Philippi. For healing a demon-possessed slave girl, the two men were dragged before the legal authorities, flogged, and chained in a prison cell. God intervened and rescued them. As a result, their jailer was converted. After complaining that they were Roman citizens and had been mistreated, Paul and Silas elicited an apology from the authorities, then left Philippi to minister in Thessalonica and then Athens. In Athens, Paul was given an opportunity to preach before the intellectual elite of Greece.

AT-A-GLANCE

1. Paul Meets Priscilla and Aquila
(Acts 18:1-4)
2. Expanding the Ministry to Ephesus
(vv. 18-24)
3. Apollos Joins the Ministry
(vv. 24-28)

IN DEPTH

1. Paul Meets Priscilla and Aquila (Acts 18:1-4)

Paul's efforts to plant a church in Athens had met with little success. However, as Acts 18 begins, he was not running for his life. Rather, he had set his sights on Corinth, the capital city of Achaia, as the place of his next missionary campaign. In Paul's day, it was customary for teachers and rabbis to minister freely and work in an occupation or trade to support themselves. Paul was trained as a tentmaker or leather worker. Once in Corinth, Paul sought out the local synagogue and began teaching about Jesus, the long-awaited Messiah. He also took up his tentmaking occupation in order to support himself.

Shortly after arriving in Corinth, Paul met Priscilla and Aquila, who apparently were believers who had moved to Corinth from Rome. They also happened to be tentmakers by profession, and these three began a lifelong friendship as they worked and ministered together among the inhabitants of Corinth.

2. Expanding the Ministry to Ephesus (vv. 18-21)

Paul and his companions ministered for a year and a half among the Corinthians before the stirring of the Holy Spirit prompted them to travel to Syria to further the ministry. Their teaching in Corinth had caused a great stir among the Jewish population that eventually resulted in Paul's being brought before Gallio, the Roman proconsul for the region. Gallio's ruling was favorable to Paul and his ministry and helped in the establishment and growth of the Corinthian church. Now Paul leaves accompanied by Priscilla and Aquila, and sailed back across the Aegean Sea. Before he left, Paul got a haircut. He had taken a personal vow to let his hair grow while in Corinth as an indication of God's hand of protection upon him and the ministry. This vow was now complete, and Paul thanked God by allowing his hair to be cut before setting sail for the Greek coast.

The ship upon which the trio were traveling stopped in Ephesus for a short time, and Paul took advantage of the stopover to begin to teach in the local Jewish synagogue. His preaching stirred interest among the Jewish inhabitants of Ephesus, who entreated Paul to stay with them longer. However, Paul desired to return to Jerusalem in time for one of the Jewish festivals and was unable to stay. He promises, however, to return if God will permit it and left Priscilla and Aquila in Ephesus to carry on what he had begun. Priscilla and Aquila remained in Ephesus for several years and permitted their home to be used as the meeting place for the Christian church they helped to plant.

3. Apollos Joins the Ministry (vv. 24-28)

In Ephesus, Priscilla and Aquila came into contact with an Alexandrian believer named Apollos. While teaching in the synagogue, Apollos impressed the couple with his knowledge of the Scriptures and his speaking ability. However, they took note that his knowledge was incomplete in that he did not teach that people needed to be saved in the name of Jesus. Priscilla and Aquila did not embarrass Apollos publicly, but took him into the privacy of their home and began to share with him what they no doubt had learned from their time with Paul. Apollos learned that Jesus is the long-awaited Messiah and that eternal life can be found only in Him. Apollos received their instruction and became a strong voice for Christ among the Ephesian believers.

In time, Apollos sought to cross the Aegean Sea and preach in Corinth. This idea was embraced by the church in Ephesus, which wrote a letter of introduction for Apollos to the believers in Achaia.

The believers who were acquainted with Apollos were probably reminded of Paul. He shared Paul's zeal to share Christ and was able to argue effectively through the Scriptures that Jesus was the Messiah. Through Apollos's efforts, the churches in Ephesus and Corinth were strengthened and encouraged in Paul's absence. In later writings, Paul would embrace Apollos, Aquila, and Priscilla as colleagues in the ministry.

SEARCH THE SCRIPTURES

1. Why did Priscilla and Aquila leave Rome and settle in Corinth (Acts 18:2)?

2. How often did Paul visit the synagogue to try to persuade the Jews and Greeks (v. 4)?

3. What characteristics distinguished Apollos as a believer (vv. 24-25)?

DISCUSS THE MEANING

1. In what ways did Priscilla and Aquila benefit from their association with Paul? How did Paul benefit?

2. What does it mean that Apollos knew "only the baptism of John?" What did the married couple do to help Apollos?

3. Why did Paul feel the need to make a vow? How do you suppose his faithfulness to that vow affected Priscilla and Aquila?

LESSON IN OUR SOCIETY

Loneliness is a universal experience that all people share. It has been suggested that our leaders are among the loneliest people in the world. God created us as a community. We enjoy the fellowship and companionship of others. Think about those times when you are happiest and most content with your life. Now think about how you would feel if you had no one to share that happiness with.

MAKE IT HAPPEN

Spend some time in prayer this week and ask God to guide you to a person who is lonely. Perhaps this person will be in a nursing home or simply a shut-in in their own home. Perhaps this person is a leader in your church or community. After you have selected the person, ask God to help you find five ways to help relieve his or her loneliness. Or consider engaging in a team ministry project to serve your church or community.

FOLLOW THE SPIRIT

What God wants me to do:

_____

_____

REMEMBER YOUR THOUGHTS

Special insights I have learned:

_____

_____

MORE LIGHT ON THE TEXT
Acts 18:1-4, 18-21, 24-28

While in Athens, Paul seized the opportunity to minister in the synagogue and in the marketplace. In the synagogue he taught and discussed matters of faith in Christ Jesus with devout Jews and God-fearing Greeks. In the marketplace, Paul took it upon himself to debate with the elite members of the *Areopagus* (Gk. **ar-i'o-pag-os**), a vast gathering of philosophers, religious leaders, and learned men and women who came together regularly just to hear and exchange new thoughts on various matters. After teaching and preaching and debating for some time there, it is recorded that among the converts were many members of the Areopagus, including a man named Dionysius and a woman named Damaris.

1 After these things Paul departed from Athens, and came to Corinth;

The Greek name for the city of Athens is *Athenai* (**Ath-ay-nahee**), which means uncertainty. What an odd name for a capital city in Greece acclaimed for education and development of civilization during the height of Greek culture. What an appropriate place, on the other hand, for Paul to minister to the lonely, difficult, and unfruitful (1 Corinthians 2:3).

The city of Corinth (Gk. *Korinthos*, **KOR'-in-thos**) means satiated or satisfied. Located about 40 miles (65 km) west of Athens, Corinth was the political and economic bedrock of Greece. Its infamy, however, was its reputation of sexual immorality. There were a dozen temples of worship specializing in lewd and lascivious sexual accommodations. This city of ill-repute founded the Greek idiom "to corinthianize," which means to practice sexual wantonness.

Paul's missionary journey preaching the Gospel seems to have taken him from one challenging place of ministry to another. Still, we note that Paul moved as the Spirit led, demonstrating his faithfulness and commitment to spread the Gospel was more important than seeking ease and comfort in ministry. Rather than regarding Corinth as a morally desolate wasteland—Paul seized the opportunity to minister in this city and to its inhabitants with the very grace and love of God that had compelled him to know and accept Jesus as Lord. In his two letters to the Corinthians, Paul undertakes extensive teaching regarding sexual purity.

2 And found a certain Jew named Aquila, born in Pontus, lately come from Italy, with his wife Priscilla; (because that Claudius had commanded all Jews to depart from Rome:) and came unto them.

When Paul arrived in Corinth, he again sought out Christian community and colaborers in Christ. While ministering in Athens alone, Paul had no doubt learned the hard way that companionship in ministry affords increased spiritual and physical strength. Going it alone leads to burnout compounded with loneliness (1 Corinthians 2:3). Paul's first order of business was to find believers!

Aquila, along with his wife Priscilla, were Jewish Christian converts, tentmakers, or leather workers by vocation, and missionary partners with Paul near the end of this two-year journey. They are described as residents of Italy, but it is made clear that they were Jewish, or *Ioudaios* (Gk. **lee-oo-DAH'-yos**), implying that they are orthodox or fully Jewish in birth, race, and religion. All Jewish converts were exiled from Rome at this time because of their belief in Christ the Messiah. It was from this edict of religious persecution that the Gospel spread wherever converts and disciples dispersed.

3 And because he was of the same craft, he abode with them, and wrought: for by their occupation they were tentmakers.

Priscilla and Aquila modeled for believers an egalitarian paradigm for partnership in vocation and ministry. Emphasizing community and companionship rather than gender competitiveness, they complemented each other as tentmakers and teachers. Priscilla and Aquila opened their homes in Ephesus (1 Corinthians 16:10) and in Rome (Romans 16:3-5) to found house churches. Paul could relate to both their transportable vocation and their passion for teaching. Within this partnership of marriage and ministry, Paul found companionship and community among Christians.

Alongside one another, the three of them took pride in their craft and enjoyed Christian fellowship as they made tents to house the very Roman soldiers who were their adversaries. This model of bi-vocational ministry is useful even today when ministers labor to meet their own needs more, becoming a financial burden to their congregations or exploiting those of new faith and little understanding of giving to the preacher.

4 And he reasoned in the synagogue every sabbath, and persuaded the Jews and the Greeks.

Paul worked throughout the week, but on every Sabbath, he headed to the synagogue. Ever diligent to the cause of the Gospel, Paul "reasoned" (Gk. *dialegomai*, **dee-al-EG'-om-ahee**), or engaged in the act of lively, thoughtful, passionate discussion continually and repeatedly with the Jews and the Greeks regarding the Christ. Paul taught the Gospel to convince and convert Jews well-versed in Old Testament theology and God-fearing Greeks well-versed in philosophy but who had not converted to Judaism.

18:18 And Paul after this tarried there yet a good while, and then took his leave of the brethren, and sailed thence into Syria, and with him Priscilla and Aquila; having shorn his head in Cenchrea: for he had a vow.

While teaching a good number of those gathering in the synagogue weekly, Paul "tarried" (Gk. *prosmeno*, **pros-MEN'-o**) meaning "to continue" or "to remain with" them for an unspecified length of time, but for what is understood to be a considerable number of days. Paul stayed put, preaching and teaching among them, even after a plot to kill him had failed (18:12-17). Because the people were receptive, the preached Word was effectual in convicting and convincing that Jesus is the Christ. Note that in the previous verse, those gathered were called Jews and Greeks. After Paul's effective and persuasive ministry to them, he now calls them "brethren" (Gk. *adelphotes*, **ad-el-fot'-ace**), which explicitly means a male brother by birth, national origin or friendship. However, within Christian community, the term became all-inclusive to refer to all who believed, whether Jew or Greek, bond or free, and male or female.

Priscilla and Aquila, a husband and wife, were present in the synagogue and had found Paul's invitation to join his evangelistic journey irresistible. Companionship and partnership in ministry is empowering, encouraging, and refining. As believers, we should seek accountability and good company in one another—both male and female. In this account, as was also in last week's lesson with Lydia, women are mentioned as central players in the spread of the Gospel. There is no apology needed to defend a woman's place in the church as preachers and teachers of this Good News!

The "vow" (Gk. *euche*, **yoo-KHAY'**) that Paul made earlier was most likely a 30-day fast and prayer of thanksgiving to God when he did not shave or drink wine. Shaving his head was simply an outward Jewish expression of his inward sincerity when this period of consecration had ended.

19 And he came to Ephesus, and left them there: but he himself entered into the synagogue, and reasoned with the Jews.

The name of the Roman city Ephesus (Gk. *Ephesos*, **EF'-es-os**) means permitted; it was located on the sea between Smyrna and Miletus—the place from which Paul would call the elders of the church). While in port at Ephesus, Paul left his companions, Priscilla and Aquila, and went directly to the synagogue to again debate with the Jewish religious and philosophical leaders assembled there. Paul was ever ready and ever seeking to persuade, convince, debate, and prove that Jesus Christ is the Messiah to all who would listen.

The Greek word *sunagoge* (**soon-ag-o-GAY'**) is used in various grammatical forms. As a verb, "to synagogue" means to bring together (a harvest or a group of men). As a noun, "synagogue" is a formal assembly of Jewish men gathered to pray, read, and discuss Scripture, which met weekly, every sabbath and feast day. (Christians also adapted the word "synagogue" to describe their formal gathering in the early church). "Synagogue" also refers to the very buildings where these religious Jewish assemblies, as well as trials and torture, were held. There was at least one synagogue in every town.

20 When they desired him to tarry longer time with them, he consented not;

Paul's teaching was so efficacious that Jewish religious leaders, some now converts to Christianity, asked him to stay or tarry with them a while longer. Whereas Paul hastened from the port of Ephesus to meet with those in the synagogue, he was compelled by the Holy Spirit to decline their persistence that he extend his stay. Here, Paul demonstrates that his calling and ministry is unto God's will and not for man's desire. The best good to be found among these new believers paled in comparison to the ministry before Paul as he journeyed to Jerusalem for the Feast of the Passover.

21 But bade them farewell, saying, I must by all means keep this feast that cometh in Jerusalem: but I will return again unto you, if God will. And he sailed from Ephesus.

Paul gave them an explanation for resisting their hospitality: he had to go to the place of worship. Paul held fast to his conviction to move on; however, he did leave them with a caveat. He promised to come back and continue in ministry and fellowship only if God needed him more there! "God willing," was a shared understanding among the pious Jews and Greeks. We must take care to use it, not as doubting God's will for our lives or buffeting a weak promise, but as a faithful declaration to do God's will, in God's time, at God's appointed place!

18:24 And a certain Jew named Apollos, born at Alexandria, an eloquent man, and mighty in the scriptures, came to Ephesus.

Apollos, in all of his intellect and eloquence, also modeled notable humility. This renaissance man of culture and law readily received instruction from these mere artisans, a couple of blue-collar workers, and most commendably, submitted himself to the learned, wise teachings from a woman.

Before meeting Priscilla and Aquila, Apollos had received a privileged education reserved for elite students in rhetoric and philosophy. "Eloquent" (Gk. *logios*, **LOG'-ee-os**) describes one very well educated in literature and the arts, particularly history and the antiquities, with exceptional reasoning and extraordinary speaking skills. Apollos was one such student who had become an expert in Old Testament Jewish theology and whose eloquence gained him the reputation described as "mighty" (Gk. *dunatos*, **doo-nat-OS'**) or one who is powerful and excellent and influential through oratorical prowess.

25 This man was instructed in the way of the Lord; and being fervent in the spirit, he spake and taught diligently the things of the Lord, knowing only the baptism of John.

Apollos was indeed knowledgeable and persuasive when he spoke and taught as evidenced by the use of the word "instructed" (Gk. *katecheo*, **kat-ay-KHEH'-o**), meaning to teach, instruct, and inform, specifically by speaking. While his natural gift was certainly honed throughout his formal education, Apollos was not simply given to flowery philosophical discourse. He used his gift and training to fervently and diligently, systematically and repeatedly teach about the Lord.

Apollos taught with passion about the Lord (the Greek noun *kurios*, **KOO'-ree-os**, meaning one who is the owner who has control of a person, the master). The Lord, in this case, is also the Messianic title of Jesus.

The prepositional phrase "in the way of the Lord" is the Greek word *hodos* (**hod-OS'**, which metaphorically means to teach the manner of thinking, feeling, and deciding as another. Apollos, then, taught what he had learned through John the Baptist about the Lord: "repent and be saved!" And he was "fervent" (Gk. *zeo*, **DZEH'-o**), meaning to be full of zeal for what is good in his teaching. This fervency and passion is the image of hot water boiling over! It is a passion to emulate as we teach this Good News!

Apollos was not only passionate about teaching, he systematically or "diligently" (Gk. *didasko*, **did-AS'-ko**) taught and instructed all who gathered. His passion was accompanied with preparation and appealed even to the most stalwart intellectuals.

26 And he began to speak boldly in the synagogue: whom when Aquila and Priscilla had heard, they took him unto them, and expounded unto him the way of God more perfectly.

"To speak boldly" (Gk. *parrhesiazomai*, **par-hray-see-AD'-zom-ahee**) is to show confidence, assurance, boldness, and freedom when speaking. This had become Apollos's custom and reputation. However, Apollos lacked "perfect" (Gk. *akribesteron*, **ak-ree-BES'-ter-on**) or complete knowledge about God through Jesus Christ.

When Priscilla and Aquila took Apollos aside, they did not merely write the pastor a letter criticizing his sermon and sign it anonymously. No! They "took" (Gk. *proslambano*, **pros-lam-BAN'-o**) him by the hand, lead him aside, received him into their home, showed kindness toward him, and confirmed Christian love to him. They did all this that they might further explain, or "expounded" (Gk. *ektithemi*, **ek-TITH'-ay-mee**, meaning to set forth, declare, or clarify) the Gospel of Christ Jesus (Acts 20:21). Through their instruction, Apollos learned that many of the Old Testament prophecies had indeed been fulfilled in the birth, life, death, and resurrection of Jesus and in the coming of the Holy Ghost!

Apollos responded to their hospitality and instruction wholeheartedly. By submitting himself to Priscilla and Aquilla's correction and instruction, Apollos became better equipped and emerged as a highly-acclaimed minister in the Christian church (1 Corinthians 1:12).

27 And when he was disposed to pass into Achaia, the brethren wrote, exhorting the disciples to receive him: who, when he was come, helped them much which had believed through grace:

The Greek word *boulomai* (**BOO'-lom-ahee**) means to express will, purpose, and desire. Apollos expressed his desire to go preach next in Achaia, a Roman city whose name means "trouble." The believers in Ephesus wrote to the believers in Achaia appealing to the grace that saved them to show kindness toward Apollos upon his arrival. Their letters of recommendation served to encourage him (Gk. *protrepomai*, **prot-REP'-om-ahee**), and to give confidence to the believers to receive Apollos as an able-bodied teacher full of grace and truth. Apollos's teaching and preaching would no doubt help them better understand and apply tenets of faith in Christ Jesus, which they had professed to believe.

The Greek word *charis* (**KHAR'-ece**) is God's merciful kindness through the Holy Spirit that compels one to repent and turn to Christ. It is grace that keeps, strengthens, and empowers Christians to live holy and serve joyfully. The Achaian "disciples" (Gk. *mathetes*, **math-ay-TES'**) were students of Christianity. Although they lived in a town named "trouble," they were blessed nonetheless because they were receptive to the preached Word.

28 For he mightily convinced the Jews, and that publickly, shewing by the scriptures that Jesus was Christ.

"Mightily" (Gk. *eutonos*, **yoo-TON'-oce**) connotes the image of something done with forceful passion, intense heat, and vigor. This had become Apollos's reputation and model of presentation (1 Corinthians 1:12; 3:4-6; 4:6). Demonstrating this passion, he "convinced" (Gk. *diakatelegchomai*, **dee-ak-at-el-ENG'-khom-ahee**), thereby challenging, disproving, and refuting all philosophical competitors and religious adversaries to Christianity.

Apollos preached and proved "shewing" (Gk. *epideiknumi*, **ep-ee-DIKE'-noo-mee**) that Jesus is Christ! (1 Corinthians 4:1-6)

DAILY BIBLE READINGS

M: Jesus Sends Disciples Out in Pairs
Luke 10:1-11
T: Go and Find a Colt
Luke 19:28-34
W: Paul Preaches in Corinth
Acts 18:1-8
T: Paul's Preaching Stirs Up Controversy
Acts 18:9-17
F: Paul, Priscilla, and Aquila Travel Together
Acts 18:18-23
S: Priscilla and Aquila Help Apollos
Acts 18:24-28
S: Paul Thanks Priscilla and Aquila
Romans 16:3-16

TEACHING TIPS

November 27
Bible Study Guide 13

1. Words You Should Know

Elders (Acts 20:17) *presbuteros* (Gk.)—The recognized leadership within the Christian church; usually men of outstanding reputation.

2. Teacher Preparation

A. Pray for the students in your class, asking God to open their hearts to today's lesson.

B. Read and study the FOCAL VERSES, paying attention to how the elders responded to Paul's address.

C. Carefully review the BIBLE STUDY GUIDE, making notes for clarification.

D. Share a personal thought with the class about being separated from a loved one. How did it make you feel?

3. Starting the Lesson

A. Before the class arrives, write the word "elders" on the board.

B. After the students arrive and are settled, lead the class in prayer. Pray specifically for godly insights from the lesson and blessings on the lives of the students.

C. Ask for a volunteer to read the IN FOCUS story, and then spend time applying the principles to the LESSON AIM.

4. Getting into the Lesson

A. Ask volunteers to read THE PEOPLE, PLACES, AND TIMES and BACKGROUND sections.

B. Ask the students to read the FOCAL VERSES together, and then have a student read the corresponding IN DEPTH section. Allow time for discussion between each section.

5. Relating the Lesson to Life

A. Spend time answering the questions in the DISCUSS THE MEANING section.

B. Ask if any student has an insight that he/she would like to share regarding today's lesson.

6. Arousing Action

A. Read the LESSON IN OUR SOCIETY section to the class. Ask the class to share personal encounters with loss they might have had. Direct the students to the MAKE IT HAPPEN section, and discuss it in class.

B. Tell the students to complete the FOLLOW THE SPIRIT section as a review during the week.

C. End the class with prayer.

WORSHIP GUIDE

For the Superintendent or Teacher
Theme: Paul's Farewell
Theme Song: "When We All Get to Heaven"
Scripture: Romans 8:38-39
Song: "My Jesus, I Love Thee"
Meditation: Holy Father, You taught us that anyone who tried to save his life would surely lose it, but that those who lose their life for Your sake will find it. Accept my life as a living sacrifice for You.
Amen.

PAUL'S FAREWELL

Bible Background • ACTS 20:17–38
Printed Text • ACTS 20:17-28, 36–38
Devotional Reading • ACTS 20:31–35

LESSON AIM

By the end of the lesson, we will:

KNOW the things Paul did that endeared him to the church at Ephesus;

FEEL the need to establish and value relationships with fellow believers; and

COMMIT to expressing appreciation and respect to someone today and during the upcoming week.

KEEP IN MIND

"Take heed therefore unto yourselves, and to all the flock, over the which the Holy Ghost hath made you overseers, to feed the church of God, which he hath purchased with his own blood" (Acts 20:28).

LESSON OVERVIEW

LESSON AIM
KEEP IN MIND
FOCAL VERSES
IN FOCUS
THE PEOPLE, PLACES, AND TIMES
BACKGROUND
AT-A-GLANCE
IN DEPTH
SEARCH THE SCRIPTURES
DISCUSS THE MEANING
LESSON IN OUR SOCIETY
MAKE IT HAPPEN
FOLLOW THE SPIRIT
REMEMBER YOUR THOUGHTS
MORE LIGHT ON THE TEXT
DAILY BIBLE READINGS

23 Save that the Holy Ghost witnesseth in every city, saying that bonds and afflictions abide me.

24 But none of these things move me, neither count I my life dear unto myself, so that I might finish my course with joy, and the ministry, which I have received of the Lord Jesus, to testify the gospel of the grace of God.

25 And now, behold, I know that ye all, among whom I have gone preaching the kingdom of God, shall see my face no more.

26 Wherefore I take you to record this day, that I am pure from the blood of all men.

27 For I have not shunned to declare unto you all the counsel of God.

28 Take heed therefore unto yourselves, and to all the flock, over the which the Holy Ghost hath made you overseers, to feed the church of God, which he hath purchased with his own blood.

20:36 And when he had thus spoken, he kneeled down, and prayed with them all.

37 And they all wept sore, and fell on Paul's neck, and kissed him,

38 Sorrowing most of all for the words which he spake, that they should see his face no more. And they accompanied him unto the ship.

FOCAL VERSES

Acts 20:17 And from Miletus he sent to Ephesus, and called the elders of the church.

18 And when they were come to him, he said unto them, Ye know, from the first day that I came into Asia, after what manner I have been with you at all seasons,

19 Serving the Lord with all humility of mind, and with many tears, and temptations, which befell me by the lying in wait of the Jews:

20 And how I kept back nothing that was profitable unto you, but have shewed you, and have taught you publickly, and from house to house,

21 Testifying both to the Jews, and also to the Greeks, repentance toward God, and faith toward our Lord Jesus Christ.

22 And now, behold, I go bound in the spirit unto Jerusalem, not knowing the things that shall befall me there:

IN FOCUS

Angela's face was wet with tears as she wrote, Dear 83V7158, . . . may you and God forgive me. It was her father's prison ID number. He had been serving a life sentence since Angela was 14. Angela's mother died in childbirth, and after her father's

115

arrest, she was adopted first by friends, then by her foster parents. She harbored great bitterness toward her biological father.

On Thanksgiving morning, he died unexpectedly. The grief she felt upon hearing the news of his passing surprised and overwhelmed her. She felt a deep sense of guilt because over the past 15 years she had refused to communicate with him and had left his many letters to her unopened. Deeply troubled, she carried her burden to her pastor.

"Pastor, I have been estranged from my father for over 15 years. Why do I feel so bad? The crime he committed was horrible!" Angela sobbed.

"If we are alienated from someone, once they die, we feel the relationship can never be healed. Even though you have denied it, you still yearn for a father's love," said the pastor as he handed her a tissue.

"But I didn't want his love. I hated him for leaving me!" she cried.

"Neither you nor he can change the past, but you can learn from it. You must reconcile with your father," the pastor instructed.

"But he is dead. How is that possible?" Angela asked.

"That doesn't matter. Do you still have any of his letters?"

"Yes, I keep them all in a trunk."

"Go home and pray, then read each letter. Afterward, write a letter to your father expressing whatever is on your heart."

That evening, Angela pulled out the old trunk and started reading the letters her father had written her over the years. She discovered that her father had accepted Christ 10 years earlier and was actually a minister behind prison walls. He had prayed for her many times and had sent many positive messages to her. He apologized for having left her alone and asked her to forgive him. Angela was ashamed that she had never prayed for him.

People who care for one another feel great sadness when they must part. Today's lesson shows us how Paul prayerfully helped the elders at Ephesus say good-bye to him for the last time.

THE PEOPLE, PLACES, AND TIMES

Miletus. About 30 miles south-southwest of Ephesus, Miletus was the southernmost of the major Greek cities on the west coast of Asia Minor (now Turkey). During the 8th, 7th and 6th centuries B.C., it was a thriving commercial center. By the time of Paul's visit, the city was in decline, mainly because its harbor bad became clogged with silt from the Maeander river.

BACKGROUND

After Apollos departed from Ephesus for Corinth, Paul returned and ministered first in the synagogue, then in a rented hall. He ministered from this hall for two years, teaching about Jesus, healing the infirmed, and helping to spread the Gospel across Asia Minor. Eventually, his teaching set off a riot in the city when merchants involved in making charms for the goddess Diana felt that their livelihood was threatened. After the riot was quieted by a city magistrate, Paul left Ephesus to travel through Macedonia and Greece. He did so in order to collect money for the poverty-stricken church in Jerusalem. During this year of travel, Paul stayed with friends in Corinth and Philippi. Finally, he determined that he would like to spend Pentecost in Jerusalem, even though he had been warned that hardships awaited him there. Paul and his friends board a ship bound for the Holy Land. Because he did not have time to make the journey to Ephesus himself, Paul asked the elders from the Ephesian church to travel the 30 miles to Miletus to meet him as his ship spent a few days in port there.

AT-A-GLANCE

1. Paul Asks to See the Elders from Ephesus (Acts 20:17)
2. Paul's Farewell to the Ephesian Church (vv. 18-28)
3. An Affectionate Parting (vv. 36-38)

IN DEPTH

1. Paul Asks to See the Elders from Ephesus (Acts 20:17)

As Paul's ship, bound for Jerusalem, harbored for a few days in the port of Miletus, Paul took the opportunity to ask to address the elders from the Christian church at Ephesus. His request was probably carried to Ephesus by able-bodied mes-

Paul's farewell to the Ephesian Church

sengers from Miletus and would have been delivered to the head of the local church, possibly Priscilla and Aquila. The elders who would have responded to Paul's invitation would have been recognized as such by everyone in the region.

2. Paul's Farewell to the Ephesian Church (vv. 18-28)

Paul knew from the testimony of prophets during his last journey that this would be the last time he had an opportunity to speak to the churches in this part of the world. It is not surprising that he opened his heart to them. His message began with his reminding them of how eagerly he had sought to impart Christ to them. He explained that he had done so because he was a slave of Jesus Christ for their benefit. Prophetic words that danger, trials, and even death awaited him did not disturb him so long as he could finish the work Christ had given him to do. Paul's fearlessness and courage were well known to the leaders; now, he gave them the reason for his resolve.

Paul was seeking to encourage the elders by reminding them of his example. He then looked to the future of the church in Ephesus and counseled the elders that they could expect opposition and trials as well. However, they were to remember his life and testimony for the Lord and to take care of those who were charged to their keeping. Paul encouraged the leaders not to focus on themselves but to stay focused on Christ and the people they were safeguarding for the kingdom.

Paul's address to this body of Christian believers was the only one recorded for us. In it, the writer of Acts revealed Paul's deep love and sensitive spirit.

3. An Affectionate Parting (vv. 36-38)

After his address to the elders, Paul kneeled and prayed with them. They bade one another an affectionate and sorrowful farewell, for they realized that this would be the last time they would see each other this side of heaven. The sorrow is genuine, and the tears that flowed were real. They had come to love Paul for his life and ministry, and he had loved them as the fruit of his labors for the Lord.

SEARCH THE SCRIPTURES

1. How was Paul tested during his ministry in the province of Asia (Acts 20:19)?

2. What grieved the elders most as they said good-bye to Paul (v. 38)?

DISCUSS THE MEANING

1. In what way did Paul's desire to get to Jerusalem resemble the Lord's thinking on His last trip to Jerusalem?

2. Are Christians today indebted to Paul in any way for his life and ministry? If your answer is yes, how do you suppose Paul would ask you to repay that debt?

LESSON IN OUR SOCIETY

It is an axiom in our society that if you live long enough, eventually you will lose something or someone really important to you. One of the most important lessons we have to learn in life is that it is the quality of our living that matters and not what we are able to acquire. What things are you doing in your life to make sure that your life counts?

MAKE IT HAPPEN

Take a few minutes to prepare a short list of phrases that describe what you think people will say about you after you are departed from them. Make each phrase no more than six words. Share your list with two friends and ask them to circle the one they most agree with. Reflect on and pray over your life's message as reflected in their choices.

FOLLOW THE SPIRIT

What God wants me to do:

_____

_____

REMEMBER YOUR THOUGHTS

Special insights I have learned:

_____

_____

MORE LIGHT ON THE TEXT

Acts 20:17-28, 36-38

The book of Acts reads like a travelogue of Paul's second missionary journey and historical eyewitness account of the spread of the Gospel across geographical, ethnic, cultural, and gender boundaries. Empowered by the Holy Spirit, Paul and his various companions and colaborers in the ministry of teaching and preaching were diligent in their duties. They were fervent to follow up with new converts and church plants in spite of mere inconveniences to outright persecution. Through their faithfulness, the church grew from a few of little faith meeting behind closed (and often, locked) doors to a worldwide explosion of faithful disciples. The church matured from a few following Jesus to many being led by the Holy Spirit. On the occasion of this farewell speech, Paul was heading to Rome, the center of the Gentile world. We approach this lesson with the advantage of historical awareness of Paul's past effectiveness and his future persecutions (before

the Jews in Acts 22 and 23; before the Romans in Acts 24 and before Herod in Acts 25).

20:17 And from Miletus he sent to Ephesus, and called the elders of the church.

"Miletus" (**MIL'-ay-tos**) was a maritime city located 35 miles (55 km) from Ephesus. Ephesus was a maritime Roman city situated on the Aegean Sea between Smyrna and Miletus. It would take about a day's journey one way on land to get to Paul.

The "elders" (Gk. *presbuteros*, **pres-BOO'-ter-os**) were men among the Jews selected to sit on the Sanhedrin (the judges and rulers of the people) and among the Christians who presided over the churches (see Acts 1 with the election of the disciple to replace Judas among the Twelve). Also note that in the New Testament, the terms "bishop," "elders," and "presbyters" are used interchangeably. It was these elders of the Christian church who Paul summoned to advise and exhort as he prepared to move on in ministry.

18 And when they were come to him, he said unto them, Ye know, from the first day that I came into Asia, after what manner I have been with you at all seasons,

After arriving and assembling before Paul, he began his farewell speech reminding the elders of his faithful and ethical reputation among them. Paul opened himself to their examination by calling them to "know" (Gk. *epistamai*, **ep-IS'-tam-ahee**) him, implying that they were well-acquainted with him and had grown to understand him based on his reputation before them over a prolonged period of time. This "season" (Gk. *chronos*, **KHRON'-os**) was quantifiable by the calendar and changing of seasons. A significant amount of time had passed from when Paul first came to Asia to preach up until the time of this farewell gathering.

19 Serving the Lord with all humility of mind, and with many tears, and temptations, which befell me by the lying in wait of the Jews:

Paul then reviewed or recounted his character and ministry as he lived among these elders and before all of the disciples. Paul went on to remind them that he served sacrificing the privileges afforded him; he instead chose to serve in the manner of "humility of mind" (Gk. *tapeinophrosune*, **tap-i-nof-ros-OO'-nay**), meaning with modesty and being humble and unpretentious. Even with a highly successful and reputable ministry, Paul was ever aware that in his inherent weakness that God would work mightily through him (2 Corinthians 12:9).

Paul also served the Lord in tears and urgent intercessory prayers (Acts 20:31, Hebrews 5:7), demonstrating fervent passion for the ministry and loving compassion for the church. He also served the Lord through "temptations" (Gk. *peirasmos*, **pi-ras-MOS'**), which is the trial or testing of one's fidelity, integrity, virtue, and constancy in the faith. In Paul's case, he continued to serve faithfully, especially when facing those who "were lying in wait" (Gk. *epiboule*, **ep-ee-boo-LAY'**) plotting against him to prevent him from preaching salvation in Christ Jesus. Paul poured out and endured much to advance the cause of Christ.

20 And how I kept back nothing that was profitable unto you, but have shewed you, and have taught you publickly, and from house to house,

Paul continued his speech, reminding the elders that neither fear nor opportunity for personal gain held him "back" (Gk. *hupostello*, **hoop-os-TEL'-lo**) from bringing the Good News with constancy, clarity, and power. He was equally apt and faithful to preach the Gospel in the synagogue, in the marketplace, and in the house churches of the converts and new disciples.

21 Testifying both to the Jews, and also to the Greeks, repentance toward God, and faith toward our Lord Jesus Christ.

Paul went on to show how he was testifying (Gk. *diamarturomai*, **dee-am-ar-TOO'-rom-ahee**, meaning to declare emphatically) solemnly and believably about Jesus the Christ. He was not selfish in his teaching but taught the Jews and the Greeks (and in a broader interpretation, naming one a Greek was to include all non-Jews who had adopted and adapted to Greek culture and cus-

toms). To whomever had a heart to hear, Paul preached the same message: "repentance" (Gk. *metanoia*, **met-AN'-oy-ah**), meaning to have a change of mind and have "faith" (Gk. *pistis*, **PIS'-tis**) in the conviction that God provided eternal salvation through Christ the Messiah.

22 And now, behold, I go bound in the spirit unto Jerusalem, not knowing the things that shall befall me there:

Paul transitioned from recalling his ministry and reputation among them and turn their attention to what was bound to happen next. Paul asserted that it was the Holy Spirit who had "bound" him (Gk. *deo*, **DEH'-o**, meaning to bind, to tie or to put under obligation to go) to go, to Jerusalem. The "Spirit" (Gk. *pneuma*, **PNYOO'-mah**) is God's power and agency apart from one's own self that influences and guides. Bound by the Spirit, under obligation to God's will, Paul set out to face unknown persecution, but persecution nonetheless.

23 Save that the Holy Ghost witnesseth in every city, saying that bonds and afflictions abide me.

The Greek *diamarturomai* (**dee-am-ar-TOO'-rom-ahee**) means to confirm a thing by testimony and cause it to be believed. The Holy Spirit, Paul's constant companion, spoke to him, testified to him, and showed him that imprisonment and oppression were lying in wait to ambush him upon his arrival to Jerusalem (Romans 15:31).

24 But none of these things move me, neither count I my life dear unto myself, so that I might finish my course with joy, and the ministry, which I have received of the Lord Jesus, to testify the gospel of the grace of God.

However, Paul was not moved. Considering his natural life of lesser value than obeying God and facing threats that would prevent him from preaching the Good News with power, Paul asserted that his purpose was to fulfill his calling. His greatest desire was to "finish" (Gk. *teleioo*, **tel-i-O'-o**), meaning to carry through completely this footrace of faith set before him (2 Timothy 4:7) and to do it with *chara* (Gk. **khar-AH'**, joy and gladness).

The ministry of which Paul speaks is the Greek noun *diakonia* (**dee-ak-on-EE'-ah**) meaning service, help, or support. He further asserted that he received this ministry of preaching the Gospel directly from Jesus and that he testified of the efficaciousness of the Gospel through "grace" (Gk. *charis*, **KHAR'-ece**), which is the merciful kindness by which God draws us to Christ and empowers us to keep steadfast in the faith.

25 And now, behold, I know that ye all, among whom I have gone preaching the kingdom of God, shall see my face no more.

Shown through revelation by the Holy Spirit, Paul told the elders that he was certain that they would not see him again. All present had heard Paul "preach" (Gk. *kerusso,* **kay-ROOS'-so**), meaning to publish and proclaim openly the Gospel and matters pertaining to it, and would now have to continue in the faith even in Paul's absence and after his demise.

In preaching the Gospel, Paul spoke of preaching the kingdom of God. The Greek noun for "kingdom" is *basileia* (**bas-il-I'-ah**) and refers to the right, authority, and reign of the Messiah. God's kingdom must never be confused with or limited to geographical boundaries and human territorial constructs.

26 Wherefore I take you to record this day, that I am pure from the blood of all men.

Having called to mind his faithfulness in suffering and forewarning the elders of his dreadful fate, Paul charged them to record this farewell speech with witness of the Holy Spirit. He was confident that the Spirit would reveal to them that all that he had said and done in the name of Jesus was "pure" (Gk. *katharos,* **kath-ar-OS'**) and free from corruption and guilt.

27 For I have not shunned to declare unto you all the counsel of God. 28 Take heed therefore unto yourselves, and to all the flock, over the which the Holy Ghost hath made you overseers, to feed the church of God, which he hath purchased with his own blood.

Paul's next movement in this farewell speech was an emphatic exhortation that the elders pay close attention to themselves, the flock, and their purpose. A further reading of verses 29 and 30 reveals the threat and cause for Paul's ardency. In these verses, we learn that wolves in sheep's clothing will arise from among the elders themselves, attack the church from the outside, and target those weak in the faith.

"Overseers" (Gk. *episkopos,* **ep-IS'-kop-os**) are those charged with the duty of seeing that things done by others are done rightly, and in this case, done with the same Christian integrity that Paul modeled and now reminded them. He reminded them that the Holy Spirit has anointed and appointed them to govern and protect, nourish and nurture the church. Because they were the leaders of the church, they could expect to be attacked first and hit hardest when the enemy came in against them.

The "flock" (Gk. *poimnion,* **POYM'-nee-on**) is shepherding terminology referring to any group of Christ's disciples as well as to the collective Christian church in the Diaspora. After first taking care to guard their own hearts and minds from discord and deception, the elders were charged to pay attention to outside agents seeking to distract and discourage new disciples. The primary functions of the pastors (elders, shepherds, overseers) were to protect, direct and defend the sheep from contrary doctrine and practices.

In addition to watching out for or protecting the disciples and the church, elders were entrusted with the task of feeding the flock. This provision was intricately dependent upon the elders following Paul's paradigm of preaching and teaching the whole counsel or complete truth about the grace of God and salvation through Jesus Christ. The church of God, Paul reminded them, was "purchased" (Gk. *peripoieomai,* **per-ee-poy-EH'-om-ahee,**) with Christ's blood.

36 And when he had thus spoken, he kneeled down, and prayed with them all. 37 And they all wept sore, and fell on Paul's neck, and kissed him,

As Paul brought his farewell speech to a close, the atmosphere and mood of the moment was no doubt heavy with sadness. In this poignant scene of Christian fellowship, Paul knelt in a final gesture of humility before the people while demonstrating dependency on God and prayer. All of the elders present joined Paul in bowing down, and they openly and lovingly wept. The elders mourned and lamented and they "kissed" (Gk. *kataphileo*, **kat-af-ee-LEH'-o**). This unrestrained display of affection in the midst of abject grief was in comparable measure to the ministry Paul had poured out while among them.

38 Sorrowing most of all for the words which he spake, that they should see his face no more. And they accompanied him unto the ship.

The elders wept most, as if Paul's death was imminently upon him, because this would be the last time they would hold this beloved brother in person. The very thought of never seeing Paul again made them "sorrowing" (Gk. *odunao*, **od-oo-NAH'-o**), meaning to be tormented with anguish. Having prayed and wept, kissed and lamented, all of the elders kept Paul company until his ship sailed. As Paul's ship sailed beyond the horizon, it is likely that the elders remained at port comforting and consoling one another as their friend, brother, mentor and spiritual leader departed for the final time. Still, it is easy to imagine that these were people of hope, holding firmly to the hope and faith that in the Great Resurrection they would see him again.

In the meantime, when spiritual leaders who have served God well and loved us deeply move from among us to their next appointment in ministry—even when we know that it is unlikely that we would see them again in the natural—let us be inspired, like these elders, to hope in God.

DAILY BIBLE READINGS

M: Naomi and Ruth Part with Orpah
Ruth 1:6-14
T: David and Jonathan Part
1 Samuel 20:32-42
W: Paul Stops in Greece and Macedonia
Acts 20:1-6
T: Paul's Farewell Visit to Troas
Acts 20:7-12
F: Paul Speaks to the Ephesian Elders
Acts 20:17-24
S: Paul Warns Elders to Be Alert
Acts 20:25-31
S: Paul and Elders Say Good-bye
Acts 20:32-38

DECEMBER 2005
QUARTER AT-A-GLANCE
God's Commitment—Our Response

Because a holy God loves us so much—so unconditionally—He sent His one and only Son to die on a cruel Cross at Calvary in atonement for our sins. This should prove beyond a shadow of a doubt that God was and is committed to His people.

UNIT 1.
GOD'S REDEEMING LOVE

Four lessons based on passages from Isaiah and Luke articulate how God brings His Good News of salvation to whomever will hear and believe. Believers experience God's redeeming love in the birth of Jesus Christ, the Lamb without blemish.

LESSON 1: December 4
Justice for All
Isaiah 42:1-8

In this Scripture, the prophet Isaiah foretells Jesus' first coming in what is called a "Servant Song." It announced the coming of the Servant-Messiah hundreds of years before He actually came in the flesh. Isaiah also spoke of Jesus as the "Chosen Servant," who would epitomize encouragement, gentleness, love, justice, and truth.

LESSON 2: December 11
Strength for the Weary
Isaiah 49:5-6; 50:4-9

These Scriptures continue to proclaim the coming of the Servant-Messiah. Before Jesus was born, God had chosen Him to bring His light to the darkness of a lost and dying world. The prophet Isaiah declared that He would offer His great salvation to all nations. However, His disciples must commit to take it to the ends of the earth.

LESSON 3: December 18
Hope for Those Who Suffer
Isaiah 53:1-3; Luke 1:47-55

Isaiah continues to speak of Jesus, the coming Messiah, the suffering Servant, who would pay His people's sin-penalty through His own death. God chose to save the world through the suffering of His only begotten Son. This defines "true servant-hood."

In Luke's gospel, the "Magnificat"—"Mary's Song"—expresses what our response should be for the great thing God has done and is doing.

LESSON 4: December 25
Good News for the World
Isaiah 61:1-2; Luke 2:8-20

Isaiah proclaims that the time of the Lord's favor has indeed come. Again, this is a prophecy of the coming Messiah—Jesus Christ. He brings good news to the poor in heart, mind, spirit, and soul. Then, in Luke's Gospel, the prophecy is fulfilled.

UNIT 2. GOD'S GIFTS
OF LEADERSHIP

This unit, with its five lessons, focuses on 1 Timothy, which is one of Paul's pastoral letters.

LESSON 5: January 1
God Gives Strength
1 Timothy 1:12-20

In counseling and instructing young Timothy, Paul shares how grateful he is for God's mercy. He remembers his own violent, anti-Christian past and shares with Timothy what his life was like before he met Christ on the Damascus Road and how it is now that He has accepted Jesus as His Saviour and Lord.

LESSON 6: January 8
Pray for Everyone
1 Timothy 2:1-8

Paul recognizes that prayer promotes godliness and that godliness certainly should be a very important part of Timothy's ministry. Paul also knows that even though God is all-powerful and all-knowing, He has chosen to let His people help Him change the world through our prayers. Therefore, Paul urges Timothy and all believers to pray with holy hands lifted up to God—free from anger and controversy.

LESSON 7: January 15
God Calls Church Leaders
1 Timothy 3:2-15

This Scripture reminds the church that God calls those who are in leadership. He has guidelines, or requirements, for those who will represent Him. This epistle teaches that to be a church leader or elder is a grave responsibility, and the leader has to give an account to God for how he has shepherded God's lambs and sheep.

LESSON 8: January 22
Guidance for Teaching
1 Timothy 4

This part of Paul's epistle to Timothy gives instructions for elders (leaders) and also warnings against false teachers. Paul counsels that preaching and teaching for God includes setting an example in conduct, faith, purity, and speech. These ministries also require reflection on God's Word and spiritual discernment.

LESSON 9: January 29
God Desires Justice and Mercy
1 Timothy 5:1-8, 17-24

Here Paul gives advice on how leaders in the church can treat all church members compassionately and fairly. He instructs that, for the good of the whole body, the Christian community must not only provide care for her members, but also provide just resolutions of problems that may arise within the church.

UNIT 3. FAITHFUL FOLLOWERS, FAITHFUL LEADERS

This unit focuses on 1 Timothy and Titus. The lessons in this unit encourage all believers to live godly lives.

LESSON 10: February 5
Be True to Your Christian Heritage
2 Timothy 1:3-14

Even though Paul is in prison, facing death himself, he seeks to pass on the torch to this new generation of church leaders. Therefore, in his second letter to Timothy, Paul seeks to strengthen Timothy's faith for his difficult ministry to the troubled Ephesus church. Paul suffered much in carrying the Gospel to the Gentiles, so he reminds Timothy of his woes and invites Timothy to accept his own hardships, which will surely come as he boldly proclaims the Gospel of Jesus Christ to an antagonistic world.

LESSON 11: February 12
Develop Christian Character
2 Timothy 2:14-26

Paul expresses concern that believers develop the character of Christ, and that we walk the walk of Christ. Therefore, he teaches about being faithful to God and His church and cultivating self-discipline so that our lives will not invalidate our preaching and teaching—our witness.

LESSON 12: February 19
Follow a Good Mentor
2 Timothy 3:10-4:8

These are very important Scriptures in that they offer a foundation for Christian ministry. They advocate that God's Word be boldly and fearlessly proclaimed to the church as well as to those who are lost. Paul summarizes his lifetime of suffering for the Good News in these verses so that believers can see the contrast between false teachers and those who are truly faithful to God.

LESSON 13: February 26
Live the Truth, Teach the Truth
Titus 2

In this letter to Titus, Paul again expresses concern that leaders in God's church do their job well—walk worthy of their calling. Here Paul advises Titus regarding his responsibility as overseer of the churches on the island of Crete. Paul promotes right living in the church by teaching that God expects from His called-out ones self-control and spiritual and moral fitness.

GOD CALLS US TO COMMIT TO HIM

What Is Our Response?

by Evangeline Carey

Out of God's unconditional love for us, His inerrant Holy Word tells us that "he gave his begotten Son, that whosoever believeth in him should not perish, but have everlasting life" (John 3:16). As we explore God's role in His salvation plan this quarter, let's look at what our response should be in order to have a real walk with God and be a witness to a lost and dying world that He is calling for us to be.

God's commitment to us. God is so committed to His people that He sent His one and only Son to die in order to redeem us from the penalty of sin. Jesus, 100% God and 100% man, accomplished our salvation by satisfying God's justice and exhausting God's wrath for His people. He did this by shedding His own blood as He died a criminal's death on a cross at Calvary. He knew no sin, yet He took on our sins. The Bible says that He became sin for us so that we might become the righteousness of God in Him (2 Corinthians 5:21). Jesus' gracious and merciful act bridged the chasm between sinful man and a holy God. Through His death and resurrection, Jesus Christ delivered the "coup de grace" to Satan's bondage and demonstrated His eternal authority over creation. He proclaimed who He really is: King of the universe and King of kings. He was and still is the Sovereign God!

Jesus, the Greatest Sacrifice. The Scriptures tell us that Jesus was innocent according to Jewish and Roman law and did not deserve death, even though both Jewish and Roman authorities tried Him six times (see Luke's gospel). Make no mistake: He did not have to die! He *chose* to die! His love for His people, the commitment, and His obedience to God the Father led Him to endure His betrayal and crucifixion. His great love for believ-ers caused Him to agonize in prayer to the Father until His sweat resembled drops of blood (Luke 22:44). He was beaten to a pulp, spat upon, humiliated, mocked, tortured, was physically unable to carry His own cross, stripped, and executed in public view. He was stretched wide, hung high and nailed to that cross and the blood came streaming down. *Because He was so committed to His people, He suffered, bled, died, and rose again.*

The Old Testament predicted His suffering. Even the prophetic vision of Isaiah illuminated the suffering of the then-coming Messiah. God gave this Old Testament sage a revelation of the suffering, death, and resurrection of the Christ. At the time of his prophecy, the nation of Israel was divided into two kingdoms: Israel in the north and Judah in the south. Both were guilty of perverting justice, oppressing the poor, and idol worship. They were seeking things from others than from the one true God, who had established a covenant with them and repeatedly stated that He would be their God and they would be His people. But the people were immersed in sin and didn't even care that they were disobeying the God who had been so faithful to them. They responded to God's faithfulness with disobedience. They were a hardheaded, stiff-necked people.

However, Isaiah's spiritual eyes were open to God's personification of the coming Messiah, and Isaiah reported that "Surely he hath borne our griefs, and carried our sorrows: yet we did esteem him stricken, smitten of God, and afflicted. But he was wounded for our transgressions, he was bruised for our iniquities: the chastisement of our peace was upon him; and with his stripes we are healed. All we like sheep have gone astray; we have turned every one to his own way; and the LORD hath laid on him the iniquity of us all. He was oppressed, and he was afflicted, yet he opened not his mouth: he is brought as a lamb to the slaughter, and as a sheep before her shearers is dumb, so he openeth not his mouth" (Isaiah 53:4-7).

Isaiah understood the ramifications of Jesus Christ dying for our sins long before Jesus even came. Do we understand today what Jesus did on Calvary? Do we comprehend that Jesus is so committed to us that He took all the blame and punishment that we deserve? God gave us mercy, when we deserve justice. Jesus paid it all! We owe all to Him because through Him forgiveness of sin is made available to all mankind.

The apostle Paul tells the church how to respond to God's great salvation. The apostle Paul, in his letters to Timothy, tells us that the church must not only know God's truth, but respond by being compelled to act upon it (1 and 2 Timothy). In essence, we, too, must obey God and show our commitment to Him by living out His Word and modeling right living. We should keep a proper attitude toward God and others at all times, showing our devotion and dedication to Him. He wants us to be so committed to Him that He becomes first in our lives. He wants us to be so committed that we come to the end of our own self-sufficiency. He wants us to know unequivocally that we need and can depend on Him.

Again, Paul declared that, because we are witnesses for Christ and the awesome sacrifice He made for us on Calvary, we should let our Christian character be evident in every aspect of our worship. Remember that our worship is not just activity inside the church walls, but it is in our everyday walk with God on the streets of this world. Everything we do in life we can do as unto God. Our conduct should show onlookers that we have indeed met the risen Christ on our own Damascus Road. Unbelievers should readily see that our bodies are not our own, but temples of the Holy Spirit.

In both 1 and 2 Timothy, Paul recognized the role of the Holy Spirit in the face of opposition and persecution of the church, as well as in daily spiritual growth and living. He informed us that our Christian journey will often be filled with suffering and hardships. However, these trials and tribulations should make us lean on the Lord and mature in Him. While in the valley, we can always turn the gaze of our soul to Almighty God. He loves us always and beyond measure. We can daily bathe our lives in Scripture, prayer, and praises to our Lord and Saviour, who promised never to leave us or forsake us in our time of need (Hebrews 13:5). The Holy Spirit will help us to live wisely and be strong in the Lord. He enables us to maintain loyalty to the risen Saviour and diligence in serving God with endurance and total commitment.

Paul stressed that if we are to carry out the Great Commission to share the Gospel and remain solidly grounded in Christian service, we must be prepared by fortifying ourselves with God's Word and possessing His Spirit of wisdom and discernment. Then we can readily recognize wolves in sheep's clothing and reject error when false teachers come to lead us astray.

Paul further states that church leaders must be wholly committed to God by teaching sound doctrine. They must not lead His flock astray by their own improprieties. This could not only compromise the believers' walk with God but could also be a stumbling block to new Christians and bring disgrace on the Christian community. Paul, then, saw that all believers must have personal discipline. This includes guarding our motives, serving faithfully, and living above reproach. In showing our commitment to God, we exemplify being Christlike.

In essence, the apostle Paul, God's proclaimer of the Good News, stressed that it is fundamental that we have a strong foundation in God to show a needy world what true Christian commitment is. *We can't show what we don't know or talk where we don't walk. This would be hypocrisy.* Therefore, we must tread in the holy standards of a holy God in order to make a positive impact on our world. This commitment to God speaks volumes to unbelievers.

It is clear that Jesus is committed to us. However, will we take up our cross and follow Him? What, then, will be our response to the kind of unconditional love that God has shown us?

Evangeline Carey is a staff writer at UMI.

GOD'S SONG OF LOVE, OUR SONG OF PRAISE

by Michael Washington

Gospel choirs fascinate me. As a singer in my childhood, I remember learning songs, practicing parts, and, of course, singing with others. Along with warm-ups and learning material, watching, submitting to, and obeying the choir director makes music happen. Whether the choir is clapping, swaying, or moaning, attention to a director enables and empowers any choral group. Without the direction of a conductor, the group flounders without vision, motivation, or effectiveness.

Following leaders not only equips choirs for singing, but also empowers disciples of Jesus Christ to live faithfully by God's Word. Faithfulness remains the goal of Christian leaders, too. Striving to live under the Spirit's direction, leaders watch, submit to, and obey God. Effective leaders live and serve in response to the Gospel's claim on their lives. The Gospel invites and challenges Christians to embody the words and truths in Scripture. As a starting point for life, the Gospel empowers leaders to serve the people of God.

Once we encounter the life and ministry of Jesus, we are changed, gradually but totally. Where our thoughts and insights were once instruments of God's enemies, they now become tools for God's use and purpose.

God's presentation of love in Jesus Christ compels us to respond. As Christian leaders respond to God's love, they also demonstrate ways that Christians can represent God's love to others.

God Loves Us

Love reveals itself. Often love changes the complexions of our relationships, or it alters relationships between two people. Love energizes life. Love illuminates people. It challenges our words. In romantic relationships, we may hide love until it seems best to confess it. The lover gathers facts as he or she considers whether their love will be received and reciprocated. Only when a person is comfortable with vulnerability (the inherent risk that comes with devotion) will one reveal his/her love and the other disclose his/her care.

How we speak about human love provides our language for discussing divine love. However powerful, the love that people have for each other weakens our language about God's perfect love. Still, our language works toward a good description of God's love for us, a love we know because of Jesus Christ. God shares love with us in that, when we were farthest from God, Jesus gave the most to us. Because of His love, Jesus affords us communion with God.

The Lord's example is clear in Scripture, giving us opportunity to have fellowship with God. Jesus prayed, worshiped, and gave of Himself. Jesus sent us the Holy Spirit, and we come to know God as we receive the Holy Spirit. Capturing that great Spirit of Christ happens when we follow Him. Certainly the only way to discover what it means to follow and be a disciple of Christ is to yield ourselves to His Lordship. Jesus performed acts of service to humankind, and we follow after Him when we do the same.

Because of God's radical grace, we can know God in Christ. We look to Him and see the image of God without blemish, sin, or brokenness. In Jesus Christ, we see perfect divinity and impeccable humanity. He discloses who we are and who God is.

Responding to God's Grace

There have always been responses to God's gracious acts of revelation. From the earliest moments when the creative Word brought life from nothing, life has reacted in varied ways. Chief among those reactions is praise to our God and Creator.

Creation responds to God in worship. When God spoke and created life out of nothing, creation's response to God's Word was worship. Everything in the created order pleased God by giving its best in praise to the Creator. What God brought forth met its destiny in the worship of God. Humankind included, the world and all that dwells therein still meets its destiny when blessing God.

Worship settles the matter of lordship. It redirects the affections of our hearts and reaffirms the sovereignty of God over our lives. In worship, we express our belief that God manages our time and that we live by grace and in God's grace. In moments of reflection, singing, and praying in the church, with prayer partners or during our daily commute, God works into our hearts His perfect love.

A second response to God's actions in our lives is faithful service to God and others. While worship takes different forms, service is always discernible to the eyes. Serving opens itself to the scrutiny and examination of others. Never internal, service moves outward, ensuring that we mirror God's works in our daily lives.

In the early church, the apostles and followers of the Way were devoted to more than worship and teaching. A main concern was the spread of this new message that had at its core the ministry of a Jewish carpenter who died and rose from the dead. Teaching the implications of Jesus' ministry was a concern that the apostles and leaders after them took seriously. Among their other primary concerns, however, were justice when applying doctrines, fairness in acknowledging the gifts of all persons, and equity in the distribution of food and resources to the people. These ethical concerns colored the service of our apostolic fathers and mothers. Still, they continue to reintroduce themselves in the contemporary church.

As in the early apostolic days of Christian history, the Black church in America faces issues of justice, fairness, and equity. Acknowledgment of the contributions of Black people rested at the core of particular leaders' decisions to form separate denominations where Black men and women were welcomed and embraced as the body of Christ. The involvement of women of color in positions of leadership continues to emerge. The willingness and gifts of sisters and the record of their enormous contributions to the development of the church (past and present) during its various embryonic stages remains challenged by many and silently embraced by few. The question as to whether the political, social, and economic structures of our day present Black Christians with similar opportunities as they do other Christians is continually debated by the best thinkers in our wide community.

All these issues leave us at the door of the church, at the foot of the altar, if you will. They provide us with the hunger to pursue justice, peace, and love in tangible ways. Our hunger and thirst for righteousness is not without challenges. In addition to the structural challenges already mentioned, systemic hindrances stop the progress of many individuals in the form of psychological challenges. The greatest of these is fear.

We fear change in our personal and corporate lives. Therefore, growth approaches impossibility. Fear, then, cancels faith, that necessary element to please God. Without faith, movement toward God is impossible. Dedicated worship and service remedies fear, granting us a clear vision of Jesus Christ and His love for us. In the words of that gospel hymn, it is His love that lifts us when nothing else can help.

Michael Washington holds a B.S. in psychology from the University of Illinois, an M.A. in theological studies from Wheaton College, and is completing a M. Div. at Garrett-Evangelical Theological Seminary.

CALLING, CHARACTER, AND COMPASSION

by Dena Dyer

John met Sam, one of the local youth pastors, at his health club. At first, John scoffed at Sam's profession and made fun of the minister's commitment. But after a while, their surface relationship took a deeper turn as Sam answered John's questions about faith with sincerity and thoughtfulness. Soon they were meeting for breakfast once a week to discuss their lives and "shoot the breeze."

"Commitment" is defined as a binding, as by a promise or pledge. When we invite Christ to be Lord of our lives, we promise, or bind, ourselves to Him. This pledge changes our lives and, if we follow Christ daily, it can change our relationships and the world.

Many times Christians are taught that commitment is the fruit of belief in Christ. However, I believe that commitment is the seed (planted by belief) that leads to other fruits like calling, character, compassion, and, ultimately, converts.

First of all, Scripture teaches us that we are chosen or *called* from the womb. Psalm 139:16 (NIV) says, "All the days ordained for me were written in your book before one of them came to be." And Isaiah 49:1 (NIV) affirms, "Before I was born the LORD called me...."

Our calling leads us to a cause: bringing justice, mercy, and hope to a broken planet, one person at a time. When the Holy Spirit reigns in us, God helps us not to falter or be discouraged in our own wounds. Then, as part of His perfect plan, God transforms and uses our hurts as healing tools.

In 2 Corinthians 1:3-4 (NIV), Paul writes, "Praise be to the God and Father of our Lord Jesus Christ, the Father of compassion and the God of all comfort, who comforts us in all our troubles, so that we can comfort those in any trouble with the comfort we ourselves have received from God." In other words, God holds our hand through our trials so that we can hold others' hands when they go through pain.

Several years ago, my friend Jamie lost her daughter in a tragic car accident on Christmas Day. Though she would never have chosen to suffer such a loss, she has seen God use her suffering many times to help other grieving parents and families. In my own life, God has brought good out of a miscarriage and depression by opening doors to ministry that otherwise would have been closed.

Several months into his friendship with Sam, John's wife, Amy (who was pregnant with their second child), had to be hospitalized to try to prevent premature labor. Sam rallied his church members (most of whom didn't even know John) to provide meals for the family. In addition, Sam's youth group took turns mowing the family's lawn, babysitting, and keeping groceries in the refrigerator.

"Why are you doing this?" John asked his buddy during one of Sam's visits to the hospital.

"I've been where you are," Sam said. "And my church family took care of me and my wife and kids. That's what we do as brothers and sisters in Christ."

In Isaiah, God says over and over that He is our strength, and that He will equip us to help the weary and downtrodden. When Isaiah draws a portrait of the suffering servant, we can find comfort in knowing we are not abandoned during painful seasons in our lives. Jesus was despised, rejected, and spat upon so that He could identify fully with us. Praise God; we are never alone!

As the apostle Peter wrote, "Dear friends, do not be surprised at the painful trial you are suffering, as though something strange were happening to you. But rejoice that you participate in the sufferings of Christ, so that you may be overjoyed when his glory is revealed" (1 Peter 4:12-13, NIV). Part of that glory is a new depth of character, the second fruit of comnitment, which emerges out of the flames of suffering. James wrote, "Consider it pure joy, my brothers, whenever you face trials of many kinds, because you know that the testing of your faith develops perseverance. Perseverance must finish its work so that you may be mature and complete, not lacking anything" (James 1:2-4, NIV).

Other facets of character that come from the seed of commitment include temperance, self-control, kindness, hospitality, gentleness, contentment, sincerity, and sound doctrine, which are all qualities that Paul urges Timothy to develop and to seek out in potential church leaders. That's what we'll become if we continue to seek after Christ and model ourselves after Him.

What man or woman of faith do you admire? It's likely that they have gone through intense grief. Former missionary and prolific author Elisabeth Elliot tells the story of one of her fans coming up to her and saying, "Oh, I wish I could write like you do!" Elisabeth replied, "Do you want to suffer as I have?"

Like Elliot or biblical heroes such as Shadrach, Meshach, and Abednego, we can become strengthened in faith, prayer, and holiness through the fiery furnaces (death, divorce, despair, etc.) in our lives. In those times, we are more likely to rely on God and cling to His hand. And if we submit to God's chisel and the heat of the flame, other people will come to believe in Jesus, too.

As John and Amy faced the fact that they were not in control of what happened to their unborn child, they began to cling to each other and to question their former resistance to God and the church. Each act of kindness by Sam's youth group pried their spirits open a little bit more. By the time the baby was born—small but healthy—they had agreed to visit the church.

"I'm floored by the people I've met," John told Sam. "I can't believe they would sacrifice so much for someone they don't know."

Sam smiled and replied, "Jesus died for us, and He never met us." John let the words sink in.

Truly, our commitment to Christ leads to the fruit of compassion for others. Like our Saviour, we have been anointed by the Holy Spirit to preach the Good News, bind broken hearts, free prisoners, comfort the mourning, and proclaim God's favor. A tall order? Perhaps. But God's gifts (mercy, grace, faith, and love) make sharing His salvation, often through the meeting of practical needs, possible.

What is amazing is that our compassion for others can even spark a revolution. In the book entitled *A Revolution of Compassion: Faith-Based Groups As Full Partners in Fighting America's Social Problems* by Dave Donaldson and Stanley W. Carlson-Thies, the authors quote J.C. Watts Jr. as saying, "There is a revolution of compassion in our nation to unite Americans who want to help the poor, addicted, hungry, and homeless no matter what their race, religion, or background happens to be....I am convinced more than ever that the foundation of our country must be laid upon strong family values, unflappable *character,* and the determination to make life better for every citizen regardless of race or creed."

Indeed cooperation, dedication, and humility are vital because whether it's done by groups or individuals, the true meeting of needs is the heart of the Gospel. And since we model Christ when we clothe the naked, feed the hungry, or visit prisoners, our faithfulness makes the person of Jesus attractive to nonbelievers.

James writes, "Religion that God our Father accepts as pure and faultless is this: to look after orphans and widows in their distress and to keep oneself from being polluted by the world" (1:27, NIV).

John and Amy visited Sam's church with their young family. Slowly, they began to get involved in Bible studies and small groups. One Sunday morning, John and Amy accepted Christ as their Saviour. Not long after, their oldest son made a profession of faith as well. Sam's commitment (and that of his church body) was the seed that bore fruit in calling, character, and compassion. Ultimately, it flowered into John and Amy's conversion. Now the new believers are taking their commitment seriously, and there is no telling what fruits will follow.

What fruit has God developed in you? Have you viewed commitment as an end in itself, rather than a means to other ends? Maybe it's time to discern your calling, discipline your character, deepen your compassion, and develop converts for Christ.

Dena Dyer is a writer, speaker, and actress from Granbury, Texas.

ROD ZIEGLER

Christian Comedian

Whether helping in the neighborhood or volunteering his time as a youth counselor at the Center for Drug Free Living, Rod Ziegler always finds a way to make people laugh and enjoy living. In more reflective moments, he consistently strives for the best in humankind, urging today's young people to take pride in themselves and to never stop reaching for the stars.

The students of Bethune Cookman College where Rod majored in Mass Communications thought he was the "cat's meow." During his time there, he was constantly sought after to do campus events and continues to do so to this day.

In his development as a comedian, he admits to being greatly influenced by Bill Cosby, Sinbad, and Jonathan Slocum. Notwithstanding such great names in the comedic world, Rod's greatest influence by admission is God. Rod believes his sense of humor is a gift from God, whose inspiration helps him to write the plethora of hilarious jokes he comes up with.

In a short time, he has opened for such notables as God's Property, Trinity 5:7, and others. He has appeared on national television. Rod also received rave reviews for his performances in the theatrical productions of *The Colored Museum* and *Soldiers Play.*

The second artist to sign with the newly formed *Allen and Allen Music Group,* Rod was extremely excited about his first comedy album release, *Stop Me If I'm Lyin'.* Filmed before a live, packed audience at the Potter's House Church in Orlando, Florida, the video sold like hotcakes, highlighting in a big way his connection with the audience. He appears to slip into and out of character effortlessly. One woman lost count of how many of the videos she bought and gave away to friends who were depressed or, in one instance, suffering from rheumatoid arthritis. Viewing the video lifted their spirits. She had given away her last video and when she attempted to order more, she was told they were no longer available. Seeing Mr. Ziegler in person, she told him what she'd been doing with the videos. He was humbled almost to tears to discover his video was being used to minister to the needs of others, and gave her an autographed video to keep for herself.

One of the benefits of celebrity status is being asked to do what he loves: speak with young people. They gravitate toward Rod because he is informative *and* funny. One of the headliners for whom Rod opened said that he appreciates Rod's clean, comedic style and that when you're funny, you're just funny! Through all his successes, Rod keeps it clean and gives God the glory and all the credit, keeping his eyes on Jesus.

December 4
Bible Study Guide 1

1. Words You Should Know

A. Judgment (Isaiah 42:1) *mishpat* (Heb.)—A sentence or formal decree.

B. Covenant (v. 6) *briyth* (Heb.)—An agreement, alliance of friendship, pledge, or obligation.

2. Teacher Preparation

A. Prayerfully read Isaiah 41 and 42 so that you will be familiar with the lesson's background and contents in order to impart God's Word effectively to the students.

B. Begin to pray that if any of your students don't have a personal relationship with Jesus Christ that God will prepare their hearts and use this lesson to cause them to accept Jesus Christ as their Saviour.

3. Starting the Lesson

A. Ask a student to read the IN FOCUS section. Point out the connection between today's story and the LESSON AIM.

B. Read the LESSON AIM and ask the students what they hope to learn from the lesson.

C. Read the FOCAL VERSES and discuss how they apply to us today. Ask the students to share their born-again experience, and ask if they have led anyone to Jesus Christ. Allow the students to share their experiences with the rest of the class.

4. Getting into the Lesson

A. Write the AT-A-GLANCE outline on the chalkboard or on newsprint for the students to review. Divide the class into three groups and assign one topic to each group. Give the students at least 10-15 minutes to discuss the topic as a group. Have one person from each group take five minutes to summarize their group's discussion for the rest of the class.

B. After you have finished the lesson, spend the next few minutes answering the SEARCH THE SCRIPTURES and DISCUSS THE MEANING questions.

5. Relating the Lesson to Life

A. Discuss creative ways of reaching others with the Gospel. Write these methods on the chalkboard or on newsprint.

B. Discuss some of the things that should be avoided when sharing the Gospel with the lost.

C. After the discussion, select two students to role-play the right and wrong ways to share the Gospel. Encourage them to utilize what they have learned.

6. Arousing Action

A. Give the students ample time to discuss the LESSON IN OUR SOCIETY and THE PEOPLE, PLACES, AND TIMES sections of the lesson.

B. Close the class in prayer.

WORSHIP GUIDE

For the Superintendent or Teacher
Theme: Justice for All
Theme Song: "Our God
Is an Awesome God"
Scripture: Proverbs 11:30
Song: "Lord, I'm Available to You"
Meditation: Lord, give me Your heartbeat
to reach the lost and to share the Good
News of the Gospel in creative ways so
others will realize how You have provided
salvation for all who believe in Your Son,
Jesus Christ. Amen.

JUSTICE FOR ALL

Bible Background • ISAIAH 41–42
Printed Text • ISAIAH 42:1–8
Devotional Reading • ISAIAH 41:8–13

LESSON AIM

By the end of the lesson, we will:

DESCRIBE the work of God's Servant, Jesus Christ, in bringing redemption and justice to earth;

BE CONVINCED that as redeemed followers of Jesus Christ, we should share His Gospel and work for justice in our society; and

SHARE the Good News with someone during the coming week.

KEEP IN MIND

"I the LORD have called thee in righteousness, and will hold thine hand, and will keep thee, and give thee for a covenant of the people, for a light of the Gentiles" (Isaiah 42:6).

FOCAL VERSES

Isaiah 42:1 Behold my servant, whom I uphold; mine elect, in whom my soul delighteth; I have put my spirit upon him: he shall bring forth judgment to the Gentiles.

2 He shall not cry, nor lift up, nor cause his voice to be heard in the street.

3 A bruised reed shall he not break, and the smoking flax shall he not quench: he shall bring forth judgment unto truth.

4 He shall not fail nor be discouraged, till he have set judgment in the earth: and the isles shall wait for his law.

5 Thus saith God the LORD, he that created the heavens, and stretched them out; he that spread forth the earth, and that which cometh out of it; he that giveth breath unto the people upon it, and spirit to them that walk therein:

LESSON OVERVIEW

LESSON AIM
KEEP IN MIND
FOCAL VERSES
IN FOCUS
THE PEOPLE, PLACES, AND TIMES
BACKGROUND
AT-A-GLANCE
IN DEPTH
SEARCH THE SCRIPTURES
DISCUSS THE MEANING
LESSON IN OUR SOCIETY
MAKE IT HAPPEN
FOLLOW THE SPIRIT
REMEMBER YOUR THOUGHTS
MORE LIGHT ON THE TEXT
DAILY BIBLE READINGS

6 I the LORD have called thee in righteousness, and will hold thine hand, and will keep thee, and give thee for a covenant of the people, for a light of the Gentiles;

7 To open the blind eyes, to bring out the prisoners from the prison, and them that sit in darkness out of the prison house.

8 I am the LORD: that is my name: and my glory will I not give to another, neither my praise to graven images.

IN FOCUS

What is meant by redemptive work? It is personal work by an individual to lead others to an acceptance of our Lord and Saviour. It is different from mass or united effort. It is the impact of your personality upon another personality, with the *definite* objective of leading a person to Christ, and to the power and simplicity of His Gospel.

What are some of the promises God fulfills when we serve others using the message of Jesus Christ? Your own soul will be blessed, people will be saved, your congregation will become dynamic, the Word of God will be honored, Jesus Christ will be glorified, the Holy Spirit will not be grieved, you will be ready for any work, you will become more devoted to Jesus Christ, the Bible will be studied more thoughtfully, your influence will be more telling, your life will be less selfish, your expectations will be heavenly, your joy will be lasting, your hope will be brighter, your courage will become undaunted, and your service will be more acceptable to God. Today's lessons will help us identify and commit to ways to work for God's justice.

THE PEOPLE, PLACES, AND TIMES

Prophets in Hebrew History. The Old Testament prophets were men and women of God who towered spiritually over their contemporaries. No category of people in all literature presents a more dramatic picture than the Old Testament prophets. The prophet was not simply another religious leader in Hebrew history, but one who had "the word of God in his mouth" (Deuteronomy 18:15-19; Jeremiah 1:6-19). Because the Spirit and the Word were in him, the Old Testament prophet manifested the following three characteristics: (1) Divinely revealed knowledge. The primary purpose of this knowledge was to encourage God's people to remain faithful to Him and His covenant. Out of the soil of Israel's and Judah's dark history came the specific prophecy about the Messiah and the kingdom of God, as well as predictions about future world events. (2) Divinely given powers. The prophets were drawn into the sphere of the miraculous as they were filled with God's Spirit. (3) A distinctive lifestyle. The prophets abandoned the ordinary pursuits of life to live exclusively for God. They were activists for holy and righteous changes in Israel. The prophets, always on the offensive for God's kingdom and His righteousness, championed the will of God without thought of personal risk.

Stamps, Donald C., ed. The Full Life Study Bible. Grand Rapids, Mich.: Zondervan Publishing House, 1992, 1002-1004.

BACKGROUND

More than 150 years before the birth of Cyrus, God gave the prophet Isaiah the ability to foresee that He would raise up Cyrus to do His will by conquering the nations and protecting Judah, God's covenant people (Isaiah 41). Cyrus was the King of Persia from 559 to 530 B.C. (see Isaiah 45:1). God used Cyrus to free the Jews from their Babylonian exile. Scripture records Cyrus as being righteous, not in himself, but because God had selected him to carry out His righteous plan of redemption on the earth.

IN DEPTH

1. The Servant's Call and Anointing (Isaiah 42:1)

The prophet Isaiah wrote about the person and ministry of Jesus Christ (see Matthew 12:18-

---

AT-A-GLANCE

1. The Servant's Call and Anointing (Isaiah 42:1)
2. The Servant's Determination to Bring Justice to the Earth (vv. 2-5)
3. The Servant's Ability to Redeem (vv. 6-8)

---

21). Through the inspiration of the Spirit of God, Isaiah prophesied that the Messiah would be anointed with the Holy Spirit in order to perform His work of redemption. We can learn several important truths from this prophecy.

First, believers are called to be servants of the Lord. As servants, we have a tremendous responsibility to completely surrender to our Lord Jesus Christ and to the Father's call upon our lives. We must be willing to totally trust Him. The Messiah was anointed with the Spirit of God to perform His task of redemption. Likewise, His followers are called to continue the work Jesus Christ began, in the power of the Holy Spirit (see Acts 1:8; 2:4). Only through the Holy Spirit can believers effectively minister for the kingdom of God. Also, the Spirit's wisdom, illumination, and power give believers the ability to make an impact on the lives of others.

Second, the Holy Spirit's power in Jesus also brought the standards of holy justice and the principles of God's divine truth to the world. Therefore, the work that Jesus did while on earth was missionary in nature. This same task is the responsibility of all who bear the name of Jesus Christ. God baptizes and empowers Christians with the Holy Spirit to carry out the Great Commission, that is to "Go ye into all the world, and preach the gospel to every creature" (Mark 16:15).

2. The Servant's Determination to Bring Justice to the Earth (vv. 2-5)

Jesus Christ was the prophesied Messiah from the tribe of Judah (see Revelation 5:5), who brings great spiritual blessings to those who accept, believe, and follow Him. When Christ returns to the earth, He will punish all wicked nations (Revelation 19:15). Today, wickedness, evil, and ungodliness are escalating at a rapid pace. Sometimes Christians wonder whether or not God is aware of what's going on and, if He is, how long it will be before justice will prevail.

As we pray and seek the Lord, He will give us illumination knowledge through the Holy Spirit and help us realize that God is in control despite what's going on in the world. We will also realize that a day is coming when the wicked will be judged and the faithful will be rewarded. Until that time, we are called to represent Jesus Christ, who came to save all who are lost (Luke 19:10).

We must remember that salvation comes by grace through faith (Ephesians 2:8), and without God's salvation, we would be "condemned already" (John 3:18). One way for believers to demonstrate their gratitude is by doing all they can to reach all mankind with the message of salvation. On the other hand, knowing that God has total control over His creation will motivate believers to trust Him and His timing to bring about justice.

We serve an awesome God, who is totally aware of everything. He has already stepped into tomorrow before we arrive. He has the power to sustain His creation and to provide for His people. The light affliction we endure can't compare to everything God has in store for His people (2 Corinthians 4:17).

We may never experience popularity, fame, and honor in this world; however, by accepting Jesus Christ and being fruitful in our covenant relationship, we need not fear, because whatever God doesn't deliver us from, He gives us the grace to go through.

3. The Servant's Ability to Redeem (vv. 6-8)

The Messiah's mission involved bringing the covenant of salvation to both Jews and Gentiles (Hebrews 8:8-12). The New Testament believer understands the fulfillment of Jeremiah's word in the New Covenant instituted by Jesus Christ for everyone who repents of their sins and accepts Him as Saviour and Lord (Jeremiah 31:31-34). However, Scripture teaches that Jeremiah's prophecy would not be completely fulfilled until the end of the age, when many in the nation of Israel will turn to Jesus Christ and accept Him as their Messiah (Romans 11:25-27).

God's promise of a new covenant was accomplished through the death, burial, and resurrection of Jesus Christ and the outpouring of the Holy Spirit. The covenant was established with all followers of Jesus Christ, Jews and Gentiles alike. We enter into a covenant relationship with the Lord, and through faith in Jesus Christ we become children of Abraham (Galatians 3:7-9, 29).

Through the redemptive work of Jesus Christ, salvation and hope have been made available to all human beings. The community of God's people has been enlarged in the household of faith (Acts 15:13-18). God has taken from all nations a people unto Himself, separated to Him for His name's sake. He is gathering out of this present world system the body of Christ—a people who will worship Him in Spirit and truth and are no longer separated by nationality, gender, or social status.

The regenerating work of the Holy Spirit will also motivate believers to be lights in a dark world that draw others to the Lord and help to lead them to a saving knowledge of Jesus Christ. The redemptive work of Christ can free people from the darkness of sin and guilt and release them from Satan's power (see Isaiah 42:7; Romans 5:12; 1 John 3:8).

Sin has gained entrance into the human race because of Adam's fall. Because of sin, death entered the world, subjecting human beings to spiritual death (see Romans 3:23; 12:14). But God's people have been transferred out of the kingdom of darkness into the glorious kingdom of Jesus Christ (Acts 26:18). Therefore, we are no longer slaves to sin, but servants of righteousness (Romans 6:18). Believers no longer have to walk in darkness or suffer from guilt. We have been forgiven and washed clean by the blood of Jesus Christ. Satan no longer has power over us; believers have been given power to live an overcoming life and to resist temptations.

The Lord redeemed and set us free that we might be His disciples and have an intimate relationship with Him. Jesus wants to manifest Himself through us and use us as instruments of light, love, grace, compassion, healing, and deliverance in a lost and dying world.

SEARCH THE SCRIPTURES

1. Who is the servant Isaiah writing about (Isaiah 42:1)?

2. The Spirit upon God's servant would bring what to the Gentiles (v. 1)?

3. God is described as being responsible for six things. What are they (v. 5)?

4. What two things did God call His servant to be (v. 6)?

5. In what way would deliverance take place for people (v. 7)?

DISCUSS THE MEANING

1. As New Testament believers, what do we need to do to be effective in reaching the lost?

2. What is our primary responsibility now that we have come to the light of Christ?

3. Why does Jesus Christ desire to baptize His followers with the Holy Spirit?

4. How does Isaiah 42:1-8 relate to our present situation and the role the church plays in the redemption of the world?

LESSON IN OUR SOCIETY

Many in the church are satisfied with just going to worship service once or twice a week. Many are in their comfort zones and have forgotten the reason why God has given them His Spirit. So many of us have become very busy in the ministry and have forgotten that our primary responsibility is to minister to the lost. If we take the time to look around us, the Holy Spirit will point out people in our families, workplaces, and communities who are in need of salvation and deliverance from the power of sin and darkness and will give us the ability to present the Gospel to them. The world is looking for love in all the wrong places. They are looking for answers, truth, and acceptance. They realize something is missing in their lives. We have been given the awesome responsibility of helping them understand that the answer is Jesus Christ. God has given us His Spirit and anointing that we may minister life and healing to others.

MAKE IT HAPPEN

This week, pray and ask the Holy Spirit to help you witness to at least three people. Pray for creative ways to share the Gospel with them. Don't allow fear to cause you to miss the way God answers your prayer by setting up divine appointments. Listen for and obey the prompting of the Holy Spirit and begin to give God praise for allowing you to play a part in His redemptive plan.

FOLLOW THE SPIRIT

What God wants me to do:

_____

_____

REMEMBER YOUR THOUGHTS

Special insights I have learned:

_____

_____

MORE LIGHT ON THE TEXT
Isaiah 42:1-8

1 Behold my servant, whom I uphold; mine elect, in whom my soul delighteth; I have put my spirit upon him: he shall bring forth judgment to the Gentiles.

The Hebrew word for "servant" (Heb. *ebed*, **EH-bed**) means "to work" (in any sense), and by implication "to serve." But God "upholds" his servant (Heb. *tamak*, **taw-MAK**) and causes him to be sustained. This servant is also "elect" (Heb. *bachiyr*, **baw-KHEER**), which means to "select" by trial because God "delighteth" (Heb. *ratsah*, **raw-TSAW**) in him and is pleased with him. It is God who "put" (Heb. *nathan*, **naw-THAN**), which means to "give His Spirit" (Heb. *ruwach*, **ROO-akh**)—a "wind" or "breath"—that is, a sensible, even violent, exhalation. In other words, God is delighted in or has been pleased with this servant; therefore, God placed His spirit on him. God will "bring forth" or, literally, cause to "go" (Heb. *yatsa*, **yaw-TSAW**). "Judgment" (Heb. *mishpat*, **mish-PAWT**, also translated "justice") is a verdict pronounced judicially to the nations of the world. The Jews referred to all non-Jews as Gentiles because they were aliens from the worship, rites, and privileges of Israel. The word "Gentiles" was used contemptuously by those who were Jewish.

2 He shall not cry, nor lift up, nor cause his voice to be heard in the street.

God's servant shall not "cry" in the future (Heb. *tsa'aq*, **tsaw-AK**), which means to "shriek" (utter a sharp shrill sound)—by implication, to "proclaim" (in assembly), especially for help. He is also told not to "lift up" in the future (Heb. *nasa*, **naw-SAW**) either himself or his voice. And he is not to cause "his voice" (Heb. *qowl*, **kole**), which means "to call aloud" or "to be heard" (Heb. *shama'*, **shaw-MAH**)—that is, to hear intelligently, with the implication of trying to get people to pay attention or to be obedient. All of these prohibitions should not be done in the "streets" (Heb. *chuwts*, **khoots**).

3 A bruised reed shall he not break, and the smoking flax shall he not quench: he shall bring forth judgment unto truth.

The word for "reed" mentioned here is in the singular absolute and stands alone and independently; thus, it could most logically refer to a single shoot from a whole reed plant. This "bruised" (Heb. *ratsats*, **raw-TSATS**) reed is cracked in many places, or has breaks. God says to His servant that he should not "break" (Heb. *shabar*, **shaw-BAR**) this reed; that is, he should not "burst it," or "break it down," or "break it off" (or into pieces) any further. In keeping with the botanical theme, God says that the "smoking flax" (Heb. *keheh*, **kay-HEH**; *pishtah*, **pish-TAW**), which is feeble or obscure, is not to be "quenched" (Heb. *kabah*, **kaw-BAW**, meaning "cause to expire" or "extinguish") by His servant. The servant is to "bring forth" (Heb. *yatsa'*, **yaw-TSAW**) or bring out "judgment" (Heb. *mishpat*, **mish-PAWT**), or a "verdict" pronounced judicially, especially a sentence or formal decree.

4 He shall not fail nor be discouraged, till he have set judgment in the earth: and the isles shall wait for his law.

God's servant shall not "fail" in the future (Heb. *kahah*, **kaw-HAW**), and shall not "be discouraged" (Heb. *ratsats*, raw-TSATS), which means to be "crushed" or "to crack into pieces" (figuratively speaking). In other words the servant would not get discouraged before he had

"set" (Heb. *siym*, **seem**) or put "judgment" (Heb. *mishpat*, **mish-PAWT**) "in the earth" (Heb. *erets*, **EH-rets**). "The isles" (Heb. *iy*, **ee**), meaning "a habitable and desirable spot," will be waiting for "his law." The phrase "his law" (Heb. *towrah*, **to-RAW**) refers to the precepts, statutes, and laws contained in the Decalogue, or Pentateuch (first five books of the Old Testament: Genesis, Exodus, Leviticus, Numbers, Deuteronomy).

5 Thus saith God the LORD, he that created the heavens, and stretched them out; he that spread forth the earth, and that which cometh out of it; he that giveth breath unto the people upon it, and spirit to them that walk therein:

Thus "saith" (Heb. *amar*, **aw-MAR**) God (Heb. *el*, **ale**), which means "strength," but this word also has a prefix letter and is the definite article, and should be expressed as "the Almighty." The word that follows is "LORD" (Heb. *Yehovah*, **yeh-ho-VAW**), which means (the) self-existent or eternal *Jehovah* that others translate as *Yahweh*. The basic meaning for the word "create" (Heb. *bara*, **baw-RAW**) is to make something exist that did not exist before. The "heavens" (Heb. *shamayim*, **shaw-MAH-yim**) means "lofty" or "the sky" (as "aloft," perhaps alluding to the visible arch in which the clouds move as well as to the higher ether where the celestial bodies revolve).

The grammatical form of the word for "heavens" suggests more than one sky, but it also describes the totality of everything that is above the earth. These heavens have been "stretched" (Heb. *natah*, **naw-TAW**). God has also "spread forth" (Heb. *raqa*, **raw-KAH**), which means "to pound," the "earth" (Heb. *erets*, **EH-rets**) as a sign of passion, literally making it spread out. The description of the acts of the Almighty *Yahweh* continues with "and that which cometh out" (Heb. *tseetsa*, **tseh-ets-AW**), which means "to issue," "to come forth (out)," or "to produce children or offspring." The Almighty Yahweh "giveth" (Heb. *nathan*, **naw-THAN**) "breath" (Heb. *neshamah*, **nesh-aw-MAW**), which means "a puff of wind" to the "people." The Almighty Yahweh has given the "spirit" (Heb. *ruwack*, **ROO-akh**) to them that go or walk in the earth.

6 I the LORD have called thee in righteousness, and will hold thine hand, and will keep thee, and give thee for a covenant of the people, for a light of the Gentiles;

The first word in this verse is the singular personal pronoun "I." It is the Lord, or the self-existent or eternal One, who is speaking. He will in the future "hold" (Heb. *chazaq,* **khaw-ZAK**) your hand. God will more than hold your hand; He will not let go of it. He will also "keep" (Heb. *natsar,* **naw-TSAR**) or "guard" you in a good sense to protect and maintain you. Yahweh will "give" (Heb. *nathan,* **naw-THAN**) His servant as a "covenant" (Heb. *beriyth,* **ber-EETH**), which means a "cutting," according to the custom of cutting or dividing animals in two and passing between pieces of flesh in ratifying a compact or covenant. The word that follows, "people" (Heb. *am,* **am**), speaks of a congregated unit and specifically of a tribe, as those of Israel. Yahweh says His servant will be a "light" (Heb. *owr,* **ore**), or an illumination, of the masses of the foreign nations or "Gentiles" (Heb. *gowy,* **GO-ee**).

7 To open the blind eyes, to bring out the prisoners from prison, and them that sit in darkness out of the prison house.

This verse begins with the imperative "to open" (Heb. *paqach,* **paw-KAKH**), which means to open the senses, especially the "eyes." But these eyes need more than just having their eyelids raised because they can't see anything; they are blind (Heb. *ivver,* **iv-VARE**). Yahweh gives further prophecy about what His servant is to accomplish, with the phrase "to bring out" (Heb. *yatsa,* **yaw-TSAW**). The word for "prisoner" (Heb. *acciyr,* **bas-SERE**) is singular and receives the action from the previous word (to cause to go out). Thus, the prisoner is going to be brought out of the "prison" (Heb. *macger,* **mas-GARE**), or "dungeon," literally, a "fastener" of something. Included in this release are the ones that "sit" (Heb. *yashab,* **yaw-SHAB**) in the "darkness" (Heb. *choshek,* **kho-SHEK**). They will come out from the prison "house" (Heb. *bayith,* **BAH-yith**) of confinement or imprisonment (Heb. *ecuwr,* **es-COR**).

8 I am the LORD: that is my name: and my glory will I not give to another, neither my praise to graven images.

The most sacred name of God ("LORD" in the KJV) is used again in this verse and is to be translated as "Jehovah" or "Yahweh." This verse begins the same as verse 6 with the personal pronoun "I." But this time, God is much more emphatic because He follows with the phrase "that is my name" (Heb. *huw,* **hoo** and *shem,* **shame**). The phrase "and my glory" (Heb. *kabowd,* **kaw-BODE**) has the idea of weight and the sense of splendor or copiousness; hence, His glory "to another" (Heb. *ach,* **awkh**) Jehovah "will not give." "Praise" (Heb. *tehillah,* **teh-hil-LAW**) means "laudation," specifically and concretely, a hymn; thus, the word can be translated as "a hymn/praise of me." The last words in verse 8 refer to "graven images" (Heb. *peciyl,* **pes-EEL**) and mean an idol as a carved graven image.

DAILY BIBLE READINGS

M: An Eastern Victor Is Roused
Isaiah 41:1-7

T: God Will Strengthen Israel
Isaiah 41:8-13

W: God Will Care for the People
Isaiah 41:14-20

T: God Is Greater Than Babylon's Deities
Isaiah 41:21-29

F: My Servant Will Bring Forth Justice
Isaiah 42:1-9

S: Sing Praise to God
Isaiah 42:10-17

S: Blind and Deaf to God's Instruction
Isaiah 42:18-25

TEACHING TIPS

December 11
Bible Study Guide 2

1. Words You Should Know

A. Gentiles (Isaiah 49:6) *gowy* (Heb.)—A foreign nation or person. The non-Israelite nation or heathen peoples. It is often used to refer to the pagan nations that surrounded Israel and are defined politically, ethnically, and territorially.

B. Ashamed (50:7) *buwsh* (Heb.)—To be confounded, disappointed, or disgraced. This is a root meaning "to become pale." When failure or sin occurs, there is a disconcerting feeling, causing a drain of color from the face.

2. Teacher Preparation

A. To begin this lesson, read the following sections: BIBLE BACKGROUND and LESSON IN OUR SOCIETY.

B. Read selected portions of Matthew's Gospel, such as Matthew 26-27, to gain a clear understanding of the character of the Servant.

C. Pray and ask God to help you stay focused on the LESSON AIM so the students will be able to achieve the objectives outlined in the aim.

3. Starting the Lesson

A. When the students arrive today, ask several of them to share about a time when they were able to help someone who may have been weary and hopeless in life. Encourage them to express how the experience made them feel.

B. Read the FOCAL VERSES and give the students an opportunity to write down the answers to the SEARCH THE SCRIPTURES questions before getting into the lesson.

C. Read the IN FOCUS story and discuss how it applies to today's lesson.

4. Getting Into the Lesson

A. Ask three students to read the lesson based on the AT-A-GLANCE outline and solicit comments from the rest of the class about what they have heard in the reading.

B. Read THE PEOPLE, PLACES, AND TIMES

section and invite the students to share its implications for today's lesson.

5. Relating the Lesson to Life

A. Have the students make comments on LESSON IN OUR SOCIETY and the SEARCH THE SCRIPTURES questions. Give them a few moments to share specific areas in the local and national communities where hopeless and weary people may be.

B. Motivate the students to put together a project that will be instrumental in helping people not only to know Jesus Christ but also to see Jesus in the actions of the class.

6. Arousing Action

A. Challenge the students to be more cognizant of their gifts and ability to serve others, rather than focusing so much on their own needs.

B. Close the class with prayer, focusing on the KEEP IN MIND verse.

WORSHIP GUIDE

For the Superintendent or Teacher
Theme: Strength for the Weary
Theme Song: "I Will Trust in the Lord"
Scripture: Romans 8:30-36
Song: "God Has Been Good to Me"
Meditation: Thank You, Lord, for Your help.
Even when I am weary and hopeless, Your
strength is available to me. Help me to give
that strength to those I meet this week who
are hopeless and weary. Amen.

STRENGTH FOR THE WEARY

Bible Background • ISAIAH 49–50
Printed Text • ISAIAH 49:5–6; 50:4–9
Devotional Reading • ISAIAH 49:7–13

LESSON AIM

By the end of the lesson, we will:

IDENTIFY God's Servant from the text;

LIST at least three ways God's Servant provides strength; and

COMMIT to become one of God's servants in helping other people find strength in their situations.

KEEP IN MIND

"For the Lord GOD will help me; therefore shall I not be confounded: therefore have I set my face like a flint, and I know that I shall not be ashamed" (Isaiah 50:7).

FOCAL VERSES

Isaiah 49:5 And now, saith the LORD that formed me from the womb to be his servant, to bring Jacob again to him, Though Israel be not gathered, yet shall I be glorious in the eyes of the LORD, and my God shall be my strength.

6 And he said, It is a light thing that thou shouldest be my servant to raise up the tribes of Jacob, and to restore the preserved of Israel: I will also give thee for a light to the Gentiles, that thou mayest be my salvation unto the end of the earth.

50:4 The Lord GOD hath given me the tongue of the learned, that I should know how to speak a word in season to him that is weary: he wakeneth morning by morning, he wakeneth mine ear to hear as the learned.

5 The Lord GOD hath opened mine ear, and I was not rebellious, neither turned away back.

6 I gave my back to the smiters, and my cheeks

LESSON OVERVIEW

LESSON AIM
KEEP IN MIND
FOCAL VERSES
IN FOCUS
THE PEOPLE, PLACES,
AND TIMES
BACKGROUND
AT-A-GLANCE
IN DEPTH
SEARCH THE SCRIPTURES
DISCUSS THE MEANING
LESSON IN OUR SOCIETY
MAKE IT HAPPEN
FOLLOW THE SPIRIT
REMEMBER YOUR THOUGHTS
MORE LIGHT ON THE TEXT
DAILY BIBLE READINGS

to them that plucked off the hair: I hid not my face from shame and spitting.

7 For the Lord GOD will help me; therefore shall I not be confounded: therefore have I set my face like a flint, and I know that I shall not be ashamed.

8 He is near that justifieth me; who will contend with me? let us stand together: who is mine adversary? let him come near to me.

9 Behold, the Lord GOD will help me; who is he that shall condemn me? lo, they all shall wax old as a garment; the moth shall eat them up.

IN FOCUS

Tamika was abducted from her birth parents when she was 5 years old. Now, as an adult, she often experienced disturbing nightmares. Her dreams always ended the same—with her waking up in a cold sweat.

Recognizing she needed help, Tamika relayed the events of her dream to her pastor. "Pastor, I have terrible nightmares almost every night." Tamika sighed. "I know they are a result of the trauma of being abducted as a child. In my dream, my arms are outstretched trying to touch the face of a woman. All of a sudden I feel a tightening in my chest and I tumble into a dark hole so narrow that I can't breathe. As I fall, I struggle to protect my arm from crashing against the jagged rocks in an effort to prevent breaking my bracelet. The bracelet is the only thing I have that connects me with my birth mother. The next thing I know, I wake up in a cold sweat. I love my foster parents, but I pray every day that God can give me the strength to continue to search for the woman who gave me this bracelet—my birth mother."

"Tamika, you must trust and have faith that God will answer your prayers. I have the number of a support group that specializes in reuniting lost children with their parents. Maybe you should consider volunteering to help them out while you continue your search," said her pastor.

Tamika was physically drained after the counseling session. On the way to pick up her daughter, she decided that maybe the pastor's suggestion was a good idea. She didn't know how it would help her, but maybe in helping others like herself, she could find comfort and her nightmares would cease.

As Tamika left the pastor's office, she noticed the time and realized she was late for picking up her daughter from school. As she climbed into her car, she did not pay attention to the oncoming traffic and pulled away from the curb. Her car was broadsided and she was knocked unconscious. She awoke in the hospital to see her daughter with a woman who seemed curiously familiar peering down at her as she lay on the hospital gurney. The teary-eyed woman clung to the ruby bracelet that once belonged to Tamika as a child. The woman wept as she explained that she recognized the bracelet as her own last gift to her daughter before she was abducted 25 years earlier. Her daughter was Tamika.

Do you trust that God will and can deliver us out of every situation? Do you believe servanthood is the source of our Christian strength? Today's lesson will explore how God, through Isaiah, brings strength to the weary.

THE PEOPLE, PLACES, AND TIMES

The Suffering Servant. This enigmatic figure arises out of the complex prophecies of Isaiah. Four "songs" celebrate the fate of the servant of Yahweh: He would bring justice to the nations, bring light to the nations, bring healing and forgiveness, and, most of all, He would suffer (see Isaiah 42:1-4; 49:1-7; 50:4-11; 52:13-53:12). But the Servant's suffering would be redemptive, for "with his stripes we are healed" (Isaiah 53:5).

In their original context, these songs seem to have been an attempt to explain the harsh suffering the nation of Israel would pass through during their exile: It was not for sins, but for the healing of the nations. One song explicitly identifies the servant and Israel: "And [he] said unto me, Thou art my servant, O Israel, in whom I will be glorified" (Isaiah 49:3).

But the servant was also God's perfect Servant. Isaiah described exactly the fate of Jesus: "He is despised and rejected of men; a man of sorrows, and acquainted with grief...Therefore will I divide him a portion with the great, and he shall divide the spoil with the strong; because he hath poured out his soul unto death: and he was numbered with the transgressors; and he bare the sin of many, and made intercession for the transgressors" (Isaiah 53:3, 12).

This paradigm made sense of the most difficult aspect of the Jesus tradition—His suffering—and transcended the Messianic title in another way: It pointed to the Gentiles, the nations, as the object of healing and forgiveness. It is no accident that the first story account in Acts that portrays an outreach to Gentiles uses this paradigm: Philip uses the passage about the suffering servant to tell the Ethiopian eunuch "the good news of Jesus" (see Acts 8:26-35; 1 Corinthians 15:3; Philippians 2:7; Matthew 12:18-21).

On the positive side, this model showed Jesus' suffering to be part of the divine plan, purposeful and redemptive. Yet, it lacked a way to deal with His life and teachings [as] other paradigms [are] needed.

Barr, David L. The New Testament Story: An Introduction. Belmont, Calif.: Wadsworth Publishing Company, 1987, 27.

BACKGROUND

In this lesson, the prophet Isaiah shares with his readers the ministry of God's Servant Israel. From the historical perspective, God visited the patriarch Jacob and changed his name from one that figuratively means "one who deceives" to "one who prevails with God and Man" (see Genesis 35:6-15). God also encouraged Jacob, telling him that because of his metamorphosis, kings and nations would be produced from his loins that would be instrumental in changing the world. In the New Covenant, believers in Jesus Christ are called "a royal priesthood" and a "holy nation," chosen by God to declare His praises to a darkened and sinful world (see 1 Peter 2:9).

From a spiritual perspective, God's Servant is the Lord Jesus Christ, who came to the earth for the purpose of healing the brokenhearted, preaching deliverance to the captives, recovering sight to the blind, and setting at liberty those that are oppressed (Luke 4:18). The Gospel writer affirms that God's Servant came to help the nation of Israel be restored to their proper place with Him as well as to strengthen the people who put their trust in their Redeemer and Deliverer. God does the same today for those who have been "grafted" into God's family and receive His promises by faith in Jesus Christ.

As the passage in Isaiah 49:7 begins, the prophet Isaiah slowly but surely identifies God's Servant as the preserver and restorer of both Jews and Gentiles alike.

AT-A-GLANCE

1. The Servant's Ministry to God's People Is Identified (Isaiah 49:5-6)
2. The Servant's Message for God's People Is Declared (50:4-6)
3. The Servant's Determination to Help God's People Is Affirmed (vv. 7-9)

IN DEPTH

1. The Servant's Ministry to God's People Is Identified (Isaiah 49:5-6)

In Isaiah's writing, God does not specifically identify His servant by name, other than to call Him Israel. But the text gives us several clues letting us know that the Servant is someone who has an intimate relationship with God the Father such as: a) God called the Servant from His mother's womb and declared His name among many people (Isaiah 49:1); b) the Servant has been given a mouth like a sharp sword that He might judge the nations of their sins (v. 2); c) the Servant's work and ministry is God-ordained and the Father has chosen Him to be the light to the nations (vv. 4, 7).

From these clues, we conclude that the Servant is Jesus Christ, the One who came to the world to redeem and save the lost (Luke 19:10). However, the prophet identifies the Servant as "Israel, in whom [God] will be glorified" (Isaiah 49:3).

In Hebrew, Israel literally means "God prevails" and is a symbolic name for Jacob. God gave Jacob that name after his encounter with the Angel of the Lord. During the encounter, the socket of Jacob's hip was wrenched out of joint. In declaring the name change the angel said, "hast thou [struggled] with God and with men, and hast prevailed" (Genesis 32:28).

In like manner, God's glory is seen in the Person of Jesus Christ. In fact, Jesus declared the same in His high priestly prayer: "Father, the hour is come; glorify thy Son, that thy Son also may glorify thee: As thou hast given him power over all flesh, that he should give eternal life to as many as thou hast given him. And this is life eternal, that they might know thee the only true God, and Jesus Christ, whom thou hast sent. I have glorified thee on the earth: I have finished the work which thou gavest me to do. And now, O Father, glorify thou me with thine own self with the glory which I had with thee before the world was" (John 17:1-5).

The prophet unveiled the ministry of God's Servant and declared both His humanity and deity. Thus, Isaiah affirmed His Personhood and ministry. First, he declared that God "formed [him] from [His mother's] womb to be his servant" (Isaiah 49:5). The Gospel writer also affirmed that before Joseph and Mary became husband and wife that she became pregnant by the power of Holy Spirit to "bring forth a son, and thou shalt call his name JESUS: for he shall save his people from their sins" (Matthew 1:21). Paul declared that for Jesus to fulfill God's work on the earth, He took on the "form" of a servant and was made in the likeness of men (see Philippians 2:5-9). Also David affirmed the mission of Jesus Christ when he writes "Then said I, Lo, I come: in the volume of the book it is written of me, I delight to do thy will, O my God: yea, thy law is within my heart" (Psalm 40:7-8). Christ came to the earth to bring redemption, establish righteousness, and obey the Father unto death. Because of His obedience, we have salvation and access to the Father. However, God also desires that every believer make the same declaration as Christ: "I come to do thy will, O God."

Isaiah explained the ministry of the servant: "to bring Jacob again to [God]" (v. 5). Jesus stated that He was sent to the lost sheep of the house of Israel to bring them back to the Father (see Matthew 15:21-28). Yet, the apostle John made it clear that the Jews did not receive the earthly ministry of Jesus (John 1:10). In like manner, many of the people outside the doors of our churches are the ones to whom God has sent us to reach. Believers are called to leave their comfort zones and penetrate our urban communities with the Gospel of Jesus Christ and share God's love with the homeless, drug addicts, and even with those who believe that the church is irrelevant to our communities. They may reject us, but we need to be vigilant in our ministry and witness to the lost and weary.

Israel eventually rejected God's message of salvation and hope. Because of their hard and impenitent hearts, the Pharisees and Jewish leaders did not believe that Jesus Christ came from God the Father, and did not accept His ministry. In fact, Jesus made it clear that "A prophet is not without honor except in his own country, among his own relatives, and in his own house" (Mark 6:4, NKJV). Their disbelief and rejection of His ministry in Nazareth prevented Jesus from healing multitudes of people.

But the Servant has hope. Though Israel rejected Him, Jesus' ministry was ordained by the Father. With Jesus' baptism by John, God spoke from heaven to declare Jesus' "Sonship" and God's favor to do His will (Matthew 3:17). On the Mount of Transfiguration, God spoke to Jesus' disciples to tell them that Jesus is the beloved Son with whom He was well pleased (Matthew 17:5).

From the eyes of the world, Jesus' ministry may have been a failure. After all, Jesus didn't have many followers, and He died a cruel death on the Cross. But from God's perspective, Jesus had God's seal of approval and gracious purpose to restore humanity to the Father. "For God so loved the world, that he gave his only begotten Son, that whosoever believeth in him should not perish, but have everlasting life" (John 3:16).

The Servant gave His life as a ransom for many people. Though the Jews refused to accept the Messiah, John said "as many as received him, to them gave he power to become the sons of God, even to them that believe on his name" (John 1:12). God made it known that the Jewish nation would not only take Jesus' ministry for granted ("a light thing"), but would also be instrumental in His crucifixion. Yet, their loss was the world's, "the Gentiles" gain.

After His resurrection, Jesus returned to His disciples and gave them the commission to reach the world with the Good News of the Gospel of the kingdom (see Matthew 28:18-20). God has made His salvation available to everyone. Indeed, Jesus' ministry and work has been a source of comfort to all who have accepted Him as their Saviour, regardless of their race, ethnicity, culture, or background.

The apostle Paul affirmed this same principle while visiting the Gentiles in Athens. When he observed them ignorantly worshiping the Lord God and many other false deities, the apostle said that God the Father had "made of one blood all nations of men for to dwell on all the face of the earth....That they should seek the Lord... though he be not far from every one of us: For in him we live, and move, and have our being" (Acts 17:26-28). We can trust that God's Servant has fulfilled His work, bringing hope and comfort to the weary who have accepted Him as their Saviour and Lord.

2. The Servant's Message For God's People Is Declared (50:4-6)

In this section of Isaiah's writing, the prophet continues the discourse of God's Servant, who demonstrates His obedience to the Father by bringing hope to the nations. The servant affirmed that "The sovereign LORD has given me an instructed tongue, to know the word that sustains the weary" (v. 4, NIV). The word "instructed" ("learned," KJV) has the idea of one who is trained and skilled in wisdom and truth—a disciple of God's immutable decrees. From this definition, we can attest the Servant to be Jesus Christ. While talking to the Jewish leaders who sought to kill Him, Jesus said, "For as the Father hath life in himself; so hath he given to the Son to have life in himself; And hath given him authority to execute judgment also, because he is the Son of man... I can of mine own self do nothing: as I hear, I judge: and my judgment is just; because I seek not mine own will, but the will of the Father which hath sent me" (John 5:26-27, 30).

God gave the Servant the ability to declare His truths to the weary and hurting in ways they had never been taught before. In fact, when Jesus shared in the synagogue of His own country, many people were astonished at the wisdom and maturity of His teachings (Matthew 13:53-56). Jesus came to earth to "preach the gospel to the poor...to heal the brokenhearted, to preach deliverance to the captives, and recovering of sight to the blind, to set at liberty them that are bruised, (oppressed) [and] To preach the acceptable year of the Lord" (Luke 4:18-19).

The prophet affirmed that the Servant never took for granted His relationship with the Father. Though He was able to heal and deliver God's people, Jesus took time to commune with the Father in solitude and prayer (see Mark 1:35; Luke 4:42). Jesus knew the awesome responsibility of being intimately connected with God so He could hear His Father and obey His commands. In like manner, it is important for the believers to spend intimate time with the Father so they too can hear and respond to His commands.

God's Servant was obedient. Not only did He listen to God at all times, but He was obedient and fully committed to doing the will of the Father, even though it cost Jesus His life. In Isaiah 50:5, the prophet uses the word "rebellious," which has the idea of being resistant and disobedient to God's divine will. Unlike Jesus, the nation of Israel constantly rebelled against God's purpose. After their deliverance from Egyptian slavery, their rebellion caused that generation to miss out on the Promised Land (see Numbers 20:7-13). But Jesus was "sold out" to His Father and refused to do anything that would dishonor or bring shame on God (see John 8:49-50).

God's Servant knew his purpose. Though Jesus came to earth to share God's love and redemption for the nation Israel, He would suffer and face humiliation by the hands of the religious leaders who refused to accept Him as the Saviour of the world. The Pharisees' hatred of Jesus so blinded them that they turned Him over to Pilate and the Roman soldiers who spat on Jesus and violently beat Him before leading Him to Calvary and the Cross (see Matthew 27:1-44).

3. The Servant's Determination to Help God's People Is Affirmed (vv. 7-9)

The Servant was determined that nothing would move Him from His purpose and destiny as the deliverer of God's people. Despite the shame and abuse, He affirmed that "the Lord GOD will help me" (v. 7). In His earthly ministry, Jesus knew His power and authority to bless and heal people. Even while dying on the Cross in agony, Jesus declared "Father, into thy hands I commend my spirit" (Luke 23:46). No matter how difficult and excruciating His situation had become, Jesus never stopped trusting His Father to help Him. God wants the church to trust and depend on Him despite the problems we may face.

As God's Servant, Jesus knew He had a date with Golgotha. In one instance, Luke wrote that Jesus set His face toward Jerusalem even though He knew that the Pharisees and religious leaders would oppose Him at every turn (see Luke 9:51, 53). But that didn't deter Jesus from destiny. In fact, Isaiah wrote, "I set my face like a flint, and I know that I shall not be ashamed" (v. 7). Jesus affirmed that His determination to help and redeem God's people was sure and that nothing or no one would change Him despite the shame He faced.

The Servant knew that because of His obedience and submission to the Father, God would justify him (v. 8). However, Jesus did not need to be made righteous as we did. By using the word "justifieth," the Servant was affirming that God would approve Him, even if men did not. None of the servant's enemies or adversaries would be able to nullify the work or ministry of the Servant.

The Servant knew that God Himself would help Him; therefore, He was not afraid of anyone who would seek to condemn Him. When the soldiers came to arrest Him in the Garden of Gethsemane, Jesus had already communed with the Father and was ready for whatever He would face (see Matthew 26:36-56). Through His death and resurrection, God would restore His Servant to His proper place with the Lord. Of His adversaries and enemies, the Servant said, "who is he that shall condemn me? lo, they all shall wax old as a garment; the moth shall eat them up" (Isaiah 50:9). Scriptures prove that all who reject Jesus have no part in eternal life. Their lives have been "eaten up" by hopeless despair because of their refusal to accept Him as their Healer and Deliverer.

Today the Servant gives strength for those who are hurting and weary. Our privilege is to receive His strength and blessing so we can be vindicated from our enemies just as Jesus was vindicated.

SEARCH THE SCRIPTURES

1. What is one of the purposes of the Servant, Jesus Christ (Isaiah 49:5)?

2. To whom does God give the Servant for revelation and salvation (v. 6)?

3. How does the Servant affirm His servanthood to the Father (50:5-6)?

4. The Servant says He shall not be ashamed because of what (v. 7)?

5. Why can the Servant be sure that God will help Him (vv. 8-9)?

DISCUSS THE MEANING

1. Why doesn't the prophet Isaiah identify the Servant by name?

2. How can we be certain that the Servant is the Lord Jesus Christ?

3. On what basis can we determine that God's Servant, as identified by Isaiah, is capable of helping God's people through their difficulties?

4. What reason does the Servant set His face like a flint? What can we learn from this example that will help us be determined in our walk with God?

LESSON IN OUR SOCIETY

Our urban communities are full of weary and hopeless people who are struggling physically, emotionally, and spiritually. God has given us gifts and abilities to help struggling people outside the church walls, but we must first commit our time to the Lord. Even though the Servant knew the dangers and uncertainty of the work God had

called Him to, He was determined to bring light and hope to mankind. Today, God wants the church to commit to His work despite the dangers we may face. Remember, the greatest among us must be God's servants, who are committed to bring light and hope to the weary.

MAKE IT HAPPEN

This week, examine the FOCAL VERSES again for specific clues about what you can do to bring strength to the weary. Perhaps spending an afternoon at a nursing home or ministering to the incarcerated may be a good place to start. Write down specific truths that God will give you this week so you can share with your classmates. Make a comment and serve someone who is less fortunate this week.

FOLLOW THE SPIRIT

What God wants me to do:

_____

_____

REMEMBER YOUR THOUGHTS

Special insights I have learned:

_____

_____

MORE LIGHT ON THE TEXT

Isaiah 49:5-6; 50:4-9

5 And now, saith the LORD that formed me from the womb to be his servant, to bring Jacob again to him, Though Israel be not gathered, yet shall I be glorious in the eyes of the LORD, and my God shall be my strength.

The opening phrase, "And now" (Heb. *attah*, at-TAW), has the meaning of "at this time." The word that is rendered "formed me" (Heb. *yatsar*, yaw-TSAR) means through the squeezing into shape or to mold into a form, especially as a potter. David recalled how God also knew him even before he was in the womb.

God's servant is to "bring again" (Heb. *shuwb*, shoob) or turn back "Jacob" (Heb. *Ya'aqob*, yah-ak-OBE) to Him. "Israel" (Heb. *Yisra'el*, yis-raw-ALE), which means "he will rule as God," is also the symbolic name of Jacob and typically refers to his posterity. Jacob was given the name Israel

(Genesis 32:28) after wrestling with the angel. The word "glorious" (Heb. *kabed*, **kaw-BADE**) is a primary root word that means "to be heavy" in a good sense (i.e., numerous, rich, or honorable). This servant will be honored heavily in "the eyes" of "the LORD" (Heb. *atsah*, **aw-TSAW**; *Yehovah*, **yeh-ho-VAW**), who is Yahweh.

My "strength" (Heb. *azaz*, **aw-ZAZ**) is a primary root word that means to be "stout" (literally or figuratively). This person, possibly the Lord Jesus Christ, will be totally dependent upon His God/Yahweh.

6 And he said, It is a light thing that thou shouldest be my servant to raise up the tribes of Jacob, and to restore the preserved of Israel: I will also give thee for a light to the Gentiles, that thou mayest be my salvation unto the end of the earth.

"It is a light (Heb. *qalal*, **kaw-LAL**) thing" is from the primary root word meaning "to be light" in a figurative way (easy or trifling).

The phrase "my servant" (Heb. *amad*, **aw-MAD**) precedes "to raise up" (Heb. *quwm*, **koom**) "the tribes of" (Heb. *shebet*, **SHAY-bet**), which is from an unused root word probably meaning "to branch off" (figuratively), as in a clan of Jacob (Heb. *Ya'aqob*, **yah-ak-OBE**).

The word "restore" (Heb. *shuwb*, **shoob**) comes from a primary root word meaning "to turn back or away" and does not necessarily include the idea of a return to the starting point. The "preserved (Heb. *natsiyr*, **naw-TSERE**) of Israel" (Heb. *Yisrael*, **yis-raw-ALE**) comes from a primary root word that means "to guard" (in a good sense). Then Yahweh says, "I will also give thee" (Heb. *nathan*, **naw-THAN**).

The word "light" (Heb. *owr*, **ore**) refers to illumination or a luminary in every sense, including lighting, happiness, etc. The term "Gentiles" (Heb. *gowy*, **GO-ee**) is used to refer to a member of a foreign or heathen nation or people.

The phrase "that thou mayest be" (Heb. *hayah*, **haw-YAW**) comes from the primary root word meaning "to exist." "My salvation" (Heb. *yeshuwah*, **yesh-OO-aw**) can also be thought of as something saved, that is, deliverance. Thus, the Servant will bring the salvation of Yahweh unto the uttermost parts of the earth.

50:4 The Lord GOD hath given me the tongue of the learned, that I should know how to speak a word in season to him that is weary: he wakeneth morning by morning, he wakeneth mine ear to hear as the learned.

The "Lord" (Heb. *Adonay*, **ad-o-NOY**) is an emphatic form of the word meaning to rule "as a sovereign."

"Hath given me" (Heb. *nathan*, **naw-THAN**) "the tongue" (Heb. *lashown*, **law-SHONE**) is clearly used here in a literal sense (as of speech) because the phrase ends with "of the learned" (Heb. *limmuwd*, **lim-MOOD**), or the instructed, accustomed disciple. This person, perhaps it is Jesus Christ, has been given this tongue in order that He may "speak" (Heb. *uwth*, **ooth**) or hasten in season to the "weary" (Heb. *ya'ph*, **yaw-AFE**), fatigued, or faint.

The word "wakeneth" (Heb. *'uwr*, **oor**) is a primary root word having the idea of opening the eyes or waking.

The word "morning" (Heb. *boqer*, **BO-ker**) is properly translated as "dawn" or "break of day" and occurs in the Hebrew text twice together in this verse. He "wakeneth" (Heb. *uwr*, **oor**) his "ear" (Heb. *ozen*, **O-zen**) communicates the idea of broadness, that is, (concretely) the ear to "hear" (Heb. *shama'*, **shaw-MAH**).

5 The Lord GOD hath opened mine ear, and I was not rebellious, neither turned away back.

This is the second occurrence of the names of God as Adonai Yahweh. He "hath opened" (Heb. *patuwr*, **paw-TOOR**) previously or sometime before this prophecy. The testimony continues by saying that he was not previously "rebellious" (Heb. *marah*, **maw-RAW**) or bitter and he did not "turn away back" (Heb. *cuwg*, **soog**).

6 I gave my back to the smiters, and my cheeks to them that plucked off the hair: I hid not my face from shame and spitting.

His testimony says that he previously "gave" (Heb. *nathan*, **naw-THAN**) his "back" (Heb. *gav*, **gav**), which is the rear part of the human body, especially from the neck to the end of the spine, "to the smiters" (Heb. *nakah*, **naw-KAW**), or the men who were striking him. "Cheeks" (Heb. *lechiy*, **lekh-EE**) means "to be soft."

The word "plucked" (Heb. *marat,* **maw-RAT**) is from a primary root word that means "to polish," and, by implication, "to make bald." His testimony is that he "hid" (Heb. *macter,* **mas-TARE**) not his "face" (Heb. *paniym,* **paw-NEEM**) from "shame" (Heb. *kelimmah,* **kel-im-MAW**) and "spitting" (Heb. *roq,* **roke**), which is spittle. This description is similar to what the Lord Jesus Christ endured and suffered just before He was crucified.

7 For the Lord GOD will help me; therefore shall I not be confounded: therefore have I set my face like a flint, and I know that I shall not be ashamed.

He "will help" (Heb. *azar,* **aw-ZAR**) means "to protect" or "aid." "Shall I not be confounded" (Heb. *kalam,* **kaw-LAWM**) literally means "to wound" and figuratively means "to taunt or insult."

The phrase "like a flint" (Heb. *challamiysh,* **khal-law-MEESH**) is translated from a word that communicates a sense of hardness (like a rock) and has a prefix that means "like this" or "thus" (or "so").

That I shall not be "ashamed" (Heb. *buwsh,* **boosh**) is a primary root word that means "to pale" or "to be disappointed."

8 He is near that justifieth me; who will contend with me? let us stand together: who is mine adversary? let him come near to me.

The word "near" (Heb. *qarowb,* **kaw-ROBE**) has the sense of close or proximate in place, kindred, or time. The phrase "who will contend" (Heb. *riyb,* **reeb**) means "to toss," that is, "to grapple," "to wrangle," or "to hold a controversy."

In the phrase, "Let us stand together," the word "together" (Heb. *yachad,* **YAKH-ad**) means "as a unit." The phrase "who is mine adversary" (Heb. *baal,* **bah-AL**) might more accurately be translated as "Who is the master judge of me?"

9 Behold, the Lord GOD will help me; who is he that shall condemn me? lo, they all shall wax old as a garment; the moth shall eat them up.

This verse begins with the interjection "Behold." The writer says that God "will help"

(Heb. *azar,* **aw-ZAR**) me. In the phrase "shall condemn me," the word "condemn" (Heb. *rasha,* **raw-SHAH**) has the meaning of "to be wrong" and, by implication, "to disturb or violate."

The word "garment" (Heb. *beged,* **BEHG-ed**) means "covering" or "clothing." The phrase "shall wax old" (Heb. *balah,* **baw-LAW**) is from a primary root word meaning "to fail" or "to wear out." "The moth" (Heb. *ash,* **awsh**) is certainly understood to be a clothes moth by the context. In its caterpillar state, the moth is especially destructive to woolen clothing and furs. Whoever attempts to condemn or prove this person (probably the Lord Jesus Christ) wrong will both fail and be eaten up.

Davidson, Benjamin. The Analytical Hebrew and Chaldee Lexicon. Grand Rapids, Mich.: Zondervan Publishing House, 1970, 19.

DAILY BIBLE READINGS

M: Comfort, O Comfort My People
Isaiah 40:1-5

T: God Strengthens the Powerless
Isaiah 40:27-31

W: My God Has Become My Strength
Isaiah 49:1-7

T: The Lord Has Comforted His People
Isaiah 49:8-13

F: I Will Not Forget You
Isaiah 49:14-18

S: I Am the Lord, Your Saviour
Isaiah 49:22-26

S: The Lord God Helps Me
Isaiah 50:4-11

TEACHING TIPS

December 18
Bible Study Guide 3

1. Words You Should Know

A. Sorrows (Isaiah 53:3) *makob* (Heb.)—Anguish, affliction, grief, and pain.

B. Saviour (Luke 1:47) *soter* (Gk.)—To save, deliver, preserve; used of God and of Christ and of His return to receive the church to Himself.

2. Teacher Preparation

A. Pray and ask the Holy Spirit to give you understanding as you prepare and study the lesson for today.

B. Read the FOCAL VERSES and the BIBLE BACKGROUND section to become familiar with today's Scripture lesson.

C. Be prepared to share your own experiences with the students as they relate to the lesson. Encourage and bring hope to those who may be hurting or suffering for Christ.

3. Starting the Lesson

A. When the students arrive for class, select one of them to open in prayer.

B. Have another student read the KEEP IN MIND verse and share briefly what this verse means to him or her.

C. Have the students read the IN FOCUS story and discuss it as a group.

D. Read the LESSON AIM and ask the students what they hope to learn from the lesson.

4. Getting into the Lesson

A. Write the AT-A-GLANCE outline on the chalkboard and read the FOCAL VERSES according to the outline.

B. Discuss the BACKGROUND section for the lesson and how it relates to what you are about to study today.

C. Select three students to read the IN DEPTH section of the lesson, and discuss each section as a group.

D. After you have completed the lesson, spend some time discussing the SEARCH THE SCRIP-TURES and DISCUSS THE MEANING questions. Allow the students to participate by answering the questions.

5. Relating the Lesson to Life

A. Encourage the students by affirming that God knows, sees, and cares about His children.

B. Encourage the students to keep their eyes on Jesus Christ and to guard their hearts against bitterness and unforgivingness. Remind the students how important it is to stay prayerful and close to the Lord and to trust Him to move on their behalf according to His divine will and purpose.

6. Arousing Action

A. Give the students time to discuss the LESSON IN OUR SOCIETY and THE PEOPLE, PLACES, AND TIMES sections.

B. Challenge the students to be more sensitive to others who may be suffering around them.

C. Ask the students if there is anyone in the class who is currently enduring suffering, persecution, rejection, disappointment, or injustice. Pray for those students as a group.

WORSHIP GUIDE

For the Superintendent or Teacher
Theme: Hope for Those Who Suffer
Theme Song: "His Eye Is on the Sparrow"
Scripture: Psalm 91:1-4
Song: "I Will Trust You Lord"
Meditation: Lord, thank You for speaking to my heart and giving me a better understanding of how suffering for Christ is a part of Your redemptive plan for my life. Amen.

HOPE FOR THOSE WHO SUFFER

Bible Background • ISAIAH 53; LUKE 1
Printed Text • ISAIAH 53:1–3; LUKE 1:47–55
Devotional Reading • ROMANS 12:9–16

LESSON AIM

By the end of the lesson, we will:

UNDERSTAND that suffering is a part of God's redemptive plan through Jesus Christ;

LOOK at the suffering God allows in the life of faithful believers from a different perspective; and

BE ENCOURAGED to trust God in the midst of the most trying circumstances.

KEEP IN MIND

"And his mercy is on them that fear him from generation to generation" (Luke 1:50).

FOCAL VERSES

Isaiah 53:1 Who hath believed our report? and to whom is the arm of the LORD revealed?

2 For he shall grow up before him as a tender plant, and as a root out of a dry ground: he hath no form nor comeliness; and when we shall see him, there is no beauty that we should desire him.

3 He is despised and rejected of men; a man of sorrows, and acquainted with grief: and we hid as it were our faces from him; he was despised, and we esteemed him not.

Luke 1:47 And my spirit hath rejoiced in God my Saviour.

48 For he hath regarded the low estate of his handmaiden: for, behold, from henceforth all generations shall call me blessed.

49 For he that is mighty hath done to me great things; and holy is his name.

50 And his mercy is on them that fear him from generation to generation.

LESSON OVERVIEW

LESSON AIM
KEEP IN MIND
FOCAL VERSES
IN FOCUS
THE PEOPLE, PLACES, AND TIMES
BACKGROUND
AT-A-GLANCE
IN DEPTH
SEARCH THE SCRIPTURES
DISCUSS THE MEANING
LESSON IN OUR SOCIETY
MAKE IT HAPPEN
FOLLOW THE SPIRIT
REMEMBER YOUR THOUGHTS
MORE LIGHT ON THE TEXT
DAILY BIBLE READINGS

51 He hath shewed strength with his arm; he hath scattered the proud in the imagination of their hearts.

52 He hath put down the mighty from their seats, and exalted them of low degree.

53 He hath filled the hungry with good things; and the rich he hath sent empty away.

54 He hath holpen his servant Israel, in remembrance of his mercy;

55 As he spake to our fathers, to Abraham, and to his seed for ever.

IN FOCUS

One Saturday morning, Terry was helping deliver food to a homeless shelter when a gunshot tore into his minivan and struck his oldest daughter, Betty, killing her instantly. Terry and his wife Stephanie could not believe what had happened. Their pain was unbearable; no amount of words provided comfort or peace.

Lying in bed that night, Terry heard Stephanie softly crying, "How could this have happened? Is there any way to explain this evil act? What do we tell our other children?"

Terry had no answers for his wife. He was just as hurt and confused as she was. He turned to his wife and tried to comfort her, reassuring her that God was with them and that everything would be all right—although he didn't know how. He suggested they pray together and ask God to relieve their suffering.

Terry prayed, "Dear Lord, we come before You tonight thanking You for the life of our daughter, Betty. She was truly a blessing to all who knew her.

Thank You for the love we would never have known without her. Father, during this time of despair and grief, I ask for Your grace, mercy, guidance, and strength. Give me and my wife the strength to encourage our other children and a blessed hope for tomorrow. In Jesus' name. Amen."

Suffering is an inescapable aspect of human life. What hope can we have in the midst of our suffering? In today's lesson, Isaiah's words affirm that Jesus suffered even more than we do. The passage from Luke celebrates Mary's release from that suffering in the anticipated birth of Christ.

THE PEOPLE, PLACES, AND TIMES

Servant. In the English Bible, a servant is often described as a slave or a hired attendant. In the Old Testament, the chief characteristic of the servant is that he or she belongs to another and therefore has no legal rights of his own. The servants/slaves must also participate in Israel's religious practices in terms of circumcision (Genesis 17:12), the Sabbath (Exodus 20:10), sacrifice (Deuteronomy 12:18), and the Passover (Exodus 12:27). The word "servant" is also used as a term of humble self-designation (2 Kings 8:13) and as a way of expressing political submission (Joshua 9:11).

Achtemeier, Paul J., ed. The Harper's Bible Dictionary. San Francisco: Harper and Row Publishers, 1985, 929-930.

BACKGROUND

The Gospel of Luke begins with an expression of the author's desire to write about the things he witnessed as a disciple and follower of Jesus Christ (Luke 1:1-4).

In the city of Nazareth, the angel Gabriel appeared to Mary, a virgin girl who was promised to Joseph. The message that Gabriel delivered to Mary troubled her and she didn't understand its meaning. But the angel instructed Mary not to fear. He assured her that she was highly favored by God and that she would bring forth a son and name Him Jesus. He went on to give her a prophetic word about the destiny of Jesus (see Luke 1:26-33). When Mary questioned the angel, wondering how a virgin could give birth, the angel revealed that the Holy Spirit would overshadow her and

impregnate her with the One called the Son of God.

Mary acknowledged that she was the handmaid of the Lord and accepted God's divine purpose for her life to give birth to Jesus the Messiah (Luke 1:34-38).

AT-A-GLANCE

1. The Suffering Messiah (Isaiah 53:1-3)
2. The Proclamation of the Messiah (Luke 1:47-50)
3. The Blessing of the Messiah (vv. 51-55)

IN DEPTH

1. The Suffering Messiah (Isaiah 53:1-3)

As today's lesson begins, Isaiah gives prophetic revelation about the Lord Jesus Christ hundreds of years before He comes to earth to be the Saviour and Deliverer of humankind.

Though Jesus was the true Messiah and Saviour of the world, there were relatively few believers among the Jews at His first coming. Many chose not to believe in Him and therefore failed to receive the free gift of salvation. There were several reasons why the Jews did not believe what was prophesied by Isaiah (John 12:38-39). However, their decision about Jesus Christ brought God's judgment. The hardening of their hearts concerning the Word of God demonstrates that Israel was broken off because of their unbelief (Romans 11:20; Psalm 95:8; Hebrews 3:8).

The Gospel will never leave unchanged the people who hear it. It will cause people either to repent and receive Jesus Christ as Saviour and Lord, or to reject Him and continue to be condemned (John 3:18). Even though many of the Jews rejected Jesus at His first coming, many believed in Him and became His followers after Pentecost (Acts 2:41).

John the Baptist was a forerunner of Jesus. John was given the assignment of awakening the people and preparing them for the Messiah. Jesus' ministry came at a time of spiritual drought on earth;

the hearts of the people were hardened. They were walking in darkness as slaves to sin, as Satan's demonic strongholds, and as those who easily succumbed to the traditions of the religious leaders.

Because Jesus lacked physical attractiveness and earthly grandeur or status, many despised and

though He came to earth to bring salvation and healing to many. The suffering Messiah was even rejected and betrayed by one of His own disciples, even though they had been taught by Jesus Himself and had witnessed many of the miracles He performed.

Jesus' mission involved great pain and suffering. He experienced grief and disappointment because of the sins of humankind. Jesus gave His life that we may experience the free gift of salvation through receiving Him as Saviour and Lord.

The suffering Messiah was crucified because humankind was guilty and had sinned against God (Psalm 22:16; Zechariah 12:10; John 19:34). Jesus became our substitute and took our punishment, paying the penalty for our sins so that we may be forgiven and have peace with God the Father (Romans 5:1; 6:23).

2. The Proclamation of the Messiah (Luke 1:47-50)

This Scripture passage focuses on the verses identified as the "Song of Mary" in the Gospel of Luke. Mary's proclamation begins when her soul magnifies the Lord (Luke 1:46). Mary's song reveals her need for salvation (v. 47). She acknowledged God as her Saviour and realized that she was a sinner who needed Christ as her Redeemer. Not only did Mary accept her mission, but she was excited about what God wanted to do through her. What an honor it is to be chosen to give birth to Jesus the Messiah. In like manner, we should have the same excitement when God wants to use us to "birth" His vision and purpose in our lives.

God's mercy for all generations.

rejected Him. He was hated and mocked by Israel's religious leaders. He was often misunderstood and accused of blasphemy as He preached throughout Jerusalem. The religious leaders even accused Jesus of casting out demons by the work of Satan. His authority was challenged and questioned many times. His life was threatened constantly, even

Mary's humility and God's choosing her to give birth to His Son would motivate generations of people to consider Mary as a blessed servant of the Lord. Indeed, Mary realized that this awesome blessing was directly from God's hands. She didn't take any of the praise for herself, but rejoiced, "For He that is mighty hath done to me great things" (v. 49). This great blessing would cause others to be attracted to her and would present an opportunity for Mary to speak of God's power and might.

Mary was in a position to make others aware of the name of the Lord as holy, a name not to be taken in vain, and to speak of God's mercy because she had experienced it herself, having been chosen for this awesome assignment. Mary affirmed that God's mercy comes to those who fear (reverence, trust or have faith) in Him, and that this mercy would be made available, not only in her generation, but also for future generations of those who are willing to work in obedience to the truth (v. 50).

3. The Blessing of the Messiah (vv. 51-55)

As Mary's prophetic word continued, she shared about the Messiah and the characteristics of the covenant blessings He would bestow upon God's people. Mary praised the Lord for His victory and salvation that would be made available to Israel and all the nations. The coming of the Messiah to His faithful people would not only bring the blessing of salvation and comfort; He would also come in power and authority with the ability to scatter the conceited in the imagination of their hearts. By His life, the Messiah would expose the real motives of the heart (v. 51).

The blessed coming Messiah would establish God's kingdom based on righteous standards. The existing social order would be radically reversed (vv. 52, 53). In this kingdom, the humble would be exalted to positions of honor while the arrogant and powerful would be brought down and humbled. In life there are many who may be overlooked or considered outcasts, as Mary was. However, in God's kingdom, all of the different racial, ethnic, and gender groups will have the opportunity to partake of the blessings of the Messiah by simply receiving Him as Saviour and Lord.

The blessed coming Messiah promised to fill the hungry with good things. Those who truly hunger for the truth and desire to be set free from

religious bondage and sin will come to know truth and freedom in Jesus Christ. There is no need to envy the world or seek its riches, fame, and/or popularity. Instead, we should pity the world and pray for ways to reach them with the Gospel of Jesus Christ.

There are many people who strive for greatness and wealth. But nothing can take the place of a personal relationship with Jesus Christ. "For what is a man profited, if he shall gain the whole world, and lose his own soul? or what shall a man give in exchange for his soul?" (Matthew 16:26).

The blessed Messiah is the One to whom we look. He has promised to help us. He takes delight in helping His people and wants us to call on Him in every situation. We can also depend on the Lord and totally trust Him to help us in our time of need. Far too often, we put our trust in people instead of trusting the Lord. Whatever situation we find ourselves in, we must remember that the Lord is our help. In Him, we find the answers we need. Even at times when it seems He has forgotten us or that our prayers are not answered, if we walk in obedience, He has promised that He will not forget us and will show mercy toward us.

Just as the blessed Messiah spoke to our father Abraham and his seed, He still speaks to the church, the body of Christ, today. As God gave promises to Israel, He gives those same promises to us. However, just as Jesus had to suffer, so do we. In the same manner, just as Israel saw the fulfillment of God's promises, so, too, will the church of Jesus Christ. Our God keeps His promises.

SEARCH THE SCRIPTURES

1. What words does Isaiah use to describe the suffering Messiah (Isaiah 53:3)?

2. How does Mary respond to the angel's announcement (Luke 1:46)?

3. How does Mary describe God (vv. 44-49)?

4. On what type of people does God show mercy (v. 50)?

5. Who does God exalt (v. 52)?

DISCUSS THE MEANING

1. How should we respond when we suffer according to God's Word?

2. Because Jesus gave His life for us, what should be our attitude toward those who are lost?

3. How should we respond to God's call on, or mission, for our lives?

4. As African Americans and God's children, what part do we play in the Lord's redemptive plan?

LESSON IN OUR SOCIETY

People are often taught that when a Christian suffers, we either have sin in our lives or we lack faith in God. However, God's Word tells us that we must enter into the kingdom of God through much tribulation (Acts 14:22) and that those who are godly will suffer persecution (2 Timothy 3:12). The persecution we suffer can come in a variety of ways, including as a result of our refusal to compromise our Christian convictions. We may be rejected, despised, and mocked because of our devotion to and love for Jesus Christ. The persecution will not only come from the world, but also from lukewarm Christians. Because God's kingdom and His principles are usually in opposition to the world, committed Christians may sometimes face injustice and unfair treatment. However, we must not lose hope; instead, we must look to Jesus for our help and strength. He is our example and suffering Messiah, the One who has stayed true to His calling, and the One who blesses His people.

MAKE IT HAPPEN

The next time you suffer for the kingdom of God, pray and ask the Holy Spirit to help you view your suffering from an eternal point of view. Pray for God's strength and grace to help you endure. Ask God to show you ways to witness and bless others in the midst of the inevitable trials you may face. Remember that nothing can happen to a faithful child of God without His approval. He works everything together for His good, for those who love Him and are called according to His purpose (Romans 8:28).

FOLLOW THE SPIRIT

What God wants me to do:

_____

_____

REMEMBER YOUR THOUGHTS

Special insights I have learned:

MORE LIGHT ON THE TEXT

Isaiah 53:1-3; Luke 1:47-55

1 Who hath believed our report? and to whom is the arm of the LORD revealed?

In this verse of Scripture, Isaiah made an inquiry for those who believed the message he proclaimed. The Hebrew word *aman* (**aw-MAN**) means "to believe." It implies support or confirmation, with an acceptance of what was said.

Isaiah called out for those who supported his message by their acceptance of it. He proclaimed redemption; he prophesied the coming of the Saviour. This is the message that needed corroboration. The Hebrew word translated as "report" is *shemuwah* (**shem-oo-AW**), meaning "something heard." A report on the coming of a Saviour is Good News, and Isaiah inquired about those who had heard this Good News.

Isaiah was asking for those to whom the arm of the Lord had been revealed. The Hebrew word *galah* (**gaw-LAW**) means "to reveal." The "arm of the LORD" refers to God's power or strength. Those who have experienced a revelation of the arm of the Lord are those who have experienced His mighty power.

2 For he shall grow up before him as a tender plant, and as a root out of a dry ground: he hath no form nor comeliness; and when we shall see him, there is no beauty that we should desire him.

Here Isaiah describes the growth of the Saviour. In the phrase "he shall grow up before him," the "he" refers to the Saviour, while "him" refers to God. This gives us a picture of the Saviour emerging and growing under the Fatherhood of God. The Hebrew word *yowneq* (**yo-NAKE**), translated as "tender plant," means "twig." It is a branch or sucker sprouting from the main tree. This main tree is therefore a parent to the twig.

The descriptive phrase "as a root" could be speaking of the Saviour as the "root of Jesse" (Isaiah 11:10). A root is parallel to a foundation. Jesus, the Saviour, is the root out of which the child of God originates by spiritual birth. He is the foundation upon whom the works and lives of believers are being built (1 Corinthians 3:11). "A dry ground," which refers to soil that lacks nutrients and water, could mean the earth devoid of heavenly conditions. This means that the Saviour, who is from heaven, is growing up in a place that lacks the riches and goodness of heaven.

Isaiah further remarks on His physical appearance. The Hebrew word *hadar* (**haw-DAWR**), translated as "comeliness," means "beauty" or "majesty." The Saviour relinquished His glory upon coming to the earth; thus, He came without beauty. Isaiah tells us that He is not attractive or good-looking; in fact, He is marred to the point of being formless, thereby having a repulsive appearance. No touch of beauty was on Him to qualify Him to receive human attention and admiration.

While the lack of material effects and deplorable conditions can cause distress, a very immediate cause of distress can be a bad bodily condition—a body plagued by sickness and disease, a body marred in form. That Jesus, the Saviour, knows it all by experience and offers help is enough to give hope to those believers who are having similar experiences.

3 He is despised and rejected of men; a man of sorrows, and acquainted with grief: and we hid as it were our faces from him; he was despised, and we esteemed him not.

Against the Saviour is the expression of the human tendency to treat with contempt what is not appealing to the eyes. The Hebrew word *maac* (**maw-AS**), meaning "to despise, abhor, reject, or treat with disdain," tells us how the Saviour is treated. It also means "to refuse." This implies that the Saviour is unaccepted and looked at with contempt.

Makob (**mak-OBE**), the Hebrew word for "sorrows," means "anguish." Isaiah presents Jesus to us as a man burdened with sorrows and "acquainted" (*yada*, **yaw-DAW**), or "familiar," with grief (*choliy*, **khol-EE**).

Jesus did not have the pleasure of being admired; He was not esteemed. The Hebrew word for "esteemed" is *chashab* (**khaw-SHAB**), which involves a mental process of thinking, regarding, or valuing something. He was not well regarded. Similarly, the worth of the believer's personality is

secured in Christ, who suffered and died but was raised up in glory. For in Christ is the manifestation of a personality metamorphosis—a transformation from the deplorable to the glorious.

Christ, the Saviour, knew sorrows and became familiar with grief through the hardship He underwent. The sufferings and hardship of a believer are very much unlike those of the sinner. It is the very life of Christ, which features sufferings, death, resurrection, and glory, that is being poured into the believer (2 Corinthians 4:8-12).

Luke 1:47 And my spirit hath rejoiced in God my Saviour.

As the effusion of Mary's breath magnifies the Lord, her spirit (Gk. *pneuma*, **PNYOO-mah**) rejoices in God. The Greek word *agalliao* (**ag-al-lee-AH-o**), translated as "rejoice," means "to be exceedingly glad" or "to be filled with exceeding joy."

The Song of Mary is a celebration of God's favor and mighty works by a woman who became instrumental in the fulfillment of the Good News of the coming Saviour. Likewise, because we are beneficiaries of God's favor, praises ought to emanate from our heart as evidence of the deposits of His grace in our lives. Praising God and giving Him glory is a supreme duty for the believer. With praise, the believer offers unto Him the fruit of his or her lips. With praise, God is magnified. With praise, the believer receives victory over every opposition (2 Chronicles 20:22). With praise, the believer creates a habitation for God (Psalm 22:3).

48 For he hath regarded the low estate of his handmaiden: for, behold, from henceforth all generations shall call me blessed.

There could be a number of reasons why Mary's spirit rejoices in God; but in this verse, she states one reason that alludes to one of God's attributes—His graciousness. Mary rejoices in God's acknowledgment and esteem of her low estate. The Greek word *epiblepo* (**ep-ee-BLEP-o**), translated as "regarded," means "to gaze upon with favor." Conscious of her "low estate" (Gk. *tapeinosis*, **tap-I-no-sis**), she rightly sees the enduring nature of this divine favor and realizes that news about her will endure to all times.

God's act of regarding the person of low estate is based on His grace. God is gracious. He gives grace to the lowly (Proverbs 3:34). There is hope for the lowly and the downtrodden. He is the Father to the fatherless. He delivers us from the "horrible pit, [and] out of the miry clay (Psalm 40:2). He is close to the brokenhearted and delivers those who are crushed in spirit (Psalm 34:18). He rescues the weak from the hands of powerful enemies.

By His grace, God worked the plan of redemption for man. Colossians 1:13-14 says, "Who hath delivered us from the power of darkness, and hath translated us into the kingdom of his dear Son: In whom we have redemption through his blood, even the forgiveness of sins."

It is a great privilege to be a child of God and a recipient of God's blessings. We are highly esteemed and fortunate to have Christ, who died for our sins.

49 For he that is mighty hath done to me great things; and holy is his name.

As Mary progresses in her song, she acknowledges that Almighty God has done great things for her. The Greek word *dunatos* (**doo-nat-OS**), meaning "mighty," is used to describe God's inherent ability to perform anything. Obviously the outcome of God's inherent and unrestrained ability ought to be great. While the Greek word *megas* (**MEG-as**) is translated as "great," the word *megaleios* (**meg-al-I-os**) is translated here as the phrase "great things," referring to magnificent or wonderful works. Only God, with inherent and unrestrained ability, can do such wonderful works capable of overwhelming human understanding (cf. Psalm 111:2).

Mary also makes reference to another of God's attributes—holiness. The Greek word *hagios* (**HAG-ee-os**), which means "holy," is used by Mary to acknowledge the inherent quality of God's name and to connect it to His wonderful works. Only a holy God can perform such wonderful works, which bestow blessings on the recipient and are devoid of sorrows (cf. Proverbs 10:22).

50 And his mercy is on them that fear him from generation to generation.

Mary now mentions yet another of God's attributes—mercy. The Greek word *eleos* (**EL-eh-os**),

translated as "mercy," denotes compassion. It is pity outwardly manifested, a special regard, or compassionate inclination toward misery, resultant of sin, extended for the alleviation of its consequences. God's mercy is infinite. He is rich in mercy, and He reserves His exclusive right to bestow it.

Mary further says that God's mercy is bestowed on those who fear His name. The Greek word *phobeo* (**fob-EH-o**), which means "to fear" or "to be in awe of," brings to mind reverential fear. This means that those who revere Him in every generation become objects of His covenant mercy.

The mercy of God is also shown to those who are in distress. The hope of the hurting and distressed obtaining relief is based on their expectation of God's mercy. The mercy of God eases the burdens of sorrow, guilt, and misery, thereby rekindling a new zeal, strength, and inclination toward doing right. David says in Psalm 79:8, "let thy tender mercies speedily prevent us: for we are brought very low." Based on this, the apostle Paul also besought the Romans that, by the mercies of God, they should present their bodies as living sacrifices, holy, and acceptable unto God (Romans 12:1). It is important that believers be merciful to one another in response to the mercy they have received (Matthew 5:7).

51 He hath shewed strength with his arm; he hath scattered the proud in the imagination of their hearts.

Mary tells us of God's accomplishments. She reveals to us that God has shown strength with His arm—the arm of the Lord spoken of by the prophet Isaiah in Isaiah 53:1, and used figuratively to mean God's power or strength. While Mary could be referring to the power of God coming against those filled with pride, her reference to the arm of God showing strength connects this statement with the prophecy of Isaiah. She tends to reiterate that God has revealed the Good News (the Gospel), which is the power of God, and insinuates that this Gospel causes a scattering (Gk. *rhipto* **HRIP-to**), meaning "to throw," "to hurl," or "to be cast down."

The Greek word *huperephanos* (**hoop-er-AY-fan-os**) means "conceited" or "haughty," showing one's elf above others, despising or even treating them with contempt. The Greek word *dianoia* (**dee-AN-oy-ah**), translated as "imagination," refers to the thoughts and ideas of the proud, who are opposed to God. This is why they are scattered by His strength. The proud with their contrary imaginations could be those who are wise and prudent by worldly standards.

52 He hath put down the mighty from their seats, and exalted them of low degree.

Mary, with her song, expresses the awesome and wonderful acts of God in the exercise of His sovereignty. The Greek word translated as "put down" is *kathaireo* (**kath-ahee-REH-o**), meaning "to lower with the application of violence" or "to demolish, to cast down, or to destroy." The Greek word *dunastes* (**doo-NAS-tace**), translated as "mighty," means "possessor of power or authority; one who demolishes the thrones of rulers and kings, casting them down from their high positions of authority."

Mary further says that God exalts them of low degree. The Greek word *hupsoo* (**hoop-SO-o**), translated as "exalted," means "to lift up." This gives us the picture of God lifting up or raising to dignity those who are of low degree. The Greek word *tapeinos* (**tap-I-NOS**), translated "of low degree," means "low" or "humble." Here we see the different treatments God metes out to two opposing categories of people—the mighty and the lowly. On one side, we see the mighty, which refers to rulers and kings. On this same side, we can also find the conceited who are spoken of in verse 51. There the conceited are said to be cast down; here in verse 52, the mighty are also cast down. On the opposing side, we find the humble, the contrite at heart, or the poor in spirit who are always beneficiaries of God's favor and grace. Those who recognize their spiritual poverty are always acceptable sacrifices to God (Psalm 51:17; Proverbs 3:34). They are esteemed by God (Isaiah 66:2).

This is talking about spiritual brokenness. It is a condition in which one is broken at heart and overwhelmed by the reverential fear of God. The fear of or reverence for God keeps one from error. It also keeps one responsive to God in absolute obedience, trembling at His Word, vested with the grace of humility, and yielding to the Holy Spirit.

There could be the coercive form of brokenness brought about by grief, sorrows, and a series of traumatic experiences one goes through in life; however, there is also the form that is personally developed over time from deliberately and consistently living a life of contrition and humility. It is achieved through a persistent servant-consciousness before God and a sense of inadequacy without the help of God.

53 He hath filled the hungry with good things; and the rich he hath sent empty away.

God provides for the hungry, filling them with good things. The Greek word *empiplemi* (**em-PIP-lay-mee**), translated as "filled," means "to fill full" or "to satisfy." This implies that God provides for the hungry, filling them to the fullest until they are satisfied.

The word *agathos* (**ag-ath-OS**), translated as "good," describes something that is good in its character or essence; something that is beneficial. This describes the quality of what God gives to the hungry—nothing short of that which is good.

The "hungry" (Gk. *prospeinos*, **PROS-pi-nos**) can also refer to persons of low estate or low degree, since conditions of depravity are common among them. God fills their vacuum of need to satisfaction. On the other hand, he sends the rich away empty.

Those who are overfed and self-satisfied not acknowledging their need for the things of God are sent away empty. Those who hunger for the things of God will be filled and satisfied. Thus, God gives grace to the humble.

54 He hath holpen his servant Israel, in remembrance of his mercy; 55 As he spake to our fathers, to Abraham, and to his seed for ever.

Mary points out that God helps. The Greek word *antilambanomai* (**an-tee-lam-BAN-om-ahee**), translated as "holpen," gives us the idea of one taking hold of another and, in turn, of someone participating or partaking while in the process of helping another. God renders help to Israel in remembrance of His mercy to fulfill the promise He made to Abraham, Isaac, and Jacob and their descendants forever. God's help is intrinsically prompted by His mercy. In addition, God expresses His love and faithfulness. He is faithful to maintain His

Word on behalf of the descendants after speaking it to their fathers.

God is absolutely committed to bringing His Word to pass in the lives of His children. His love, mercy, faithfulness, power, and might are bestowed on His children to work deliverance, to make provision, to strengthen and encourage, and to create distinctions between the saints and the ungodly. To such a loving, merciful, and faithful God, believers owe the duty to serve, praise, and worship. Thus, believers should take up the responsibility to zealously be witnesses for Christ, pursue peace with all men, bring people to the saving knowledge of Christ, show His love, shine His light, become filled with all wisdom, and demonstrate the power of God through righteous action and holy living in our homes, churches, and the community at large.

DAILY BIBLE READINGS

M: Despised, Rejected, a Man of Suffering
Isaiah 52:13-53:3
T: He Bore the Sins of Many
Isaiah 53:4-12
W: John the Baptist's Birth Foretold
Luke 1:5-17
T: The Birth of Jesus Foretold
Luke 1:26-38
F: Mary Visits Elisabeth
Luke 1:39-45
S: Mary's Song of Praise
Luke 1:46-55
S: Hope Comes Through Suffering
Romans 5:1-11

TEACHING TIPS

December 25
Bible Study Guide 4

1. Words You Should Know

A. Proclaim (Isaiah 61:1) *qara* (Heb.)—To cry aloud, preach, celebrate, or pronounce.

B. Joy (Luke 2:10) *chara* (Gk.)—To rejoice; cause or matter of rejoicing in exultation, exuberance, excitement, good cheer, and gladness of heart.

2. Teacher Preparation

A. Before you begin to study the lesson, pray and ask the Lord to give you wisdom and insight on how to teach the lesson, especially for visitors and strangers who may come to your class on this Christmas Day.

B. Read and study the DEVOTIONAL READING. Then get into the lesson by reading the FOCAL VERSES. Make some notes for yourself that will help you convey certain truths that you want your students to remember.

C. Read the LESSON IN OUR SOCIETY and MAKE IT HAPPEN sections.

3. Starting the Lesson

A. Ask a student to read the IN FOCUS story. Connect the story to the LESSON AIM.

B. As the students arrive, ask them to share their experiences from last week's MAKE IT HAPPEN assignment.

C. Read the FOCAL VERSES according to the AT-A-GLANCE outline and spend a few moments discussing what you have read.

D. Have a student lead the class in prayer, using the LESSON AIM as the foundation of the prayer.

4. Getting into the Lesson

A. Select at least four volunteers to read IN DEPTH, according to the AT-A-GLANCE outline.

B. After the lesson is read, have the students read and answer the SEARCH THE SCRIPTURES questions one at a time.

5. Relating the Lesson to Life

A. Ask the students to share what Christmas means to them, how they plan to celebrate Christ's birth, and how it has a significant impact on their spiritual lives.

B. Direct the students to the LESSON IN OUR SOCIETY section and have them share their ideas about how to incorporate it into their lives.

C. Give ample time for visitors to share their impressions of today's lesson.

D. Read the KEEP IN MIND verse in unison and ask each student to share its meaning for him or her with the rest of the class.

6. Arousing Action

A. Give the students a few moments to read the MAKE IT HAPPEN section and reflect on what they will do to make the lesson a reality in their lives.

B. Before the students leave today, encourage them to read the DAILY BIBLE READINGS for the week.

C. Close the class by asking each student to share a brief prayer relating to the theme of Christmas.

WORSHIP GUIDE

For the Superintendent or Teacher
Theme: Good News for the World
Theme Song: "Hark, the
Herald Angels Sing"
Scripture: Matthew 1:21-23
Song: "It Came Upon The
Midnight Clear"
Meditation: Lord, we thank You for sending Your Son Jesus Christ as a babe in a manger. We trust that You will motivate us to share Your love and redemption with those who may not know that You are the Good News for the world. We ask in faith for power to witness of Your love to the world. In Jesus' name. Amen.

GOOD NEWS FOR THE WORLD

Bible Background • ISAIAH 61:1–3; LUKE 2:8–20
Printed Text • ISAIAH 61:1–2; LUKE 2:8–20
Devotional Reading • ISAIAH 52:7–12

LESSON AIM

By the end of the lesson, we will:

EXPLORE the truth that God's redeeming love is for all;

BECOME PERSUADED that the Good News of God's kingdom should be shared with our family and friends; and

COMMIT to work out the principles of God's Good News in the community we serve.

KEEP IN MIND

"For unto you is born this day in the city of David a Saviour, which is Christ the Lord" (Luke 2:11).

LESSON OVERVIEW

LESSON AIM
KEEP IN MIND
FOCAL VERSES
IN FOCUS
THE PEOPLE, PLACES, AND TIMES
BACKGROUND
AT-A-GLANCE
IN DEPTH
SEARCH THE SCRIPTURES
DISCUSS THE MEANING
LESSON IN OUR SOCIETY
MAKE IT HAPPEN
FOLLOW THE SPIRIT
REMEMBER YOUR THOUGHTS
MORE LIGHT ON THE TEXT
DAILY BIBLE READINGS

FOCAL VERSES

Isaiah 61:1 The Spirit of the Lord GOD is upon me; because the LORD hath anointed me to preach good tidings unto the meek; he hath sent me to bind up the brokenhearted, to proclaim liberty to the captives, and the opening of the prison to them that are bound;

2 To proclaim the acceptable year of the LORD, and the day of vengeance of our God; to comfort all that mourn;

Luke 2:8 And there were in the same country shepherds abiding in the field, keeping watch over their flock by night.

9 And, lo, the angel of the Lord came upon them, and the glory of the Lord shone round about them: and they were sore afraid.

10 And the angel said unto them, Fear not: for, behold, I bring you good tidings of great joy, which shall be to all people.

11 For unto you is born this day in the city of David a Saviour, which is Christ the Lord.

12 And this shall be a sign unto you; Ye shall find the babe wrapped in swaddling clothes, lying in a manger.

13 And suddenly there was with the angel a multitude of the heavenly host praising God, and saying,

14 Glory to God in the highest, and on earth peace, good will toward men.

15 And it came to pass, as the angels were gone away from them into heaven, the shepherds said one to another, Let us now go even unto Bethlehem, and see this thing which is come to pass, which the Lord hath made known unto us.

16 And they came with haste, and found Mary, and Joseph, and the babe lying in a manger.

17 And when they had seen it, they made known abroad the saying which was told them concerning this child.

18 And all they that heard it wondered at those things which were told them by the shepherds.

19 But Mary kept all these things, and pondered them in her heart.

20 And the shepherds returned, glorifying and praising God for all the things that they had heard and seen, as it was told unto them.

IN FOCUS

David sat in his Sunday School class on Christmas Day and pondered the question asked by the Sunday School teacher: "What good news can you share today?" David reflected on where he was one year ago today. Last Christmas he was a United States Marine stationed in Iraq. With him he carried many things—a machine gun, hand grenades, and other weapons of war. But his most treasured possession was the Bible his grandfather had given him the day he left for Iraq. He had never taken much stock in the stories of the Bible that his grandfather used to tell him as a child, but as he found himself in a foreign land—the land where Jesus was born—he began to read and study the Bible. Smiling, David told the class what had happened to him one year ago on Christmas Day after reading the story of Christ's birth in the book of Luke.

Christmas morning found his unit in combat for control of a major bridge that spanned the Euphrates River around Baghdad. After securing the bridge, David was on patrol and heard the whimpering of a baby coming from inside a waste dump. As he lifted the top of the garbage can, to his surprise he discovered a large cardboard box with a newborn baby girl barely alive inside. David carried the baby for seven miles wrapped in his fatigue jacket to the army medical unit. He prayed for her recovery while the doctors fought to keep her alive; miraculously, she survived. The doctors said it was a miracle that the baby survived given the circumstances under which she was found.

After telling his story, David told the class, "It's because of the birth of that tiny baby girl that I sit here today. God used a seemingly insignificant thing—a tiny, helpless baby—to bring His Word to life. I'm thankful to have walked on the same ground as Jesus and His disciples. I am thankful that I serve a mighty God who gives me strength and courage to face the unknown every day."

Today, as we celebrate Jesus' birth, what good news can you share with others?

THE PEOPLE, PLACES, AND TIMES

The City of David. This name was given to the part of Jerusalem that was the Jebusite city after its capture by David (2 Samuel 5). This oldest part of Jerusalem had been an urban site since the early third millennium B.C. and was located in the southeastern part of present-day Jerusalem on a land peninsula that was formed by the Kidron Valley on the east and the Tyropoeon Valley on

the west. The City of David comprised no more than 7.5 to 10 acres and was no more than a medium-sized village.

Other than the Jebusite water shaft and some of the walls of the Jebusite-Davidic city, almost nothing survives in Jerusalem today from the period of David or Solomon. Neither David's palace nor his tomb has ever been found.

Frick, Frank S. Old Testament Studies. San Francisco: Harper, Collins and Row, 1988, 211-12.

BACKGROUND

In today's lesson, we learn that the prophet Isaiah wrote of an important aspect of God's ministry to His people. This particular revelation was used by Jesus Christ, who began His ministry to the nations after His wilderness experience (Luke 4:19-20). The prophet assures us that Jesus Christ came to share the Good News of the kingdom and to restore God's righteousness to fallen humanity.

We are introduced to Jesus Christ, who came into the world as a baby in a manger. Jesus is the Word of God made flesh, and He has become the focal point of human history.

AT-A-GLANCE

1. The Good News of God's Kingdom Is Declared (Isaiah 61:1-2)
2. The Good News of Jesus Is Announced (Luke 2:8-12)
3. The Good News for Humanity Is Proclaimed (vv. 13-15)
4. The Good News of the World Is Seen by the Shepherds (vv.16-20)

IN DEPTH

1. The Good News of God's Kingdom Is Declared (Isaiah 61:1-2)

The prophet Isaiah wrote one of the most powerful passages of Scripture in the Old Testament that directly relates to the ministry and work of Jesus Christ. In fact, when Jesus entered the synagogue in Nazareth, He read this passage of

Scripture and declared that He was the fulfillment of that Word (Luke 4:16-21).

The Servant made an emphatic statement to affirm His relationship with God the Father. "The Spirit of the Lord GOD is upon me; because the LORD hath anointed me to preach good tidings unto the meek" (Isaiah 61:1). Who is the Spirit of the Lord? He is the Second Person of the triune God and very instrumental in the work of creation (Genesis 1:2, 26-27). It was the Spirit of God that brought life to human beings (Genesis 2:7; Ezekiel 37:1-14). Specifically, Isaiah used the term "the Spirit of the Lord" to describe the future empowering work of the Messiah.

The primary difference between the Spirit's work in the Old Testament and that in the New Testament is the way in which the Holy Spirit empowered God's servants. In the Old Testament, His work was for a select few—chosen for special service for God. However, in the New Testament, God's Spirit baptizes and comes to live in believers as they ask in faith for His presence.

The Servant has been anointed for a specific purpose. The phrase "hath anointed" literally means to be chosen and separated by God. The Servant made it clear that He had a tremendous responsibility to share the good news of God's saving faith, especially with those who had lost hope. What can we do to stem the tide of hopelessness? The church must be willing to become the good news for a brokenhearted, captive, and spiritually shackled humanity, just as Jesus committed His life to helping the less fortunate.

The word "captive" (v. 1) has the idea of being exiled and banished to a faraway country. We know that sin separates and "exiles" us from God. But the good news is that God took the initiative to bring the exiles and captives back to Himself through the death and resurrection of Jesus Christ.

Jesus' primary message was to declare "the acceptable year of the LORD" (v. 2). In the Old Testament, "the acceptable year" coincides with Jubilee, the year of release for God's people (Leviticus 25:8-24). In the New Testament, this term refers to the time of Jesus' ministry, which spanned three years and encapsulated God's saving message of redemption. The apostle Paul

describes the acceptable year as "the fulness of the time" (Galatians 4:4).

In Isaiah 61:2, "the day of vengeance of our God" makes reference to the final days of human history, when God Himself will pour out His wrath on the wicked and unrepentant during the time of the Great Tribulation just before the return of Jesus Christ. Jesus made reference to this day in the parable of the sheep and the goats (Matthew 25:31-46). Those who obey the Lord and share the Gospel with those who are hurting and hopeless will receive their place in eternity—that's Good News!

Jesus didn't just preach the Word of the kingdom. He was committed to sharing God's healing and miraculous power, which demonstrated God's love and concern for humankind. We have a tremendous opportunity to share God's healing and miraculous power with people in our community so that they will know that God is a healer today. This Christmas season, let's commit our lives to bringing Good News to people so that they, too, can experience the love of God.

2. The Good News of Jesus Is Announced (Luke 2:8-12)

Our lesson now turns to the Gospel of Luke. Luke was a Gentile convert whose sole purpose for writing this Gospel was to share the life and ministry of Jesus Christ. It is in this light that Luke focuses on some shepherds who were watching over their sheep at almost the same moment that the Son of God was born to Mary and Joseph in Bethlehem (Luke 2:1-7).

We are not told how far away these shepherds were from Bethlehem, but Luke assures us that they were nearby. Yet, as close as they were to the city, these shepherds were as ambivalent about God's miracle as the rest of Bethlehem. But that was about to change.

It may have been cold and dreary the night the shepherds were in the field tending their flock. They were so accustomed to their routine that they may have even drifted off to sleep. However, this night would be different from all others because these shepherds were visited by an angelic messenger who quickly got their attention.

The angel of the Lord declares the birth of Jesus.

From Luke's writing, we can surmise that the angel suddenly appeared before the shepherds in a way that startled them. The shepherds probably wondered why this angelic being would come to them, especially at night. But the angel quickly allayed their fears by sharing the "good tidings of great joy" (v. 10). They would be the first to receive the announcement of the birth of Jesus as the anointed Saviour and Deliverer of God's people (vv. 11-12).

Jesus' birth happened on "this day," indicating that God's message of redemption and hope was immediate. As soon as Jesus was born, the message of His arrival was broadcast to men of no reputation. It is interesting that the announcement of Jesus' birth was given to these humble shepherds, even as Jesus took on the form of a humble Servant to come to earth (Philippians 2:6-7).

Jesus' birth happened in "the city of David," indicating that the prophecy of Micah had come true (Micah 5:2). No doubt these shepherds had heard of the prophecy of the "ruler in Israel" who would come out of Bethlehem. Thus, the angel's declaration confirms the prophecy.

Jesus' birth affirms God's promise of a Saviour to the nations (Matthew 1:21). The word "Saviour" comes from the Greek word *soter* (**so-TARE**), which means "deliverer" and "preserver." Jesus' primary reason for being born into the world was to give His life as payment for our sins and to deliver us from the sinful nature that separates us from God (Isaiah 19:20; John 4:42; Acts 4:12; 5:31; 13:23).

The shepherds were told that the One born would be called "Christ the Lord." The name "Christ" comes from the Greek word *Christos*

(**Khris-TOS**), meaning "the anointed one." In the Old Testament, the high priest was anointed with holy oil to perform his task as God's representative for the people. In like manner, Christ has been anointed by God to become the representative of the New Covenant of righteousness. The angel made sure that these shepherds would have no trouble identifying the Saviour. Once they made their way to the city, they would find the baby in an animal stable "lying in a manger" (v. 12).

What a paradox! Here was the Saviour of the world, the Lord of the universe, born in humble surroundings. Perhaps that is why God chose these humble shepherds to announce the Good News of Jesus' birth.

3. The Good News for Humanity Is Proclaimed (vv. 13-15)

The angelic messenger was not alone. In a moment, he was joined by "a multitude of the heavenly host" [angels] (v. 13), who raised their voices in one accord to declare God's glory and praise for what He had done in Bethlehem. Jesus' birth was predicted long before it occurred (Deuteronomy 18:15, 18; Isaiah 7:14). Now the fulfillment of God's prophetic word compelled these angels to worship the Father.

The angels acknowledged that Jesus' birth affirmed God's honor in heaven and peace on earth. Jesus is the expression of God's glory (Ephesians 3:21; Revelation 5:13). The apostle Paul says that Jesus is our peace because He abolished all enmity and confusion between human beings and God (Ephesians 2:14-16).

As quickly as the angels had appeared, they returned to heaven, leaving the shepherds still wondering about the vision. But the shepherds agreed to leave their flock of sheep and go to Bethlehem to see the miracle that God had shared with them through the angelic messengers.

The birth of Jesus reflects more than just a babe in a manger. God gave His Son to the world so that we may experience God's glory and peace in our own lives. Sometimes we will have to leave the traditional and familiar to experience the powerful miracles that God wants to share with us. That is the Good News of the Christmas message.

4. The Good News of the World Is Seen by the Shepherds (vv. 16-20)

Scripture does not say how the shepherds knew what barn to look in to find Jesus. But they made a diligent search until they found Joseph, Mary, and the baby, just as the angels said they would.

The shepherds acknowledged the family and immediately left the barn to spread the Good News throughout the land. They were excited about hearing the message of love and redemption that was shared with them, and they had the opportunity to share that message with others. God gives us His Word, not to keep it for ourselves, but to share it with as many people as possible. Christmas is a wonderful opportunity to share God's love with family and friends.

The shepherds' message was not readily received by others. In fact, the Bible says that the people "wondered" about the shepherds' excitement (v. 18). During that time, the Bethlehemites were more concerned about the required enrollment imposed by the government than a baby being born in the city. Though the shepherds declared God's Word of hope, the people were unconcerned. Even Mary understood the birth of Jesus to be very significant to the human race, but she "kept all these things, and pondered them in her heart" (v. 19).

The people's lack of concern for God's miracle didn't seem to bother these shepherds. They left the city, returning to the countryside and their flock of sheep, excited about what they had just experienced; not only had they heard from the angelic messengers but they had also had the opportunity to see the Christ child in person. The shepherds rejoiced and praised God, no doubt because they had been chosen by the Father to receive the Good News of Jesus Christ on the day of His birth.

The prophet Isaiah and Luke the physician give us powerful reminders that Jesus Christ came into the world as a babe in a manger to give His life to redeem sinful humankind by proclaiming the acceptable year of our Lord. The good news is that we can receive and incorporate that message into our lives 365 days a year.

SEARCH THE SCRIPTURES

1. What is salvation compared to (Isaiah 61:1)?
2. What shall the Gentiles see (v. 2)?

3. To whom did the angelic messenger give God's Good News (Luke 2:8-12)?

4. Where did the shepherds go to find the fulfillment of the message (v. 15)?

5. What happened after the shepherds saw Jesus Christ in the manger (vv. 17-18)?

6. How did the shepherds react to God's Good News (v. 20)?

DISCUSS THE MEANING

1. In what way does the Gospel message today reflect Isaiah's prophetic word?

2. In what way is the passage in Isaiah connected to Luke's passage in today's lesson?

3. How should the church react to God's Good News for the world today?

4. In what way are people in the world today similar to the people in Bethlehem in Jesus' day?

5. Why was it important for Mary to keep the message in her heart?

LESSON IN OUR SOCIETY

Today is perhaps the most significant date of the Christian calendar, and yet for many people it is just another day to celebrate. Isaiah's prophetic word gives us a glimpse of what we can do to help people understand the significance of Christmas. After studying today's lesson, what specific steps can you take to share with confused and/or hopeless people the Good News of the "acceptable year of the Lord"?

MAKE IT HAPPEN

There are many people who are in need of the Good News of God's love for the world and His gift of Jesus Christ. On this Christmas Day, be prepared to share with someone who may not understand that the babe in the manger represents God's gift of love and redemption for lost and hurting humanity.

FOLLOW THE SPIRIT

What God wants me to do:

_____

_____

REMEMBER YOUR THOUGHTS

Special insights I have learned:

_____

_____

MORE LIGHT ON THE TEXT
Isaiah 61:1-2; Luke 2:8-20

1 The Spirit of the Lord GOD is upon me; because the LORD hath anointed me to preach good tidings unto the meek; he hath sent me to bind up the brokenhearted, to proclaim liberty to the captives, and the opening of the prison to them that are bound;

This is a prophetic declaration about the Saviour that reveals His commission. The Hebrew word *ruwach* (**ROO-akh**) is translated as "spirit" and means "breath." The breath that comes upon the Saviour empowers Him to make divine proclamations. This function is enabled by the anointing. The Hebrew word *mashach* (**maw-SHAKH**) is translated as "anointed" and means "to rub with oil, besmear, or consecrate." The act of anointing signifies the separation of an individual, placing him or her in a position of authority to function in the specified office.

In this passage of Scripture, the prophet Isaiah declares Jesus' earthly mission. First, he says it is "to preach good tidings unto the meek." The Hebrew word *anav* (**aw-NAWV**), translated as "meek," refers to the poor, humble, and needy people of the society. They are people who are financially constrained and socially defenseless. The word *anav* describes their social status, and, as a result of their condition, they are considered afflicted. They are consistently subjected to oppression, and, because of this, God pays special attention to them. The Bible says that whatever kind of treatment is given to them is also given to God (Proverbs 14:31; Matthew 25:40). These are the people to whom the Saviour was sent to preach good news. By virtue of their social status, they are more likely to receive the good news that brings redemption.

The Hebrew word for "brokenhearted" is *shabar* (**shaw-BAR**). It refers to an emotional disposition and means "to break or shatter." The brokenhearted are afflicted in the sense that they are crushed by grief; they are continually filled with agony and pain. The brokenhearted might not be the poor and needy alone; they might also be those who have had an unbearable share of trauma that renders them continually sorrowful. In other words, the Saviour was sent to build up the brokenhearted and to heal the emotionally wounded.

The proclamation "to proclaim liberty to the captives, and the opening of the prison to them that are bound" pertains to the year of Jubilee. The Israelites were required to count seven Sabbath years multiplied by seven years, totaling 49 years. The fiftieth year was proclaimed to be the year of Jubilee, or the year of liberty. The year of Jubilee is a time when all debts are cancelled, slaves are set free or redeemed, and sold properties are returned to their original owners.

2 To proclaim the acceptable year of the LORD, and the day of vengeance of our God; to comfort all that mourn;

This is a proclamation of the era of God's favor—the era of grace. The Hebrew word *rat-sown* (**raw-TSONE**), translated as "acceptable," means "favor, goodwill, or pleasure." The acceptable year is the year of God's favor. This implies the period or era that God is favorably disposed to—a time when He makes the fullness of His blessings available to His people. This is the year the Saviour has come to proclaim.

The Hebrew word *naqam* (**naw-KAWM**), translated as "vengeance," is the retributive punishment God will mete out to His enemies. The day of vengeance refers to a set time when God will avenge Himself on His enemies.

Consequently, the Saviour's proclamation points out the concentration of two distinctive acts of God in two different eras, one coming after the other. First, there is the concentration of God's favor, goodwill, and pleasure, signifying His full covenant blessings, on an era designated as "the acceptable year of the Lord." Second, there is the concentration of retributive punishment on a set time He calls "the day of vengeance of our God."

The Saviour speaks of another function in this verse; He says "to comfort all that mourn." The Hebrew word translated as "comfort" is *nacham* (**naw-KHAM**), while the Hebrew word for "mourn" is *abal* (**aw-BAL**). Mourning occurs when there is a loss of a loved one or relative. It could be synonymous with "lamentation," which occurs when there is loss, destruction, or desolation. Therefore, the Saviour brings consolation to those who have experienced a kind of loss that causes them to mourn.

Luke 2:8 And there were in the same country shepherds abiding in the field, keeping watch over their flock by night. 9 And, lo, the angel of the Lord came upon them, and the glory of the Lord shone round about them: and they were sore afraid.

Here we are introduced to shepherds—a group, or audience, who heard the Good News of the birth of Jesus brought to them by an angel.

The shepherds have a similar vocational calling, on the earthly plane, as the Lord Jesus Christ, who is actually the Good Shepherd from heaven (John 10:11). Jesus is the Good Shepherd who lays down His life to redeem mankind from sin and death.

The presence of the angel brought the glory of the Lord, which shone around them. The Greek word for "glory" is *doxa* (**DOX-ah**). This could also be referring to the supernatural brightness and splendor from the presence of God. The angel conveyed this divine splendor that acted upon the natural surroundings. The appearance of the angel and the majesty of God's glory caused fear to awaken in the hearts of the shepherds—their response to a divine visitation.

10 And the angel said unto them, Fear not: for, behold, I bring you good tidings of great joy, which shall be to all people.

The Greek word *phobeo* (**fob-EH-o**) means "fear." In this sense, it means "to be terrified" or "to be frightened." The shepherds were terrified of the presence of the angel, but the angel quickly allayed their fears and strengthened their hearts to enable them to receive the Good News. The word *phobeo* also means "reverential fear." Reverence for God is a form of response coupled with faith, which opens up people's hearts to Him. This verse contains the preamble to the Good News and serves to make the shepherds early contacts for and witnesses to the good tidings of great joy meant for all people.

11 For unto you is born this day in the city of David a Saviour, which is Christ the Lord.

164

This verse reveals the actual Good News, the birth of the Saviour. The phrase "for unto you" could be referring to the inhabitants of the earth generally. It also could be interpreted as "for your sake" or "as a gift to you." Jesus Christ is truly given for the sake of a dying world. He is a gift to the world. One of the best-known verses of the Bible tells us that Jesus is a gift given out of God's unconditional love for humankind. John 3:16 says, "For God so loved the world, that he gave his only begotten Son, that whosoever believeth in him should not perish, but have everlasting life."

12 And this shall be a sign unto you; Ye shall find the babe wrapped in swaddling clothes, lying in a manger.

The babe wrapped in swaddling clothes and lying in a manger was a sign for the shepherds to enable them to identify the infant Jesus when they went to look for Him in Bethlehem, the City of David. The Greek word translated as "sign" is *semeion* (**say-MI-on**); it refers to a mark, indication, or token that distinguishes someone or something from others.

The Greek word translated as "swaddling clothes" is *sparganoo* (**spar-gan-O-o**), which means to strap or wrap with strips or bandages. The swaddling clothes were narrow bandages wrapped around the infant Jesus. Instead of a crib, the Baby Jesus lay in a stable in a box or trough to feed cattle or horses.

The nativity scene usually portrays Christ wrapped in swaddling clothes and lying in a manger in a stable. These cirucumstances are peculiar to Christ alone, and together they constitute a "sign" that distinguishes His birth from the birth of any other child born in Bethlehem at that time. These distinguishing features were sure to aid the shepherds in identifying Him. This "sign" was a mark of Christ's humble beginnings and conforms to Scripture in that it expresses the enclosure of a great and significant end in an ignoble beginning. The Scripture says, "Though thy beginning was small, yet thy latter end should greatly increase" (Job 8:7). This points to the fact that this babe, wrapped in swaddling clothes and lying in a manger, would be the Saviour of the world. He would grow up to redeem mankind from the powers of sin and death and from eternal damnation.

13 And suddenly there was with the angel a multitude of the heavenly host praising God, and saying, 14 Glory to God in the highest, and on earth peace, good will toward men.

After the angel delivered the Good News to the shepherds, a praise session started, performed by a multitude of angels who joined the heavenly emissary. The Greek word translated as "praise" is *aineo* (**ahee-NEH-o**); it means "to speak in praise of" or "to praise." The angels praised God; they sang of His Majesty and offered Him glory.

The birth of Christ, the Saviour, is the revelation of God's redemptive plan, which established peace and goodwill for mankind—according to the lyrics of the angelic "praise" team. The Greek word translated as "peace" is *eirene* (**i-RAY-nay**). It describes a harmonious relationship, friendliness, and freedom from molestation. The birth of Christ brought about peace. This means there is an opportunity for man to be reconciled to God (2 Corinthians 5:18), to be on friendly terms with Him in a harmonious relationship, and to enter into His rest, free from molestation (Hebrews 4:9-10). Isaiah 53:5 also reveals that "the chastisement of our peace [that chastisement that brought us peace] was upon him."

The Greek word translated as "good will" is *eudokia* (**yoo-dok-EE-ah**). It means to think well of or have good thoughts toward someone. This tells us that, as a result of the birth of Christ, there will be peace on earth to all people on whom God's goodwill rests.

15 And it came to pass, as the angels were gone away from them into heaven, the shepherds said one to another, Let us now go even unto Bethlehem, and see this thing which is come to pass, which the Lord hath made known unto us.

After the departure of the heavenly choir, the shepherds went seeking the Saviour. Believing what they had been told, they went to Bethlehem to see what had happened. The Greek word *ginomai* (**GHIN-om-ahee**), which is translated as "to come to pass," means "to become" or "to take place." This word is used frequently in the

Synoptic Gospels and refers to something that is done, has taken place, or has already happened. The message of the angels roused curiosity and faith in the shepherds, and this motivated them to go to Bethlehem.

The Greek word translated as "made known" is *gnorizo* (**gno-RID-zo**), which means "to come, know, or discover." With this message, the angel brought the shepherds to the point of having knowledge of the birth of the Saviour. They came to know, they came in contact with knowledge—the knowledge of the Word of God—and this roused faith in them. We have to respond to God in faith.

16 And they came with haste, and found Mary, and Joseph, and the babe lying in a manger. 17 And when they had seen it, they made known abroad the saying which was told them concerning this child.

Roused by curiosity, acting in faith, and filled with an intense desire, the shepherds hastily arrived at the scene of the birth of Christ. The Greek word *speudo* (**SPYOO-do**), translated as "with haste," means "speed." Literally, it implies immediate action on the part of the shepherds; thus, the phrase "they came with haste" can be interpreted as "they came immediately or expeditiously."

Upon coming to the scene of Christ's birth, they found the babe lying in a manger just as the angel had said. The second part of their faith at work was the fact that "they made known abroad the saying." The Greek word translated as "made known abroad" is *diagnorizo* (**dee-ag-no-RID-zo**). The prefix "dia," which means "through" modifies the verb *gnorizo* and denotes information that is "sent through all ears" or that "cuts across" to all people.

The Greek word *rhema* (**HRAY-mah**), translated as "saying," means "a word" or "that which is proclaimed." After they had seen the babe, the shepherds went, disseminating what they had been told by the angel concerning the Lord. They went out to proclaim the message, thereby increasing the number of those who heard the Good News of Christ's birth and becoming evangelists and soul winners.

It is the spiritual responsibility of believers to be witnesses for Christ. All believers should take their place in this end-time harvest. Commendable witnessing is done effectively when one expresses the power, love, and wisdom of God through service. This is done through missions work and various Christian outreach programs that pervade the home, the church, and the entire community.

18 And all they that heard it wondered at those things which were told them by the shepherds. 19 But Mary kept all these things, and pondered them in her heart.

It was a thing of wonder to those who heard the story proclaimed by the shepherds. The Greek word translated as "wondered" is *thaumazo* (**thou-MAD-zo**), which means "amazement." The hearers of the proclamation expressed amazement at the message of the shepherds. When we witness to people around us, we can hold them in wonder and awe of God as they see the power of God's might in the very things we say and do.

The Greek word translated as "pondered" is *sumballo* (**soom-BAL-lo**), which means to put things together in the process of considering. Mary "put the events together" in her heart as she experienced an internal awakening to divine truth and manifestation, which kept her in constant bewilderment. The Good News must have an amazing impact on the soul and cause an awakening.

20 And the shepherds returned, glorifying and praising God for all the things that they had heard and seen, as it was told unto them.

The shepherds had been awakened. They heard the Good News, went to Bethlehem and saw for themselves, and returned with praises for God. The amazing effect of the Good News is that it awakens you to the reality of life, enlightens you on how to live life, and enlivens you to conform your life to Christ. This is the transformation process that leads sinners to conversion.

This verse tells us that the shepherds heard, believed, acted, saw, proclaimed, and, finally, glorified and praised God. The way the shepherds responded to the Good News is commendable. Upon hearing the news, they believed—this was an expression of faith. The shepherds acted based upon what they had heard by going to Bethlehem to see for themselves what had been told to them; this is faith backed by actions. When we go out to evangelize and proclaim what we believe so that others can be saved, we back up our faith with actions. James (2:17) says, "Even so faith, if it hath not works, is dead, being alone."

When the shepherds got to Bethlehem, they actually saw the baby lying in a manger as they had been told by the angel. Because they believed and acted upon their belief, they saw with their eyes. Jesus said to Martha, "Said I not unto thee, that, if thou wouldest believe, thou shouldest see the glory of God?" (John 11:40). If we believe, we will behold the glory of God.

What they received, they proclaimed. The shepherds heard the Good News and actually saw the Saviour. They had received the divine information and believed it in their hearts, and they proclaimed it: "for of the abundance of the heart his mouth speaketh" (Luke 6:45). Let us fill our hearts with the Word of God so that we will speak gracious words that edify, strengthen, and bring about the salvation of lost souls.

Finally, the shepherds glorified God and offered praises to Him. We are called to praise God.

DAILY BIBLE READINGS

M: God's Justice and Deliverance Never End
Isaiah 51:1-6

T: God's Messenger Brings Good News
Isaiah 52:7-12

W: God Will Be Your Glory
Isaiah 60:17-22

T: Good News for the Oppressed
Isaiah 61:1-7

F: God Gives Salvation and Righteousness
Isaiah 61:8-62:3

S: Mary Has a Baby
Luke 2:1-7

S: The Angels Bring Good News
Luke 2:8-21

TEACHING TIPS

January 1
Bible Study Guide 5

1. Words You Should Know

A. Mercy (1 Timothy 1:13, 16) *eleeo* (Gk.)—Kindness in excess of what may be expected or demanded by fairness; God's loving-kindness toward humankind.

B. Blasphemer (v. 13) *blasphemos* (Gk.)—One who speaks evil or speaks irreverently or profanely of or to God or anything held as divine.

C. Pattern (v. 16) *hupotuposis* (Gk.)—A model, example, or prototype; a person or thing to be imitated.

2. Teacher Preparation

A. Pray for understanding before engaging in the lesson.

B. Read the BIBLE BACKGROUND.

C. Read BIBLE STUDY GUIDE 5 and record any insights you might want to share with the students.

D. Collect and make copies of doxologies. Examples are: "Glory to God in the highest," "Glory be to the Father," and "Praise God from Whom All Blessings Flow."

3. Starting the Lesson

A. Before the students arrive, write the words from the WORDS YOU SHOULD KNOW section on the board or on newsprint.

B. Lead the class in prayer. Focus your prayer on the main themes in the LESSON AIM.

C. Instruct the students to silently read the IN FOCUS section. Then discuss the story as a group.

4. Getting into the Lesson

A. Have the students read the words on the board. Ask them to use each word in a sentence or give the definition of each word.

B. Ask volunteers to read THE PEOPLE, PLACES, AND TIMES and the BACKGROUND section.

C. Ask a couple of students to take turns reading the FOCAL VERSES as outlined in the AT-A-GLANCE section.

D. Ask for volunteers to read the IN DEPTH section. Then discuss the key themes.

5. Relating the Lesson to Life

A. Ask volunteers to read the SEARCH THE SCRIPTURES questions. Next, ask for volunteers to share their answers.

B. Help the students apply the lesson to their lives by leading them in the examination of the DISCUSS THE MEANING questions and the LESSON IN OUR SOCIETY section.

C. Call the students' attention to the MAKE IT HAPPEN section and give them time to complete the assignment.

6. Arousing Action

A. Ask the students to select one thing they will do this week to show their gratitude for what God has done in their lives.

B. Remind the students to read the DAILY BIBLE READINGS.

C. Close the class with prayer.

WORSHIP GUIDE

For the Superintendent or Teacher
Theme: God Gives Strength
Theme Song: "All Glory, Laud, and Honor"
Scripture: Philippians 4:13
Song: "Your Grace and Mercy"
Meditation: Dear God, thank You for redeeming me from my sins. Please give me the strength to overcome any obstacles that would prevent me from following the path You have set before me. Amen.

GOD GIVES STRENGTH

Bible Background • 1 TIMOTHY 1
Printed Text • 1 TIMOTHY 1:12–20
Devotional Reading • ROMANS 16:17–27

LESSON AIM

By the end of the lesson, we will:

UNDERSTAND that God offers mercy, grace, and strength to all who believe in Jesus Christ;

BE ENCOURAGED by Christ Jesus, who gives us strength for His service; and

SET an example for those who have been strengthened by faith in Jesus Christ.

KEEP IN MIND

"And I thank Christ Jesus our Lord, who hath enabled me, for that he counted me faithful, putting me into the ministry" (1 Timothy 1:12).

FOCAL VERSES

1 Timothy 1:12 And I thank Christ Jesus our Lord, who hath enabled me, for that he counted me faithful, putting me into the ministry;

13 Who was before a blasphemer, and a persecutor, and injurious: but I obtained mercy, because I did it ignorantly in unbelief.

14 And the grace of our Lord was exceeding abundant with faith and love which is in Christ Jesus.

15 This is a faithful saying, and worthy of all acceptation, that Christ Jesus came into the world to save sinners; of whom I am chief.

16 Howbeit for this cause I obtained mercy, that in me first Jesus Christ might shew forth all long-suffering, for a pattern to them which should hereafter believe on him to life everlasting.

17 Now unto the King eternal, immortal, invisible, the only wise God, be honour and glory for

LESSON OVERVIEW

LESSON AIM
KEEP IN MIND
FOCAL VERSES
IN FOCUS
THE PEOPLE, PLACES,
AND TIMES
BACKGROUND
AT-A-GLANCE
IN DEPTH
SEARCH THE SCRIPTURES
DISCUSS THE MEANING
LESSON IN OUR SOCIETY
MAKE IT HAPPEN
FOLLOW THE SPIRIT
REMEMBER YOUR THOUGHTS
MORE LIGHT ON THE TEXT
DAILY BIBLE READINGS

ever and ever. Amen.

18 This charge I commit unto thee, son Timothy, according to the prophecies which went before on thee, that thou by them mightest war a good warfare;

JAN 1ST

19 Holding faith, and a good conscience; which some having put away concerning faith have made shipwreck:

20 Of whom is Hymenaeus and Alexander; whom I have delivered unto Satan, that they may learn not to blaspheme.

IN FOCUS

Sonny sat in his living room chair dressed for a New Year's celebration at his home. His thoughts focused on his pastor's call for him to teach Bible class. Sonny used every imaginable excuse not to teach. Even though he felt he was called by God to teach, he ignored His calling. He continually asked himself, "Why am I making it so hard to do what God has placed on my heart?"

As he got up and went into the kitchen, he opened the liquor cabinet, poured himself a drink, and reflected on his last meeting with his pastor.

"Sonny, you're a great student of the Word. If God told you to teach, what makes you feel so inadequate?" the pastor asked.

Sonny felt ashamed. Since his release from prison four years ago, Sonny's life had begun to unfold beautifully. He owned his own home, had a good job, and was a true believer in the righteousness of Christ Jesus. His eyes must have shown his hopelessness and sadness. From the outside, there appeared to be no reason for Sonny's sadness.

"The Lord asks us not to be afraid. What is it you fear?" asked the pastor.

Before he could swallow the words in his throat, Sonny's secret fell out of his mouth so loudly it startled him. "I drink alcohol!"

Startled, the pastor asked, "Are you saying you are an alcoholic?"

"Never!" Sonny said. The pastor read the conviction in his voice as truth.

"Sonny, you are a walking testimony of God's grace and mercy. You must realize that we all fall short and learn to use our struggles and hardships for God's glory and to serve His people."

What do you need from God to provide you with the strength for better service? Today's lesson will focus on Paul's message to rely on God for strength to serve.

THE PEOPLE, PLACES, AND TIMES

The apostle Paul. Paul was born to Jewish parents in the first century A.D. in Tarsus, a rich, cosmopolitan city located in modern-day Turkey. Greek culture and language dominated the Mediterranean world in the first century. Therefore, as a young boy Paul learned the Scriptures from the Septuagint (LXX), the Greek translation of the Hebrew Bible. "Paul" was his Greek name. However, his Hebrew name was Shaul or Saul. Paul was a devout Jew and a Pharisee, who strictly observed the Jewish law. His devotion to Judaism led Paul to persecute Jewish Christians, whom he viewed as a threat to the Jewish religion. Jesus Christ convicted Paul on the road to Damascus, and Paul became a follower of Christ. Paul founded several churches and trained many church leaders, both male and female.

Blasphemy. A transliteration of a Greek word meaning literally "to speak harm." In the biblical context, blasphemy is an attitude of disrespect that finds expression in an act directed against the character of God. The New Testament use of the term is understood in relation to the Old Testament concept. Blasphemy was the use of God's name along with an improper attitude. It

was an offense punishable by death (Leviticus 24:14-16). The New Testament broadens the concept of blasphemy to include actions against Christ and against the church as the body of Christ. Christ equates Paul's persecution of the church with his persecution of Christ (Acts 9:5). Paul later refers to his persecution of Christians as blasphemy (1 Timothy 1:13).

BACKGROUND

First Timothy is one of three letters referred to as the "pastoral letters" because of their concern for the pastoral office and other church leadership positions. The others are 2 Timothy and Titus. This letter addresses the problem of false teachings within the community. Certain members of the church at Ephesus were promoting doctrine that Paul opposed, such as asceticism, Gnosticism, and attention to myths and genealogies. Paul writes to Timothy to encourage him to confront the false teachers and eradicate their false doctrine and to prepare Timothy for the spiritual battle that will ensue.

AT-A-GLANCE

**1. Paul's Conversion and Call
(1 Timothy 1:12-17)
2. Paul's Charge to Timothy
(vv. 18-20)**

IN DEPTH

1. Paul's Conversion and Call
(1 Timothy 1:12-17)

Paul's letter is addressed to Timothy, but it was intended to be read to the entire congregation at Ephesus. Paul reviews his life as Saul of Tarsus, the zealous Jew who once opposed the Christian faith so vehemently that he pursued Christians, male and female, to destroy them (Acts 9:1-2). While on a mission to capture Christians fleeing persecution and return them to Jerusalem for sentencing, Paul encountered the risen Christ and was converted to Christianity himself. Jesus Christ called Paul to preach the Gospel to high officials and ordinary citizens alike.

Paul conveys his thankfulness to Christ for trusting him enough to call him to be His messenger and giving him the grace and strength to accomplish his mission. He also expresses his gratitude to God for showing him mercy even when he uttered strong language against Christ and pursued Christians for execution. Paul declares the trustworthiness of the message that he has been preaching about the salvific activity of Jesus Christ by stating, "This is a faithful saying." This introductory phrase appears four other times in the pastoral letters (1 Timothy 4:9; Titus 3:8).

Even though Paul considers himself the greatest of sinners, he attests to the mercy of God in forgiving such a chief transgressor. He states that his life is an example of Christ's abundant grace revealed through Christ. Paul lifts up his life as an example for such persons who might come to believe on Jesus Christ and receive eternal life.

Paul concludes his summary of his conversion and call with a doxology, words or expressions of glory to God in response to His mercy and grace. Paul's doxology follows traditional Jewish prayers or praise that was often recited or sung at the end of a psalm or prayer; this was likely a doxology used in Jewish synagogue worship during the first century. Doxologies include praise to God and attest to the infinite nature of God. The "amen" at the end anticipates the hearers' assent to the truthfulness of the statement. In other words, "amen" means "Let it be so."

2. Paul's Charge to Timothy (vv. 18-20)

Paul had previously implored Timothy to remain in Ephesus to deal with certain people in the congregation who were spreading doctrine contrary to that which Paul had taught (1 Timothy 1:3, 5). Now Paul renews his charge to Timothy by recalling the prophecies spoken about him at the time of his ordination and encouraging him to "fight the good fight" against the false teachers in their midst. The "good fight" was a common phrase used by Greek philosophers and moralists in their intellectual skirmishes with their opponents for the truth. The meaning of the phrase was not lost on Timothy, who was gearing up for his own battle for truth.

Paul identifies by name certain individuals who, having abandoned a good conscience, had strayed from the faith. He uses the familiar maritime metaphor of a ship that has gone off course and crashed among the rocks to describe the situation of his opponents, Hymenaeus and Alexander. Their false teachings had led them to depart from the path of true doctrine, with disastrous results. Paul expels them from the community of believers in Ephesus. However, the excommunication of Hymenaeus and Alexander is not for the purpose of excluding them permanently from the church. Rather, their exclusion is intended to help them see the error of their ways and repent.

SEARCH THE SCRIPTURES

1. For what does Paul give thanks to Christ Jesus (1 Timothy 1:12)?

2. What reason does Paul give for his past transgressions (v. 13)?

3. What does Paul say is a faithful saying (v. 15)?

4. For what situation is Paul trying to prepare Timothy (v. 18)?

DISCUSS THE MEANING

1. Paul describes the trust that Jesus Christ placed in him to carry the Gospel to nations and peoples. Paul was able to fulfill his mission because Christ enabled him to do so. Do you believe that Christ has given you the strength to accomplish His will in your life?

2. Paul lists some major transgressions that he committed for which God had forgiven him as evidence of God's mercy. Do you think that believers should publicly acknowledge their past offenses to help nonbelievers come to accept that Jesus Christ came into the world to save sinners from eternal condemnation?

3. Paul was trying to prepare Timothy to combat the false teachings that had infiltrated the church in Ephesus. Why do you believe that it was important for Timothy, as the pastor of the church, to confront false doctrines being spread in the congregation?

LESSON IN OUR SOCIETY

More than 50 years ago, the United States Supreme Court decided the landmark case *Brown v. Board of Education* (Topeka, Kansas). Many children and their families endured harassment, humiliation, loss of employment, and loss of their homes to desegregate public schools in the United States. Many of these individuals expressed that their faith in God was what inspired them and gave them the courage to take on such a lofty endeavor. Moreover, they explained that it was God who gave them the strength to carry on in such difficult times.

At the time, this task of desegregating American schools by African American parents for the sake of their children's education and future seemed insurmountable. However, we can look back and see how God was working through certain individuals to demolish segregation. Persons born after 1965 probably have no recollection of the segregation of public institutions by race. In fact, many young people complain that either their parents did not share with them their civil rights struggles in the past, or that there are no struggles to participate in today. What are some of the social issues of concern today that you can identify? How does your faith inform you how you should respond to these issues?

MAKE IT HAPPEN

Paul closed the summary of his conversion and call to Christian discipleship and leadership with a doxology, or words of glory (1 Timothy 1:17). Write your own doxology. Be sure to include words of praise for the mercy and grace God has shown in your life and examples of God's infinite nature. Don't forget the "Amen."

FOLLOW THE SPIRIT

What God wants me to do:

_____

_____

REMEMBER YOUR THOUGHTS

Special insights I have learned:

_____

_____

MORE LIGHT ON THE TEXT
1 Timothy 1:12-20

12 And I thank Christ Jesus our Lord, who hath enabled me, for that he counted me faithful, putting me into the ministry;

Saturating this verse is the spirit of thankfulness. Paul was thankful to Jesus, who enabled him to serve and entrusted him with his ministry. The Greek word for "thank" is *charis* (**KHAR-ece**), meaning "graciousness" or "gratitude." Paul served with a tremendous sense of gratitude for all God had done for him.

One of the key Greek words to note in this verse is *endunamoo* (**en-doo-nam-O-o**), meaning "to empower" or "enable." Paul acknowledged that his ministry was by no means accomplished through his own strength. All he ever achieved was through God's empowerment. This echoes Paul's testimony in Philippians 4:13, where he notes the following: "I can do all things through Christ which strengtheneth me."

God counted Paul faithful. The word "counted" comes from the Greek word *hegeomai* (**hayg-EH-om-ahee**), and means "to deem or consider." God gave him grace to be trustworthy. Man looks at the outward appearance to determine whether a person will be successful or is worthy to be trusted. God, however, uses other criteria. In a day in which image is everything, God regards character as more important.

The Greek word for "faithful" is *pistos* (**pis-TOS**), which means "trustworthy or trustful." We often hear politicians tell us that one's private life has no bearing on public service, yet the teaching of this verse clearly is otherwise. Because he was a man of integrity, Paul found strength to preach the Gospel as God chose him and enabled him to serve.

God found Paul faithful and put him into ministry. The word "put" comes from the Greek word *tithemi* (**TITH-ay-mee**), which means "to appoint or place." Paul was keenly aware that his ministry was not something he sought and secured for himself. Rather, God had positioned him in his ministry and he served daily with this knowledge.

Paul considered his efforts for God to be a ministry. The word "ministry" comes from the Greek word *diakonia* (**dee-ak-on-EE-ah**), which means "attendance as a servant." Paul viewed himself as God's servant. It is also apparent from this verse that Paul accepted the responsibilities that went along with his appointment to ministry. Penetrating his mind was the thought that he was accountable to God and that he must fulfill God's expectations for his life.

13 Who was before a blasphemer, and a persecutor, and injurious; but I obtained mercy, because I did it ignorantly in unbelief.

Not only did Paul serve with a sense of gratitude for all the blessings he received, but he also knew how far God had brought him. He said he was formerly a blasphemer. The word "before" comes from the Greek word *proteron* (**PROT-er-on**), meaning "earlier" or "in former times." Before Paul came to Christ, he lived a life that denied the teachings of Christ. Even though he was a Pharisee of Pharisees, his life was motivated by selfish ambition; but through the power of the Gospel, his life was changed.

Before Paul came to Christ, he was a "blasphemer." The Greek word is *blasphemos* (**BLAS-fay-mos**), which means "slanderous or scurrilous." Blasphemy is speaking evil of God and was punishable by death in the Old Testament. Paul was also a "persecutor." The Greek word is *dioko* (**dee-O-ko**), which means "subject to harassment or cruel treatment." Prior to his conversion, Paul was "injurious." The Greek word is *biaios* (**BEE-ah-yos**), which means "violent." Acts 9:1 records that Paul visited the high priest with murderous intent. Shortly after this, in the same chapter, Paul was converted on the Damascus Road.

Paul then explains how his life was changed. He says he obtained God's mercy. The phrase "obtained mercy" comes from the Greek word *eleeo* (**el-eh-EH-o**), which means "to be compas-

sionate" by word or deed. The noun form of this word, *eleos* (**el-eh-os**), is usually defined as the outward expression of pity. Even though Paul was a despicable person, God looked beyond that and showed him grace and mercy.

Paul makes a surprising admission in this verse. He says that his violent past was lived ignorantly in unbelief. The word "ignorantly" comes from the Greek word *agnoeo* (**ag-no-EH-o**), which means "not to know." Does he make an excuse for his lifestyle prior to trusting Christ as Saviour?

Jesus gives us strength to serve.

Not at all. He simply admits that his unbelief prevented him from acting any differently. The word "unbelief" comes from the Greek word *apaistia* (**ap-is-TEE-ah**), meaning "faithlessness" or "disbelief." Paul confesses that his violent abuse of Christians was compelled by his disobedience. This prevented him from understanding his actions. However, God was able to work around his disobedient spirit and bring him to Christ.

14 And the grace of our Lord was exceeding abundant with faith and love which is in Christ Jesus.

The Greek word for "grace" is *charis* (**KHAR-ece**), meaning "favor." This word is used as an expression of gratitude or thanks. It is used in this verse to describe God's gracious favor toward His children. Paul describes God's grace as being "exceeding abundant." The word "exceeding" comes from the Greek word *huperpleonazo* (**hoop-er-pleh-on-AD-zo**), meaning "beyond measure" or "superabundant." God's grace transcended anything Paul had ever imagined. Paul's salvation, as well as strength for service, was rooted in God's grace, which was found in his Saviour and Lord.

Paul not only found God's grace to be beyond measure, but God's faith and love were also superabundant. "Faith" comes from the Greek word *pistos* (**pis-TOS**), meaning "trustworthy." "Love" comes from the Greek word *agape* (**ag-AH-pay**), meaning "affection" or "benevolence." These qualities are rooted in God's character and are immeasurable because of His infinite nature.

These superabundant realities are in Christ Jesus. Jesus Christ is the source of all spiritual truth, and this theme is announced throughout Scripture. Paul notes in Ephesians 1:3 that we have been blessed with every spiritual blessing in Christ. These blessings, which are beyond measure, are made available through our infinite Saviour. Jesus Christ is unlimited and illimitable. Everything about Him is outside the limits placed upon common man. His infinite nature also extends to His attributes.

15 This is a faithful saying, and worthy of all acceptation, that Christ Jesus came into the world to save sinners; of whom I am chief.

Because Paul experienced the life-changing power of the Gospel, he affirmed its claims to be true. He referred to the message of the Gospel as a faithful saying. The word "faithful" comes from the same Greek word found in verse 12. "Saying" comes from the Greek word *logos* (**log-os**), meaning "communication." In other words, Paul says that this message about the Word is worthy to be believed. It can be believed because he had personally witnessed Christ change his life. Paul demonstrated the most effective endorsement of the Gospel—a changed life. This testimony is worthy of all acceptance. The word "acceptance"

comes from the Greek word *apodochomai* (**ap-od-EKH-om-ahee**), meaning to "receive favorably." Paul said that all who hear it should welcome the message of salvation.

The message of this faithful saying is that Jesus came into the world to save sinners. This is a clear reference to His birth. The reason for His birth was to save sinners. Paul contemplated this and reflected on his own great sinfulness. As he did this, he realized the primary purpose of Christ's coming. It was not to teach great morals or to provide an example of a sacrificial life spent helping others. Neither did Jesus come to present to the world great philosophical truths. Instead, the clear purpose of Jesus' birth was to save sinners like himself.

The word "save" comes from the Greek word *sozo* (**SODE-zo**), meaning "to deliver or protect." This was the focus of Paul's ministry. His life was spent teaching the message of the Gospel to others and leading them to the One who saved him. Who needs to be saved? All need to be delivered from sin because all are sinners. Paul declared in the book of Romans that all have sinned and fall short of the glory of God. Therefore, all need to be saved.

Paul called himself the chief of sinners. The word "chief" comes from the Greek word *protos* (**PRO-tos**), meaning "foremost." Paul viewed his own sinfulness in the present tense, not the past tense, because the force of the Greek is the significant present. In other words, Paul stated, "I am the foremost sinner." He was keenly aware of his own sinful tendencies, even after coming to Christ and knowing salvation, and he lived with a certain degree of regret for his persecution of the church.

16 Howbeit for this cause I obtained mercy, that in me first Jesus Christ might shew forth all longsuffering, for a pattern to them which should hereafter believe on him to life everlasting.

Paul viewed his salvation as a part of God's greater plan. For him, there was a cause for his coming to faith in Christ. The word "cause" comes from the Greek word *dia* (**dee-AH**), meaning the "channel" of an act. Paul realized he was brought to Christ, not only because of his own deep spiritual need, but for a greater purpose. His salvation served as evidence to others of what God is able to do in the life of even the most violent of sinners.

How is Christ's long-suffering revealed through Paul's coming to faith in Him? The word "long-suffering" comes from the Greek word *makrothumia* (**mak-roth-oo-MEE-ah**), meaning "forbearance" or "patience." Jesus Christ patiently calls people to come to Him. He did the same with Paul, who violently opposed the Gospel for many years.

Paul's conversion served as a pattern for others to follow. The word "pattern" comes from the Greek word *hupotuposis* (**hoop-ot-OOP-o-sis**), meaning a sketch for imitation or a form. Paul knew that if God could reach him, considering his state of unbelief, then his conversion experience could be used to reach others also. It is important to realize the impact of Paul's coming to faith in Christ. His use of the Greek word *hupotuposis* shows us that not only was his life after his conversion a witness and testimony to others, but his actual conversion experience was also a witness for others to follow.

Paul never lost sight of the greater purpose of his life and the reason why he was so blessed to experience God's grace. He had in view the greater vision of those who still needed to believe in Christ. He kept the hereafter in mind. The word "hereafter" comes from the Greek word *mello* (**MEL-lo**), which carries with it the idea of expectation. Paul lived in a state of expectation, knowing that others needed what he had. Because of his unbelieving past, Paul was keenly aware that others lived in ignorance of the grace and mercy of God, and he prayed constantly that God would use his testimony so that others might also believe in Christ for salvation.

The greatest result Paul desired to see was for others to believe on Christ for everlasting life. The word "believe" comes from the Greek word *pisteuo* (**pist-YOO-o**), meaning to have faith in a person or thing. Paul's ministry included the deep needs of others to believe in Christ for salvation. His ministry brought others to a trust in Christ, which leads to life everlasting.

17 Now unto the King eternal, immortal, invisible, the only wise God, be honour and glory for ever and ever. Amen.

Paul's reflection upon the grace of God, realizing its power in his personal life and ministry to lead others to it, compelled him to declare a doxology of praise. He declared God to be his King. The word "King" comes from the Greek word *basileus* (**bas-il-YOOCE**), meaning "sovereign." Paul's doxology briefly contemplated God's attributes.

God is eternal. The word "eternal" comes from the Greek word *aion* (**ahee-OHN**), meaning "perpetuity." God is eternal in that He exists forever and ever. He is immortal. The word "immortal" comes from the Greek word *apthartos* (**AF-thar-tos**), meaning "undecaying." God, because He is eternal, never decays or corrupts. He is also invisible. The word "invisible" comes from the Greek word *aoratos* (**ah-OR-at-os**), meaning "unseen." And He alone is wise. In light of these divine attributes, Paul declared that God is worthy of honor. The word "honour" comes from the Greek word *time* (**tee-MAY**), meaning "to esteem in the highest degree." And God is worthy of glory. The word "glory" comes from the Greek word *doxa* (**DOX-ah**), meaning "dignity."

18 This charge I commit unto thee, son Timothy, according to the prophecies which went before on thee, that thou by them mightest war a good warfare;

Paul reminded Timothy of his charge. "Charge" comes from the Greek word *paraggelia* (**par-ang-gel-EE-ah**), meaning "mandate." The mandate given to Timothy related to his ministry. Paul recalled the words spoken at the inception of Timothy's ministry. These words, as well as Paul's reminder, served to guide Timothy through the treacherous waters of life and ministry. Service for God is difficult, and His servants need constant reminders of the trust and responsibilities given to them.

Paul delivered his mandate to Timothy in the form of a commitment. The Greek word for "commit" is *paratithemi* (**par-at-ITH-ay-mee**), meaning "to deposit or present." Timothy had been handed a commitment. Since ministry is often difficult, commitment is especially important. Paul realized this and sought to communicate this concept to his young disciple, Timothy.

When times are tough, those who are truly committed will pursue their mandate at any cost. Those who are not committed will ultimately drop out.

Timothy is encouraged to wage the good warfare. The Greek words used in this verse refer to military terminology. The verb "to war" comes from the Greek word *strateuomai* (**strat-YOO-om-ahee**), meaning "to serve in a military campaign." Paul used current military terms to discuss spiritual warfare. He encouraged Timothy to wage spiritual warfare as a good soldier of Jesus Christ.

19 Holding faith, and a good conscience; which some having put away concerning faith have made shipwreck:

God provides strength for ministry, and this strength comes through faith and a good conscience. As we read earlier, faith comes from the Greek word *pistos* (**PIS-tos**), meaning "trust or confidence" in God. The good soldier prepares for spiritual warfare by faith and confidence in God, not in self.

Along with faith, a good conscience is also required. The word "conscience" comes from the Greek word *suneidesis* (**soon-I-day-sis**), meaning "moral consciousness." Paul also described the conscience needed for effective ministry. It must be good. The word "good" comes from the Greek word *agathos* (**ag-ath-os**), meaning "worthy of admiration and respect."

Why is a good conscience important for effective ministry? A good conscience is a sign of personal integrity and inward character. The person who claims to follow Christ, but whose personal life does not back that up, lives in denial of what they say they believe. Therefore, this person lacks personal integrity. When these persons teach Christian principles and urge others to pursue personal integrity, while lacking it themselves, their teaching will not be received positively. The result is disastrous on both a personal and public level.

Paul described the result as a shipwreck. The word "shipwreck" comes from the Greek word *nauageo* (**now-ag-EH-o**), meaning "to be stranded" or "to suffer severe damge or destruction." Who were these whose faith was shipwrecked? They were false teachers Timothy had to deal with.

20 Of whom is Hymenaeus and Alexander; whom I have delivered unto Satan, that they may learn not to blaspheme.

Paul revealed how he handled Hymenaeus and Alexander, who were false teachers he encountered in his ministry. Their ways had become so serious that he delivered them to Satan. The word "delivered" comes from the Greek word *paradidomi* (**par-ad-ID-o-mee**), meaning "to give over or yield up." Paul apparently had these false teachers excommunicated from the church.

What was the ultimate goal of their excommunication? Paul desired that they would learn from this action. "To learn" comes from the Greek word *paideuo* (**pahee-DYOO-o**), meaning "to train up a child" or, by implication, "to discipline." Even in the case of false teachers, Paul wanted to teach them and restore them. His solution was severe, but it was required since the effect of their teaching was so disastrous.

Paul wanted to stop their blasphemy. As these false teachers spoke evil teachings, they defamed the name of Christ. Therefore, Paul chose to deal with them by removing them from fellowship, but he maintained hope that they would learn the error of their ways and repent.

DAILY BIBLE READINGS

M: Strengthen Me, O God
Psalm 119:25-32
T: God Is Able to Strengthen You
Romans 16:17-27
W: We Sent Timothy to Strengthen You
1 Thessalonians 3:1-5
T: May God Strengthen Your Hearts
1 Thessalonians 3:6-13
F: Paul, Silas, and Timothy Strengthen Churches
Acts 16:1-5
S: Paul Writes to Timothy
1 Timothy 1:1-11
S: Strengthened by Christ
1 Timothy 1:12-20

TEACHING TIPS

January 8
Bible Study Guide 6

1. Words You Should Know

A. Supplications (1 Timothy 2:1) *deesis* (Gk.)—A humble seeking, asking, or entreaty to God or to man, usually on behalf of oneself.

B. Prayers (v. 1) *proseuche* (Gk.)—Attempted communication with God designed to affect the course of the relationship with the divine.

C. Intercessions (v. 1) *enteuxis* (Gk.)—Entreaty in favor of another, especially a prayer or petition to God on behalf of another.

2. Teacher Preparation

A. Following prayer, read the FOCAL VERSES in a modern translation (TEV, CEV, NIV) to increase your understanding of the text.

B. Read THE PEOPLE, PLACES, AND TIMES and the BACKGROUND section. Write down questions that might be raised in class. Study the SEARCH THE SCRIPTURES and DISCUSS THE MEANING questions and prepare the answers.

C. Review the LESSON AIM. Write down each point and keep it in mind throughout the lesson.

3. Starting the Lesson

A. Prior to the students' arrival, write the words "supplications," "prayers," and "intercessions" from the WORDS YOU SHOULD KNOW section on the board or on newsprint.

B. Before opening the class with prayer, ask if the students have any prayer requests, and pray for those concerns.

4. Getting into the Lesson

A. Assign two to three students to read THE PEOPLE, PLACES, AND TIMES and the BACKGROUND section.

B. Ask a couple of students to take turns reading the FOCAL VERSES according to the AT-A-GLANCE outline.

C. Have the students read the words on the board. Ask them to explain the differences between the words. Then define each word.

D. Invite someone to read the LESSON AIM aloud. Ask the students to silently read the IN FOCUS section.

5. Relating the Lesson to Life

A. Have the students discuss the LESSON IN OUR SOCIETY section.

B. Call the students' attention to the MAKE IT HAPPEN section. Remind them of the difference between the words "intercessions" and "supplications."

C. Give the students time to read the IN DEPTH commentary. Then discuss any questions.

D. Lead the students in answering the SEARCH THE SCRIPTURES and DISCUSS THE MEANING questions.

JAN 8TH

6. Arousing Action

A. Ask that each student select one person to pray for this week who he or she would not have prayed for before studying this lesson.

B. Remind the students to complete the DAILY BIBLE READINGS, and the REMEMBER YOUR THOUGHTS and FOLLOW THE SPIRIT sections.

C. Close the class with prayer.

WORSHIP GUIDE

For the Superintendent or Teacher
Theme: **Pray for Everyone**
Theme Song: **"Acceptable to You"**
Scripture: **Luke 11:1-13**
Song: **"I Know the Lord Will Answer Prayer"**
Meditation: **Dear God, help us to remember our leaders in government as we pray for our loved ones and ourselves. Amen.**

PRAY FOR EVERYONE

Bible Background • 1 TIMOTHY 2
Printed Text • 1 TIMOTHY 2:1–8
Devotional Reading • 1 THESSALONIANS 5:16–22

LESSON AIM

By the end of the lesson, we will:

KNOW that God desires that we pray for everyone, including people in authority such as parents, supervisors, community and world leaders, and ourselves;

BE CONVINCED that by praying for others we can affect the outcome of certain situations; and

COMMIT to further develop and deepen our prayer lives.

KEEP IN MIND

"I exhort therefore, that, first of all, supplications, prayers, intercessions, and giving of thanks, be made for all men" (1 Timothy 2:1).

FOCAL VERSES

1 Timothy 2:1 I exhort therefore, that, first of all, supplications, prayers, intercessions, and giving of thanks, be made for all men;

2 For kings, and for all that are in authority; that we may lead a quiet and peaceable life in all godliness and honesty.

3 For this is good and acceptable in the sight of God our Saviour;

4 Who will have all men to be saved, and to come unto the knowledge of the truth.

5 For there is one God, and one mediator between God and men, the man Christ Jesus;

6 Who gave himself a ransom for all, to be testified in due time.

7 Whereunto I am ordained a preacher, and an

LESSON OVERVIEW

LESSON AIM
KEEP IN MIND
FOCAL VERSES
IN FOCUS
THE PEOPLE, PLACES,
AND TIMES
BACKGROUND
AT-A-GLANCE
IN DEPTH
SEARCH THE SCRIPTURES
DISCUSS THE MEANING
LESSON IN OUR SOCIETY
MAKE IT HAPPEN
FOLLOW THE SPIRIT
REMEMBER YOUR THOUGHTS
MORE LIGHT ON THE TEXT
DAILY BIBLE READINGS

apostle, (I speak the truth in Christ, and lie not;) a teacher of the Gentiles in faith and verity.

8 I will therefore that men pray every where, lifting up holy hands, without wrath and doubting.

IN FOCUS

Oftentimes, people say they don't know how to pray to affect the outcome of certain situations. If you want to develop or deepen your prayer life, all you need is the prayer that our Lord Jesus taught His disciples:

The Disciples' Prayer:
"Our Father which art in heaven,"

Jesus stresses the bond between God in heaven and mankind on earth, which is that of the Father and child.

"Hallowed be thy Name."
We should recognize that God is reverend, pure, blameless, and holy.

"Thy kingdom come."
Here we pray persistently for the Lord to establish His everlasting kingdom, even though we know it will not occur perfectly until Jesus returns.

"Thy will be done in earth, as it is in heaven."
Jesus said that He came to offer abundant life to the whole world! Jesus said we should *hunger* and *thirst* for righteousness and justice to prevail in the earth (Matthew 5:6).

"Give us this day our daily bread."

God provides for all of us. We can pray for our daily needs.

"And forgive us our debts, as we forgive our debtors."

The Bible says that every living soul has sinned and fallen short of the glory of God. We can pray for God to forgive our sins. We should forgive others in order to facilitate better interpersonal relationships.

"And lead us not into temptation, but deliver us from evil."

We pray that God helps us and others to avoid sin, and be delivered from the evil one, Satan.

"For thine is the kingdom, and the power, and the glory, for ever. Amen" (from Matthew 6:9-13).

Prayer is powerful. Prayer can be as multifaceted and varied as the people we pray for. Notice, however, the priority: worship of God precedes petitions. In today's lesson, we learn that prayer is for everyone. God's power is sovereign, and when we give God the glory, our prayers will have a miraculous effect.

THE PEOPLE, PLACES, AND TIMES

Emperor worship. The practice of assigning the status of deity to a Roman emperor—usually conferred by the Senate upon the emperor's death, but living emperors could be unofficially recognized as deity. The worship of kings or rulers was conceivable since male and female rulers were frequently portrayed as the earthly representatives of the divine. Emperor worship was especially prevalent during the Roman era. Under the emperors' rule, Christians, like other Roman subjects, were permitted to worship their own gods. However, they also had to demonstrate their loyalty by offering prayers, sacrifices, wine, and incense to the Roman ruler. Persons who did not comply with this decree were suspected of disloyalty and viewed as a threat to the peace in the land. This presented a problem for Christians because they worshiped God exclusively. Many Christians were severely persecuted because they refused to worship the emperors.

Prayer. The act of communion or conversation with God; a calling on God. Prayer comes in several different forms, including petition, confession, thanksgiving, praise, meditation, and intercession. The views on prayer reflected in the Old Testament varied during the different phases of biblical history. During the monarchic period, God is largely portrayed as dangerous, but also as One who acts on behalf of His people. Inquiries of God were made by Urim and Thummim (by lot). During the period of the major prophets, prayer acquired an ethical dimension. The prophets preached that Israel was taken into exile because it had broken its covenant with God. Therefore, true prayer according to the prophets required a recollection of God's past favor and repentance. Confession led to a renewed relationship with God (Psalm 51). Prayers of praise and thanksgiving are portrayed throughout the Old Testament.

BACKGROUND

Nearly 50 years had passed since the birth of the Christian faith, and the church was growing and changing rapidly. Paul's mission to the Gentiles had been a success, and the number of Gentile Christians began to eclipse the number of Jewish Christians. Around A.D. 70, Judaism and Christianity were irrevocably separated, further increasing the Gentile influence on the church. Judaism, however, was an officially recognized religion in the empire and Christianity was recognized as a Jewish sect. The split with Judaism placed the church in a precarious situation. Nero, the emperor during this time, was very hostile toward Christians. The church was forced to confront two very pressing issues: (1) the need to demonstrate its loyalty to the Roman state while practicing Christianity in a hostile environment, and (2) the need to institute "manuals of church order" for believers to preserve sound doctrine and practices for future Christians.

Roetzel, Calvin J. *The Letters of Paul: Conversations in Context. Fourth Edition.* Louisville, Ky.: Westminster/John Knox Press, 1998.

Schnelle, Udo. *The History and Theology of the New Testament Writings.* Minneapolis, Minn.: Fortress Press, 1998.

1. The Instructions Concerning Prayer
and Worship (1 Timothy 2:1-4)
2. The Universal Offer and Sufficiency of
Salvation (vv. 5-6)
3. The Herald of Truth (vv. 7-8)

IN DEPTH

1. The Instructions Concerning Prayer and Worship (1 Timothy 2:1-4)

Christianity faced several internal and external challenges at this time. Internally, the church faced opposition from so-called Christians who were spreading false doctrine. Externally, the Roman government viewed the church with suspicion because of its unfamiliarity with Christianity and misunderstanding of certain Christian practices. Paul had left instructions for the church at Ephesus to embrace Timothy as their leader in his absence. As the leader, Timothy was responsible for confronting the internal conflicts as well as instructing the congregation in proper worship.

Paul's instructions to Timothy concerning public prayer and worship sound much like the books of worship used by many contemporary Christian congregations. His instructions included directions for public prayer as well as examples of exemplary Christian conduct. The insistence of prayers on behalf of the king or emperor and all others in high offices probably struck the hearers as unusual because of emperor worship. However, Paul's commands may have been meant to keep the peace between Christians and the Roman government. The Christian resolution of this conflict was to pray and offer thanksgiving *for* the well-being of the emperor, while avoiding praying and sacrificing *to* him. Such public displays of loyalty could demonstrate that Christians led respectable and godly lives. Such exemplary lives lead others to salvation.

2. The Universal Offer and Sufficiency of Salvation (vv. 5-6)

Verses 5 and 6 may be remnants of an extend-ed confession of faith recited by worshipers in the early church. Paul inserts this liturgical piece in his letter to Timothy to emphasize the universal goal of salvation and Jesus' role in God's plan. Although God's plan of salvation is for everyone, regardless of race, gender, age, or nationality, all have sinned and are in need of being reconciled to God. Jesus gave Himself as a ransom to redeem, or buy us back, from sin. Jesus is also our mediator, standing between God and us to intercede on our behalf.

3. The Herald of Truth (vv. 7-8)

Paul attests that Jesus' self-sacrifice on our behalf is a testimony to God's plan of salvation. Jesus Christ appointed Paul an apostle, a herald, and a teacher of the Gospel to bring knowledge of the truth to the Gentiles. Paul's response to God's redemption was to become a missionary to the Gentiles. This mission was in fulfillment of God's promise to bring salvation to the Jews and non-Jews alike. Paul repeatedly stresses that he speaks the truth concerning the Gospel since certain members have fallen under the influence of false teachings.

SEARCH THE SCRIPTURES

1. List the four types of prayers that Paul names (1 Timothy 2:1).

2. For whom does Paul urge the believers to pray (v. 1)?

3. What does Paul say is "good and acceptable in the sight of God" (vv. 2-3)?

4. For what purpose does Paul say he was sent (v. 7)?

DISCUSS THE MEANING

1. Paul's letter to Timothy provides written instructions to the congregation on how to pray. How important do you believe it is for congregations to have access to written resources regarding prayer and worship?

2. Universality is a major theme in Paul's opening instructions concerning prayer and worship. Paul urged the believers to pray for everyone. Why do you believe that it is important to include everyone in our prayers, even people whose beliefs and lives are different from our own?

3. Paul's prayers for kings or emperors reflected

his desire for effective leadership, peace in the world, and religious tolerance for Christians. Do you believe that your prayers can affect the outcome of certain situations? How should we pray for our mayor, legislators, and president?

LESSON IN OUR SOCIETY

Throughout American history, the relationship between Blacks and the government has often been tenuous at best. At times, the government has demonstrated open hostility toward African Americans. During the Reconstruction period, the government declared that Whites did not have to respect the rights of Blacks, and elected officials conspired to revoke the few gains made by Blacks. Law enforcement officials have often appeared to disregard the rights of Blacks rather than protect them. We might ask, "How do you offer prayers on behalf of those who seem antagonistic toward you? Why does God want us to pray for people in positions of authority?" Looking back on our past provides us with clues to the answer. God has responded to the prayers of our ancestors as people of faith, and changed people and circumstances to improve the situation of African Americans. We need to pray for everyone because we do not know what God will do through our prayers.

MAKE IT HAPPEN

By now you should know that God wants us to offer prayers of intercession, supplication, and thanksgiving for ourselves and others (1 Timothy 2:1). Practice praying these various types of prayers using a model such as "ACTS" (Adoration, Confession, Thanks, and Supplication). Praise God and give Him glory, repent from sins, express your gratitude, and ask in humility for your needs. Then pray for others.

FOLLOW THE SPIRIT

What God wants me to do:

_____

_____

REMEMBER YOUR THOUGHTS

Special insights I have learned:

_____

_____

MORE LIGHT ON THE TEXT

1 Timothy 2:1-8

1 I exhort therefore, that, first of all, supplications, prayers, intercessions, and giving of thanks, be made for all men;

Paul knew the value of prayer and sought to impress its significance upon his young disciple, Timothy. This is why he begins this passage with the expression "first of all." Paul elevated the importance of prayer during church services that Timothy was responsible to lead.

He exhorted Timothy, and all who read his words, to pray. The word "exhort" comes from the Greek word *parakaleo* (**par-ak-al-EH-o**), meaning "to invite or invoke." He didn't want prayer to become a legalistic practice. Rather, Paul wanted prayer to pervade the heart and soul of every believer. He didn't command that prayer be made for all men. If that were his intention, other Greek words would have better reflected that desire. Instead, he used *parakaleo* so that the true spirit of prayer would be nurtured and encouraged.

Paul called for prayers to be uttered for all men. There are at least seven different terms for prayer in the New Testament, and four are used in this verse. The Greek word for "supplications" is *deesis* (**DEH-ay-sis**), meaning "petition." This prayer is offered in the form of a request that expresses a desire or need. The Greek word for "prayers" is *proseuche* (**pros-yoo-KHAY**), which is a general term for both public and private prayer. The Greek word for "intercessions" is *enteuxis* (**ent-YOOK-sis**), meaning "supplication." This term is used to describe prayer that is both bold and confident. The Greek word for the fourth type of prayer is *eucharistia* (**yoo-khar-is-TEE-ah**), meaning "gratitude" or "gratefulness." We express our prayer of gratitude to God as we praise and thank Him.

Paul insisted that prayer be offered for all men. To whom does all men refer? "All" comes from the Greek word *pas* (**pas**), meaning "every, whatsoever, or whoever." The word for "men" is derived from the Greek *anthropos* (**ANTH-ro-pos**), meaning "human being." Thus, we can safely assume that Paul wanted prayer to be offered for everyone, and not be limited by race, gender, or nationality.

2 For kings, and for all that are in authority; that we may lead a quiet and peaceable life in all godliness and honesty.

Paul specifically identified kings and others in authority as those who needed prayer for direction and discernment. Rather than protest against and complain about politicians, we should pursue the alternative of concerted prayer and intercession for them to an even greater degree. We should pray for those in authority to make wise decisions that will contribute to a stable social order, allowing us to live in peace and tranquility.

What is the source of a quiet and peaceable life? It is prayer. Such prayer impacts our lives on a personal level. As we pray, we learn to lead more reflective lives. This is what Paul refers to when he speaks of a quiet and peaceable life. The word "lead" comes from the Greek word *diago* (**dee-AG-o**), meaning "to pass time or life." Paul told Timothy that the key to a more reflective life was to spend time in prayer and intercession, rather than wasting one's life on frivolous activities. In other words, you determine how you live your life. The most effective way to live your life is to commit yourself to prayer. As you pray, you reflect upon what God says to you through His Word. And if you listen closely, you can hear Him speak to you, and you can respond in obedience.

People who pray are more fully able to live godly and reverent lives. "Godliness" comes from the Greek word *eusebeia* (**yoo-SEB-i-ah**), meaning "piety or respect toward God." Honesty comes from the Greek word *semnotes* (**sem-NOT-ace**), meaning "venerableness." To "venerate" means to regard someone with great respect or to revere. As we learn to reflect upon God through prayer and the study of His Word, we gain insight into who deserves our veneration and respect. It is God, not man, who is worthy of our worship.

3 For this is good and acceptable in the sight of God our Saviour;

To what does "this" refer? And what is good and acceptable? The word "this" refers to the kind of prayer Paul urges Timothy, and all disciples, to engage in before God. The word "good"

comes from the Greek word *kalos* (**kal-OS**), meaning "useful, praiseworthy, or advantageous." The word "acceptable" comes from the Greek word *apodektos* (**ap-OD-ek-tos**), meaning "to be agreeable."

Prayer is useful and agreeable to God because it is in conformity with His will. He wants His children to be devoted to prayer, and He finds pleasure in this. He longs to see His children calling out to Him and praising Him. Inherent in this verse is the truth that God finds joy in His children who commune with Him.

The Greek word for "sight" is *enopion* (**en-O-pee-on**), meaning "in the face of" or "in the presence of." All that we do is in God's sight, and we never escape this reality. As a result, it brings God pleasure when His children engage in prayer because prayer is powerful and is our way to communicate with our God and Saviour.

4 Who will have all men to be saved, and to come unto the knowledge of the truth.

According to Paul, God would have all men to be saved. The Greek word reflecting God's thinking is *thelo* (**THEL-o**), meaning "a wish of desire or want." When we say that God desires all men to be saved, does this mean He has determined that all *will* be saved? No, because each person must come to a personal knowledge of the truth.

Why doesn't God guarantee that His desires become reality? His desires don't always become reality because of man's choice. God wants all to enjoy the blessings of salvation, but only those who come to the knowledge of the truth will know them.

The Greek word for "knowledge" is *epignosis* (**ep-IG-no-sis**), meaning "recognition" or "full discernment." What is the knowledge one must have to be saved? This knowledge is simply the reality of the Gospel of Jesus Christ—that He died on the cross, arose on the third day, and offers forgiveness and pardon to all who believe this. The Greek word for truth is *aletheia* (**al-AY-thi-a**), which means "verity" or "truth."

The world is under the influence of the devil, who distorts the truth. Those who desire to be saved must personally recognize the truth, which is found in the message of the Gospel. When we arrive at knowledge of the truth, we come to Christ, who is the source of all that is true.

5 For there is one God, and one mediator between God and men, the man Christ Jesus;

Paul explains the reason God desires all to come to the knowledge of the truth. Paul includes a qualifier in this verse to emphasize that there is only one God and one Mediator. The Greek word for "one" is *heis* (**hice**), meaning the numeral 1, "the only one," or "a single one." The theological significance of this verse should not be overlooked. There are not many different ways to God. There is only one.

Neither are there a variety of mediators between God and man. The Greek word for "mediator" is *mesites* (**mes-EE-tace**), meaning a go-between or reconciler. A mediator is someone who works with two parties to reconcile them or to work out their differences. Various religious systems claim to offer a variety of means to be reconciled to God. But because they are dependent on the efforts of sinful humans beings, they all are doomed to failure. However, as Paul explains within the context of this verse, there is only one mediator—Jesus Christ. What makes this unique is that Jesus came from the Father; thus, through Him, God is reconciled to us. That is why He, being God, can reconcile us.

Paul notes that the man Jesus Christ serves as our mediator. Why does Paul emphasize Jesus' manhood? Jesus Christ took on the form of a servant, became a man, and served as our substitute when He offered Himself on the cross for our sins. By doing this, He fulfilled the requirements to serve as our mediator.

Why can't others serve as mediators between God and man? No one else can serve as a mediator because none has ever been qualified to serve in that position. According to Scripture, God spelled out what was needed for someone to serve in the position of mediator. In the Old Testament, the priest served as a go-between before God for the people. However, the priesthood was an imperfect system and merely a shadow of things to come. Jesus Christ fulfilled the priesthood and the requirements to serve as our

mediator when He shed His blood upon the cross. To do so, Jesus had to be the perfect sacrifice for sin. No one else can fulfill these righteous requirements. Therefore, Jesus alone mediates for us before the Father. To be sure, Jesus is the only way to God.

6 Who gave himself a ransom for all, to be testified in due time.

The Greek word for "ransom" is *antilutron* (**an-TIL-oo-tron**), meaning a redemption price. His death served as an atonement for our sins. There are several terms that clarify how Jesus served as a ransom for all. Each of these theological concepts explores one of the many facets of ransom as seen in the death of Jesus upon the cross.

Reconciliation: As our ransom, Jesus ended the hostility that existed between God and man. When He died on the cross, He removed the hostility. God was offended by our sin, yet because of His love for us, He gave His Son, who was sinless, to make our reconciliation possible through Christ's death.

Substitution: Jesus took our place when He gave Himself as a ransom. Many passages in Scripture describe how our sins were laid upon Him. For example, He "was made sin" for us, and He bore "our iniquity" upon Himself (cf. 2 Corinthians 5:21; Isaiah 53:10).

Propitiation: Jesus' death fulfilled God's righteous demands as He served as our ransom. It turned God's wrath aside, taking away sin. The concept of propitiation is seen in Paul's writings elsewhere in the New Testament. We can also see the concept in the Old Testament: the priest presented the sacrifice on the altar, and his offering made atonement for the sins of the people (Leviticus 4:35).

Sacrifice: The New Testament teaches that Jesus served as our High Priest. He entered the Holy of Holies to offer Himself as a living sacrifice to make atonement for the sins of the world. His sacrifice differed from the one offered by the priests who served before Him. Jesus sacrificed His own body and blood, shed on the cross. His sacrifice and the sacrifice of other high priests differ also in permanence. His offering was once for all, instead of the daily sacrifice brought by the priest. His sacrifice was offered on Calvary's cross for the sins of the world.

7 Whereunto I am ordained a preacher, and an apostle, (I speak the truth in Christ, and lie not;) a teacher of the Gentiles in faith and verity.

Paul viewed his life and ministry within the context of Christ's death for the sins of the world. He saw his ministry as an appointment. The word "ordained" comes from the Greek word *tithemi* (**TITH-ay-mee**), meaning "to appoint or place." He echoes the thought he expressed in 1 Timothy 1:12 as he reflected upon how God had put him in ministry.

In this verse, Paul says that he was ordained a preacher. The word "preacher" comes from the Greek word *kerux* (**KAY-roox**), meaning "herald." This word is used primarily to refer to heralds of divine truth, especially the Gospel. Paul elevated the significance of his position as a herald or preacher of the Gospel of Jesus Christ. This is not some lowly position he held, nor is his message something that could be casually disregarded; it was priceless information he communicated through his preaching.

He was not only ordained as a preacher, but also as an apostle. The Greek word for "apostle" is *apostolos* (**ap-OS-tol-os**), meaning a "delegate." Paul had been given multiple responsibilities in his service for his Lord. He was a herald and a delegate. As a delegate, he was an ambassador of the Gospel. In a general sense, an apostle is one who is sent with a special message or commission. Jesus is called "the Apostle and High Priest of our profession" in Hebrews 3:1. The Jews referred to the person who collected the half shekel, which all Israelites paid to the temple on a yearly basis. The original 12 disciples were called apostles. This designation distinguished them from the other disciples. They were the first to be sent out to preach and to have authority to drive out demons (Mark 3:14-15).

Along with his responsibilities as a preacher and apostle, Paul carried an additional responsibility as a teacher of the Gentiles. The word "teacher" comes from the Greek word *didaskalos* (**did-AS-kal-os**), meaning an instructor. He was assigned the responsibility of instructing the Gentiles in the truths of the Gospel. However, he had witnessed others who did not teach faithfully. Therefore, he further explained how he taught. Paul instructed the Gentiles in faith and veracity. The word "faith" comes from the Greek word *pistis* (**PIS-tis**), meaning "persuasion" or "moral credence." The word "verity" comes from the Greek word *aletheia* (**al-AY-thi-a**), meaning "truth" or "truly."

These words explain how Paul conducted his teaching ministry among the Gentiles. He taught with integrity so that those who heard him could trust his words. In other words, his students never had to fear that Paul would use his position as a teacher to persuade them to do what was wrong. He never abused his position as their teacher.

Paul also taught the truth. He instructed them

Prayer and Supplication for all.

in the plain, simple truths of the Gospel. In a culture where the truth is often viewed as politically incorrect, Paul's testimony regarding how he approached his ministry is extremely helpful. We would do well to follow his example.

8 I will therefore that men pray every where, lifting up holy hands, without wrath and doubting.

Paul ended this section with a return to the central teaching of the chapter. He desired that men everywhere pray. The Greek word for "will" is *boulomai* (**BOO-lom-ahee**) meaning "to be willing or disposed." A better translation of this word in this context is "to desire." Paul expressed his desire to see men everywhere committing themselves to prayer. The Greek word for "pray" is the same word used in the first verse of this chapter. Paul included two added thoughts regarding prayer. First of all, he wanted men to pray in all places. Second, he instructed them to lift holy hands.

The Greek word for "every where" is actually three Greek terms added together; the original reads "in all places." The thought, however, remains the same. Men are to pray wherever they are.

In addition, Paul desired to see men pray as they lifted up holy hands. The word "holy" comes from the Greek word *hosios* (**HOS-ee-os**), meaning "right due to intrinsic character." Paul described these men who pray as men who lived "right" lives. Their hands were not used for evil intentions, and they had a desire to please God through pure lives.

Following God's deliverance of him from Saul, David rehearsed God's work in his life in the following manner in Psalm 18:20: "The LORD rewarded me according to my righteousness; according to the cleanness of my hands hath he recompensed me." Once again, David is concerned that God find him living a righteous life. His description of a right life before God included clean or holy hands.

Paul further defined holy hands by adding the following thought: "without wrath and doubting." The Greek word for "wrath" is *orge* (**or-GAY**), meaning "violent passion." According to Paul's

definition, "holy hands," cannot include anger that leads to violence. Anger and violence never contribute to an effective prayer life. Violent men are not prayerful men.

Men who pray are not motivated by wrath, nor are they motivated by doubt. The Greek word for "doubt" in this verse is *dialogizomai* (**dee-al-og-ID-zom-ahee**), meaning an "internal discussion" or "reasoning." In other words, men who pray do not spend time debating within themselves whether they should pray about certain things or whether God even hears them.

Paul wanted men to be committed to prayer, live clean lives, and not waver in their faith. Because they didn't vacillate, these men prayed effectively and God did awesome things through them. The book of James provides some insights that contribute to a better understanding of doubt. James described doubt in this manner: "But let him ask in faith, with no doubting, for he who doubts is like a wave of the sea driven and tossed by the wind. For let not that man suppose that he will receive anything from the Lord; he is a double-minded man, unstable in all his ways" (James 1:6-8, NKJV).

The HAND of GOD is Holy > ALSO, see page 273

DAILY BIBLE READINGS

M: Paul Prays for the Philippians
Philippians 1:3-11
T: Pray Without Ceasing
1 Thessalonians 5:16-22
W: God Hears Our Prayers
1 Peter 3:8-12
T: A Parable About Praying
Luke 18:1-8
F: Pray for Your Enemies
Matthew 5:43-48
S: Pray for Everyone
1 Timothy 2:1-7
S: Prayer Is Powerful and Effective
James 5:13-18

TEACHING TIPS

1. Words You Should Know

A. Bishop (1 Timothy 3:2) *episkopos* (Gk.)—Overseer of persons who have a definite function or a fixed office within a group; the superintendent, elder, or overseer of a Christian church.

B. Novice (v. 6) *neophutos* (Gk.)—Newly planted in the Christian church; newly converted.

C. Deacons (v. 8) *diakonos* (Gk.)—Servant or helper; servant of apostles and other prominent Christians; servant of the Gospel; an official of the church.

D. Doubletongued (v. 8) *ilogos*—Lack of sincerity in speech; deceitful; repetitive or saying something twice.

2. Teacher Preparation

A. Ask the Holy Spirit to guide you in preparing for this lesson.

B. Read the FOCAL VERSES in at least three or four different translations since there are variations in each textual reading.

3. Starting the Lesson

A. Begin the class with prayer. Be sure to lift up church leaders in your prayer.

B. Ask the students to write down the names of the leaders in their church or denomination and list the criteria or responsibilities of these offices.

C. Discuss the answers in class.

4. Getting into the Lesson

A. Ask the students to compare the criteria for and responsibilities of their church leaders with the list in 1 Timothy 3:2-15.

B. Have volunteers take turns reading the FOCAL VERSES, the KEEP IN MIND verse, and the IN DEPTH section.

C. Discuss the SEARCH THE SCRIPTURES questions as a group.

D. Ask a volunteer to read the IN FOCUS section. Lead the class in a brief discussion of the relationship of Jessica's situation to the LESSON AIM.

5. Relating the Lesson to Life

A. Divide the class into three groups. Assign each group one of the DISCUSS THE MEANING questions, and ask them to answer the question. Reconvene the class and share the group discussions.

B. Discuss the LESSON IN OUR SOCIETY section as a group.

6. Arousing Action

A. Encourage the class to reflect on the MAKE IT HAPPEN section.

B. Ask the students to select one thing they will do to show support for the leaders in their church.

C. Remind the students to complete the DAILY BIBLE READINGS, REMEMBER YOUR THOUGHTS, and FOLLOW THE SPIRIT sections.

D. Close the class with prayer.

WORSHIP GUIDE

For the Superintendent or Teacher
Theme: God Calls Church Leaders
Theme Song: "Order My Steps"
Scripture: Hebrews 13:20-21
Song: "Lead Me, Guide Me"
Meditation: Dear God, You called women and men to serve Your church in the world. Equip them, strengthen them, and bless them for Your work. Amen.

GOD CALLS CHURCH LEADERS

Bible Background • 1 TIMOTHY 3
Printed Text • 1 TIMOTHY 3:2–15
Devotional Reading • MARK 9:33–37

LESSON AIM

By the end of the lesson, we will:

UNDERSTAND the qualifications necessary to become an effective church leader both inside the church and in the community,

BE CONVINCED these qualifications should be the standard to strive for in church leadership today; and

DETERMINE to use these standards in selecting leaders for church.

KEEP IN MIND

"Holding the mystery of the faith in a pure conscience" (1 Timothy 3:9).

FOCAL VERSES

1 Timothy 3:2 A bishop then must be blameless, the husband of one wife, vigilant, sober, of good behaviour, given to hospitality, apt to teach;

3 Not given to wine, no striker, not greedy of filthy lucre; but patient, not a brawler, not covetous;

4 One that ruleth well his own house, having his children in subjection with all gravity;

5 (For if a man know not how to rule his own house, how shall he take care of the church of God?)

6 Not a novice, lest being lifted up with pride he fall into the condemnation of the devil.

7 Moreover he must have a good report of them which are without; lest he fall into reproach and the snare of the devil.

8 Likewise must the deacons be grave, not dou-

LESSON OVERVIEW

LESSON AIM
KEEP IN MIND
FOCAL VERSES
IN FOCUS
THE PEOPLE, PLACES, AND TIMES
BACKGROUND
AT-A-GLANCE
IN DEPTH
SEARCH THE SCRIPTURES
DISCUSS THE MEANING
LESSON IN OUR SOCIETY
MAKE IT HAPPEN
FOLLOW THE SPIRIT
REMEMBER YOUR THOUGHTS
MORE LIGHT ON THE TEXT
DAILY BIBLE READINGS

bletongued, not given to much wine, not greedy of filthy lucre;

9 Holding the mystery of the faith in a pure conscience.

10 And let these also first be proved; then let them use the office of a deacon, being found blameless.

11 Even so must their wives be grave, not slanderers, sober, faithful in all things.

12 Let the deacons be the husbands of one wife, ruling their children and their own houses well.

JAN 15TH

13 For they that have used the office of a deacon well purchase to themselves a good degree, and great boldness in the faith which is in Christ Jesus.

14 These things write I unto thee, hoping to come unto thee shortly:

15 But if I tarry long, that thou mayest know how thou oughtest to behave thyself in the house of God, which is the church of the living God, the pillar and ground of the truth.

IN FOCUS

Jessica saw herself praying in the pulpit with her head down. The muscles in her toes tightened until they cramped with increasing pain. She felt her calves aching as the choir sang the last stanza of the hymn. She wanted to scream at the top of her lungs—not shout hallelujah. Her ears and neck began to hurt from the clenching of her jaw. The only relief she felt was that she was no longer aware of the nausea and pressure against her throat. Suddenly, she awakened, and she realized she had been dreaming. Nevertheless, she felt weak and exhausted. As she loosened her grip on the bed pillow, her eyes sprang open and tears ran down her cheeks. She realized it was Sunday morning, and today she would teach her first lesson.

If you are called by God for a difficult position of church leadership, would you measure up to the task in the face of any opposition? Today's lesson will review Paul's description to Timothy of the characteristics of good church leaders.

THE PEOPLE, PLACES, AND TIMES

Bishop. An overseer or guardian. "Overseer" was a title for both civil and religious officials charged with the oversight of buildings, provisions, and finances. Overseers were usually equated with elders (Acts 20:17, 28; Titus 1:6-9; 1 Peter 5:1-2), which has led some scholars to conclude that the position is Jewish in origin, even though the term was fairly common in the Greco-Roman world. Translators of ancient Hebrew texts—discovered near the Dead Sea—known as the Dead Sea scrolls, have found the Hebrew equivalent of the term "overseer" used to describe individuals responsible for admitting new members into the community, looking after the concerns of all members, and handling financial transactions.

By the end of the first century A.D., the term "overseer" in the Christian church described an official ministerial office. There were likely several overseers/bishops who were each responsible for overseeing a congregation.

Deacon. A servant, usually in a civil or religious position. The office of deacon was developed in the Christian church in response to the needs within the body of Christ. Deacons assisted the elders in caring for widows and orphans, visiting and ministering to the sick, and assisting with baptism of new converts. Deacons later assisted the bishop in liturgical and pastoral duties, including serving at the Lord's Supper or Holy Communion by receiving the offerings of the people and administering the elements. Deacons also visited the sick, the poor, and the indigent, taking communion to them and reporting back to the bishop their various needs. Instructed by the bishop, the deacon would bring portions of the offerings collected to those in need. The ordination of deacons in the New Testament is ambiguous. Acts 6:1-6 refers to the selection and ordination of certain members to assist the apostles with caring for the Greek widows.

However, the function rather than the term was used in the text.

By the second century, extra biblical Christian writings provided specific directions for the ordination of deacons.

House or household. The household was the basic unit of Greco-Roman society. A household consisted of a husband, wife, and children. It might also include other relatives and servants and slaves, depending on the family's economic status. The husband was responsible for providing for the family's needs, but the wife managed the day-to-day affairs of the household. Everyone had his or her place and function within the household, which was determined by the strict "household codes" in place at the time. References to household codes are mentioned throughout the New Testament (Ephesians 5:21-6:9; Colossians 3:18-4:1). The household was also the basic unit of and metaphor for the church. The early church met in the homes of individuals.

BACKGROUND

The focus of attention in 1 Timothy 3 is on the qualifications within the church for the offices of "overseer," or "bishop," and "server," or "deacon." Paul discusses the qualities that individuals seeking these positions should have. Among the qualifications that Paul lists, overseers, bishops, and deacons must be blameless in character inside and outside of the church, a mature Christian who is also discreet, a good household manager, and, most importantly, faithful to Christ. The leadership begun by Paul and exercised by Timothy in Paul's absence is now being passed on through church leaders to preserve the truth of Paul's teachings in the face of false doctrine and to ensure the survival of the church.

Ferguson, Everett. Backgrounds of Early Christianity. Grand Rapids, Mich.: Eerdmans Publishing Company, 1987.

1. Credentials for Bishops
(1 Timothy 3:2-7)
2. Credentials for Deacons
(vv. 8-13)
3. Conduct in God's House
(vv. 14-15)

IN DEPTH

1. Credentials for Bishops (1 Timothy 3:2-7)

A bishop in the early church was responsible for seeing that things went smoothly in the community for which he was responsible. Therefore, individuals called to this position had to exhibit exemplary behavior in the church and community. No fewer than 16 specific virtues to embody and vices to avoid are listed. First on the list is that a bishop be blameless (v. 2). The church's precarious position as a minority religious group in the community required that Christians be above reproach in the public's eye.

The list also includes that a bishop should be the husband of one wife. Most biblical commentaries state that this passage refers to fidelity in marriage. Some believe this qualification means that widowed or divorced men should remain single. We take for granted in our contemporary society that a married man, particularly a religious leader, is expected to exercise marital fidelity, avoiding any sexual indiscretion. However, in Greco-Roman society, extramarital relations were both acceptable and common. Men married to produce legitimate heirs but were known to enjoy the company of concubines.

Hospitality was widely encouraged as a Christian virtue. Christians opened their homes to traveling missionaries, other Christians, and traders who carried letters back and forth between Christian communities. Bishops should also be able teachers of the faith, which comes with Christian maturity and experience. Vices the bishop should avoid include drunkenness, addiction to wine, conflict, and indiscretion. Bishops were expected to be low-key and well-mannered,

not given to being embroiled in quarrels (v. 3). The absence of greed was another important qualification. Bishops received the offerings from the congregations to provide for the members' needs. A person who exhibited poor financial management at home would not be expected to maintain the church's finances.

Christian worship in the early church was held in members' homes. A church leader was likely to conduct worship in his or her home. Since the household was the basic unit of society, a bishop who could demonstrate that he was able to manage his household proved that he could oversee the affairs of the church (vv. 4-5). Husbands and fathers exercised absolute authority over everyone in their household. Therefore, a man whose children were submissive and behaved admirably at home was to be commended. In contrast, a man's wife and children could bring him shame in the eyes of the public by their behavior. Wives or children who transgressed the approved social roles demonstrated a man's lack of control over his dependents.

A man could demonstrate his qualifications for the position of bishop by holding lesser offices in the church. Over time, experience and reputation could determine whether or not a candidate was qualified. A newly converted Christian, on the other hand, might view his selection to such a prominent position as a sign of his stature in the community and be boastful (v. 6). Finally, Paul emphasizes again that the candidate for bishop should be highly regarded by persons outside the Christian community (v. 7).

2. Credentials for Deacons (vv. 8-13)

The deacon's qualifications are similar to the bishop's. Persons wishing to serve as deacons must likewise be above reproach, sober or clear-headed, moderate in drink, free of greed, and the husband of one wife, and should supervise his children and manage his household well (vv. 8, 12). The deacon's responsibilities made such credentials important. The deacon administered the Lord's Supper in the homes of individuals who were unable to attend worship. They might visit more than one home in a short time period. The consumption of wine during this sacred meal could lead a deacon to acquire a tolerance for this strong drink. The deacons also dispensed charity to members in need. Therefore, it was important that they could be trusted with the church's funds. A married man was also probably less vulnerable to indiscretions when visiting widows.

A new addition to the list is the qualification that a deacon not be double-tongued. The visits to individuals' homes made the deacon privy to individuals' confidences, and put him at risk for gossip and slander. Therefore, it was essential that a deacon be discreet and speak well of people. It was also required that a deacon possess a genuine faith and not be one who could be persuaded to believe differently by the false teachers in the church (v. 9). As with a bishop, an individual was required to demonstrate an ability to function well in a lesser office before being elevated to the office of deacon (v. 10).

Scholars have debated whether the "women" mentioned in verse 11 refers to the wives of male deacons or to female deacons. Female deacons are attested elsewhere in the New Testament and in extra-biblical Christian and non-Christian writings (Romans 16:1). Pliny the Younger, a Roman government official, wrote about female Christian deacons. However, the meaning here is ambiguous. The term *gunaikeios* (**goo-nahee-KI-os**) is Greek for both "adult woman" and "wife." The Greek word immediately preceding it is *hosautos* (**ho-SOW-toce**), which means "in the same way," "similarly," or "likewise." Thus, the verse could be translated, "women (deacons) similarly must be serious, not slanderers, but temperate, faithful in all things," or "wives likewise."

The former is more likely because of the textual context as well as the concern expressed previously by Paul that church members' behavior in the eyes of the public be above reproach. New converts in the early church were baptized without their clothes on and dressed in white robes following baptism. Female deacons assisted female converts and male deacons assisted males. Any appearance of impropriety by the public would have been avoided. Anyone, male or female, who serves the office of deacon well earns a good reputation in the Christian community (v. 13).

3. Conduct in God's House (vv. 14-15)

This section concludes with Paul's anticipated return to the community. In the meantime, he has provided the church with written instructions on how members should behave in the household of God, modeled on the house churches. The house of God, or church, is the assembly of believers in the presence of the living God. Wherever believers meet to worship God, there God dwells. The leaders or "pillars" of the community were expected to uphold the high standards of conduct expected of members and to maintain the truth of the faith (vv. 14-15).

SEARCH THE SCRIPTURES

1. List at least three qualifications that are required of both bishops and deacons (1 Timothy 3:1-4, 8-9, 12-13).

2. What reason does Paul give for not selecting new converts to be bishops (v. 6)?

3. Who must think well of bishops (v. 7)?

4. What are the qualifications for a female deacon (v. 11)?

5. What is gained by deacons who serve well in their position (v. 13)?

DISCUSS THE MEANING

1. The ability to manage one's household well is a qualification required of both bishops and deacons. Why do you believe it is important that individuals seeking a leadership position in the church also manage their household affairs well?

2. Paul places a great deal of emphasis on church leaders being well-respected both inside and outside the church. Why do you believe that it is as important to have a respectable reputation in one's community as in the church?

3. The list of qualifications for both offices is very long. Do you believe that the qualifications in the first century A.D. should still apply to individuals called to lead the church in the twenty-first century? Why or why not?

LESSON IN OUR SOCIETY

The African presence in the episcopacy goes back to the first bishops chosen to oversee the church. Cyprian, Bishop of Carthage (A.D. 190-258), worked for Christian unity in North Africa;

Augustine, Bishop of Hippo (A.D. 354-430), is a major North African figure in church history and theology. The Vatican appointed James Augustine Healy the first African American bishop in the United States in 1875. Each of these men was highly regarded in the church and advanced the work of Christianity in the world. The number of men and women in church history who have served as deacons is too numerous to single out any particular one. However, our congregations continue to function today in large part because of the sacrificial service of all of our church leaders. Controversies arise from time to time when it becomes public that certain church leaders have committed some impropriety. The church is often portrayed as having gone wrong when a minority commits an infraction. This is why church leaders are held to such a high standard. What is your attitude toward or your perception of church leaders?

MAKE IT HAPPEN

Ask God if your present role is where He wants you to serve in the church. If the answer is "no," then pray about ways you can increase your service in the church. For example, God might be calling the Sunday School teacher to become superintendent. How would one prepare to become superintendent of Sunday School? Or how can you support other church leaders? Think of areas in the church where you can volunteer if you do not already. You might serve on a search committee looking for a church leader or on a personnel committee that evaluates church leaders.

FOLLOW THE SPIRIT

What God wants me to do:

_____

_____

REMEMBER YOUR THOUGHTS

Special insights I have learned:

_____

_____

MORE LIGHT ON THE TEXT

1 Timothy 3:2-15

2 A bishop then must be blameless, the husband of one wife, vigilant, sober, of good behaviour, given to hospitality, apt to teach;

God's call to ministry may be subjective and personal; there are, however, objective criteria by which anyone called can be measured. Paul here outlines these criteria for Timothy to employ in considering candidates for the office of bishop at Ephesus. The word "bishop" is translated as the Greek word *episkopos* (**ep-IS-kop-os**). It designates a church officer charged with overseeing the affairs of a local church.

Everyone aspiring to the position of bishop must meet certain criteria. The candidate must be considered "blameless" (Gk. *amemptos*, **AM-emp-tos**) by members of the congregation. He must not be someone liable to accusation of wrongdoing by members. Being blameless in this sense does not mean being perfect; otherwise, no one could meet the standard.

The candidate must also be "the husband of one wife." The literal rendering in Greek is "a one-woman man." Some have taken this difficult phrase to refer to monogamy, i.e., having one wife at a time. Others see it as implying that the elder must be a married man.

A leader should also be "vigilant." The Greek word behind this is *nephaleos* (**nay-FAL-eh-os**), which can also mean "temperate," "sober," or "watchful." It is only to be expected that a leader, whose primary function is overseeing the affairs of the church, be watchful and vigilant lest false teachers or doctrines infiltrate the church and lead members astray.

Another quality of an overseer is sobriety. The Greek word for "sober" is *sophron* (**SO-frone**), which also means "self-controlled" or "temperate." This quality is demonstrated by having mastery over one's nature.

The next quality on Paul's list is from the Greek word *kosmios* (**KOS-mee-os**). It means "good behavior," "orderly," or "modest." This quality brings out publicly other inward qualities like sober-mindedness, self-control, etc. A candidate for church leadership may claim to have the virtue of self-control, but the only way this can be verified is by observing his behavior. The life of a church leader must not only reflect his status in the Christian community, but it must also reflect the work of grace that has

God calls godly men to lead.

taken place in that life.

It is also required that a church leader be "given to hospitality." The Greek word for "hospitality," *philoxenos* (**fil-OX-en-os**), is self-revealing. It literally means "lover of strangers." A church leader is to be one who keeps an open door, not just for relatives and friends, but especially for strangers.

A functional requirement in the list is to be "apt to teach," which translates the Greek word *didaktikos* (**did-ak-tik-OS**). The spiritual gift of teaching the Word is a biblical requirement for anyone who desires to be a leader in the church. Today, this quality is wrongly applied only to pastors. Other church elders are virtually exempt from it. Ministry of the Word is the primary duty of all Christian leaders, not just the pastor. The most effective ministry of the Word is by lifestyle.

3 Not given to wine, no striker, not greedy of filthy lucre; but patient, not a brawler, not covetous;

In the previous verse, Paul deals with what a church leader should be. Here, he deals with what a church leader should not be. A leader must not be someone who is given to wine (Gk.

paroinos, **par'-oy-nos**) or drunkenness. The implication is that such a person habitually spends a long time consuming wine until he becomes tipsy and loses self-control. Since wine causes many to stumble in walking with the Lord, it is only proper for a Christian leader to abstain from it altogether (1 Corinthians 10:31-32).

A leader must not be a striker, i.e., one who is physically violent toward others. It is bad enough for a Christian to have the reputation of being violent, and inconceivable for a church leader to be so known. There is a correlation between the previous vice of drunkenness and being violent. It is not uncommon for brawling to erupt after one is drunk. In the Greek text, the virtue of "patience" follows as the opposite of "striker." It takes inward maturity to exercise patience when provoked, whereas all it takes to resort to violence is brute force. A church leader must be one who resorts to inner strength to resolve conflict rather than one whose first recourse is his physical strength. There is no place for a bully in the leadership of the church. The church needs leaders who would rather settle disputes through gentle words than through violent deeds.

The next negative is "not greedy of filthy lucre," which translates the Greek phrase *me aischrokerdes* (**may ahee-skhrok-er-dace**). The phrase literally means "not a lover of money." A church leader who loves money can easily fall victim to other vices, as Paul makes very clear later (1 Timothy 6:10). The lover of money sees money as an end and every other thing as a means to that end. A church leader who is in the grip of such a love exploits the ministry as a means of financial gain. While church leaders must not be lovers of money, neither should the church they serve exploit them for financial gain by saying, in essence, "Lord, keep our pastor humble. We'll make sure on our part; we'll keep him poor." For a church to care for her employed leaders in a manner less than it can afford is not only against Scripture (1 Timothy 5:17-18), but it also exposes the leaders to the love of money. Churches should not tempt their leaders to evil.

It is also expected of a church leader not to be a brawler. According to the NIV, a church leader must be someone who is "not quarrelsome." If this quality is to be summarized in one word, that word is "peaceable." The leader is not to be a contentious person who never misses an opportunity to pick a fight; rather, he should be one who abstains from fighting.

The quality "not covetous" found in Greek is *aphilarguros* (**af-il-AR-goo-ros**). The remaining three qualities are a mixture of positive and negative requirements for a church leader, with particular emphasis on his family life.

4 One that ruleth well his own house, having his children in subjection with all gravity;

According to this criterion, a prospective church leader must rule or manage his family affairs well. The Greek word translated as "ruleth" is *proistemi* (**pro-IS-tay-mee**), which also means "to preside or be over." The emphasis of this requirement is on "his own house," suggesting that it is possible for one to be an astute manager and leader outside the home and yet be a total failure in managing the home front. Many have achieved great success in various endeavors but cannot replicate the same success at home. Too often we make the mistake of thinking that achieving success in a profession qualifies a person for a leadership position in the church; this is not true at all. Leadership in the church, unlike leadership in other organizations that put a high premium on financial and professional achievements, requires a different measure of success. The emphasis here also shows that the church is to be managed more like a family than like a business or other social institutions.

The evidence for this quality is seen in the children's attitude toward their father as an authority figure. He should discipline his children so that they obey him "with all gravity." The Greek word rendered "gravity" is *semnotes* (**sem-NOT-ace**), which also denotes dignity and honesty.

5 (For if a man know not how to rule his own house, how shall he take care of the church of God?)

Paul asks a rhetorical question in order to make a logical point. If one cannot "rule" (manage) his own home, he should not be expected to properly care for God's church. The Greek word translated as "rule" is *proistemi* (**pro-IS-tay-mee**), meaning to "be over," "superintend," or "to be a protector or guardian." Paul's argument is from the lesser to the greater; it is a clear case that is difficult, if not impossible, to refute.

6 Not a novice, lest being lifted up with pride he fall into the condemnation of the devil.

The word rendered "novice" is from the Greek *neophutos* (**neh-OF-oo-tos**). Its literal meaning is "newly planted." It is used here of one who is a recent convert to Christianity. While there is a place for such a person in the body of Christ, it is certainly not at the helm of affairs. It is therefore in the interest of the new convert that he be exempt from a leadership position in the church, so that he does not swell with arrogance and incur the same judgment as the devil for the same sin of arrogance. Rather than being immune to sin, church leaders can easily yield to the strong temptation to become conceited due to their position. Church leadership is for service, not to boost one's ego. That is an abuse of office.

7 Moreover he must have a good report of them which are without; lest he fall into reproach and the snare of the devil.

A positive testimony or witness from non-believers is no less important a criterion for church leadership. The reason for this is in order not to give the devil, i.e., "the accuser," grounds to accuse the leader through those outside the church. Today, members of a local church come from near and far; thus, it is nearly impossible to know each person's reputation in their community. Care must be taken that this is done within the provisions of the legal system. A local church that disregards this criterion not only opens her leadership to possible criticism, but also risks damaging the image of the church before outsiders.

8 Likewise must the deacons be grave, not doubletongued, not given to much wine, not greedy of filthy lucre;

The focus here is on the qualifications for the office of deacon. The Greek word for "deacons" is *diakonos* (**dee-AK-on-os**) and generally denotes one who serves. This service can be in various capacities, such as domestic servants (John 2:5, 9), civil rulers (Romans 13:4), followers of Christ (John 12:26), and ministers of the Gospel (1 Timothy 4:6). The term is also used with specific reference to certain officers in the church whose primary duty is characterized by service and administration of the church's material resources (Philippians 1:1).

Most of the qualifications for a deacon are the same as those for an elder, which were covered earlier. The first quality of a deacon is to be "grave." The Greek word is *semnotes* (**sem-NOT-ace**), which also denotes dignity and honesty. The church must not be so desperate for service that it allows just anyone to fill this office. Rather, people who are honorable and honest should be made deacons in the church.

A deacon is not to be "doubletongued" (Gk. *dilogos*, **di-LOG-os**). The term literally means "two words." It describes one who says one thing to one person and a different thing to another. Today, we call it being two-faced. The words of a doubletongued person can't be trusted. A person who can't be trusted in speech should not be trusted with the resources of the church. For example, when a double-tongued person gives a report on the financial state of the church, not many will be inclined to accept it at face value. To prevent such an embarrassment, the church must avoid making such a person a deacon. The qualities relating to wine and love of money have already been discussed (see earlier comments on verse 3).

9 Holding the mystery of the faith in a pure conscience.

A candidate for the position of a deacon must be someone who believes in the "mystery" (Gk. *musterion*, **moos-TAY-ree-on**) of the faith. As used here, the phrase "mystery of the faith" refers to revealed truth of the Gospel. Today, this truth is contained in Scripture. Paul makes clear that this biblical truth must be held in a pure conscience, i.e., a conscience that has been cleansed and made pure by the blood of Christ.

10 And let these also first be proved; then let them use the office of a deacon, being found blameless.

The church must be cautious that candidates are not approved hastily to serve as deacons. It is necessary for a candidate to be screened first before being accepted to serve. The screening should not be just to fulfill all righteousness; the candidate must be deemed "blameless" (Gk. *anegkletos*, **an-ENG-klay-tos**) with respect to the screening standards.

11 Even so must their wives be grave, not slanderers, sober, faithful in all things.

The wives of the deacons are not left out of the equation, since their reputation would rub off on their husbands, either positively or negatively. So, like their husbands, they are to be "grave," i.e., dignified and honest in their conduct. They are not to be "slanderers," from the Greek word *diabolos* (**dee-AB-ol-os**), meaning "false accuser" or "devil." In other words, they should not partner with the devil in falsely accusing others with the intent to destroy.

The word translated "wives" here (Gk. *gune*, **goo-NAY**) can mean either "wives" or "women." More commentators and translators opt for "wives" in light of the context, which focuses on deacons and not deaconesses. This does not rule out the role of deaconesses, as is evidenced by Phebe's example in Romans 16:1.

12 Let the deacons be the husbands of one wife, ruling their children and their own houses well.

Like the overseers, the deacons are to exhibit exemplary leadership in their homes before they are appointed to serve in the church. This qualification requires that the candidate not be a polygamist.

13 For they that have used the office of a deacon well purchase to themselves a good degree, and great boldness in the faith which is in Christ Jesus.

Deacons who distinguished themselves by their quality of service gained two things for themselves that must not be confused with the salvation that they already had. First, they gained a respectable position or standing in the community of believers. Second, they gained great assurance regarding their faith in Jesus. Their quality of service was a confirmation of the saving quality of their faith in Jesus. Theirs is not a dead faith in Christ; their faith is proven by their service.

14 These things write I unto thee, hoping to come unto thee shortly: 15 But if I tarry long, that thou mayest know how thou oughtest to behave thyself in the house of God, which is the church of the living God, the pillar and ground of the truth.

Paul writes these instructions to his young associate, Timothy, who is with the church at Ephesus. These instructions are given to help Timothy know how to regulate conduct in the Ephesian church in the event that Paul is delayed in coming to Ephesus. The church is described as God's house, thus showing the relevance of a house code of conduct. It is also the church of the living God, as contrasted with the many temples of idols in Ephesus. And finally, as the pillar and ground of the truth, the church, based on Scripture, has an authoritative claim to truth that is unequaled. Therefore, members of the church must not discredit by misconduct the truth entrusted to them; instead, they must conduct themselves and their affairs in a manner worthy of the truth they uphold.

DAILY BIBLE READINGS

M: Moses Appoints Israel's Tribal Leaders
Deuteronomy 1:9-18
T: Paul Is Welcomed as a Leader
Galatians 2:1-10
W: Respect Those Who Labor Among You
1 Thessalonians 5:6-15
T: Qualities of a Leader
Titus 1:5-9
F: The Greatest Is Servant of All
Mark 9:33-37
S: Qualifications of Overseers
1 Timothy 3:1-7
S: Qualifications of Helpers
1 Timothy 3:8-15

TEACHING TIPS

1. Words You Should Know

A. Doctrines (1 Timothy 4:1) *didaskalia* (Gk.)—Instruction (the function or the information).

B. Hypocrisy (v. 2) *hupokrisis* (Gk.)—Dissimulation or disguise.

C. Minister (v. 6) *diakonos* (Gk.)—Those who serve. This word emphasizes the humility of Christian service. It emphasizes responsibility rather than privilege. In the Old Testament, ministry was performed by the priests and Levites. The New Testament speaks of each believer as a priest before God.

2. Teacher Preparation

A. Prayerfully read the FOCAL VERSES and DAILY BIBLE READINGS.

B. Prayerfully study the entire BIBLE STUDY GUIDE. Highlight parts to emphasize.

C. Be prepared to discuss the questions and the challenges from the MAKE IT HAPPEN section.

D. Recall some examples of false teaching and their effect on the church.

3. Starting the Lesson

A. Assign a student to lead the class in prayer, focusing on the LESSON AIM.

B. Ask a student to read the IN FOCUS section.

C. Initiate a discussion among the students regarding areas of perceived personal accountability to God.

4. Getting into the Lesson

A. Allow each student to read some portion of THE PEOPLE, PLACES, AND TIMES, BACKGROUND, KEEP IN MIND, and AT-A-GLANCE.

B. Allow each student to read one of the FOCAL VERSES. As each verse is read, discuss and instruct using the portions of IN DEPTH and MORE LIGHT ON THE TEXT that you highlighted in your time of teacher preparation.

C. Ask the students to respond to the SEARCH THE SCRIPTURES questions.

5. Relating the Lesson to Life

A. Have someone read the LESSON IN OUR SOCIETY section.

B. Ask the students to respond to the DISCUSS THE MEANING questions.

6. Arousing Action

A. Ask individual students to express what they are committed to doing.

B. Allow a student who did not respond to read the MAKE IT HAPPEN section.

C. Encourage the students to be prepared for next week's lesson.

WORSHIP GUIDE

For the Superintendent or Teacher
Theme: Guidance for Teaching
Theme Song: "Ring Out the Message"
Scripture: Romans 12
Song: "Stand Up For Jesus"
Meditation: Heavenly Father, our Sovereign Lord, we desire Your rule in our lives. Compel us to read, study, and meditate on Your Word. Speak to our hearts. Give us wisdom and boldness to share with others, and let our hearts be ruled by Your love. Amen.

GUIDANCE FOR TEACHING

Bible Background • 1 TIMOTHY 4
Printed Text • 1 TIMOTHY 4
Devotional Reading • 1 CORINTHIANS 3:6–11

LESSON AIM

By the end of the lesson, we will:

KNOW the purpose and benefit of accurate Bible study;

BE CONVINCED that the application of sound doctrine is essential to eternal salvation, Christian growth, and making disciples; and

APPLY sound doctrine and encourage others to do the same.

KEEP IN MIND

"Take heed unto thyself, and unto the doctrine; continue in them: for in doing this thou shalt both save thyself, and them that hear thee" (1 Timothy 4:16).

LESSON OVERVIEW

LESSON AIM

KEEP IN MIND

FOCAL VERSES

IN FOCUS

THE PEOPLE, PLACES, AND TIMES

BACKGROUND

AT-A-GLANCE

IN DEPTH

SEARCH THE SCRIPTURES

DISCUSS THE MEANING

LESSON IN OUR SOCIETY

MAKE IT HAPPEN

FOLLOW THE SPIRIT

REMEMBER YOUR THOUGHTS

MORE LIGHT ON THE TEXT

DAILY BIBLE READINGS

these things, thou shalt be a good minister of Jesus Christ, nourished up in the words of faith and of good doctrine, whereunto thou hast attained.

7 But refuse profane and old wives' fables, and exercise thyself rather unto godliness.

8 For bodily exercise profiteth little: but godliness is profitable unto all things, having promise of the life that now is, and of that which is to come.

9 This is a faithful saying and worthy of all acceptation.

10 For therefore we both labour and suffer reproach, because we trust in the living God, who is the Saviour of all men, specially of those that believe.

JAN 22ND

FOCAL VERSES

1 Timothy 4:1 Now the Spirit speaketh expressly, that in the latter times some shall depart from the faith, giving heed to seducing spirits, and doctrines of devils;

2 Speaking lies in hypocrisy; having their conscience seared with a hot iron;

3 Forbidding to marry, and commanding to abstain from meats, which God hath created to be received with thanksgiving of them which believe and know the truth.

4 For every creature of God is good, and nothing to be refused, if it be received with thanksgiving:

5 For it is sanctified by the word of God and prayer.

6 If thou put the brethren in remembrance of

11 These things command and teach.

12 Let no man despise thy youth; but be thou an example of the believers, in word, in conversation, in charity, in spirit, in faith, in purity.

13 Till I come, give attendance to reading, to exhortation, to doctrine.

14 Neglect not the gift that is in thee, which was given thee by prophecy, with the laying on of the hands of the presbytery.

15 Meditate upon these things; give thyself wholly to them; that thy profiting may appear to all.

16 Take heed unto thyself, and unto the doctrine; continue in them: for in doing this thou shalt both save thyself, and them that hear thee.

IN FOCUS

Since her first year in high school, Jamie had prayed that her friend Kisha would stop experimenting with drugs. What really troubled Jamie was that Kisha was very active in all the young adult programs at church. She gave Kisha Scripture after Scripture to no avail.

The night before their graduation, Jamie decided to break off their friendship if Kisha wouldn't listen.

"Kisha it is illegal—and you know it is not biblical!"

Kisha argued back. "A lot of spiritualists use drugs to get to a higher consciousness."

"But you are a Christian."

"So. I don't hang around drug people. I just use marijuana recreationally."

Jamie made one last attempt to bring Kisha back to reality. "What if your little brother knew? How would you explain it to him?"

"I'm careful around him—he'll never know."

"But God knows you are being a hypocrite."

That night, Kisha went to bed devastated by Jamie's decision to break off their friendship. In the middle of the night she was awakened by the voice of a beautiful young woman on television giving her testimony about overcoming a life scarred by drugs. The whole time, the woman held out her arms as if she might touch Kisha's face. "If you are using drugs—stop! Your body is the temple of the Holy Spirit."

Kisha listened to the woman's testimony for over an hour in the darkness of her bedroom, crying. At the close of the program, she felt the correcting power of the Holy Spirit purging her desire for drugs. She called Jamie and told her how the Scriptures she had shared had helped guide her to a true Christian walk. Kisha finished college without ever touching drugs again.

First Timothy encourages us to pay close attention to Christian doctrine in order to ensure salvation for ourselves and for those around us. Is your lifestyle helping others by example?

THE PEOPLE, PLACES, AND TIMES

Ephesus. The capital of the Roman province of Asia, located at the mouth of the Cayster River on the west coast of Asia Minor. Its location, roads, and harbors made it an important commercial center. It was known for the temple of Artemis (Diana, KJV), one of the seven wonders of the world.

BACKGROUND

The apostle Paul spent more than two years in Ephesus on his third missionary journey (Acts 19). Timothy was later stationed there as an apostolic representative, giving assistance to local church leaders. Timothy was one of Paul's most active coworkers, having traveled extensively with him (Acts 16:1-3; 19:22; 20:4; 2 Corinthians 1:1, 19) and as his representative on numerous missions (1 Corinthians 16:10; 1 Thessalonians 3:6). He was greatly trusted and beloved by Paul (Phillippians 2:19-22).

AT-A-GLANCE

1. The Minister Warned About False Teachers (1 Timothy 4:1-5)
2. The Minister's Response to False Teachers (vv. 6-10)
3. The Minister's Commitment to Spiritual Maturity (vv. 11-16)

IN DEPTH

1. The Minister Warned About False Teachers (1 Timothy 4:1-5)

The apostle Paul, writing to Timothy, his spiritual "son in the faith," now continues to address issues in the church at Ephesus as he had previously done in the first chapter.

The opening phrase, "Now the Spirit speaketh expressly," means that on this issue the Holy Spirit is speaking distinctly and clearly, and He is speaking on it now. The expression "the latter times" does not have the same meaning as the expression "the last days" found elsewhere in Scripture. According to Hebrews 1:2, "the last days" commenced with the advent of Jesus Christ, the Messiah. The apostle Peter also calls these present times "the last days" in Acts 2:17 and "the last times" in 1 Peter 1:20. The apostle John says the same thing in 1 John 2:18. Therefore, the term "the last days" does not refer only to the time of the second coming of Jesus Christ, but to the entire period from His first coming to His second coming. Believers today are living in "the last days."

The word "times" in 1 Timothy 4:1 carries the idea of a plurality of fixed times or seasons—in other words, something set to occur again and again at its proper time. When the text says "latter times," it means times or seasons that will happen going forward. So the Holy Spirit is saying that at the time of Paul's writing and after that, there will be times when some will depart from the faith. Sometime earlier, before the apostle Paul had written this letter to Timothy and was in Miletus (a city about 30 miles south of Ephesus), he had sent for the elders of the church of Ephesus and warned them that this falling away could occur (Acts 20:29-31). It was happening then, and it is happening now. It continues to occur throughout this present church age. The agents of this deception are evil spirits and those persons who are used by them spread the doctrine of evil (James 3:15). Those who accept the doctrine of devils are victimized by these false teachers. They seduce by deception. The Scriptures speak of evil spirits influencing people (John 8:44; 1 John 4:1-6). The enemy of God and His people is constantly at work in the world, seeking to distort and deny the truth of God (cf. Matthew 24:11-12; 2 Thessalonians 2:1-12; 1 John 2:18-27).

The false teachers use hypocritical teaching to victimize those who fall away. These false teachers make themselves appear to be something they are not. They hide their sinfulness behind a mask portraying righteousness. This is what hypocrisy is. They are comfortable doing this because their conscience is cauterized, or burned as with a hot iron. When this is done to flesh, the flesh becomes desensitized. The action described here is not gradual but swift and decisive.

When the false teachers allowed the doctrine of demons to enter their hearts, a radical act of perversion against the truth of God took place, resulting in total absence of sensitivity to the Holy Spirit. When Christians receive the indwelling of the Holy Spirit and are taught the Word of God, a proper standard develops by which the conscience can operate. The expression "a good conscience" is used in Scripture to describe a condition of the believer in which the conscience, based on a good moral standard and a clean life, does not condemn. However, if the conscience condemns and the person continues in that act of condemnation, his or her life is hypocritical, or a false portrayal of righteousness. Ephesians 4:19 speaks of those "who being past feeling have given themselves over unto lasciviousness, to work all uncleanness with greediness." They became callous from the constant violation of the ways of God. Sincere Christians must not allow this to happen.

These false teachers would forbid marriage, an institution ordained by God. Marriage is the basis of family formation, and the family is the foundation of society. This emphasis on asceticism began to creep into the church in the first century. It was the result of the influence of Gnosticism—the belief that all matter is evil. Thus, anything associated with the human body was seen as evil and to be an ascetic was seen as being holy. They would also forbid the eating of certain solid foods (rendered "meat" in the KJV) which God called good of creation (Genesis 1:31; 9:3).

Both marriage and food are necessary for procreation and life. It is the will of God that His people be fruitful and multiply, both naturally and spiritually. Good things should be received by those who know and serve God and are thankful to Him. In Colossians 2:18-23, the apostle Paul writes that these errors are the result of a false concept of self-abasement. These practices are of no value against fleshly indulgence. Punishing the physical body does not make a person spiritually strong. Here again, we see the enemy attempting to steal the provisions that God gives to His people. Christians should be dead to things that hinder their growth in God. Jesus said, "For out of the heart proceed evil thoughts, murders, adulteries, fornications, thefts, false witness, blasphemies: These are the things which defile a man" (Matthew 15:19-20).

Celibacy and fasting have their place, but they are not meritorious in themselves. Those who are celibate for the kingdom's sake do so in order to devote more of themselves to kingdom work.

Those who fast do so when there is a heartfelt need to get God's attention.

All that God provides is good. By God's grace, people receive life-sustaining provisions; therefore, all people should be thankful... "for he maketh his sun to rise on the evil and on the good, and sendeth rain on the just and on the unjust" (Matthew 5:45). God does this because He loves people.

God spoke to Peter in a trance and told him that whatever He had cleansed, Peter was not to call unclean (Acts 10:15). The things that God provides for His people fulfill the purpose of God. They are sanctified (set apart or dedicated) for His holy purpose. But they only fulfill that purpose if they are used according to His Word and guidance in prayer. By the Word of God, Christians understand God's design for marriage and the proper treatment of their body in a general sense. Through prayer, they receive guidance and assistance that enables them to have Christ-centered families and productive lives.

2. The Minister's Response to False Teachers (vv. 6-10)

The good minister (servant) of Christ guards his people from the vicious attacks of the enemy. Since the enemy will come disguised, with evil cloaked in an appearance of righteousness, appearing even as an angel of light (2 Corinthians 11:13-15), the people of God must be kept in remembrance of these things. They must be sober and vigilant (alert) because their adversary, the devil, walks about like a roaring lion, seeking whom he may devour. The believer resists or stands up against him by being steadfast in the faith (1 Peter 5:8-9). This requires the believer to know sound doctrine and obey the instruction of God.

Christians are encouraged to be "as newborn babes, desire the sincere milk of the word, that ye may grow thereby" (1 Peter 2:2). The Word of God is as essential to spiritual life and growth as milk is to the proper development of newborn babies. The good minister will instruct his people in the words of faith and good "sound" doctrine. The expression "words of faith" is a reference to the Scriptures, which is the spoken Word of God

revealed. The theology that the Word of God teaches is called "good doctrine."

The good minister keeps himself "nourished up" in the words of faith and good teaching (doctrine) so that he may be a workman that need not be ashamed, rightly dividing (literally, "cutting it straight" with precision and with accuracy) the word of truth (2 Timothy 2:15). He is responsible to himself and to those he serves.

The good minister must remind his people that the Holy Spirit speaks the words of God and not the fables and myths of individuals. The fables, myths, speculations, and imaginations of individuals serve no useful purpose; rather, they are a distraction and a waste of time. Therefore, the good minister refuses to entertain them. Though he must vigorously challenge false teaching with sound teaching, he must not bother to even argue against myths and old wives' tales that can lead to endless debates about nothing of spiritual value.

Rather than wasting time, the good minister should keep on exercising godliness (piety). All effective ministry must start with a proper attitude and response toward God. The effort required on the part of the good minister is comparable to the effort and training of a serious athlete. The extent and duration of athletic training is limited and temporal. Its benefit is limited to the physical body. Though some great athletes have their time of glory, it soon comes to an end. But godliness is of benefit in this life for an entire lifetime and for all eternity in the next life, and godliness benefits all aspects of life—soul, body, and spirit as well as the circumstances of life. Godliness is consistent with the great message of the Gospel (1 Timothy 3:16). The benefits of godliness are trustworthy and far-reaching.

Since godliness is profitable, it is the goal toward which all believers labor (work hard; exhaust themselves) and suffer abuse. Their faith and trust are in the one living and active God who is the hope of salvation for the entire world and the eternal Saviour for those who trust Him in faith and believe. The expression "Saviour of all men" does not mean, as some might suggest, that all mankind is saved from eternal punishment (Matthew 7:14; Revelation 20:12-15). God is a

Saviour to all in this temporal world to the extent that He sustains life and provides its desirable attributes (theologians call this "common grace"), but His salvation is complete and eternal for those who accept Jesus Christ as Lord and Saviour.

3. The Minister's Commitment to Spiritual Maturity (vv. 11-16)

The diligent minister should command and teach "these things" on an ongoing basis. "These things" are the study and proclamation of sound doctrine, a life of reverence toward God, and an aggressive repudiation of false doctrine. He is authorized to command and teach continually what the Holy Spirit expressly says in order to secure the believers.

Timothy lived in a world that respected elders (overseers) older than himself. So as a younger minister, he would have to earn the admiration and respect of others by example. The word "youth," as used in verse 12, is a relative term and could apply to anyone under 40 years of age. He was considered young for the position and had responsibility, but he certainly was not without experience or examination by Paul since he had been with Paul during the second missionary journey perhaps some 13 years earlier. There was no legitimate reason for anyone to despise (to think against or look down upon) him. Nevertheless, so that he may give no cause for disdain, Timothy is urged to live above reproach by being an example in the things he says (word), in the way he lives and conducts himself (conversation), in self-sacrificial giving to others (charity), in spirit, in steadfast dependability (faith), and in moral living (purity). This is good counsel for any good servant.

The good minister is commanded to keep on (as a general habit) participating in public worship, reading the Scriptures, encouraging the application and practice of the Scriptures that are read, and teaching the meaning of Scripture in a systematic and practical way. Exhortation appeals to the will and the emotions. Teaching appeals more to the rational faculties.

The word "gift" (literally "grace-gift"), in verse 14, means a divinely bestowed grace used to perform a Spirit-empowered service for the body of Christ (the church). It is a gift that comes only from God and can never be attained or developed by man's own efforts (Romans 12:3). It is given for the equipping of the saints for the work of service, to the building up of the body of Christ (Ephesians 4:12; 1 Peter 4:10). It is given for the common good (1 Corinthians 12:7). God knows the needs of the church (12:11). When the "grace-gift" is not functioning according to the wisdom of God, the members suffer and the body suffers. The servant must never neglect the "grace-gift" and function given by God. The "grace-gift" given to Timothy was revealed by a God-inspired utterance (prophecy). In obedience to this, the elders confirmed it by the laying of hands. As Timothy is diligent in these matters ("grace-gifts") and gives himself wholly to them continually, the ever-increasing benefit becomes evident to all.

Finally, in verse 16, there is a summation of the responsibilities of a good servant. First and foremost, before he can minister to others, he must take heed to himself and his personal life. He must take heed to studying the Scriptures, godliness, the teaching and preaching (exhortation) of sound doctrine, and the work of the ministry. By doing so continually, the mature servant will allow God to work salvation in himself and in those his ministry reaches (Philippians 2:12-13).

SEARCH THE SCRIPTURES

1. Explain the difference between the "the latter times" and "the last days" (1 Timothy 4:1).

2. How were the false teachers able to teach lies without conviction (v. 2)?

3. What can a relatively young servant do to gain the approval of those served (vv. 6, 12)?

4. Can a ministry be effective and grow if only natural talents are used? Please explain (vv. 14-16).

5. Summarize the responsibilities of a good servant (vv. 4-16).

DISCUSS THE MEANING

1. What are some false teachings unique to the Black community that cause Blacks to abandon the Christian faith?

2. What "grace-gifts" are evident in the church today? In what ways have these gifts benefited believers in the local church? What evidence can be presented to suggest that believers are neglecting their gifts?

3. What can the student do to prevent a "falling away" of those who attend the local church?

LESSON IN OUR SOCIETY

On the eve of his assassination in Memphis, Tennessee, Dr. Martin Luther King Jr. issued a challenge in much the same way as the apostle Paul did to Timothy—"And you know what's beautiful to me, is to see all of these ministers of the Gospel. It's a marvelous picture. Who is it that is supposed to articulate the longings and aspirations of the people more than the preacher? Somehow the preacher must be an Amos, and say, 'Let justice roll down like waters and righteousness like a mighty stream.' Somehow, the preacher must say with Jesus, 'The spirit of the Lord is upon me, because he hath anointed me to deal with the problems of the poor.'" How is this statement similar to this apostle Paul's charge to Timothy? How do the statements differ?

MAKE IT HAPPEN

Christians must be accountable to themselves and to their brothers and sisters in Christ. Family members can be accountable to one another by setting aside time to study the Bible and pray together and by the example they portray in the home. As a servant to others, you are first of all accountable for knowing your assignment from God and the gift(s) He has graced you with in order to accomplish your assignment. Identify needs that are not being met in your church and community. Ask God to show you what you can do to address those needs. Be faithful to what He assigns you to do. Periodically, evaluate your progress and take action to correct any deficiencies.

FOLLOW THE SPIRIT

What God wants me to do:

_____

_____

REMEMBER YOUR THOUGHTS

Special insights I have learned:

_____

_____

MORE LIGHT ON THE TEXT

1 Timothy 4

1 Now the Spirit speaketh expressly, that in the latter times some shall depart from the faith, giving heed to seducing spirits, and doctrines of devils;

Paul here appeals to the prophetic voice of the Spirit to confirm what was already happening in his day, specifically in the Ephesian church; i.e., some Christians were abandoning their faith. The Greek word is *aphistemi* (**af-IS-tay-mee**) and means "to draw away, fall away, or apostatize." Some people depart from the faith by going after deceitful spirits and their demonic teachings. These deserters became agents of demonic false teachings. Sometimes Christians are unaware that false teachings originate from demons who seek to lead believers astray. Combating false teachings is a spiritual battle. One needs to put on the whole armor of the Spirit, which includes the Word of God as the sword of the Spirit (Ephesians 6:17).

2 Speaking lies in hypocrisy; having their conscience seared with a hot iron; 3 Forbidding to marry, and commanding to abstain from meats, which God hath created to be received with thanksgiving of them which believe and know the truth.

These false teachers present their falsehood in a hypocritical manner that rings true to their audience. Their tactics are similar to Satan's, who presents himself as an "angel of light" (2 Corinthians 11:14). The false teachers had first "seared" their consciences, thereby rendering themselves insensitive to the falsehood they knowingly peddled. It is important to test new teachings before our minds are desensitized by them.

Demonic teaching prohibits marriage and promotes abstinence from certain foods. This ascetic lifestyle is based on an Ephesian worldview that sees matter as evil and the spirit as good.[1]

Marriage is the union of two bodies, and food is used to sustain the body. Since both body and food are material, both are evil, according to this heresy. The heretics missed the truth that God created foods and marriage and intends for them to be enjoyed to His glory. Since these things derive from God, they cannot be evil in themselves unless God Himself is the Author of evil, which cannot be! God created matter and put it under man's dominion for His own glory. However, this fact does not give man the liberty to exploit this matter for his own selfish ends, but for the glory of God.

4 For every creature of God is good, and nothing to be refused, if it be received with thanksgiving: 5 For it is sanctified by the word of God and prayer.

Paul offers Timothy two reasons why the heretics are wrong. First, they are wrong because the things God created for our pleasure are inherently good and not evil as long as they are received with thanksgiving. Created things can become evil if they are abused or used in a manner that does not glorify God. The second reason the heretics are wrong is that created things are also sanctified—"hagiazo" (Gk. **hag-ee-ad-zo**)—i.e., set apart for God. Genesis 1 declares creation good no less than six times, and Jesus in Mark 7:18-19 declared all foods clean in themselves.

6 If thou put the brethren in remembrance of these things, thou shalt be a good minister of Jesus Christ, nourished up in the words of faith and of good doctrine, whereunto thou hast attained.

In light of the threat posed by false teachers in Ephesus, Paul encouraged Timothy to call the believers' attention to the truth of the matter. The Greek word *epios* (**AY-pee-os**) is suggestive of a gentle, humble, and modest instruction rather than a harsh, dogmatic chastisement. Timothy's ability to take such a corrective measure against false teaching would be a test of the quality of his service for Christ. It would also serve as evidence of Timothy's nurture and maturity in the Word. It is not enough for a leader to know the Word; it is also important to know how to apply it to differ-

ent life situations. The church does not need ministers who only entertain with the Word, but ministers who can correct, encourage, and challenge through the Word.

7 But refuse profane and old wives' fables, and exercise thyself rather unto godliness.

To qualify as a good minister of Christ requires spiritual exercise. Just as an athlete must avoid certain lifestyles to be in top form, so must the minister of Christ avoid certain things. He must avoid things that are "profane." The Greek term is *bebelos* (**BEB-ay-los**). It refers to that which lacks all relationship or affinity to God. Here, it has particular reference to, but is not limited to, godless speech. The other thing to be shunned is "fables" (Gk. *muthos*, **MOO-thos**), which is a reference to myths or a fictitious story that has no factual basis. That is how Paul regards the false teachings of the previous verses. Instead of dabbling in these, Timothy was to discipline himself to achieve godliness.

8 For bodily exercise profiteth little: but godliness is profitable unto all things, having promise of the life that now is, and of that which is to come.

Paul compares physical exercise with spiritual exercise and concludes that, while the former has some temporary benefit, spiritual exercise is much more profitable in terms of both quantity and quality. Unlike physical exercise, which affects only certain aspects of life on earth, spiritual exercise affects every aspect of life here on earth and makes one fit for life in the hereafter. Whatever the sphere of our ministry, be it teaching, preaching, or service, it is profitable for here and eternity that we cultivate a disciplined life that is inclined toward God.

9 This is a faithful saying and worthy of all acceptation. 10 For therefore we both labour and suffer reproach, because we trust in the living God, who is the Saviour of all men, specially of those that believe.

Here, as in 1 Timothy 1:15, the formula "this is a faithful saying" is a common way of presenting the reliability of a doctrine or practice. And we believe that in this context, the phrase refers back to Paul's claim in verse 8 regarding the superior benefit of spiritual exercise compared with physical exercise. While Paul's conclusion in verse 8 might not have attained the status of a maxim (a generally accepted saying), he says that it is worthy of such recognition.

Therefore, given the established benefit of spiritual exercise that cultivates godliness, Paul and his associates were willing to "labour and suffer reproach." The Greek word for "labour" is *kotaponeo* (**kat-ap-on-EH-o**) and denotes hard work that results in weariness such as a laborer experiences after a hard day's toil under the sun. The Greek term for "suffer" is the more familiar word *adikeo* (**ad-ee-KEH-o**), which refers to agony or the kind of energy that athletes exert in their struggle to win a prize. All of this goes to show that a life aimed at godliness to which the minister of the Word is called has no room for laziness, just as there is no room for an undisciplined athlete in the hall of fame.

11 These things command and teach. 12 Let no man despise thy youth; but be thou an example of the believers, in word, in conversation, in charity, in spirit, in faith, in purity.

Timothy was charged to command and teach the instructions in this epistle. A command calls for obedience, while teaching calls for understanding. Timothy's task as a pastor was to make sure these instructions were obeyed and understood. Timothy was to discharge these pastoral duties in an exemplary way that would not cause people to disrespect him because of his age. Though Timothy was young, if he led an exemplary life, it would earn him the respect of the believers, thereby making it easier for him to teach and enforce the instructions of Paul. To be effective, ministers must teach by both words and conduct.

Timothy was to be an example to the believers. The Greek word for "example" is *tupos* (**TOO-pos**) and is used to refer to a model to be imitated by others. It also refers to an instance to be avoided. Timothy was to be a model for others to imitate in his speech, in conversation (i.e., the way he lived), in charity (referring to the objects of his affection, like not loving money), in spirit (his inner quality, which would find expression in his speech and conduct), in faith (the object of his belief, like not holding to false teachings), and in purity (which refers to holiness in act and thought). We all function as an example.

13 Till I come, give attendance to reading, to exhortation, to doctrine.

Pending the arrival of Paul in Ephesus, Timothy's pastoral duties were to include three things. The first was public reading of Scripture. This was a practice that had been adopted by the early church from Jewish worship in the synagogue (compare the examples in Luke 4:16; Acts 13:27; 15:21). There is an urgent need for reading sizable portions of Scripture in our services today, for that is the only encounter many have with Scripture for the rest of the week.

The second duty for Timothy was exhortation, which is encouraging believers through the Word. Believers need to be inspired from the truth of Scripture.

The third duty was doctrine. The Greek word for "doctrine" is *didaskalia* (**did-as-kal-EE-ah**), which means "that which is taught." All three functions are centered around the ministry of the Word. The Word, rather than human tradition, philosophy, or psychology, should be the basis of our ministry.

14 Neglect not the gift that is in thee, which was given thee by prophecy, with the laying on of the hands of the presbytery.

Timothy was probably making light of a spiritual gift he had received earlier, not finding relevant use for it while he was an associate of Paul. The Greek word used here for "gift" is *charisma* (**KHAR-is-mah**). It denotes a freely given gift. In this case, the gift is spiritual endowment for service. Timothy now finds himself alone in a leadership position in the strategic church of Ephesus. He was charged to stop neglecting his gift and step up to the plate.

The giving of the gift to Timothy was initiated through a prophetic utterance,[2] thereby showing that the Spirit dispenses His gifts to believers as He deems fit. The Spirit also deemed it appropriate to bestow the gift on Timothy through the instrument of the elders' laying hands on him. In this way, Timothy's consecration and authority for ministry were given public recognition. Like Paul, believers should be a source of inspiration rather than discouragement to those called to lead the church of Christ.

15 Meditate upon these things; give thyself wholly to them; that thy profiting may appear to all.

Finally, Timothy was called to meditate on the instructions given to him. The word translated "meditate" is the Greek word *meletao* (**mel-et-AH-o**) and has the force of practicing or caring for something. As a leader, Timothy was expected to practice the instructions given to him. It is a common temptation of ministers to approach the Word only as a source of preaching and teaching, forgetting that it is also designed to shape their own conduct. Many pastors are so preoccupied with what they can do with the Word that they are missing out on what the Word can do for them.

Timothy was also to give himself wholly to the instructions of this epistle. When a teacher is absolutely sold on the veracity of his teaching, it is apparent in his tone, his passion, his commitment, and his endurance to get the message across.

16 Take heed unto thyself, and unto the doctrine; continue in them: for in doing this thou shalt both save thyself, and them that hear thee.

In caring for others, Timothy must not neglect to pay attention to himself. It has been rightly observed that a Christian must first watch his/her own inner life as well as the outer life. Too often, ministers of the Gospel are so busy caring for others that they take no time to pay attention to themselves. In addition, Timothy was to pay attention to his teaching and continue doing it. This was necessary to ensure that what he taught corresponded to revealed truth. In this case, it is not only the buyer (student) who needs to beware; but even the seller (teacher) needs to beware, making sure his products have not been adulterated.

Endnotes
1. William Barclay, *The Letters to Timothy, Titus, and Philemon* (Philadelphia, Penn.: Westminster Press, 1975), 93.

2. Walter Lock, *A Critical and Exegetical Commentary on the Pastoral Epistles* (New York, N.Y.: Charles Scribner's Sons, 1924), 49.

DAILY BIBLE READINGS

M: Moses Teaches Israel to Obey
Deuteronomy 4:1-8
T: Give Ear to My Teaching
Psalm 78:1-8
W: Rules for the New Life
Ephesians 4:25-5:2
T: The Teacher's Gift Is Teaching
Romans 12:3-8
F: A Warning Against False Teaching
1 Timothy 4:1-5
S: Train Yourself in Godliness
1 Timothy 4:6-10
S: —Put All These Things into Practice
1 Timothy 4:11-16

TEACHING TIPS

January 29
Bible Study Guide 9

1. Words You Should Know

A. Rebuke (1 Timothy 5:1) *epiplesso* (Gk.)—To chastise with words; to upbraid; figuratively, to strike out with words.

B. Muzzle (v. 18) *phimoo* (Gk.)—To make speechless, reduce to silence; to be kept in check.

2. Teacher Preparation

A. Prayerfully read the FOCAL VERSES and the DEVOTIONAL READING.

B. Prayerfully study the entire BIBLE STUDY GUIDE. Highlight parts to emphasize.

C. Be prepared to discuss the questions and challenges from the MAKE IT HAPPEN section.

D. Name some procedures in place in your church that maintain accountability for purity and charity, or note some actions that need to be taken in your church.

3. Starting the Lesson

A. Assign a student to lead the class in prayer, focusing on the LESSON AIM.

B. Ask a student to read the IN FOCUS section.

C. Initiate a preliminary discussion about how the congregation can determine who requires the most help from them.

4. Getting into the Lesson

A. Allow each student to read some portion of THE PEOPLE, PLACES, AND TIMES, BACKGROUND, KEEP IN MIND, and AT-A-GLANCE section.

B. Allow each student to read one of the FOCAL VERSES. As each verse is read, discuss and instruct using the portions of IN DEPTH and MORE LIGHT ON THE TEXT that you highlighted in your time of teacher preparation.

C. Ask the students to respond to the SEARCH THE SCRIPTURES questions.

5. Relating the Lesson to Life

A. Ask the students to respond to the DISCUSS THE MEANING questions.

B. Have someone read the LESSON IN OUR SOCIETY section.

6. Arousing Action

A. Allow the students to meditate on the MAKE IT HAPPEN section.

B. Ask the students to take a few minutes to respond to the FOLLOW THE SPIRIT and REMEMBER YOUR THOUGHTS sections.

C. Encourage the students to be prepared for next week's lesson.

GOD DESIRES JUSTICE AND MERCY

Bible Background • 1 TIMOTHY 5
Printed Text • 1 TIMOTHY 5:1–8, 17–24
Devotional Reading • MATTHEW 23:23–28

LESSON AIM

By the end of the lesson, we will:

KNOW how church members should be treated;

BE CONVINCED that God requires justice and mercy among His people; and

DETERMINE to preserve one another with love, truth, and provisions.

KEEP IN MIND

"Rebuke not an elder, but intreat him as a father; and the younger men as brethren; The elder women as mothers; the younger as sisters, with all purity" (1 Timothy 5:1-2).

FOCAL VERSES

1 Timothy 5:1 Rebuke not an elder, but intreat him as a father; and the younger men as brethren;

2 The elder women as mothers; the younger as sisters, with all purity.

3 Honour widows that are widows indeed.

4 But if any widow have children or nephews, let them learn first to shew piety at home, and to requite their parents: for that is good and acceptable before God.

5 Now she that is a widow indeed, and desolate, trusteth in God, and continueth in supplications and prayers night and day.

6 But she that liveth in pleasure is dead while she liveth.

7 And these things give in charge, that they may be blameless.

8 But if any provide not for his own, and specially for those of his own house, he hath denied

LESSON OVERVIEW

LESSON AIM
KEEP IN MIND
FOCAL VERSES
IN FOCUS
THE PEOPLE, PLACES, AND TIMES
BACKGROUND
AT-A-GLANCE
IN DEPTH
SEARCH THE SCRIPTURES
DISCUSS THE MEANING
LESSON IN OUR SOCIETY
MAKE IT HAPPEN
FOLLOW THE SPIRIT
REMEMBER YOUR THOUGHTS
MORE LIGHT ON THE TEXT
DAILY BIBLE READINGS

the faith, and is worse than an infidel.

5:17 Let the elders that rule well be counted worthy of double honour, especially they who labour in the word and doctrine.

18 For the scripture saith, Thou shalt not muzzle the ox that treadeth out the corn. And, The labourer is worthy of his reward.

19 Against an elder receive not an accusation, but before two or three witnesses.

20 Them that sin rebuke before all, that others also may fear.

21 I charge thee before God, and the Lord Jesus Christ, and the elect angels, that thou observe these things without preferring one before

JAN 29TH

another, doing nothing by partiality.

22 Lay hands suddenly on no man, neither be partaker of other men's sins: keep thyself pure.

23 Drink no longer water, but use a little wine for thy stomach's sake and thine often infirmities.

24 Some men's sins are open beforehand, going before to judgment; and some men they follow after.

IN FOCUS

When the police came knocking at the door of 80-year-old Rosa's house, she was fast asleep. The State Drug Enforcement Agency heaved a stun grenade into the bungalow, where it exploded with a blinding white flash, a deafening bang, and a thunderous concussion.

Her 26-year-old grandson, Julius, who had been staying temporarily at his grandmother's home, came charging out of the basement disoriented and confused. Two officers handcuffed and arrested him for trafficking in cocaine and selling illegal assault weapons.

Rosa suffered a mild heart attack from the effects of the stun grenade and lay semiconscious on her bedroom floor. The police dispatched an ambulance and rushed her to the hospital.

Afterward, her solidly Christian family surrounded her hospital bedside. They began to heap blame on Julius, who had been in trouble since his early teens.

His sister recounted the things he had stolen from her over the years.

His mother said, "He ain't never going to amount to nothing."

His uncle declared, "He can no longer count him as part of the family."

Finally, Rosa spoke in a weakened voice, "I forgive Julius."

The uncle asked why she would say such a thing when he had brought her so close to death's door. She replied, "Because my prayers are fixed on my hope in God. I pray to heaven every night and morning that he might become a strong man of God. If the charges are true, Julius must suffer the consequences of his actions, and if it is jail time, so be it." Then she narrowed her brow and gave a gentle rebuke aimed at each of them. "If we can't forgive Julius, how can we draw him closer to the salvation that Christ offers everyone?"

Rosa's gentle rebuke of her family reminds us of Paul's letter to Timothy, which requires Christians to provide for our own, and especially for those in our household. Our Christian walk requires that we practice justice and mercy in all life situations. Are there people in your life that you believe are beyond salvation?

THE PEOPLE, PLACES, AND TIMES

Widows and Orphans. In the Mosaic law, special regard was given to widows and orphans. They were partly dependent on family, especially the eldest son, who received a double portion of the inheritance. They also participated in the third type of tithe, which occurred every three years (Deuteronomy 26:12-13); in gleaning produce left in the field (24:19-21); and in religious feasts (16:14). God proclaimed Himself "married" to the widow and orphan (Psalm 68:5) and condemned those who oppressed them (Malachi 3:5). The New Testament church continued to support widows, as can be seen in the lesson today.

Laying Hands. The laying on of hands was done as part of the ceremony of appointment and consecration of persons to a sacred function (Numbers 27:18-20; Acts 6:6; 13:3). It was also used for the bestowal of blessing (Genesis 48:14; Mark 10:16), healing (Mark 5:23), and supernatural gifts (Acts 19:6). This action was accompanied by prayer to God, who alone could effect the desired results. It was a point of contact by which identification was made with the request for or charge to the recipient.

BACKGROUND

Most traditional Bible historians agree that the apostle Paul was released from his first Roman confinement some time between A.D. 62 and 64. After his release, he revisited several cities where he had previously ministered, including Ephesus. Apparently, he saw a need to leave his trusted co-worker Timothy there while continuing on to Macedonia. In all probability, he witnessed conditions in and around the local church that he would later address under the inspiration of the Holy Spirit in his letter to Timothy. One can imagine Paul taking these concerns to God, and God, in His infinite wisdom, providing specific instruction for the church then and now. Some of the themes addressed included false doctrine, false teachers, prayer, requirements for public worship, requirements for spiritual leaders, godliness, and, as seen in today's lesson, justice and mercy.

AT-A-GLANCE

1. Proper Correction for Believers
(1 Timothy 5:1-2)
2. Proper Support for the Destitute
(vv. 3-8)
3. Proper Treatment for Pastor-Teachers
(vv. 17-24)

IN DEPTH

1. Proper Correction for Believers (1 Timothy 5:1-2)

The apostle Paul now turns to the practical application of love within the body of Christ. God so loved the world that He gave His Son, the Living Word. The Word of God serves a number of purposes, including rebuke for wrong belief or behavior and correction (restoration back to godly living). The body of believers are the "pillar and ground of the truth" (1 Timothy 3:15), so purity (godliness) must be maintained. The love of God demands it. It is not His will for His children to suffer spiritual devastation (Matthew 18:14). Those He loves, He chastens, as parents do their children (1 Peter 4:17; Hebrews 12:10-11). Believers must be accountable to one another as well. Jesus provides guidelines for restoring a believer (Matthew 18:15-19), which are echoed in this lesson's text. Rebuke and correction should not be done in an offensive way (Romans 14:13, 19, 21; 15:2). A self-righteous, vindictive attitude is not appropriate. The goal is to draw the errant believer into godliness, not to drive him out into more sin. This is accomplished through exhortation.

As used in 1 Timothy 5:1, the word "intreat" (exhort) carries the same connotation as one of the functions of the Holy Spirit, i.e., to call near or to come alongside in order to assist or comfort. The use of the word "elder" here does not mean an official, but rather is part of specific age groups. Not being offensive requires taking into consideration the type of person being addressed. What is appropriate is determined by age and function. This is a wakeup call to a society that abandons the manners God deems as appropriate. An adult is not spoken to like a child, and a mature person is not addressed harshly (upbraided) or with disrespect. Instead, approach a mature person as a parent and a younger adult as a sibling while not compromising the truth. God's design for a family provides a model for the relationship between believers, who make up the family of God. No one is exempt from correction appropriately done.

2. Proper Support for the Destitute (vv. 3-8)

Paul next turns his attention to the most needy group in the church. The need to provide assisted living became apparent early in the church in Jerusalem (Acts 6:1). The society of that day provided no honorable work for women. Women relied on the support of their families, which could be a father, a husband, a family business, or children. For this reason, God gave special consideration to widows and orphans (Exodus 22:22-24; James 1:27). Catastrophic events such as famines, persecutions, and relocation increased the numbers of those in need beyond just widows. The apostles placed a high priority on daily distributions by establishing a new ministry for this purpose. Those chosen to do this were called deacons. The source of these distributions were offerings from the believers, who were of one heart and mind (Acts 4:32; 11:29). They understood that everything they had belonged to God and that they were obligated to share what belonged to God with the needy. They were enthusiastic about doing this (2 Corinthians 9:7). The apostle John said that love for God is demonstrated by the way we treat those in need (1 John 3:17). The apostle James added that faith in God is demonstrated by the way we treat the destitute (James 2:15-16).

Paul defines four types of widows in 1 Timothy 5:

a. Widows indeed (vv. 3, 5, 16) are widows who are desolate (without a husband or family to provide support), trust in God (true believers), and continue in supplications and prayers night and day (spiritual or godly women). They are dependent on God to provide benefactors. These widows are to be honored (valued and respected) by the church. This includes financial assistance from believers.

b. Widows not completely destitute (left alone) are those who should receive their support from existing children or descendants (family). This can include support from other women (vv. 4, 8, 16). Doing this is consistent with God's moral law (Exodus 20:12; Matthew 15:4-6; Mark 7:9-13). Not to do so is to live a life inconsistent with one's profession of faith and the lordship of Jesus Christ. It denies the testimony of Christ to a fallen world. Even unbelievers do acts of love for those they love (Matthew 5:46). In this sense, believers who neglect their duty to their own family are worse

Show honor to one another.

than unbelievers. Though the issue is not addressed here by Paul, widows who are totally abandoned by their family should be able to appeal to their church family.

c. Widows who are pleasure seekers (v. 6) are those living promiscuously, those satisfying lustful or sensual desires, or those having immoral and worldly hearts. These widows are spiritually dead and unregenerate. The church is not obligated to support their lifestyle. Believers are obligated to evangelize them like all other unregenerate people. In this sense, Christian love is still exercised.

d. The final type of widow Paul identifies is enrolled widows (vv. 9, 10). Although the meaning is obscure, some view this group as a subset of widows indeed who should be given the highest priority or perhaps be eligible for permanent daily distributions, while support for the rest (younger) who potentially could work or get married would be temporary. Church resources were limited, so they had to be managed in the most sympathetic way. Others view this group as a subset of widows indeed who qualified for ministry assignments reserved for mature widows.

Paul instructs chargers or commands the believers that these things be done (v. 7).

3. Proper Treatment for Pastor-Teachers (vv. 17-24)

The elders discussed in this section are officials in the church, not merely the mature men discussed in verse 1. They are referred to as elders that rule (1 Timothy 3:5; 5:17). The word "rule" means to preside over, oversee, or manage like a superintendent. Prayer and the ministry of the Word are of the highest priority for spiritual leaders (Acts 6:4; James 5:14). These are their primary functions in the local church (Titus 1:5-9). These men are the pastor-teachers (Ephesians 4:11), bishops, overseers, and shepherds (Acts 20:28). They are those responsible, as 1 Timothy 4:13 says, for reading, exhortation, and teaching with God-given authority. They labor to the point of exhaustion, stand before the people to lead them in godliness (Hebrews 13:7, 17), and admonish the people (1 Thessalonians 5:12). Their qualifications are given in 1 Timothy 3.

The church at Ephesus had a number of elders (Acts 20:17). Here, Paul provides guidelines for their treatment in terms of honoring, protecting, correcting, and selecting. Those who rule "full well," or excellently, and those who put all their energy into preaching (word) and teaching (doctrine), should be recognized and commended. Their efforts should not go unnoticed or be taken for granted, but they are to be observed and remembered. These men are worthy of "double honour." There is room for discussion of the meaning of "double honour," but it is doubtful that this term means double pay. More likely, it means a distinction in recognition and compensation between the more excellent and hardworking elder and the elder whose effort is not as extensive. The verses that follow support the conclusion that compensation is included in being honored.

Paul appeals to both Old and New Testament Scripture (Luke 10:7) to confirm that the Lord has commanded that those who preach the Gospel should get their living from the Gospel (1 Corinthians 9:14). Elsewhere, he effectively argues that the willingness of people to pay for material things should be superseded by a willingness to pay for spiritual things that have eternal value (v. 11). Another noteworthy point made by Paul is that God includes in the law a command concerned with the proper treatment of a beast of burden. It was humane for an animal who labored tirelessly to be allowed to eat while working.

Pastor-teachers are not above reproach. They are admonished to carefully watch themselves; nevertheless, they can and do err. In such cases, correction is required. On the other hand, their function makes them desirable targets of slander from the enemy. When this happens, they are entitled to the same protection as any believer. Jesus set forth this process in Matthew 18:15-20. First, the believer considered to be in error is confronted privately. If the issue is not resolved, the believer considered to be in error is confronted with sufficient evidence by two or three witnesses who are in agreement. In the absence of evidence, no accusations should be made. Disciplinary proceedings should not be based on rumors. Finally, the believer considered to be in error is taken before the entire local assembly. Correction should be witnessed by the entire congregation so that all may know that sin cannot be tolerated regardless of whose sin it is. If repentance is warranted but is not forthcoming, the guilty believer is removed from the local assembly. Again, as taught in the first two verses of this chapter, the goal is restoration.

All discipline of pastor-teachers is to be done without partiality or prejudice. This means that no one is exempt from correction, nor should anyone be singled out because of prejudice (judgment prior to consideration of the facts) or dislike. Paul stressed the importance of justice on the part of the believers by reminding them that they function before God the Father, the Lord Jesus Christ, and the elect angels.

Pastor-teachers must not be appointed hastily; rather, a thorough evaluation must be done. The appointed person should also have attained a proper level of maturity (1 Timothy 3:6). Those who neglect to do this are liable for any misconduct on the part of the one appointed. Imagine the scandal an appointment committee suffers by appointing a spiritual leader who misleads the people. Instead, leaders should keep themselves pure by following the instruction given in 1 Timothy 3:1-13 and Titus 1:5-9.

Jesus says that people are known by the fruit they bear. Some candidates for leadership can be either eliminated or supported on the basis of what has been observed prior to consideration.

More time is required to observe and evaluate others. The character of a person eventually becomes evident. A patient, methodical, and discerning approach results in wise selections.

Paul encouraged Timothy to maintain his physical health with a little wine. Overseers were cautioned against the consumption of wine to satisfy personal desire (1 Timothy 3:3); however, the use of wine in place of polluted drinking water or for medicinal reasons was warranted.

SEARCH THE SCRIPTURES

1. What is meant by the word "elder" in 1 Timothy 5:1? Does the word "elders" have the same meaning in verse 17?

2. What model is given for how believers should relate to one another in the church (vv. 1-2)?

3. How should mercy be shown toward widows (vv. 3-8)?

4. Who is worthy of double honor (v. 17)?

5. What serious charge does the apostle Paul give in verse 21?

DISCUSS THE MEANING

1. What obligation do believers have toward the homeless and the beggars on the street?

2. Think of at least three different ways believers can neglect their duty to their spiritual leaders. What needs to be done in your church to correct this?

LESSON IN OUR SOCIETY

Churches were among the first Black organizations established. They were the primary institutions serving the community's religious, social, and political needs. As early as the 1780s, African Americans in northern cities established hundreds of mutual aid societies, churches, and fraternal organizations. Cooperative organizations provided benefits for burials and for the support of widows, orphans, the sick, and the unemployed. One of the first examples was the Free Africa Society, which was founded by Richard Allen and Absalom Jones in 1787 in Philadelphia, Pennsylvania. When we consider the obstacles that our ancestors overcame to love God and people through acts of mercy, should we not be stirred to do the same?

MAKE IT HAPPEN

Review the attitude you have toward church leaders and individual church members. Are there some believers you just don't like? Are there some believers you look down upon? Could you consciously or unconsciously be part of a clique? Perhaps you see a need but don't feel obligated to help. Be honest with yourself and try in your heart to relate to others God's way. Admit to God areas that need correction in your life and ask Him to help you as you labor to do the right thing.

FOLLOW THE SPIRIT

What God wants me to do:

_____

_____

REMEMBER YOUR THOUGHTS

Special insights I have learned:

_____

_____

MORE LIGHT ON THE TEXT

1 Timothy 5:1-8, 17-24

1 Rebuke not an elder, but intreat him as a father; and the younger men as brethren; 2 The elder women as mothers; the younger as sisters, with all purity.

Paul continues his pastoral instruction to Timothy. The focus here is on relating to the various groups in the Ephesian church in a just and merciful way. The instruction begins with how Timothy should treat an older person. Timothy is not to rebuke an older person. The Greek word translated "rebuke" here is *epiplesso* (**ep-ee-PLACE-so**), which literally means "to strike upon." Figuratively, it denotes harsh rebuke or verbal chastisement. In a cultural context where respect for elders was valued, Timothy was to show respect for the elderly by not rebuking them harshly as he would a child. Instead, he was to intreat an older person as he would his father or mother. The word "intreat" is from the Greek word *parakaleo* (**par-ak-al-EH-o**), meaning "to comfort or exhort." This is a milder and more respectful way to correct an older person. The noun form of the Greek word *parakletos* (**par-ak-LAY-tos**) is used for the Holy Spirit with

respect to His ministry of comforting believers (John 14:16, 26; 15:26; 16:7). While Timothy is to act in such a way that no one will look down upon him because he is younger, neither should he disrespect the older members of his church.

Timothy is to exhort or urge younger men and women as he would his own siblings. He should correct them in ways that will encourage them when they are wrong, rather than reprimand them with a severe tongue-lashing. He is to correct them in a manner that does not compromise or call in to question his purity in terms of his motives, attitude, or conduct.

3 Honour widows that are widows indeed.

There are widows who by virtue of remarriage are not real widows as far as meeting their material needs is concerned. Such are the responsibility of their second husbands. But the church is to honor widows who have not remarried. The word "honour" is from the Greek word *timoreo* (**tim-o-REH-o**), which means to honor, but also "to price, value, or revere." In this context, it refers especially to the material support that real widows are to be given by the church. Some widows are in such a good financial situation that they do not need the assistance of the church; otherwise, Christian love requires that poor widows be assisted by the church. This is not to totally exclude from the church's assistance widows who have remarried; rather, such can be assisted as the need arises.

4 But if any widow have children or nephews, let them learn first to shew piety at home, and to requite their parents: for that is good and acceptable before God.

While the church is to help widows in need, it is not to be burdened by the material needs of widows who have children or grandchildren who are capable of providing for their parents or grandparents. The term "piety," from the Greek word *eusebeo* (**yoo-seb-EH-o**), refers to pious or godly duties. Supporting one's parents or relatives who are not capable of providing for themselves is considered a key religious duty of children. It is assumed that the children are believers who take seriously their walk with God.

All our religious favor, activities, tithing, and offerings are acceptable to God only after we fulfill our duties at home, which include supporting older family members who need our help.

5 Now she that is a widow indeed, and desolate, trusteth in God, and continueth in supplications and prayers night and day.

Paul further describes who a real widow is. She is one who is left "desolate." The Greek word for this is *monos* (**MON-os**), and it means "to leave alone." A real widow is one who has not remarried and is, therefore, alone, having no husband to support her. Finding herself in such a situation, her only recourse is to put her trust in God, to whom she prays constantly to provide her needs.

6 But she that liveth in pleasure is dead while she liveth.

The opposite of a real widow who depends solely on the Lord is one who lives a wanton life, dedicated to physical gratification outside the context of marriage. This by no means discourages a widow from remarrying. The term "pleasure" is from the Greek word *spatalao* (**spat-al-AH-o**), which refers to a lifestyle given to pleasure, especially of the sensuous type. These widows see their state as freedom to engage in self-indulgence instead of a challenge to cultivate an inner quality of dependence on the Lord.

7 And these things give in charge, that they may be blameless.

Timothy's duty in all of this was to provide instruction for the believers on how to care for the needy, especially the widows. The reason for the instruction is so the believers may not be open to blame for failing to care for the needy among them.

8 But if any provide not for his own, and specially for those of his own house, he hath denied the faith, and is worse than an infidel.

A true believer who practices his/her faith will provide, within his/her ability, first for members of his/her immediate family. Second, provision is to be made for those relatives who do not live with each other as members of the immediate family. Failure to meet this obligation not only opens one to blame before the Lord, but it also opens to question one's standing in the Lord.

5:17 Let the elders that rule well be counted worthy of double honour, especially they who labour in the word and doctrine.

The phrase "elders that rule well" refers to the leaders who are charged with overseeing the leadership affairs of the church. Apart from directing the affairs of the church, their duties also include teaching and preaching the Word. While ability to minister the Word is a requisite for all church leaders (1 Timothy 3:12), some who distinguish themselves by working extra hard on their teaching and preaching are recommended for special honor. Honoring all the leaders is assumed. But those who do extra work in ministering the Word are singled out for additional honor.

Most scholars agree that the double honor recommended here refers to two types of honor—not necessarily double remuneration. The Greek word for "honour" is *time* (**tee-MAY**) and can also stand for two types of honor—not necessarily double remuneration, esteem, or dignity. Leaders who distinguish themselves by their ministry of the Word are to receive both esteem and financial recognition. Today, full-time pastors who minister the Word as well as administer the affairs of their congregations fall under this category. Given what the average preacher is paid today in the African American Church, can it be said that the average Black church honors those who preach the Word in accordance with this instruction?

18 For the scripture saith, Thou shalt not muzzle the ox that treadeth out the corn. And, The labourer is worthy of his reward.

Paul supports his assertion concerning rewarding leaders who excel by quoting Deuteronomy 25:4 and Jesus' teaching in Luke 10:7 (cf. 1 Corinthians 9:9). These quotations show unmistakably that more than abstract honor is envisaged by Paul; he is thinking of honorariums for leaders who also minister the Word in the church. The Greek word for "reward" is *misthos* (**mis-THOS**) and primarily refers to wages, hire, or pay. Of course, while the laborer deserves his hire, it is also expected of him to contribute an equitable share of labor. It is a common temptation for some pastors today to put in less hours than they are actually being paid for, thereby milking the sheep. Neither the church nor the pastor should take advantage of the other in the matter of remuneration.

19 Against an elder receive not an accusation, but before two or three witnesses.

Being a leader exposes one to more criticisms than otherwise. Sometimes the criticisms are justified and well-intentioned. Other times they are not. Unless there are witnesses to establish the veracity of an accusation against a leader, the church should not entertain it. An accusation not corroborated by at least two independent witnesses is difficult to resolve because it boils down to the accuser's word against the defendant's, unless the defendant admits to the accusation. The Greek term for "accusation" is *kategoria* (**kat-ay-gor-EE-ah**). It denotes a criminal charge requiring official investigation by the church rather than a malicious accusation, which in Greek is *diaballo* (**dee-AB-al-lo**), such as the devil levels against believers.

20 Them that sin rebuke before all, that others also may fear.

Paul is not trying to give the leaders a privilege that places them above the law, but rather to protect them from frequent and frivolous accusations. But once a leader's guilt is established, he should be rebuked publicly before the church, not to humiliate him, but to deter others. Such public rebuke also shows that the church does not condone sin, not even among its leaders. Now, if the leaders are thus rebuked, how much more should be those who are led? Public or any rebuke of erring members seems to be unfashionable today. Some don't do it for fear of litigation, others for fear of losing members. If we love our members, we will rebuke them when they sin, for love casts out fear.

21 I charge thee before God, and the Lord Jesus Christ, and the elect angels, that thou observe these things without preferring one before another, doing nothing by partiality.

Timothy had his hands full. He was to instruct the believers, model his instruction, and enforce its requirements. To this end, he was charged very solemnly to be impartial in applying the instructions. The solemnity of the charge is further heightened by the divine quality of the witnesses before whom it was made, i.e., God, Christ, and the elect angels. This should motivate Timothy to do his best.

Leaders can easily be liable to partiality and favoritism in dealing with their members. Paul, therefore, strongly warns Timothy against such vices. It has been rightly observed that nothing does more harm than when some people are treated as if they could do no wrong and others as if they could do no right.

22 Lay hands suddenly on no man, neither be partaker of other men's sins: keep thyself pure.

The practice of laying on of hands symbolizes the ordination of elders. Since Timothy was to oversee the establishment of the office of elders in the Ephesian church, Paul advised him to be cautious in ordaining elders. The word "suddenly" translates the Greek word *tacheos* (**tahk-EH-oce**), which suggests the idea of being hasty. Timothy was not to be hasty in ordaining elders; rather, he was to be cautious, following the instructions outlined in this letter, particularly in chapter 3, which lists the qualifications of an elder.

It is a sin to assume the office of an elder unworthily. It is also a sin to ordain a candidate who does not meet the requirements for such an office. While it is a noble thing to serve as an elder in the church, it is nevertheless a sacred function that should not be undertaken in an unworthy manner.

23 Drink no longer water, but use a little wine for thy stomach's sake and thine often infirmities.

It is apparent from this that Timothy did not enjoy optimum health, at least not during his ministry at Ephesus. He had frequent stomach and other health problems. Paul therefore recommends the medicinal use of a little wine to Timothy. The Greek word for "wine" is *oinos* (**OY-nos**) and refers to fermented drink (Matthew 9:17;

Ephesians 5:18). But this is for medicinal purposes and provides no basis for the abusive use of wine, which is prohibited in 1 Timothy 3:3, 8.

The health of the minister is important. The tendency for some ministers to overwork themselves to the detriment of their health is not in the interest of the Gospel or of the church. The minister is human and therefore liable to work-related stress, which accounts for a lot of ministerial burnouts today.

24 Some men's sins are open beforehand, going before to judgment; and some men they follow after.

In considering candidates for church leadership, care must be taken that sin is not condoned. Now the sins of some men are no secret. They are so well known that they hardly call for serious investigation. The sins of other men are carefully concealed, requiring careful investigation to uncover them. So, while some candidates may appear pious and innocent, they should not for that reason be exempt from careful scrutiny before they are ordained. Just because a sin is not apparent does not mean it does not exist. The Lord cautions against judging by appearance; rather, our judgment and investigation should be based on righteousness (John 7:24).

Bibliography

Barclay, William. *The Letters to Timothy, Titus, and Philemon.* Philadelphia, Penn.: Westminster/John Knox Press, 1975, 117.

DAILY BIBLE READINGS

M: God Loves Righteousness and Justice
Psalm 33:1-5
T: Show Justice, Integrity, Righteousness, and Mercy
Proverbs 28:4-13
W: Jesus Demands Justice and Mercy
Matthew 23:23-28
T: Mercy Triumphs over Judgment
James 2:8-13
F: Show Mercy to All Believers
1 Timothy 5:1-8
S: Show Justice to the Widows
1 Timothy 5:9-16
S: Show Justice to the Elders
1 Timothy 5:17-25

TEACHING TIPS

February 5
Bible Study Guide 10

1. Words You Should Know

A. Forefathers (2 Timothy 1:3) *progonos* (Gk.)—A word used in association with parents, grandparents, and ancestors.

B. Unfeigned (v. 5) *anupokritos* (Gk.)—Unfeigned, undisguised, sincere.

C. Stir up (v. 6) *anazopureo* (Gk.)—To kindle up, inflame one's mind, strength, zeal.

2. Teacher Preparation

A. Pray for your students.

B. Read all the FOCAL VERSES for the lesson.

C. Read through the entire BIBLE STUDY GUIDE. Make a note of specific highlights you may want to emphasize.

3. Starting the Lesson

A. Choose a student to read the LESSON AIM.

B. Choose another student to lead the class in prayer.

C. Ask a student to read the IN FOCUS story then ask the students to share how their ancestors contributed to their Christian heritage. Point out the relationship of the discussion to today's lesson.

4. Getting into the Lesson

A. Read THE PEOPLE, PLACES, AND TIMES, as well as the BACKGROUND section to help set the stage for today's lesson. Have the students silently read the sections and write down their thoughts in the REMEMBER YOUR THOUGHTS section.

B. Refer to the SEARCH THE SCRIPTURES questions as you begin the discussion of the lesson.

5. Relating the Lesson to Life

A. Engage in conversation with your students as you answer and discuss the questions in the DISCUSS THE MEANING section.

B. The LESSON IN OUR SOCIETY section should be used to help the students apply the lesson to their present-day situation. Ask the students about the legacy their forefathers left them. What type of legacy are they leaving the next generation? Ask the students if they are sharing their Christian heritage with the next generation.

6. Arousing Action

A. Sum up the lesson with the KEEP IN MIND verse. Ask the students to read it in unison while contemplating how they can apply the verse to their everyday lives.

B. Challenge the students to follow through on the MAKE IT HAPPEN assignment.

C. Close the class with prayer.

BE TRUE TO YOUR CHRISTIAN HERITAGE

Bible Background • 2 TIMOTHY 1
Printed Text • 2 TIMOTHY 1:3–14
Devotional Reading • 2 THESSALONIANS 2:13–17

LESSON AIM

By the end of the lesson, we will:

KNOW how our faith is often directly tied to or derived from our ancestors;

FEEL the responsibility of passing our faith onto the next generation; and

DECIDE to implement the MAKE IT HAPPEN section.

KEEP IN MIND

"When I call to remembrance the unfeigned faith that is in thee, which dwelt first in thy grandmother Lois, and thy mother Eunice; and I am persuaded that in thee also" (2 Timothy 1:5).

FOCAL VERSES

2 Timothy 1:3 I thank God, whom I serve from my forefathers with pure conscience, that without ceasing I have remembrance of thee in my prayers night and day;

4 Greatly desiring to see thee, being mindful of thy tears, that I may be filled with joy;

5 When I call to remembrance the unfeigned faith that is in thee, which dwelt first in thy grandmother Lois, and thy mother Eunice; and I am persuaded that in thee also.

6 Wherefore I put thee in remembrance that thou stir up the gift of God, which is in thee by the putting on of my hands.

7 For God hath not given us the spirit of fear; but of power, and of love, and of a sound mind.

8 Be not thou therefore ashamed of the testimony of our Lord, nor of me his prisoner: but be

LESSON OVERVIEW

LESSON AIM
KEEP IN MIND
FOCAL VERSES
IN FOCUS
THE PEOPLE, PLACES, AND TIMES
BACKGROUND
AT-A-GLANCE
IN DEPTH
SEARCH THE SCRIPTURES
DISCUSS THE MEANING
LESSON IN OUR SOCIETY
MAKE IT HAPPEN
FOLLOW THE SPIRIT
REMEMBER YOUR THOUGHTS
MORE LIGHT ON THE TEXT
DAILY BIBLE READINGS

thou partaker of the afflictions of the gospel according to the power of God;

9 Who hath saved us, and called us with an holy calling, not according to our works, but according to his own purpose and grace, which was given us in Christ Jesus before the world began,

10 But is now made manifest by the appearing of our Saviour Jesus Christ, who hath abolished death, and hath brought life and immortality to light through the gospel:

11 Whereunto I am appointed a preacher, and an apostle, and a teacher of the Gentiles.

12 For the which cause I also suffer these things: nevertheless I am not ashamed: for I know whom I have believed, and am persuaded that he is able to keep that which I have committed unto him against that day.

13 Hold fast the form of sound words, which thou hast heard of me, in faith and love which is in Christ Jesus.

14 That good thing which was committed unto thee keep by the Holy Ghost which dwelleth in us.

IN FOCUS

Dean got out of bed late Sunday morning. He stayed in bed as long as he could, but the noise his three younger brothers and sister made getting ready for church was too much for him. When his father came knocking at the door, he

FEB
5TH

was ready with the excuse that would keep him home; he was 16 and determined.

"Why aren't you dressed, young man? It's Sunday, and we always go to church. Are you sick?"

"Dad, I'm tired of going to church Sunday after Sunday."

"Tired!" His father's eyes showed a little fire. "Why would you say something like that?"

Dean straightened himself on his bedside. "My point is this: I been going to church since I was 5 or 6 years old. I've heard something like 2,000 sermons, and I can't remember a single one of them. So I think we are wasting our time and the pastors are wasting theirs by giving all those sermons."

His father's voice became a little stern. "Listen, son, your mother and I have been married for 25 years now. In that time, she has cooked over 25,000 meals. But just like the sermons you can't remember, I can't recall every course of even one of those meals. But I do know that each meal nourished me and gave me the strength I needed to provide for this family. If your mother had not prepared those meals, I might be dead today. Likewise, if this family was not a church-going family and was not receiving the nourishment that the church offers, we would be spiritually dead today!"

In 2 Timothy, we are blessed with the understanding that faith is the bread of immortality. Do you understand the importance of passing the faith along from generation to generation?

THE PEOPLE, PLACES, AND TIMES

Timothy. He was a disciple of Jesus Christ and a co-laborer with the apostle Paul in the ministry. Timothy worked extensively with Paul, traveling and preaching the Gospel. Paul often refers to Timothy as his son in the faith (1 Timothy 1:2, 18; 2 Timothy 1:2). Timothy was the product of a mixed union. His mother was Jewish, and his father was Greek (Acts 16:1). However, it appears that at some point Timothy's mother became a Christian, and she ensured that her son was instructed in the Scriptures. The Bible gives us various insights into the life and character of Timothy. Timothy, from the scriptural account, was faithful, loyal, and trustworthy. Paul entrusted him to instruct the saints in Thessalonica, Ephesus, and Corinth.

BACKGROUND

Second Timothy is known as one of the pastoral epistles (letters) written by the apostle Paul. Paul uses this second letter to Timothy, as an opportunity to encourage his young protégé in the Gospel. This letter was written during Paul's second imprisonment in Rome, shortly before his death. Paul's love for and trust in Timothy is evident in his correspondence to him, and he longs to see his son in the faith one more time. While this second epistle is predominantly a letter of encouragement, Paul does not neglect the opportunity to warn Timothy to be aware of false teachers and inaccurate doctrine.

AT-A-GLANCE

1. Paul Expresses Love Toward Timothy (2 Timothy 1:3-4)
2. Paul Reminds Timothy of His Heritage of Faith (vv. 5-7)
3. Paul Reminds Timothy of His Purpose and Calling (vv. 8-10)
4. Paul Speaks of His Personal Afflictions (vv. 11-12)
5. Paul Admonishes Timothy to Continue in the Work (vv. 13-14)

IN DEPTH

1. Paul Expresses Love Toward Timothy (2 Timothy 1:3-4)

Paul was imprisoned, and others, who had once served faithfully, had forsaken him. It was during this time that he was especially grateful to Timothy for his faithfulness to him and the Gospel of Jesus Christ. Paul remembered Timothy in his petitions and supplications to the Lord, and his times of prayer reflected on Timothy and all they had experienced as co-laborers in the ministry. As Paul remembered the tears of Timothy, he longed to see his son in the faith so that he could once again experience the joy they shared together.

Paul and Timothy are examples of how to build a Christian family and leave an eternal spiritual legacy. The apostle Paul took time with his disciple to encourage him in ministry, allowing Timothy to travel with him and experience the pain and joy that comes with serving the Lord. Paul's work would not go unrewarded. Because this elder was willing to take time to pour himself into the next generation, Timothy was now equipped to continue the work which the apostle started. God showed righteousness toward Paul and remembered his labor of love toward the saints (Hebrews 6:10). He reminded Timothy that he was praying for him continuously because he knew firsthand the persecution that comes with being an ambassador for Christ. As Paul prepared to pass the torch of ministry to this next generation, he was not neglectful in his prayers for Timothy. Paul was aware that the task set before Timothy was too big for him alone, but that through Christ Jesus he could do all things (Philippians 4:13).

2. Paul Reminds Timothy of His Heritage of Faith (vv.5-7)

Paul took time to encourage Timothy in the faith. He reminded Timothy of the heritage of his faith and the source of his gift. Paul spoke of Timothy's faith as unfeigned, meaning that Timothy's faith was honest and sincere. Timothy did not have to be timid in his faith. He could find strength in knowing that the same faith that had sustained and equipped his ancestors was present in him to sustain and equip him also.

The faith within Timothy had been tried and proven over generations. So Paul admonished him to stir up the gift of God inside him and refrain from walking in fear. In essence, Paul was simply instructing Timothy to rekindle the flame of his passion to serve the Lord. It seems as though Timothy had been discouraged by various events. It could have been the mission in Corinth, the rise of Gnosticism, or other false teachings in the church. Paul does not tell us the actual events that may have contributed to the young man's discouragement. Paul did not judge, belittle, or degrade him for becoming discouraged. On the contrary, he simply encouraged Timothy to rekindle the flame. Paul reminded the young pastor that the God he served does not deal in fear or timidity. He

is a God of faith. The spirit of fear does not come from God. The Spirit of God is one of power, love, and sound mind (v. 7). Fear comes to rob you of your power, your love, and your soundness of mind. The apostle John reminds us that there is no fear in love and that perfect love (that is, the love from God) removes fear (1 John 4:18). It is the love that we receive from God that enables us to overcome fear and to walk in the power, love, and sound mind that He provides for us.

3. Paul Reminds Timothy of His Purpose and Calling (vv. 8-10)

Timothy did not have to be ashamed of the trials and persecutions that came with serving Jesus Christ. Nonbelievers and false teachers would say that Christ's death on the Cross proved He was not the Messiah. So they would work to shame those who served and followed Him. However, Paul encouraged Timothy to not be ashamed of the Gospel of Christ, but to partake in His afflictions. It is an honor to share in Christ's afflictions.

The same power that raised Christ from the dead is at work in us (Romans 8:11). Paul reminded Timothy that the power of God had saved him and called him to do a work in the ministry. Now Timothy was called to fulfill the purpose of God by the grace of God. Such purpose and grace had been designed for Timothy before the foundation of the world and was made available to him through Jesus Christ. So Timothy did not need to be ashamed of Christ, for Christ was his Source. Similarly, it is through Him that we now have access to the grace and purpose of God. Everything we need to do the will of God is available to us through Christ.

4. Paul Speaks of His Personal Afflictions (vv. 11-12)

Paul reminded Timothy that he (Paul) was not alone in his suffering. However, this was not because of anything he had done; it was simply because of the One he served, Jesus Christ. Paul was aware that his appointment and service to ministry came from Jesus Christ. Isn't it ironic that the source of his appointment is also the source of his pain and affliction? Paul was writing this letter to Timothy from a Roman jail. He was in jail because he was a

Christian, a follower of Jesus Christ. This did not bring Paul shame. His hope was in Christ Jesus (Colossians 1:27), and he was fully persuaded (confidently believed and trusted) that Christ would keep all that Paul had given in service to Him.

5. Paul Admonishes Timothy to Continue in the Work (vv. 13-14)

Our study of this passage ends with Paul admonishing Timothy to follow after sound doctrine. Some of Paul's previous followers had succumbed to false teachers and erroneous doctrine (2 Timothy 1:15). However, Paul warned Timothy to not turn toward any teaching different than what he (Paul) had taught him about Jesus Christ. However, Paul knew that this could not be done on Timothy's own accord. It was only with the assistance of the Holy Spirit that Timothy could discern sound teachings and hold fast to the truth given to him by Paul.

SEARCH THE SCRIPTURES

1. What does Paul tell Timothy to do with the gift that has been given to him by God (2 Timothy 1:6)?

2. What does the Holy Spirit give to those who follow after Him (v. 7)?

3. What is the role of the Holy Spirit in the life of Timothy as stated in verse 14?

DISCUSS THE MEANING

1. Why do you think Paul felt the need to remind Timothy of the heritage of his faith?

2. What do you think Paul meant when he told Timothy to stir up the gift of God he had received by the laying on of hands?

LESSON IN OUR SOCIETY

The themes of heritage and legacy are prevalent in Jewish culture and are referred to on numerous occasions in both the Old and New Testament writings. God is often referred to as "the God of our forefathers" or "the God of Abraham, Isaac, and Jacob." Genealogy was not just a listing of kinsmen. Genealogy represented one's identity. The Children of Israel would find strength and encouragement as they read about the battles and struggles of their forefathers. In Jewish culture, the prevailing attitude was, "If it happened to my forefathers, it happened to me."

There is a great sense of strength and pride that comes from knowing one's heritage. Take time during the celebration of Black History Month to learn more about an African or African American ancestor who changed the course of history or made a positive contribution to society. Think about what things you can learn from him or her. Ask yourself about the legacy you are leaving for the next generation.

MAKE IT HAPPEN

Using the principles of today's lesson and in commemoration of Black History Month, develop a project that puts your faith into action and allows you to share your Christian heritage with someone of a younger generation.

FOLLOW THE SPIRIT

What God wants me to do:

_____

_____

REMEMBER YOUR THOUGHTS

Special insights I have learned:

_____

_____

MORE LIGHT ON THE TEXT
2 Timothy 1:3-14

Timothy's mother and grandmother created a culture and heritage of faith, from which Paul encouraged Timothy to draw strength and courage. The theme of the importance of family continued throughout this text. Paul shows Timothy the love and affection that a father shows a son. Paul also reminds Timothy of the faith that his mother and grandmother possessed and expresses belief that Timothy also possessed that same faith. Throughout the passage, Paul shows Timothy how to use that faith to reach the masses with the Gospel.

3 I thank God, whom I serve from my forefathers with pure conscience, that without ceasing I have remembrance of thee in my prayers night and day;

Paul started by using words of thanks and service at the beginning of this letter. The word "serve" in 2 Timothy 1:3 in Greek is *latreuo* (**lat-RYOO-o**), which means "to minister to God" or "to do service." Paul establishes a tradition of heritage when he mentions his "forefathers," which in Greek is *progonos* (**PROG-on-os**) and means "ancestor." Paul also shows the affection and concern of a parent for Timothy. The phrase "without ceasing" in Greek is *adialeiptos* (**ad-ee-al-IPE-toce**), which means "uninterrupted." The word "remembrance" is *mneia* (**MNI-ah**), which means "recollection," and the word "prayers" is *deesis* (**DEH-ay-sis**), which means "petition." Paul expressed how he constantly remembered Timothy when he petitioned the throne in prayer.

4 Greatly desiring to see thee, being mindful of thy tears, that I may be filled with joy;

Paul continues to express his care for Timothy in verse 4. The phrase "greatly desiring" in Greek

is *epipotheo* (**ep-ee-poth-EH-O**), which means "to long after." Paul could not see Timothy because he was in prison, but he still longed to see Timothy. Paul then uses the phrase "being mindful of thy tears, that I may be filled with joy." In Greek, "being mindful" is *mnaomai* (**mnah'-om-ahee**), meaning "having remembered." Also, to be "filled" is *pleroo* (**play-RO-o**) in Greek, which means "complete." Paul is saying that his joy was made complete by Timothy's tears and suffering for the Gospel.

5 When I call to remembrance the unfeigned faith that is in thee, which dwelt first in thy grandmother Lois, and thy mother Eunice; and I am persuaded that in thee also.

The word for "remembrance" in the phrase "When I call to remembrance" is similar to the word used in verse 3 that is similarly translated. The Greek word for "remembrance" in this verse is *hupomnesis* (**hoop-OM-nay-sis**) and means "a reminding or recollection." The words "unfeigned faith" in Greek are *anupokritos pistis* (**an-oo-POK-ree-tos PIS-tis**), which means "sincere conviction." Paul remembered the sincere faith that was a part of Timothy's lineage through his mother and grandmother. Paul also used the word "persuaded," which is *peitho* (**PI-tho**) in Greek and is translated as "convinced." Paul is convinced that the unfeigned faith in Lois and Eunice was in Timothy also.

6 Wherefore I put thee in remembrance that thou stir up the gift of God, which is in thee by the putting on of my hands.

Paul continues stressing the importance of recollection by repeating the word "remembrance." This time, the word "remembrance" in the phrase

Holding fast to sound words is godly advice.

"I put thee in remembrance" comes from *anamimnesko* (**an-am-im-NACE-ko**), which means "to remind." The phrase "stir up" in Greek is *anazopureo* (**an-ad-zo-poor-EH-o**), meaning "to stir into flame." The word "gift" is *charisma* (**KHAR-is-mah**), and one of its meanings is "spiritual endowment." Paul told Timothy to ignite the spiritual endowment that God had already placed in Timothy. Paul says that the gift of God had been placed in Timothy by his laying hands on Timothy. Timothy had a history of having "the gift" in his family with his mother and grandmother. In verses 5 and 6, Paul encourages Timothy to look at his family heritage and see how God had worked through the faith of Timothy's mother and grandmother. Timothy was to use the knowledge of their faith to help him "stir up the gift of God" that was inside of him.

7 For God hath not given us the spirit of fear; but of power, and of love, and of a sound mind.

Paul contrasts what God has not given us (spirit of fear) with what He has given us (power, love, and a sound mind). The word for "spirit" is *pneuma* (**PNYOO-mah**). One of the translations of *pneuma* is "breath." This suggests that God never breathed into us or gave us "fear," which in Greek is *deilia* (**di-LEE-ah**) and means "timidity." Verse 7 tells us that God did give us power, love, and a sound mind. The Greek word for "power" is *dunamis* (**DOO-nam-is**), which means "miraculous power." The word "love" in this verse comes from the Greek word *agape* (**ag-AH-pay**) and means "godly love or affection." Finally, the word for "sound mind" in Greek is *sophronismos* (**so-fron-is-MOS**), which means "discipline" or "self-control." God has given us the ability to have miraculous power, godly love, and self-control.

8 Be not thou therefore ashamed of the testimony of our Lord, nor of me his prisoner: but be thou partaker of the afflictions of the gospel according to the power of God;

This verse continues the point that Paul made in verse 7. Since God has not given us the spirit of fear, we should not be ashamed of the Lord's testimony, which includes the suffering and crucifixion of Jesus. Paul even referred to himself as the

Lord's prisoner, since he was writing this from prison. Despite all of this, Paul encouraged Timothy to be a "partaker of the afflictions." In Greek, this phrase is *sugkakopatheo* (**soong-kak-op-ath-EH-o**), which means "to suffer hardship in company." Although Paul talked about suffering, he also reminded Timothy of why he was to suffer when he talked about the Gospel and the power of God. The word for "gospel" in Greek is *euaggelion* (**yoo-ang-GHEL-ee-on**), which means good message. The word for "power" is the same Greek word that is used in verse 7.

9 Who hath saved us, and called us with an holy calling, not according to our works, but according to his own purpose and grace, which was given us in Christ Jesus before the world began,

The Greek word for "saved" is *sozo* (**SODE-zo**), which means "to deliver." The Greek word for "called" is *kaleo* (**kal-EH-o**), and it means "to call forth." The phrase "an holy calling" is *hagios klesis* (**HAG-ee-os KLAY-sis**) in Greek and literally means "a sacred invitation." Paul reminds Timothy that they were delivered and invited by God to do a sacred work. Paul also reminds Timothy that the calling was not due to their works, but because of Christ's purpose and grace given to them from the beginning.

10 But is now made manifest by the appearing of our Saviour Jesus Christ, who hath abolished death, and hath brought life and immortality to light through the gospel:

The phrase "made manifest" comes from the Greek word *photizo* (**fo-TID-zo**), which means "to bring to light." The word for "abolished" (Gk. *katargeo*, **kat-arg-EH-o**) means "to render entirely useless." Paul says that Christ's death, burial, and resurrection rendered the power of death useless and brought life and immortality to light.

11 Whereunto I am appointed a preacher, and an apostle, and a teacher of the Gentiles.

In verses 8 through 11, Paul reminds Timothy of the purpose of the call of God on their lives. The word for "appointed" in Greek is *tithemi* (**TITH-ay-me**), which means "to ordain" or "to purpose." The word for "preacher" (Gk. *kerux*,

KAY-roox), refers to a herald of divine truth. The word for "apostle" in Greek is *apostolos* (**ap-OS-tol-os**), which is translated "ambassador of the Gospel." Finally, the word "teacher" (Gk. *didaskalos*, **did-AS-kal-os**) simply means "instructor or master." Paul and Timothy had been purposed to be speakers of divine truth, ambassadors who spread the Gospel around the world, and instructors of the Word.

12 For the which cause I also suffer these things: nevertheless I am not ashamed: for I know whom I have believed, and am persuaded that he is able to keep that which I have committed unto him against that day.

Paul again adds to the theme of suffering for the Gospel. He reminds Timothy that he was suffering, but he was in no way ashamed. Paul knew what he believed, and he was willing to suffer for it. As a matter of fact, when Paul used the word "persuaded," he used the Greek word *peitho* (**PI-tho**), which means "convinced." This is the same word that he used in verse 5 when he said that he was convinced that the unfeigned faith that was in Lois and Eunice was also in Timothy. This shows how much Paul believed that God was able to keep that which he had committed unto Him. The word "keep" in Greek is *phulasso* (**foo-LAS-so**), which means to be "on guard." The Greek word *paratheke* (**par-ath-AY-kay**), which means "trust," is the word translated as "committed." Paul was convinced that God was able to guard everything that Paul had entrusted to Him until His return.

13 Hold fast the form of sound words, which thou hast heard of me, in faith and love which is in Christ Jesus.

The word "form" (Gk. *hupotuposis*, **hoop-ot-OOP-o-sis**) means "pattern." The word for "sound" (Gk. *hugiaino*, **hoog-ee-AH-no**) means "uncorrupted." Paul was imploring Timothy to hold on to the doctrine that he had taught Timothy in Christ Jesus. Despite the false doctrines that were spreading around the world, Timothy was to remain in the true doctrine that had been taught to him by Paul himself.

14 That good thing which was committed unto thee keep by the Holy Ghost which dwelleth within us.

The "good thing" in this verse refers to the sound words of true doctrine that Paul talked about in the previous verse. The word for "dwelleth" is *enoikeo* (**en-oy-KEH-o**) in Greek, which means "inhabit." Paul says that the power to hold on to sound doctrine comes from the Holy Ghost, who inhabits us.

DAILY BIBLE READINGS

M: God Gives the Heritage
Psalm 111

T: We Can Lose Our Heritage
Jeremiah 17:1-8

W: Stand Firm, Hold Fast
2 Thessalonians 2:13-17

T: Timothy's Mother Was a Believer
Acts 16:1-5

F: Lois and Eunice Passed On Faith
2 Timothy 1:1-5

S: Be Not Ashamed of Your Heritage
2 Timothy 1:6-10

S: Guard the Good Treasure Given You
2 Timothy 1:11-18

TEACHING TIPS

February 12
Bible Study Guide 11

1. Words You Should Know

A. Shun (2 Timothy 2:16) *periistemi* (Gk.)—To change or turn around for the purpose of avoiding something; to avoid.

B. Canker (v. 17) *gaggraina* (Gk.)—A disease that continually spreads, attacks, and eats away at the body.

2. Teacher Preparation

A. Pray for your students. Ask God to give them the tools to hear the lesson and develop godly Christian character.

B. Read and study the FOCAL VERSES. Draw attention to those things that represent Christian character.

C. Share with your class things you do to develop Christian character within yourself. Also share any struggles you may have in developing a particular area as you try to become more Christlike.

3. Starting the Lesson

A. Begin class with prayer. Thank God for your students, praying that they will continue to grow and develop into Christians who represent Christ in every area of their life.

B. Ask a student to read the IN FOCUS section, then ask class members to examine their lives and look at areas in which they have developed Christian character.

C. Ask class members to examine and share areas in their lives in which they struggle to be more Christlike.

4. Getting into the Lesson

A. Read THE PEOPLE, PLACES, AND TIMES section. Share with the students how the righteousness we receive in Christ should be evident in our daily living.

B. The BACKGROUND section will help set the stage for today's lesson. Have the students read this section silently and write down any thoughts or questions in the REMEMBER YOUR THOUGHTS section.

5. Relating the Lesson to Life

A. Give the students the opportunity to answer the questions in the SEARCH THE SCRIPTURES section.

B. Engage in conversation with your students as you answer and discuss the questions in the DISCUSS THE MEANING section.

6. Arousing Action

A. Sum up the lesson with the KEEP IN MIND verse. Have the students read the verse in unison while contemplating how they can apply the verse to their everyday lives.

B. Have one student read the LESSON IN OUR SOCIETY section. Ask the students to share how this lesson applies to them.

C. Challenge the students to follow through on the MAKE IT HAPPEN assignment.

D. Close the class with prayer.

WORSHIP GUIDE

For the Superintendent or Teacher
Theme: Develop Christian Character
Theme Song: "Give Me A Clean Heart"
Scripture: Psalm 51:10
Song: "Blessed Be The Name"
Meditation: Dear Lord, as I walk through this life, give me the strength to discipline myself and develop Christlike character as I follow your Word. Help me to become a doer and not just a hearer of your Word.

DEVELOP CHRISTIAN CHARACTER

Bible Background • 2 TIMOTHY 2
Printed Text • 2 TIMOTHY 2:14–26
Devotional Reading • 1 PETER 2:1–10

LESSON AIM

By the end of the lesson, we will:

KNOW that our inward redemption should manifest itself in outward change;

FEEL the need to live godly before Christ and others; and

DECIDE to acknowledge one ungodly habit and align it with our confession of Christ.

KEEP IN MIND

"Flee also youthful lusts: but follow righteousness, faith, charity, peace, with them that call on the Lord out of a pure heart" (2 Timothy 2:22).

FOCAL VERSES

2 Timothy 2:14 Of these things put them in remembrance, charging them before the Lord that they strive not about words to no profit, but to the subverting of the hearers.

15 Study to shew thyself approved unto God, a workman that needeth not to be ashamed, rightly dividing the word of truth.

16 But shun profane and vain babblings: for they will increase unto more ungodliness.

17 And their word will eat as doth a canker: of whom is Hymenaeus and Philetus;

18 Who concerning the truth have erred, saying that the resurrection is past already; and overthrow the faith of some.

19 Nevertheless the foundation of God standeth sure, having this seal, The Lord knoweth them that are his. And, Let every one that nameth the name of Christ depart from iniquity.

20 But in a great house there are not only vessels of gold and of silver, but also of wood and of earth; and some to honour, and some to dishonour.

21 If a man therefore purge himself from these, he shall be a vessel unto honour, sanctified, and meet for the master's use, and prepared unto every good work.

22 Flee also youthful lusts: but follow righteousness, faith, charity, peace, with them that call on the Lord out of a pure heart.

23 But foolish and unlearned questions avoid, knowing that they do gender strifes.

24 And the servant of the Lord must not strive; but be gentle unto all men, apt to teach, patient,

25 In meekness instructing those that oppose themselves; if God peradventure will give them repentance to the acknowledging of the truth;

26 And that they may recover themselves out of the snare of the devil, who are taken captive by him at his will.

LESSON OVERVIEW

LESSON AIM
KEEP IN MIND
FOCAL VERSES
IN FOCUS
THE PEOPLE, PLACES, AND TIMES
BACKGROUND
AT-A-GLANCE
IN DEPTH
SEARCH THE SCRIPTURES
DISCUSS THE MEANING
LESSON IN OUR SOCIETY
MAKE IT HAPPEN
FOLLOW THE SPIRIT
REMEMBER YOUR THOUGHTS
MORE LIGHT ON THE TEXT
DAILY BIBLE READINGS

IN FOCUS

FEB 12TH

The park was under a blazing hot sun where Jamal, his wife Karen, and a few friends picnicked one summer afternoon. Their 7-year-old son Patrick ran from his screaming young friends and sat on his father's lap, announcing that he wanted to have lunch with God. He said he had seen God sitting all alone. Giving her husband a wink, Karen placed a few cookies and two cans of soda in a small bag.

The couple watched as their son walked two picnic tables over and sat next to an older woman who was sitting alone staring at some birds. Patrick sat on the bench next to her and opened his bag. His parents looked on as he offered the elderly woman one of his cookies. She accepted them and beamed. Then he offered her a soda. Again, she smiled at him. Patrick seemed so happy to be sitting with her.

Patrick and the old woman sat there eating, drinking, and watching the birds as his parents looked on. Neither Patrick nor his elderly friend said a word. After awhile, Patrick got up to leave. After he had gone just a few steps, he turned around, ran back to the old woman, and gave her a big hug. Laughing, the old woman hugged him back.

Patrick ran to his parents excited and giggling aloud. Karen asked, "Why did your visit make you so happy?"

Patrick replied, "Because she was God!"

Development of our Christian character should start early in life. How often do we let our children express the love of Christ toward others?

THE PEOPLE, PLACES, AND TIMES

Righteousness. Often defined as describing one who is aligned or in right standing with God. Man's righteousness is an expression of God's grace. Righteousness comes to the Christian through Jesus Christ (Romans 5:17; Philippians 3:9). Since righteousness is based on what Christ did for us on the Cross, we strive continuously to live a life that reflects our righteous status in God through Christ Jesus. Therefore, "the extrinsic righteousness imputed through the Cross finds inevitable expression in the intrinsic righteousness of a life that in a new way conforms to the will of God."

BACKGROUND

When the apostle Paul penned this letter to Timothy, Gnosticism and other heretical teachings had begun to surface in the church. Some people started to embrace false doctrine, and those once associated with the Lord Jesus Christ started to reject the truth. It is in these matters that the apostle Paul instructed young Timothy to lead the church toward the Lord Jesus. Paul knew the importance of godly character and growth in the life of the Christian; therefore, he instructed Timothy to remind the believers of those things that produce godliness as well as these things that produce ungodliness.

AT-A-GLANCE

1. Strive to Win God's Approval
(2 Timothy 2:14-15)
2. Stay Away from False Teaching
(vv. 16-21)
3. Stick with Those Who Practice
Godliness (vv. 22-23)
4. Show Gentleness to Those Who
Oppose the Truth (vv. 24-26)

IN DEPTH

1. Strive to Win God's Approval (2 Timothy 2:14-15)

The apostle tells his son Timothy he should make every effort to win the approval of God. God wants His children to develop godly character in both word and deed. Words are living and powerful. Proverbs 18:21 tells us that "death and life are in the power of the tongue." Empty, vain talk does not lead to godliness. Arguing over what is right or wrong does not bring someone to righteousness. Truth does not come through vain babbling. We can only access truth by taking time to study the Word of God.

The apostle Paul tells Timothy to instruct the saints to refrain from arguing with each other. Such arguments only work to undermine the faith of those who hear them. Timothy was instructed to teach the saints, not to argue about the truth, but to study. Jesus also spoke about the need to be cautious about the words we speak. Matthew 15:18-20 reminds us that the words that proceed from the mouth come from the heart and can work to defile the one speaking. Such vain babbling leads to ungodliness, including evil thoughts, fornication, and blasphemy.

2. Stay Away from False Teaching (vv. 16-21)

Empty words led to a falling away from the truth for Hymenaeus and Philetus. They had once walked in the truth of the Gospel. Now, however, they embraced false teachings and walked in error instead of continuing in the Word of God. Strife, false teachings, and vain babblings eat away at the truth and open the door for erroneous doctrine to grow, take root, and eventually bring destruction in the body of Christ.

Many Christians put great effort into separating their church life from their non-church life. However, God wants to be involved in every aspect of a Christian's life. Stay away from useless arguments and strife. Instead build a strong foundation in the Lord.

A vessel of honor is a vessel of character. We have the ability to choose what we will and will not do; we choose what we will and will not say. Many of us are familiar with the saying, "If you can't say anything nice, don't say anything at all." We also have the ability to choose the type of Christians we will be. Will we choose to be weak Christians, walking after the things of the flesh? Or will we choose to be strong Christians, guided by the Holy Spirit—a vessel of honor that can be used by the Master?

In pursuit of righteousness.

3. Stick with Those Who Practice Godliness (vv. 22-23)

In order to be a vessel of honor, we must choose to follow after righteousness. As New Testament believers, we understand that righteousness is a result of what Christ has done, not our works. However, every individual who has confessed Christ as Lord and Saviour should seek to develop character that reflects such a confession.

Righteousness is the position of the believer in Christ Jesus. We are made righteous not because of our own actions, but because of the actions of Christ. While our actions do not make us righteous, our righteousness should be visible in our actions. The moment we confess with our mouth and believe with our heart (Romans 10:9) that Christ died and was resurrected, we are saved. While we are immediately saved from the guilt of sin, we are not yet completely saved from the power of sin. The physical nature of man does not immediately reflect one's new status in the Lord. Thus, believers become committed to the process of having their lives reflect their position in Christ. To do so, we must choose to walk in faith, love, and peace. There are times when we must choose to walk in love instead of proving a point or being "right." There are times when we have to choose to not partake in certain conversations because they will lead to strife or other forms of ungodliness.

In his letter to the church in Corinth, the apostle Paul spoke about not being carnal Christians (1 Corinthians 3). A carnal Christian is a Christian who gives in to the desires of the flesh and who is not committed to a lifestyle that reflects Jesus Christ. God does not want His children to be carnal or remain immature. For example, a daughter of just 18 months old exhibits behavior that is typical of someone her age. However, the parent does not desire her to continue with the same behavior when she is 7, 12, or 18 years old. It is expected that with proper nurture and teaching, she will mature, grow, and learn. The same is true of the spiritual growth and development of the Christian. Some level of immaturity is expected when we are newly saved and young in the Lord. However, it is expected that we study the Word of God and develop character that is more representative of Him. Just as natural growth and maturity require proper nurturing, so it is with spiritual growth and maturity.

4. Show Gentleness to Those Who Oppose the Truth (vv. 24-26)
Paul instructs Timothy to avoid quarreling over God's Word and to be gentle toward those who respect the truth.

In certain Christian circles, the title "servant of the Lord," is reserved for a special group of people, usually clergy or other church leaders. However, all Christians are servants of the Lord. As such, Christians are instructed to conduct their lives in gentleness and meekness. Notice that verse 24 does not say "the preacher, the pastor, or the Sunday school teacher." It simply says "the servant of the Lord." That includes every believer. So every believer should be kind to others. Every believer should be able to teach someone something about the Word of God, even if they have had the chance to attend seminary, and be a preacher or pastor.

However, the responsibility that comes with being a Christian is yours. Such responsibility is outlined in verse 24: Be kind to all men, be able to teach, and be patient. As a workman (v. 15), or servant of the Lord, we are expected to study the Word and develop the ability to "divide" or share it properly with others.

Studying the Word of God is not reserved for the pastor. It is for everyone, from the pulpit to the pew. As more Christians begin to own the responsibility that comes with being a Christian, they become vessels that God can use to bring salvation to others. No, Christians should not argue with others about the Word of God. Instead, we are called to teach the Word with gentleness and meekness and leave the results up to God. As we humbly teach God's truth, God through the Holy Spirit can provide illumination to the one who hears the teaching.

SEARCH THE SCRIPTURES
1. What is it that every Christian is expected to do with the Word of God (2 Timothy 2:15)?
2. What do empty words and vain babbling pro-

duce in the lives of those who engage in idle talk (vv. 16-18)?
3. What is the outcome or reward for someone who chooses to become a vessel of honor in the house of the Lord (v. 21)?
4. What is it that the Christian is told to avoid (v. 23)?

DISCUSS THE MEANING
1. Why do you think idle talk has such a negative effect on both the one speaking and the one listening?
2. Suppose that you are out with some friends from church. You all begin to engage in conversation about another lady from church who is not present. The conversation is very unkind, and the facts of the conversation may or may not be true. How should you respond? What does God expect you to do?
3. Think about a time when you have taken part in or listened to a negative conversation about someone else. What did you do? How did you feel? What type of atmosphere did the conversation produce?

LESSON IN OUR SOCIETY
Godly character is not a very popular topic in many Christian circles. It is great to hear messages on purpose, healing, destiny, and other topics of interest. However, we cannot afford to continue to neglect the role of godly character in the life of a Christian. God is concerned about the character of His children. He wants us to allow His Spirit to permeate every area of our lives, including our speech. I am sure that every one of us, if we would examine our lives, can find an area in which gossip or idle chatter produced a negative outcome for us or for someone we know. Let me challenge you to take a stand against that which does not produce godly fruit in your life. It is not always the popular thing to do, and it can take a lot of courage to follow after righteousness. However, as you follow after righteousness, you will become a vessel of honor in the house of the Lord.

MAKE IT HAPPEN
On a sheet of paper, list those areas in your life in which you have seen tremendous growth since

giving your life to Christ. On a separate sheet of paper, list those areas in your life in which you are struggling to follow after righteousness. Then, list several things you can do to change those areas in which you are presently struggling to produce righteousness. It is said that it takes 21 days to break an old habit and make a new one. Therefore, make it a goal to work on one area for a month, choosing a new area each month, and watch righteousness develop in your life.

FOLLOW THE SPIRIT
What God wants me to do:

_____
_____
_____

REMEMBER YOUR THOUGHTS
Special insights I have learned:

_____
_____

MORE LIGHT ON THE TEXT
2 Timothy 2:14-26

In this passage, Paul gives Timothy instructions on how to maintain Christian behavior. Throughout the text, Paul instructs Timothy to tell the people of God about the importance of good character. He constantly emphasizes meekness, righteousness, and the avoidance of sin as signs of godly character.

14 Of these things put them in remembrance, charging them before the Lord that they strive not about words to no profit, but to the subverting of the hearers.

The phrase "these things" in verse 14 refers back to previous verses in this chapter (vv. 11-13). In those verses, Paul talked about the importance of remaining faithful in suffering. Paul also said that even if we do not remain faithful, God will be faithful because He cannot deny Himself. Paul tells Timothy to "put these things in remembrance." This phrase comes from the Greek word *hupomimnesko* (**hoop-om-im-NACE-ko**), which literally means "to put in mind" or "remind." Paul tells Timothy to keep in mind or remind others in the church of the things that he said in the previous verses. The word "charging" in Greek is *dia-*

marturomai (**dee-am-ar-TOO-rom-ahee**), which means to "attest or protest earnestly." The Greek word *logomacheo* (**log-om-akh-EH-o**) means "to quarrel about words." Interestingly, the word for "subverting" in Greek is *katastrophe* (**kat-as-trof-AY**), which is where we get the word "catastrophe," and means "demolition." Paul instructs Timothy to command the people to stop fighting over words because it does nothing but bring destruction to the hearers of the argument.

15 Study to shew thyself approved unto God, a workman that needeth not to be ashamed, rightly dividing the word of truth.

The Greek word for "study" is *spoudazo* (**spoo-DAD-zo**), which can be translated as "to endeavor" or "to labour." "To show thyself approved" is the Greek phrase *paristemi dokimos* (**par-IS-tay-mee DOK-ee-mos**). This phrase can be loosely translated as "to present yourself as acceptable." The word for "workman" is (Gk. *ergates*, **er-GAT-ace**), and means "laborer." The phrase "rightly dividing" in Greek is *orthotomeo* (**or-thot-om-EH-o**), and it means to "cut straight," to "hold a straight course," or to "handle right." Paul tells Timothy to present himself as an acceptable workman to God by intensely studying Scripture and by handling it correctly.

16 But shun profane and vain babblings: for they will increase unto more ungodliness.

The word for "shun" in Greek is *periistemi* (**per-ee-IS-tay-mee**) meaning "to keep away from." The phrase "vain babbling" comes from the Greek word *kenophonia* (**ken-of-o-NEE-ah**), which means "fruitless chatter." The explanation that Paul gives is that vain babblings would only "increase unto more ungodliness." The Greek word for "increase" in this verse is *prokopto* (**prok-OP-to**), which means "advance." The Greek word for "ungodliness" is *asebeia* (**as-EB-I-ah**), which means "wickedness." Paul says that not only will vain babblings not bear fruit for God's kingdom, but they will also advance wickedness.

17 And their word will eat as doth a canker: of whom is Hymenaeus and Philetus;

The Greek word for "canker" is *gaggraina*

(**GANG-grahee-nah**). This word refers to an ulcer, or something similar to gangrene. With such strong language, Paul showed Timothy what type of damage fruitless discussion can do. Paul even points out Hymenaeus and Philetus as false teachers.

18 Who concerning the truth have erred, saying that the resurrection is past already; and overthrow the faith of some.

The word for "erred" in Greek is *astocheo* (**as-tokh-EH-o**), which means "to miss the mark." Paul declares that Hymenaeus and Philetus are guilty of missing the mark of the truth in Scripture. The "resurrection" that Paul refers to is the raising of the dead in Christ at His return. These two men claimed that this resurrection had already taken place. Paul says that this false teaching has overthrown the faith of some of the believers in the church. The word Paul uses for "overthrow" is *ana-trepo* (**an-at-REP-o**) and means "to subvert." Unfortunately, this false teaching could subvert the faith of some of the followers of Christ.

19 Nevertheless the foundation of God standeth sure, having this seal, The Lord knoweth them that are his. And, Let every one that nameth the name of Christ depart from iniquity.

Paul begins to address the character of the Lord and the character that the Lord's people should have. He begins by saying that "the foundation of God standeth sure." The Greek word that Paul uses for "sure" is *stereos* (**ster-eh-OS**), which means "solid" or "stable." The Greek word for "knoweth" is *ginosko* (**ghin-OCE-ko**), which means "to know or understand." Paul states that God has a strong character and a steady foundation, and that He knows and understands His people. Paul also says that God's people should depart from iniquity. The word for "iniquity" in Greek is *adikia* (**ad-ee-KEE-ah**), which can be translated as "wrongfulness of character." Just as God has a strong character, Paul says God's people should avoid things that develop a wrong character.

20 But in a great house there are not only vessels of gold and of silver, but also of wood and of earth; and some to honour, and some to dishonour.

Paul uses this verse to form an analogy to describe the importance of turning away from wickedness. The "great house" that Paul mentions in this verse is a reference to the house of any wealthy person. The wealthy people of Paul's day, not unlike today, had utensils and dishes used for special guests and those for everyday use. The gold and silver vessels are vessels of "honour," while the wood and earthen vessels are vessels of "dishonour." Paul uses the Greek word *time* (**tee-MAY**), which means "dignity or esteem," when the word "honour" appears in this text. Paul will continue to build on this analogy in the next few verses.

21 If a man therefore purge himself from these, he shall be a vessel unto honour, sanctified, and meet for the master's use, and prepared unto every good work.

The word for "purge" in Greek is *ekkathairo* (**ek-kath-AH-ee-ro**), which means "to cleanse thoroughly." Paul says that if one shuns "vain babblings" (v. 16) and follows Paul's instructions in the verses to come, that person would become "a vessel unto honour, sanctified, and meet for the master's use, and prepared unto every good work." The Greek word for "sanctified" in this verse is *hagiazo* (**hag-ee-AD-zo**), which can be translated as "made holy." The Greek word *euchrestos* (**YOO-khrays-tos**), which means "useful," is the word translated here as "meet." Those who want to be vessels that are made holy and ready to be used in the kingdom of God should take Paul's advice in the following verses.

22 Flee also youthful lusts: but follow righteousness, faith, charity, peace, with them that call on the Lord out of a pure heart.

The Greek words for "youthful lusts" are *neoterikos epithumia* (**neh-o-TER-ik-os ep-ee-thoo-MEE-ah**), which mean "juvenile longings." Paul says to flee the juvenile longings and pursue godly things. The Greek word for "righteousness" is *dikaiosune* (**dik-ah-yos-OO-nay**), which means "equity." The Greek word for "charity" is the same as one of the words for "love," namely, *agape* (**ag-AH-pay**). The word *agape* means "godly love." Paul says to pursue equity and justice, faith, godly love, and peace with a pure heart and motives.

23 But foolish and unlearned questions avoid, knowing that they do gender strifes.

The words for "foolish" and "unlearned" in Greek are *asonetos* (**as-OON-ay-tos**) and *apaideutos* (**ap-AH-ee-dyoo-tos**), respectively. The word *moros* (**mo-ROS**) means "absurd," while *apaideutos* is translated as "uninstructed." The phrase "gender strifes" in Greek is *gennao mache* (**ghen-NAH-o MAKH-ay**). These two words together in this text mean "to bring forth controversy." Paul advises Timothy to not allow fruitless and unnecessary questions that only cause division among the people in the church.

24 And the servant of the Lord must not strive; but be gentle unto all men, apt to teach, patient,

The word used for "servant" in this verse is *doulos* (**DOO-los**) in Greek. This word is also translated as "slave." As Christians, we are bought with a price (1 Corinthians 7:23) by the blood of Jesus Christ. As a result, we should be obedient to the way the Master wants to develop our character. Paul says that the Lord's servant "must not strive." The Greek word for "strive" is *machomai* (**MAKH-om-ahee**), which means "to quarrel." Paul is saying that the people of God should not fight against one another. Instead, he says we are to be "gentle unto all men, apt to teach, patient." The Greek words for "gentle," "apt to teach," and "patient" are *epios* (**AY-pee-os**), *didaktikos* (**did-ak-tik-OS**), and *anexikakos* (**an-ex-IK-ak-os**), respectively.

25 In meekness instructing those that oppose themselves; if God peradventure will give them repentance to the acknowledging of the truth;

Paul continues to accentuate the traits of godly character. In verse 22, he talked about how true Christians are righteous, faithful, loving, and peaceful. Then he talks about how Christians should know God's Word and have servants' hearts (vv. 23-24). Now Paul calls for Christians to be meek and able to train others. The Greek word *paideuo* (**pahee-DYOO-o**) is translated as "instructing" and means "to train a child." Paul tells Timothy to teach those who are young in the faith with the truth of Scripture. The word "peradventure" comes from the Greek word *mepote* (**MAY-pot-eh**), which simply means "perhaps." Paul says that maybe those who are new Christians or those who have been given false doctrine will repent when they learn the truth of Scripture.

26 And that they may recover themselves out of the snare of the devil, who are taken captive by him at his will.

Finally, Paul says that Christians who have embraced false doctrine will come to their senses and avoid falling into the enemy's trap. The Greek word that Paul uses for "recover" is *ananepho* (**an-an-AY-fo**), which literally means "to become sober again." The Greek word for "snare" is *pagis* (**pag-ECE**), which means "trick." The Greek word *zogreo* (**dzogue-REH-o**) is translated as the phrase "taken captive" and refers to someone who is taken alive as a prisoner of war. Paul realizes that Christians still make bad decisions and make mistakes in life. By using the word *zogreo* here, as well as in some of the other texts that he wrote, Paul showed that he realized that, as humans, we constantly struggle with sin (Romans 7:21). However, he also said that it is a sign of godly character to recover from sinfulness and return to righteousness.

DAILY BIBLE READINGS

M: God's Promise Is Realized Through Faith
Romans 4:13-25

T: So You May Grow into Salvation
1 Peter 2:1-10

W: Grow in the Knowledge of God
Colossians 1:3-10

T: A Good Soldier of Christ Jesus
2 Timothy 2:1-7

F: Remember Christ Jesus
2 Timothy 2:8-13

S: Be a Worker Approved by God
2 Timothy 2:14-19

S: Pursue Righteousness, Faith, Love, and Peace
2 Timothy 2:20-26

TEACHING TIPS

February 19
Bible Study Guide 12

1. Words You Should Know

A. Seducers (2 Timothy 3:13) *goes* (Gk.)—A deceiver or imposter.

B. Itching Ears (4:3) *knetho akoe* (Gk.)—A term used to refer to those who turn away from the truth and want to hear only those things that are pleasing to them.

2. Teacher Preparation

A. Pray for the students in your class. Ask God to give your students ears to hear and a heart to receive today's lesson.

B. Read and study the FOCAL VERSES. Give close attention to Paul's tone and to his instructions to young Timothy.

C. Be prepared to share with your class personal examples about how having a mentor and/or being a mentor have changed your life.

3. Starting the Lesson

A. Begin class with prayer. Thank God for your students and for those who have taken time to serve as mentors in their lives, offering wise advice and godly counsel.

B. Ask a student to read the IN FOCUS section, then allow the students to share how mentoring has affected their lives. Ask the students to share their experiences with having or being a mentor. How did such experiences change their lives?

4. Getting into the Lesson

As you begin the lesson, remind your students that the focus is on the importance of having and being a good mentor. Open a discussion with your students, focusing on the role of Paul in the life of young Timothy. Discuss how Timothy's life could have been different without the encouragement and wise counsel of Paul. Also, discuss how Paul must have felt when he took young Timothy "under his wing."

5. Relating the Lesson to Life

A. Give the students the opportunity to answer the questions in the SEARCH THE SCRIPTURES section.

B. Engage in conversation with your students as you answer and discuss the questions found in the DISCUSS THE MEANING section.

6. Arousing Action

A. Encourage your students to thank those who have served as mentors in their lives.

B. Encourage your students to find someone to mentor.

C. Close the class with prayer.

WORSHIP GUIDE

For the Superintendent or Teacher
Theme: Follow a Good Mentor
Theme Song: "He Leadeth Me"
Scripture: Luke 9:23
Song: "Follow Jesus"
Meditation: Dear Lord, as I follow Your Word, help me to set an example that others may want to emulate. We realize that in the community of faith, we all must lead by example and that Your Son, Jesus Christ, is the ultimate example for all that we do.

FE
19

FOLLOW A GOOD MENTOR

Bible Background • 2 TIMOTHY 3–4
Printed Text • 2 TIMOTHY 3:10–4:8
Devotional Reading • PSALM 119:9–16

LESSON AIM

By the end of the lesson, we will:

BECOME AWARE of the importance and impact of a mentor in the life of someone else;

REALIZE we have a responsibility to share our experiences with others; and

DECIDE to become a mentor to someone in your church or neighborhood.

KEEP IN MIND

"But continue thou in the things which thou hast learned and hast been assured of, knowing of whom thou hast learned them" (2 Timothy 3:14).

FOCAL VERSES

2 Timothy 3:10 But thou hast fully known my doctrine, manner of life, purpose, faith, longsuffering, charity, patience,

11 Persecutions, afflictions, which came unto me at Antioch, at Iconium, at Lystra; what persecutions I endured: but out of them all the Lord delivered me.

12 Yea, and all that will live godly in Christ Jesus shall suffer persecution.

13 But evil men and seducers shall wax worse and worse, deceiving, and being deceived.

14 But continue thou in the things which thou hast learned and hast been assured of, knowing of whom thou hast learned them;

15 And that from a child thou hast known the holy scriptures, which are able to make thee wise unto salvation through faith which is in Christ Jesus.

16 All scripture is given by inspiration of God,

LESSON OVERVIEW

LESSON AIM
KEEP IN MIND
FOCAL VERSES
IN FOCUS
THE PEOPLE, PLACES, AND TIMES
BACKGROUND
AT-A-GLANCE
IN DEPTH
SEARCH THE SCRIPTURES
DISCUSS THE MEANING
LESSON IN OUR SOCIETY
MAKE IT HAPPEN
FOLLOW THE SPIRIT
REMEMBER YOUR THOUGHTS
MORE LIGHT ON THE TEXT
DAILY BIBLE READINGS

---

and is profitable for doctrine, for reproof, for correction, for instruction in righteousness:

17 That the man of God may be perfect, throughly furnished unto all good works.

4:1 I charge thee therefore before God, and the Lord Jesus Christ, who shall judge the quick and the dead at his appearing and his kingdom;

2 Preach the word; be instant in season, out of season; reprove, rebuke, exhort with all longsuffering and doctrine.

3 For the time will come when they will not endure sound doctrine; but after their own lusts shall they heap to themselves teachers, having itching ears;

4 And they shall turn away their ears from the truth, and shall be turned unto fables.

5 But watch thou in all things, endure afflictions, do the work of an evangelist, make full proof of thy ministry.

6 For I am now ready to be offered, and the time of my departure is at hand.

7 I have fought a good fight, I have finished my course, I have kept the faith:

8 Henceforth there is laid up for me a crown of righteousness, which the Lord, the righteous judge, shall give me at that day: and not to me only, but unto all them also that love his appearing.

IN FOCUS

Sonny's brush with the law began when he was just 14. He lived the life of a gangbanger throughout his teenage years. It all came to a halt when he got involved in a major gang war that resulted in the death of a rival gang member. Although Sonny wasn't directly linked with the crime, he was given a three-year prison sentence on his 25th birthday.

Three years after his release, the pastor, who had carefully shepherded him in his Christian walk, asked him to organize a mentoring program aimed at teenage gang members.

The pastor chuckled a little as he examined the stunned expression in Sonny's eyes, and said, "I know; you want to ask 'Why me,' right?"

"No, pastor, that's not it. I can see that I might be able to point out the dangers to those who are headed down the wrong path. But I question whether I'm ready to take that kind of leadership role in the midst of the lifestyle that I have been dodging, retreating, and hiding."

"Sonny, let me tell you this: If these youngsters connect with a person who has been through the trenches of life and survived, they will grow to appreciate your wisdom.

"It's also important to understand that you have much to gain in your personal walk. Mentoring is a form of discipleship in which you can use the Scriptures for the training of others in righteousness. If we give what we learn to others, ultimately we strengthen our own relationship with Christ. Now can you see the importance of mentoring?"

Sonny's apprehension lifted and he accepted his mentoring role.

In Timothy, we see that followers of God are equipped for every good work. Are you using your God-given gifts to help mentor another person?

THE PEOPLE, PLACES, AND TIMES

Mentor. A mentor is a person who is looked to for wise advice and guidance; a wise and trusted counselor or teacher; an influential senior sponsor or supporter; an adviser, master, guide, preceptor.

BACKGROUND

In this section of Paul's pastoral epistle to Timothy, the apostle speaks about his persecution as a servant of Jesus Christ. He also reminds

Timothy that he, too, can expect to suffer persecution for the sake of the Gospel. Paul realizes that his service in this life was coming to an end, and he was awaiting his crown of glory. Yet, he reminds Timothy to continue preaching the Gospel of Jesus Christ. He encourages Timothy to preach even when people don't want to hear the Word of God.

AT-A-GLANCE

1. An Example of Faith Under Fire
(2 Timothy 3:10-11)
2. A Warning of Persecution to Come
(vv. 12-13)
3. An Exhortation to Remain Faithful
(vv. 14-17)
4. A Charge to Proclaim the Gospel (4:1-5)
5. A Testimony of a Well-lived Life
(vv. 6-8)

IN DEPTH

1. An Example of Faith Under Fire (2 Timothy 3:10-11)

Paul was imprisoned, and he was revisiting, in his letter to Timothy, his time of service for the Lord Jesus Christ. He recounts how he had always tried to live a life that followed what he taught. He also reminds Timothy of the persecution he had faced as an ambassador for Jesus Christ.

Like Paul, many of our Christian brothers and sisters in various parts of the world endure persecution today. Many of us have or may face similar opposition. As Paul mentors Timothy, he also instructs us to be brave and patiently persevere against the hindering physical and spiritual forces arrayed against us, whether they be persecutions, temptations, or other types of opposition.

Paul knew that Timothy would also face the kind of persecution the apostle faced in Pisidia, Antioch, Iconium, and Lystra (Acts 13:50; 14:2, 5, 19). Because the Lord delivered Paul and restored him to health, he wanted to encourage Timothy through his experiences of God's faithfulness. Paul knew that his time on earth was coming to an end. So he used this letter as an opportunity to guide and exhort Timothy in the faith one final time.

2. A Warning of Persecution to Come (vv. 12-13)

Paul had experienced persecution for the sake of the Gospel, and he knew that Timothy would experience persecution as well. He encourages Timothy by reminding him that all who choose to serve Christ will be persecuted.

Just as Paul encouraged Timothy, he encourages us to endure persecution for the sake of the Gospel. The writer James also encourages us. He writes, "Blessed is the man that endureth temptation: for when he is tried, he shall receive the crown of life, which the Lord hath promised to them that love him" (James 1:12). Likewise, Jesus said, "There is no man that hath left house, or brethren, or sisters, or father, or mother, or wife, or children, or lands, for my sake, and the gospel's, But he shall receive an hundredfold now in this time, houses, and brethren, and sisters, and mothers, and children, and lands, with persecutions; and in the world to come eternal life" (Mark 10:29-30). Therefore, we should remain encouraged whenever we are persecuted for the sake of the Gospel.

While religious persecution is less severe in America than in other places, it is appropriate that we remember our brothers and sisters who live in lands where it could cost them their lives to be Christians. We can hold them up in prayer that their faith will not fail and that they, like Paul and Timothy, will continue to declare the Gospel and live for Jesus Christ.

3. An Exhortation to Remain Faithful (vv. 14-17)

Paul and Timothy provide us with a great example of how a mentoring relationship can and should work. While Timothy did not feel prepared for the task at hand, he was encouraged by his mentors. There are times when we may not believe that God can use us. However, knowing that someone we admire has confidence in what God can do through us can serve as a great encouragement. Notice what Paul wrote to the Corinthians, "Blessed be God, even the Father of our Lord Jesus Christ, the Father of mercies, and the God of all comfort; Who comforteth us in all our tribulation, that we may be able to comfort them which are in any trouble, by the comfort wherewith we ourselves are comforted of God." (2 Corinthians 1:3-4).

Paul was able to encourage and comfort Timothy based on his experience and the comfort he himself had received. This speaks to our responsibility to give back that which has been given to us. The Bible says, "Give, and it shall be given unto you" (Luke 6:38). This is not just referring to money; it relates to everything we receive. We have an obligation as Christians to give back. We need to give encouragement and assistance to those in our families, our neighborhood, and our church community.

4. A Charge to Proclaim the Gospel (4:1-5)

Paul encourages Timothy to remain focused on his assignment. Timothy had been assigned to "be instant," that is to be prepared, to proclaim the Gospel in all circumstances. Just as a fireman must be prepared to respond to emergencies, so too, Timothy should be ready to reprove, rebuke, and exhort. He is to do this with longsuffering and sound doctrine.

People are not always open to hear the truth. On the contrary, people often turn to false teachings and false doctrine. However, this did not excuse Timothy from the responsibility of his ministry, nor does it excuse us from our ministry as the children of God. We are all called to serve in some capacity or another, and we have a responsibility to represent God and remain strong in the faith, not wavering from sound doctrine.

5. A Testimony of a Well-lived Life (vv. 6-8)

Paul realized that his earthly ministry was coming to an end, and he prepared himself and Timothy. Good mentors usually know when their season is up and when it is time to pass the torch to the next person in line. Paul did this very well. He placed full confidence in Timothy and was able to conclude his earthly ministry in peace, knowing that Timothy would continue to preach the Gospel and promote the cause of Christ.

When we have served the Lord faithfully we can know we have not worked for Him in vain. God remembers our service, and reserves a reward for our obedience. While we might not always see the benefits of our service while on this earth, we must be confident that our labor of love is not in vain.

SEARCH THE SCRIPTURES

1. What does Paul say will happen to all those who choose to live godly (2 Timothy 3:12)?

2. Who is the source of all Scripture and what is the purpose of the Word of God (vv. 16-17)?

3. What does Paul instruct Timothy to do (2 Timothy 4:2)?

DISCUSS THE MEANING

1. Why do you think Paul spoke of the persecutions he endured while preaching the Gospel?

2. What do you think Paul meant when he told Timothy that people will have "itching ears"?

3. Do you think it is important to have a mentor? Why or why not?

4. What lessons can we learn from Paul and Timothy about mentoring and the discipling of others in the faith?

LESSON IN OUR SOCIETY

We have a responsibility to witness to others about the Gospel of Jesus Christ. In addition, we have a responsibility to give back to and encourage others in the faith. The mentoring relationship is essential in fulfilling our divine purpose and advancing the kingdom of God in the earth. This relationship model is prevalent in the Bible, and its benefits cannot be ignored. Such biblical examples include Eli and Samuel, Elijah and Elisha, and Paul and Timothy.

Our experiences are not just for us. We are to serve others through them and continue the legacy and promises planted in us by God. Mentors encourage, listen, guide, and advise. They often share common experiences and can serve as great comforters during times of difficulty. While many of us recognize the importance of having a mentor, few choose to serve as a mentor. As you examine the relationship between Paul and Timothy, ask yourself how you are working to encourage those who are coming behind you.

MAKE IT HAPPEN

Do you have a mentor? Do you serve as a mentor? If not, determine to develop these relationships with others in the body of Christ. If so, connect with your mentor and find someone to disciple.

FOLLOW THE SPIRIT

What God wants me to do:

_____

_____

REMEMBER YOUR THOUGHTS

Special insights I have learned:

_____

_____

MORE LIGHT ON THE TEXT

2 Timothy 3:10-4:8

10 But thou hast fully known my doctrine, manner of life, purpose, faith, longsuffering, charity, patience, 11 Persecutions, afflictions, which came unto me at Antioch, at Iconium, at Lystra; what persecutions I endured: but out of them all the Lord delivered me.

In this verse, the apostle Paul uses himself as an example for Timothy to emulate. The Greek word for the phrase "hast fully known" is *parakoloutheo* (**par-ak-ol-oo-THEH-o**), which means "to examine thoroughly or investigate." Because Timothy was mentored by Paul, he was able to testify that what Paul preached was completely in line with the way Paul lived his life. Timothy was able to thoroughly examine Paul's life while under his tutelage. Timothy also witnessed the persecutions Paul suffered for living a Christian life and doing good. Paul warns Timothy that just as he had suffered persecution for following Jesus Christ and living a righteous life, so would Timothy. Paul also encourages Timothy that God is on his side and will deliver him out of every persecution.

12 Yea, and all that will live godly in Christ Jesus shall suffer persecution.

Paul wanted his young disciple to know that he too would suffer persecution. He was clear that everyone who wants to live a "godly" (Gk. *eusebos*,

yoo-seb-oce,' meaning pious, having or showing an earnest reverence toward God) life in Christ Jesus will be "persecuted" (Gk. *dioko,* **dee-o'-ko,** meaning to pursue in a hostile manner, to harass, trouble or molest).

The Christian lifestyle is not always popular in today's society. Today's youth are constantly under peer pressure to do what is popular and follow the crowd. Many men and women have given their lives for Christ and suffered persecution. In fact, everyone who lives for Christ will suffer persecution at one time or another. The kind of suffering may vary, but eventually persecution will come in some form or fashion. Paul reminds Timothy that there will be hard times.

13 But evil men and seducers shall wax worse and worse, deceiving, and being deceived.

Paul cautions Timothy concerning the actions of evil men. The Greek phrase for "shall wax" is *prokopto* (**prok-OP-to**), which means "to go forward, advance, proceed, or increase." Evil men

In the pursuit of knowledge.

will become worse and worse through their own corruption, and those who lead others down the path of destruction will themselves be destroyed in the process.

As Christians, when we see our brother or sister in Christ headed down the path of destruction, it is our responsibility to help guide them back to the path of righteousness. It is especially important that we watch out for new Christians who are eager to learn and practice their faith.

14 But continue thou in the things which thou hast learned and hast been assured of, knowing of whom thou hast learned them; 15 And that from a child thou hast known the holy scriptures, which are able to make thee wise unto salvation through faith which is in Christ Jesus.

Paul did not want Timothy to be led astray by the "seducers" (impostors) mentioned in verse 13. He was to be faithful to what he had learned from his trustworthy teachers, namely his grandmother Lois and his mother Eunice—things he had been "assured (convinced) of" because of their faithfulness to the Scriptures (Old Testament). Timothy apparently learned the law and committed much of it to memory at an early age. This was common Jewish custom.

Timothy was raised in the nurture and admonition of the Lord. As such, he learned to have faith in God's saving grace as he learned to walk, talk, and run. In other words, as he grew, he was discipled by Lois and Eunice. This is what we must do with our children and grandchildren. It is important that we give our children this kind of heritage, especially in this day of social and cultural opposition to the biblical Gospel.

During times of persecution, trials, and afflictions, it is important to continue in the things that we have learned and know to be true. We are to trust God and stand on the Word of God. Many of us have been raised in Christian homes and learned the Bible when we were children. It is through faith that our knowledge and understanding of the Bible will keep us walking on the path of righteousness. It is the Word of God that will keep us. Psalm 119:11 says, "Thy word have I hid in mine heart, that I might not sin against thee." As we study and meditate on the Word of God, it is important that the Word of God becomes part of who we are.

As we mature in Christ, there will be many people who inspire us and contribute to our learning and growth. We must also remember to pass on to others the wisdom, knowledge, and understanding that we have received.

16 All scripture is given by inspiration of God, and is profitable for doctrine, for reproof, for correction, for instruction in righteousness: 17 That the man of God may be perfect, throughly furnished unto all good works.

Paul encouraged Timothy by reminding him that his scriptural heritage is not the product of human tradition, it is of divine origin. We should always keep this in mind as we navigate through the complexities of life. The phrase "inspiration of God" comes from the Greek word *theopneustos* (**theh-op'-nyoo-stos**). This is a compound word that includes *theos* (**theh-os**), meaning God and *pneo* (**pne-o),** meaning breathed. Thus, the literal meaning of the word is "God breathed." When we read our Bibles, we receive the very words that proceeded from the mouth of God. Therefore, for the believer, the Scriptures must have a very high position of authority in our lives. It must govern our whole outlook on life—our worldview. We exercise poor stewardship of this priceless scriptural treasure if we do not apply it in every area of life. Why? Because the Word of God is "profitable," (useful) especially in the areas of "doctrine" (Gk. *didaskalia*, **did-as-kal-ee'-ah**, meaning teaching), "reproof" (Gk. *elegwos*, **el'-eng-khos,** meaning rebuking conviction of a sinner), "correcting" (Gk. *epanorthosin*, **ep-an-or'-tho-sis**, literally restoration to an upright position or a right state), and "instruction (Gk. *paideia*, **pahee-di'-ah**, meaning training) in righteousness. The root of the word *paideia* is *pais* (Gk. **pahees**),

meaning child. Thus, the original use of *paideia* was for "the nurturing of a child." For the child of God the Scripture is indispensable in "training in righteousness," both internally and externally.

The Bible will equip us for ministry. The Greek word for the phrase "thoroughly furnished" is *exartizo* (**ex-ar-tid-zo**), which means to complete or finish. This word contains an adjective and a verb in the form of a perfect passive participle. The adjective is *artios* (**ar-tee-os**), and means complete, capable, and proficient—able to meet every demand. The verb *exartizo* (**ex-ar-tid-zo**) means to equip. The Bible gives everything we need to do the work of the ministry.

4:1 I charge thee therefore before God, and the Lord Jesus Christ, who shall judge the quick and the dead at his appearing and his kingdom; 2 Preach the word; be instant in season, out of season; reprove, rebuke, exhort with all longsuffering and doctrine.

In these verses, the apostle Paul commissions Timothy into the service of God. The Greek word *diamartyromai* (**dee-am-ar-too'-rom-ahee**) means "I solemnly charge." This charge has the weight of the most sacred earnest of testimonies, confirming a thing to be believed. The confirmation of Paul's sacred charge is none other than Jesus Himself, the returning Judge of the living and the dead. Timothy was not to base his thinking on the present reality, which was temporal, but on the coming reality of the eternal kingdom of Christ. Like Timothy we are also commissioned into the service of God. And like Timothy, we are charged by the apostle Paul to govern ourselves in such a way that we do not sacrifice the permanent (eternal) on the altar of the temporary.

The Greek word for the phrase "be instant" is *ephistemi* (**ef-IS-tay-mee**), which means "to stand by," "be present" or "be prepared." Timothy was commissioned to preach the Word of God and to always be ready to give an account of the Gospel of Jesus Christ. Similarly, we must also be ready to speak on Christ's behalf whenever the opportunity arises. We are not to let any opportunity slip by. As Christians, we must make sure that we speak the truth of the Gospel; this will sometimes require reproof and correction, and we must correct in love. The Gospel message is used to draw men and women to God through encouragement and patience.

3 For the time will come when they will not endure sound doctrine; but after their own lusts shall they heap to themselves teachers, having itching ears; 4 And they shall turn away their ears from the truth, and shall be turned unto fables.

Paul assures Timothy that there will be times when some who claim to be Christians will not "endure sound doctrine." The Greek word translated "endure" is *anechomai* (**an-ekh'-om-ahee**), meaning to hold up, to sustain, or to bear. The Greek word for "sound" is *hugiaino* (**hoog-ee-ah'-ee-no**), meaning to be well or to be in good health. In essence, these heretics will not tolerate healthy (biblical) teaching. They will only be interested in hearing what they want to hear, namely, false doctrines that will eventually bear the fruit of spiritual sickness or even spiritual death. Thus, they will look to and follow those who will teach these heresies, not those who speak truth. To guard against false teaching, we must be like the Bereans who examined the Scriptures every day to see if what is being taught is true (Acts 17:11).

Greed and the possibility of free or cheap labor seduced America to participate in grave injustices against the African people. Our national core values were rooted in Judeo-Christian principles, yet we were never completely true to them. One result was the horrible practice of slavery. Many religious leaders compromised their integrity by accepting the horrible practice of slavery. Many ministers hid the truth of a liberating Gospel from the slaves in order to try to keep them submissive. Slaves were denied access to the Bible because they were not allowed to read. Whole denominations split because of this divisive issue of slavery. However, God had other plans. Like the Children of Israel, who were always singing, African American slaves developed a rich oral tradition that carried many biblical truths. Some slaves taught themselves to read the Bible and conducted secret services away from the watchful eyes of slave owners. Black preachers were able to preach and teach slaves

the true liberating Gospel message, which gave them a blessed hope of better days to come.

5 But watch thou in all things, endure afflictions, do the work of an evangelist, make full proof of thy ministry.

The Greek word for "watch" used in this verse is *nepho* (**NAY-fo**), which means "to be sober" or "to be calm and collected in spirit." Paul tells Timothy to always be sober and calm in everything, even when enduring affliction. Paul informs Timothy that there will be times when he will suffer, and he urges him not to be discouraged during the difficult times but to hold on to the task set before him. Timothy had to continue his work as an evangelist by watering and nurturing the church that was planted by Paul. The Greek word for the phrase "make full proof" is *plerophoreo* (**play-rof-or-EH-o**), which means "to cause something to be shown to the full." Timothy is to fulfill the ministry in every aspect. He must get all the members in the church to work together to stop heresy from coming into the church and corrupting the new Christians.

6 For I am now ready to be offered, and the time of my departure is at hand. 7 I have fought a good fight, I have finished my course, I have kept the faith:

The Greek word for "ready to be offered" is *spendo* (**SPEN-do**), which means to be poured out as a drink offering and refers to one whose blood is to be poured out in a violent death for the cause of God. In this verse, Paul views his life as a sacrificial drink offering to God. Paul was ready to give his life for the cause of Christ. Paul had dedicated his life to the service of Jesus Christ; thus, as his life drew to an end, he did not fear death, but faced it head on, knowing he had labored faithfully for the cause of Christ.

What a blessing to be able to look back over your life and know that you have fulfilled the call given to you by God. Many African Americans throughout history have devoted their lives to the cause of Christ. For example, the members of the Underground Railroad, Catherine Harris, Thomas James, Frederick Douglass, Harriet Tubman, Jermain Loguen, and Sojourner Truth were all associated with the Zionite activity against slavery. Daniel Alexander Payne visited President Abraham Lincoln, urging him to sign a bill passed by Congress on August 14, 1862, abolishing slavery. President Lincoln signed the bill on August 22, 1862. Shortly afterward, Payne penned a welcoming address to all the freed slaves entitled "Welcome to the Ransomed." In 1916, Rosa Young, upon graduation from college and led by the Holy Spirit, returned home to the poor community of Rosebud, Alabama and opened a school for poor Blacks. Dr. Martin Luther King Jr. dedicated his life to the achievement of civil rights for all humankind through the concept of nonviolent social change. There are many who have gone before us and been found faithful. Let us also persevere in our calling as good and faithful servants of the risen Lord (cf. 2 Corinthians 4:2; Matthew 25:21).

8 Henceforth there is laid up for me a crown of righteousness, which the Lord, the righteous judge, shall give me at that day: and not to me only, but unto all them also that love his appearing.

When Paul says that a crown is "laid up" for him, he is not referring to a crown of royalty. The "crown" Paul speaks about is *stephanos* (Gk. **ste-fan-os**) a laurel wreath given to the winner of the marathon race. The same crown is mentioned by Paul in 1 Corinthians 9:25. Similar crowns were awarded to great athletes such as Jesse Owens in the Olympic games of 1936. As Paul was pressing toward the finish line, God was waiting to award him the prize for victory in the marathon of life. God is ready to award the same crown of righteousness to all Christians who victoriously run the marathon of lifetime ministry.

We need not seek earthly rewards for our service to God because they will not last. Matthew 6:19-21 (NRSV) tells us, "Do not store up for yourselves treasures on earth, where moth and rust consume and where thieves break in and steal; but store up for yourselves treasures in heaven, where neither moth nor rust consumes and where thieves do not break in and steal. For where your treasure is, there your heart will be also." As Christians, we need not seek earthly rewards because we have already received the ultimate treasure: the gift of salvation through the blood of our Lord and Saviour Jesus Christ.

DAILY BIBLE READINGS

M: Treasure God's Word in Your Heart
Psalm 119:9-16
T: Turn Your Heart to God's Decrees
Psalm 119:33-40
W: An Example to Imitate
2 Thessalonians 3:6-13
T: Avoid Godless People
2 Timothy 3:1-9
F: Continue in What You Have Learned
2 Timothy 3:10-17
S: Carry Out Your Ministry Fully
2 Timothy 4:1-8
S: Final Instructions
2 Timothy 4:9-22

TEACHING TIPS

February 26
Bible Study Guide 13

1. Words You Should Know
A. Sober (Titus 2:2) *nephaleos* (Gk.)—Temperate; to abstain from wine, either entirely or at least from its immoderate use.

B. Purloining (v. 10) *nosphizomai* (Gk.)—To set apart, separate, divide; to set apart or separate for one's self.

2. Teacher Preparation
A. Pray for your students.

B. Read the FOCAL VERSES for the lesson.

C. Read through the entire BIBLE STUDY GUIDE; make a note of specific highlights you may want to emphasize.

3. Starting the Lesson
A. Select a student to read the LESSON AIM.

B. Select another student to lead the class in prayer.

4. Getting into the Lesson
A. As you begin the lesson, remind your students that the focus is on the importance of living a life that represents God. Remind the students of the old saying, "Don't just talk the talk, but make sure you walk the walk." Begin a discussion with your students on the importance of living a life that is in line with the words we speak.

B. Read THE PEOPLE, PLACES, AND TIMES as well as the BACKGROUND section to help set the stage for today's lesson. Have the students silently read the sections and write down their thoughts in the REMEMBER YOUR THOUGHTS section.

C. Refer to the SEARCH THE SCRIPTURES questions as you begin the discussion of the lesson.

5. Relating the Lesson to Life
A. Encourage discussion among your students as you answer and discuss the questions in the DISCUSS THE MEANING section.

B. The LESSON IN OUR SOCIETY section should be used to help the students apply the lesson to their present-day situation. How much weight do you give to the words or promises of others? Why?

6. Arousing Action
A. Sum up the lesson with the KEEP IN MIND verse. Ask the students to read it in unison while contemplating how they can apply the verse to their everyday lives.

B. Challenge the students to follow through on the MAKE IT HAPPEN assignment.

C. End the class with prayer.

WORSHIP GUIDE

For the Superintendent or Teacher
Theme: Live the Truth, Teach the Truth
Theme Song: "An Evening Prayer"
Scripture: Psalm 51:1-2
Song: "Lord, I Want To Be A Christian"
Meditation: Dear Father, it is in you that
I live, move, and have being. Help me
each day to be a living epistle providing
a shining example to others of faithful,
righteous living. Amen

FEB
26TH

LIVE THE TRUTH, TEACH THE TRUTH

Bible Background • TITUS 2
Printed Text • TITUS 2
Devotional Reading • EPHESIANS 4:11–16

LESSON AIM

By the end of the lesson, we will:

FEEL strongly that God desires and expects us to live godly;

COMMIT to display faith in God through acts and deeds, living out God's Word; and

SET a godly example for others to follow.

KEEP IN MIND

"In all things shewing thyself a pattern of good works" (Titus 2:7).

FOCAL VERSES

Titus 2:1 But speak thou the things which become sound doctrine:

2 That the aged men be sober, grave, temperate, sound in faith, in charity, in patience.

3 The aged women likewise, that they be in behaviour as becometh holiness, not false accusers, not given to much wine, teachers of good things;

4 That they may teach the young women to be sober, to love their husbands, to love their children,

5 To be discreet, chaste, keepers at home, good, obedient to their own husbands, that the word of God be not blasphemed.

6 Young men likewise exhort to be sober minded.

7 In all things shewing thyself a pattern of good works: in doctrine shewing uncorruptness, gravity, sincerity,

LESSON OVERVIEW

LESSON AIM
KEEP IN MIND
FOCAL VERSES
IN FOCUS
THE PEOPLE, PLACES, AND TIMES
BACKGROUND
AT-A-GLANCE
IN DEPTH
SEARCH THE SCRIPTURES
DISCUSS THE MEANING
LESSON IN OUR SOCIETY
MAKE IT HAPPEN
FOLLOW THE SPIRIT
REMEMBER YOUR THOUGHTS
MORE LIGHT ON THE TEXT
DAILY BIBLE READINGS

8 Sound speech, that cannot be condemned; that he that is of the contrary part may be ashamed, having no evil thing to say of you.

9 Exhort servants to be obedient unto their own masters, and to please them well in all things; not answering again;

10 Not purloining, but shewing all good fidelity; that they may adorn the doctrine of God our Saviour in all things.

11 For the grace of God that bringeth salvation hath appeared to all men,

12 Teaching us that, denying ungodliness and worldly lusts, we should live soberly, righteously, and godly, in this present world;

13 Looking for that blessed hope, and the glorious appearing of the great God and our Saviour Jesus Christ;

14 Who gave himself for us, that he might redeem us from all iniquity, and purify unto himself a peculiar people, zealous of good works.

15 These things speak, and exhort, and rebuke with all authority. Let no man despise thee.

IN FOCUS

Today we can see how Dr. King's strong Christian attitudes and sound doctrine guided his single-minded efforts to break down Jim Crow laws of the South. Often we forget how difficult it was for Dr. King to fulfill his calling.

We tend to forget the throngs of influential people who told him, "Wait." But it's important we remember that part of his story.

Many older Black ministers in the early years thought he was too radical, that his marches and sit-ins caused too much violence. White church leaders who had never felt the stinging darts of segregation wrote, telephoned, and pleaded with him to wait. They argued that the time was not right, or that this was not how one handled the Southern problem.

Dr. King's posture remained dignified even while some tried to hold him back. He wasn't mean-spirited when he spoke out against vicious mobs who were lynching mothers and fathers and drowning "insolent" teenagers on a whim. Dr. King demonstrated how the gospel of Christ could combat police filled with so much hate; they would kick, brutalize, and kill marchers who wanted to vote. It was the tireless example Dr. King set that finally won over all of his detractors.

The book of Titus reminds us regardless of the circumstances or how many well-meaning persons we find ourselves at odds with, we must teach the truth by example, and like Dr. King hold fast to the characteristics of a Soldier of Christ.

THE PEOPLE, PLACES, AND TIMES

Titus. He was a minister of the Gospel and a co-laborer with Paul in the ministry. Titus was a Greek who served with Paul on several missionary journeys. In other writings, Paul refers to Titus as his partner and fellow helper. Titus had served with Paul on a mission to Corinth and was sent to Crete to continue his service in the ministry. Paul wrote while Titus was on assignment in Crete. Paul's pastoral epistle to Titus seems to have been written from Corinth after his first imprisonment. Paul's epistle to Titus was similar to Paul's first epistle to Timothy and is believed to have been written around the same time from the same place.

BACKGROUND

Contaminated teachings began to develop within the Cretan church. Paul left Titus in Crete to establish proper church government and to ordain other ministers in the Gospel. In his letter to Titus, Paul speaks of the qualifications for elders and warns Titus to be aware of false teachers.

AT-A-GLANCE

1. The Need for Sound Doctrine (Titus 2:1)
2. The Call to Teach the Next Generation (vv. 2-6)
3. The Responsibility to Live the Life You Teach (vv. 7-8)
4. The Duty to Comply with the Social Structure (vv. 9-10)
5. The Mandate for Godly Teaching and Righteous Living (vv. 11-15)

IN DEPTH

1. The Need for Sound Doctrine (Titus 2:1)

Paul urged Titus to faithfully teach sound doctrine. Paul was aware of how different doctrines serve to bring division and confusion in the body of Christ. He tells us to not be like children, tossed to and fro by every wind of doctrine (Ephesians 4:14). Sound doctrine always results in a life centered around Jesus Christ. The first chapter of Titus ends with Paul's warning against false teachers. He then goes on in chapter 2 to remind Titus to not be moved by false teachers and their inaccurate doctrine.

False teachers began to deny that Jesus was the Son of God. They doubted the reality of the resurrection of Christ from the dead. Such teachings caused many to turn away from sound doctrine and begin to embrace the doctrine espoused by the false teachers. While false teachers may say that they represent Jesus and that they know God, their actions often contradict a faith in God. One cannot claim to be a representative of God and deny the resurrection of Christ.

2. The Call to Teach the Next Generation (vv. 2-6)

Each generation has a responsibility and an obligation to teach the next generation. Paul extorts Titus to teach the aged men to be calm and patient and to teach the younger men in both word and deed. In addition, older women are instructed to teach younger women to live a life according to holiness. Older women are to instruct younger women in matters of personal conduct as well as concerning their relationships with their spouse and children.

Oftentimes we see younger couples make mistakes early in marriage that could have been avoided if an older couple had taken the time to mentor and teach them. The body of Christ will benefit as we fulfill our responsibility to give to others, share what we have learned, and train others in the faith and teachings of Jesus Christ.

3. The Responsibility to Live the Life You Teach (vv. 7-8)

"Do as I say, and not as I do" is a popular quote within our society. However, Paul reminds Titus of the importance of living a life that is in line with what we teach. "Faith without works is dead also" (James 2:26). Therefore, we can't just *say* we believe in Christ and in the Word of God. We must follow the teachings of God if we say we are children of God. Genuine faith moves from belief to action. Our actions of faith produce fruit. Jesus tells us, "A good tree cannot bring forth evil fruit, neither can a corrupt tree bring forth good fruit" (Matthew 7:18). Therefore, if we teach Christ, we must also live Christ. Our actions prove what we believe.

4. The Duty to Comply with the Social Structure (vv. 9-10)

Being a Christian does not negate our social responsibilities. Paul urged Christian slaves to remain compliant to the social laws of the land. Servants were to obey their masters and not respond to them with backtalk or sarcasm. Christian slaves in that culture were expected to follow the law and allow their lives to serve as godly examples as a testimony to their masters. However, this duty is not limited to just slaves and masters. Paul goes on to speak of a respect for those in authority. In 1 Timothy 2:2, we are instructed to pray for those in authority. Such godly instructions apply to all who rule over us in one capacity or another.

5. The Mandate for Godly Teaching and Righteous Living (vv. 11-15)

God does not discriminate. He is not partial to a particular group or to those from a particular background. It is the will of God that all should receive salvation. As followers of Christ, we should take every occasion to live a righteous life. We must live for Christ in this present age while we await the return of our Lord and Saviour. Don't allow anyone to despise you for teaching the truth. Speak the Word of God, encourage, and correct with authority.

SEARCH THE SCRIPTURES

1. What role should older men assume in the lives of young men (Titus 2:2)?

2. What behavior is befitting of a Christian woman (vv. 4-5)?

3. How should Christian slaves interact with their masters (vv. 9-10)?

4. Why did Christ give His life for us (v. 14)?

DISCUSS THE MEANING

1. Why do you think Paul admonishes Christian slaves to remain obedient to their masters?

2. Imagine that you work in an environment that is hostile to Christianity. How can you continue to practice your faith and remain employed at this particular company? What is your greatest witnessing tool?

3. Imagine that your best friend was recently married and is experiencing difficulty with his or her new spouse. Who could he or she turn to for godly counsel? How might Paul's letter to Titus provide guidance in this particular area?

LESSON IN OUR SOCIETY

Recent scandals in the business world have caused people to question the integrity of others. Individuals often say one thing and do another. This has become so common in our society today that less and less weight is given to a person's word. In fact, it almost seems expected that an individual will break a promise. Think about times when you have said that you were going to do something and failed to do it. What kept you from following up on your promise? How can you avoid a similar situation in the future?

MAKE IT HAPPEN

Think about a time when you have followed after godliness in both word and conduct. Then think of another time when your actions didn't represent righteous, godly living. Write down the reasons you believe you followed after godliness. Then write down the reasons you believe you didn't follow after godliness. What steps could you have taken to behave in a manner that follows the teachings of Christ? Make a commitment to take the steps that are necessary to behave in ways that will please the Lord.

FOLLOW THE SPIRIT

What God wants me to do:

_____

_____

REMEMBER YOUR THOUGHTS

Special insights I have learned:

_____

_____

MORE LIGHT ON THE TEXT

Titus 2

Chapter two, concerned with the pastoral care of the Cretan Christians, is the second main division. In verses 1-10 Paul gives Titus instructions on how the various groups in the congregations are to govern themselves ethically. In verses 11-14 Paul points out that the empowering motivation for the Christian life is the grace of God.

1 But speak thou the things which become sound doctrine: 2 That the aged men be sober, grave, temperate, sound in faith, in charity, in patience.

In these verses Paul outlines the manifestations of spiritual healthiness as it applies to different groups, designated by age and gender. The "aged men" referred to here, are not necessarily the "elders" of the church. This is a designation of longevity, not office. Because these senior male members were looked up to for leadership, their example had great influence. It was imperative that they had moral character. As such, they were to be "sober" (Gk. *nephaleos,* **nay-fal'-eh-os**, meaning temperate, clear-minded, having presence of

mind in all circumstances), "grave" (Gk. *semnos,* **sem-nos'**, meaning honorable, worthy of respect), "temperate" (Gk. *sophron,* **so'-frone**, meaning of a sound mind, sane, self-controlled—curbing one's desires and impulses), "sound" (Gk. *hugiaino,* **hoog-ee-ah'-ee-no**, meaning to be in good spiritual health), "in faith (Gk. *pistis,* **pis'-tis**) "in charity" (Gk. *agape,* **ag-ah'-pay**, meaning brotherly affection and benevolence), "in patience" (Gk. *hupomone,* **hoop-om-on-ay'**, meaning steadfastness, constancy or perseverance).

3 The aged women likewise, that they be in behaviour as becometh holiness, not false accusers, not given to much wine, teachers of good things;

"The aged women likewise" indicates that the apostle expects the same kind of demeanor from them as he did from the "aged men." Basically, they are to have "behavior as becometh holiness." The NIV says that they "be reverent in the way they live." The word "holiness" comes from the word *hieroprepes* (**hee-er-op-rep-ace'**), meaning reverent, befitting the sacred things to God. Such behavior springs from a spiritually healthy inner character and displays a life totally dedicated to God.

Reverence like this requires that they not be "false accusers" (Gk. *diabolos,* **dee-ab'-ol-os**, meaning slanderous). In essence, they are not to engage in gossip, spreading unfounded rumors about people. Also they should not be "given (Gk. *douloo,* **doo-lo'-o,** meaning to make a slave of, reduce to bondage) to much wine." Slander (gossip) and intoxication are grouped together in this verse to show that there is a connection between the two. On the contrary, these older women in the church are to be "teachers of good things" or "teach what is good" (NIV) by example and speech.

4 That they may teach the young women to be sober, to love their husbands, to love their children, 5 To be discreet, chaste, keepers at home, good, obedient to their own husbands, that the word of God be not blasphemed. 6 Young men likewise exhort to be sober minded.

The older women who are spiritually healthy are qualified to teach the younger women to love their husbands and children. The word translated as "teach" is *sophronizo* (**so-fron-id'-zo**) and means to train in the lessons of self-control, to moderate or to admonish earnestly.

They are to encourage the younger women to be "discreet" (temperate or self-controlled), "chaste" (Gk. *hagnos*, **hag-nos'**, meaning exciting reverence or pure from carnality), "keepers at home" ("busy at home," NIV). The stresses of the constant demands of home management can lead to exasperation. Therefore, she must cultivate the quality of being "good" (Gk. *agathos*, **ag-ath-os'**, meaning pleasant, agreeable, or joyful). Finally, the older women should train the young wives to be "subject to their husbands, so that no one will malign the word of God" (NIV). The idea here is not that of a dictatorship, but a voluntary acceptance of their husband's headship. This supportive role is an expression of the love the young wives are to give to their husbands.

These duties grew out of the patriarchal society that existed during that time when the roles of men and women were strictly defined. Today many women are no longer just administrators of the home; many work full-time jobs outside of the home. There are many single parent homes, and the roles once assigned to women have changed. Most women today have duties in the church and society that extend beyond the home. Women's cultural status has evolved over the years. Yet, the basic principles of self-control outlined by Paul still apply.

In a similar way, Titus was to encourage the young men to be "sober minded" (Gk. *sophroneo*, **so-fron-eh'-o**, meaning to exercise self-control). As a young man, Titus was in a good position to deal directly with other young men. Thus, he was to do more than "teach," but to exhort them. The Greek word for "exhort" is *parakaleo* (**par-ak-al-eh'-o**), meaning to call to one's side or admonish.

Model good works.

7 In all things shewing thyself a pattern of good works: in doctrine shewing uncorruptness, gravity, sincerity

Now Paul reminds Titus that his teaching will be confirmed by how he carries out his ministry: "in all things shewing thyself a pattern (Gk. *tupos*, **too'-pos**, meaning the mark or figure formed by a stroke or impression) of good (Gk. *kalos*, **kal-os'**, meaning beautiful, excellent, surpassing, or commendable) works." The NIV renders this, "set them an example by doing what is good." Seriousness and integrity must be the mark of Titus's ministry in Crete. In light of the sacred nature of his commission, Titus's motives must be pure (integrity) and his conduct must reflect high moral standards with dignity (seriousness). The same should be true of us as ambassadors of Christ (Ephesians 6:20).

8 Sound speech, that cannot be condemned; that he that is of the contrary part may be ashamed, having no evil thing to say of you.

"Sound speech" must mark the ministry of Titus. His teaching and conversation must be in accord with "healthy doctrine." Thus, he would be beyond condemnation to such an extent that his critics will be put to shame, having nothing on which to base their diatribes. This is especially crucial in light of the false teachers who constantly tried to undercut the ministry of Paul and Titus.

Like Titus, our teaching may not be popular. Sometimes being true to "healthy doctrine" will lead us to take a stand that is not politically correct. But, with dignity and integrity, we will be able to persevere and outlast any opponent.

9 Exhort servants to be obedient unto their own masters, and to please them well in all things; not answering again;

The church in Crete had a cross section of society in its ranks. This included servants. In his instructions to Titus, the apostle Paul lays down guidelines for how they should represent who they are as members of the body of Christ.

We must remember that the servanthood Paul referred to bore no resemblance to American slavery. There have been those who used Paul's words to teach that he would have been in full agreement with the American slave system. Nothing could be further from the truth. In fact, when addressing Christian slaves in Corinth, Paul stated, "...if you can gain your freedom, do so" (1 Corinthians 7:21, NIV). The closest contemporary equivalent to the master/servant relationship is the employer/employee relationship.

When Paul instructs Titus to "exhort (encourage) servants to be obedient unto their own masters," the aim is to demonstrate the Gospel of Jesus Christ, not to endorse the institution of slavery. To maximize the effectiveness of their witness, they were to seek to "please them well" (Gk. *euarestos,* **yoo-ar'-es-tos**), meaning their masters, in "all things." They were not to perform their duties with bad attitudes. The only exception to obedience in "all things" would be if the master demanded that the Christian servant do something contrary to healthy doctrine or clear biblical teaching. Otherwise, they were to perform their assigned tasks with dignity, "not answering again" (Gk. *antilego,* **an-til'-eg-o,** meaning to speak against or to talk back).

10 Not purloining, but shewing all good fidelity; that they may adorn the doctrine of God our Saviour in all things.

Like Titus, the Christian servant must also demonstrate integrity. Honesty was to distinguish the work of children of God. For example, they were not to be guilty of "purloining" (Gk. *nosphizomai,* **nos-fid'-zom-ahee,** meaning to set apart or separate for one's self, to steal or embezzle) from their masters. In Roman households petty theft among servants was common. This was not to be the case for followers of Christ. They were to show "all good fidelity" (Gk. *pistis,* **pis'-tis,** meaning conviction of the truth of anything, faith). To show such good faith is to demonstrate that one can be fully trusted. By this they "adorn the doctrine of God our Saviour in all things." If we are motivated by true Christian spirituality, it will show in ethical conduct. In other words, the teaching about God's salvation through Christ is made attractive through the integrity of the Christian servant.

Those of us who are employees would do well to implement these principles in our various careers and professions. For many of our employers, the quality and integrity of our character and work may be the only Bible they will ever read.

11 For the grace of God that bringeth salvation hath appeared to all men, 12 Teaching us that, denying ungodliness and worldly lusts, we should live soberly, righteously, and godly, in this present world;

The grace of God is the foundation for godly living and this grace has appeared (Gk. *epiphaino,* **ep-ee-fah'-ee-no,** meaning to become visible or clearly known) in the person of Jesus Christ—His birth, life, death, and resurrection.

Mankind could never have accomplished redemption. Why? Because human nature is sinful and weak. Only Jesus was able to bring salvation and it is applied to us by grace through faith. God's grace not only saves us, but it empowers us to rise above the ethical merditrocarcy that surrounds us. It teaches us to say no to "ungodliness" (Gk. *asebeia,* **as-eb'-i-ah,** meaning the lack of reverence toward God) and worldly "lusts" (Gk. *epithumia,* **ep-ee-thoo-mee'-ah,** meaning desire for what is forbidden). This transforming grace leads us to live soberly (self-controlled—the inward dimension), righteously (the outward dimension), and godly in our present circumstances. Grace is not visible until it becomes visible in the way we live.

13 Looking for that blessed hope, and the glorious appearing of the great God and our Saviour Jesus Christ; 14 Who gave himself for us, that he might redeem us from all iniquity, and purify unto himself a peculiar people, zealous of good works. 15 These things speak, and exhort, and rebuke with all authority. Let no man despise thee.

As we receive instruction from God's grace and seek to demonstrate it in the present reality, we eagerly anticipate the fulfillment of our "blessed hope," glorious return of our Lord and Saviour. This is what gives meaning to all the sacrifices we make in our pursuit of righteousness.

It is Jesus, the only perfect man who ever lived, who gave himself for us. We were hopelessly lost in guilt and shame, but He redeemed "us from all iniquity (Gk. *anomia*, **an-om-ee'-ah,** meaning wickedness), to purify unto himself a peculiar (Gk. *periousios*, **per-ee-oo'-see-os,** meaning that which is one's own possession) people, zealous (Gk. *zelotes*, **dzay-lo-tace',** meaning most eagerly desirous of) of good works."

From the beginning, God has been after a people to call His own who are eager for good works. In Christ, God has brought forth such a people. We are able to become God's own people in Christ by grace through faith. Having received such a privilege, we are to live the rest of our lives in gratitude to God. How then are we to express our gratitude to God for His saving grace? By following Paul's instruction, it means being eager for good works.

DAILY BIBLE READINGS

M: Speak the Truth in Love
Ephesians 4:11-16
T: Be Established in the Truth
2 Peter 1:3-12
W: Walk in the Light of Truth
1 John 1:5-10
T: Support All Believers in the Truth
3 John 2-8
F: Teaching Older Men and Women
Titus 2:1-5
S: Teaching Younger Men and Slaves
Titus 2:6-10
S: Teach What God Expects of Believers
Titus 2:11-15

MARCH 2006
QUARTER AT-A-GLANCE
LIVING IN AND AS GOD'S CREATION

This quarter examines the "wisdom literature" that is found in the books of Psalms, Job, Ecclesiastes, and Proverbs. These texts emphasize our relationship to God, since we are the work of His hands, as well as our relationship to God's larger world. These Scriptures also help us to not only appreciate how mighty God is, but how we are made in His own image and should give Him continuous glory and praise.

UNIT 1. THE GLORY OF GOD'S CREATION

There are four lessons based on selected psalms. Lesson 1 highlights the special qualities that God gave humans as part of His larger creation. Lesson 2 shows how God made the different parts of creation and made them to work together and support one another. Lesson 3 emphasizes the fact that God knows us intimately. Finally, lesson 4 extols the abiding love and tender mercies of God for His creation, showing that He is indeed worthy to be praised.

LESSON 1: March 5
God Made Us Special
Psalm 8

Even though Jesus is the only person who perfectly reflects God's image, still the psalmist, King David, appreciates that human beings are made in the image of the all-knowing, all-powerful, all-present God. In this text, David proclaims our special place in God's created order and how God, Himself, gave us tremendous authority to be in charge of His whole earth.

LESSON 2: March 12
God Created Wonderful Things
Psalm 104:1-13

The anonymous author of this psalm appreciates God through God's beautiful creation. He understands that God designs and God maintains, as well. To help us appreciate and rejoice over what God has done, this psalmist summarizes God's creation of the world according to Genesis 1.

LESSON 3: March 19
God Created and Knows Us
Psalm 139:1-3, 7-14, 23-24

King David hails the fact that God is all-knowing, all-present, and all-seeing. He explains that God knows us intimately. David reminds us that because God is present everywhere, there is no place that we can go and hide from His Spirit. In fact, no matter what we do or where we go, we cannot escape His love or His comforting presence.

LESSON 4: March 26
A Hymn of Praise to the Creator
Psalm 145:1-13

In this psalm, David meditates on the goodness of God. He reflects on God's majesty, glorious splendor, wonderful miracles, and His awe-inspiring deeds. All of these attributes caused David to continuously praise and worship the Lord of lords and King of kings.

UNIT 2. LIVING WITH CREATION'S UNCERTAINTY

There are five lessons based on passages from Job and Ecclesiastes. Lessons 5 and 6 reintroduce us to Job's story. Lesson 7 affirms that the resurrection of our Lord and Saviour should give our faith and hope a boost as we face life's many challenges, including tragedies. Lesson 8 highlights the search for meaning in life and deals with the post-Resurrection theme by combining passages from John and Ecclesiastes. Finally, in lesson 9, Ecclesiastes helps us to examine our lives and appreciate the fact that our lives are set within God's timetable.

LESSON 5: April 2
When Tragedy Occurs
Job 1:14-15, 18-19, 22; 3:1-3, 11

These Scripture passages deal with the age-old question, "Why do Christians or good people suffer?" It acknowledges the fact that even God said that Job was "perfect, upright, and eschewed evil" (Job 1:1). However, these facts did not keep Job from being tried in the crucible of suffering.

LESSON 6: April 9
When All Seems Hopeless
Job 14:1-2, 11-17; 32:6, 8; 34:12; 37:14, 22

These Scripture passages deal with the fact that humanity is frail, and life is short and it is full of trouble. We come to understand that Job laments in his suffering, but still does not blame a holy and just God. This lesson shows us that even when friends offer no consolation in our suffering, we can still hope in God.

LESSON 7: April 16
God Responds with Life
Job 38:1, 4, 16-17; 42:1-2, 5; Mark 16:1-7, 9-14, 20

This lesson further shows the humanity of Job. Still hurting in the trial, he seeks answers from God about his plight. God responds by challenging Job. He questions Job's knowledge and wisdom in the arena with that of the Creator. By comparison, the passages from Mark illustrate that regardless of what we are going through, Jesus' birth, death, and Resurrection brings hope to all believers.

LESSON 8: April 23
Finding Life's Meaning
Ecclesiastes 1:1-9; John 20:19-23

King Solomon had God's favor. It was shown in extraordinary wisdom, honor, power, reputation, and riches. However, Solomon concluded that true satisfaction in life came from knowing that what we are doing is a part of God's purpose for our life. He taught that we should strive to know and love God: the one who holds the key to life and death. Like Solomon, John says in his gospel that we should bank on Jesus, who arose from the dead.

LESSON 9: April 30
In God's Time
Ecclesiastes 3:1-8, 14-15

These Scriptures teach that timing is important. God has a declared season for everything under the sun, including our lives. King Solomon, the teacher, wants us to know that the secret to our peace is with God.

UNIT 3. LESSONS IN LIVING
Many people seek guidance that will help them successfully navigate through life. In this unit we have four lessons from Proverbs that discuss wisdom. Lesson 10 presents wisdom as a priceless treasure. Lessons 11 and 12 explore wisdom's invitation to us to make wise choices and to follow the path of integrity. Lesson 13 focuses on living a balanced life that exudes the wisdom, faithfulness, and integrity of God.

LESSON 10: May 7
A Treasure Worth Seeking
Proverbs 2:1-5; 3:1-6, 13-18

In these Scriptures, Solomon gives fatherly advice to young people so that they will not negatively impact or shorten their days by making costly mistakes.

LESSON 11: May 14
Wisdom's Invitation
Proverbs 8:1-5, 22-31

God created wisdom before creating the earth. Solomon declares that godly wisdom cries out to us—asking for our attention. God approves of those who embrace wisdom, and therefore, Solomon concludes that we should seek wisdom and live.

LESSON 12: May 21
The Path of Integrity
Proverbs 11:1-14

This passage includes proverbs that give people practical wisdom for godly living at every stage of life. In fact, they disclose the path of integrity—walking through life with Christlike character.

LESSON 13: May 28
Living Out Wisdom
Proverbs 31:8-14, 25-30

The teachings of King Lemuel end the book of Proverbs with a picture of what may be a composite portrait of ideal womanhood.

CHRISTIANS LIVING IN AND AS GOD'S CREATION

by Evangeline Carey

We owe our lives, our entire being, to a loving, merciful, infinite God who said, "Let us make man in our image, after our likeness" (Genesis 1:26). "And the LORD God formed man of the dust of the ground, and breathed into his nostrils the breath of life; and man became a living soul (being)" (2:7). God made us to reflect His glory, and we can mirror His character by possessing the fruit of His Spirit: love, joy, peace, long-suffering, gentleness, goodness, faith, meekness, and temperance (Galatians 5:22-23). The Holy Spirit produces these character traits in us. He is the Gardener. We cannot plant them within the conservatories of our spirit, no matter how hard we try. They become evident when we make Jesus Christ the center of our life—when He controls our everyday living. The fruit of the Spirit is the by-product of a Spirit-filled life—a life that is lived in harmony with God the Father—when we walk *in* and *as* God's creation.

Once we have received Jesus Christ as Lord and Saviour, we need to daily cultivate an intimate relationship with Him. He made us to reciprocate love and have a relationship with Him. In fact, He loved us so much that He sent His one and only Son to pay our penalty for sin. Therefore, we show our love and reverence for and to Him by studying, meditating, and walking in His Word through prayer and praises to God. Whatever tasks we do—even the small ones—should be done to the glory of God. According to Rick Warren, author of *The Purpose Driven Life,* this is true worship. Worship of God is our Christian lifestyle, and everything we do, we should do unto Him.

God made us a little lower than the angels, thereby proving that we are highly valued by Him.

In fact, Peter made the observation, "But ye are a chosen generation, a royal priesthood, an holy nation, a peculiar people; that ye should shew forth the praises of him who hath called you out of darkness into his marvellous light" (1 Peter 2:9).

God showed our worth to Him again when He gave humans His stamp of approval and great authority. God entrusted humankind with the care of His opus—the works of His hands—and "put all things under his feet" (Psalm 8:6). However, He holds us personally responsible, or accountable, for how we treat God's creation. Certainly, then, we should worship and magnify the Creator in caring for His handiwork.

We are sinners. We are not like Jesus Christ, who knew no sin. However, because we have been redeemed by the atoning work of Jesus, we are joint heirs with Him. We should draw daily on the Holy Spirit's power to overcome sin, which estranges us from God. Again, we cannot do this on our own. It is the Spirit of God living in us that empowers us to overcome. If we try to live a sin-free life in our own strength, we will surely fail. Many Christians can attest to this truth. In fact, every aspect of our lives must be submitted to God if we want to please Him. He is indeed omniscient (all-knowing), omnipresent (present everywhere), and omnipotent (all-powerful). He is the God who is more than enough for anything that we are going through!

God is everywhere. We cannot hide from Him no matter where we go. He knows everything, so we cannot conceal any sin from Him. He is all-powerful; therefore, He can cleanse every sin from us. God sets the standards for Christian living. As children of God, we can and should live by the power of God's Holy Spirit. His Word is our guide. In fact, He commands us to "Sanctify yourselves therefore, and be ye holy: for I am the LORD your God" (Leviticus 20:7). He goes on to say, "And ye shall keep my statutes, and do them: I am the LORD which sanctify you" (v. 8).

The word "sanctify" is derived from the Hebrew verb *qadash* (**kaw-dash'**). It means to be set apart or consecrated. We set ourselves apart when we purposely obey God's commands. The apostle Peter tells us, "all malice, and all guile, and hypocrisies, and envies, and all evil speakings, As newborn babes, desire the sincere milk of the word, that ye may grow thereby: If so be ye have tasted that the Lord is gracious" (1 Peter 2:1-3).

King David, the second king of Israel, was a man whom God referred to as a "man after his own heart" (1 Samuel 13:14). Even though David made many mistakes, he knew how to acknowledge his sin and confess the greatness of God. David had a good understanding of how God wanted him to live. On one occasion David proclaimed, "O LORD our Lord, how excellent is thy name in all the earth! who hast set thy glory above the heavens" (Psalm 8:1). David respected God's majesty—who God is. He said "Bless the LORD, O my soul. O LORD my God, thou art very great; thou art clothed with honour and majesty. Who coverest thyself with light as with a garment: who stretchest out the heavens like a curtain: Who layeth the beams of his chambers in the waters: who maketh the clouds his chariot: who walketh upon the wings of the wind" (Psalm 104:1-3). God created the entire universe, and nothing exists without Him. Surely, this should engender our own healthy respect for the one and only God as we walk daily in and as His creation!

Job was a wealthy, blameless, and upright man—according to God's own assessment (Job 1:6-8). Job reverenced God so much that even in his suffering, he would not sin with his lips. Even after God permitted Satan to destroy Job's children, possessions, and health, he still refused to curse God Almighty

(2:10). Throughout his suffering, Job was unaware of what was going on between God and Satan in the realms of heaven. Job's faith was on trial, and by grace Job persevered. Through it all, he knew his place and recognized God as His majestic Creator.

At the end of his long life, King Solomon also recognized that our living is in vain if God is not the focus of our life. He had all the wealth and women he wanted, yet he realized that everything is indeed futile unless we seek to know God. Unless we receive Jesus Christ as Lord and Saviour and live for Him in and as His creation, all is vanity. The writer of Ecclesiastes asserted after an exhaustive narration on the vainglory of everything, "Let us hear the conclusion of the whole matter: Fear God, and keep his commandments: for this is the whole duty of man. For God shall bring every work into judgment, with every secret thing, whether it be good, or whether it be evil" (12:13-14). In other words, God is going to judge whether or not we have lived in and as His creation.

We should always remember that Jesus is coming back the second time as our Judge, not our Saviour. Indeed, "Blessed is the man who finds wisdom, the man who gains understanding" (Proverbs 3:13, NIV). Living in and as God's creation is finding happiness, wisdom, and understanding.

Bibliography

Warren, Rick. *The Purpose Driven Life.* Grand Rapids, Mich.: Zondervan Publishing Company, 2002, 63-68.

Evangeline Carey *is a staff writer at UMI.*

TECHNOLOGY IN CHRISTIAN EDUCATION

by Virginia Stith

Technology greatly affects the education of all humankind. The way we live, work, and learn is continuously changing. It has created different needs for our society than those of past generations. Increased knowledge has improved our quality of life, thereby extending life expectancy. Technology extends from new and improved medicines to wireless communications. Computers and health technology have been accepted as a tremendous advancement for society in general. However, it often appears that the field of Christian education is moving at a slower pace, particularly in the African American community. While it is the nature of humans to fear the unknown, the Scriptures encourage us to seek knowledge. Solomon tells us to "Cry out for insight and understanding. Search for them as you would for lost money or hidden treasure" (Proverbs 2:3-4, NLT). Technology, when used in any one of its many forms, influences the learning process of all ages, from preschool to retirement age, from private devotional study to Bible scholar study.

A Christian philosophy of education is the communication of the eternal Word of God as revealed in Scripture and in creation. Christian education is not about running or hiding from the world system, but rather about embracing and pursuing the mind of Christ. It is founded on the biblical truth that all that can be discovered, studied, fathomed, created, adorned, or enjoyed exist first in the mind of God, and is sustained by Christ's power and revealed through the Holy Spirit's presence. "He is the image of the invisible God, the firstborn over all creation. For by him all things were created: things in heaven and on earth, visible and invisible, whether thrones or powers or rulers or authorities; all things were created by him and for him. He is before all things, and in him all things hold together. And he is the head of the body, the church; he is the beginning and the firstborn from among the dead, so that in everything he might have the supremacy." "For in Christ all the fullness of the Deity lives in bodily form, and you have been given fullness in Christ, who is the head over every power and authority" (Colossians 1:16-18; 2:9-10, NIV).

According to Elliot W. Eisner, the increased accessibility of the Internet offers a challenging vehicle for Christian education. Schools for all ages are using the Internet. The question for us should be: How can Christian schools make use of the Internet? Christian schools can benefit from the Internet in the same ways as non-Christian schools. According to the book *Literature Distribution Through the Internet*, schools can use the Internet to add to their library resources. They can supplement or replace printed textbooks and handouts with web sites for each course. It can be used to help students communicate with their instructors, as well as aid in discussion, both among the students themselves and with those outside the school community. E-mail also allows those associated with Christian education to quickly share ideas and concerns.

While there are many ways the Internet affects Christian education, Christian schools have unique needs. According to Ian G. Barbour, Christian schools seek to teach students to view everything in light of the self-attesting Christ of Scripture. They seek to prepare students to live their entire lives in terms of Christ's Great Commission. It is unfortunate that Christian schools often have tight budgets as they frequently operate without state or corporate funding and in the shadow of hostile governments.

Technology must be placed in context with a curriculum, teachers, and a community to support real learning. On most of today's college campuses, students have the use of wireless networks, laptops, and high-speed computing labs. They are able to use video conferencing to study with experts in any field with the use of high-speed connections. The ways in which the Internet is able to contribute to Christian education are many and varied.

Church school teachers incresingly have at their disposal many aids. The CD-ROM that accompanies *Precepts For Living*™ is an excellent tool that should definitely be used in the preparation of the lesson. This CD-ROM contains virtually every resource that anyone studying the Scriptures might need. It is regrettable that some educators fear the computer and all that accompanies it. We are encouraged by the apostle Paul to make every effort "to shew [ourselves] approved unto God, a workman that needeth not to be ashamed, rightly dividing the word of truth" (2 Timothy 2:15); technology can certainly help us to do that.

In the future, other applications of technology for Christian education will be discovered. Breakthroughs of this kind in Christian education have given this field of study great potential and the ability to reach students both far and near. Of course educators must be willing to accept the ever changing world of technology and its superhighway to knowledge, particularly as it relates to research and mastering inquiry itself, thereby in many instances generating the answer before the question is asked. Technology in Christian education is an enabling tool when used with the guidance of the Holy Spirit in our search for wisdom, which ultimately brings happiness to those who find it. "Happy is the person who finds wisdom and gains understanding" (Proverbs 3:13, NLT).

Bibliography

Barbour, Ian G. *Ethics in an Age of Technology: The Gifford Lectures. Vol. 2.* New York, N.Y.: HarperSanFrancisco, 1930.

Eisner, Elliot W. *The Educational Imagination: On the Design and Evaluation of School Programs.* Indianapolis, IN: Prentice Hall Professional Technical Reference, 1994.

Virginia Stith *is the pastor of Saint Peter African Methodist Episcopal Church in Cameron, South Carolina. She is also an adjunct professor at Claflin University in Orangebury, South Carolina.*

WISDOM LITERATURE: PERPENDICULAR PATH

by Barbara Carr-Phillips

I am a perpetual goal setter. I'm always charting a path to where I want to be. I teach others how to use a personal journal to help them meet their goals. It's important to define a clear path by writing it down.

Last summer, my journalized goals included accomplishing tasks at the law firm where I worked, and helping abused and neglected children as a volunteer of the court. The family vacation was my husband's idea, or so we thought. If my husband hadn't insisted I schedule vacation time, I wouldn't be alive today. Looking back, we both feel God called us away.

God's nature is to care for His children. I see His love through wisdom literature, the tangible evidence of His deep and infinite knowledge. My nature as a child of God is to go about my business, and call on God if I fall. Last summer, God did not allow me to fall. "Thou compassest my path and my lying down, and art acquainted with all my ways" (Psalm 139:3). The path I designed went straight to my goals, but after a few quiet days at the ocean, I noticed another path emerging . . . a path perpendicular to mine. Indeed, God did chart another path for me and He eliminated the distractions of my daily schedule with a vacation so I would find it.

I remember sitting alone on the balcony of our rented beach apartment. I opened my prayer journal, surprised that my last entry was dated three weeks ago—no wonder my life felt so unmanageable. Time alone with God had been replaced with excuses: "I'll make one more call, and then I'll spend time in prayer." "I'll squeeze in one more appointment, then maybe I'll have time for Bible study." Of course, I was usually too tired to do either by the end of the day.

I began to pray and ask the Lord to direct me. I thought of my mother, who had just finished treatment for breast cancer. I wrote in my journal that I'd schedule a mammogram when I returned home. I surprised myself when I wrote the words. After all, my mother's doctor said a hormone treatment she took years ago probably initiated her cancer. I'd never taken any type of medicine other than an occasional aspirin. I had no reason to believe I was at risk for breast cancer.

As I soaked up a few minutes alone with God each day, I knew He wouldn't allow the mammogram to weigh on my mind without reason. Psalm 145:14-15 illustrates that God gives me what I need as I need it. As I need it—not before and not after: "The LORD upholdeth all that fall, and raiseth up all those that be bowed down. The eyes of all wait upon thee; and thou givest them their meat in due season."

Each day of my vacation, I spent time alone with the Lord in prayer and study. I did not know why I felt such urgency to schedule the mammogram as soon as I returned home; I just knew I needed to do it. I revised my goals, adding the mammogram appointment and daily time with God to my list. Returning home, I felt very relaxed and energized, confident in my written goals. I scheduled and completed a mammogram, but my resolution to spend time each day with the Lord was quickly replaced with soccer schedules, overtime, and volunteer work. At the office, I was annoyed by the interruption when I received a call from the mammogram technician. "We need you to come in for a follow-up test," she said. "It's no big deal, but you have some dense tissue we need to look at more closely since you have a family history of breast cancer."

If it's no big deal, why bother? I wondered. Reluctantly, I added the follow-up appointment to my schedule.

The second test was inconclusive. An ultrasound was scheduled just to be "on the safe side." The dense tissue appeared as a tiny spot on the ultrasound screen. I couldn't understand all of the concern over a one-centimeter sized spot, but my doctor encouraged me to have a biopsy. I hesitated to add another appointment to my schedule, but I remembered the urgency I felt at the beach to schedule the first appointment. I decided to go ahead with the procedure.

I can't remember exactly what the doctor said to me when he called me at the office with the biopsy results. I heard the words "malignant," "chemotherapy," "radiation" . . . strange, unbelievable words that floated around my thoughts and spilled out in silent tears across my pillow that night.

How could a tiny spot be cancer? How could it be that it was already starting to spread to my other organs? I was only 41 and my youngest child was only 4! I focused on the diagnosis and that focus increased my fear. I had accepted Jesus in my heart as a young child, yet I refused to lift my eyes from the disease, so I could not see down the path. Ecclesiastes 3:11 (NIV) teaches: "He has made everything beautiful in its time. He has also set eternity in the hearts of men; yet they cannot fathom what God has done from beginning to end."

I learned that cancer treatment is much more debilitating to the human body than cancer itself. Chemotherapy kills bad cells. . .but it kills good cells too. My immune system was wiped out, and I couldn't be around people because they could unintentionally infect me with a virus that could kill me. I took a leave of absence from work. There were many days my husband would carry me from the bathroom floor to my bed because I was too weak to stand. When my 4-year-old daughter stroked my hair, it fell out into her hand.

A lifelong Christian, I believed I would be exempt from such pain. If only I had paid attention to Job 1:7: "And the LORD said unto Satan, Whence comest thou? Then Satan answered the LORD, and said, From going to and fro in the earth, and from walking up and down in it." The enemy was always awake, looking to attack. I was unprepared.

Isolated from my friends and family, I turned to my journal more and more, praying and recording Scripture. I knew from God's Word that He would receive my questions. Proverbs 2:2-3: "So that thou incline thine ear unto wisdom, and apply thine heart to understanding; Yea, if thou criest after knowledge, and liftest up thy voice for understanding." One day, my body broke out into a cold sweat and I lay in my bed trembling. I could not lift my head from my pillow nor could I lift a phone to call for help. I shut my eyes and asked God if I was going to die.

God answered my question, just as He said He would in Proverbs 8:17: "I love them that love me; and those that seek me early shall find me." Once again, God had set aside a time just for the two of us when He would plant a small seed of knowledge for what was ahead. I felt a warm rush of blood through my veins. Uncertainty vanished. I could breathe without pain for the first time in weeks. I knew I had received His healing touch because He allowed me to see a bit farther down the path He prepared for me last summer. Physical healing began.

I learned that the meaning of life is not revealed by my job or my good intentions. The meaning of life is revealed to me in the Resurrection story. When faith begs for renewal, the resurrection of Jesus provides the answer. When I am not listening, my ever-present Father will bring me to a place where I will have no choice.

Staying grounded through wisdom literature reminds me of God's faithfulness even during the attack of the enemy (as in Job's story). My responsibility is to focus on His Word so that I will understand He is not only with me through every season of life, but He will also prepare the correct path for me. I never want to forget that His infinite knowledge lies ahead of me on this path, waiting to receive me through every circumstance. I am a cancer survivor. As much as I believe in the power of journalizing my path to success, ultimate success is achieved by staying on a path paved by the wisdom of God's Word: God's perpendicular path.

Barbara Carr-Phillips is a freelance writer who has published many short stories, articles, and essays.

MARY ANN SHADD CARY

Abolitionist • Attorney • Editor • Educator

by Judith St.Clair Hull, Ph.D.

"The first of Harriet and Abraham Shadd's 13 children, Mary Ann Shadd was born October 9, 1823. Like her parents and grandparents, Mary Ann would reap the benefits of a mixed ancestry that offered certain privileges (they were mulatto)—they were free born, they worked in skilled trades, and they owned property. The Shadds escaped the worst of slavery while living in a slave state, and benefited from a color-conscious social system in which light-skinned blacks had more status, wealth, and power than their dark-skinned counterparts" (Rhodes 5).

Because the education of Blacks was forbidden in Delaware, the Shadds relocated to Pennsylvania. Mary was educated by Pennsylvania Quakers from 1833-1839; shortly after that, Mary committed to educating Black children. She was only 16 years of age when she returned to Wilmington to sponsor a private school for Black children. The school's motto was careful to imply that both light-skinned and dark-skinned children would be treated the same and educated in the same manner. She spent the next 12 years of her life educating Black children in Pennsylvania, Delaware, and New York.

Once the Fugitive Slave Law had been passed in the United States, Mary and her brother Isaac relocated to Windsor, Canada. It was believed that Blacks had better opportunities to gain wealth and employment there. While in Canada, Mary developed a weekly periodical designed to appeal to free Blacks. As editor of the *Provincial Freeman*, Mary became the first Black woman in North America to edit a weekly newspaper. The newspaper was used to admonish others to relocate to Canada, and to cover stories pertaining to Blacks already living in Canada. The National Archives of Canada notes that Mary "complemented her active anti-slavery efforts and editorials with articles on women and their contributions." At a time when it was still uncommon for women to speak in public, she lectured frequently in the United States against slavery and for Black emigration to Canada in an effort to keep the paper viable. Despite her efforts, the *Provincial Freeman* fell victim to the economic depression of the day and ceased publication in 1858.

Mary Ann Shadd Cary was somewhat of a rebel, and many of her friends and family members referred to her in that way. In 1858, when John Brown held a secret meeting in Isaac's home, Mary attended the meeting. As a result of her encounter with John Brown, Mary's concern for slaves grew all the more, and her abolitionist efforts increased. She used a paper entitled "Notes on Canada West" to admonish Blacks to come to Canada. According to the African American Almanac, Cary's "Notes on Canada West" was nearly 50 pages of information concerning jobs and other opportunities for Blacks in Canada. It appeared that the pamphlet had been widely circulated in the United States, and many Blacks became aware that Canada was an option for those who feared for their freedom.

As the first woman to speak at a national Negro convention, Cary began to speak to Black audiences all over the United States and in some parts of Canada, and became a friend to the fugitive slave. In 1856, she married Thomas F. Cary (a barber from Toronto). He shared Mary's beliefs and ideals, especially those things relating to freeing Blacks and embracing salves. To their union, two children were born, and in 1860 Thomas F. Cary preceded his wife in death. After the loss of her husband, Mary Ann Shadd Cary relocated to Washington, D.C., and began to teach in the public school system pursuing a law degree at Howard University. She would be among the first Black women to ever receive a Juris Doctorate. The Mary Ann Shadd Cary House in Washington, D.C., has been dedicated in memory of this legendary woman.

Though actual details about Mary's life are sketchy at best, many viewed her as a feminist. Her promotion of self-reliance oftentimes fueled that image of her. The National Women's Hall of Fame reports that Mary Ann Shadd Cary fought alongside Susan B. Anthony and Elizabeth Caddy Stanton in the Women's Suffrage Movement, and that she became the first woman of color to cast a vote in a national election.

Mary Ann Shadd Cary once said that "self-reliance is the fine road to independence." Though Cary was self-reliant and ambitious, she served as the backbone for many entangled by the bonds of slavery. Like her father, Thomas F. Cary, who was instrumental in the Underground Railroad, Mary Ann Shadd Cary devoted much of her life to the abolition and eradication of slavery.

Bibliography

Rhodes, Jane. *Mary Ann Shadd Cary: The Black Press and Protest in the Nineteenth Century.* Bloomington, Ind.: Indiana University Press, 1998.

Judith St.Clair Hull, Ph.D. *is the Senior Editor at UMI.*

March 5
Bible Study Guide 1

1. Words You Should Know

A. Glory (Psalm 8:1) *howd* Heb.—Grandeur and imposing form; beauty, comeliness, excellency, and majesty. The splendor of God; His perfection and honor.

B. Suckling (v. 2) *yanaq* Heb.—To suckle; to give milk or nurse. Refers to an infant or young animal not yet weaned from its mother's milk.

2. Teacher Preparation

A. Read BIBLE STUDY GUIDE 1. Study Ephesians 1, 2, and 3.

B. Purchase 3 x 5" index cards (seven or more per student), pencils, one large poster board (or use a chalkboard), and journals.

C. Write in capital letters on the poster board, "WHY I AM SPECIAL TO GOD."

3. Starting the Lesson

A. Before the students arrive to class, place the poster board where the students can see it.

B. Ask one student to lead the class in prayer.

C. Give a brief synopsis of the BACKGROUND section, read the IN FOCUS story, and discuss the LESSON AIM.

D. Have the students read the KEEP IN MIND section and the FOCAL VERSES. After reading the IN DEPTH section, have a discussion.

E. Draw the students' attention to the poster board. Ask them to use words that express "WHY I AM SPECIAL TO GOD." Discuss responses.

4. Getting into the Lesson

A. Pass out the pencils and 3 x 5" index cards.

B. Ask the students to read the SEARCH THE SCRIPTURES and DISCUSS THE MEANING sections. Allow them to write their responses on the cards and share out loud.

5. Relating the Lesson to Life

A. Have the students read the LESSON IN OUR SOCIETY section.

B. Ask the students to write how they feel about praise and worship and their perception of God on a 3 x 5" index card.

C. Ask the students to share their responses out loud.

6. Arousing Action

A. Direct the students' attention to the MAKE IT HAPPEN section.

B. Ask the students to read Ephesians 1:3-7, 10-13; 2:6, 10, 13; 3:12. Ask them to write the Scriptures on a 3 x 5" index card, pray, and memorize the verses.

C. Give each student a journal. Ask the students to write daily meditations on God's Word.

WORSHIP GUIDE

For the Superintendent or Teacher
Theme: God Made Us Special
Theme Song: "I Stand Amazed in the Presence"
Scripture: Psalm 8
Song: "I Sing the Almighty Power of God"
Meditation: Lord Jesus, we love, honor, and praise Your holy name. Help us to see how special we are in Your eyes. In Your name we pray. Amen.

GOD MADE US SPECIAL

Bible Background • PSALM 8
Printed Text • PSALM 8
Devotional Reading • GENESIS 1:26–31

LESSON AIM

By the end of the lesson, we will:

KNOW that God's act of creation inherently endows us with value;

REALIZE that God considers us special in His sight; and

COMMIT to praise and worship God daily.

KEEP IN MIND

"What is man, that thou art mindful of him? and the son of man, that thou visitest him? For thou hast made him a little lower than the angels, and hast crowned him with glory and honour" (Psalm 8:4-5).

FOCAL VERSES

Psalm 8:1 O LORD our Lord, how excellent is thy name in all the earth! who hast set thy glory above the heavens.

2 Out of the mouth of babes and sucklings hast thou ordained strength because of thine enemies, that thou mightest still the enemy and the avenger.

3 When I consider thy heavens, the work of thy fingers, the moon and the stars, which thou hast ordained;

4 What is man, that thou art mindful of him? and the son of man, that thou visitest him?

5 For thou hast made him a little lower than the angels, and hast crowned him with glory and honour.

6 Thou madest him to have dominion over the works of thy hands; thou hast put all things under his feet:

7 All sheep and oxen, yea, and the beasts of the field;

8 The fowl of the air, and the fish of the sea, and whatsoever passeth through the paths of the seas.

LESSON OVERVIEW

LESSON AIM
KEEP IN MIND
FOCAL VERSES
IN FOCUS
THE PEOPLE, PLACES, AND TIMES
BACKGROUND
AT-A-GLANCE
IN DEPTH
SEARCH THE SCRIPTURES
DISCUSS THE MEANING
LESSON IN OUR SOCIETY
MAKE IT HAPPEN
FOLLOW THE SPIRIT
REMEMBER YOUR THOUGHTS
MORE LIGHT ON THE TEXT
DAILY BIBLE READINGS

9 O LORD our Lord, how excellent is thy name in all the earth!

IN FOCUS

From planet Earth, about 5,000 stars are visible to the human eye. The Hubble telescope recently sent back pictures of the Helix Nebula. It is the closest example of a sun-like star at the end of its existence. Interestingly, it has been referred to as the "eye of God" because the formation of gases around the hot stellar core gives the impression of a huge eye (thousands of miles high and wide) floating trillions of miles from Earth.

Reading the article about the Hubble brought to mind the psalmist who exalted God, referring to the Being who filled the heavens, and who was amazed that He should waste a thought on such a creature as man. David said, "When I consider thy heavens, the work of thy fingers, the moon and the stars, which thou hast ordained; What is man, that thou art mindful of him?" (Psalm 8:3-4).

Suppose David had looked through a modern telescope that brings five million stars within our field of vision. What if he had been told that some of those stars were shining with 5,000 times the magnitude and splendor of our sun and were so far away that light, traveling at the inconceivable speed of 186,000 miles a second, still takes 14,000 years to reach this little speck of earth? If David had known all these revelations of modern science, how much greater his amazement would have been that God condescends to commune with man.

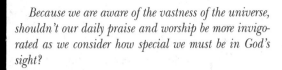

Because we are aware of the vastness of the universe, shouldn't our daily praise and worship be more invigorated as we consider how special we must be in God's sight?

THE PEOPLE, PLACES, AND TIMES

Angels. Angels are created spiritual or heavenly beings. Angels are not God and should not be ntified with God Himself. God created angels, bey the commands and directives given by lm 103:20). Angels are God's couriers, arth to help humans. Angels have various ctions in serving humans, such as being God's messengers to His people (Luke 1:13), being providers of relief for human thirst and hunger (Genesis 21:17-19), and being protectors of God's people (Daniel 3:28). Also, angels listen to the voice of God (Psalm 103:20-21).

Before the world existed, there were angels who disobeyed God. These angels were cast out of heaven. Satan was one of these angels. Theologians believe that Satan was once a beautiful angel and a divine worship leader. To his demise, Satan wanted equal footing with God and led a revolt against the Lord in heaven; hence, he was evicted from heaven, along with his group of rebellious angels (Revelation 12:7-9).

Certain angels are mentioned by name in the Bible: the archangels Gabriel and Michael. Gabriel was sent by God to Daniel (Daniel 8:15-16), Zacharias (Luke 1:18-19), and the Virgin Mary (Luke 1:26-27). Michael was sent to the people of Israel to serve as guardian and prince (Daniel 10:21; 12:1).

Ordained. The means to be dedicated, consecrated, and set aside for a special service. After Judas's death, Matthias was ordained as an apostle (Acts 14:23). Jesus ordained His disciples to produce fruit that would last (John 15:16). Jesus Christ was ordained as our great High Priest (Hebrews 4:14) who will judge both the living and the dead (2 Timothy 4:1).

BACKGROUND

The Psalms are a collection of poems written to be accompanied by the harp in worship. When we read the Psalms, we experience the "heart" of the psalmist. The Psalms express the heartfelt sentiment of the composer. In them, we "see" these emotions expressed through love, anger, fear, and disappointment. Sometimes these feelings are aimed at the writer, sometimes at his enemy, and sometimes at God Himself. Many of the Psalms esteem the beauty, majesty, and splendor of God by exalting His name and declaring His sovereignty among the nations.

Theologians believe King David wrote at least 73 psalms. Moses wrote Psalm 90 and Ethan penned Psalm 89. Other contributors were Solomon (Psalms 72, 127), Asaph, and the sons of Korah. There are 51 psalms whose authors are unidentifiable; these psalms are referred to as "orphan psalms."

Although the Psalms are not written in any particular order, they are grouped into five sections, each of which conveys a particular theme that corresponds to one of the five books of Moses. For example, in the book of Genesis, the creation of the world and its inhabitants, the fall of man, and deliverance from sin are themes that are paralleled in the first 41 psalms. King David and the sons of Korah are credited with writing the majority of Psalms 42-72. These psalms describe emotions and incidencts similar to those in the book of Exodus, in which the nation of Israel is devastated and restored. Psalms 73-89, written by Asaph and his descendants, talk about God's awesome holiness, His enthronement, and the tabernacle, much like the book of Leviticus. Psalms 90-106, written by unknown authors, have themes similar to those treated in the book of Numbers, in which relationships among the Israelites and other nations are discussed. The authors also discussed God's prevailing kingdom and sovereignty. The Davidic Psalms (Psalms 107-150) are a blueprint from the book of Deuteronomy. In these latter psalms, the psalmist is preoccupied with God and His Word. These psalms represent songs of praise and thanksgiving for God and His unfathomable love (Romans 8:39).

The Psalms remind us that, in trying times, God is our refuge and strength, an ever-present help in times of trouble (Psalm 46:1). In times of trepidation, the Lord is our deliverer (Psalm 34:4). In times of weakness, the Lord is our strength and we can take courage in Him (Psalm

27:14). Yet, in all that God is and does for us, His greatest desire is to have fellowship with mankind. He has chosen us as His object of affection. It is humans to whom He has given the greatest responsibility on earth and with whom He desires an intimate covenant relationship.

AT-A-GLANCE

1. God's Glory Reigns (Psalm 8:1)
2. God's Ordained Praise (v. 2)
3. God's Creative Power (v. 3)
4. God's Most Valuable Possession (vv. 4-5)
5. God's Call to Accountability (vv. 6-9)

IN DEPTH

1. God's Glory Reigns (Psalm 8:1)

The Lord's name is synonymous with power and preeminence. These qualities of God are confirmed throughout the earth! The Bible instructs us to exalt the name of the Lord! In Christian circles, the praises of God are expressed in music and song. The writers of the Bible have recorded glorious works accomplished through His name, including the manifestation of God's glory through deliverance of His people (Exodus 13:21-22) and the glory of the Lord appearing to Moses in a cloud and fire (Exodus 19:9-16:18; 24:15-18; Deuteronomy 5:5, 22-24). There is no other name besides the name of Jesus by which man can be saved (Acts 4:12).

Glory signifies the majesty, honor, and splendor of God; it reflects His beauty and perfection. God's glory on earth is evident in all He produces. When we look at the magnificent works of the Lord, we see His presence everywhere. God's beauty is experienced through all we can see, taste, smell, hear, and touch. The flowers, birds, and trees were all created by Him; even the things not visible to the human eye are God's handiwork, bearing His awesome signature.

God's glory reigns not only on earth, but in and above heaven! His splendor ranks superior to everything and pales in comparison to nothing! God's power and abilities rise above and beyond all we can ever imagine. His exalted position demands our attention and commands our praise. God's commanding posture may intimidate some Christians by causing them to feel uneasy in approaching Him and spurring feelings of unworthiness. However, the more we study God's Word, the more we realize how God made every human being special. When we deepen our understanding of who God is and enlarge our view of who we are in Him, it lessens our apprehension in approaching Him (Ephesians 3:12).

2. God's Ordained Praise (v. 2)

When something is ordained, it is set aside and consecrated for special service. The Bible tells us that from the mouths of children come ordained praise—exaltation that honors and glorifies God. Children are not ashamed to praise the Lord. Their innocence facilitates worship; they are not embarrassed to publicly raise their arms, lift their hands, and open their mouths to give God glory. Sincere praise pleases the heart of God. The Lord requires this same "childlike" response from all His people. Our praise and worship should be void of hidden agendas, deception, and manipulation.

Fear, guilt, arrogance, and shame can hinder our praises to God. We can overcome these feelings of inadequacy by admitting our shortcomings to the Lord. He is faithful and willing to help us in our weaknesses. We do not necessarily have to dance, shout, and run around the pews to give God His well-deserved praise; however, at some point in our Christian walk, we should feel and display heartfelt praise and admiration for our Lord.

Children may not understand why they sing praises to God, but the Lord delights in their gestures of love! When we operate from a "childlike" worship, seeking only to exalt our Lord, the power of God undergirds us with strength! This strength silences our enemies!

The Bible tells us that if we lift up the name of the Lord, our enemies are scattered (Psalm 68:1). Genuine praise invites God's presence and defeats our enemies. God answers the cries of His people when we praise Him with a thankful heart. Praise is an expression of admiration and exaltation. Worship is an expression of reverential love and allegiance to God. Both are necessary and commanded by God.

3. God's Creative Power (v. 3)

When we consider the breathtaking and mysterious handiwork of our God, we are baffled by His grandeur. God is the Creator of heaven and Earth. He shaped the universe, set the moon and stars in place, and created every living thing in and on the earth. All that God has created validates His existence. Most scientists will agree that human beings are meticulously designed. Science experts tell us that our DNA (deoxyribonucleic acid) confirms our uniqueness and that no two individuals have identical fingerprints. Not all scientists may agree that we are created beings who are made in the image of God, but even the most intellectual individual, when pondering the formation of the human anatomy, would doubt that such a well-oiled machine was created by accident. There are no accidents with God. Everything was created by God, and everything made by Him was superbly designed and deliberately produced.

When we look at all that God has created and compare ourselves to His greatness, we tend to

God's most valuable possession is man.

feel small in comparison. It is proper to maintain a healthy perspective of God—to respect and honor Him. Reverencing His position keeps us humble. Yet, the Lord does not want us to reside in our smallness. God has made each one of us special; even the hairs on our heads are numbered (Matthew 10:30). This kind of craftsmanship comes only from a loving and caring Heavenly Father (Ephesians 2:12). Our uniqueness is God's way of letting us know how much He adores us! So the next time you are feeling unloved and unworthy, remember to look up! Raise your eyes toward heaven and realize that you have a wonderful Heavenly Father who loves you dearly.

4. God's Most Valuable Possession (vv. 4-5)

To examine the origin of man, we must visit the book of Genesis, where God first created man. God placed man and woman in the Garden of Eden and made them responsible for taking care of the garden. God permitted the man to name every kind of bird that flew in the air, every creature that crawled on the earth, and every living thing that swam in the ocean. Man had God's favor; he was the creme de la creme on earth. Man lost this prime position when he was deceived by Satan. However, God's unfailing love for man was not shaken; although human disobedience grieved the heart of God, the Lord's mercy prevailed. God removed Adam and Eve from the garden, and the plan of redemption began. Redemption came to us through the shed blood of Jesus Christ on the Cross. In Christ, we have forgiveness for sin and the gift of salvation. Through our Lord Jesus Christ, we've regained favor with God (Genesis 2:7-9, 15-20; 3:23; Romans 3:22-26).

God crowns us with glory and honor. What an awesome revelation! Accepting this truth will help us see our value in the eyes of God. It is no wonder the enemy spends countless hours trying to defeat us in our thinking, telling us we are not loved by God. The enemy knows that if a believer grasps the full knowledge of who Christ is and how much the Lord loves us, he or she will no longer fall victim to his deceptive strategies. Unfortunately, so many believers fail to take hold of this revelation and consequently live defeated Christian lives. When we recognize our position in Christ, we will walk victoriously in Him. Instead of living this Christian life we feel, we start living our lives according to what we know about Jesus. What we know about Christ comes from reading, studying, and meditating on the Word of God.

Honor is a noble quality, marked with dignity. Yet, most believers would not equate their position in Christ with this kind of distinction. Nevertheless, God has crowned us with honor and given us a prominent place in His heart! It is mind-boggling to think that the God of this universe would esteem humans with this kind of nobility. God has been gracious toward us. It is a privilege to serve Him. We should reverence the Lord, and our place in Him should make us humble. We are not to be arrogant or condescending toward others. Our attitude should be sprinkled with grace so that people will see the love of Christ in us, and this love will draw others closer to Him.

5. God's Call to Accountability (vv. 6-9)

God has placed tremendous responsibility in our hands. We must take care of His property on Earth—with accountability comes challenges. We can successfully deal with these challenges if we remember the following: First, everything we own belongs to God, and we are only stewards over what He has given us (Psalm 24:1). Second, we must practice good stewardship. This means using godly wisdom. We've all heard the saying, "heavenly minded but no earthly good." This means we should not be so "spiritually deep" that we throw common sense out the window. For example, if our homes have termites, we should pray and ask the Lord for a solution. The solution may come in the form of an exterminator, but if we refuse to accept this solution and ignore the problem, we risk the possibility of ruining our homes. A home destroyed by termite invasion is an exercise in poor stewardship.

God has given man dominion over the beasts of the fields. Does this mean we are responsible for all the animals on earth? No, but we should offer benevolence toward animals, especially those under our care. If you have pets, do you take care of them, or do you neglect and abuse them? God will give us the wisdom to manage our responsibilities well and be good stewards when we ask Him for guidance.

God's purpose in revealing humanity's superiority over the rest of His creation is to help us realize our importance to Him. This revelation is important for four reasons. First, when we begin to grasp the width, depth, height, and length of God's love for us, we respond to Him differently. Second, when we believe that the One who is seeking our affection protects, cherishes, and adores us, it builds our self-esteem. Third, when we know that God made us in His image, we realize our self-worth comes from Him alone. Fourth, when we see how God loved us by giving His only begotten Son to die on the Cross for our sins, we realize there is nothing God will not do to keep us in intimate fellowship with Him. Gaining knowledge about our rightful standing with God facilitates an intimate walk with Him and teaches us to trust Him to take care of all our needs (Ephesians 3:17-19; Psalm 91:11-16; Genesis 1:27; John 3:16).

SEARCH THE SCRIPTURES

1. Why is it important to maintain a humble and realistic perspective of ourselves in relation to God? How do we do this without self-depreciation (Psalm 8:1-2)?

2. God "made us a little lower than the angels." What does this statement mean to you? How does this revelation change your view of yourself and your feelings toward God (vv. 3-5)?

3. After studying Psalm 8, do you feel you are a good steward over the things the Lord has given you (vv. 6-9)?

DISCUSS THE MEANING

1. We are special in the eyes of God. What are some hindrances and life experiences that keep many adults from accepting this truth?

2. We should be good stewards over God's property. This includes taking care of our pets. Read the following scenario, then discuss problems and solutions that stem from the situation: An individual neglects to discipline his or her pet and allows the animal to run unleashed in the community.

LESSON IN OUR SOCIETY

Church fellowship facilitates corporate worship. Fellowship bonds members in unity and helps individuals express open praise to God. Yet, if an individual is unsure of his or her rightful position in God, worship and praise can become an exercise in defeatism. Our perception of God and how we view ourselves in the light of His Majesty have a great deal to do with how we praise and approach Him. Consider your response and participation in corporate praise and worship. Are you often hindered by self-doubt, negativity, and low self-esteem? Do you doubt that the Lord hears your prayers? Do you feel unworthy to approach God?

MAKE IT HAPPEN

Read Ephesians 1: 3-7, 10-13; 2:6, 10, 13; 3:12. Highlight these Scriptures in your Bible. Start a prayer journal with daily meditations on God's Word. Next, ask God to make you a better steward. Share your results with the class next week.

FOLLOW THE SPIRIT

What God wants me to do:

_____

_____

_____

REMEMBER YOUR THOUGHTS

Special insights I have learned:

_____

_____

MORE LIGHT ON THE TEXT

Psalm 8

Unique in all of Scripture, the Psalms speak to us today through the voices of those who spoke and sang to God in ancient Israel. The Psalms were Israel's hymnal. When explaining such musical poems, the able interpreter proceeds within their context, being careful not to overexplain or "atomize" them, as one of my seminary professors put it. Their most common structural element consists of parallelism, usually of a type called synonymous, in which two lines complement each other and together make a single point, as opposed to saying two separate things.

Keeping in mind the Psalms' unique literary and very functional genre—with which the Israelites were extremely familiar—one will find sufficient depth, beauty, and inspiration for countless applications. However, only by respecting their intended, original purposes and not planting meaning (thus committing the hermeneutical crime of "I-sigesis") may one properly hear God's voice through the Psalms.

Psalms 8 and 104 (along with 19 and 148) are hymns of praise; more specifically, they praise God as Creator (along with 33 and 145). Unlike Thanksgiving Psalms (e.g., 65, 67, 75, 107), which stem from particular circumstances or events, Psalms 8 and 104 are timeless, transcultural "pure praise" psalms. Their specific, functional purpose was to help Israel praise God as the Creator of everything, both in heaven and on Earth.

Written around 1015 B.C., Psalm 8 is attributed to David in the Masoretic text, and Psalm 104 is attributed to David in the Septuagint, with no reason to assume otherwise, especially since the latter so strongly resembles other known Davidic Psalms (such as 103, which uses very similar wording).

1 O LORD our Lord, how excellent is thy name in all the earth! who hast set thy glory above the heavens.

Not only is He God, but "Lord" (Heb. *Yahweh,* **yah-way,** meaning "existing one"). The truth that He is our Lord is a sweet reminder of a very special and very personalized excellence. Not only is His name "excellent" (Heb. *addiyr,* **ad-deer,** meaning mighty, noble, worthy; also rendered "majestic" in Psalm 93:4, NASB) in the earth, but there is no place where He is not, or better, where His "glory" (Heb. *howd,* **HODE,** meaning "grandeur" or "majesty") is not. Our glorious Lord is greater than His greatest creation (Psalm 57:5, 11; 97:5; 113:4), and His glory is revealed throughout creation (Psalm 19:1; Isaiah 6:3) whether we accept it or not (Romans 1:20).

If the psalmist saw God beyond the visible "heavens" (Heb. *shamayim,* **shaw-mah'-yim,** meaning the visible sky and where celestial bodies revolve), imagine his rapture today with the aid of our powerful electronic "eyes," such as the Hubble telescope. God's name was not only great in Israel, it is great throughout the earth. People throughout the world worship the true and living God. As the great preacher Spurgeon aptly said, "Space is too narrow for the Eternal's rest, and time is too short a footstool for His throne."

The first and last verses of Psalm 8 are bookends between which the glory of the Creator is thoroughly celebrated. One commentator writes, "He, the glorious One, has endowed the earth with glory!" How else could the glory of God be expressed, except with such a hymn of praise?

2 Out of the mouth of babes and sucklings hast thou ordained strength because of thine enemies, that thou mightest still the enemy and the avenger.

Anyone who has been corrected, inadvertently or directly, by a child is familiar with the principle of this verse (see also Matthew 21:15-16). God cares for children in a very real and practical way—He protects and defends them (Matthew 18:6). The fact that God protects the innocent and defends the defenseless is something every adult should respect and appreciate about God's nature.

In a spiritual sense, even the apostles were unsophisticated and uneducated spiritual "babes" yet the arm of the Lord was powerful through them and they accomplished great things. It is when God uses weak vessels to confound, confuse, and shame the wise that His glory most brightly shines (Psalm 29:1; 118:14). God "ordained" (Heb. *yacad,* **yaw-sad,** meaning to appoint or establish) strength because His enemies are arrogant and haughty. Thus, it is with His strength at work in weak vessels that He chooses to silence and humble them. The NIV renders the phrase "ordained strength" as "ordained praise."

Satan is the enemy "avenger" (Heb. *naqam,* **naw-kam,** meaning to take revenge or to punish; see Psalm 44:16) who is stilled only by the pure praises of God's children or the Word of God uttered through the simplest of lips. God's Word truly is a light shining into a dark place (Isaiah 9:2), exposing lies and dismissing the darkness (2 Peter 1:19; 1 John 1:5).

3 When I consider thy heavens, the work of thy fingers, the moon and the stars, which thou hast ordained;

To "consider" (Heb. *raah,* **raw-aw,** meaning to see, perceive, or discern; see Psalm 111:2), requires that one review or meditate or reflect on things greater than oneself and has the effect of reminding us of our place in the created order (v. 3 sets up v. 4). This contemplation promotes healthy humility while confronting our ridiculous arrogance. The stress is on the size and grandeur of creation versus the size of arrogant man. When observing the revealed glory of God, we should be led to contemplate God's coming and greater glory. We really cannot praise God enough when we truly consider the full extent of His glory.

In this nighttime psalm, the lesser, reflected light of the moon and the distant, twinkling stars are no less a reflection of the greatness of the Creator, who provides the night for rest and also provides lights for the night (Psalm 136:9). The work of His "fingers" (Heb. *etsba,* **ets-bah;** see Psalm 89:11) implies both sensitive care and effortlessness, like an artist flicking his brush on a canvas, a guitarist deftly picking strings, or a sewer skillfully weaving a tapestry. All that is above, under, or around us is part of the generous gift of our beautiful home, which is shared by all men and all nations (Deuteronomy 4:19). Our generous God has ordained all this for us, and through it, His glory, wisdom, and power are eloquently revealed in the grandeur of space (Job 36:29; 38:33; Isaiah 40:26).

4 What is man, that thou art mindful of him? and the son of man, that thou visitest him?

After considering, with the sweeping, incomprehensible grandeur of creation (the set up of v. 3), one naturally asks questions like those in verse 4. These rhetorical questions are poetic tools designed to elevate God and put man in proper perspective (see also Job 7:17; Psalm 144:3): "What is man (Heb. *'enowsh,* **en-oshe',** meaning a mortal, a person; see Psalm 9:20; 90:3; 103:15) that thou art mindful (Heb. *zakar,* **zaw-kar',** meaning to remember, to think on) of him, and the son of man (Heb. *ben,* **bane**) that thou visitest him" (Heb. *paqad,* **paw-kad',** meaning to care for or to bestow upon).

Who is this mortal, fallible creature made from clay who receives such loving attention and lavish care as God eminently bestows on us? Such good and generous visitation or bestowed caring rightly gives us pause and fresh incredulity at the magnitude of God. Instead of visiting us with the judgment we deserve, God extends His goodness to us and to all living creatures under His fatherly care (Matthew 5:45). The purpose of these questions, however, isn't to make man smaller, but by contrast to better see God's greatness. The verse is also a reminder that God hasn't forgotten His children in the past and won't forget us in the future.

5 For thou hast made him a little lower than the angels, and hast crowned him with glory and honour.

Even though glory and honor uniquely belong to God (Psalm 29:1; 104:1), man's pre-Fall position was high and noble. Even in our fallen state, God's royal image greatly enhances our status (Genesis 1:26). Man is only a little lower (Heb. *chacer,* **khaw-sare',** meaning to make lower or to decrease) than the "angels" (Heb. *elohiym*) because our situation is temporary. The Septuagint interprets the word as "angels," as does Hebrews 2:7-9, quoting this psalm. After we are transformed at the second coming of Christ (1 Corinthians 15:52-53), we will be in a position to judge angels (1 Corinthians 6:3).

Verse 5 is difficult to explain due to its divided application. Some theologians argue that the verse applies wholly to Jesus. Even if this is true (as seems to be the case from Hebrews 2:6-8; see also 1 Corinthians 1:15-20), one could argue that it is not a reach at all to imply our shallow human footprints become enclosed in Christ's, however faintly, and from there to read a parallel meaning in the sharing of our humanity and His humanity (but not at the expense of His deity).

Christ was, for awhile, made lower than the angels (made like us) but now is restored to His former "glory" (Heb. *kabod,* **kaw-bode',** meaning splendor, copiousness) and "honor" (Heb. *hadar,* **haw-dawr',** meaning glory, excellency; these two are interchangeable words; see also Psalm 21:5). He had nothing personal to gain when He already had everything, and no one can rise higher than to the right hand of the Father—the posi-

tion Christ left to become like us. In our case, not only will we return to our former glory as it was in the garden, but our redemption will make us eligible to obtain bodies like His glorious body (Philippians 3:21).

6 Thou madest him to have dominion over the works of thy hands; thou hast put all things under his feet:

With the exception of power over nature or natural laws, clearly man, who alone in creation has the stamp of the image of God (Genesis 1:26-27), was given dominion, or governorship, over all the earth (v. 28; 9:2)—the works of God's fingers (Psalm 8:3). Here, God's creative digits are rendered "hands" (Heb. *yud,* **kaf,** meaning hands that are open and giving, as opposed to closed hands), as if granting us dominion, just as we are under the dominion of the God who created both us and all other living things (1 Corinthians 15:27).

Our position as caretaker didn't change with the Fall (Job 35:11). Unlike the animals, we can observe and appreciate the heavens and know that they are God's and belong to no other because He made them (Psalm 115:16). Not only is all of creation His, but every corner of it is subject to His control. God sets the paths of the planets and the life span of the stars, and He ordains a time, place, and purpose for everything.

Again, the parallel is apparent—Christ has dominion over all, including us (Ephesians 1:22; Hebrews 2:8), while we have been given dominion over all on Earth except ourselves. There is a strong contrast between David's previous diminution of man over the vast wonders of creation and his present exaltation of man over creation. Even so, ultimately Christ alone is the supreme ruler, as evidenced in the Messianic overtones of the passage.

7 All sheep and oxen, yea, and the beasts of the field; 8 The fowl of the air, and the fish of the sea, and whatsoever passeth through the paths of the seas.

This is an ongoing thought from verses 5-6 concerning all the animals, which are represented here by a few. The "paths of the seas" represent the ocean currents. No doubt the larger sea animals mystified the ancient people, thus, the almost fearful reference ("whatsoever passeth") to them as if they were intimidating, wandering giants who deserved special acknowledgment. It was an act of homage in Genesis 2:19-20 when all the animals presented themselves to Adam for naming, confirming his assigned (and our inherited) dominion over them. Putting things at someone's feet is a symbol (or "insignia" as Matthew Henry put it) of royalty or the power to rule. From the beginning, man clearly has ruled, and to this day continues to rule over the animal kingdom (James 3:7). May we be faithful to that with which we've been entrusted, which is nothing less than the right to rule the earth. Without diminishing man's role in creation, all this, of course, remains married to the contextual, overriding parallel of Christ's superior dominion over us and the rest of creation, including nature and the laws of nature.

9 O 'LORD our Lord, how excellent is thy name in all the earth!

Returning to the beginning thought is the sign of a good writer or composer—to bring something full circle and tie it back together without leaving loose ends. In sum, the worldly mind sees God nowhere, but the spiritual mind sees Him everywhere. In a recent tour to Israel, our highly educated and articulate guide said, "If your eyes are open, you can learn from everything you see." Many who live in the Holy Land are so close to so much, but they seem to see so little—missing entirely the much-prophesied Christ, their Messiah, their Lord and God!

This psalm is also an excellent argument for a basic intelligent design theory, to which even some atheists and agnostics are willing to subscribe, leaving the ranks of evolutionism in droves. The unenlightened may argue over whose God it was who created the universe, but the numbers of those believing there is no God (or intelligent being) are rapidly dwindling. Intelligent, scientific people realize that the voluminous evidence and numerous impossibilities just don't fit the once-heralded theory anymore, especially since in all its years it produced literally

zero evidence in favor of an accidental creation and the random evolution of man.

If creation is great, how great must creation's Creator be, who flung it into existence for His glory and for man's enjoyment? We, who are mere clay, are reminded by the psalmist that we have been graced with the care of the eternal God. This is excellence indeed apart from all the other generous wonders of our God and Lord! In the words of Charles Spurgeon, "O for grace to walk worthy of that excellent name which has been named upon me, and which we are pledged to magnify!"

Bibliography

Spurgeon, Charles. *The Treasury of David: Classic Reflections on the Wisdom of the Psalms.* Peabody, Mass.: Hendrickson Publishers, 1988, 80.

VanGemeren, Willem A. *Psalms. Vol. 5, The Expositor's Bible Commentary,* edited by Frank E. Gaebelein. Grand Rapids, Mich.: Zondervan Publishing Co., 1991, 110.

DAILY BIBLE READINGS

M: God Creates Humankind
Genesis 1:26-31
T: God Creates Man and Woman
Genesis 2:7, 15-25
W: God Establishes a Covenant with Noah
Genesis 9:8-17
T: God Is Our Help and Strength
Psalm 63:1-8
F: God Is Our Guide and Refuge
Psalm 73:21-28
S: God Leaves Nothing Outside Our Jurisdiction
Hebrews 2:5-10
S: Created a Little Lower Than God
Psalm 8

TEACHING TIPS

March 12
Bible Study Guide 2

1. Words You Should Know

A. Majesty (Psalm 104:1) *hadar* (Heb.)—Magnificent, ornament, or splendor; beauty, comeliness; excellency, gloriousness, and honor. A term referring to the dignity, power, and authority of a king or other high official.

B. Rebuke (v. 7) *g'arah* (Heb.)—A reprimand; reproof.

2. Teacher Preparation

A. Pray for the students in your class, asking God to open their hearts to today's lesson.

B. Study the FOCAL VERSES, BIBLE BACKGROUND, THE PEOPLE, PLACES, AND TIMES, and IN DEPTH.

C. Read and study the SEARCH THE SCRIPTURES and DISCUSS THE MEANING questions.

D. Bring writing paper and pens to class.

3. Starting the Lesson

A. Before the students arrive to class, write the words, "Authority," "Order," and "Provisions" on the board.

B. Ask one student to lead the class in prayer.

C. Ask a student to read the IN FOCUS story aloud. Then draw students' attention to the words, "Authority," "Order," and "Provisions" written on the chalkboard. Ask them to keep these words in mind when reading the lesson.

4. Getting into the Lesson

A. Read the FOCAL VERSES and the KEEP IN MIND verse together in class.

B. Ask for volunteers to read the IN DEPTH section. Generate a thorough discussion around class responses.

5. Relating the Lesson to Life

A. Use the LESSON IN OUR SOCIETY section as an opportunity for students to discuss God's boundaries and our dependence on Him.

B. Ask the students to read the MAKE IT HAPPEN section. Encourage the students to share their feelings about enjoying God's creation.

6. Arousing Action

A. Divide the students into small groups. Give each group writing paper and pens. Ask each group to read and answer the SEARCH THE SCRIPTURES and DISCUSS THE MEANING questions. Give the students about 10-20 minutes to complete the exercises. Ask each group to share their responses with the class.

B. Remind the students to read the DAILY BIBLE READINGS and the REMEMBER YOUR THOUGHTS and FOLLOW THE SPIRIT sections for the week.

WORSHIP GUIDE

For the Superintendent or Teacher
Theme: God Created Wonderful Things
Theme Song: "God that Madest the Earth and Heaven"
Scripture: Psalm 104:1-13
Song: "O Splendor of God's Glory Bright"
Meditation: Lord, we thank You for all You've created. Teach us to love You as our wonderful Creator. Give us a heart that is filled with genuine praise for all Your glorious works. In Jesus' holy name we pray. Amen.

GOD CREATED WONDERFUL THINGS

Bible Background • PSALM 104
Printed Text • PSALM 104:1–13
Devotional Reading • PSALM 104:31–35

LESSON AIM

By the end of the lesson, we will:

KNOW that God has authority over all He creates;

UNDERSTAND that God makes provisions for His creations; and

COMMIT to rely on God's divine order for all He creates.

KEEP IN MIND

"Bless the LORD, O my soul. O LORD my God, thou art very great; thou art clothed with honour and majesty" (Psalm 104:1).

FOCAL VERSES

Psalm 104:1 Bless the LORD, O my soul. O LORD my God, thou art very great; thou art clothed with honour and majesty.

2 Who coverest thyself with light as with a garment: who stretchest out the heavens like a curtain:

3 Who layeth the beams of his chambers in the waters: who maketh the clouds his chariot: Who walketh upon the wings of the wind:

4 Who maketh his angels spirits; his ministers a flaming fire:

5 Who laid the foundations of the earth, that it should not be removed for ever.

6 Thou coveredst it with the deep as with a garment: the waters stood above the mountains.

7 At thy rebuke they fled; at the voice of thy thunder they hasted away.

8 They go up by the mountains; they go down by the valleys unto the place which thou hast founded for them.

9 Thou hast set a bound that they may not pass

LESSON OVERVIEW

LESSON AIM
KEEP IN MIND
FOCAL VERSES
IN FOCUS
THE PEOPLE, PLACES, AND TIMES
BACKGROUND
AT-A-GLANCE
IN DEPTH
SEARCH THE SCRIPTURES
DISCUSS THE MEANING
LESSON IN OUR SOCIETY
MAKE IT HAPPEN
FOLLOW THE SPIRIT
REMEMBER YOUR THOUGHTS
MORE LIGHT ON THE TEXT
DAILY BIBLE READINGS

over; that they turn not again to cover the earth.

10 He sendeth the springs into the valleys, which run among the hills.

11 They give drink to every beast of the field: the wild asses quench their thirst.

12 By them shall the fowls of the heaven have their habitation, which sing among the branches.

13 He watereth the hills from his chambers: the earth is satisfied with the fruit of thy works.

IN FOCUS

With reference to the "Science and the Spiritual Quest" conference held at the Center for Theology and Science in Berkeley, California, a recent cover of *Newsweek* boldly announced: "Science Finds God." The article reported that several hundred scientists and theologians were virtually unanimous in agreeing that science and religion are now converging, and what they are converging on is God. The consensus at the conference was: "There is a huge amount of data supporting the existence of God. The question is how to evaluate it."

It is worthy to note how wonderful it is that science has collected enough data to believe they have located God. Ironically, the article also triggers laughter, since God had never been lost in the first place.

Because scientists can only examine things around them, they evaluate the data in the following manner: by working on the same principle as the average person who might examine a beautifully cut diamond or well-designed piece of furniture and instantly recognize that it was created by a master craftsman. This same logic should be used by the scientist who discovers the complexity of the cell world and the encoded language of DNA. There is only one logical explanation for its existence: God, the Master Craftsman of the universe.

We can always rely on God's sustaining power and divine order. If you ever feel that you have lost God, ask yourself the question: Who moved?

THE PEOPLE, PLACES, AND TIMES

Heaven. In the Old Testament, the most frequent association with heaven is that it is the place where God dwells. The epithet "God of heaven" occurs several times (e.g., Genesis 24:7; 2 Chronicles 36:23; Nehemiah 2:4). In Isaiah's vision of heaven, the train of God fills the temple (Isaiah 6:1). In the parallel passage in Ezekiel, the vision of what the prophet sees "above the firmament" is likewise dominated by the figure of God (Ezekiel 1:26-28). Throughout the heavenly visions of Revelation, the presence of God and Christ is a constant reference point for what happens in heaven. Heaven is nothing less than the "holy and glorious habitation" of God (Isaiah 63:15; Deuteronomy 26:15). At the top of the ladder joining heaven and earth in Jacob's vision stands God (Genesis 28:13). When the dying Stephen gazes into heaven, he sees God and Christ (Acts 7:55-56).

God is the central inhabitant of heaven, but not its only resident. The angels live there as well, as more than a dozen verses tell us and as Jacob's vision with its imagery of angels ascending and descending the ladder (Genesis 28:12) makes clear. The company of the redeemed also live in heaven: At the end of Elijah's earthly life, God took him up to heaven by a whirlwind (2 Kings 2:1), and the book of Revelation repeatedly portrays glorified saints as inhabiting heaven. A preponderance of the Bible's pictures of heaven show it to be a crowded place. Crowded scenes along the lines of Micaiah's sight of God "sitting on his throne, with all the host of heaven standing beside him on his right hand and on his left" (1 Kings 22:19, RSV; 2 Chronicles 18:18) are common.

In the New Testament, Jesus claimed heaven as His dwelling place (John 3:13; 6:33-51). On three occasions, a voice from heaven confirmed Jesus' claim (Matthew 3:16-17; 17:5; John 12:28). God will create a new heaven (Isaiah 65:17), the future home of all believers, who will dwell with the Lord eternally (Colossians 1:5-6).

Bibliography

Ryken, Leland, James C. Wilhoit, and Tremper Longman III, eds. *Dictionary of Biblical Imagery.* Downers Grove, Ill. and Leicester, England: InterVarsity Press, USA, InterVarsity Press, England, 1998.

Elwell, Walter A., and Philip W. Comfort, eds. *Tyndale Bible Dictionary.* Wheaton, Ill.: Tyndale House Publishers, 2001, 579-580.

BACKGROUND

The Psalms are the literary centerpiece of the Bible, a masterful compilation of prayers and songs that express the very essence of the human heart and soul. In this particular psalm, the creative works of God are articulated by the psalmist giving praise and honor to the Lord for His ingenious abilities. This psalm is similar to what we read in the book of Genesis: God created heaven and earth, water, vegetation, the sun and moon, fish, animals, and eventually man (Genesis 1:1-31). God has the ability to speak any directive He chooses, and the recipient of His command has to obey His Word. Even nature must comply with God's Word, and only God can reverse a command. When He speaks, the earth is formed and the waters flee to their permanent location. Everything the Lord creates is satisfied with the fruit of His work.

In this psalm, we will learn that God is not only the Creator but is also the Sustainer of what He creates. He ensures that every need is met. As children of God, we rest in His assurance and know that He will take care of our needs. God promises to meet our needs when we seek His righteousness, trust Him, and wait on His provisions (Psalm 23; 40:1-4; 91; 121; 127; Matthew 6:33).

AT-A-GLANCE

1. God's Divine Authority (Psalm 104:1-4)
2. God's Divine Order (vv. 5-9)
3. God's Divine Provisions (vv. 10-13)

IN DEPTH

1. God's Divine Authority (Psalm 104:1-4)

The writer describes the Lord as majestic,

emphasizing His splendor and beauty. The brilliance of God's light shines luminously throughout the universe, reflecting God's magnificent glory, which radiates across heaven and earth. This light is supreme, outshining the brightest star (vv. 1, 2)! The psalmist tells us that God "walketh upon the wings of the wind" (v. 3). This literary conceit gives us a glimpse of God's power and superiority over the things He creates. God has all power and authority in His hands. When we look at nature—for example, the wind—we know that it can be devastating and powerful. Tornadoes, twisters, and hurricanes can rip through neighborhoods, destroying homes, towns, and communities. Sometimes the challenges we face in life feel like these powerful winds, disrupting our peace and shaking our faith in God. The Lord is sovereign and has more power than any "windstorm" that blows into our lives. When we bring our concerns to the Lord in prayer, we can trust Him to guide us in every situation and can take comfort in His ability to handle our problems.

The writer informs us that the Lord "maketh the clouds his chariot" (v. 3). It may be difficult to imagine God riding on the clouds; however, this visual concept may help us understand God's authority. His authority ranks above every demonic influence. No matter what "cloud of treachery" the enemy tries to use against us, the power of God is supreme. The enemy is defeated and trampled under our feet. For example, if the "clouds" in our life are fear and hopelessness, we can fix our eyes on our Lord Jesus Christ, who is "the author and finisher of our faith" (Hebrews 12:2). By His strength we can "ride" the chariots of difficult times.

2. God's Divine Order (vv. 5-9)

The Lord established the earth. He fashioned the foundation upon which it was formed and created vegetation and every beast and fowl that roams the earth. He created the stars, sun, and moon and placed them in divine order. The Bible tells us that the earth cannot be moved unless God moves it. It cannot be destroyed unless God so commands (v. 5). God's Word tells us that He is a God of order. He meticulously synchronized the universe and put everything in its place. God orchestrated the four seasons, the rising and setting of the moon and sun, the rotation of the earth, the migration of geese, and even the hibernation of bears.

At one point in time, the waters ruled and covered the mountains; yet, by the command of God's voice, the waters fled to the valley, making the ravine its permanent location. Thus, it was forbidden for water to rise above the mountains again (vv. 6-9). This illustrates the power of God's Word and His divine authority. Everything God creates is arranged according to His plan. All that God produces has a specific purpose and function; for example, the water quenches our thirst, nourishes plants, and provides a habitat for fish. We may not understand the purpose for all of God's creation; nevertheless, we can respect the work of His hand and appreciate His goodness.

The Lord sets boundaries for His creation. These limitations are

God created wonderful things.

"confirmation"

designed by God for our protection. Obviously if the waters covered the mountains, we could not live on earth. God has restrained the activities of nature, and human beings are no exception! We are also governed by God's commands; God uses boundaries to protect us from the consequences of sin. For example, the Bible tells us not to engage in fornication or adultery. Sexual sin can lead to divorce, abortion, and venereal diseases. When we rebel against God's commands, we find ourselves outside the will of God.

The Lord sets limitations not only on His creation, but also on situations and circumstances in our lives. When the Lord decides a situation must end, it is prohibited from continuing beyond that point! When God lifts the enemy's restraints from our paths, the stumbling blocks must crumble! God can open and shut doors of opportunity for us! The Lord uses boundaries to show us our dependence on Him.

3. God's Divine Provisions (vv. 10-13)

Developing a God-centered perspective will keep our heart and mind in a state of praise. When we view God in the light of His divine creativity, we are mystified by His greatness. When we are in tune with His ability to provide for our needs, a greater appreciation for God should emerge.

The caring and loving heart of our God is displayed throughout nature. God's sustaining power is evident in all He creates and in all He does. His greatest love is bestowed upon the human race. Unfortunately, we sometimes forget to appreciate what God has done for us. During the hustle and bustle of life, we neglect to thank the Lord for His goodness. We take for granted the daily functions of our bodies, such as eating, sleeping, and breathing. We forget to smell the flowers, appreciate the autumn breeze, adore the fresh morning dew, or look in awe at the rising of the sun! God has given us so many wonderful things to enjoy.

Some Christians find it difficult to praise the Lord unless He is meeting some material need. God desires to meet our needs and always provides the very best for us. If we would take inventory of what we currently possess, we would see the blessings of God in our life. If we would compare our material "wealth" to the situations of those who are starving and suffering in unindustrialized countries—where electricity and food are scarce and public worship is forbidden—we would fall down on bended knees, praising God for His mercy! It is the heart of God to take care of His people. When God provides comfort, He provides it perfectly; when God gives us His rest, He gives it totally; His provisions are altogether sufficient and completely satisfactory. Yet, in all that He provides for us, we must find solace in praising Him just because He is God. He created us, breathed life into us, and redeemed us from sin! He is worthy of our praise!

God feeds the birds of the air, nourishes the wild donkeys, and tends to the animals in the fields. From the contentment of their hearts come songs of thanksgiving. All God's creations are satisfied with the fruit of His work (vv. 11-13). If the birds can sing "praises" to the Lord for what He has done, we certainly have no excuse! As believers, we've received the greatest portion of God's love: His only begotten Son, our Lord Jesus Christ. As children of God, our posture toward Him should be one of gratitude. We should thank the Lord on a daily basis for His loving-kindness toward us. A grateful heart pleases God.

SEARCH THE SCRIPTURES

1. What is meant by the statement, "God walketh upon the wings of the wind" (Psalm 104:3)?

2. Why did the Lord set boundaries for the water (vv. 5-11)?

3. What is meant by the statement, "The earth is satisfied with the fruit of thy works" (v. 13)?

DISCUSS THE MEANING

1. Why would some Christians find it difficult to trust God as their ultimate provider?

2. Why is it important to understand that God is a God of order? What does this tell us about chaos and confusion?

3. God is "bigger" than what we imagine Him to be. What are some consequences of thinking our problems are bigger than God?

LESSON IN OUR SOCIETY

The Lord gives us His Word so we can learn of Him and resist the temptation to sin. If we view God's boundaries as harnesses that restrict our independence, we will miss the opportunity to experience an intimate relationship with Him— one that is established on our dependence upon Him. Are you depending on God or yourself? Are you struggling with issues concerning His provisions?

MAKE IT HAPPEN

Rediscover the beauty of God. Make plans to go to the beach or park, or enjoy any outdoor activity where you can appreciate nature. Take time to sit, pray, and meditate on God's creation. Smell the roses and dance in the rain! Refurbish a "childlike" appreciation for the things of God.

FOLLOW THE SPIRIT

What God wants me to do:

_____

_____

REMEMBER YOUR THOUGHTS

Special insights I have learned:

_____

_____

MORE LIGHT ON THE TEXT
Psalm 104:1-13

Charles Spurgeon writes that this psalm presents a "complete cosmos" and is "a poet's version of Genesis." These 13 verses describe the first six days of Creation in the order of events from the first chapter of Genesis. Verses 1-4 are about the light of the first day and the sky and land of the second day. Verses 5-6 are about the formation of land of the third day. Verses 7-10 are about the waters receding from the land and the growth of greenery and fruit-bearing vegetation of the third day (the separation of day and night of the fourth day of creation is implied as God clothes Himself in light and all else is darkness). Verses 11-13 mention the birds and animals that were created on the fifth and sixth days. All was good, all were satisfied—and praise comes naturally when God satisfies.

1 Bless the LORD, O my soul. O LORD my God, thou art very great; thou art clothed with honour and majesty.

Starting and ending just like Psalm 103 (a fact that underscores David's authorship), this psalm gives God the worship He is due. To "bless" (Heb. *barak,* **baw-rak'**) means to kneel, praise, or adore the Lord or to communicate to Him that He is loved, trusted, and adored (some versions render this word as "praise").

The word "great" in Hebrew is *gadal* (**gaw-dal'**), which means "magnified" or "exalted" (see Genesis 12:2; Psalm 34:3). The word "very" in Hebrew is *m'od* (**meh-ode'**), which means "especially" or "exceedingly "(see Genesis 1:31; Psalm 96:4). Such added superlatives are appropriate within the context; indeed, God is worthy of every superlative and expression of praise and blessing.

We can't physically reach God, but by His visible glories we can see Him "darkly" (1 Corinthians 13:12); indeed, we, like Moses, couldn't survive the full brilliance of His person (Exodus 34:29). Thus, because we could not bear His full appearance, God clothes Himself with the "fabric of the world," in the choice words of John Calvin. The phrase "thou art clothed" in Hebrew is *labash* (**law-bash'**) and means simply to put on a garment; the same Hebrew word is used to describe God dressing Adam and Eve (Genesis 3:21). While earthly kings adorn themselves with royal finery of every kind, none can compare to God's infinitely greater "robes" of exceeding honor and majestic excellence (Psalm 93:1; 1 Timothy 6:16).

2 Who coverest thyself with light as with a garment; who stretchest out the heavens like a curtain:

In the previous verse, God clothed Himself with honor and majesty; in this verse His attire is light itself. If one of the garments in God's wardrobe is "light" (Heb. *'owr,* **ORE,** meaning a lightning type of brilliance or a bright morning sun), one can't help but ask how bright His being is (Habakkuk 3:4). If "the heavens" (Heb. *shamayim,* **shaw-mah'-yim**) implies that either the visible arch in which the clouds move or the larger space where celestial bodies revolve is merely a curtain, one can only wonder how grand God's royal pavilion—His heavenly tabernacle is. Other verses such as Isaiah 40:12; 54:2; and Job 37:18 refer to the heavens in a similar manner. Isaiah 34:4 and Revelation 6:14 refer to the sky (or heavens) being rolled up like a scroll.

Light and fire (see Psalm 104:4) are co-symbols of God used throughout Scripture: for example, the fire of the burning bush (Exodus 3:2), the light of the guiding pillar of fire (13:21), the light of the temple candles (25:37), the brilliant light of His presence on Mount Sinai (34:29), and the light of the cloud of God's presence in the tabernacle (40:35). At His transfiguration, Jesus' face "shone like the sun" and His clothes became "white as the light" (Matthew 17:2). Jesus said, "I am the light of the world" (John 8:12), and throughout Scripture, God's angels (Acts 12:7), His children (Ephesians 5:8), and even the Gospel (2 Corinthians 4:4) are couched in terms of light. In 1 Timothy 6:16, God is described as living in "unapproachable light."

3 Who layeth the beams of his chambers in the waters: who maketh the clouds his chariot; Who walketh upon the wings of the wind:

God's construction materials are vastly different from ours (Amos 9:6); everything is supported by His awesome power. His "beams" (Heb. *qarah,* **kaw-raw'**, meaning beams or supporting structures as for flooring or roofing) in footings of water are infinitely more stable than our strongest steel and concrete. [Note: Here the reader must follow good hermeneutics by staying within the boundaries of a Scripture's unique literary genre, type, purpose, and structure. When metaphor and poetry are the tools of the author, we as commentators should not override the author's intent by reading these great metaphors in an overly literal way.]

Our great King doesn't require chariots or limousines to define His royalty; rather, He rides on the "clouds" (Heb. *ab,* **awb**, meaning a thick cloud) and the "wind" (Heb. *ruwach,* **roo-akh**, meaning spirit; also, a blasting breath or violent exhalation) is harnessed for His traveling needs; the sky itself obeys His every whim like a plane obeys its pilot. If the beams of His tabernacle are stabilized in the oceans, the clouds are His equally firm floorboards, and the wind provides His corridors.

4 Who maketh his angels spirits; his ministers a flaming fire:

Both "spirit(s)" and "wind" are translated from the same Hebrew word (*ruwach*). If "angels" (Heb. *malak,* **mal-awk'**, meaning "messenger") are made into spirits, they are also made into wind, upon which God is transported (see also Hebrews 1:7). In a real sense, God speaks words or breathes out life (wind), and angels (messengers) take His breath or words of life to deliver them (Psalm 103:20). We must remember the incredible power and importance of all God's countless angels (Matthew 25:31; 2 Thessalonians 1:7; Hebrews 12:22; Revelation 5:11), especially guardian angels (Psalm 91:11), harvesting angels (Matthew 13:39), ministering angels (Hebrews 1:14), cherubim (Genesis 3:24; Exodus 25:20), seraphim (Isaiah 6:2, 6), the four living creatures (Ezekiel 1:5), and the archangels (1 Thessalonians 4:16; Jude 9).

Hebrews 1:7 also refers to God's ministers or servants (which includes angels) as a "flame of fire," again drawing on the image of God as both light and fire; the angels who do His bidding are referred to as beams of light emanating from Him or flames extending from His brilliant, fiery presence. In verse 2, God's brilliance is brighter than light, brighter than what humans can see and live to describe; our sun is probably the closest visible element but is surely only a dim ember compared to the eternally blazing essence of God. Indeed, in heaven there will be no need for a sun, as God Himself will be our light (Revelation 22:5).

5 Who laid the foundations of the earth, that it should not be removed for ever.

Ancient mariners and mapmakers once envisioned the world as being both flat and resting on huge pillars (what supported the pillars went unexplained). Today, we know that the earth spins silently, smoothly, and seamlessly through space. Yet no matter how many volcanoes, earthquakes, or other natural disasters occur, nothing is able to shake the earth from its preordained (Job 38:4), God-established path and foundation

(Heb. *makown,* **maw-kone**', meaning a settled habitation). In constancy of rotation and stability of axis and orbit, our globe is held securely in God's hand and obeys His pleasure.

6 Thou coveredst it with the deep as with a garment: the waters stood above the mountains.

Before the oceans and waters of the world receded to their appointed place, water covered even the mountains. Most geologists and archaeologists affirm the truth that Scripture told centuries before. How can we help but think in terms of praise when we consider these things? The context defines this verse as a reference to the chaos at Creation (2 Peter 3:5-6), rather than to the Flood (Genesis 7:19), yet both are grand demonstrations of God's power and control over nature.

7 At thy rebuke they fled; at the voice of thy thunder they hasted away.

Scripture labels God's commanding the waters to recede from covering the earth as a "rebuke" (Heb. *g'arah,* **gheh-aw-raw**, meaning a chiding or reproof; see also Isaiah 50:2; Nahum 1:4). In this case, it was with thunder representing His power (Psalm 18:13). Similarly, Moses rebuked the Red Sea (Exodus 14:21), Joshua rebuked the Jordan River (Joshua 3:15-16), and Jesus rebuked the storm on the Sea of Galilee (Matthew 8:26). The point of the psalm ultimately is that God is sovereign over all and thus worthy of praise.

8 They go up by the mountains; they go down by the valleys unto the place which thou hast founded for them.

Every form of water—stream, river, ocean, dew, waterfall, ocean—is subject to God's command. Even when water completely covered the entire earth, including the mountains, our Creator set the boundaries for all the waters (see also Proverbs 8:29; Job 26:10), and then at His rebuke (Psalm 104:7) sent each of them to their ordained places, where they will remain essentially unmoved until He speaks to them again. In the end, He'll rebuke evil and send it to its appointed place just as easily as He sent the oceans, lakes, rivers, and springs to theirs (Psalm 9:5).

9 Thou hast set a bound that they may not pass over; that they turn not again to cover the earth.

Again, the earlier context in the psalm (v. 5) refers to Creation, but the principle of God's control over nature applies both to the boundaries set in the beginning, and to the implied context of Noah's Flood, after which God promised never again to cover the earth with water (Genesis 9:15). There would have been no flood had God not personally removed the restraints set at Creation. Likewise, since God once again rebuked the water, it remains to this day firmly bound, unable to break free from its divinely ordained perimeters.

Virtually all of human life depends on the waters of the world remaining where they are; even a few feet of difference would be cataclysmic, decimating huge populations on many continents. Hollywood likes to speculate about our destiny, as if huge meteors could randomly strike the planet and cause devastation to all of human life, not understanding that even meteors would need permission from the Lord of the universe before entering our atmosphere.

10 He sendeth the springs into the valleys, which run among the hills.

Those familiar with the landscape of Israel know well the extremely hilly terrain, the lack of precipitation, especially in the south (as little as 2" per year), and the incredibly important and welcome rains that race down the steep hills and into the many wadis (dry river beds), providing life's most essential ingredient for all living creatures. Springs also appear from below the surface, from within bedrock, as rainwater, and as snow melt-off from the northern mountains, which travels underground toward the Judean wilderness and all points on the eastern side of the water divide. Numerous springs bubble up out of the surface, grow into rivers, and race downward, creating oases and nourishing everything within reach. It was at an oasis called En Gedi in some of the Judean foothills next to the Dead Sea where David hid from Saul. Some speculate that he wrote many psalms there, possibly even this one, because of the lush waterfalls, pools, and greenery as well as the plentiful hiding places in numerous nearby caves.

11 They give drink to every beast of the field: the wild asses quench their thirst.

God, the great gardener and farmer, takes care of His creation, even in the most desolate of places. He cares for the least of the animals and the least of the vegetation. So what about us who are made in His image? Will He forget His most beloved creation? It shouldn't be a stretch to infer from this verse a spiritual analogy as God sends spiritual water rushing into even the most humble of dry souls and quenches their thirst.

12 By them shall the fowls of the heaven have their habitation, which sing among the branches.

Happy are those creatures that know that their Creator feeds and waters them; how lovely are their voices of praise—and what better representatives of them than cheerful, chirping birds? Likewise, when we drink of the water of life and eat of the fruit of the vine, we, too, sing for joy.

13 He watereth the hills from his chambers: the earth is satisfied with the fruit of thy works.

Only God can cause the rain; only God can hover over the mountains to start the water flowing to all lower parts; as a result, all receive and are satisfied—none are neglected. The word "chambers," indicating God's habitation, in Hebrew is *aliyah*, **al-ee-yaw'**, meaning "upper chamber." This Hebrew word is significant in light of a parallel to the New Testament Greek word *katalama*, **kat-AL-oo-mah**, meaning a guest chamber or an upper room reserved for one's most important guests, such as the site of Jesus' Passover meal (Luke 22:11).

In a spiritual parallel, those who feed and water the flock are themselves fed and watered from the highest points in the spiritual chain of command. It is by the obedient caring for everyone within their reach, which is then duplicated "downhill," that God's master plans and purposes are fulfilled.

Bibliography

Spurgeon, Charles. The Treasury of David: Classic Reflections on the Wisdom of the Psalms. Peabody, Mass.: Hendrickson Publishers, 1988, 314.

DAILY BIBLE READINGS

M: The Firmament Proclaims God's Handiwork
Psalm 19:1-6

T: Make a Joyful Noise to God
Psalm 66:1-9

W: God's Steadfast Love Endures Forever
Psalm 136:1-9

T: God, the Great Creator
Psalm 104:1-13

F: God's Creation Is Balanced and Orderly
Psalm 104:14-23

S: Manifold Are God's Works
Psalm 104:24-30

S: Rejoice in the Lord
Psalm 104:31-35

TEACHING TIPS

March 19
Bible Study Guide 3

1. Words You Should Know

A. Wonderfully (Psalm 139:14) *palah* (Heb.)—To distinguish or set aside; to make marvelous or wonderful.

B. Everlasting (v. 24) *'olam* (Heb.)—Always, eternal; lasting a long time; something that is perpetual or without end.

2. Teacher Preparation

A. Pray for the students in your class, asking God to open their hearts to today's lesson.

B. Study the FOCAL VERSES, BIBLE BACKGROUND, THE PEOPLE, PLACES, AND TIMES, and IN DEPTH sections.

C. Read and study the SEARCH THE SCRIPTURES and DISCUSS THE MEANING questions.

D. Purchase 3 x 5" index cards. Write "warm fuzzies" (things that are nice to say to someone) on each of the cards (e.g., "You are beautiful," "You are intelligent," "You are special," "You are wonderful"). Fold the cards and place them in a hat or box. Make enough cards for your entire class.

3. Starting the Lesson

A. Ask one student to lead the class in prayer.

B. Read the KEEP IN MIND verses together in class.

C. Ask the students to read the IN FOCUS story and the BACKGROUND section. Then allow the students to share their comments and opinions.

4. Getting into the Lesson

A. Ask for volunteers to read the IN DEPTH section. Generate a thorough discussion around class responses.

B. Bring out the box of 3 x 5" cards. Ask each student to randomly pick a card from the box and read aloud what is written on the card. Encourage the students to express how they feel about the "warm fuzzies." Explain to the students that this is how the Lord views us.

5. Relating the Lesson to Life

A. Use the LESSON IN OUR SOCIETY section as an opportunity for the students to discuss issues regarding concealment and honesty.

B. Ask the students to read the MAKE IT HAPPEN section. Encourage the students to share their feelings in developing a more intimate relationship with God.

6. Arousing Action

A. Ask the students to pair up. Then ask each pair of students to take turns interviewing each other using the DISCUSS THE MEANING questions. Encourage the students to share their responses with the class.

B. Ask the students to respond to the SEARCH THE SCRIPTURE questions, sharing their insights with the entire class.

C. Remind the students to read the DAILY BIBLE READINGS and the REMEMBER YOUR THOUGHTS and FOLLOW THE SPIRIT sections for the week.

WORSHIP GUIDE

For the Superintendent or Teacher
Theme: God Created and Knows Us
Theme Song: "O Perfect Love"
Scripture: Psalm 139:3, 7-14, 23-24
Song: "Praise, My Soul, the King of Heaven"
Meditation: Lord, thank You for creating me. I am fearfully and wonderfully made in Your sight. Help me to understand and appreciate how much You love me. In Jesus' name we pray. Amen."

GOD CREATED AND KNOWS US

Bible Background • PSALM 139
Printed Text • PSALM 139:1–3, 7-14, 23–24
Devotional Reading • PSALM 100

LESSON AIM

By the end of the lesson, we will:

KNOW that God is omniscient, omnipotent, and omnipresent;

DEVELOP a greater sense of self-worth and intimacy with God; and

SURRENDER to God those areas of our life in which we experience personal struggles.

KEEP IN MIND

"I will praise thee; for I am fearfully and wonderfully made: marvellous are thy works; and that my soul knoweth right well" (Psalm 139:14).

FOCAL VERSES

Psalm 139:1 O LORD, thou hast searched me, and known me.

2 Thou knowest my downsitting and mine uprising, thou understandest my thought afar off.

3 Thou compassest my path and my lying down, and art acquainted with all my ways.

139:7 Whither shall I go from thy spirit? or whither shall I flee from thy presence?

8 If I ascend up into heaven, thou art there: if I make my bed in hell, behold, thou art there.

9 If I take the wings of the morning, and dwell in the uttermost parts of the sea;

10 Even there shall thy hand lead me, and thy right hand shall hold me.

11 If I say, Surely the darkness shall cover me; even the night shall be light about me.

12 Yea, the darkness hideth not from thee; but the night shineth as the day: the darkness and the light are both alike to thee.

LESSON OVERVIEW

LESSON AIM
KEEP IN MIND
FOCAL VERSES
IN FOCUS
THE PEOPLE, PLACES, AND TIMES
BACKGROUND
AT-A-GLANCE
IN DEPTH
SEARCH THE SCRIPTURES
DISCUSS THE MEANING
LESSON IN OUR SOCIETY
MAKE IT HAPPEN
FOLLOW THE SPIRIT
REMEMBER YOUR THOUGHTS
MORE LIGHT ON THE TEXT
DAILY BIBLE READINGS

13 For thou hast possessed my reins: thou hast covered me in my mother's womb.

14 I will praise thee; for I am fearfully and wonderfully made: marvellous are thy works; and that my soul knoweth right well.

139:23 Search me, O God, and know my heart: try me, and know my thoughts:

24 And see if there be any wicked way in me, and lead me in the way everlasting.

IN FOCUS

At dinner with her mother, 11-year-old Margie pulled a letter of suspension from somewhere beneath the table, her hand trembling. Her mother gasped in disbelief as she read it. "What's going on, Margie?" she asked.

Margie related her story with tears washing her cheeks, "After lunch the substitute teacher told the class that Kara, a new girl, had lost her ring, and that if someone had taken or found the ring, they should return it."

"Next period, I found the ring in the girls' locker room. I didn't see Kara in gym, so when I got back to homeroom I put the ring on her desk. The trouble started when Roger and Joey told her they saw me with the ring."

Margie's tears started up again. This time her mother wiped her tears away with a napkin.

Sniffling, Margie went on. "Kara was really, really angry and went straight up to the substitute teacher and said that I stole her ring and the boys saw me do it. I was so upset that the more I tried to explain, the more I cried. Roger and Joey just kept giggling and pointing at me. Now everybody thinks I'm a thief!"

"Everybody?" her mother asked.

"Well, not my girlfriends."

"And not me," her mother added, "because I have known you from birth. I was searching your eyes while you talked, and I know you didn't steal the ring." Her mother went on, "Margie, you have to learn to be strong in truth. Don't be so easily upset when you are wrongly accused. You must believe that God's all-seeing eyes know the whole story and that His truth will penetrate every lie."

The psalmist in the lesson focuses on the knowledge that God knows all things and that His wonderful omniscience can protect us in all situations. Are you willing to surrender to God's intimate care when you experience personal struggles?

THE PEOPLE, PLACES, AND TIMES

Darkness. A word that describes the absence of light. Darkness ruled the world before God's creation of light (Genesis 1:2). Thus, darkness is symbolic of man's sin, rebellion, and ignorance (Job 24:13-17). When we are in sin, we are walking in darkness. When we accept Jesus as our personal Saviour, we should walk in His light because His Spirit lives in us. If we habitually walk in darkness, we know that His Spirit is not in us, and "if any man have not the Spirit of Christ, he is none of his" (Romans 8:9).

Light. Metaphorically or symbolically, "light" is used in the Bible to denote the absence of darkness or sin. It signifies holiness, purity, righteousness—all attributes of God Himself. God, then, is the light giver. He is the epitome of righteousness and holiness. In fact, 1 John 1:5 says, "This then is the message which we have heard of him, and declare unto you, that God is light, and in him is no darkness at all." Jesus, then, is the light giver as well as the giver of eternal life.

BACKGROUND

The Lord knows everything and sees everything. He is omnipresent (everywhere, therefore always with us), omnipotent (all-powerful), and omniscient (all-knowing). The writer of this Psalm gives us a clear picture of the extent to which God is involved in our lives. He is with us from the onset. He knows when we are conceived in our mother's womb. He knows our whereabouts, our thoughts, and our actions. He knows our past, present, and future. Serving a God of this caliber would prove to be very beneficial if we would adopt the proper attitude. For example, it is unwise to assume that because God already knows our needs, we should not present our concerns to Him in prayer. On the contrary, God, who loves us unconditionally, knows all our issues, and is able to meet all our needs; it is to our advantage that we bring all our petitions to Him in prayer (Philippians 4:4-7).

The writer reminds us that God desires intimacy with His children. It is important for believers to understand that we are "beautiful" in the eyes of God. God created us wonderfully. Even when we don't "feel" beautiful, we are magnificent in the eyes of God! This psalm inspires us to seek God earnestly and honestly, asking Him to search the contents of our hearts and remove any impediments that hinder our walk with Him.

AT-A-GLANCE

1. God, the Omniscient One
(Psalm 139:1-3)
2. God, the Omnipresent One (vv. 7-14)
3. God, the Omnipotent One (vv. 23-24)

IN DEPTH

1. God, the Omniscient One (Psalm 139:1-3)

This text is powerful. The omniscience (all-knowingness) of Almighty God is emphasized throughout this psalm. The writer gives indication that God is well-acquainted with each individual. He knows us so well, even the number of hairs on our heads (Matthew 10:30). He observes our behavior. He knows every action we take and every word we speak. He "compassest" our comings and goings (v. 3). The Lord has the supernatural ability to surround us. We cannot hide from God. Our geographical location will not stifle God's ability to find us, and we are never outside the realm of God's presence. This does not mean that God intentionally spies on us so He can condemn us later. It means He lovingly watches over us. His surveillance is similar to the kind of tender observation a loving mother extends to her infant child. The word "compassest" can also express God's understanding and comprehension. The Lord understands our motives. He knows why we act or react to situations and people around us. He has ownership of our history! He may not agree with our behavior, but He is aware of the core underpinnings of our actions. The purpose for God's watchful eye over His children is to allow us to know Him, to become familiar with the Lord we serve. Once we realize that our God loves us in spite of what He knows about us, we can rejoice and freely serve Him.

"Acquaintance" is a term used to express personal knowledge or information about someone or something. Scripture tells us that God is acquainted with all our ways, which means He knows our habits; our background; our socioeconomic, marital, and educational status; our gender; and everything that makes us who we are! God is knowledgeable about our high school graduation, our trips to the Caribbean, our desires to have children, and the birth of our grandchildren. He is also aware of the tragic events that may have taken place in our lives, such as divorce, drug abuse, debilitating injuries, financial ruin, and the loss of our loved ones. God is not the originator or instigator of all these terrible events. We have an adversary, the devil, who seeks to steal, kill, and destroy (1 Peter 5:8). Yet, when we cast all our cares, disappointments, and hurts on God's shoulders, we can experience healing and restitution, thereby allowing the Lord to use our experiences to deepen our intimacy with Him. God is a doting Father who seeks nothing but the best for His children. Recognizing that God is no stranger to our predicaments or successes in life can strengthen our relationship with Him.

2. God, the Omnipresent One (vv. 7-14)

The Lord is always with us, even in times of tremendous pressure, trials, and tribulations.

God promised that He would never leave or forsake us. God will never violate His own Word, for it is impossible for Him to lie (Joshua 1:5; Hebrews 6:18). Scripture tells us that no matter where we go, God is close at hand. We cannot hide from the Spirit of God, nor can we at any time elude His presence. There are times when we act as if this truth did not exist—for example, when we curse out our neighbor, pocket company stationery, or lie about a car accident. No matter how much we try to justify our actions; say, "No one will ever know the truth; or think *It's their word against mine*, God is the ultimate eyewitness. He sees and hears everything, and it is God to whom we will eventually have to give an account (Matthew 12:36; Romans 14:12; Hebrews 4:13).

Fortunately, the Lord has given us a Helper who guides us in the things of God and reminds us of His Word. He is called the Holy Spirit, and He lives in the heart of every believer. Wherever we go, we take Him with us. This truth should remind us to be "God-conscious" in every situation and encourage us to ask the Holy Spirit to guide us in our daily activities.

Anger is a typical response at the beginning of most hardships. We feel victimized and wonder, "Why me?" As we grow in the Lord and become spiritually mature Christians, we learn that God is worthy of praise because He is God. Our current situation does not dictate our response to Him. He was worthy before the problem arrived and will remain worthy whether the problem stays or goes away. Spiritually mature Christians have learned to appreciate God in both good and bad times. Their response to Him is not based on superficial or temporary circumstances; they have learned to praise Him during seasons of prosperity and seasons of adversity. Developing a "God-centered" attitude, where the Lord is the focus of praise, will help us get through the "highs" and "lows" that come with living this Christian walk.

According to the Word of God, we are made wonderfully! Our "wonderful" status is not based on how we feel about ourselves because much of what we feel about ourselves has been prescribed to us by the world. We do not judge ourselves according to the world's standards. We do not view ourselves according to the world's viewpoint.

Our self-worth is based on the standards of God. God's Word defines who we are, and His Word has much to say about us. For example, the Bible tells us that we are righteous and holy in Christ (1 Corinthians 1:30), we are justified through Him (Romans 3:24), we are a new creation (2 Corinthians 5:17), we are adopted as God's children (Ephesians 1:5-6), and we are forgiven by God through Christ Jesus (Ephesians 1:7). Who we are in Christ does not make us better or less than anyone else. Our position in Him is given to us by God's mercy and grace, not by our good deeds. This truth should remind us to walk humbly before others.

3. God, the Omnipotent One (vv. 23-24)

The power of God searches our hearts and examines our motives. That's why it is important to give the Lord access to our hearts. The reason why so many believers fail to see changes in their personal walk is that they are either unaware of the need, afraid, or have refused to ask the Lord to inspect their hearts. A heart examination is crucial and beneficial. It is crucial because we cannot effectively serve the Lord with an impure heart. It is beneficial because a godly inspection is for our own spiritual growth and well-being. God already knows what is lodged in our heart, but He wants us to ask Him to expose its contents to us. Most of the time we may think it is one particular issue that is hindering our walk with Him, when in reality it is something else entirely. We may think we have resolved an issue completely, but through God's thorough investigation, we've discovered that we've only hit the tip of the iceberg. We do not have the capacity to see the hidden source of most of our issues. We tend to gloss over our "stuff" and glance at our issues through rose-colored lenses. Self-examination is difficult. The painful reality of what may motivate our actions is hard to digest. That is why God is better equipped than anyone else to expose our "stuff" to us. He knows how to present the truth in love. There may be times when godly counsel from an outside source is necessary. However, the best counselor afforded to us is our Lord and Saviour Jesus Christ, for He is our Wonderful Counselor (Isaiah 9:6).

When we approach the Lord in sincerity, asking Him to examine our hearts and remove any "wickedness or offenses," He is faithful and will oblige. Our loving Heavenly Father does not intend to expose our issues in a public forum for all to see. In love and with concern, God gingerly reveals our weakness to us. God's purpose is to purify our hearts. When we ask God, He will show us why we act or speak in a manner that is offensive to others. He will reveal our lack of forgiveness and the areas of our lives that are not surrendered to Him. He will show us the anger and resentment we harbor, the deceitfulness we practice, and the tools we employ for self-pity and manipulation. He also reveals to us the source of these impurities.

The ultimate source is sin; however, the Lord will bring to our memory the critical events that triggered our rejection, hatred, and self-depreciation (e.g., a blind date, bullying episodes in grammar school, a disapproving parent, an abusive childhood, or abandonment). Whatever issue we face, God is willing and able to help us deal with our problem. When we turn our "stuff" over to Him, He is readily available to lovingly heal us from all feelings of inadequacy.

David asked God to search his heart and know his thoughts. When we yield our thought processes to God (v. 23), He transforms our minds. God's Word will rectify our perceptions so that our thinking is in line with His Word. It is important that we study the Bible, meditate on the Word of God, and pray for understanding. God will lead us in His paths of righteousness when we walk according to His Word. He will guide us by His divine plan into His perfect will (v. 24).

SEARCH THE SCRIPTURES

1. Explain what is meant by, "If I ascend up into heaven, thou art there" (Psalm 139:8).

2. What is meant by the statement, "I am fearfully and wonderfully made" (v. 14)?

3. What did the writer of this psalm ask God to search, and why (vv. 23-24)?

DISCUSS THE MEANING

1. What are the benefits of asking God to examine our hearts? What are some of the consequences of not asking?

2. What insights have been gained in recognizing that God is omnipotent, omnipresent, and omniscient?

3. When experiencing difficulties in life, why do some adults blame God?

LESSON IN OUR SOCIETY

Some of us can remember sneaking out of the house as teenagers to attend a friend's party. Knowing we were forbidden to go, we would pretend to be asleep in our beds by stuffing our pillows under our sheets. We thought we'd outsmart our parents, only to discover that they knew our whereabouts, as they beat our butts with a belt all the way back home. Ouch! Just as with our parents, God's "radar" can detect our "comings and goings." He may not correct us with a belt like a disciplining parent, but His disciplinary tactics have the same stinging effect. Ask yourself these questions: "Are there things in my life I am trying to conceal from God?" "Am I running away from God, or am I moving closer to Him?"

MAKE IT HAPPEN

Pray and ask the Lord to reveal areas of your life that are not totally surrendered to Him. Ask Him to reveal to you the steps necessary for a more intimate relationship with Him. Write down what He tells you on paper. Share your insights with the class next week.

FOLLOW THE SPIRIT

What God wants me to do:

_____

_____

REMEMBER YOUR THOUGHTS

Special insights I have learned:

_____

_____

MORE LIGHT ON THE TEXT

Psalm 139:1-3, 7-14, 23-24

The theme of this psalm is that God created us and knows us. The psalm is a personal prayer in which the psalmist expresses his knowledge of the attributes of God. The psalmist is confident that God has examined him and knows him. As the psalmist reflects on the past and on his present situation, he expresses a profound knowledge of God and a conviction that God is deeply concerned about individuals. Because God loves and knows His people, they do not have to be worried that He knows their innermost secrets.

1 O LORD, thou hast searched me, and known me.

There are two key Hebrew words in this verse: "searched" (*chaqar*, **khaw-kar'**), which means to examine thoroughly or to investigate, and "known" (*yada'*, **yaw-dah'**), which means to have knowledge of or to find out and discern. In this verse, the psalmist contends that God created us and knows us individually and intimately, inside and out. He knows us better than we know ourselves. God looks beyond the external man (which is revealed to humankind) into the heart, which reveals everything about us. "The Lord knows those who are his" (2 Timothy 2:19, NIV). God not only knows the facts about His people (the number of hairs on our heads, etc.), He also knows us relationally.

2 Thou knowest my downsitting and mine uprising, thou understandest my thought afar off. 3 Thou compassest my path and my lying down, and art acquainted with all my ways.

God is omniscient (all-knowing). He not only knows our actions, our "going out and coming in" (Psalm 121:8), but He knows when we sit and when we stand, when we go out and when we lie down. He also knows the deep motivations behind our actions. God discerns righteousness from wickedness, even when the line between them is ever so thin. We can hide our true feelings and thoughts from other people but not from God. In this verse, the psalmist reminds us that even though God seems to be far, off but He sees and knows everything. God not only knows us, but He understands us. We may not always feel God's presence in our lives, but He is always with us. God knows every step we take and directs our path. God alone is capable of such discernment. Only God is qualified to be the Judge of all mankind. The fact that this great God scrutinizes us so thoroughly yet loves us is "too wonderful" (v. 6).

139:7 Whither shall I go from thy spirit? or whither shall I flee from thy presence?

God is omnipresent (everywhere). It is foolish to think there is any place we can go to escape God's presence. We may think that because we can't see or feel God's presence, He is not with us. Jonah is the perfect example of our inability to escape God. Jonah refused to obey God and decided to flee to Tarshish away from God's presence (Jonah 1:3). Jonah found himself in serious trouble and, finally, in the belly of a large fish (Jonah 1:17). Jonah cried out to God for help, and God rescued him (Jonah 2:10).

8 If I ascend up into heaven, thou art there: if I make my bed in hell, behold, thou art there. 9 If I take the wings of the morning, and dwell in the uttermost parts of the sea; 10 Even there shall thy hand lead me, and thy right hand shall hold me.

There is nowhere we can go to escape God's presence. The universe belongs to God and everything in it, so whether we are in heaven or hell, God is there. God loves us, and through the power of the Holy Spirit, He is ever present with us, guiding, directing, teaching, and protecting us. The apostle Paul states, "For I am convinced that neither death nor life, neither angels nor demons, neither the present nor the future, nor any powers, neither height nor depth, nor anything else in all creation, will be able to separate us from the love of God that is in Christ Jesus our Lord" (Romans 8:38-39).

11 If I say, Surely the darkness shall cover me; even the night shall be light about me. 12 Yea, the darkness hideth not from thee; but the night shineth as the day: the darkness and the light are both alike to thee.

The Hebrew word for "darkness" is *choshek* (**kho-shek'**), which means secret place or obscurity. As Christians, we will experience some trials in our lives that can make us feel totally isolated from God, but He assures us that even in the darkness, when we cannot see our way, He is there. God's promise is, "Never will I leave you; never will I forsake you" (Hebrews 13:5, NIV), and it is through faith that we trust Him.

13 For thou hast possessed my reins: thou hast covered me in my mother's womb. 14 I will praise thee; for I am fearfully and wonderfully made: marvellous are thy works; and that my soul knoweth right well.

God knew us even before we were formed in our mother's womb. Jeremiah 1:5 (NIV) states, "Before I formed you in the womb I knew you, before you were born I set you apart; I appointed you as a prophet to the nations." We were created in the image of God (Genesis 1:27), and as our Creator, God is worthy to be praised. In Psalm 139:13, the psalmist expresses the awesomeness of being created by God. It is our spiritual act of worship to praise God, not just for what He has done but also for who He is.

139:23 Search me, O God, and know my heart: try me, and know my thoughts: 24 And see if there be any wicked way in me, and lead me in the way everlasting.

In this prayer the psalmist expresses his recommitment to God. He prays that the Lord would justify him before his accusers. He asks the Lord to thoroughly investigate him, his actions and motivations, and make a legal judgment of innocence. Having been justified by the Lord, the psalmist gives his testimony that the Lord is a righteous judge. He does so by writing this psalm.

His personal relationship with the Lord has moved to a new level. God has "searched" him through and through and (v. 1), knows him in every way (vv. 1-2, 4), perceives and discerns his deepest thoughts (v. 2), and is familiar with his every move (v. 2). This kind of examination is bound to reveal an abundance of wickedness, yet the psalmist has nothing to fear from the righteous Judge. For His covenant name is "HWEH; the compassionate and gracious God, slow to anger, abounding in love and faithfulness, maintaining love to thousands, and forgiving wickedness, rebellion and sin" (Exodus 34:6-7, NIV).

The divine Judge does much more than settle disputes between opposing parties. He is also the one in whom the psalmist finds refuge, protection, and blessing. In his prayer of gratitude, he says, "You hem me in—behind and before; you have laid your hand upon me" (Psalm 139:5, NIV).

"Search me"... "try me," says the psalmist. "Thoroughly examine me." He wants God to see his loyalty and his rejection of evil. He is asking God to discern his motives and his actions. Evil and vicious men had falsely accused him, but he does not directly address his foes. Instead, he cries out to God, "the compassionate and gracious," the righteous Judge who alone can discern his "heart" and "thoughts." All he wants is to do God's will. He abhors the "wicked way"—the offensive way that leads to destruction and death. He desperately desires "the way everlasting"—the way that leads to intimate fellowship with God.

Having experienced God's examination, the psalmist has a greater understanding of God's amazing grace. He knows that he could never meet God's perfect, righteous standards. Yet he knows that God has shown great favor to those who are His—those who are loyal to Him. In other words, the psalmist has gotten an Old Testament glimpse of justification by faith. What a blessing! Truly, God's grace is too wonderful to fully comprehend!

DAILY BIBLE READINGS

M: We Belong to God
Psalm 100

T: Our Help Comes from the Lord
Psalm 121

W: Our God Watches Over All
Psalm 146

T: God Is Acquainted with My Ways
Psalm 139:1-6

F: God, You Are Always with Me
Psalm 139:7-12

S: Fearfully and Wonderfully Made
Psalm 139:13-18

S: Search Me, O God
Psalm 139:19-24

TEACHING TIPS

March 26
Bible Study Guide 4

1. Words You Should Know

A. Dominion (Psalm 145:13) *memshalah* (Heb.)—The power to rule.

B. Generations (v. 13) *dowr* (Heb.)—A revolution of time; an age or dwelling; a single step or stage in a line of descent from one's ancestor.

2. Teacher Preparation

A. Pray for the students in your class, asking God to open their hearts to today's lesson.

B. Study the FOCAL VERSES, BIBLE BACKGROUND, THE PEOPLE, PLACES, AND TIMES, and IN DEPTH section.

C. Read and study the SEARCH THE SCRIPTURES and DISCUSS THE MEANING questions.

3. Starting the Lesson

A. Ask one student to lead the class in prayer.

B. Read the FOCAL VERSES and KEEP IN MIND verse together in class.

C. Ask the students to read the IN FOCUS story and the BACKGROUND section.

4. Getting into the Lesson

A. Ask for volunteers to read the IN DEPTH section. Generate a thorough discussion around class responses.

B. Share a personal testimony about achievements and the Lord's provisions.

5. Relating the Lesson to Life

A. Use the LESSON IN OUR SOCIETY section as an opportunity for the students to discuss expressing gratitude toward God.

B. Ask the students to read the MAKE IT HAPPEN section. Encourage the students to incorporate the exercise into their daily routine, devoting quality time to praying and praising the Lord.

6. Arousing Action

A. Divide the students into groups. Ask each group to prepare a skit that demonstrates God's mercy to others. Give each group 10 minutes to prepare the skit and 5 minutes to present the skit in front of the class. Ask the students to share their observations with the class.

B. Ask the students to respond to the SEARCH THE SCRIPTURES and DISCUSS THE MEANING questions. Ask them to share their insights with the entire class.

C. Remind the students to read the DAILY BIBLE READINGS and the REMEMBER YOUR THOUGHTS and FOLLOW THE SPIRIT sections for the week.

WORSHIP GUIDE

For the Superintendent or Teacher
Theme: A Hymn of Praise to the Creator
Theme Song: "To God Be the Glory"
Scripture: Psalm 145:1-13
Song: "O Worship the King"
Meditation: Lord, thank You for all Your magnificent creations, Your mercy, and Your love. You are wonderful and worthy of praise. Teach us to show genuine gratitude for all You have done. In Jesus' name we pray.
Amen.

A HYMN OF PRAISE TO THE CREATOR

Bible Background • PSALM 145
Printed Text • PSALM 145:1–13
Devotional Reading • PSALM 150

LESSON AIM

By the end of the lesson, we will:

KNOW that God is wonderful, merciful, everlasting, and worthy of praise;

FEEL appreciation for all the things God does for us; and

COMMIT to spending time each day praising God for the things He has done in our life.

KEEP IN MIND

"The LORD is gracious, and full of compassion; slow to anger, and of great mercy" (Psalm 145:8).

FOCAL VERSES

Psalm 145:1 I will extol thee, my God, O king; and I will bless thy name for ever and ever.

2 Every day will I bless thee; and I will praise thy name for ever and ever.

3 Great is the LORD, and greatly to be praised; and his greatness is unsearchable.

4 One generation shall praise thy works to another, and shall declare thy mighty acts.

5 I will speak of the glorious honour of thy majesty, and of thy wondrous works.

6 And men shall speak of the might of thy terrible acts: and I will declare thy greatness.

7 They shall abundantly utter the memory of thy great goodness, and shall sing of thy righteousness.

8 The LORD is gracious, and full of compassion; slow to anger, and of great mercy.

9 The LORD is good to all: and his tender mercies are over all his works.

10 All thy works shall praise thee, O LORD; and thy saints shall bless thee.

MAR 26TH

11 They shall speak of the glory of thy kingdom, and talk of thy power;

12 To make known to the sons of men his mighty acts, and the glorious majesty of his kingdom.

13 Thy kingdom is an everlasting kingdom, and thy dominion endureth throughout all generations.

IN FOCUS

Paul's son Jeremy caught him off guard with a typical "5-year-old" question. While waving a celery strip like a symphony conductor, he asked, "Where does music come from?"

Paul was in his home office listening to his favorite music station and organizing his notes for an important business meeting the next day. So Paul did what all good fathers do when they can't be distracted: He told his son to ask his mother.

Minutes later, Jeremy came to the door again. Smiling from ear to ear, with his celery stick beating in rhythm, he asked, "What is music anyway?"

Paul sat down at his desk, lifted his son onto his lap, and scratched his head. Looking into the expectant eyes of his offspring, he took a stab at the question. "Music is the words our hearts make...and —"

Before he could finish, Jeremy's attention went off in another direction. "Do angels sing like people?" Jeremy asked.

Paul was a little perplexed about where his son's questions were coming from. "Jeremy, why are you asking all these questions about music and songs?"

"Last night after I said my prayers and Mommy turned off the light, I thought I heard angels singing, like Grandma used to say; so I started singing with them. When I told my friend at school, he said music can't come from nowhere; you need a CD player. And angels can't sing because they don't have lips."

His father hugged him and said, "Don't listen to your friend. Music comes from God. And angels in heaven sing praises to God all the time."

In Psalm 145, we are taught a hymn of praise to God for His greatness about which one generation tells the next. The more we praise the Lord, the more we can appreciate the little things He does in our lives.

THE PEOPLE, PLACES, AND TIMES

Kingdom. The phrase "kingdom of God" is not found in the Old Testament; however, the concept is echoed from the mouths of prophets and psalmists. The Lord is referred to as "King," both of Israel and of earth. The Old Testament prophets looked forward to the day when the entire world would acknowledge God's rule (Numbers 23:21; 2 Kings 19:15; Psalms 29:10; 47:2; 93:1-2; 96:10; 97:1-9; 99:1-4; 145:11-13; Isaiah 6:5; 43:15; Jeremiah 46:18). The word "kingdom" also refers to the spiritual reign of God in the hearts of believers (Luke 17:20-21). In the New Testament, Jesus frequently preached and instructed His disciples to seek after the kingdom (Matthew 6:33; Mark 1:14). Believers are encouraged to pray for God's kingdom; sinners who have not repented cannot enter the kingdom of God, which is reserved for the saints of God (Ephesians 5:5).

BACKGROUND

This particular Davidic psalm expresses the sentiment of praise to God for all He has done. In the book of Psalms, praise is usually directed to God and often shared with others. When we praise the Lord, we are conveying appreciation, respect, and gratitude toward Him. When studying this psalm, keep in mind all that God has

done on earth and in our lives. Praise is the vehicle by which believers express thankfulness for God's creativity, blessings, and forgiveness. Praise also communicates our heartfelt love for our Lord. God is just, loving, and faithful and deserves our praise. Christian songs tell us that when we praise the Lord, He inhabits the praises of His people. God adores praise, and His heart is pleased when genuine praise is articulated from the hearts of His children.

AT-A-GLANCE

1. God Is Worthy (Psalm 145:1-3)
2. God Is Wonderful (vv. 4-7)
3. God Is Merciful (vv. 8-10)
4. God Is Everlasting (vv. 11-13)

IN DEPTH

1. God Is Worthy (Psalm 145:1-3)

The word "worthy" means having merit or value. As mentioned in our earlier lessons, God is worthy of our praise. He is deserving of our honest admiration because He is God. In the first four verses of this psalm, the psalmist gives a few reasons why we should praise the Lord. The writer offers no explanation for his praise; he simply says, "I will extol and bless the name of the Lord forever." To "extol" means to worship God. To bless the name of the Lord requires exaltation, lifting His name above every name. Praise suggests that we pay tribute to God and declare His righteousness throughout the world.

"Forever" means without end and implies that praising God should never cease. There are no set limitations on the amount of time we should dedicate to honoring the Lord. We are to engage in active, perpetual praise. Inexorable admiration for God is very important. We should maintain a standard of praise in front of our children and allow our offspring to experience the art of worship. As worship becomes a way of life, a tradition is formed and values are transferred from one generation to the next. Ultimately, praising God becomes a lifelong and long-lasting experience that is practiced by each generation. It is also imperative that the church teach its congregants to praise the Lord.

The psalmist writes, "Every day will I bless thee" (v. 2). This precept tells us that on a daily basis our lips should honor the Lord with praise. When we think about praise, some of us can attest to the many different forms of worship, such as giving, serving, and stewardship. However, all these different avenues of devotion are called for and required by God, but none should take the place of blessing God through genuine praise. Praise is our heart's response to God. Praise tells God that we love Him. Praise grabs God's attention and whispers how wonderful He is in His ear. Praise pulls on the heartstrings of God and lets our enemies know that God is supreme.

The psalmist describes the Lord's greatness as "unsearchable" (v. 3). The word "unsearchable" indicates that something is imponderable, inscrutable, and beyond search. God is immeasurable. We can earnestly study the Word of God; yet, during our lifetime we will never comprehend all there is to know about God. The Bible informs us that God's ways are superior to our ways and His thoughts are higher than our thoughts (Isaiah 55:8). The magnitude of our Lord is beyond research. It is His unfathomable and mystifying qualities that draw us closer to Him. We yearn for a deeper and more meaningful relationship with Him. Although we will never know everything about God, Scripture encourages us to seek the Lord with all our heart. Through diligent pursuit of God, we will find Him (Jeremiah 29:13). However, in our search for God, what will the Lord find us to be like? Will He find that we are harboring a contrite spirit—or animosity in our hearts? The Lord is aware of all our issues; this understanding should quicken a reverent attitude in our approach to Him.

God's preeminence is worthy of praise. He does not have to prove His worthiness. The evidence of why we should adore Him is exemplified through all He creates. The Lord is not required to prove His credibility. Just read the Bible. All we need to do is open our eyes or recall where we were prior to salvation; then we can confirm His greatness. God's "work ethic" is impeccable, His character flawless, and His position unimpeachable. No one or nothing compares with Him.

2. God Is Wonderful (vv. 4-7)

In order for a whole generation of people to declare the work of one individual, the accomplishments of that person would have to be extraordinary. Historians write books about the achievements of great men and women who have made significant contributions to society. We learn of these noteworthy achievements from reading books and going to school. Our society employs a variety of forums to pay tribute to prominent people (e.g., presidential faces are printed on currency, the names of war heroes are engraved on memorial walls, handprints of Hollywood legends are cemented in concrete, athletic superstars are eulogized in a hall of fame).

All these forums are wonderful, and these people are great. Nonetheless, man's achievements pale in comparison to the accomplishments of God. God still holds "first place" in the hall of fame of success. His handprint may not be molded on the streets of Hollywood, but from His hand, dust gave birth to man, and in the Potter's hands, we are transformed into the image of His Son, Jesus Christ. His name may not be engraved on the walls with those of fallen heroes, but His name is esteemed from the lips of every believer. It is at the name of Jesus that every knee shall bow, and every tongue will confess that He is Lord (Philippians 2:10-11).

God is always true to His promises, and the wonderful achievements of the Lord benefit the entire world. This is not always the case with man's efforts. For example, there are some laws created by man that offer temporary solutions to ongoing problems. God gives us a permanent solution to every problem in the form of His Son, Jesus Christ. Man establishes world records that will be broken by contenders. God's record is indestructible. There are no contenders with God. There will always be faster cyclists and speedier runners and quarterbacks who will break world records, but there will never be another authority who can outproduce what God has created. We cannot outshine God's track record. When we look at what God has performed through our lives, we can stand as a personal witness to His extraordinary achievements.

He works in every event and situation to shape and transform our lives according to His Word. The Lord is a wonderful God.

3. God Is Merciful (vv. 8-10)

The compassionate acts of God are endless. The Psalms echo God's divine mercy in His treatment of His people. Despite the times when God's people disobeyed and had a rebellious attitude, the Lord had compassion on them. The Bible is full of events that demonstrate God's unyielding mercy. The Word of God reminds us that He has removed our transgressions and iniquities to the east and west of us, never shall the two meet (Psalm 103:11-12). God's love reaches to the highest heaven. This kind of agape love is impossible for us to fathom. God is patient and slow to anger. He desires to see all come to repentance. The Bible illustrates God's leniency toward His people and provides numerous examples of the Lord protecting His sheep against "ferocious wolves." God is the good and perfect Shepherd. He meticulously watches over His sheep, ensuring that not even one little sheep is lost. The Lord does not treat us as our sin deserves; He remembers that we were formed from the dust of the earth (Psalm 103:10, 14). The Lord loves us unconditionally and has the divine capacity to look beyond our faults. When God looks at us, He sees us according to the perfect righteousness of Jesus Christ—a righteousness provided by His blood applied by our faith in Him. The blood of Jesus cleanses us from all impurities. It is only by the blood of the Lamb that we have access to the throne of God. It is by God's mercy and our Lord Jesus Christ that we are presented faultless before almighty God (Jude 1:24-25). The love of God should provoke us to praise His precious name, thanking Him for all He has done for us.

As children of God, we should regularly pray for God's mercy on the unsaved. At one time we all stood on the other side of salvation as enemies of God. The Lord is our perfect example of how to extend mercy to those who don't know Him. Jesus sternly warned His disciples that the mercy of God is poured unto the lives of those who show mercy toward others (Matthew 5:7).

4. God Is Everlasting (vv. 11-13)

To ensure that effectual and continuous praise comes from our souls, our hearts should be filled to capacity with the Word of God. The Word of God introduces us to God's will and His ways. Genuine praise comes from knowing who God is and understanding that His kingdom continues forever. God is the Alpha and the Omega, the first and the last. He is the beginning and the end (Revelation 22:13; Exodus 3:14). It is difficult to picture perpetuity. Eternity is something we cannot grasp. Our minds take miniature snapshots of what eternity looks like, but the concept remains vague. When we read the Psalms, we get a heavenly glimpse of the kingdom of God. When we read the Scriptures, our minds are tantalized by a taste of paradise, which is revealed by the splendor, beauty, and perfection of heaven. We know heaven is where God and Jesus live and the place allocated for all believers. We hear sermons preached on God's authority on Earth and in heaven and about how His kingdom will last forever; yet, we are not quite sure what all that entails. Nevertheless, we take comfort in knowing, as ambassadors for Christ, that we have the "kingdom of God" living inside of us. We are co-laborers with Jesus and are commissioned to make disciples for God's kingdom on earth. Our lives are the closest some people may ever come to reading the Bible. Our lives are the only "mighty acts" some people will ever experience. To that end, we should let the light of Jesus shine brightly wherever we go and display the everlasting love of the God we serve (Matthew 28:18-20; Luke 17:21; Romans 8:17; 2 Corinthians 5:20).

SEARCH THE SCRIPTURES

1. What is meant by "I will extol thee, my God, O king" (Psalm 145:1)?

2. What does the psalmist say about the greatness of God (v. 3)?

3. What will endure forever and have dominion throughout all generations (v. 13)?

DISCUSS THE MEANING

1. If praise is essential and important to God, why do some adults struggle with giving God praise?

2. What insights have been gained in recognizing that God is worthy, wonderful, and merciful?

3. What are the difficulties some adults may have in conceptualizing the everlasting attributes of God?

LESSON IN OUR SOCIETY

The number of traffic tickets issued to motorists has skyrocketed. Our hectic lifestyles and the need to be in two places at the same time are contributing factors for the increase. Similarly, we speed in our cars like we speed through our walk with God. Our busy schedules perpetuate this forgetfulness, and we neglect to pause and give God thanks. If it had not been for the Lord's mercy, we would not have the car, the house, or the job to pay for everything we own. Ask yourself these questions: "Do I take time on a daily basis to thank God for all He has done for me?" "Do I take His mercy for granted?" "Am I speeding through life and not giving Him well-deserved praise?"

MAKE IT HAPPEN

Pray and ask the Lord to check your heart "speedometer." Make arrangements to spend at least five minutes a day thanking and praising the Lord for all He has done. Increase the time by 5 minutes each week until you are spending at least 20 minutes a day praising God and meditating on His Word. Share your insights with the class next week.

FOLLOW THE SPIRIT

What God wants me to do:

_____

_____

REMEMBER YOUR THOUGHTS

Special insights I have learned:

_____

_____

MORE LIGHT ON THE TEXT

Psalm 145:1-13

The theme of this psalm is the praise of God, for His magnificent attributes and marvelous deeds. It is written in the acrostic form; every verse begins with a successive letter of the Hebrew alphabet. This acrostic scheme was used to help memorize specific psalms.

1 I will extol thee, my God, O king; and I will bless thy name for ever and ever. 2 Every day will I bless thee; and I will praise thy name for ever and ever.

In verse 1, the psalmist exhibits a deep and personal relationship with his Creator and King. He displays a total devotion to God. "I will bless the LORD at all times: his praise shall continually be in my mouth" (Psalm 34:1). The Lord is always faithful and loyal to His covenant people. Therefore, the psalmist calls on the people of God to praise Him without ceasing. We should praise our God and King every day regardless of the cares and challenges we may face.

3 Great is the LORD, and greatly to be praised; and his greatness is unsearchable.

Here, the psalmist provides a reason why we should praise the Creator. God is great; therefore, He is to be praised greatly. Every fiber of our being is called to glorify God because He is worthy of our praise. Psalm 150:6 states, "Let every thing that hath breath praise the LORD." This psalm summons us as living, breathing creatures to give praise to our Creator and King. God's greatness is so vast that we cannot begin to explore or fully comprehend it.

4 One generation shall praise thy works to another, and shall declare thy mighty acts.

The praise of God's wonderful works shall be handed down from generation to generation. His "mighty" acts (*Heb. geburah,* **gheb-oo-raw'**, meaning strength, valor, and bravery) are unparalleled. We must remember the importance of sharing with the next generation our own personal experiences of God's love, justice, patience, and chastisements. Many of the old Negro spirituals that were handed down to us from our ancestors were born out of pain and a sense of comfort and assurance that God loved us and was faithful to His salvation promises.

5 I will speak of the glorious honor of thy majesty, and of thy wondrous works.

The psalmist testifies to God's "glorious" (*kabowd*) "honour" (*hadar*). The Hebrew word *kabowd* (**kaw-bode'**) means glorious, abundance, and riches, and the Hebrew word *hadar* (**haw-dawr'**) means splendor and majesty. The psalmist speaks of God's "wondrous" (*pala'*) "works" (*dabar*). The Hebrew word *pala'* (**paw-law'**) means marvelous, wonderful, surpassing, or extraordinary, and the Hebrew word *dabar* (**daw-baw'**) means speech, word, utterance, or acts. The psalmist does not make a distinction between the words of God and the acts of God. Why? Because they are interwoven.

Not only is God's Word meaningful in what it says, but it is powerful in what it does. It is truly efficacious. God's Word created the universe (Psalm 33:6). The Word of God is omnipotent. It will not return void but shall accomplish its purpose (Isaiah 55:11). There is no word (promise) that is too hard for God to fulfill (Genesis 18:14; Jeremiah 32:27). No word of God shall be void of its power (Luke 1:37). No word of God shall be void of its meaning. God's Word is always an expression of His character, wisdom, and plan (Deuteronomy 4:5-8).

The Bible gives numerous accounts of God's wondrous works. Hebrews 1:10 (NIV) states, "In the beginning, O Lord, you laid the foundations of the earth, and the heavens are the work of your hands."

6 And men shall speak of the might of thy terrible acts: and I will declare thy greatness. 7 They shall abundantly utter the memory of thy great goodness, and shall sing of thy righteousness.

The Hebrew word for "might" is *'ezuwz*, **ez-ooz'**, meaning strength, power, or fierceness. The Hebrew word for "terrible acts" is *yare'*, **yaw-ray'** and means awesome, fearful, or astonishing. The Bible gives us numerous displays of God's fierceness. The plagues of Egypt (Exodus 9:14) and the Passover (Exodus 12:11-13) are excellent examples. God's justice and wrath are equal and fair for all. Romans 2:6-8 (NIV) states, "God 'will give to each person according to what he has done.' To those who by persistence in doing good seek glory, honor and immortality, he will give eternal life. But for those who are self-seeking and who reject the truth and follow evil, there will be wrath and anger."

The Hebrew word for "utter" is *naba* (**naw-bah'**), which means to gush forth or bubble up. The psalmist wants us to know that the many memories of God's great goodness will flow from the lips of men. These abundant utterances constitute joyful celebration. Thus, His people will celebrate "the memory of God's great" and abundant goodness, and shall joyfully "sing of His righteousness" to the whole world.

8 The LORD is gracious, and full of compassion; slow to anger, and of great mercy.

The psalmist continues to share the great attributes of God, which gives us reason and purpose to praise Him. He leads us to celebrate the Lord's goodness and righteousness because of His great Name (Exodus 34:6-7). In other words, He is "gracious" (Heb. *channuwn*, **khan-noon'**) and full of "compassion" (Heb. *achuwm*, **rakhoom'**); slow to "anger" (Heb. *'aph*, **af**), and of great "mercy" (Heb. *checed*, **kheh'-sed**, meaning goodness, kindness, or faithfulness). This Name is not just a label; His Name is who He is.

God knows our sorrows and forgives our sin infinitely. First John 1:9 states, "If we confess our sins, he is faithful and just to forgive us our sins, and to cleanse us from all unrighteousness."

9 The LORD is good to all: and his tender mercies are over all his works. 10 All thy works shall praise thee, O LORD; and thy saints shall bless thee.

In this verse, the Hebrew word for "works" is *maaseh* (**mah-as-eh**), which means deeds or labor. God's goodness and compassion extend to the entire creation. His goodness is exhibited in many ways. His kingship is glorious, His sovereignty is benevolent, and His countless acts are redemptive.

God is praised by all His creations. This is evident and revealed in nature by His awesome majesty displayed in the rising and setting of the sun, the heavenly display of stars at night, the splendor of a snowcapped mountain range, or an afternoon breeze that blows through the trees. For Christians, praise is a natural response to God's love.

11 They shall speak of the glory of thy kingdom, and talk of thy power; 12 To make known to the sons of men his mighty acts, and the glorious majesty of his kingdom.

Praise will come from all He has made because all things were made to praise Him. Praise for God's mighty deeds will be passed from one generation to the next. All power comes from God, and it is through God's awesome power that we live and move and have our being. We will never find balance in life until God is at the center of all our education, proclamation, celebration, and meditation. What is the mark and passion of God's people (the saints)? To bless God. God's covenant love evokes the praise and thanksgiving of His saints.

The saints make known the mighty acts of God by all means at their disposal. God's kingdom, power, and glory are matchless in all the universe, and the saints will not be silent about this. They will not be satisfied until all mankind knows about God's mighty acts and the glorious splendor of His kingdom. Here the psalmist gives us the *doxological* basis for the Great Commission. In other words, the *glory of God* should be a central motivation for the saints in making disciples of all nations.

13 Thy kingdom is an everlasting kingdom, and thy dominion endureth throughout all generations.

The Hebrew word for "dominion" is *memshalah* (**mem-shaw-law'**), which is translated as "rule" or "realm." God's kingdom will last forever. The governments of humankind will one day cease to exist, but God's reign is eternal.

Unlike the present temporal reality, which is subject to change and decay, the kingdom of God is stable and permanent. It is "everlasting." The dominion of God is not only magnificent, glorious, and powerful (mighty), but it is loving, compassionate, and faithful—with God showing great concern for the needs of His creatures.

The Lord Jesus beautifully expressed this truth in His Sermon on the Mount: "Look at the birds of the air; they do not sow or reap or store away in barns, and yet your heavenly Father feeds them. Are you not much more valuable than they? Who of you by worrying can add a single hour to his life? And why do you worry about clothes? See how the lilies of the field grow. They do not labor or spin. Yet I tell you that not even Solomon in all his splendor was dressed like one of these. If that is how God clothes the grass of the field, which is here today and tomorrow is thrown into the fire, will he not much more clothe you, O you of little faith? So do not worry, saying, 'What shall we eat?' or 'What shall we drink?' or 'What shall we wear?' For the pagans run after all these things, and your heavenly Father knows that you need them" (Matthew 6:26-32, NIV).

How then should we respond to God for His matchless covenant faithfulness? With thanksgiving and praise. How can we best express thanksgiving and praise? By doing what Jesus told us to do: "...seek first His kingdom and His righteousness." Because God's generosity is more than abundant, we have nothing to fear or worry about, for in seeking His kingdom, all the things we need will be given to us as well (Matthew 6:33).

DAILY BIBLE READINGS

M: Glory in God's Holy Name
Psalm 105:1-11

T: I Sing Your Praise
Psalm 138

W: Sing to God a New Song
Psalm 149

T: Praise the Lord!
Psalm 150

F: I Will Extol You, O God
Psalm 145:1-7

S: Your Kingdom Is an Everlasting Kingdom
Psalm 145:8-13a

S: God Is Faithful
Psalm 145:13b-21

TEACHING TIPS

April 2
Bible Study Guide 5

1. Words You Should Know

A. Sabeans (Job 1:15) *Sheba* (Heb.)—A Semitic people known to be "men of stature" (Isaiah 45:14) who settled in Sheba, known today as Marib, located in Yemen.

B. Cursed his day (3:1) *qalal yowm* (Heb.)—Job "cursed his day" as a rhetorical wish to escape life's adversities, hardships, and difficulties "without having lived." To curse one's day was a way of lamenting the worthlessness of one's life.

C. Give Up the Ghost (v. 11) *gava'* (Heb.)—To be ready to die; to be about to die; to expire.

2. Teacher Preparation

A. Read and memorize the KEEP IN MIND verse. Read the FOCAL VERSES until you begin to feel Job's sense of loss and appreciate his loyalty and commitment to God.

B. Read IN FOCUS, THE PEOPLE, PLACES, AND TIMES, and BACKGROUND.

C. You will need newsprint or a chalkboard for this lesson.

3. Starting the Lesson

A. Review the LESSON AIM. Then ask the students to read the IN FOCUS story silently.

B. With your students' assistance, list on newsprint or a chalkboard 10 to 15 national or international tragedies that have occurred within the past two or three years.

C. Have two or three of your students share a personal tragedy that has occurred in their own lives. Remind your students that tragedy is a part of living in a world where evil and human error exist. The question is: "How can we best manage and live with tragedy?"

4. Getting into the Lesson

A. Remind the students that Job's story teaches several lessons about "living with tragedy." Have one of your students read the FOCAL VERSES aloud.

B. Discuss the question, "How was Job able to manage and live with his tragedy?" Expand the discussion to include some of the other questions under DISCUSS THE MEANING.

5. Relating the Lesson to Life

A. Ask the students to share any personal experiences concerning how their faith in God has helped them to manage and live with personal tragedies.

B. Guide the students in praying for those who may be struggling with unresolved issues relating to some tragedy.

6. Arousing Action

A. Remind the students that while God does not send our tragedies, He can use them as occasions for our spiritual strengthening and growth.

B. With some encouraging and affirming words, close the session by calling the students' attention to the KEEP IN MIND verse.

WORSHIP GUIDE

For the Superintendent or Teacher
Theme: When Tragedy Occurs
Theme Song: "Great Is Thy Faithfulness"
Scripture: Psalm 27:1-5
Song: "Joyful, Joyful, We Adore Thee"
Meditation: We thank You, Lord, for Your presence with us during our darkest hours. Be patient with us, and help us to trust You when tragedy occurs. Amen.

WHEN TRAGEDY OCCURS

Bible Background • JOB 1–3
Printed Text • JOB 1:14–15, 18–19, 22; 3:1–3, 11
Devotional Reading • PSALM 22:1–11

LESSON AIM

By the end of the lesson, we will:

KNOW and discuss some of the insights for living with suffering caused by tragedy;

BE CHALLENGED to share our feelings about specific tragedies in our own lives; and

IDENTIFY ways to work with God to use our suffering to serve a higher purpose.

KEEP IN MIND

"Shall we receive good at the hand of God, and shall we not receive evil? In all this did not Job sin with his lips" (from Job 2:10).

FOCAL VERSES

Job 1:14 And there came a messenger unto Job, and said, The oxen were plowing, and the asses feeding beside them:

15 And the Sabeans fell upon them, and took them away; yea, they have slain the servants with the edge of the sword; and I only am escaped alone to tell thee.

1:18 While he was yet speaking, there came also another, and said, Thy sons and thy daughters were eating and drinking wine in their eldest brother's house:

19 And, behold, there came a great wind from the wilderness, and smote the four corners of the house, and it fell upon the young men, and they are dead; and I only am escaped alone to tell thee.

1:22 In all this Job sinned not, nor charged God foolishly.

3:1 After this opened Job his mouth, and cursed his day.

2 And Job spake, and said,

3 Let the day perish wherein I was born, and the night in which it was said, There is a man child conceived.

3:11 Why died I not from the womb? why did I not give up the ghost when I came out of the belly?

LESSON OVERVIEW

LESSON AIM
KEEP IN MIND
FOCAL VERSES
IN FOCUS
THE PEOPLE, PLACES, AND TIMES
BACKGROUND
AT-A-GLANCE
IN DEPTH
SEARCH THE SCRIPTURES
DISCUSS THE MEANING
LESSON IN OUR SOCIETY
MAKE IT HAPPEN
FOLLOW THE SPIRIT
REMEMBER YOUR THOUGHTS
MORE LIGHT ON THE TEXT
DAILY BIBLE READINGS

APR
2ND

IN FOCUS

After Terry lost his daughter in a drive-by shooting, he still remained a faithful believer. He even forgave the shooters. But he continued to struggle with the mission that God had given him. God wanted him to evangelize the unprivileged children in the community where his daughter was murdered.

He went to his minister for counseling, where he hoped to find answers that might reconcile his rebellion against God.

After engaging in small talk, Terry released his well of emotions. "I want to continue the work God set out for me, but I can't. I keep asking myself, Why did God let this happen? And why should I go back into that community?"

His minister listened to Terry's pain and let the Holy Spirit guide his words. "Listen, Terry, you must lean on the fact that all the promises of God are endless but they all end with a period. We cannot change God's periods."

Terry, confused, asked, "What do you mean?"

"Death is a period; let me explain. God has an eternal story that He has written. When acts of

God, like a death in the family, floods, or tornadoes come a believer's way, we cannot help but ask God, "Why? We are good people. Why did you allow that to happen to us?" What I'm suggesting is that instead of bringing up the question marks, we all must strive to scratch out a comma."

Terry's mouth sagged in disappointment and his eyes bored into the minister's face "What does a comma have to do with the questions that are weighing so heavy on my heart?"

"A comma means to wait and take a breath—wait for the answer. Sometimes the answers to life's questions come only by trusting what God has written on the next page in eternity. If God wants you in that community, He may very well use your suffering for His higher purpose."

One of the many lessons from the book of Job is living with tragedy. When we continually focus only on our pain, we may be missing God's divine purpose in our adversity.

THE PEOPLE, PLACES, AND TIMES

Job. The central character in the book of Job may have lived during the time of Abraham, Isaac, and Jacob. He was "perfect and upright." He "feared God, and eschewed evil" (Job 1:1). He was a responsible husband and father (vv. 2, 5) and was richly blessed with material goods (v. 3). He had good health and was highly respected by others. In short, Job "was the greatest of all the men of the east" (v. 3). "God's intimate friendship blessed his house" (29:4, NIV).

The Land of Uz. Bible scholars tell us that the location is uncertain. Some believe, however, that it was in the Arabian or Syrian Desert, east of Palestine—east of the Jordan River near Canaan (Israel) where the Israelites would later live. Lamentations 4:21 and Genesis 36:28 suggest that Uz was in the vicinity of Edom. From the Scriptures, most scholars know that Uz had succulent, thriving pastures and crops (Job 1:3). They also know that it lay close to the Sabeans and Chaldeans, who raided them (vv. 14-17).

Eliphaz. He was the first and most prominent of Job's three friends. He had come from a great distance to comfort an ailing buddy (Job 2:11).

Scriptures describe him as a distinguished thinker or sage of Teman in Edom, which was known for its wisdom (Jeremiah 49:7).

Bildad. He was the second friend to visit Job, a Shuhite (one of the sons of Abraham and Keturah from Genesis 25:2; Job 2:11; 8:1, 18:1; 25:1; 42:9). Bible scholars believe that Bildad's home was the Assyrian land of *Shuhu*, south of Haran, near the middle Euphrates River.

Elihu. He was Job's young friend, who raised the discussion of Job's suffering to a higher theological level. He tried to show a hurting Job that greater wisdom comes by inspiration, instead of human experience and tradition (Job 32:2-6, 8-9; 34:1; 35:1; 36:1).

Zophar. He was also a friend and counselor of Job (2:11; 11:1; 20:1; 42:9). His home is unknown, but Bible scholars surmise that it was in Edom or northern Arabia. He agreed with Job's other friends in attributing Job's suffering to his sins and spoke bluntly and harshly to Job.

Bibliography
Pfeiffer, Charles F., Howard F. Vos, and John Rea, eds. *Wycliffe Bible Dictionary.* Peabody, Mass.: Hendrickson Publishers, 1998, 257-258, 517, 520, 931, 1762, 1850.

BACKGROUND

In Job's day, trouble and suffering were viewed as the consequence of one's sin. It was believed that since God is love and all-powerful, He cannot be the source or cause of suffering. Moreover, it was reasoned that since God is holy and has zero tolerance for sin, He cannot let those who sin go unpunished. This line of thought led to the conclusion that sin is at the root of all suffering, trouble, and pain.

Each of Job's peers, Eliphaz, Bildad, and Zophar, speak from this vantage point. From their perspective, Job's tragic situation was evidence of some unconfessed sin in his life.

For example, Eliphaz questions Job (Job 4:7-8; 22:5, 6). Bildad also voices the perspective that sin is behind all suffering (Job 8:3-6, 13; see also Job 18:21). Zophar affirms the thought that Job's suffering is because of some sin in Job's life (Job

11:6). In fact, Zophar proceeds to plead with Job to confess his sin in order that he might again experience God's peace (Job 11:14-19).

These assumptions, however, do not speak to Job's situation. Job is innocent! His defense begs the question, "Why do the righteous suffer?" Why do bad things happen to good people? And what are good people who suffer to do—curse God, or embrace their pain and recommit their lives to His care? What are good people to do when tragedy occurs and leaves in its wake a torrent of suffering and trouble?

Job is confident that God will eventually come to his aid and give him the resources he needs to go on trusting God and to live creatively with the suffering and pain occasioned by tragedy. What faith! This is the faith that overcomes the world. This is the faith that overcomes anything and everything that life may hurl at those who dare to place their lives in God's hands.

AT-A-GLANCE

1. Job's Tragedies (Job 1:14-15)

2. Job's Nonverbal Response to His Tragedies (vv. 18-19)

3. Job's Faith Response to His Tragedies (v. 22)

4. Job's Faith Bogs Down in Despair (3:1-3, 11)

IN DEPTH

1. Job's Tragedies (Job 1:14-15)

Truly, Job was a godly man who left no stone unturned in his devotion to God; yet, within a matter of seconds, he received the worst possible news from four messengers, one on the heels of the other. He was wiped out by natural calamity and the vicious attacks of men. All these tragedies were the work of the Accuser, Satan. Job had no idea that Satan was using him to challenge God. Nor did Job know that his suffering would be used by God to defeat Satan. Job's life had become a combat zone where God and Satan battled for Job's allegiance.

God was pleased to announce to Satan that Job was His unique and most faithful servant. Satan countered God's boast by charging that Job was faithful only because he enjoyed God's favor. In short, Satan told God that when His blessings ceased to flow in Job's direction, "he will curse thee to thy face"' (Job 1:11). For reasons known only to Him, God responded to Satan's challenge in a way that would ultimately test Job's resolve to be faithful in the absence of divine blessings.

As soon as God released Job into Satan's power, Job was struck with a terrible series of tragedies. The writer uses four different scenes to illustrate that over an unknown period of time, Job was deprived of every material blessing and nearly all family and friendship ties. Job was completely stripped of all God's favors. Eventually his health failed and he was left destitute (2:7). Satan had Job where he wanted him, namely, outside of God's apparent protection.

We should note, however, that Job's destitute position was due, not to Satan's power, but to God's power. The writer wants his readers to know that Satan could do nothing to Job without God's permission. While Job may not have been immediately aware of God's active and continuing intervention, he was aware of God's availability. Suffering may blind us to God's active intervention, but it need not blind us to His availability. God is always available to us even though we may not be able to see any evidence of His intervention. Faith enables us to see that God is always keeping watch over His own.

2. Job's Nonverbal Response to His Tragedies (vv. 18-19)

Upon hearing the reports of his tragic losses, Job remained silent. The reader is informed of Job's silence by the writer's use of the poetic device, "While he (i.e., the messenger of Job's bad news) was yet speaking" (Job 1:16-18). This phrase implies that Job's first response to the tragedies reported to him was one of complete silence. The sudden news about the successive tragedies renders Job speechless. He says nothing. Job is deeply shaken. He is able to express himself only with the mourning gestures known in ancient Israel. He "rent his mantle [tore his robe], and shaved his head, and fell down upon the ground" (v. 20).

Silence is a natural first response to tragedy,

which affects us personally. We cannot immediately put our feelings into words. We are shocked, stunned, and, in some ways, traumatized. Words elude us. We can only cry and groan inwardly. We may even express ourselves in a primordial scream that expresses our sense of helplessness in the face of circumstances that we wish were different but know we cannot change. Our emotions swing back and forth between anger and denial.

3. Job's Faith Response to His Tragedies (v. 22)

Faith in God is a tremendous source of strength when one is facing tragic loss. Handling the personal stress occasioned by loss is one of life's greatest challenges, and it requires a strong and viable faith.

William E. Hulme has helpfully noted that Job went "from a position of prominence in the community to becoming the butt of scoffers." It is instructive to note, however, that "In all this Job sinned not, nor charged God foolishly" (Job 1:22). This statement, which summarizes Job's faith response to the tragedies that had befallen him, teaches at least two things about faith. The first is that faith is not dependent upon the constant flow of God's blessings. Second, while faith may be tested and is often severely shaken, it is not necessarily destroyed by tragic loss.

Although the culmination of Job's losses did not destroy his faith, it did create for him a religious problem, best summarized in the question: What kind of God would allow these tragic things to happen to me when I have been so faithful to Him?

4. Job's Faith Bogs Down in Despair (3:1-3, 11)

The religious problem that Job faced brought him to the very edge of despair. His days of silence had ended. His days of questioning God's mysterious ways with those who trusted Him had begun. Job began to entertain thoughts that caused him to have some doubts about God's fairness and justice. Job knew that he had done everything he could to sustain an ever-growing and intimate relationship with God. What he could not understand, however, was why God had ceased bestowing His blessings. Job wanted desperately to know why God had withdrawn His care and favor.

We tend to be well versed in faith's capacity to believe. We have much homework to do, however, if we are to embrace faith's capacity to doubt, or to at least question God's ways with us. Doubt is not faith's enemy, nor is it the opposite of faith. The opposite of faith is unbelief. Unbelief says, "There is no God with whom to discuss the tragedies of life." Faith that dares to doubt says, "There is a God whose ways I do not fully understand. Therefore, I will be honest about my doubts and pray that God will entertain my questions and in His own time reassure me of His care and guidance."

Job's religious problem is common to all who are challenged to live with the terrible consequences of tragedy. Have you ever been in a tragic situation and asked God for help, only to feel that He was not helping at all? You waited and waited, you kept on petitioning God to intervene and change your circumstances, and things grew worse.

Job is not hesitant about exercising the faith to engage with doubt. His first step toward dealing with his doubts involves being honest with himself, honest enough to admit his sense of anguish and despair over God's treatment of him. Job is to be commended for having the kind of faith that takes doubt seriously. He "opened. . . his mouth, and cursed his day" (Job 3:1). In other words, Job's situation of loss coupled with his bewilderment about God's ways result in his desire to die without having lived. Job is not threatening suicide here. Rather, he is lamenting the day of his birth. He reasons that if he had not been born, he would not have experienced the tragedies that had brought him to the point of despair.

Tragedy is a part of living in a fallen world. Moreover, God has not promised people of faith a life free of tragedy. He has promised, however, to be with us when tragedy occurs. In the face of tragedy, we may, like Job, rue the day of our birth. But let us pray that at the end of the day our faith, and our continued dialogue with God about our doubts, will give us the spiritual resources necessary to live victoriously with the consequences of tragedy.

SEARCH THE SCRIPTURES

1. In whose house were Job's sons and daughters partying (Job 1:18)?

2. "And, behold, there came a great wind from the _____, and smote the four corners of the _____, and it fell" (v. 19).

3. "After this opened Job his mouth, and _____ his day" (3:1).

4. "Why did I not give up the _____ when I came out of the belly?" (v. 11).

DISCUSS THE MEANING

1. What can faith do to help us live with tragedy?

2. What was the common thought or theological perspective of the times when tragedy visited Job?

3. What two things have you learned about living with tragedy?

LESSON IN OUR SOCIETY

Few, if any, people live tragedy-free lives. Tragedy comes with the territory of living in a fallen world, a world where sin and human error abound. Everyone is a potential recipient of some kind of tragedy. We would all do well, therefore, to develop a faith that does not give up on God when tragedy occurs. God is with us when we celebrate on the mountain peaks of life. He is also with us when we walk through the valley of the shadow of death. His guidance and His care are always at our disposal.

Therefore, we would do well to entrust our all, including our doubts, to God's care, and to dare to believe that He will work with people of goodwill to make tragedy's consequences serve some higher purpose. When we do this, our faith will live and grow all the more when tragedy occurs.

MAKE IT HAPPEN

This week, identify someone with whom you are acquainted who is living with the terrible consequences of some tragedy. Take the time to pray for them. Visit or call them and listen to their story. Raise with them the kinds of questions that will encourage them to discuss their doubts and questions with you and in prayer with God. Listen to them. Empathize with them. You will probably not have answers for their questions. You can, however, encourage them to share their feelings with God in the confidence that He cares and understands.

FOLLOW THE SPIRIT

What God wants me to do:

_____

_____

REMEMBER YOUR THOUGHTS

Special insights I have learned:

_____

_____

MORE LIGHT ON THE TEXT

Job 1:14-15, 18-19, 22; 3:1-3, 11

The title of this week's lesson isn't *if* tragedy occurs, but *when*. Unexpected tragedies are realities in all of our lives. Accidents, acts of nature, and deliberate criminal behavior are often the causes. Of the four tragedies that befell Job, two resulted from human actions and two from acts of nature. None occurred because of something Job had done.

The crush of crimes and calamities that confronted Job forced him to make a choice. Could he justify trusting God when faced with the unfairness of life? Or was the pain of tragedy a sufficient reason to deny God's love or His power to overcome evil, or both? People have struggled with this question in the past, and every living person must still seek answers for it today.

The setting of the book of Job appears to be before the formation of the nation of Israel. None of the main characters in the story, including Job, was from Israel. There is no reference to the patriarchs Abraham, Isaac, or Jacob, to Moses, the lawgiver, or to David, Israel's greatest king. In the 42 chapters of this book, there is only one mention of the law, or *torah* (Heb. **TOHR-ah,** meaning "instruction" (Job 22:22).

This point has led some scholars to suggest that Job could be the oldest book in the Bible. Three clues indicate that the story of Job was initially transmitted orally. It was not put into writing until long after Job's trials took place. First, many foreign words are used in Job that did not appear in the Hebrew language until after the captives returned from the exile. Second, the last three servants who arrived to announce disaster are introduced by the same phrase (Job 1:16, 18) and their announcements end with the exact same word (Job 1:15, 17, 19). This is typical of information that was told and retold over a long stretch of time. Third, Job's name means "the assailed," "the hated one," or "the persecuted one." This suggests that "Job" may be a nickname given in light of what he endured. In addition, almost the entire book of Job was written in the Hebrew form of poetry. This poetic form helped Hebrews memorize the parts of the Bible that God had inspired at that time. Unlike English poetry that rhymes, Hebrew poetry repeats words and makes use of emphases and parallel thoughts.

Job was a godly man. God described him to Satan as a "perfect (blameless) and upright" man (Job 1:1). He lived a blessed life. The second verse in chapter 1 tells us that Job had 10 children. Ten was not symbolic of perfection but of fullness or sufficiency. Seven of his children were sons; the number seven was symbolic of perfection. So with 10 children, 7 of whom were sons, Job had all a man could ask for in a family. In addition, Job was enormously rich. Verse 3 lists his possessions—sheep and camels in the thousands. Owning one camel was a sign of wealth and status. To have thousands of camels suggests that Job was a caravan operator or a dealer in camels. Job had 500 yoke of oxen. A yoke holds two oxen; thus, "500 yoke" means he owned 1,000 oxen. Taken together, these details tell us that Job was a highly successful, well-respected, happy, godly man. Yet all that was about to change.

14 And there came a messenger unto Job, and said, The oxen were plowing, and the asses feeding beside them.

This verse tells us that it was not winter, since the servants had the oxen out in the field plowing. All of Job's children had gathered for a family meal, which they took turns hosting. This shared responsibility suggests close family ties since the meals were not always held at the house of the eldest son, who traditionally became head of the family at his father's passing.

On the day of the dinner, a servant "messenger" (Heb. *mal'ak,* **mal-awk'**) rushed up to Job. This same word is translated "angel" when referring to a heavenly messenger. As one servant after another comes and reports another loss, Job does not realize that these calamities are evidence of God's confidence in him, rather than His displeasure.

15 And the Sabeans fell upon them, and took them away; yea, they have slain the servants with the edge of the sword; and I only am escaped alone to tell thee.

The Sabeans were a nomadic people from an area called Sheba about 1,000 miles from Job's region. Sheba was at the extreme southern tip of the Arabian peninsula. The queen of that desert kingdom traveled to Israel to inquire about Solomon's great wisdom (1 Kings 10:1-2). Elsewhere in the Bible, the Sabeans are known as traders and merchants (Job 6:19; Ezekiel 27:22), but nowhere else as robbers.

The messenger described a peaceful farm scene. Fields were being plowed to turn the soil after seed had been sown. Job's huge herd of donkeys were grazing in an adjoining pasture. Who would bother someone so rich, so prominent, "the greatest of all the men of the east" (Job 1:3)? Suddenly an army of vicious cutthroats swarmed over both herds, hacking down one servant after another. The Hebrew word for "slain" is *a'kah* (**haw-kaw'**), which means "slay" or "kill." The same word was used to describe savage, deadly attacks by bears or lions. In Deuteronomy 19:11, it is used to describe a vengeful, intentional murder.

People both then and now often make godless choices and behave in sinful ways that are contrary to what we would expect of them. As a result, innocent victims today are beaten, robbed, or murdered, just like Job's servants were.

1:18 While he was yet speaking, there came also another, and said, Thy sons and thy daughters were eating and drinking wine in their eldest brother's house: 19 And, behold, there came a

great wind from the wilderness, and smote the four corners of the house, and it fell upon the young men, and they are dead; and I only am escaped alone to tell thee.

Undoubtedly, Job's children shared in their father's prosperity. Verse 18 says that they were "eating and drinking wine." The word "eating" here means more than taking nourishment; the Hebrew word used is 'akal (aw-kal') and means to consume or devour. This indicates they were having a great feast.

Although our lesson is focused on the first and last of Job's tragedies, there were actually four. As the first servant came to announce a disaster, another servant came in and interrupted the servant who was giving his report. This interruption of the servant that was speaking was not an act of rudeness, but a result of his sense of urgency and alarm.

The first three events wiped out Job's wealth, but the fourth, the death of all his children, broke his heart. The "wind" (Heb. ruwach, roo'-akh) here implies a strong wind similar to that of a whirlwind or tornado. Job's sons and daughters were killed when the house "fell" on them (Heb. naphal, naw-fal').

Satan and evil are free to inflict harm and heartbreak only to the extent God allows. God didn't cause Job's problems to take place, but He did allow them. These tragedies caused Job to confront a question that we still struggle with today: Is suffering a good enough reason to deny God's love or power? NO!

1:22 In all this Job sinned not, nor charged God foolishly.

After all the tragedy he had gone through, Job still didn't sin! He didn't blow up at God or curse the Sabeans or Chaldeans who had stolen his oxen, donkeys, and camels.

In fact, despite his deep grief, Job proved his faith in God by praising Him while confessing the loss he was feeling (v. 21).

Verse 22 shows that although Job grieved terribly, he didn't sin when learning of his losses, nor did he sin later. "Sinned" here comes from the Hebrew word chata' (khaw-taw'), which means to miss a target or get off track. Job did not let these

disasters cause his faith in God to get off track. Instead, he fell face down on the ground in worship as a sign of submitting himself to God's will.

Job didn't charge God "foolishly" (Heb. tiphlah, tif-law'). Tiphlah is derived from the Hebrew word taphel meaning "unsavory" or "untempered." In other words, despite all he had lost, Job didn't accuse God of being angry or offended with him.

3:1 After this opened Job his mouth, and cursed his day. 2 And Job spake, and said,

Job was not using vulgar language. The word "cursed" (Heb. qalal, kaw-lal), as used here, means to make something unworthy, of no consequence, or contemptible. Job does not *curse* God; he simply despises the day he was born.

This verse occurs after a week of Job's silence. After Job's initial shock at his losses and reasons for grief, he had time to reflect. During that time, his wife came and told him he must have done something that she wasn't aware of. She ordered him to quit trying to act righteous and "curse God, and die" (2:9). Job broke his silence and expressed his bitterness and frustration over what had happened to him and his family. Although his answer might seem to be toward his wife, it was more likely that he was just responding to the situation.

Some Christians still think that anger about injustice or the tragic unfairness of life is evidence of spiritual immaturity. The book of Job does not support that attitude. Job 1:8; 2:3; and 42:7 show God's positive view of Job as a righteous man both *before* and *after* the tragedies he went through.

3 Let the day perish wherein I was born, and the night in which it was said, There is a man child conceived.

Here Job is shown at his lowest point. He felt there was nothing left that was worth living for. Job wished that the day he was born had never happened. The Hebrew word translated as "perish" is 'abad (aw-bad'), which means to vanish or to be forgotten or blotted out. Because of his anguish, Job wanted the day of his birth announcement forgotten and blotted out from the minds of men.

3:11 Why died I not from the womb? why did I not give up the ghost when I came out of the belly?

Job questions God. The word "died" (Heb. *muwth,* **mooth**) means to die as a result of a penalty or to be put to death. Here Job seems to be asking God, "If I was to suffer like this, why was I born? Why didn't I come out of the womb, take a breath, and die?" He was asking why he had to be born if he had to go through all this and come to this end.

Many people have asked questions as they coped with heartbreaking losses, agonizing pain, or vicious brutality. For the next two Sundays, churches all over the world will stop to remember the Cross God allowed His Son to endure and the Resurrection that followed. As Christians recall the Easter events, perhaps we will find a new sense of God's love and power in spite of the tragedies God allows, and find faith to trust His will and wisdom.

DAILY BIBLE READINGS

M: Job, A Blameless and Upright Man
Job 1:1-5
T: Satan Determines to Strike Job
Job 1:6-12
W: Job Loses All, But Remains Faithful
Job 1:13-22
T: Job Falls Ill, But Praises God
Job 2:1-10
F: Job Curses His Day of Birth
Job 3:1-10
S: Job Wishes for Death
Job 3:11-19
S: Job Questions God's Benevolence
Job 3:20-26

TEACHING TIPS

April 9
Bible Study Guide 6

1. Words You Should Know

A. Man that is born of woman (Job 14:1) *'adam yalad ishshah* (Heb.)—Since everyone is born of a woman, this is the author's way of saying "every person is mortal."

B. Fail (v. 11) *'azal* (Heb.)—To go away; to evaporate; to be used up.

C. Buzite (32:6) *Buwziy* (Heb.)—The name given to the Aramean tribe of the country of Buz, the location of which is uncertain.

2. Teacher Preparation

A. After reading the printed text, read it again from two modern translations (e.g., the *New International Version* and the *New Living Translation*).

B. Recall a time in your own life when you or a close friend faced what, at the time, appeared to be a hopeless situation. Identify and think about some of the questions that occupied your thoughts.

C. Review the LESSON AIM and study all sections of BIBLE STUDY GUIDE 6.

3. Starting the Lesson

A. Remind your students that this is Palm Sunday, the beginning of Holy Week—the week that we remember our Lord's Passion. Note also that Jesus was very much aware of the agony, the suffering, and the inevitable death that awaited Him as He rode into Jerusalem.

B. Write this question on the chalkboard or newsprint: "How do you think Jesus felt entering Jerusalem, knowing that in a few days He would be condemned as a criminal and crucified on a shameful cross?"

C. Without comment, give the students time to read the question silently.

D. Offer prayer, asking that God would teach us how to respond "when all seems hopeless."

4. Getting into the Lesson

A. Referring to last week's lesson, review the circumstances of Job's situation and his accompanying feelings of despair.

B. Remind the students that today's lesson teaches at least two things: 1) despair is part of human existence, and 2) we can count on God to be good, just, and all-powerful.

C. Have a student read the FOCAL VERSES.

D. Read and discuss the IN FOCUS story, THE PEOPLE, PLACES, AND TIMES, and the BACKGROUND section.

5. Relating the Lesson to Life

APR 9TH

A. Lead a discussion focusing on the DISCUSS THE MEANING questions.

B. Have the students share what they like about Job's faith and what his faith teaches us about handling despair.

6. Arousing Action

A. Review what is suggested in MAKE IT HAPPEN, and encourage the students to do it this week.

B. Close the session with prayer, thanking God for a faith that dares to believe that He will be our God, our source of strength and courage, even when all seems hopeless.

WORSHIP GUIDE

For the Superintendent or Teacher
Theme: When All Seems Hopeless
Theme Song: "My Faith Looks Up to Thee"
Scripture: John 16:33
Song: "Have Faith in God"
Meditation: When all seems hopeless, O God, help us to know that Your grace is sufficient. Amen.

WHEN ALL SEEMS HOPELESS

Bible Background • JOB 14; 32:1–8; 34:10–15; 37:14–24
Printed Text • JOB 14:1–2, 11–17; 32:6, 8; 34:12; 37:14, 22
Devotional Reading • JOB 36:24–33

LESSON AIM

By the end of the lesson, we will:

KNOW that faith alone does not prevent us from encountering hopeless situations;

REALIZE that faith does arm us to live creatively in what may seem to be hopeless situations; and

BE ENCOURAGED to develop the kind of faith that acknowledges and questions, yet makes a prayerful decision to trust God's ways.

KEEP IN MIND

"If a man die, shall he live again? all the days of my appointed time will I wait, till my change come" (Job 14:14).

LESSON OVERVIEW

LESSON AIM
KEEP IN MIND
FOCAL VERSES
IN FOCUS
THE PEOPLE, PLACES, AND TIMES
BACKGROUND
AT-A-GLANCE
IN DEPTH
SEARCH THE SCRIPTURES
DISCUSS THE MEANING
LESSON IN OUR SOCIETY
MAKE IT HAPPEN
FOLLOW THE SPIRIT
REMEMBER YOUR THOUGHTS
MORE LIGHT ON THE TEXT
DAILY BIBLE READINGS

FOCAL VERSES

Job 14:1 Man that is born of a woman is of few days, and full of trouble.

2 He cometh forth like a flower, and is cut down: he fleeth also as a shadow, and continueth not.

14:11 As the waters fail from the sea, and the flood decayeth and drieth up:

12 So man lieth down, and riseth not: till the heavens be no more, they shall not awake, nor be raised out of their sleep.

13 O that thou wouldest hide me in the grave, that thou wouldest keep me secret, until thy wrath be past, that thou wouldest appoint me a set time, and remember me!

14 If a man die, shall he live again? all the days of my appointed time will I wait, till my change come.

15 Thou shalt call, and I will answer thee: thou wilt have a desire to the work of thine hands.

16 For now thou numberest my steps: dost thou not watch over my sin?

17 My transgression is sealed up in a bag, and thou sewest up mine iniquity.

32:6 And Elihu the son of Barachel the Buzite answered and said, I am young, and ye are very old; wherefore I was afraid, and durst not shew you mine opinion.

32:8 But there is a spirit in man: and the inspiration of the Almighty giveth them understanding.

34:12 Yea, surely God will not do wickedly, neither will the Almighty pervert judgment.

37:14 Hearken unto this, O Job: stand still, and consider the wondrous works of God.

37:22 Fair weather cometh out of the north: with God is terrible majesty.

IN FOCUS

The police station's clock was ticking. Jessica looked at it and realized that it was 2:30 p.m. Only 45 minutes ago, she was in the midst of praising God for the Palm Sunday sermon she had preached. Now she was numb. While racing home to cook dinner, her brakes had failed as she turned into a major intersection, and her car had plowed into a crowd of pedestrians. One little boy was in critical condition, hanging on for his life. Now Jessica sat hunched over in the small jail cell waiting for her bond to be set

She sank to her knees on the cement floor and prayed for the healing of the child.

After her sister posted bond, they went to Jessica's house, sat on her sofa, and talked. In the middle of the conversation, the phone rang; it was the police. The little boy had died from his injuries.

Jessica hung up the phone and blurted out, "I'm scared, Sis; I killed the little boy. I don't know what this means."

Her sister tried to comfort her. "Come on, you didn't kill anyone. You had an accident. You were not drunk; you did not run a red light. It was an accident."

Distressed, Jessica continued to mumble, "What is God saying? What can I say to the little boy's parents? Why has God abandoned me?"

Her sister pushed away from her. "Wait a minute!" her sister screamed. "I don't believe you. You preach forgiveness, so forgive yourself and accept God's forgiveness. You preach that faith is rooted in the knowledge that God is always in control; now is the time to practice what you preach."

In the book of Job, we recognize that tragedy is no respecter of persons, position, or age. Do you encourage others to develop the kind of faith that helps them through situations that seem hopeless?

THE PEOPLE, PLACES, AND TIMES

Each of Job's friends was sincere in his desire and efforts to console Job. Their intended words of consolation, however, were more condemning than consoling and more harmful than helpful. Their good intentions made Job's situation worse. Eliphaz was concerned that Job did not practice what he preached (Job 4:1-6). Bildad was concerned to uphold the prevailing theological perspective of the day, which made a person's sin the direct cause of his or her suffering (Job 8:1-7). Zophar reminded Job that things could be worse (Job 11:1-6). Although Eliphaz, Bildad, and Zophar sought to console Job from different perspectives, they shared several things in common. They each tried to tell Job why he was suffering. Neglecting Job's feelings and ignoring his pain, they each took issue with what Job said. They each spoke from their own limited perspective and

personal experience. None of them attempted to feel Job's pain or to understand his perplexity. They were more judgmental than empathetic. None of these perspectives produces encouragement or helpful counsel for hurting people.

Having heard and responded to his intended comforters, Job summarized his view of their counsel: "Ye are forgers of lies, ye are all physicians of no value" (Job 13:4). Job wished that his friends would exercise wisdom and be silent (v. 5). Instead of being a source of comfort for Job, they had become a part of Job's burden. Without help from his friends, Job faced what seemed to be a hopeless situation.

Free of his miserable comforters, Job decided to present his own argument to God. He risked putting his relationship with God on the line and confronted Him with a question: "Wherefore hidest thou thy face, and holdest me for thine enemy?" (v. 24). Job confronted God in the faith and confidence that even if God condemned him, he would continue to trust God and to defend his own ways before Him (v. 15).

While Job continued his dialogue with God, a fourth friend, Elihu, approached. The text introduces Elihu as being angry (32:2). Elihu's anger suggests that he was aware of the conversations Job had already had with his three friends. Elihu was angry with both Job and Job's three friends. He was angry with Job's three friends because they had failed to convince Job of his sins (v. 3). Elihu was angry with Job for attributing the cause of his troubles to God (v. 2).

Elihu was not always in agreement with Job, nor was he any more professional than Job's other three friends. He was, however, successful in getting Job to open himself up to the possibility that God may choose to speak to us through our troubles.

Job's story affirms the truth that despair is part of human existence, and that when all seems hopeless we can still count on God to be good, just, and all-powerful.

BACKGROUND

In Job 14, Job was very frustrated and weary of talking with his three friends, Eliphaz, Bildad, and Zophar. Their counsel was anything but helpful.

Telling Job, as Eliphaz did, that sinners reap what they sow (Job 4:7-11) is hardly the way to help hurting people, nor is pontificating about one's own experience (vv. 12-21). Neither is self-righteously pressuring someone to repent (4:5-8) and to accept God's correction for some undesignated sin (5:17) the way to help hurting people. Discussing delicate points of theology (8:1-7), past tradition (vv. 8-10), and the natural laws of cause and effect (vv. 11-22), as Bildad did, is not a healing approach to hurting people. Exhorting those who hurt to repent, keep quiet, and be thankful that their situation is not as bad as it could have been, as Zophar did (11:1-15), is cruel.

This is the counsel that Job received before he decided to take his case directly to God. Having made this decision, Job now had to decide how best to approach God. He recognized that God has the upper hand (Job 9:32), and this being the case, Job reasoned that it may be better for someone to arbitrate between them (v. 33). Job concluded, however, that utilizing an arbitrator was not possible.

After giving considerable thought to his approach to God, Job opted to soften his language and talk with God about the general human condition. His focus shifted from himself specifically to humankind in general. In other words, Job chose to project his situation onto all of humanity.

Job then set his mind to tell God that righteous people do not deserve the kind of treatment he was receiving from God.

AT-A-GLANCE

1. Job's Situation Described in Universal Terms (Job 14:1-2, 11-12)
2. Job Hopes for a Change in His Situation (vv. 13-17)
3. Elihu Speaks about Job's Situation (32:6, 8; 34:12; 37:14, 22)

IN DEPTH

1. Job's Situation Described in Universal Terms (Job 14:1-2, 11-12)

Job opened his conversation with God by noting that everyone is born to die. We live a "few days," and the few days we live are full of trouble. Life is transient, fleeting, temporary, short-lived, and full of strife and tribulation. Using universal images from nature, Job illustrated the transitory and grievous nature of life. Life, he observed, "cometh forth like a flower, and is cut down" and "fleeth also as a shadow, and continueth not" (Job 14:2).

Reflecting upon his own experience, Job actually lamented, with some degree of anger, the transient quality of life. Job seemed to be taking issue with God's sovereignty over life. Although it is not a part of the printed text for today's lesson, this point is affirmed in the following verses: "Seeing his days are determined, the number of his months are with thee, thou hast appointed his bounds that he cannot pass; Turn from him that he may rest, till he shall accomplish, as an hireling, his day" (vv. 5-6).

In verses 11 and 12, Job used another universal image from nature to describe the human condition. He spoke of "waters [that] fail from the sea, and the flood [that] decayeth and drieth up." This image is not that of a riverbed that dries up because of seasonal drought due to a lack of rain; there is always the chance that it will rain again and replenish the riverbed with water. The image Job references here indicates that even if it rains, the contours of the riverbed will have been so irreversibly disrupted, by either an earthquake or some other freak of nature, it will make it impossible for the riverbed to hold or receive water.

So it is with humankind. When one "lieth down," or, more accurately, when one dies, he "riseth not" again. "They shall not awake, nor be raised out of their sleep" (v. 12). Once one dies, Job reasoned, they are forever dead "till the heavens be no more" (v. 12). It is as though Job saw death as a part of the human condition. Death for Job was a part of the burden and pain he was experiencing. From Job's perspective, death cannot, therefore, be a means of escape from the terrible situation in which God had placed him. Obviously, Job felt trapped between a rock and a hard place. He felt trapped between death, which provided no escape, and an angry God who had surrounded him with untold trouble and pain.

Since death offered no way of escape, and since God seemed unrelenting in His treatment of Job, what was Job to do? What can anyone who faces what seems to be a hopeless situation do?

2. Job Hopes for a Change in His Situation (vv. 13-17)

Feeling trapped between death, which offers no hope, and an angry God (Job 14:13), Job took a giant step of faith toward a hope he was prepared to wait for. In spite of his reasoning, Job reached for hope and continued to trust in the God whom he believed would yet act in his defense. Thus, Job's question and resolve was: "If a man die, shall he live again? all the days of my appointed time will I wait, till my change come" (v. 14).

Job seemed to carry in the back of his mind the thought that God's anger would not last forever. It may be that Job understood what the psalmist later wrote: "For his anger lasts only a moment, but his favor lasts a lifetime" (Psalm 30:5, NIV). Job seemed to express a hope that God's anger would relent (v. 15). With this hope was Job's desire for his relationship with God to be restored: "You shall call, and I will answer you." Job's experience bordered on suggesting that when all seems hopeless, talking with God, even debating with God, could ignite a deeper hunger and love for God. This was a spiritual truth about which we sometimes sing:

I may have doubts and fears, my eyes be filled with tears.
But Jesus is a friend who watches day and night.
I go to Him in prayer; He knows my every care.
And just a little talk with Jesus makes it right.

Job's hunger for a renewed relationship with God did not give him the assurance, however, that God would cease to afflict him. Job wanted a relationship with God that was free of the suffering he thought God had imposed upon him. Job was concerned about how God would deal with sin in a renewed relationship. Job knew that his whole life was known by God (his steps were numbered), but he also somehow knew that God did not keep track of his sin (v. 16). For his sins were 'sealed up in a bag and covered' (v. 17).

When it comes to our sins, Job's hope is a hope we all have. We hope that God will deal mercifully with us and that He will not withhold his grace and forgiveness.

3. Job's Lecture from Elihu (32:6, 8; 34:12; 37:14, 22)

Elihu, as was noted earlier, was the fourth of Job's friends who tried to console him. He was also the youngest. Elihu's comments suggest that he was present when Job's three other friends offered their counsel, but, that out of what was presumed to be respect for his elders, Elihu had remained silent (Job 32:6).

In a polite move to qualify himself to engage in conversation with his elders, and as a camouflage for his youthfulness, Elihu introduced his comments with an axiom known by his elders. In short, Elihu said, "the inspiration of the Almighty giveth them understanding" (v. 8). Elihu wanted his elders, including Job, to know that what he was about to say ought not to be discredited because of his youth. After all, God, who is not partial, can give wisdom and understanding without regard to age.

Elihu had a lot to say. The gist of his comments, however, are stated in Job 34:12; 37:14, 22. Elihu moved quickly to correct any thought that God perverts justice and treats people wickedly. This comment from Elihu flew in the face of Job's contention that God was neither fair nor just in His treatment of him. Since God is a fair and just God, Elihu advised, Job should "stand still, and consider the wondrous works of God" (37:14).

Moreover, Elihu concludes, "Fair weather cometh out of the north: with God is terrible majesty" (v. 22). Scholars continue to debate about how best to translate and interpret this verse. The NIV renders this verse, "Out of the north he comes in golden splendor; God comes in awesome majesty." Elihu had been arguing from a moral perspective, but here he brings his point home, using nature as an analogy. At the end of a storm comes clear skies and fair weather. In the same way, after life's storms, God comes from heaven, His awesome splendor and majesty bringing peace to our souls. Elihu was reminding Job how necessary it was to see God as all-powerful and perfectly righteous.

Elihu's aim is to encourage Job to show wisdom by remaining true to God and daring to believe that God is not mistreating him. Suffering comes with the territory of living in a fallen world. Despair is part of human existence. When all seems hopeless, we can count on God to be good, just, and all-powerful.

SEARCH THE SCRIPTURES

1. "Man that is born of a woman is of few days, and full of _____" (Job 14:1).

2. What images from nature does Job use to describe the brevity of life (v. 2)?

3. What images from nature does Job use to describe the irreversible reality of death (vv. 11-12)?

4. "O Job: stand still, and _____ the wondrous works of _____" (Job 37:14).

DISCUSS THE MEANING

1. Identify and discuss four things we learn from Job's friends that may help us in our efforts to encourage hurting people.

2. Discuss the difference between doubt and unbelief.

3. In what ways does doubt contribute to the development of one's faith?

4. Identify and discuss three insights you have gained from today's lesson.

LESSON IN OUR SOCIETY

The need to manage one's life, daily behavior, and thoughts in the face of hopeless situations is a common issue. No one escapes having to deal with some degree of despair and the threatening loss of hope. Despair is a part of human existence. Our challenge is to learn how to maintain faith in a gracious, fair, and just God when all seems hopeless.

We can learn much about the role of faith during times of despair from Job's experience. The question that haunted Job during the days of his despair is akin to our Lord's question during the days of His passion—my God, why? Sometimes faith has no answer. Sometimes faith can only arm us with the courage to believe that God has His reasons and that we can count on Him to be good, just, and all-powerful.

MAKE IT HAPPEN

Take the insights you have gained from today's lesson and practice them in your conversation with some hurting person during week. Remember that hurting people need your empathizing presence more than they need your words. As we have learned from Elihu, words tend to be more relevant and are certainly more helpful when we first identify with the pain of those whom we want to assist.

FOLLOW THE SPIRIT

What God wants me to do:

_____

_____

REMEMBER YOUR THOUGHTS

Special insights I have learned:

_____

_____

MORE LIGHT ON THE TEXT

Job 14:1-2, 11-17; 32:6, 8; 34:12; 37:14, 22

In last week's lesson, we saw how Job clung to his faith in God to deal with the tragedies that befell him. Today, we will look at how Job worked through the long-term effects of tragedy. Although Job refused to admit that the tragedies he went through were evidence of hidden sin in his life, he flip-flops between hope and hopelessness, between faith and despair, and between trust in the justice of God and anger at his inability to see any meaning in what he had suffered. He considered, and then rejected, the possibility that God was unconcerned about or powerless to make anything better in his life (Job 6:4; 8:3; 9:2, 18, 22; 13:15-16). Job and his friends tried to come up with a reason for what had happened. They agreed that God is not unjust (Job 8:3). They surmised that good people don't suffer injustice, and if they do, God delivers them (Job 4:6; 5:17-18). They argued that people aren't capable of seeing their own sin, but God is, and He punishes them justly.

On Palm Sunday, the church recalls how God's sinless Son was cheered one day and crucified the next. Palm Sunday reminds us that none of the beliefs held by Job and his friends was true. Jesus was innocent. Peter and Judas both recognized this, although they responded differently (Matthew 27:3-5; Luke 22:54-62). God allowed "the Just" to suffer for "the unjust" (1 Peter 3:18) so that Jesus would "be just and the one who justifies those who have faith in Jesus" (Romans 3:26 NIV).

What lasting meaning is there for us today in what Job and Elihu said? It is the understanding that our suffering unfairly cannot compare to the events of the day in Jesus' earthly life that many Christians around the world celebrate on Palm Sunday.

14:1 Man that is born of a woman is of few days, and full of trouble.

In the midst of pain in body and spirit, Job made two comments about himself and every living person. Life doesn't last long, and as short as life is, people have a lot of problems. The word "full" (Heb. sabea', **saw-bay'-ah**) means to abound. The word was sometimes used in a positive sense, meaning "excited" or "emotionally stirred up." If Job had had only a few of his animals stolen, he likely would have come to terms with the loss of his property. Or if one of his 10 children had died, in time, like a deep gash, his grief would have healed. But to lose all his property and have all 10 sons and daughters killed in one day was overwhelming; life is too short to ever accept that. Although Job was rich and respected, he wasn't immune to troubles. He had more trouble than anyone could be expected to handle. The *New Living Translation* translates this verse as, "How frail is humanity! How short is life, and how full of trouble!" Job wasn't the first person to be swamped—drowned—in one tragic event after another, and he wouldn't be the last.

2 He cometh forth like a flower, and is cut down: he fleeth also like a shadow, and continueth not.

Job collided with the reality of disaster. Isaiah 40:6 compares human life to a flower that withers: "What shall I cry? All men are like grass, and all their glory is like the flowers of the field" (NIV). Life can be beautiful for a moment, but it never stays that way forever. The word "continueth" is from the Hebrew word 'amad (**aw-mad'**), meaning to stand or to endure. Sometimes the demands of life are so heavy that people cannot continue to stand up for themselves, others, or the causes they believe in.

14:11 As the waters fail from the sea, and the flood decayeth and drieth up: 12 So man lieth down, and riseth not: till the heavens be no more, they shall not awake, nor be raised out of their sleep.

Job compares dying to a sea drying up. Some scholars have said that Job compares the sea drying up to a weak person who is dying. When rain comes, the sea will fill up again. However, oftentimes a person drowning in hardship forgets about better days ahead. Instead, the person thinks that the way life is now is how it will always be. Like many people today, Job seems to have felt hopelessly plagued by tragedy.

Often when we experience great loss or the ability to make a living, all sense of meaning seems to disappear from life. What seemed so important in our lives today is gone tomorrow, like our shadow when we move or a stream that dries up in the summer heat.

Verse 11 says, "the flood...drieth up." The word "drieth" (Heb. yabesh, **yaw-bashe'**) is also found in Proverbs 17:22: "a broken spirit drieth the bones." Tragedy often drains life of its meaning, leaving even people of faith feeling despair.

The best Job knew how to do was to hope for escape from physical, spiritual, and emotional pain. Verse 12 shows that Job hoped for some meaning beyond death but had no basis for that hope except his faith in the nature of God. This verse shows the common belief that death was the end of life and all meaning.

13 O that thou wouldest hide me in the grave, that thou wouldest keep me secret, until thy wrath be past, that thou wouldest appoint me a set time, and remember me!

Notice that the end of verse 12 refers to "their sleep." The belief was that when people died, they all went to the same shadowy place of weakness (Psalm 88:12; Isaiah 14:9-11).

In verse 13, Job identifies that place. It is often translated as "hell" and is sometimes rendered as "the grave" (Heb. sheol, **sheh-ole.'**) Almost all modern versions translate it to mean the place of the dead, rather than the place of punishment for Satan, his angels, and unbelievers after Judgment Day.

Job began to pray, "hide me in the grave." The

word "hide" comes from the Hebrew word *tsaphan* (**tsaw-fan'**), which means to conceal something of value in order to keep it from being lost or stolen. In Hebrew, the phrase "keep me secret" is translated from one word, *cathar* (**saw-thar'**, meaning to shelter someone. In essence Job was saying, "God, shelter me until all this bad stuff is over, then remember where You hid me." As Psalm 32:7 tells us, Job was not the last person who in despair and hopelessness had wished that God was his hiding place.

The phrases "until thy wrath" (Heb. *'aph,* **af**) and "be past" (Heb. *shuwb,* **shoob**), literally mean to turn back. Here, they refer to God turning His anger away.

Job prays and asks God to remember him. The Hebrew word for "remember" is *zakar* (**zaw-kar'**), meaning to call to mind or recall. In the *New Living Translation* the phrase reads, "Mark your calendar to think of me again." It was Job's desire for God to hide him among the dead until his troubles were over, but not to forget to come back and get him.

14 If a man die, shall he live again? all the days of my appointed time will I wait till my change come.

This verse contains what may be the most important question in the Old Testament: "Can there be any hope of life after death?" What made Job one of the great men of the Old Testament was that he dared to hope that something more than death awaits the person who trusts in the goodness, power, and love of God. Job had the spiritual courage to trust in the possibility of resurrection.

How much do Christians have to be thankful for because of what happened that first Easter? The heart of the Gospel, the Resurrection of Jesus, was something for which Job could only hope.

The word God inspired Job to use was "live" (Heb. *hayah,* **khaw-yaw'**), whose simplest meaning is "to have life." When used in contrast to death, "live" means to revive, to live again, or to quicken. In other words, Job said he was willing to wait and endure hardship if resurrection lay ahead.

The phrase "my appointed time" doesn't capture the meaning of the Hebrew word Job used here, *tsaba'* (**tsaw-baw'**), which carries the sense of hardship and difficulty. In comparison, the *New Living Translation* uses the phrase "my struggle,"

and the *New International Version* translates it as "my hard service." Job was saying that he didn't expect life to be easy, but was willing to wait expectantly until he was released from pain and suffering, and renewed.

The phrase "my change" (Heb. *chaliyphah,* **khal-ee-faw'**) implies someone coming to take Job's place to relieve him. Bible scholars disagree on what "my change" refers to. Some think Job meant he was willing to wait until he changed from being alive to being dead. Others believe the wording signifies Job's desire to escape the grave. However, a comparison of verse 13 with Job's answer to God's call in verse 15 seems to dictate that the natural interpretation is that Job meant changing from death to life, being relieved from this mortal body—thus, resurrection.

15 Thou shalt call, and I will answer thee: thou wilt have a desire to the work of thine hands.

This verse shows that Job believes that people are of great value to God. He says, "If God summoned, I would answer without fail." He expects the call from God. He wouldn't be surprised when it came because he believes God would "desire" (Heb. *kacaph,* **kaw-saf'**) His creation.

16 For now thou numberest my steps: dost thou not watch over my sin?

After reminding God of His desire to have the people He created with Him, Job says that God keeps track of where each person goes in life. "Thou numberest (Heb. *caphar,* **saw-far'**) my steps" means to take account or reckon. "Dost thou not watch" translates the Hebrew word *shamar* (**shaw-mar'**), meaning to guard or protect. Here, Job isn't speaking out of fear that God judges every minute of his life; rather, he is grateful that God cares enough to watch over him. He doesn't see God as constantly looking for his faults and sins.

17 My transgression is sealed up in a bag, and thou sewest up mine iniquity.

Job describes God's attitude toward his sin, in spite of his faithfulness, much like New Testament writers often describe God's attitude toward a Christian's sins. He says his sins were "sealed up" (Heb. *chatham,* **khaw-tham'**) or "locked up." Then he adds that God "sewest up" (Heb. *taphal*, **taw-fal'**), meaning to glue or to plaster over, his sin. Again, the idea is that God has put Job's sins in a bag out of sight, then shut them up where they couldn't be seen.

Job didn't pretend to be sinless or without the need for God's forgiveness. He admitted his transgressions and iniquities and commented at length on his need for forgiveness (Job 7:20-21). But in this verse, the emphasis is on the fact that God forgives those who trust Him and forgets their sins. The Bible uses a variety of comparisons to describe the nature of God's forgiveness (see Psalm 32:1; 85:2; Proverbs 17:9; Romans 4:7; James 5:20).

Job and his friends had gone back and forth trying to make sense of the disasters Job had endured. When neither he nor they could think of any more to say, a young observer who had been sitting nearby listening inserted himself into their discussion. His name was Elihu.

Elihu was from the same area as Job and his friends, a region south of Cannan on the northwest side of the Arabian Desert called Buz. Genesis 22:21 records that Buz was Abraham's nephew; it is likely that in generations before, this was his territory and was given his name. Elihu was also a relative of Ram, who may have been an ancestor of King David (Ruth 4:19) and of Jesus (Matthew 1:3-4). This may explain the connection of the book of Job to the Hebrew people, although its main characters are from the region where Edom was located.

32:6 And Elihu the son of Barachel the Buzite answered and said, I am young, and ye are very old; wherefore I was afraid, and durst not shew you mine opinion.

Elihu was much younger than Job, and thus his opinions were not counted to be as important as those of Job or his friends. Job 32:2-3 says that Elihu was offended by Job's defense of himself and his repeated complaint of his inability to confront God about the basis for God's disapproval of him. Unbeknownst to Elihu (and Job) was the fact that the disasters Job experienced occurred because of God's confidence in him, not His disapproval.

The phrase "answered and said" (Heb. *'amar*, **aw-mar'**) implies words spoken in a forceful or commanding manner. Although Elihu's words

showed humble deference for Job's age, his tone of voice did not. Elihu said he was "afraid" (Heb. *zachal*, **zaw-khal,'** meaning to crawl away or "fear") to give his "opinion" (Heb. *dea,* `**day'-ah**, meaning "knowledge"). This implies something stronger than just giving a point of view, but more like certain knowledge.

8 But there is a spirit in man: and the inspiration of the Almighty giveth them understanding.

Elihu begins this verse by expressing his certainty. He points out the difference between what he believed and what Job said. *Aken* (Heb. **aw-kane**), or "but," does not account for the Hebrew word Elihu used and translates as "surely" or "indeed."

This verse provides a good example of the Hebrew poetic form called parallelism. In parallelism, the first line parallels the second or sometimes makes a contrast with it. First, Elihu says, "there is a spirit (Heb. *ruwach,* **roo'-akh**, meaning "breath") in man." Then he "parallels" or adds to what he means by saying, "the inspiration of the Almighty" (Heb. *shadday,* **sahd-dah-ee**). In effect, what Elihu meant was that the spirit or breath of the Almighty *(shadday)* inside of man will give him understanding. The same Hebrew word is used in Genesis 2:7 to describe when God breathed into Adam's nostrils the breath of life. Elihu understood that our capacity to think, reason, and understand exists because God gave us life and created us to relate to Him and to one another.

34:12 Yea, surely God will not do wickedly, neither will the Almighty pervert judgment.

In this verse, Elihu insists that God will not act wickedly by using an even stronger word—"surely" (Heb. *'omnam,* **om-nawm'**), which means "indeed" or "no doubt." Here, Elihu was emphasizing that whenever bad things happen to us, we can trust that God was not the source of them.

In the second half of this verse, he refers to God "the Almighty," meaning "most powerful." Likewise, God does not use His power to "pervert" (Heb. *'avath,* **aw-vath'**) "judgment" (justice) (Heb. *mishpat,* **mish-pawf**). Elihu's point was that God is all-powerful. He doesn't twist or bend the affairs of life to exact judgment.

37:14 Hearken unto this, O Job: stand still, and consider the wondrous works of God.

Much that Elihu says is true. In the verses preceding verse 14, he reminds Job that weather becomes extremely hot and, at other times, freezing cold. He points out that sometimes it rains too much and sometimes too little. He urges Job to pay attention to these things that, along with much more, are under God's control.

Job had noticed these things and had commented on them more eloquently than Elihu back in 9:10-11. But Elihu told Job to stand still and stop floundering and pacing. Job was covered with boils and was trying to come to terms with the deaths of all 10 of his children. He had been bankrupted by thievery and disaster. Obviously, focusing on the greatness of God had to be difficult. When Job had considered what Elihu was urging, he asked, "Who hath hardened himself against him, and hath prospered?" (Job 9:4). Although what Elihu advised was hard to do, Job had already admitted that this was his only answer for dealing with heartbreak and despair.

37:22 Fair weather cometh out of the north: with God is terrible majesty.

Bible scholars debate what the first half of this verse means. Literally it says, that from the north, "fair weather" (Heb. *zahab,* **zaw-hawb'**), or "gold" will come. What does "gold" mean? Most translations interpret "gold" as being symbolic of beauty rather than referring to the actual metal. The *New International Version* and *New Living Translation* say "golden splendor" and "gold light," respectively.

The last half of verse 22 emphasizes that if we could see all of God's greatness we would be amazed. We would marvel, even gasp at it. Verse 22 uses the word "terrible," which to most people means something really bad. But here the idea is something that causes astonishment and creates a sense of wonder and reverence in us. In Ephesians 3:17-20, Paul wrote, "I pray that you...may have power...to grasp how wide and long and high and deep is the love of Christ...who is able to do immeasurably more than all we ask or imagine" (NIV). It is difficult to imagine that someone would be willing to die for the sinful, the unbelieving, the unfaithful (Romans 5:7-8). It is much more amazing to consider how God could or would die on the Cross and rise again to save us. It is this sacrifice of love that we celebrate on Easter Sunday.

Bibliography

Allen, Clifton J., ed. *The Broadman Bible Commentary*. Nashville, Tenn.: Broadman Press, 1971.

Andersen, Francis I. *Job: An Introduction and Commentary*. London; Downers Grove, Ill.: InterVarsity Press, 1976.

Hanson, Anthony and Miriam Hanson. "The Book of Job: A Commentary."

Torch Bible Commentaries. Edited by John Marsh, David M. Paton, and Alan Richardson. New York: Collier Books, 1962.

Rowley, H. H. *New Century Bible Commentaries*. Edited by Ronald Clements and Matthew Black. Grand Rapids, Mich.: William B. Eerdmans Publishing Company, 1976.

DAILY BIBLE READINGS

M: Job Pleads for Respite Before Death
Job 14:1-6

T: Job Petitions the Grave as Refuge
Job 14:7-17

W: Mortal Finally Overcomes Mortal Life
Job 14:18-22

T: God's Spirit Makes for Understanding
Job 32:1-10

F: God Repays According to Our Deeds
Job 34:11-15

S: Elihu Proclaims God's Majesty
Job 36:24-33

S: Around God Is Awesome Majesty
Job 37:14-24

TEACHING TIPS

April 16
Bible Study Guide 7

1. Words You Should Know

A. Whirlwind (Job 38:1) *ca'ar* (Heb.)—In the Old Testament, storms are often used to describe revelatory experiences. Here "whirlwind" might be a poetic description of Job's inner experience.

B. Foundations (v. 4) *yacad* (Heb.)— In erecting a building, the foundation is the first to be put in place. Here, the writer uses the phrase to refer to God's initial act of creation.

C. Sepulchre (Mark 16:2, 3, 5) *mnemeion* (Heb.)—A burial place such as a tomb or a grave.

D. Residue (v. 13) *loipoy* (Heb.)—Literally, that which remains after a part is removed or disposed of (i.e., the remainder, the rest, or remnant).

E. Sat at meat (v. 14) *anakeimai* (Heb.)—An old English phrase meaning "as they ate" or "as they were eating."

2. Teacher Preparation

A. Read the FOCAL VERSES and study the IN DEPTH and MORE LIGHT ON THE TEXT sections.

B. Review the LESSON AIM. Read the IN FOCUS section, THE PEOPLE, PLACES, AND TIMES, and the BACKGROUND section.

3. Starting the Lesson

A. Open the session with prayer. Thank God for what He has done for us through the life, death, and resurrection of Jesus Christ. Praise Him for the hope and new life we are able to have through faith in the resurrected Christ.

B. Have the students read the LESSON AIM in unison. Have one student read aloud the IN FOCUS story.

4. Getting into the Lesson

A. Have a student read aloud THE PEOPLE, PLACES, AND TIMES.

B. Summarize the BACKGROUND material. Remind the students that Job's story is a good example of our common need for faith in a God who can give us hope and a new lease on life.

C. Note also that Easter comes once a year to remind us that God, who raised Jesus from the dead, can also breathe new life into our hopeless situations.

5. Relating the Lesson to Life

A. Have the students, in small groups of five or six people, share any experience they may have had in which their faith in Christ helped them to find life and meaning in some difficult or hopeless situation.

B. Reconvene the entire class and have a representative from each small group share the most exciting experience that was shared in their group.

C. Discuss what these shared experiences have in common with Job's story. If necessary, use the DISCUSS THE MEANING questions to help facilitate conversation.

6. Arousing Action

Read MAKE IT HAPPEN and encourage the students to spend this week thanking and praising God for the newness of life they have come to experience in following Jesus Christ.

GOD RESPONDS WITH LIFE

Bible Background • JOB 38:1–4, 16–17; 42:1–6; MARK 16
Printed Text • JOB 38:1, 4, 16–17; 42:1–2, 5; MARK 16:1–7, 9–14, 20
Devotional Reading • LUKE 24:1–9

LESSON AIM

By the end of the lesson, we will:

EXPLORE Job's experience as a model of God's power and goodness while experiencing trouble;

REJOICE in the hope of new life found in the resurrection of Jesus Christ; and

COMMIT to finding ways in which we can use suffering and pain to forge a more meaningful life and relationship with God.

KEEP IN MIND

"And he saith unto them, Be not affrighted: Ye seek Jesus of Nazareth, which was crucified: he is risen; he is not here: behold the place where they laid him" (Mark 16:6).

FOCAL VERSES

Job 38:1 Then the LORD answered Job out of the whirlwind, and said,

4 Where wast thou when I laid the foundations of the earth? declare, if thou hast understanding.

38:16 Hast thou entered into the springs of the sea? or hast thou walked in the search of the depth?

17 Have the gates of death been opened unto thee? or hast thou seen the doors of the shadow of death?

42:1 Then Job answered the LORD, and said,

2 I know that thou canst do every thing, and that no thought can be withholden from thee.

5 I have heard of thee by the hearing of the ear: but now mine eye seeth thee.

LESSON OVERVIEW

LESSON AIM
KEEP IN MIND
FOCAL VERSES
IN FOCUS
THE PEOPLE, PLACES, AND TIMES
BACKGROUND
AT-A-GLANCE
IN DEPTH
SEARCH THE SCRIPTURES
DISCUSS THE MEANING
LESSON IN OUR SOCIETY
MAKE IT HAPPEN
FOLLOW THE SPIRIT
REMEMBER YOUR THOUGHTS
MORE LIGHT ON THE TEXT
DAILY BIBLE READINGS

Mark 16:1 And when the sabbath was past, Mary Magdalene, and Mary the mother of James, and Salome, had bought sweet spices, that they might come and anoint him.

2 And very early in the morning the first day of the week, they came unto the sepulchre at the rising of the sun.

3 And they said among themselves, Who shall roll us away the stone from the door of the sepulchre?

4 And when they looked, they saw that the stone was rolled away: for it was very great.

5 And entering into the sepulchre, they saw a young man sitting on the right side, clothed in a long white garment; and they were affrighted.

6 And he saith unto them, Be not affrighted: Ye seek Jesus of Nazareth, which was crucified: he is risen; he is not here: behold the place where they laid him.

7 But go your way, tell his disciples and Peter that he goeth before you into Galilee: there shall ye see him, as he said unto you.

16:9 Now when Jesus was risen early the first day of the week, he appeared first to Mary Magdalene, out of whom he had cast seven devils.

10 And she went and told them that had been with him, as they mourned and wept.

11 And they, when they had heard that he was alive, and had been seen of her, believed not.

12 After that he appeared in another form unto

two of them, as they walked, and went into the country.

13 And they went and told it unto the residue: neither believed they them.

14 Afterward he appeared unto the eleven as they sat at meat, and upbraided them with their unbelief and hardness of heart, because they believed not them which had seen him after he was risen.

16:20 And they went forth, and preached every where, the Lord working with them, and confirming the word with signs following. Amen.

IN FOCUS

At his wife's funeral, Nate sat on the first pew with his family. Somehow, a smile came to Nate's lips as each person walked by the casket. His wife wore a lovely silk dress, her were arms crossed over her Bible, and a spoon was placed in one hand. The spoon allowed him to gently let go of his wife of 40 years. Over and over people mumbled, "What's with the spoon?" Nate smiled each time.

During his sermon, the pastor shared the story of the spoon.

"Sharon was diagnosed with a terminal illness with three months to live. I met with her and Nate as they decided on songs, Scriptures, and what outfit she would be buried in. Just as I was leaving, she called me back very excitedly."

"There's one more thing!" she said. "I want to be buried with a spoon in my right hand."

Both of us were mystified. "Why a spoon?" we both asked.

She explained, "In my years of attending banquets and potluck dinners, after the main course I knew the best was yet to come when someone would lean over and say, 'Keep your spoon.' I would expect something like atomic cake or peach clobber—a dessert with substance!

So, I want people to see me in that casket with a spoon in my hand, and I want them to wonder what's with the spoon. Then I want you to tell them oh so gently that the next time they reach for their spoons, let it remind them that the Lord has promised that the best is yet to come!"

Nate's eyes welled up with tears of joy.

One great lesson in the book of Job and the story of

Christ's Resurrection is that new life is possible if we know God. We must remember that the Resurrection is the foundation of Christian faith and our promise that the best is indeed yet to come.

THE PEOPLE, PLACES, AND TIMES

Job. He had extensive conversations with four of his friends and with his wife. He had listened intently, hoping to gain some understanding of why God seemed to have been treating him so unfairly and unjustly.

It is reasonable to think that most people having Job's experience and receiving the counsel of friends, like Eliphaz, Bildad, and Zophar, and Job's wife would have given up on God. Job, however, was determined to find answers to questions that threatened to turn his concept of God upside down.

What was his motivation for maintaining faith? Job had at least two things going for him. First, he was keenly aware of God's past blessings. He recounted those blessings in Job 29. Given the intimate friendship between himself and God, he was unwilling to give up on God. Job reasoned, even against the counsel of his friends and his wife, that God must have had his reasons for allowing these terrible things to happen. While he searched to know and understand God's reasoning, he did not take God's past blessings for naught.

Recounting past blessings is *a spiritual discipline* that can help us to maintain faith during difficult days. During difficult days, the temptation is to neglect cultivating a remembrance of past blessings. Caught up in the pain of the moment, we do not naturally call to memory the glorious days of the past "when the secret of God was upon our tabernacle" (29:4). Recalling past blessings while treading deep waters requires intentional effort. It is a spiritual discipline which, like all spiritual disciplines, must be practiced and developed. Fortunately, Job was not above exercising this spiritual discipline.

Additionally, Job had something else going for him. In the face of the prevailing theological perspective of his day that made sin the cause of suffering, Job knew that he was innocent. Like Paul before King Agrippa, Job knew that he had not been "disobedient unto the heavenly vision" (Acts 26:19).

Obedience tends to help create the emotional freedom to question God about His mysterious ways. Children who know they have done something wrong are reluctant to approach their parents to request a favor. However, the heart of a parent is softened when a child says, "Daddy, I've been a good boy. May I go outside and play?"

Job "was blameless and upright; he feared God and shunned evil" (Job 1:1, NIV). While this may not have qualified him to debate with God, it certainly provided him with the emotional freedom necessary to question God and to tell God what he thought and how he felt.

All believers would do well to lead obedient lives so as to be free to take everything to God in prayer. It is hard, indeed well-nigh impossible, to pray while overlooking sin and filth in one's life. When there is known sin, the only prayer God hears is the prayer seeking His forgiveness.

BACKGROUND

Job had a multiplicity of questions that he hurled at God. He wanted answers from God. He wanted to know why God was using His power to afflict him when he had been so faithful to Him.

After the counsel of Job's three friends and his wife had been given, Elihu seemed to have impressed Job by helping him to think about his predicament in a wider vision. Having affirmed Job's right to hear from God, Elihu questioned Job's preconceived notions about what he wanted to hear from God. Elihu reasoned that God might have chosen to speak where Job had not chosen to listen. In other words, Elihu pushed Job to consider the possibility that God may be speaking to Job through Job's suffering and pain. It never occurred to Job to look for the answers to his questions within the context of his own tragic circumstances.

Sometimes our desire to be delivered from painful situations robs us of the opportunity to discover blessings that only pain and suffering can produce. See the introduction to Job 38: "Then the LORD answered Job out of the whirlwind" (v. 1). God, in His goodness and power, can use anything and everything that happens to us to serve our best interests. It is difficult, however, to see God's goodness and to be cognizant of His power while sitting among the ashes scraping painful sores with a piece of broken pottery (Job 2:7-8).

God, in His love, mercy, and patience, made Himself available for a conversation with Job. Before Job was able to fire off a question to God, God proceeded to question Job, which proved to be an inversion of Job's plan. Job had positioned himself to question God, but God beat Job to first base. Job found himself forced to table his agenda and consider God's agenda as God confronted Job with a series of questions that he could not answer. Job's inability to answer God's questions caused him to realize that God was still in control of his life and future. As soon as Job surrendered himself to God's care (Job 42:2), God breathed new life into his tragic situation, resulting in his renewed statement of faith in God: "I have heard of thee by the hearing of the ear; but now mine eye seeth thee" (v. 5).

AT-A-GLANCE

1. The Lord Speaks to Job (Job 38:1, 4, 16-17)
2. Job Responds to the Lord (42:1-2, 5)
3. Christ's Resurrection Shows His Power to Bring Hope to the Hopeless (Mark 16:1-7, 9-14, 20)

IN DEPTH

1. The Lord Speaks to Job (Job 38:1, 4, 16-17)

God's rhetorical questions to Job did at least two things: They reminded Job of his limitations and of God's unlimited resourcefulness, power, and wisdom. This confrontation was particularly revealing given Job's claim to know a lot about God's power and ways (see Job 27:11). How is one to answer God's question, "Where wast thou when I laid the foundations of the earth?" (Job 38:4).

Even with our current scientific knowledge about the earth, its movement, and its relationship to the other planets, there remains a certain mystery about God's creation that we may never comprehend. The more we know about the work of God's hands, the more we realize how much we have yet to learn. Those who have braved all the dangers of chasing tornadoes and who, in so doing, have reported profound insights, still stand in awe of nature's uncontrollable power and force.

We spend billions of dollars to harness the force of water to create the energy necessary to send electrical currents to heat our homes and light our city streets. Yet, every now and then, rain falls from God's heaven that swells our rivers and makes the largest dams and reservoirs look like structures made of toothpicks held together with a dab of glue. We have scientific equipment to measure the speed of wind. We can witness the effects of the wind, but no one has ever seen the wind. We do not know where wind comes from or where it goes when it blows by us.

God is really there. He who raised Jesus from the dead is resourceful enough to squeeze blessings out of our tragedies. Knowing this gives us reason to keep hope and faith in God alive. This was also Job's conclusion.

2. Job Responds to the Lord (42:1-2, 5)

When God finished speaking, Job began to see that behind God's power, and seemingly heartless handling of his life, was a God who cared. Upon pondering God's probing rhetorical questions, Job gained a new understanding of God's intentions and exercise of power. Additionally, Job discovered that there was divine purpose in his plight. His encounter with God enabled him to realize that "No discipline seems pleasant at the time, but painful. Later on, however, it produces a harvest of righteousness and peace for those who have been trained by it" (Hebrews 12:11, NIV).

Then with a radical change of heart and mind, Job decided to exchange the desire to defend his case before God for the desire to develop a deeper relationship with God. In short, Job recognized his need to repent: "I have heard of thee by the hearing of the ear: but now mine eye seeth thee" (Job 42:5). Job's repentance was evidence that all his prior doubts were wiped away. Having doubt-

ed God's care and concern, Job was now convinced that God was fair and just in all His ways. What Job wanted to believe as true, but doubted, had now been confirmed: "I know that my redeemer liveth....Whom I shall see for myself... though my reins be consumed within me" (19:25-27).

The story of Job teaches that God is in the business of resurrecting hope from seemingly hopeless situations; and this is the eternal message of Easter.

3. Christ's Resurrection Shows His Power to Bring Hope to the Hopeless (Mark 16:1-7, 9-14, 20)

Easter experiences are not limited to the New Testament era. As we have seen in our study of Job, when tragedy occurs and all seems hopeless, God responds with life. This is also a fitting summary of the life, death, burial, and resurrection of Jesus.

Jesus' death and burial, plus the sealing of the tomb, projected a tragic, hopeless situation. But God responds with life, and as we have already seen in Job, God always has the last word: "Don't be alarmed.... You are looking for Jesus the Nazarene, who was crucified. He has risen! He is not here. See the place where they laid him" (Mark 16:6, NIV).

SEARCH THE SCRIPTURES

1. What was God's first question to Job (Job 38:4)?

2. "I have heard of thee by the _____ of the ear: but now mine eye _____ thee" (42:5).

3. Was it before or after the Sabbath that the two Marys brought spices to anoint Jesus (Mark 16:1)?

4. Following His resurrection, to whom did Jesus appear first (v. 9)?

DISCUSS THE MEANING

1. In what sense are we to understand the phrase, "answered Job out of the whirlwind" in Job 38:1?

2. Identify and discuss some of the positive things that can come from suffering and pain.

3. How should we pray and what should we pray for during times of suffering? Should we

pray for deliverance, for courage, or for both? How should we pray when it seems that God is not going to deliver us?

4. In what ways can God be glorified through our suffering?

LESSON IN OUR SOCIETY

There are so many ways in which we are tempted to lose hope. Life can be very difficult, complicated, and overwhelmingly frustrating when we suffer hurts we know we don't deserve. Sometimes we seek God's help and He seems so very far away. Other times God seems near, but slow in responding to our petitions. During these times, we are sorely tempted to draw conclusions about God that may not be accurate.

Job's story teaches that no matter what may happen to us, or how we may feel about what happens to us, the Lord is good, and they who take refuge in Him are blessed (Psalm 34:8), if not in this life, then in the life to come.

MAKE IT HAPPEN

Make this week a time of thanking and praising God for the hope we have in Christ Jesus. Share this hope with others who may be enduring some stress or life-threatening disappointment. You can best do this by listening to their pain and offering to walk with them in prayer.

FOLLOW THE SPIRIT

What God wants me to do:

_____

_____

REMEMBER YOUR THOUGHTS

Special insights I have learned:

_____

_____

MORE LIGHT ON THE TEXT

Job 38:1, 4, 16-17; 42:1-2, 5; Mark 16:1-7, 9-14, 20

1 Then the LORD answered Job out of the whirlwind, and said

After 37 chapters, God finally answered Job. Nine times Job tried to convince his friends that the losses he had suffered in a single day were not caused by some unknown sin in his life. Each time, he argued his innocence and demanded that God reveal to him the reason for these devastating events. However, Job never budged from his belief that God was just. One after another, his friends' responses showed they were just as certain that he was wrong (Job 4:17-19; 8:1-6; 11:13-15). They repeatedly argued that Job wasn't being honest with himself or had some hidden sin that he was too proud or embarrassed to admit. God's response to Job was not all He had to say. His final answer came only when He sent Jesus to reveal all that people could know about God.

Notice that God responded to Job only after he had wrestled with the pain and loss and had listened to the thoughts of others who knew him and his situation. Often in Scripture, the people God used most had to wait for a clear understanding of God's will and wisdom to deal with their situation. First Kings 18:1 says of God's dealing with Elijah, "And it came to pass after many days, that the word of the Lord came to Elijah." Three times Paul prayed to be delivered from his "thorn in the flesh" before God told him that His grace was all he needed in order to live with this "thorn" (2 Corinthians 12:8-10).

Isaiah 40:31 describes the nature of God's help: "But they that wait upon the LORD shall renew their strength; they shall mount up with wings as eagles; they shall run, and not be weary; and they shall walk, and not faint." Sometimes God's wisdom or strength comes soon, as if we grow wings and fly off, leaving our problem behind. Sometimes God's help is not strength to escape our problem, but to keep going in spite of it. Other times He gives us a problem or allows a problem to enter our lives that we can't overcome. Here, God gives us enough strength to keep putting one foot in front of the other. Often Christians don't think they have received help unless God takes the problem away.

Notice also how God's reply to Job's constant demand for a personal confrontation came—in a "whirlwind" (Heb. *ca'ar,* **sah'ar**) or blinding desert windstorm. Most, but not all, of God's appearances in the Bible involved a disruption in the physical environment. Psalm 50:3 (NIV) warns, a fire devours before him." When Moses led the Hebrew leaders up to Mount Sinai, thunder and lightning erupted. With other divine appearances, earthquakes, tornadoes, or volcanic eruptions took place. When God arrived, Job got the confrontation he had demanded, but it wasn't what he expected.

38:4 Where wast thou when I laid the foundations of the earth? declare, if thou hast understanding.

When God arrived, instead of answering questions, He asked them. All of the questions He asked were beyond Job's ability to answer. When God was making the world, neither Job nor anyone else was alive.

The use of the word "foundations" (Heb. *yacad*, **yaw-sad'**) suggests construction and means to set or establish. Here God challenged Job to explain how he (Job) could question God or understand His plan if he was not there when the earth was established.

38:16 Hast thou entered into the springs of the sea? or hast thou walked in the search of the depth?

This verse showed how little Job knew of the earth. God asked if Job had seen everything that needed to be searched out in all the holes in the deepest canyons in earth's seas. The word "depth" (Heb. *tehowm*, **teh-home'**) means "abyss" or "deep place." "Walked" (Heb. *halak*, **haw-lak'**) means to traverse or to move back and forth. In other words, God asked Job, "Have you looked in the deepest, hidden parts of the earth? Have you looked everywhere there is to look?"

17 Have the gates of death been opened unto thee? or hast thou seen the doors of the shadow of death?

After asking a series of questions about the world where Job lived, God asked Job what he knew about the world beyond this one. "The gates of death" refers to the grave, the place of the dead; Job 10:20-21 describes it as a place of shadows, weakness, and gloomy emptiness.

Nowhere in God's response to Job's demands for a confrontation did God ever explain the rea-

son for Job's misfortunes. God wanted Job to trust that His love, goodness, justice, and power would see him through the bad times and hard places of life. He wants the same for us today, and sent Jesus to show perfectly what doing that means.

42:1 Then Job answered the LORD and said, 2 I know that thou canst do every thing, and that no thought can be withholden from thee.

God's questions forced Job to admit how limited his understanding was of God's plans and will for the world He created. After God finished questioning Job, Job declared his renewed faith in God's power. God's questions led Job to see that God's goodness and love meant nothing unless He had the power to make them known, and that He was able to carry out His plans and enforce His justice. When Job said, "thou canst do," he used the Hebrew word *yakol* (**yaw-kole'**), which meant "you have the power" or "you are able." God's purposes are not limited by people's ignorant hopelessness or sinful blindness.

Many modern translations interpret the second half of verse 2 differently from the King James Version. The *New International Version* translates it as, "No plan of yours can be thwarted." None of God's purposes can be stopped by us. God may allow people to think they have thwarted His purposes for a time. As a result, people like Job and Jesus, who trusted God, may suffer because they are sharing in God's patient and loving purposes for the human race. They may not understand what's happening in their lives or why. To share in the suffering by which Jesus revealed the extent of God's love for a world of sinful people might be more than many of us could sincerely pray. Job had not reached that point but had decided to trust God in spite of what he didn't know and could never understand.

42:5 I have heard of thee by the hearing of the ear: but now mine eye seeth thee.

Job was not saying that he had seen God visually. His point was that all he knew previously about God was based on what he had been told. Now he knew God because of personal experience. Job did not realize that that was how God wanted all people to know Him. He could not have even guessed that someday God would break into time and history to reveal Himself personally. Job now saw that in his arguments with his friends, he had failed to have enough understanding to argue about God's purposes.

Job declared publicly that he was unable to fully grasp God's plans. In spite of all Job's frustrated and often despairing demands for an explanation, he never renounced God as Satan had predicted that he would. Job was confused when he couldn't make sense of what had happened to him.

Mark 16:1 And when the sabbath was past, Mary Magdalene, and Mary the mother of James, and Salome, had bought sweet spices, that they might come and anoint him.

Jesus was crucified by Roman soldiers on Friday and died on Friday afternoon. The Jewish Sabbath began at sundown Friday. In order to get Jesus into a grave before the Sabbath began, Joseph of Arimathea asked permission to bury Jesus, and then rushed to complete the burial. Joseph anointed Jesus' corpse with an ointment of sweet-smelling spices, wrapped Him in linen strips (John 19:40), and put His body in a new tomb that he had just prepared for himself (Mark 15:46). Mary Magdalene and Mary, the mother of James ("the other Mary"), followed him and saw where Joseph buried Jesus' body.

Because of Joseph's haste, the women apparently assumed that Jesus had been buried without proper burial customs being followed. They were unaware that Joseph had already anointed Jesus' body and wrapped it securely in linen strips. So they came back early Sunday morning to anoint Jesus' body.

2 And very early in the morning the first day of the week, they came unto the sepulchre at the rising of the sun.

When a loved one dies, some people hardly ever go to the grave site because being there brings up such sad feelings. But in spite of their sadness, the three women went to anoint Jesus' body because the Jewish custom was to visit a person's tomb for each of the first three days after burial. Mary Magdalene had started "while it was

still dark." After picking up the other women along the way, she and the others reached the tomb at sunrise (Matthew 28:1).

3 And they said among themselves, Who shall roll away the stone from the door of the sepulchre? And when they looked, they saw that the stone was rolled away; for it was very great.

At least two of the women had been there when the tomb was sealed (Matthew 27:61). In tombs of well-to-do men, of whom Joseph of Arimathea was probably one, a channel sloping downward to the opening was dug. Then a large, flat stone would be rolled into the upper end of the trench. After a body was put in the tomb, the stone would be rolled down to the channel's deepest spot in front of the tomb's opening. The immense stone sealed out marauding animals and made it difficult for vandals to break in.

But as the women reached the tomb, they looked up to see a gaping black hole where the huge stone had been. God had moved the stone, not to let Jesus out, but to let the women go in.

5 And entering into the sepulchre, they saw a young man sitting on the right side, clothed in a long white garment; and they were affrighted.

The form of the Greek verb "entering" (*eiser-chomai*, ice-er'-khom-ahee) means to go out or come in. When the women saw the tomb standing open, they hurried inside. The most common meaning for "affrighted" (Gk. *ekthambeo*, **ek-tham-beth'-o**) is "alarmed" or "amazed." The women did not know what to make of the situation; they were confused and probably agitated.

6 And he saith unto them, Be not affrighted: Ye seek Jesus of Nazareth, which was crucified; he is risen; he is not here: behold the place where they laid him. 7 But go your way, tell his disciples and Peter that he goeth before you into Galilee: there shall ye see him, as he said unto you.

The messenger told the women to stop being upset. Instead, he instructed them to go tell Jesus' closest disciples that He had been raised victorious over death and wanted them to meet Him in Galilee.

As Job discovered in the midst of tragedy and

the women found out at the empty tomb, what God has done, is doing, and is capable of doing is beyond our ability to comprehend. Jesus had told His disciples over and over again that He would be raised from death after crucifixion (Mark 8:31; 9:31; 10:34).

16:9 Now when Jesus was risen early the first day of the week, he appeared first to Mary Magdelene, out of whom he had cast seven devils. 10 And she went and told them that had been with him, as they mourned and wept. 11 And they, when they had heard that he was alive, and had been seen of her, believed not. 12 After that he appeared in another form unto two of them, as they walked, and went into the country. 13 And they went and told it unto the residue: neither believed they them. 14 Afterward he appeared unto the eleven as they sat at meat, and upbraided them with their unbelief and hardness of heart, because they believed not them which had seen him after he was risen. 20 And they went forth, and preached every where, the Lord working with them, and confirming the word with signs following. Amen.

The greatness of God's love was proven by His willingness to send Jesus to die unjustly on the Cross for the sins of all people. Just like Job, some may question God's motives and goodness. However, the enormity of God's power was revealed in raising Jesus from death, never to die again. In spite of loss, unexpected tragedy, or injustice, we must cling in faith to God's unchanging faithfulness.

DAILY BIBLE READINGS

M: Where Were You During the Creation?
Job 38:1-7

T: Do You Understand My Creation?
Job 38:8-18

W: I Know You, and I Repent
Job 42:1-6

T: Job's Fortunes Are Restored Twofold
Job 42:10-17

F: He Is Not Here
Mark 16:1-8

S: Jesus Appears to His Followers
Mark 16:9-14

S: Go and Proclaim the Good News
Mark 16:15-20

TEACHING TIPS

April 23
Bible Study Guide 8

1. Words You Should Know

A. Vanity (Ecclesiastes 1:2) *hebel* (Heb.)—Literally, "breath" or "vapor," that which is fleeting, insubstantial, of no lasting consequence, unreliable, empty, or ineffective.

B. Labour (v. 3) *'amal* (Heb.)—Here it refers to more than just work, activity, and effort. In the context of Ecclesiastes, it refers also to the mental and emotional struggle involved in achieving some end or goal.

C. Peace (John 20:19, 21) *eirene* (Gk.)—It does not necessarily mean the cessation of war and struggle. Rather, it means inner peace and calm even in the midst of war and struggle.

D. Remit, remitted (v. 23) *aphiemi* (Gk.)—To forgive, or to have been forgiven.

2. Teacher Preparation

A. Read the printed text and all the material in BIBLE STUDY GUIDE 8, giving particular attention to WORDS YOU SHOULD KNOW.

B. Review the LESSON AIM and reflect upon how this lesson relates to your own life. For example, in what ways has your relationship with God through faith in Jesus Christ given meaning to your life? What do you think your life would be like without this relationship?

C. You will need a chalkboard or newsprint and enough 3 x 5" cards to give one to each student.

3. Starting the Lesson

A. Have the students brainstorm brief answers to the question raised in Ecclesiastes 1:3. List on the chalkboard or newsprint at least four or five of their responses.

B. Have the students develop a brief sentence summarizing what they think the writer's answer is to his own question in Ecclesiastes 1:3.

C. Have a student read the IN FOCUS story and the BACKGROUND section aloud.

4. Getting into the Lesson

A. Have a student read aloud Ecclesiastes 1:1-9.

B. Discuss how the writer's answer compares with the students' initial answers to the question of verse 3.

5. Relating the Lesson to Life

A. Ask for volunteers to read the IN DEPTH section aloud, and answer the DISCUSS THE MEANING questions.

B. Have the students discuss what they think their lives would be like without a relationship with God.

6. Arousing Action

A. Read the LESSON IN OUR SOCIETY and MAKE IT HAPPEN sections aloud.

B. Encourage the students to list on a 3 x 5 card the names of at least three of their peers who are not involved in any church and are, presumably, living their lives outside of a meaningful relationship with God through faith in Jesus Christ.

C. Discuss ways in which the students might share their faith with their unchurched peers.

D. Challenge the students to invite the people they identified on their 3 x 5 cards to next week's session. Close this session with prayer.

WORSHIP GUIDE

For the Superintendent or Teacher
Theme: Finding Life's Meaning
Theme Song: "Heavenly Sunlight"
Scripture: Hebrews 12:14
Song: "Wonderful Peace"
Meditation: May the peace of God, which transcends all understanding, guard our hearts and our minds in Christ Jesus.
Amen.

FINDING LIFE'S MEANING

Bible Background • ECCLESIASTES 1:1–11; JOHN 20:19–23
Printed Text • ECCLESIASTES 1:1–9; JOHN 20:19–23
Devotional Reading • LUKE 24:36–48

LESSON AIM

By the end of the lesson, we will:

KNOW how Jesus provides purpose and peace in our lives;

SHARE personal experiences related to our own search for peace and meaning; and

RELATE how our relationship with God through faith in Jesus Christ has affected our search.

KEEP IN MIND

"Then the same day at evening, being the first day of the week, when the doors were shut where the disciples were assembled for fear of the Jews, came Jesus and stood in the midst, and saith unto them, Peace be unto you" (John 20:19).

FOCAL VERSES

Ecclesiastes 1:1 The words of the Preacher, the son of David, king in Jerusalem.

2 Vanity of vanities, saith the Preacher, vanity of vanities; all is vanity.

3 What profit hath a man of all his labour which he taketh under the sun?

4 One generation passeth away, and another generation cometh: but the earth abideth for ever.

5 The sun also ariseth, and the sun goeth down, and hasteth to his place where he arose.

6 The wind goeth toward the south, and turneth about unto the north; it whirleth about continually, and the wind returneth again according

LESSON OVERVIEW

LESSON AIM

KEEP IN MIND

FOCAL VERSES

IN FOCUS

THE PEOPLE, PLACES, AND TIMES

BACKGROUND

AT-A-GLANCE

IN DEPTH

SEARCH THE SCRIPTURES

DISCUSS THE MEANING

LESSON IN OUR SOCIETY

MAKE IT HAPPEN

FOLLOW THE SPIRIT

REMEMBER YOUR THOUGHTS

MORE LIGHT ON THE TEXT

DAILY BIBLE READINGS

to his circuits.

7 All the rivers run into the sea; yet the sea is not full; unto the place from whence the rivers come, thither they return again.

8 All things are full of labour; man cannot utter it: the eye is not satisfied with seeing, nor the ear filled with hearing.

9 The thing that hath been, it is that which shall be; and that which is done is that which shall be done: and there is no new thing under the sun.

John 20:19 Then the same day at evening, being the first day of the week, when the doors were shut where the disciples were assembled for fear of the Jews, came Jesus and stood in the midst, and saith unto them, Peace be unto you.

20 And when he had so said, he shewed unto them his hands and his side. Then were the disciples glad, when they saw the Lord.

21 Then said Jesus to them again, Peace be unto you: as my Father hath sent me, even so send I you.

22 And when he had said this, he breathed on them, and saith unto them, Receive ye the Holy Ghost:

23 Whose soever sins ye remit, they are remitted unto them; and whose soever sins ye retain, they are retained.

IN FOCUS

Hal couldn't even find peace fishing on the

APR
23RD

323

riverbank. Hal loved fishing because it usually relieved the stress of his job.

What had the preacher said last Sunday? Hal's mind wandered with the river as he cast his line and let the hook and bait fall beneath the surface. As the ripples faded, his mind caught the words that had evaded him all morning: There is no guarantee of a positive benefit from a man's work. No peace came as he remembered the words.

He had been let go from his job for lack of performance over two months ago. He couldn't bring himself to tell his pregnant wife. Nothing in his life had hit him so hard. He hadn't spoken to his wife in weeks. His vanity made him leave home every morning in the pretense of going to work. Some days he looked for jobs, but lately he just went fishing and then changed back into his suit.

Suddenly a fish yanked at his line. Hal pulled the struggling fish into the air.

"Fear not" was another message from the sermon. "Trust God," the preacher had said.

Hal reeled the thrashing fish onto the bank and reached into its mouth to release the hook.

"'And peace will be with you,' Jesus said."

He tossed the fish back into the water and fell to his knees to repent of his self-centeredness. He realized that there would be no peace at the riverbank or in his life unless his relationship with God was right. He finally understood that his failure to trust God, not losing his job, was the cause of his turmoil.

Ecclesiastes reminds us that all our work is temporal and that we cannot depend on our accomplishments to keep us lifted up. Do you believe trusting God will provide everlasting peace?

THE PEOPLE, PLACES, AND TIMES

The author of Ecclesiastes. We cannot know for certain who wrote the book of Ecclesiastes. Ancient tradition attributes the book to Solomon because it describes as the writer "son of David, king in Jerusalem" (1:1). Some recent scholars have concluded that Solomon was not the author of the book of Ecclesiastes because the language in this book comes from a time much later than when Solomon lived. However, we must remember that Solomon was king when Israel was at its height of power, prestige, and prominence. He was exposed to the wisdom literature of civilizations such as Egypt and Babylon. This poetic literature also wrestled with the problems and issues of life. It is reasonable to assume that he collected this literature and added to this wealth of wisdom by showing how to navigate through life as a God-fearing person.

We must also remember that Solomon was world famous for His wisdom. Besides, who else but Solomon fits the profile in Ecclesiastes 1:16, NIV, "I have grown and increased in wisdom more than anyone who has ruled over Jerusalem before me; I have experienced much of wisdom and knowledge." Of course, we cannot completely rule out that the "Preacher" or "Teacher" in this remarkable book was someone other than Solomon. Scholars of goodwill differ on this issue.

We do know that "the Preacher" was a wise individual who taught and worked among the people (Ecclesiastes 12:9). Whether he was a commoner or a member of the elite, it would appear that the thoughts articulated in the book of Ecclesiastes are those of an individual who was associated and familiar with a diverse population.

Ecclesiastes 1:1-9 expresses the thought of one who is totally convinced that life is meaningless and, therefore, that any hope of experiencing peace is unlikely. One should not read these verses and conclude, however, that this is the message of the book of Ecclesiastes. It is not. These verses simply describe the author's current position in his search for meaning and peace.

Ultimately, the author reasons his way to the conclusion that life is only meaningless when God is not included in the equation. Thus, the preacher's "conclusion of the whole matter" was, "Fear God, and keep his commandments: for this is the whole duty of man" (12:13). According to the writer, to live a life of commitment and obedience to the will of God is to pursue a life of meaning and peace. This Old Testament truth, which makes the pursuit of God the path that leads to meaning and peace, is reaffirmed in the New Testament gospel of John.

The author of the fourth gospel is the apostle John. It was written in or before the last decade of the first century. Scholars have concluded that the book of John is distinct from the Synoptic Gospels (Matthew, Mark, and Luke).

A wide variety of purposes have been attributed to the book of John. The most essential purpose is given to us by John: "These are written, that ye may believe that Jesus is the Christ, the Son of God; and that believing, ye might have life through his name" (20:31). John plainly stated that he was motivated to show Jesus as the Christ, the Son of God. He did this in order that he might bring his readers to a place of faith, that is, to a new life in Christ's name.

John did not use language or historical reporting that might have distorted his theological aim, but frequently presented evidence that Jesus is indeed the Christ. John confronts us with the challenge posed by the message of Jesus, and there is no neutral ground of belief. Either you commit yourself to Christ in faith and so enter life, or you remain in darkness and in a condition of lostness. Only Jesus can give meaning and peace to one's life.

Bibliography
Towner, W. Sibley. "The Book of Ecclesiastes." The New Interpreter's Bible, Vol. 5. Nashville, Tenn.: Abingdon Press, 1997.

BACKGROUND

The crucifixion, burial, and entombment left the disciples afraid, confused, depressed, and groping to find meaning in the things that had happened. The value the disciples attributed to life with Jesus and the peace they experienced from fellowship with Him had become the organizing principles for their lives. While Jesus was alive and casting His vision about the kingdom of God, the disciples felt energized and excited. Their lives had meaning when following Jesus. Listening to Jesus' frequent words of counsel and learning about prayer and faith filled the disciples with an inner peace they deeply cherished.

Everything changed in the space of three days; Jesus was dead and buried. The meaningful dream that the disciples had been pursuing had now come to an end. The disciples were tempted to return to their previous occupations and careers. They probably would have done so, except that "at evening, being the first day of the week, when the doors were

shut where the disciples were assembled for fear of the Jews, came Jesus and stood in the midst, and saith unto them, Peace be unto you" (John 20:19). What a day and moment that must have been for the disciples.

From that day until now, disciples of Jesus have found meaning and peace while pursuing the things that pertain to God and His will. It is the hope and prayer of this writer that you are numbered among those who have chosen to follow Jesus and to pursue a growing relationship with God. This is the only way to peace and a meaningful life.

> ## AT-A-GLANCE
>
> 1. The Vanity of Life Evidenced in Nature (Ecclesiastes 1:1-8)
> 2. The Vanity of Life Evidenced in History (v. 9)
> 3. The Path to Meaning and Peace (John 20:19-23)

IN DEPTH

1. The Vanity of Life Evidenced in Nature (Ecclesiastes 1:1-8)

After a brief introduction in verse 1 and a concise statement of the preacher's thesis in verse 2, the reader is immediately confronted with a question: "What profit hath a man of all his labour which he taketh under the sun?" (v. 3).

Most people can identify with the preacher's question. Indeed, there is perhaps hardly a person alive who has not asked in one way or another, is it worth it? Am I making any progress? When will it all end? Will I ever get finished? Is this all there is? What benefit did it bring me?

All these questions imply a gloomy answer. The implied answer is NO, NEVER, NOTHING! One would like to think that toil results in profit (Proverbs 14:23) and that hard work always brings beneficial rewards, but it is not necessarily so. Pursuance of the Protestant work ethic has not always met with positive results. The early bird has not always gotten the worm, nor does the squeaky wheel always get greased. The jobs of hardworking people are known to have dried up or moved overseas, creating unemployment lines populated with hardworking people in search of jobs that don't exist. Many of the things people need to depend upon for survival in life are not dependable. Necessary foundations keep shifting, resulting in meaninglessness and a lack of peace and security. "Vanity of vanities; all is vanity" (v. 2).

The preacher's viewpoint cannot be easily dismissed. There is a certain vanity that accompanies so much of what we do and experience in life. The question is, "How does one find meaning and peace amidst the fleeting and insubstantial structures of our lives?" In order to illustrate the vanity and meaninglessness of life, the preacher of Ecclesiastes draws evidence from nature (vv. 4-8) and history (v. 9). For example, natural laws make it true that "one generation passeth away, and another generation cometh. . . the sun ariseth, and goeth down. . . The wind whirleth about continually. . .unto the place from whence the rivers come, thither they return again. . . the eye is not satisfied with seeing, nor the ear filled with hearing" (vv. 4-8). This is the writer's way of saying that what goes up, must come down.

2. The Vanity of Life Evidenced in History (v. 9)

The writer of Ecclesiastes also draws an analogy from history: what "hath been shall be that which is done shall be done there is no new thing under the sun" (v. 9). In other words, what has happened in the past will happen in the future. "The more things change, the more they stay the same." There is a certain repetitiveness that contributes to a sense of meaninglessness and a lack of peace.

Given the preacher's assessment of life, can there be meaning and peace in this life? If so, where are peace and meaning to be found? The Good News of the Gospel declares that meaning and peace can be found only through faith in Jesus Christ and in a growing relationship with God. Moreover, things done repeatedly, if done for the glory and honor of God, bring excitement, joy, meaning, and peace.

3. The Path to Meaning and Peace (John 20:19-23)

Following the crucifixion and burial of Jesus, out of "fear of the Jews" (John 20:19), the disciple cloistered themselves behind locked doors. They were more than fearful. They were also dejected. Their hopes and dreams had been destroyed. Their lives were now void of meaning and purpose. The peace they once knew had been swallowed up by their despondency and fears about their future. However, when they saw the resurrected Lord, when He appeared in their midst, and when He said "Peace be unto you," they were overjoyed (v. 19).

This episode in the disciples' life teaches us several lessons. First, only the presence of God can give meaning, purpose, and peace to our lives. Therefore, if what we do in life is not done to the glory and honor of God, our lives will be devoid of meaning, and we will not know peace. Life's meaning is found in Christ. Those who submit to His will, will have found peace. Second, there are no barriers that God cannot and will not cross to bring meaning and peace to our lives. If He can step through locked doors, He can present Himself in any place and any situation to speak peace to our souls. Third, we are taught that our experience of God's peace is not limited to our fellowship with believers behind closed doors. The peace God gives through faith in Jesus Christ will accompany us as we render service in the wider community (v. 21). Finally, we are taught that there is no greater peace than the peace that comes from knowing that one's sins have been remitted (v. 23).

SEARCH THE SCRIPTURES

1. "What profit hath a man of all his _____ which he taketh under the _____?" (Ecclesiastes 1:3).

2. "There is no new _____ under the sun" (v. 9).

3. "When the doors were shut where the _____ were assembled for fear of the Jews, came Jesus and stood in the _____, and saith unto them, _____ be unto you" (John 20:19).

4. What did Jesus say to the disciples upon appearing in their midst (vv. 21-23)?

DISCUSS THE MEANING

1. In what ways has your acceptance of Jesus Christ given meaning to your life?

2. Discuss what life might be like without a relationship with God through faith in Jesus Christ.

3. What is meant by the word "peace"?

4. Discuss how you might share Christ with those who are searching to find meaning and peace.

LESSON IN OUR SOCIETY

One of the unstated preoccupations of our time is the search for meaning and peace. Many people spend countless hours searching in all the wrong places. Money can provide a materially comfortable life. Friends can help us fill our available time with something to do and someone to do it with. Law enforcement officers and a strong national defense system can help provide us with physical protection. None of these, however, can assuage the human thirst for meaning and inner peace. More money is no substitute for a lonely heart. Friends may never understand all our hurts, nor can they save us from the sting of death.

In our search for meaning and peace, where can we go but to the Lord?

MAKE IT HAPPEN

Take the time this week to thank and praise God for the meaning and peace He gives you through faith in Jesus Christ. Share your experience with others who may not know the peace of Christ, which passes all understanding.

FOLLOW THE SPIRIT

What God wants me to do:

_____

_____

_____

REMEMBER YOUR THOUGHTS

Special insights I have learned:

_____

_____

MORE LIGHT ON THE TEXT

Ecclesiastes 1:1-9; John 20:19-23

The word "Preacher" in Hebrew is *Qoheleth*, (ko-heh'-leth). This word does not occur outside of the book of Ecclesiastes. It is believed that the word is related to the term *qahal*, meaning "assembly." The Greek translators of the Bible rendered Ecclesiasties as *ekklesiates*, hence, "the Preacher," or "the Teacher." Like Proverbs and Job, Ecclesiastes is one of the five wisdom books, but little is known for sure about its background or the history of its composition. Its author is identified as "the son of David, king in Jerusalem" (Ecclesiastes 1:1), which is Solomon.

1 The words of the Preacher, the son of David, king in Jerusalem. 2 Vanity of vanities, saith the Preacher, vanity of vanities; all is vanity.

"The Words of the Preacher" is probably the title of the book of Ecclesiastes. This phrase is also used to introduce an anthology or collection of the teachings of the one who gathered or collected written materials. The initial verse of today's text is verse 2, which states the theme of the book's argument. The key word, which occurs frequently in the book, is the Hebrew term *hebel*, meaning "vanity." The word literally means "wind," "breath," or "vapor." Used in this context, it infers that everything is either ephemeral, futile (meaningless), or both.

Ecclesiastes, unlike other wisdom literature, is not merely a collection of sayings; instead, the sayings seem to frame a life story. The book describes Solomon's experience in investigating both wisdom (the path of patience and restraint) and folly (hedonism and reckless abandon).

3 What profit hath a man of all his labour which he taketh under the sun? 4 One generation passeth away, and another generation cometh: but the earth abideth for ever. 5 The sun also ariseth, and the sun goeth down, and hasteth to his place where he arose. 6 The wind goeth toward the south, and turneth about unto the north; it whirleth about continually, and the wind returneth again according to his circuits.

Truly life is meaningless apart from finding its meaning in relationship to God. Fallen man gets caught up in his sense of self-importance, yet after his life has ended, the earth continues as it did before. History progresses without missing a beat. Nature goes through its seasons as if unconcerned with the demise of one generation and the rise of another. God calls the shots, not man. Jesus reminds us of this when He asks, "Who of you by worrying can add a single hour to his life?" (Matthew 6:27, NIV). The only way for life to make sense is to make it God-centered and God-guided, not self-centered and self-guided.

7 All the rivers run into the sea; yet the sea is not full; unto the place from whence the rivers come, thither they return again. 8 All things are full of labour; man cannot utter it: the eye is not satisfied with seeing, nor the ear filled with hearing.

Life has many paths, and not all paths lead to a purpose-filled life. Solomon, referring to himself as the "Preacher," seeks to instruct people of the emptiness of searching for the meaning of life in knowledge, money, pleasure, work, or popularity. Life is not measured quantitatively (in the abundance of material possessions), but qualitatively. One can spend an eternity searching for that "one thing" to give his or her life purpose and happiness. Yet, the more one searches, the more he or she realizes everything is vanity, says the preacher, utter vanity! If it is not God-centered, life becomes a lost enterprise of false expectations. Because we are the image bearers of God, our lives will have only purpose and meaning as God directs and empowers us with His love, Word, and abiding presence, leading us into fruitful fields of service (to God and humanity). God alone gives wisdom, knowledge, and joy.

Like Solomon taking a personal inventory and assessing the meaning of life, we need to take a sober look at our lives, determine what it really means to live, and assess the real meaning of life. We must ask: For all the hard work I have done, what have I really accomplished? The preacher asked rhetorically, "What profit do people get for all their hard work?" (v. 3, paraphrased). A comparable question posed by Jesus in Mark 8:36 is: "What shall it profit a man if he shall gain the whole world, and lose his own soul?" The Hebrew word for "profit" is *yithrown* (**yith-rone'**). This word is derived from the world of business and, means "advantage" or "excellency." In this context, it would suggest that nature and hard work have no

residuum, i.e., anything left over. There is no gain, profit, or purpose for man inherent within nature or work.

Solomon illustrates the restlessness, or tiresome nature, of life by using four examples from the realm of nature: the earth, sun, wind, and rivers. What is suggested is that while generations are coming and going, the earth stands (v. 4). The preacher, with these examples, is contrasting the permanently abiding condition of the earth with the transitory status of human existence (vv. 5-7). Nature remains permanent without deviation. Yet, this uniformity does not offer any comfort to humanity or provide the rationale for humanity's own meaning. Earth, with all of its parts, is ever hastening on. People are in a frantic pursuit of more—more possessions, more power, greater pleasure. However, no matter how much we see, we are never satisfied. No matter how much we hear, we are not content (v. 8).

The one thing that gives purpose and meaning to all human existence is not education, work, or pleasure, but it is service to God. Only by living a life devoted to the service of God will you experience the God-centered and God-empowered life that clarifies and defines who you really are. When your focus is on God and not on self, you will be able to learn the lesson of contentment. Nothing in this world can truly satisfy the hunger of the spiritual self.

9 The thing that hath been, it is that which shall be; and that which is done is that which shall be done: and there is no new thing under the sun.

Solomon was convinced that serving God was his greatest satisfaction—the place where peace is found. God measures the worth and greatness of a person's life in terms of humble service—serving others. We each need to determine whether our works, values, and service will survive the grave.

Nature remains without deviation and nothing new has ever appeared, for it had already appeared long before human existence. So what do people get for all their hard work? Is it merely the dreary rhythm of ceaseless activity? Only a God-directed and empowered life brings purpose and meaning to human existence.

The cyclic nature of human existence renews

the preacher's argument. Like a sphere, life's surface cannot be viewed or described completely from any one angle; we must gain God's perspective and understand His truths.

John 20:19 Then the same day at evening, being the first day of the week, when the doors were shut where the disciples were assembled for fear of the Jews, came Jesus and stood in the midst, and saith unto them, Peace be unto you.

This incident occurred on the evening of the first Easter. John tells us that the doors of the room where the disciples had assembled were shut and locked. They had almost been arrested with Jesus in the Garden of Gethsemane. Since Jesus was seen as a dangerous troublemaker, they knew that as the disciples of Jesus, they were targets of the religious establishment. They were probably meeting together to figure out how they could escape from Jerusalem while avoiding attracting the attention of the Roman authorities and the temple police. The doors were locked because they were afraid that the Jews would send vigilantes against them the way they had done for Jesus.

Jesus came and stood among them, presumably entering through the locked doors. The Scripture says nothing of the mode of Jesus' entry into the room. This is John's way of showing that the risen Jesus was not limited by closed or locked doors. Jesus miraculously stood in their midst and pronounced, "Peace be unto you." This was not the typical Hebrew greeting; rather, it was a pronouncement of peace upon them.

20 And when he had so said, he shewed unto them his hands and his side. Then were the disciples glad, when they saw the Lord.

The disciples did not believe the fact of the Resurrection when it was reported to them by a credible witness (Mary Magdalene), but on the evidence of a physical demonstration: "Jesus. . . stood in the midst. . .. And [without any apparent urging]. . . he shewed unto them his hands and his side." The disciples needed such proof to stabilize their faith; however, we need no such proof, for "[we] know that [our] redeemer lives" (Job 19:25). Jesus gave this demonstration in order to convince the disciples that He was the same Jesus

who was crucified, but now was resurrected and standing in their midst; hence, He was taking away their fear.

21 Then said Jesus to them again, Peace be unto you: as my Father hath sent me, even so send I you. 22 And when he had said this, he breathed on them, and saith unto them, Receive ye the Holy Ghost: 23 Whose soever sins ye remit, they are remitted unto them; and whose soever sins ye retain, they are retained.

Jesus repeated the greeting, then went on to say, "as my Father hath sent me, so send I you" (v. 21). The sending out of the church (disciples) by Jesus is parallel to the sending out of Jesus by God. As Jesus was in the perfect will of God, so too, must believers be in the will of Jesus, who commissions us. The church's (disciples') mission was identical to the mission of Jesus. Thus, Jesus' mission had not ended; it would not end. It was to be carried on in the lives of His followers whom He commissioned. Jesus had completed the work of His earthly mission (the task that the Father had given Him). He now sent His followers into the world. It was because Jesus had accomplished His mission that He sent His followers into the world. Through the empowered disciples, Jesus' ministry would continue in the world.

Now that the disciples were commissioned, Jesus "breathed on them, and saith unto them, 'Receive the Holy Ghost: Whose soever sins ye remit, they are remitted unto them; and whose soever sins ye retain, they are retained.'" The indwelling of the Spirit was the confirmation of their apostolic authority.

Some have taken verse 23 to mean that God forgives sins because we forgive sins. This is not what Jesus is saying. In the Greek construction, the verb "remit" (forgive) in the phrase, "whose soever sins ye remit," and the verb "retain" (not forgive) in the phrase "whose soever sins ye retain," are in the aorist (past) tense. This implies a one-time action. The verb "remitted" (forgiven) in the phrase "they are remitted unto them," and the verb "retained" (not forgiven) in the phrase "they are retained," are in the perfect tense. This implies an ongoing action that began before the action of the verbs in the aorist (past) tense.

Therefore, the best rendering of this verse would be, "Those whose sins you forgive have already been forgiven; those whose sins you do not forgive have not been forgiven." This is an announcement of forgiveness and non-forgiveness, not the determination of it. Whether or not someone's sins are forgiven depends on whether or not they believe the Gospel of Jesus Christ.

To do God's work, you need the guidance and power of the Holy Spirit. The Holy Spirit's presence enables you to move from personal ambition to mission, reminding you that the mission is never yours but the Lord's. Jesus has demonstrated how to accomplish the mission assigned to us. His saving work is accomplished only through the power of His divine Spirit. With the power of the Holy Spirit directing your life, you can move from fear and hopelessness to the discovery of meaning and purpose by living a life that honors God.

DAILY BIBLE READINGS

M: Nothing New Under the Sun
Ecclesiastes 1:1-11
T: The Futility of Seeking Wisdom
Ecclesiastes 1:12-18
W: The Futility of Self-indulgence
Ecclesiastes 2:1-11
T: All Is Vanity
Ecclesiastes 2:12-17
F: Of What Good Is Our-Toil?
Ecclesiastes 2:18-26
S: Jesus Gives the Disciples a Mission
Luke 24:36-48
S: Receive the Holy Spirit
John 20:19-23

Bibliography

Achtemeier, Paul J., ed. *Harper's Bible Dictionary*. San Francisco: Harper and Row, 1985.

TEACHING TIPS

April 30
Bible Study Guide 9

1. Words You Should Know

A. Cast away stones (Ecclesiastes 3:5) *shalak 'eben* (Heb.)—is probably a reference to the demolition of a building. Some argue that the phrase also refers to human relationships, thus connecting it to avoiding an embrace.

B. Time to rend (v. 7) *'eth gara* (Heb.)—A contrast that is probably a reference to tearing one's clothing as a sign of mourning.

2. Teacher Preparation

A. Read Ecclesiastes 3:1-8, 14-15 from several different translations. As you read the text, note the thoughts that come to your mind.

B. Study all sections of BIBLE STUDY GUIDE 9. Compare your initial thoughts with the content of the BIBLE STUDY GUIDE. Are your thoughts confirmed, or is there need for adjustment?

3. Starting the Lesson

A. Ask a student to read aloud the IN FOCUS story, and engage the class in a brief discussion regarding God's timetable versus man's timetable.

B. Have the students read the FOCAL VERSES in unison.

4. Getting into the Lesson

A. Inform the students of the LESSON AIM.

B. Have the students brainstorm what they think the writer of Ecclesiastes is trying to illustrate in verses 1-8 of the FOCAL VERSES.

5. Relating the Lesson to Life

A. Summarize and share the BACKGROUND content. Help the students to see that verses 1-8 present a picture of the kinds of activity that take place between the time of one's birth and one's death.

B. Remind the students that verses 14-15 confirm the fundamental biblical teaching that God controls the unfolding of human history in ways that serve His purposes.

6. Arousing Action

A. Ask the students to discuss how they see God acting in the affairs of mankind. For example, it is relatively easy to see how God is at work when good things happen in our history. In what ways is God's activity revealed during tragic events?

B. Have the students select three or four tragic events; then identify and discuss any good that has resulted from these identified tragedies.

IN GOD'S TIME

Bible Background • ECCLESIASTES 3
Printed Text • ECCLESIASTES 3:1–8, 14–15
Devotional Reading • PSALM 34:1–8

LESSON AIM

By the end of the lesson, we will:

KNOW God's thoughts on how there is a time for everything in our lives;

FEEL that God's timetable provides balance in our lives; and

EXPLORE the various ways in which God uses objectionable experiences to serve our good.

KEEP IN MIND

"To every thing there is a season, and a time to every purpose under the heaven" (Ecclesiastes 3:1).

FOCAL VERSES

Ecclesiastes 3:1 To every thing there is a season, and a time to every purpose under the heaven:

2 A time to be born, and a time to die; a time to plant, and a time to pluck up that which is planted;

3 A time to kill, and a time to heal; a time to break down, and a time to build up;

4 A time to weep, and a time to laugh; a time to mourn, and a time to dance;

5 A time to cast away stones, and a time to gather stones together; a time to embrace, and a time to refrain from embracing;

6 A time to get, and a time to lose; a time to keep, and a time to cast away;

7 A time to rend, and a time to sew; a time to keep silence, and a time to speak;

8 A time to love, and a time to hate; a time of war, and a time of peace.

LESSON OVERVIEW

LESSON AIM
KEEP IN MIND
FOCAL VERSES
IN FOCUS
THE PEOPLE, PLACES,
AND TIMES
BACKGROUND
AT-A-GLANCE
IN DEPTH
SEARCH THE SCRIPTURES
DISCUSS THE MEANING
LESSON IN OUR SOCIETY
MAKE IT HAPPEN
FOLLOW THE SPIRIT
REMEMBER YOUR THOUGHTS
MORE LIGHT ON THE TEXT
DAILY BIBLE READINGS

3:14 I know that, whatsoever God doeth, it shall be for ever: nothing can be put to it, nor any thing taken from it: and God doeth it, that men should fear before him.

15 That which hath been is now; and that which is to be hath already been; and God requireth that which is past.

IN FOCUS

When Rita walked out of the kitchen, her 6-year-old daughter, Christine, turned from the window where she had been watching the fall leaves blowing in the yard. "Mommy, why do leaves change colors?"

Drying her hands on her apron, Rita smiled and said, "Because God says it's time."

Suddenly her daughter went adult on her: "No, I mean really, Mommy. I told Amy's big sister that, but she says it's because the trees stop making stuff that makes their leaves green, something called colorfill. Is that true?"

"Oh, you mean chlorophyll."

"Yes, ma'am, colorfill," her daughter said, repeating her version.

Rita sat down on the floor and tried a different answer. "Yes, it's true that when it gets cold, God takes green away. The red, orange, and yellow colors you see are always there, but during the spring and summer they're covered by chlorophyll."

Her daughter's response was, "I wish God would let the colors stay all the time. Don't you, Mommy?"

"Sometimes," Rita answered. "But I think it's nice that God picks the time for the seasons. I could never pick the right time because if I waited too long, maybe the birds wouldn't know when to fly away."

Christine added, "And maybe the squirrels wouldn't know when to hide their nuts."

Christine stroked her teddy bear and went adult again. "Just like it was nice that God picked the time for Granddad to die," because we would have wanted to keep him here with us. But instead, God knew it was time for him to go to heaven."

Rita smiled and thought how much we can learn from the wisdom of a child. She said softly, "Christine, dear, you are absolutely right."

In Ecclesiastes, Solomon pondered God's design and divine order. When we struggle with life's events, we must remind ourselves that everything is happening in God's appointed time.

THE PEOPLE, PLACES, AND TIMES

The book of Ecclesiastes discusses the age-old question that many people continue to ask: "Is life worth living?" As we saw in last week's lesson, the writer was initially convinced that life was meaningless and without purpose. He reasoned that, much like riding a merry-go-round, so much of what we experience is repetitious, boring, and takes us nowhere except to the grave. In the language of the text, all "is vanity and vexation of spirit" (Ecclesiastes 2:26). How then are we to live life in a way that rises above the "vanity" Solomon ascribes to everything? The key is not to be found in the vicissitudes of life itself because all things have validity in their own time. The key to life is only found "under heaven," that is, under and in God Himself.

Why does life sometimes seem so empty (vain)? Is God responsible for meaninglessness? Of course not! The world we know is not the world as God created it. The world God created was "very good" (Genesis 1:31). The world in its present condition is fallen and messed up by sin. That is why the mystery of life cannot be solved from within life itself.

We cannot see God's complete purposes in life because we are finite (limited). There are some things that only God knows in His infinite (unlimited) wisdom. When we tried to pry into God's exclusive knowledge, the result was the Fall of mankind (Genesis 3:1-19). Yet, God "has also set eternity in the hearts of men" (3:11b). Thus, we desire to live life on a higher level than the animals. There is meaning to life. But how can we know it? This is the question Solomon wrestles with in this passage.

BACKGROUND

Ecclesiastes 3, which is probably the most often quoted portion of the book, announces an initial change in the writer's perspective on life. Here the writer begins to think about the sovereign rule of God. Verses 1-8 are intended to remind the reader of God's presence and His control over the affairs of mankind. While the experiences of life may toss us from one extreme to the other, we are not left dangling forever at one extreme. Things may seem erratic and arbitrary, but there is a degree of order and dependability about the events of our lives. God's sovereignty and grace arrange life's extremes in ways that give balance to what we experience.

Solomon shows us that the key to understanding life is to start with God's purpose and work out from there because God has an appropriate time for all of life's activities (3:1-8). When we recognize this, we are able to deal with the issues life can throw at us, even if our understanding is not complete. The secret to peace of mind is to be yielded to God in all things; as the apostle Paul would say, "So whether you eat or drink or whatever you do, do it all for the glory of God" (1 Corinthians 10:31, NIV).

AT-A-GLANCE

1. The Seasons of Our Lives
(Ecclesiastes 3:1-8)
2. The Power Behind the Seasons of Our Lives (vv. 14-15)

IN DEPTH

1. The Seasons of Our Lives
(Ecclesiastes 3:1-8)

The writer of Ecclesiastes uses verses 1-8 to illustrate God's sovereign activity in human affairs. The principle stated in verse 1 echoes the psalmist's testimony: "My times are in thy hand" (Psalm 31:15). In other words, the events of our lives are all under God's control and occur within the timeframe He determines.

Verses 2-8 are not intended to identify all the events that occur in one's life. Rather, they are intended to present the reader with a picture of the broad scope of God's involvement in human affairs and mankind's response to God's sovereignty.

Twenty-eight human experiences are listed. These experiences take place between the boundaries of birth and death, both of which are under God's control. The experiences listed reflect human choice to be involved in either constructive or destructive activities. These activities, in turn, give rise to joys and sorrows, love and hate, at both individual and social levels.

The first set of activities speaks of birth and dying, and of planting and plucking up what is planted. One may ask, "In what sense is birth and dying an activity of God that requires some human response?" The time of birth and the time of dying are determined by God. Expectant parents often speak about when their child is due. The reality is that under normal circumstances children come forth from the womb according to God's timing, and parents respond accordingly. Our times are in God's hands.

In like manner, under normal circumstances, God determines the time of our dying and we respond to God's timing. "Planting" and "plucking up" are metaphors aimed at reinforcing the idea of birth and dying.

Just as birth and dying represent seasons of life, so also do killing and healing. Given the metaphorical use of "breaking down" and "building up"... "killing"... is probably not the best translation. A more helpful understanding is to think in terms of demolishing and repairing, which is further pictured in the idea of breaking down and building up. The common thread is destruction and construction.

Another universal experience is listed in verse 4, weeping and laughing, with the parallel experiences of mourning and dancing. Again, one might ask, "What is the divine activity referenced in weeping and laughing?" Psalm 30:11 gives the answer: "Thou hast turned for me my mourning into dancing: thou hast put off my sackcloth, and girded me with gladness." What joy and encouragement there is in knowing that during our times of weeping and mourning, God comes at the appropriate time and turns our mourning into celebration.

While verse 5 refers to "a time to cast away stones, and a time to gather together," its meaning is difficult to decipher. Obviously, however, it is a reference to negative and positive action, or to destructive and constructive activity. We can be certain, however, that God can use both destructive and constructive events to serve His purposes and our good (Romans 8:28).

Verse 6 identifies an experience common to all: that of keeping for oneself and sharing with others. Knowing when one has enough and when to share with others is a virtue, the development of which requires prudence and a heart touched by the love of God.

Various interpretations have been given to verse 7. Some see it as a reference to mourning. Others see it as a reference to the breach and restoration of a relationship. In either event, we can be confident of God's capacity to transform our mourning and any broken relationship into a thing of beauty.

Verse 8 focuses on the human experiences of love and hate, and war and peace. Again, we can be certain that whether love or hate, war or peace, God has the last word.

2. The Power Behind the Seasons of Our Lives (vv. 14-15)

While there may be differing interpretations of the antitheses cited earlier, they all have one thing in common—they are generalized descriptions of some of the events that constitute living under the rule and reign of God. We can be grateful that God, in His providence and grace, uses the events of our lives to accomplish His purposes. Thus, those who yield themselves to God will, by His grace, see beauty in all the events of life. Like the writer of Ecclesiastes, they will come to "know that, whatsoever God doeth, it shall be for ever: nothing can be put to it, nor any thing taken from it: and God doeth it, that men should fear before him" (v. 14).

God can and does give beauty to the seasons of our lives. His activity in our midst is not new to our age. For "that which hath been is now; and that which is to be hath already been; and God requireth that which is past" (v. 15). Truly, our times are in God's hands, and He can be trusted to make the good and the bad work together for our good.

SEARCH THE SCRIPTURES

1. "A time to be born, and a time to _____" (Ecclesiastes 3:2).

2. "A time to _____, and a time to _____ from embracing" (v. 5).

3. "Whatsoever God _____, it shall be _____" (v. 14).

4. " That which hath _____ is now; and that which is to be hath already _____" (v. 15).

DISCUSS THE MEANING

1. In what ways does God's sovereignty benefit humankind?

2. According to the writer of Ecclesiastes, what gives meaning to the monotony of life?

3. What should be our response to God's activity?

LESSON IN OUR SOCIETY

All of us live on the edge of the unknown. While we may give considerable time, effort, thought, and prayer to planning certain events in our lives, some events happen without our planning and in spite of our expectations. Some events catch us by surprise and, at times when we are least prepared to handle them. Given the realities that are beyond our control, we would do well to put God center stage in our planning and in our lives. Our plans without God will inevitably send us in meaningless circles, drifting without purpose. We need not reinvent the wheel that the writer has already called to our attention. Let us learn from His experience and affirm the truth that God uses both positive and objectionable experiences for His good purposes and to keep balance in our lives.

MAKE IT HAPPEN

Identify two positive experiences and two disappointing experiences you have had within the past month. Thank God for the blessings that emerged from the positive experiences. If you have not already discovered the silver lining in your disappointing experiences, ask God to help you to do so. Dare to believe that your times and all the events of your life are both known to Him and controlled by Him.

FOLLOW THE SPIRIT

What God wants me to do:

_____

_____

REMEMBER YOUR THOUGHTS

Special insights I have learned:

_____

_____

MORE LIGHT ON THE TEXT
Ecclesiastes 3:1-8, 14-15

The statements in verses 1-8 proceed from the previous verses (2:24-26). Everything in our reality (under heaven) goes through changes, but God does not go through changes. Everything is relative to Him and His unchangeable counsel. In light of this, we are wise to live "one day at a time" because God is Lord over life. Enjoyment in life and the satisfaction we derive from work come "from the hand of God."

Since everything has its time from God, all the labor of man by itself cannot change the time or circumstance or control events. Everything has its regular time, and time moves on. God has a plan for all people. He provides cycles of life, each with its work for us to do. Many times we face problems that seem to contradict God's plan. However, problems should not cause us to disbelieve or lose trust in the providence of God. Without God, the problems we face have no lasting solution. The lesson to be learned is patience: endure whatever you face, for its time will end. War and peace, love and hate all have their time. Solomon stressed the importance of studying and learning in order to know the right time for each thing. The wise person has good timing, whether in knowing when to speak or when to plant; one could take the rhythm of time as a gift.

1 To every thing there is a season, and a time to every purpose under the heaven:

Solomon boldly stated that every action of humanity can be traced to its ultimate source: an eternal plan that is controlled and directed by God. For all the affairs of life, argues Solomon, God has set a time. Thus, we must understand that in God's economy, there is an appropriate time for every human experience and activity. If we understand the right times for the right actions and perform these actions according to God's ordained time, we will discover that in His providence "everything is beautiful in its own time" (v. 11).

2 A time to be born, and a time to die; a time to plant, and a time to pluck up that which is planted.

Solomon listed 14 pairs of opposites to illustrate the comprehensive providence of God, beginning with the most extreme opposites of all, at least with regard to human life: "A time to be born, and a time to die."

The issues raised by birth and death were important at the time of Solomon, and they are important for us today. We can try to extend life through modern medicine or shorten it through euthanasia, but ultimately God alone has the last say over birth and death.

Planting and plucking up (*'aqar*, **aw-kar'**, meaning to uproot) have an appropriate time. The call of Jeremiah involved both activities metaphorically. "See, today I appoint you over nations and kingdoms to uproot and tear down, to destroy and overthrow, to build and to plant" (Jeremiah 1:10 NIV). In 11:6, Solomon gives us a physical application: "Sow your seed in the morning, and at evening let not your hands be idle, for you do not know which will succeed, whether this or that, or whether both will do equally well" (NIV). Jesus' parable of the wheat and the tares (Matt 13:24-30) gives us and application that is both physical and metaphorical.

3 A time to kill, and a time to heal; a time to break down, and a time to build up.

God's judicial acts illustrate this statement. For example, when God brings judgment, it is often a time of death and destruction, but when the people repent, it is a time of healing. "Come, let us return to the LORD. He has torn us to pieces but he will heal us; he has injured us, but he will bind up our wounds" (Hos. 6:1, NIV).

Breaking down (*parats*, **paw-rats'**, meaning to breach or to break in pieces) and building up (*banah*, **baw-naw'**, meaning to establish, to cause to continue, or to rebuild) have their appointed times. If a building is not sound, it needs to be torn down and replaced with a structure that is stable and sturdy. This is the way it is in the walk of the Christian. The Apostle Paul teaches this truth in Corinthians: "By the grace God has given me, I laid a foundation as an expert builder, and someone else is building on it. But each one should be careful how he builds. For no one can lay any foundation other than the one already laid, which is Jesus Christ. If any man builds on this foundation using gold, silver, costly stones, wood, hay or straw, his work will be shown for what it is, because the Day will bring it to light. It will be revealed with fire, and the fire will test the quality of each man's work. If what he has built survives, he will receive his reward. If it is burned up, he will suffer loss; he himself will be saved, but only as one escaping through the flames" (1 Corinthians 3:10-15 NIV).

4 A time to weep, and a time to laugh; a time to mourn, and a time to dance; 5 A time to cast away stones, and a time to gather stones together; a time to embrace, and a time to refrain from embracing.

There is an appropriate time for "weeping" and "laughter," "mourning" and "dancing." Grief is part of the healing process, and different people handle the same grief in different ways. Paul admonishes us, "Rejoice with those who rejoice; mourn with those who mourn" (Rom 12:15 NIV). Because we are under the providential care of God, David was able to say, "Weeping may endure for a night, but joy cometh in the morning" (Psalm 30:5b). For some, the mourning period is short; for others, it is long. We exacerbate the grief of some when we flippantly say, "Get over it."

On the other hand, we must be careful to encourage those in mourning not to languish in their grief. Laughter is also therapeutic and should be encouraged. However, we must distinguish between genuine joy and silliness.

God has appointed a time for "casting away" stones (**shalak, shaw-lak**, meaning to throw, hurl, fling, or cast down). Sometimes the ground needs to be cleared of loose stones to prepare the way for something new. There are other times when "gathering" stones together is appropriate (*anac*, **kaw-nas'**, meaning to collect) for erecting a new building.

There are also times for the closeness of an "embrace" and times for keeping our distance and refraining from embracing. Affection does not apply to everybody in the same way. For close and trusted friends, an embrace is appropriate, but at first introductions, it is usually wise to play it safe with a handshake. Paul reminds married couples that the conjugal "embrace" is the norm. The only exception should be by mutual consent for spiritual purposes, and the period of abstaining must be short (1 Corinthians 7:3-5).

6 A time to get, and a time to lose; a time to keep, and a time to cast away; 7 A time to rend, and a time to sew; a time to keep silence, and a time to speak.

Like the preceding opposites, "to get" (*baqash*, **baw-kash'**, meaning to seek, require, desire, or request) and "to lose" (*'abad*, **aw-bad'**, meaning to perish, vanish, go astray, or be destroyed); "to keep" (*shamar*, **shaw-mar'**, meaning to guard, protect, or retain) and to "cast away" (*shalak*, **shaw-lak**, meaning to throw, cast, hurl, fling, or shed); "to rend" (*qara'*, **kaw-rah'**, meaning to tear or tear in pieces) and "to sew" (*taphar*, **taw-far'**, meaning to sew together or mend); "to keep silence" (*chashah*, **khaw-shaw'**, meaning to be quiet, still, or inactive) and "to speak" (*dabar*, **daw-bar'**, meaning to declare, converse, or command); all unfold under the appointment of God's providence in their time.

8 A time to love, and a time to hate; a time of war, and a time of peace.

Love and hate both have their proper place under heaven. However, it is imperative that we love and hate the right things. Like God, we should hate sin and love sinners. The Apostle Paul says, "Love must be sincere. Hate what is evil; cling to what is good" (Romans 12:9 NIV). To hate evil is to protest it and work against it. For example, racial segregation was an evil that plagued American society. The Civil Rights Movement emerged to protest and dismantle this injustice. The protestors hated segregation, yet they demonstrated love toward their segregationist oppressors.

Remember what the apostle John tells us: "If anyone says, 'I love God,' yet hates his brother, he is a liar. For anyone who does not love his brother, whom he has seen, cannot love God, whom he has not seen. And he has given us this command: Whoever loves God must also love his brother" (1 John 4:20-21, NIV).

14 I know that, whatsoever God doeth, it shall be for ever: nothing can be put to it, nor any thing taken from it: and God doeth it, that men should fear before him. 15 That which hath been is now; and that which is to be hath already been; and God requireth that which is past.

His reflection on the appropriate times for human activities brought Solomon face to face with human limits. It is not the difficulty of knowing the right time for an activity that produces the frustration and resentment, but the fact that all human times come to an end, that there is the inevitable "time to die." This awareness of death (for both the righteous and the wicked, and for animals) as the final human boundary is key to the book of Ecclesiastes.

Therefore, we must seek to do the will of God in this life because He is the only constant in reality. Everything God does will endure forever, and only that done for Him will last. In other words, "...Store up for yourselves treasures in heaven, where moth and rust do not destroy, and where thieves do not break in and steal. For where your treasure is, there your heart will be also" (Matthew 6:20-21, NIV). At the end of the day, all our "works" will be tested by fire. Only the permanent works will survive—those done in pursuit of God's will: "gold, silver, precious stones" (1 Corinthians 3:10-15).

God has given us only a glimpse of His creative genius. We are incapable of seeing into the future or comprehending the magnitude of the perfection of His creation. God has the final answer and word. Life, with all its diverse activities, can lead to frustration and resentment. Frustration and resentment will remain until humanity comes to fear God, that is, to believe and obey Him. The incomprehensibility of life as perceived by man has its purpose—the total commitment of the whole self to trust and believe the living God. The absolute lordship of God is essential to any happiness, meaning, or purpose in life. God's purpose and plan, said the writer, are final, or unchangeable (v. 14). God, in His infinite wisdom, can call back the past and connect it with the future (perhaps as a witness at the last judgment) (v. 15). "And I know," concluded the writer of Ecclesiastes, "that whatever God does is final. Nothing can be added to it or taken from it. God's purpose in this is that people should fear Him. Whatever exists today and whatever will exist in the future has already existed in the past. For God calls each event back in its turn" (vv. 14-15, paraphrased).

History is not meaningless. We have all heard the saying, "Those who fail to learn from history are doomed to repeat it." Fortunately for us, the futility viewed by the writer of Ecclesiastes has been radically changed by God sending His Son into the world. The coming of Christ makes possible a transforming experience that gives us hope for the present and hope for the future. We know that despite all the pessimism in the world today, the time will come when Christ will make all things new. We who place our confidence in Jesus Christ can overcome the obstacles we face today and share in God's wonderful plans for the future.

DAILY BIBLE READINGS

M: The Lord Is Good
Psalm 34:1-8
T: Use Moderation and Respect God's Authority
Ecclesiastes 7:15-22
W: Every Matter Has Its Time
Ecclesiastes 8:2-8a
T: Life Is in God's Hands
Ecclesiastes 9:1-12
F: For Everything There Is a Season
Ecclesiastes 3:1-8
S: Whatever God Does Endures Forever
Ecclesiastes 3:9-15
S: Judgment and Future Belong to God
Ecclesiastes 3:16-22

TEACHING TIPS

May 7
Bible Study Guide 10

1. Words You Should Know

A. Hide (Proverbs 2:1) *tsaphan* (Heb.)—To hoard or reserve.

B. Merchandise (3:14) *chokmah* (Heb.)—Gain; profit.

2. Teacher Preparation

A. Read the LESSON AIM for this week. What do you want your students to take away from this lesson?

B. Read the first three chapters of Proverbs. Pray that God would use you to create a desire for wisdom within your students.

C. Read MORE LIGHT ON THE TEXT to gain a deeper understanding of this week's passages.

D. Using the *Precepts For Living*™ CD-ROM, access the reference materials. Use the search function to look up any unfamiliar words or concepts.

3. Starting the Lesson

A. As the students enter the room, hand each student a blank index card. Instruct the students to write a definition of wisdom on their card.

B. Next, collect the cards. Read some of the definitions out loud. Ask the students to clarify the difference between knowledge and wisdom. Have some of the students confused these two concepts?

C. Ask a volunteer to read the IN FOCUS story aloud to the class.

D. Read the KEEP IN MIND verse out loud. Then ask a student to offer a prayer for the class that was based on the verse.

4. Getting into the Lesson

A. Before the students arrive, write the title of today's lesson and the AT-A-GLANCE outline on the board.

B. Ask for volunteers to read each of the three passages of the FOCAL VERSES out loud.

C. Initiate a discussion about each passage. Use the information in the IN DEPTH section to assist in the discussion.

5. Relating the Lesson to Life

A. Direct the students to the LESSON IN OUR SOCIETY section. Read and discuss the article.

B. Ask the students to share some of the benefits of wisdom they have seen in their own lives.

C. Ask for volunteers to share any new insights that they may have received from today's lesson.

6. Arousing Action

A. Give the students a few minutes to quietly reflect on today's lesson. Instruct them to record their thoughts in the REMEMBER YOUR THOUGHTS section.

B. Read the MAKE IT HAPPEN exercise aloud, and encourage the students to complete the exercise at home.

C. Close in prayer, asking God to give each student a desire for godly wisdom. Encourage the students to search for wisdom as if they were seeking a priceless treasure.

WORSHIP GUIDE

For the Superintendent or Teacher
Theme: A Treasure Worth Seeking
Theme Song: "More Precious Than Silver"
Scripture: Proverbs 3:13
Song: "Open Our Eyes, Lord"
Meditation: God, Your Word says that You are the One who gives wisdom. You are wisdom! We desire Your wisdom as we live in this sinful world. We acknowledge You in all our ways, and we thank You for directing our paths.
In Jesus' name. Amen.

A TREASURE WORTH SEEKING

Bible Background • PROVERBS 2–3
Printed Text • PROVERBS 2:1–5; 3:1–6, 13–18
Devotional Reading • PROVERBS 2:6–15

LESSON AIM

By the end of the lesson, we will:

DEFINE wisdom both in the context of Proverbs and in terms of its practical application to our own lives;

UNDERSTAND the difference between knowledge and wisdom; and

LIST some benefits of wisdom, feel a desire to gain godly wisdom, and decide to seek God's wisdom in our own lives.

KEEP IN MIND

"Happy is the man that findeth wisdom, and the man that getteth understanding" (Proverbs 3:13).

FOCAL VERSES

Proverbs 2:1 My son, if thou wilt receive my words, and hide my commandments with thee;

2 So that thou incline thine ear unto wisdom, and apply thine heart to understanding;

3 Yea, if thou criest after knowledge, and liftest up thy voice for understanding;

4 If thou seekest her as silver, and searchest for her as for hid treasures;

5 Then shalt thou understand the fear of the LORD, and find the knowledge of God.

3:1 My son, forget not my law; but let thine heart keep my commandments:

2 for length of days, and long life, and peace, shall they add to thee.

3 Let not mercy and truth forsake thee: bind them about they neck; write them upon the table of thine heart:

LESSON OVERVIEW

LESSON AIM
KEEP IN MIND
FOCAL VERSES
IN FOCUS
THE PEOPLE, PLACES, AND TIMES
BACKGROUND
AT-A-GLANCE
IN DEPTH
SEARCH THE SCRIPTURES
DISCUSS THE MEANING
LESSON IN OUR SOCIETY
MAKE IT HAPPEN
FOLLOW THE SPIRIT
REMEMBER YOUR THOUGHTS
MORE LIGHT ON THE TEXT
DAILY BIBLE READINGS

4 So shalt thou find favour and good understanding in the sight of God and man.

5 Trust in the LORD with all thine heart; and lean not unto thine own understanding.

6 In all thy ways acknowledge him, and he shall direct thy paths.

3:13 Happy is the man that findeth wisdom, and the man that getteth understanding.

14 For the merchandise of it is better than the merchandise of silver, and the gain thereof than fine gold.

15 She is more precious than rubies: and all the things thou canst desire are not to be compared unto her.

16 Length of days is in her right hand; and in her left hand riches and honour.

17 Her ways are ways of pleasantness, and all her paths are peace.

18 She is a tree of life to them that lay hold upon her: and happy is every one that retaineth her.

IN FOCUS

Dr. Craig had received his Ph.D. in theology from a prestigious University in Chicago, but now he couldn't remember whether or not it was a weekday. He was even uncertain of the date. He vaguely remembered walking through the doors and still couldn't believe that he was a patient in a rehabilitation center.

Dr. Craig tried to examine at what point he had thought his alcoholic behavior was OK. Over the last year, he had lost everything: his wife, his position in the church, and his reputation. There was no longer any evidence of pride or arrogance in his trembling body.

Dr. Craig knew the Holy Spirit had caused him to stumble through the doors of the rehab center days ago. A slight veil of soberness made him want everything back; he even had a notion to walk out of the place and change his identity. He had also contemplated suicide. Instead, he sank to his knees in the prayer position he had taught, but that he had not assumed in three years.

"Forgive me, Father, for forgetting your teaching. Lord, give me knowledge to lift me back to my position in society. Show me how to face—" Thunder began to rumble, and suddenly a lightning bolt sliced the sky. Startled, Dr. Craig opened his eyes to see the words on a small wooden plaque on the wall. "God, grant me the serenity to accept the things I cannot change, the courage to change the things I can, and the wisdom to know the difference." It was the first time that he had noticed the plaque over his bed. Dr. Craig struggled to his feet with joy, realizing that what he wanted was the serenity, courage, and wisdom to trust God again.

In the book of Proverbs, we learn that wisdom is a treasure that God gives. How blessed are those who seek God's wisdom and gain His understanding for the situations they face in life?

THE PEOPLE, PLACES, AND TIMES

Solomon. Authorship of the book of Proverbs is attributed to Solomon in 1:1; 10:1; and 25:1. However, several sections are attributed to other authors (see 22:17 24:34; 30:1 31:31). Along with Job and Ecclesiastes, Proverbs is known as Israel's wisdom literature.

In biblical times, Israel's leadership consisted of three different groups of leaders: the prophets, the priests, and the wise men. The wise men were a distinct class, probably associated with the scribes. The wise men were often involved in the politics and moral issues of the day and were usually skilled writers. Many of them were probably government officials. Generally, the wise men were far less prominent and authoritative than the other leaders. Earnest seekers of life's lessons, they drew informal disciples from the common people. The wise man often dispensed his wisdom both in a public forum and to those who sought him out privately.

In the Old Testament, the first person who was called "wise" was a woman from Tekoa (2 Samuel 14:1-20). Another wise woman is mentioned in 2 Samuel 20:14-22. Job was a wise man from this period (Job 29:7-25). And Solomon, of course, is the quintessential wise man of the Bible. But there were many other wise men and women who are unnamed in the Bible.

The teaching of the wise men (or women) was often done in public places (see Proverbs 1:20-21), such as the town gate. Later, formal schools were formed where pupils would gather as the wise man shared his wisdom. These teachings were often prefaced with "my son," directing the words of wisdom to any individual who would take heed. The wise men employed imagery, allegory, personification, and even riddles and fables to direct their listeners toward wisdom.

Bibliography

Buttrick, George Arthur, ed. The Interpreter's Bible, Vol. 4. New York: Abingdon Press, 1955.

BACKGROUND

The word "wisdom" generally connotes such ideas as skill, experience, knowledge, or good judgment. The Hebrew word used in Proverbs for wisdom is *chokmah* (**khok-maw'**), meaning "wisdom," "experience," or "shrewdness." This word can refer to technical skills or special abilities, but *chokmah* is also the knowledge and ability to make the right choices at the opportune time. This kind of wisdom, based upon the fear of the Lord (Proverbs 1:7), is the type of wisdom believers should desire.

Throughout the Old Testament and specifically in the book of Proverbs, wisdom is connected to such words as "commands," "precepts," and "laws." In the New Testament, we realize that Jesus has become the fulfillment of all wisdom. As believers today, we understand that "keeping the commandments" or "obeying the law" is accomplished through a personal relationship with Jesus Christ. Following a list of rules will never draw us into the place where we can find the hidden treasures of wisdom.

How can we approach Proverbs with the light we have as New Testament believers? Here's the gist of it: We cannot have true wisdom without knowing the Wisdom-Giver. In 1 Corinthians 1:30, the apostle Paul says that Jesus "is made unto us wisdom, and righteousness, and sanctification, and redemption." Jesus is wisdom! When we pray for wisdom, we are praying to know Jesus better! What a concept! He is all in all. Only in Him will we find what we need to live a victorious, vibrant Christian life. In Him "are hid all the treasures of wisdom and knowledge" (Colossians 2:3).

AT-A-GLANCE

1. Wisdom: What Is It? (Proverbs 2:1-5)
2. Wisdom: Why Do We Need It? (3:1-6)
3. Wisdom: What Are Its Rewards? (vv. 13-18)

IN DEPTH

1. Wisdom: What Is It? (Proverbs 2:1-5)

Godly wisdom is the ability to apply God's Word and His will to everyday situations. Wisdom is not gained by attending seminars, reading books, or taking college courses. So how do we gain wisdom? Wisdom comes from a daily, consistent, purposeful application of God's Word to everyday circumstances.

Wisdom also comes from experiencing life, with all its joys and sorrows. Many believers and unbelievers have the kind of wisdom gained from trial and error (i.e., a "learn-from-your-mistakes" kind of wisdom). But godly wisdom is a direct byproduct of walking in the Spirit. This wisdom for living is bestowed upon us as a gift from God (see Proverbs 2:6; James 1:5).

There are, however, some prerequisites to receiving wisdom. We must first desire wisdom. Small children will often plug their ears in order to block out something they do not want to hear. Sometimes, Christians, too, will childishly close their minds and their spirits to the Holy Spirit, not wanting to receive wisdom. But Proverbs 2:1 says, "If thou wilt receive my words" and thereby

implies that a teachable spirit is necessary if a person is to receive wisdom.

When we have received wisdom, we are told to "hide" it in our heart (2:1; Psalm 119:11). The Hebrew word used here for "hide" is *tsaphan* (**tsaw-fan'**), which means to treasure or store up. Many people today are focused on accumulating wealth; therefore, making more money and obtaining more "stuff" is a driving compulsion. Some will spend every waking moment and every available cent in search for more. Yet, as believers, we are exhorted to expend our time and resources to gain the riches of wisdom.

Verse 3 instructs us to cry out for knowledge and understanding! Pray for wisdom. Call out to God for His will in every situation. Be diligent in searching the Scriptures. That's the second prerequisite for gaining godly wisdom: We must be willing to do what it takes to acquire wisdom. It will take time to search God's Word. It will take time and perseverance to pray for godly wisdom. It will take a quiet heart to hear the voice of the Spirit. But in order to gain the treasure, we must be willing to dig (v. 4).

When we do find wisdom, we find God (v. 5). We begin to understand His nature. We stand in awe of who He is. We have found the treasure.

The advantages of wisdom are numerous: deliverance from evil men (2:12), blessings (v. 21), divine guidance (3:6), happiness (v. 13), long life (v. 16), riches and honor (v. 16). The list could go on and on. But the overarching prerequisite to and reward for gaining wisdom is a burning desire to know God.

2. Wisdom: Why Do We Need It? (3:1-6)

Proverbs 3:1 instructs us not to forget God's law. Practically speaking, this means we must keep our focus on God. The treasures of God are not attained by lackluster performance. Believers must be diligent in seeking, reading, and meditating on God's Word; spending time in prayer; and heeding the Spirit. Does this guarantee that we will have a long, peaceful life? Proverbs 3:2 seems to intimate that it does. Generally, of course, one can expect to reap the benefits of living a wise and prudent life. But we can't make it into a linear equation because life does not work that way. We can all think of examples to illustrate the inequity and disappointments of life.

So what is the point of gaining wisdom? As with all spiritual issues, it is a matter of the heart. If our only motive for achieving wisdom is to obtain the "perks," then we're headed for disillusionment. We have to be able to see further than that. As we focus our eyes on Jesus, He begins to mold us into His image. The wisdom that flows from Him becomes a way of life, a fiber of our very being as believers. We are then able to go forth as workers in the harvest, as builders of God's kingdom. We seek after wisdom so that we may be servants.

As we seek to know the God of wisdom, more of His characteristics will blossom within us. Proverbs 3:3 mentions mercy and truth. Along with the wisdom of God comes the knowledge of how to respond in every area of our lives, including our relationships with others. If we approached every person with mercy and truth, conducting ourselves with wisdom, we would be getting closer to the way Jesus lived. In fact, verse 4 says that if we will do so, we will find favor with God and man. The rewards of wisdom may not be minutely predictable, but they are worth searching for.

In verses 5 and 6, we find a summation of all that the writer of Proverbs has discussed so far: Trust in the Lord because He is able to care for you. In other words, God is sovereign. We must acknowledge Him in every area of our lives at all times. Though we seek His wisdom, He is the One who enables us to apply it. He is the One who gives us life and directs our steps.

Verse 5 says that we must trust in the Lord with "all" of our heart. In verse 6, the emphasis is on "all" once again: "In all thy ways acknowledge him." God desires complete obedience and surrender. But acknowledging God and accepting His direction in one's life requires humility. Humans have a tendency to think more highly of themselves than they should. As we search for and gain the wisdom of God, we must not become "wise in our own eyes" (v. 7). When we choose to go our own way, we work against God, accomplishing His will in our lives. But when we trust Him completely, He directs our paths according to His perfect plan.

3. Wisdom: What Are Its Rewards? (vv. 13-18)

The word "happy" is used at the beginning and end of this passage. These verses describe the true joy of someone who has learned the secret of godly wisdom: complete dependence upon God. To rest upon God's Word in the time of crisis, to know the Saviour intimately, and to possess inner peace throughout life's trials is truly more valuable than silver or priceless gems.

The benefits gained from this kind of wisdom are worth more than what could be gained from silver or gold (v. 14). This verse is not to be looked at in a materialistic sense, but in a spiritual sense. God's will is for every believer to grow in the knowledge of Him (2 Peter 3:18). We are to be consciously striving for the kind of wisdom that effects change and growth within ourselves and others. This wisdom brings joy that transcends the happiness attained by wealth or any other earthly pleasure. In fact, verse 15 says that nothing we could desire compares with wisdom. That's quite a statement! But even Job, one of the venerable "wise men" of the Bible, affirms that wisdom is far more precious than gold or silver, coral or pearls, rubies or sapphires or onyx (Job 28:1-28). Nothing else in this world can compare to personally knowing the sovereign God. The person who pursues this relationship gains peace (v. 17) and happiness (v. 18).

Wisdom is personified in verses 15-18, depicted as a woman holding the treasures of wisdom in her hands. In her right hand she holds life, and in her left hand are riches and honor (v. 16). Verse 17 says, "Her ways are ways of pleasantness." The word "ways" in Hebrew is *de-rek* (**deh'-rek**), meaning "course of life" or "mode of action." In other words, the person who gains wisdom will enjoy the peace and "pleasantness" of knowing God as a way of life. This daily and lifelong pleasure far outweighs the pleasures or treasures of this world.

Godly wisdom is a "tree of life" to the believer (v. 18). If we feed from this tree, we will gain abundant life. We will find wisdom's treasure—a deep and abiding relationship with the Wisdom-Giver, God Himself.

Bibliograpy

Buttrick, George Arthur, ed. *The Interpreter's Bible*, Vol. 4. New York: Abingdon Press, 1955.

SEARCH THE SCRIPTURES

1. What is one of the prerequisites for gaining wisdom (Proverbs 2:2)?

2. What else will we find when we find wisdom (v. 5)?

3. What are some of the benefits of wisdom (3:2, 13, 17-18)?

4. Why is it important for believers to rely on God's wisdom (vv. 5-6)?

DISCUSS THE MEANING

1. Discuss the difference between God's wisdom and human wisdom.

2. What are some practical ways to gain godly wisdom? What are some life situations that might require wisdom?

3. Why is it sometimes difficult to view God as the source of true wisdom? How can believers make wisdom a high priority in their daily lives?

4. What are some tangible rewards of gaining wisdom?

LESSON IN OUR SOCIETY

In today's world, we have many avenues for gaining knowledge. Formal education, online courses, books, speakers, and the news media all contribute to an overload of information. How does wisdom differ from knowledge? As believers, how can we exercise godly wisdom in everyday situations? How can we encourage others to seek the priceless treasure of wisdom?

MAKE IT HAPPEN

Plan some quiet time this week to begin your search for godly wisdom. Identify situations or areas in your life where you need wisdom. Ask God for specific wisdom for those scenarios.

FOLLOW THE SPIRIT

What God wants me to do:

_____

_____

REMEMBER YOUR THOUGHTS

Special insights I have learned:

_____

_____

MORE LIGHT ON THE TEXT
Proverbs 2:1-5; 3:1-6, 13-18

The Christian community accepts the book of Proverbs as a great book of wisdom containing many sayings and poems. The word for "proverb" implies a sense of superiority in mental action. According to 1 Kings 3:12, when bestowing wisdom and understanding upon Solomon, God said, "there was none like thee before thee, neither after thee shall any arise like unto thee." Solomon demonstrated his possession of the "wisdom of God" (v. 28) in the sayings he recorded and the way he performed his duties as king and judge of the people. Solomon begins this book by revealing his purpose for the teachings in Proverbs (Proverbs 1:1-4) and the benefits of obeying (vv. 8-9) and acquiring wisdom (3:1-6, 13-18).

1 My son, if thou wilt receive my words, and hide my commandments with thee; 2 So that thou incline thine ear unto wisdom, and apply thine heart to understanding; 3 Yea, if thou criest after knowledge, and liftest up thy voice for understanding; 4 If thou seekest her as silver, and searchest for her as for hid treasures; 5 Then shalt thou understand the fear of the LORD, and find the knowledge of God.

This passage tells us what is necessary to acquire knowledge and understanding. We must first listen to the teacher (Solomon in this discussion), then follow his instructions so much so that the student must humble him or herself to receive wisdom. The Hebrew word for "wisdom" is *chokmah* (**khok-maw'**), a feminine noun meaning to be wise in mind, word, or action.

We are taught in these verses that wisdom is as necessary as breathing. As a part of God's marvelous creation, we must do everything humanly possible to possess wisdom for ourselves; it is necessary for our very survival. When we seek something precious and are willing to search for it, we must at times use instruments, such as a pick and shovel, that will assist us in conquering whatever elements are obstructing the search. The instruments used in the hunt for wisdom are the head, heart, and voice. Many times, the elements of obstruction are the trials that we endure in this life. Nevertheless, whether we are seeking wisdom or riches, success is obtained as the instruments are used with concentration and determination on our part.

3:1 My son, forget not my law; but let thine heart keep my commandments: 2 for length of days, and long life, and peace, shall they add to thee.

Parental obedience comes with a promise of a long and peaceful life. This promise is also made in Exodus 20:12; Deuteronomy 5:16; and Ephesians 6:2-3.

While "the law" is a set of rules established for the community to live by, a commandment is prescribed by an individual in—this case, Solomon to a son. Therefore, even though the law can appear to be impersonal, a commandment can be personal and individualized. As we strive to keep God's commandments, it is the desire to demonstrate our gratitude to God for His promise of eternal life through Christ's resurrection that motivates us.

3 Let not mercy and truth forsake thee: bind them about thy neck; write them upon the table of thine heart: 4 So shalt thou find favour and good understanding in the sight of God and man.

Mercy is an aspect of God's unmerited favor, which we cannot buy, steal, or borrow. God is truth. He speaks and judges the whole universe. In knowing this, we don't want mercy and truth to walk away from us, but to stay with us continuously wherever we go. We must hide (treasure) God's Word in our hearts so that in our obedience we will please Him and establish an intimate relationship with God and a positive relationship with humankind.

5 Trust in the LORD with all thine heart; and lean not unto thine own understanding.

To trust in the Lord, we must practice patience, courage, and confidence as we yield our lives, present and future, to Him. At no time must we depend upon what we think. We should enjoy the peace of knowing that God is in control of every part of our lives. As a part of God's marvelous creation, we can be assured of His faithfulness toward us.

6 In all thy ways acknowledge Him, and he shall direct thy paths.

We must recognize that God exists and has ultimate control over every aspect of our lives. It is He who makes provision for us and allows us to accomplish the goals that we attempt to set for ourselves. God is our provider (Philippians 4:19).

3:13 Happy is the man that findeth wisdom, and the man that getteth understanding.

The Hebrew word for "happy" is *'esher* (**eh'-sher**) meaning "blessed," "fortunate," or "enviable." Understanding is drawn forth from God's Word and life's experiences. When we can take God's words and apply them to our life experiences and live our lives for God's approval, we are truly blessed. Only the knowledge and the meaning of God's Word can create in us true happiness.

14 For the merchandise of it is better than the merchandise of silver, and the gain thereof than fine gold. 15 She is more precious than rubies: and all the things thou canst desire are not to be compared unto her..

To gain wisdom is better than the gaining profit of silver and fine gold. This comparison of wisdom to precious metals and precious stones (gems) is also found in Job 28:12-18. Job asks, "But where shall wisdom be found? and where is the place of understanding?" He then gives the answer: "God understands the way to wisdom and He knows the place of it [wisdom is with God alone]" (v. 19, paraphrased). In chapter 28, Job gives a discourse similar to Solomon's as he tells his friends of man's search for wisdom and wisdom's value.

16 Length of days is in her right hand; and in her left hand riches and honour.

Solomon continues his description of wisdom in the feminine gender as he reminds his students of the promise of long life and riches. However, in this verse he adds the promise of honor.

17 Her ways are ways of pleasantness, and all her paths are peace.

The Hebrew word for "pleasantness" is *no'am* (**no'-am**), meaning "agreeableness," "delightfulness," "suitableness," "splendor," or "grace." The Hebrew word for "paths" is *nathiyb* (**naw-theeb'**), meaning "beaten path" or "traveler."

In this verse, wisdom is pictured as a graceful yet powerful lady with flowing garments. In one hand she holds that which only God can give long life, and in the other hand that which only humankind can influence. Yet those who embrace wisdom experience peace as they travel from place to place.

18 She is a tree of life to them that lay hold upon her: and happy is every one that retaineth her.

The tree of life is first mentioned in Genesis as being in the midst of the Garden of Eden (Genesis 3:22-23). The fruit of this tree, if eaten after the Fall, would have confirmed Adam and Eve in their sinful state forever. However, Solomon lets us know in this verse that God is the giver of life, and that only through the wisdom of His Word can we find eternal life, which leads to happiness—provided we continuously respect and trust in God. Remember Jesus said, "I am the way the truth and the life" (John 14:6).

DAILY BIBLE READINGS

M: Seek Wisdom
Proverbs 2:1-5
T: Wisdom Brings Knowledge, Prudence, and Understanding
Proverbs 2:6-15
W: Follow the Way of the Good
Proverbs 2:16-22
T: Trust and Honor God
Proverbs 3:1-12
F: Wisdom Is Precious
Proverbs 3:13-20
S: Wisdom Brings Security
Proverbs 3:21-30
S: Do What Is Right
Proverbs 3:31-35

TEACHING TIPS

May 14
Bible Study Guide 11

1. Words You Should Know

Dust (Proverbs 8:26) *aphar* (Heb.)—Dry earth: ground.

2. Teacher Preparation

A. Read Proverbs 7 and 8 to become familiar with the contrasts and comparisons of wisdom and folly.

B. Study the WORDS YOU SHOULD KNOW section.

C. Review the questions in the DISCUSS THE MEANING section and consider possible answers in order to effectively facilitate the class discussion.

3. Starting the Lesson

A. Lead the class in prayer, asking God to reveal His wisdom to the class through His Word.

B. Ask a student to read the IN FOCUS story aloud.

C. Write the LESSON AIM on the board on a large poster. Draw the students' attention to the LESSON AIM by reading it out loud. Ask for comments about the LESSON AIM.

D. Ask for a volunteer to read the KEEP IN MIND verse, then encourage the class to commit the verse to memory during the week.

4. Getting into the Lesson

A. Ask for volunteers to read the FOCAL VERSES.

B. Instruct the students to reflect on the availability of God's wisdom to believers. Have the students write their insights in the REMEMBER YOUR THOUGHTS section.

5. Relating the Lesson to Life

A. Divide the class into groups to answer the SEARCH THE SCRIPTURES questions.

B. Read each DISCUSS THE MEANING question out loud, encouraging discussion for each question.

C. Review the LESSON IN OUR SOCIETY section. Ask the students to share personal experiences concerning God's wisdom in their life. Ask how Christians can be ambassadors of wisdom to others. Challenge the students to choose wisdom over folly in every area of their life.

6. Arousing Action

A. Challenge the students to complete the MAKE IT HAPPEN assignment. Ask them to be prepared to share the results with the class next week.

B. Ask a student to close in prayer, thanking God for the availability of His wisdom to believers.

WISDOM'S INVITATION

Bible Background • PROVERBS 8–9
Printed Text • PROVERBS 8:1–5, 22–31
Devotional Reading • PROVERBS 8:10–21

LESSON AIM

By the end of the lesson, we will:

UNDERSTAND the availability of God's wisdom;

DESIRE to respond to God's wisdom; and

SEEK a deeper relationship with Jesus, the source and fulfillment of all wisdom.

KEEP IN MIND

"Doth not wisdom cry? and understanding put forth her voice?" (Proverbs 8:1)

FOCAL VERSES

Proverbs 8:1 Doth not wisdom cry? and understanding put forth her voice?

2 She standeth in the top of high places, by the way in the places of the paths.

3 She crieth at the gates, at the entry of the city, at the coming in at the doors.

4 Unto you, O men, I call; and my voice is to the sons of man.

5 O ye simple, understand wisdom: and, ye fools, be ye of an understanding heart.

8:22 The LORD possessed me in the beginning of his way, before his works of old.

23 I was set up from everlasting, from the beginning, or ever the earth was.

24 When there were no depths, I was brought forth; when there were no fountains abounding with water.

25 Before the mountains were settled, before the hills was I brought forth:

26 While as yet he had not made the earth, nor the fields, nor the highest part of the dust of the world.

LESSON OVERVIEW

LESSON AIM
KEEP IN MIND
FOCAL VERSES
IN FOCUS
THE PEOPLE, PLACES, AND TIMES
BACKGROUND
AT-A-GLANCE
IN DEPTH
SEARCH THE SCRIPTURES
DISCUSS THE MEANING
LESSON IN OUR SOCIETY
MAKE IT HAPPEN
FOLLOW THE SPIRIT
REMEMBER YOUR THOUGHTS
MORE LIGHT ON THE TEXT
DAILY BIBLE READINGS

27 When he prepared the heavens, I was there: when he set a compass upon the face of the depth:

28 When he established the clouds above: when he strengthened the fountains of the deep:

29 When he gave to the sea his decree, that the waters should not pass his commandment: when he appointed the foundations of the earth:

30 Then I was by him, as one brought up with him: and I was daily his delight, rejoicing always before him;

31 Rejoicing in the habitable part of his earth; and my delights were with the sons of men.

IN FOCUS

For Diane, a successful high school principal, Christ, family, and friendship were the most important things in life. She and her best friend Asia had gone to high school and college together. They used to be inseparable, and they acted as the siblings that neither had had in their fatherless homes. Asia had dropped out of college and run off with her "dream man" without marrying him. It had been a shock because Asia had been president of the College Christian Fellowship. Shortly after that, they had lost touch.

One Thursday night, Diane received a call from Asia. "Asia, is it really you?" Diana cried. "It's been 20 years."

"Girl, it's me!" said Asia. "I'm in town. I'd like to swing by your house later," said Asia.

Diane was excited as she hung up the phone. At dinner that evening, Diane shared memories of Asia with her husband and two teenage daughters. The story of how Asia had helped her memorize all the books of the Bible made tears of laughter roll down their faces. By 10 o'clock when the doorbell rang, Diane's family was eager to meet Asia.

When Diane opened the door, Asia's face stole her breath away. Asia was scarecrow thin, and her eyes reflected a life of drug abuse and pain.

Asia put her finger to her lips and then said, "Shhh. I can't come in to meet your family. I just need a little money to help me get out of town."

Shocked at Asia's appearance and her request, Diane told her to wait a minute and closed the door. She wondered if she should comply with Asia's request for money, insist that she come in, or just turn her away.

Suddenly, Diane realized that at some point in her life, Asia had chosen a life quite different from the one they had shared as young girls in Bible study. The folly of a life consumed by narcotics had blinded Asia and robbed her of the ability to make wise decisions. Diane decided that she would attempt to help Asia by offering to take her home to her family.

As Diane opened the door, an impatient Asia said, "What's up, 'D'? Can you help me out with a little cash or what?"

"I do have a few dollars, Asia, but I would rather offer you a ride home to your mom. Why don't you come in? I can call her," said Diane.

"No, girl. My mom doesn't want to see me. What about that cash?" asked Asia.

Reluctantly, Diane handed Asia some money and a Bible.

Asia took the money and refused the Bible, saying, "I still got plenty of Bible knowledge from when we were kids." With that, Asia shuffled back to the car that was waiting for her.

As Diane closed the door behind her, she prayed that she had made the right decision and that Asia would find her way back home and to God.

In Proverbs, we learn that God's wisdom is available to everyone who desires a deeper relationship with Christ. Do you have a desire to respond to God's wisdom?

THE PEOPLE, PLACES, AND TIMES

Wisdom Literature. The "wise men" of ancient times regularly employed figures of speech as they sought to disciple others in the way of wisdom. Biblical wisdom literature can be divided into three different types: The first is *mashal* (**maw-shawl'**), a Hebrew word usually translated as "proverb." The second is the riddle (see Judges 14:14), and the last is the parable (see 1 Kings 20:39-40; 2 Samuel 12:1-6).

The *mashal* is the most prominent type of wisdom literature in Proverbs. Personification (i.e., giving a thing or a concept human qualities) is a favorite figure of speech used by the wise men. In some places in Proverbs, wisdom is personified to the extent that it is almost presented as a real, tangible being. With these vivid word pictures, God reveals the availability of His wisdom to us.

BACKGROUND

The book of Proverbs was written as instructional material, to be used as a sort of a "how-to" manual for life. As such, the book of Proverbs consists of succinct statements about life and human nature. Similes, metaphors, and other figures of speech are used generously to help give the reader a memorable word picture of a particular truth. In today's passage, wisdom is portrayed as "Lady Wisdom," giving us a unique, down-to-earth perspective on an intangible commodity. And as we will see, wisdom is fulfilled in the Person of Jesus Christ. He is wisdom.

AT-A-GLANCE

1. Wisdom's Call (Proverbs 8:1-5)
2. Wisdom's Story (vv. 22-31)

IN DEPTH

1. Wisdom's Call (Proverbs 8:1-5)

Chapter 8, promoting the excellency of wisdom, is in contrast with the preceding chapter, which warns of the wiles of the adulteress. The way of the adulteress is called "folly," which is, of course, the opposite of wisdom. A person who lives for folly is like an ox headed for the slaughter or a fool going to receive his punishment (Proverbs 7:22). This person is like a bird who is flying into a snare, without realizing that it will soon be held captive (v. 23). Many strong people, God's Word says, have been ruined by the folly of adultery (v. 26), and their eternal destination is hell (v. 27). What a sobering thought!

The warnings of chapter 7 should, of course, be taken literally. We need to constantly be on guard against adultery. However, believers should also be aware of those who would seduce them away from the truth of God's Word. We must be careful that we don't commit spiritual adultery. God demands our full devotion to Him and His Word.

Moving from Proverbs 7 to Proverbs 8 is like stepping from darkness into light. The contrast between the two passages is marked and refreshing. Wisdom calls out to all people (8:1), calling them to a better life than the one described in chapter 7.

How does wisdom call out? God uses many avenues to reach those living in sin's folly. First, wisdom begins with the fear of the Lord (Proverbs 1:7). Those who fear and reverence God place themselves in a position to gain wisdom. As we sit at His feet, learning from Him, we are awed by who He is. When we submit ourselves to His sovereignty, we see ourselves for who we really are—sinners saved by His grace. Once we grasp this perspective, God can then begin to fill us with the wisdom we need.

Second, God's wisdom is revealed in His creation. Psalm 19:1-6 describes God's wisdom revealed in the sky, sun, stars, day, and night. Psalm 19:1-2 (NIV) says, "The heavens declare the glory of God. Day after day, they pour forth speech; night after night they display knowledge." God's creation is a reflection of the beauty of His nature. These verses illustrate that nature itself is a showcase for God's wisdom. Many people have been drawn to God by experiencing the works of His hands—the rivers and oceans, the mountains and deserts, the woods and the plains. He is calling to all people, even through the world around us.

Third, God's wisdom is revealed through His Word. Look at Psalm 19 again. In verses 7-10

(NIV), we see that God's Word is "perfect," "trustworthy," "right," "radiant," "pure," "sure," "righteous." God's Word makes "wise the simple" and brings "light to the eyes." And if that weren't enough, God's Word is "more precious than gold" and "sweeter than honey." Wisdom is a priceless treasure. God's Word is wisdom.

Fourth, we as believers are wisdom's voice. As we live our lives of faith before others, they will be drawn to the godly wisdom we display. Second Corinthians 2:14 (NIV) says, "But thanks be to God, who always leads us in triumphal procession in Christ and through us spreads everywhere the fragrance of the knowledge of him." As we are led by the Spirit, our lives become a tangible example of godly wisdom to those around us. We become wisdom's voice, extending her rewards to all who would desire them.

Proverbs 8:2-3 further reveals the availability of wisdom "She standeth in the top of high places... She crieth at the gates, at the entry of the city, at the coming in at the doors." God longs to give wisdom! Through these Scriptures, He is urging us to take advantage of the abundance of wisdom.

This wisdom is available to all people, regardless of age, social status, or race (v. 4). God's wisdom, found and fulfilled in Jesus, is extended to all. But until we admit that we need wisdom, we won't find it. Verse 5 urges the "simple" and the "fools" to choose understanding. In other words, we must not allow sin to blind us to the wisdom of God. We must choose to search for understanding and wisdom by submitting ourselves to God because in Him "are hid all the treasures of wisdom and knowledge" (Colossians 2:3). When we walk in the Spirit instead of the flesh, we are choosing wisdom.

Wisdom is then put into practice as a skill. As believers, we must live our wisdom out in the daily grind of life. Our godly wisdom should shine through in every decision, every word, and every action. If wisdom is not put to use, what good is it? Practicing wisdom is a choice; it is a discipline. And it is sorely needed in today's world.

2. Wisdom's Story (vv. 22-31)

In this passage, wisdom is personified to the extreme. Wisdom, as an attribute of God, is portrayed as an almost real, separate person. This is called "hypostatization"—thinking of a concept, abstraction, etc. as having real, objective existence.

In Proverbs 8, we see wisdom existing eternally. A sweeping panorama of creation is covered in verses 24-29, following the order of God's work listed in Genesis. Wisdom was with God before there was anything created. Wisdom was with God before there were oceans and rivers, before there were mountains and hills. Wisdom was there when God created the heavens and when He "set a compass" (v. 27) or "marked out the horizon" (NIV). What an indescribably beautiful picture! The everlasting wisdom of God, an intrinsic fiber of His nature and character that was with Him as He created the world, is available to us! When God set the world into motion, wisdom was there. Wisdom was there when God set the boundaries for the oceans, when He set the stars in motion. Wisdom was there when He placed the clouds in the sky (vv. 28-29). Wisdom is like a skilled craftsman, rejoicing in the Master's presence and His creation (vv. 30-31). Wisdom flowed from God's character, and His wonderful, perfect creation was the result. And God desires to give wisdom to those who seek Him. What an incredible thought!

God's creative wisdom is available for the asking. In fact, wisdom "delights" in those who choose her (v. 31). Through wisdom, God set the creation in motion; likewise, through wisdom He orders our lives. He is aware of every detail of our lives and delights in giving us the wisdom to know Him more. As we know Him more, we begin to walk in wisdom. It's a circular principle, but one that God longs for us to take hold of. The more we know Him, the more wisdom we receive. The more wisdom we receive, the more we seek Him.

So the plea goes out to all people: "Listen to me; blessed are those who keep my ways" (v. 32, NIV). Receive instruction—don't refuse it. Proverbs 19:20 (NIV) says, "Listen to advice and accept instruction, and in the end you will be wise." Only a fool rejects instruction that will improve his life. Respond to God's wisdom! He has made it available to us for our good. We will be blessed when we choose to live by God's wisdom. What kind of blessings can we expect from liv-

ing a wise life? Peace with God is certainly high on the list. A good reputation is also a benefit. Wisdom affects every area of our lives. If we conduct our interpersonal relationships with wisdom, we will have meaningful friendships and strong family ties. If we practice our business policies with wisdom, we will enjoy the blessing of a reputable business. If we live our Christian life with wisdom, we will draw others to Christ. The blessings of wisdom may not always be tangible, but they far outweigh the material blessings that we often desire. Wisdom is worth it.

Wisdom does have another aspect, however. It is not only something that God possesses and something that God gives. Wisdom is Jesus.

In the New Testament, Jesus is viewed as the ultimate fulfillment of the Old Testament. Proverbs 8:22 tells us that wisdom was with God in the beginning before any of His "works of old." Does this have a familiar ring to it? John 1:1 says, "In the beginning was the Word, and the Word was with God, and the Word was God." Who is the Word? Jesus!

Proverbs 8:23 says that wisdom was "appointed" or "set up" from eternity—before the beginning! Jesus is the anointed one, the everlasting God! He was with God in the beginning, before time began. He has always been and always will be. In fact, without Him, "nothing was made that has been made" (John 1:3, NIV). He is and was first. He is and was supreme. He was "rejoicing always before him; Rejoicing in the habitable parts" (vv. 30-31). Jesus, Wisdom Himself, rejoices over those who choose Him.

When we choose Jesus, we avail ourselves of a tremendous, infinite amount of wisdom. Christ is "the power of God, and the wisdom of God" (1 Corinthians 1:24). He has "made unto us wisdom, and righteousness, and sanctification, and redemption." Hallelujah! What a treasure! When we seek Jesus, we gain wisdom. He is our all in all.

SEARCH THE SCRIPTURES

1. What is the point of Proverbs 8:2-3?

2. To whom does "lady wisdom" extend her invitation (vv. 4-5)?

3. Describe some of the word pictures used in verses 22-26.

4. What role did wisdom play at the time of the Creation (vv. 27-30)?

5. What is the believer's responsibility toward wisdom (vv. 32-33)?

DISCUSS THE MEANING

1. Discuss opportunities that present-day Christians have to extend wisdom's invitation to those around them.

2. Discuss the availability of wisdom. How does God reveal His wisdom to us? How do we gain the wisdom that is available to us?

3. Discuss the imagery of wisdom in Proverbs 8. How does the use of such imagery help us to understand God's ways and His Word? How is Jesus the fulfillment of all wisdom?

LESSON IN OUR SOCIETY

Wisdom is a scarce commodity in today's world. Watching the evening news is like seeing the "folly" of Proverbs 7 in action. Everywhere we look, people are making bad choices, trying to live life by their own rules.

God's Word calls us to a very different life—a life of godly wisdom. Wisdom is knowing God's will and His Word, then having the ability to apply this knowledge. In short, we must walk in the Spirit. Without a Spirit-led personal relationship with Jesus, we will never truly be able to live a wisdom-filled life. Jesus is wisdom. He is our treasure worth seeking. He extends His gift of wisdom to all who would receive it.

MAKE IT HAPPEN

How would your life be different if you sought God's wisdom on a regular basis? This week, try an experiment: Make a conscious effort to gain godly wisdom before you make a decision or tackle a problem.

FOLLOW THE SPIRIT

What God wants me to do:

_____

_____

REMEMBER YOUR THOUGHTS

Special insights I have learned:

_____

_____

MORE LIGHT ON THE TEXT
Proverbs 8:1-5, 22-31

In chapter 8, we see the continued personification of wisdom. Here Lady Wisdom reaffirms her value as she did in 1:20-33 and reminds us of her role in creation as she did in 3:19-26. She presents herself as a kind of divine person yet subject to Yahweh. In a similar way, love is described with the attributes of personhood (1 Corinthians 13:4-7). Because love is an attribute of God and God cannot be divided into parts, the apostle John was able to say, "God is love." Similarly, because wisdom is an attribute of God, we can say, "God is wisdom."

1 Doth not wisdom cry? and understanding put forth her voice? 2 She standeth in the top of high places, by the way in the places of the paths. 3 She crieth at the gates, at the entry of the city, at the coming in at the doors.

In last week's lesson, we explored Solomon's instructions to us to seek after wisdom. However, in this lesson the tables are turned as wisdom calls out to humankind. In this verse, wisdom publicly speaks for herself. She testifies to her value through rhetorical questions. She is prepared to "cry [out]." Her voice is to be heard at the key intersections ("by the way in the places of the paths"). The Hebrew word for "paths" is *nathiyb* (**naw-theeb'**), meaning to tramp or trod with the feet, or a beaten track. It is clear that we are given every opportunity to encounter wisdom during our daily travels. Wisdom's voice is to be heard in the halls of power and government ("at the gates, at the entry of the city"). The gates of the ancient cities were where the people would congregate and discuss many matters. It was where the business of the city was conducted, i.e., the meeting place of the city council. Wisdom makes her plea in every known and familiar path taken by us all. This might be today's coffee shop or another place where many of us meet for fellowship.

In Deuteronomy 5:1, Moses called all the people of Israel together and said, "Hear, O Israel, the statutes and judgments which I speak in your ears this day, that ye may learn them, and keep, and do them." Listening is an important spiritual skill that we must cultivate. When we listen, we are able to absorb and accept information about

God. We listen to learn, and learning deals with understanding the meaning and implications of the information we hear.

4 Unto you, O men, I call; and my voice is to the sons of man. 5 O ye simple, understand wisdom: and, ye fools, be ye of an understanding heart.

Wisdom never discriminates. She calls out to all mankind and invites us to avail ourselves of her wealth of understanding. Even those who are "simple" (Heb. *pethiy*, **peth-ee'**, meaning "naive") or "fools" (Heb. *keciyl*, **kes-eel'**, meaning "not very bright") are not excluded from the benefits of Lady Wisdom. Whoever we are, she offers us the opportunity to get "understanding" (Heb. *biyn* **bene'**).

The Hebrew word for "sons of man" is *ben* (**bane**), which refers to a son as a builder of the family; it includes the grandson as well as the nations. Wisdom is speaking to the present as well as the past. She leaves no one out.

8:22 The LORD possessed me in the beginning of his way, before his works of old. 23 I was set up from everlasting, from the beginning, or ever the earth was.

The Hebrew word for "possessed" is *qanah* (**kaw-naw'**), meaning to acquire or create. The Hebrew word for everlasting is *owlam* (**o-lawn'**) meaning "long duration," "antiquity," or "futurity." Wisdom now began to document her credibility in this verse. She testifies that she was present with the Lord before and during the Creation (v. 23), before she gave her generous invitation to mankind (vv. 4-5). Therefore, she indeed deserved the respect that was given to an elder. Her words were words of authority, much like God gave to the prophet Ezekiel to speak to the Israelites: "But when I speak to you, I will open your mouth and you shall say to them, 'This is what the Sovereign LORD says.' Whoever will listen let him listen, and whoever will refuse let him refuse; for they are a rebellious house" (Ezekiel 3:27, NIV).

24 When there were no depths, I was brought forth; when there were no fountains abounding with water. 25 Before the mountains were settled, before the hills was I brought forth: 26 While as yet he had not made the earth, nor the fields, nor the highest part of the dust of the world.

Wisdom proclaims that she was the agent of Creation. She was established before the creation of the "depths" (Heb. *tehowm*, **teh-home'**, meaning the "deep" or "oceans").

The Hebrew word for the phrase "brought forth" is *chiyl* (**kheel**), meaning to travail or to be born. While wisdom still proclaims her existence before time began, her dialogue in these verses can be likened to that of childbirth. The surging mass of water is the "water breaking before the actual birth of the child; the writhing in pain being a part of the labor and birthing process; with the child finally being 'brought forth' or born."

27 When he prepared the heavens, I was there: when he set a compass upon the face of the depth: 28 When he established the clouds above: when he strengthened the fountains of the deep: 29 When he gave to the sea his decree, that the waters should not pass his commandment: when he appointed the foundations of the earth:

Wisdom was present with God when He "prepared the 'heavens'" (Heb. *shamayim*, **shaw-mah'-yim**, meaning, "the sky, atmosphere, visible universe, where the stars dwell), "strengthened the fountains of the deep," "gave to the sea his 'decree'" (Heb. *choq*, **khoke** meaning prescribed limit or boundary), and "appointed the 'foundations' of the earth" (Heb. *mowcad*, **mo-sawd'**).

The Hebrew word for the phrase "set a compass" is *cheshmown* (**skhesh-mone'**), meaning to cut out, decree, or inscribe. The Hebrew word for "established" is *amats* (**aw-mats'**), meaning to be alert, of good courage, steadfastly minded, or strong. The Hebrew word for "strengthened" is *'azaz* (**aw-zaz'**), meaning to be strong.

In these verses, Solomon carries us back to the beginning of time to remind us of wisdom's presence at the time of Creation. This dialogue is one that demands respect because it emphasizes our Creator's omnipotence as He establishes the boundaries of the heavens and earth.

30 Then I was by him, as one brought up with him: and I was daily his delight, rejoicing always before him; **31** Rejoicing in the habitable part of His earth; and my delights were with the sons of men.

Lady Wisdom's role paralleled the role of the preexistent "Word" (logos) of John 1:1-3. She brought joy to God and rejoiced in the Creation: "I was daily His delight, rejoicing always before Him." The Hebrew word for rejoicing is *sachaq* (**saw-khak'**) meaning to laugh or play. The Hebrew word for "delight" is *sha`shua* (**shah-shoo'ah**) The Hebrew word translated "brought up" is *amown* (**aw-mone'**). It means "architect," "master workman," or "skilled workman." The picture is that of wisdom, the faithful master craftsman, standing at God's side as He created the universe. "How many are your works, O LORD! In wisdom you made them all; the earth is full of your creatures" (Psalm 104:24, NIV).

Wisdom was ecstatic as she was able to enjoy the "handiwork" of God (Psalm 19:1). This implies a wonderful gathering of wisdom and humankind; do we dare envision a party? We celebrate God's creation in many ways. Each time we enjoy a ride through the countryside and see the beautiful colors of fall, view snowcapped mountains, or enjoy a picnic on a bright sunny day, we share wisdom's pleasure and joy in Creation. As God's creation, we should praise our Creator: "Oh that men would praise the LORD for his goodness, and for his wonderful works to the children of men!" (Psalm 107:8).

DAILY BIBLE READINGS

M: Learn Prudence and Acquire Intelligence
Proverbs 8:1-9
T: Receive Advice, Wisdom, Insight, and Strength
Proverbs 8:10-21
W: Wisdom Participated in Creation
Proverbs 8:22-31
T: Listen to Wisdom's Instruction
Proverbs 8:32-36
F: Wisdom Extends an Invitation
Proverbs 9:1-6
S: Wisdom Multiplies Our Days
Proverbs 9:7-12
S: Folly Extends an Invitation
Proverbs 9:13-8

TEACHING TIPS

1. Words You Should Know

A. False (Proverbs 11:1) *mirmah* (Heb.)—Deceitful; can also be translated as "treachery".

B. Balance (v. 1) *mo'zen* (Heb.)—Denotes scales.

C. Integrity (v. 3) *tummah* (Heb.)—Integrity or incorruptibility.

D. Upright (v. 3) *yashar* (Heb.)—Defined as "straight," or "righteous."

2. Teacher Preparation

A. Read Proverbs 11.

B. Search out current events for examples of newsworthy headlines or stories that involve integrity. Clip some of these stories to distribute to students for discussion.

C. Be prepared to elicit opinions regarding "integrity in the media."

3. Starting the Lesson

A. Open the session with prayer. Ask for wisdom in teaching the path to integrity.

B. Ask for volunteers to read Proverbs 11.

C. Ask a student to define the terms "reputation" and "integrity."

4. Getting into the Lesson

A. Have a student read the LESSON AIM.

B. Circulate news stories about integrity around the class. Invite the students to share their opinions regarding the integrity of the persons in the stories.

C. Ask the students how they would have reacted if faced with the same set of circumstances.

5. Relating the Lesson to Life

A. Ask the students to silently read the IN FOCUS story; then discuss how it relates to today's lesson.

B. Remind the students that the path of integrity isn't always the easiest road to follow.

6. Arousing Action

A. Encourage the students to travel the path of integrity this week as they face challenges in their personal or professional lives.

B. Close with prayer, specifically requesting that God provide the strength of character to stay on the path of integrity every day.

WORSHIP GUIDE

For the Superintendent or Teacher
Theme: The Path of Integrity
Theme Song: "Give of Your Best to the Master"
Scripture: 1 John 4:19
Song: "Give Me a Clean Heart"
Meditation: Dear Lord, help me to be an instrument used to build up the body of Christ. Always walking in integrity and bringing glory to Your name. Amen.

MAY 21ST

THE PATH OF INTEGRITY

Bible Background • PROVERBS 11
Printed Text • PROVERBS 11:1–14
Devotional Reading • PROVERBS 10:27–32

LESSON AIM

By the end of the lesson, we will:

REALIZE that God expects His offspring to reflect His character and walk in integrity;

ASPIRE to strengthen our integrity in all aspects of our daily lives; and

MAKE a conscious effort toward having our walk match our talk.

KEEP IN MIND

"The integrity of the upright shall guide them: but the perverseness of transgressors shall destroy them" (Proverbs 11:3).

FOCAL VERSES

Proverbs 11:1 A false balance is abomination to the LORD: but a just weight is his delight.

2 When pride cometh, then cometh shame: but with the lowly is wisdom.

3 The integrity of the upright shall guide them: but the perverseness of transgressors shall destroy them.

4 Riches profit not in the day of wrath: but righteousness delivereth from death.

5 The righteousness of the perfect shall direct his way: but the wicked shall fall by his own wickedness.

6 The righteousness of the upright shall deliver them: but transgressors shall be taken in their own naughtiness.

7 When a wicked man dieth, his expectation shall perish: and the hope of unjust men perisheth.

8 The righteous is delivered out of trouble,

LESSON OVERVIEW

LESSON AIM
KEEP IN MIND
FOCAL VERSES
IN FOCUS
THE PEOPLE, PLACES, AND TIMES
BACKGROUND
AT-A-GLANCE
IN DEPTH
SEARCH THE SCRIPTURES
DISCUSS THE MEANING
LESSON IN OUR SOCIETY
MAKE IT HAPPEN
FOLLOW THE SPIRIT
REMEMBER YOUR THOUGHTS
MORE LIGHT ON THE TEXT
DAILY BIBLE READINGS

and the wicked cometh in his stead.

9 An hypocrite with his mouth destroyeth his neighbour: but through knowledge shall the just be delivered.

10 When it goeth well with the righteous, the city rejoiceth: and when the wicked perish, there is shouting.

11 By the blessing of the upright the city is exalted: but it is overthrown by the mouth of the wicked.

12 He that is void of wisdom despiseth his neighbour: but a man of understanding holdeth his peace.

13 A talebearer revealeth secrets: but he that is of a faithful spirit concealeth the matter.

14 Where no counsel is, the people fall: but in the multitude of counsellors there is safety.

IN FOCUS

Albert walked out of his garage and across the yard after a long day at work. The yard near the porch was covered with dead sparrows with BB's deep in their bodies. Albert reached down and started picking them up. He dumped the half-dozen birds in a discarded box. Right away, he knew that Ben, his youngest son, was the culprit. He had bought him the BB gun for his birthday and had had many arguments with his wife because of it.

"He is only 10 and not responsible enough for a toy like that," she had said.

Albert had argued. "He's a good boy who gets straight A's, and goes to Sunday School and church without ever complaining. I will supervise and let him use the gun on targets." Albert hid the BB gun in his bedroom closet to ensure that Ben would have to ask permission when he wanted to use it.

"Did you do this, Benjamin?" he asked his son, while holding the box of birds.

"No, Dad. My friend Roger wanted to see the gun, and then I couldn't stop him."

"You're grounded. You took the BB gun without permission. No after school activities for a month, and no more BB gun."

Never looking his father in the eye, Ben mumbled through silent tears.

"But Dad, the Peewee baseball league starts next week, and if I don't go to practice for a month, I can't play. Why can't you just take the BB gun away?"

"Because, Benjamin, it's about integrity."

"Integrity? What's that?"

"It's when a person does what they say they will do. Jesus said it is important that we show by our actions that we can be trusted."

Sniffling, Ben looked up at his father. "Is that why you have to put me on punishment so I can have integrity?"

"Yes, son. Now you understand."

The book of Proverbs shows us that integrity means matching behavior with belief. Do your deeds line up with what Jesus taught?

THE PEOPLE, PLACES, AND TIMES

Scales. Like today, people in biblical times used scales to measure the weight of various items, including silver and other metals, sold in marketplaces. Sometimes an unscrupulous merchant would rig a scale so that the weighing mechanism would not accurately reflect the weight of the purchased item. The result was that customers would actually receive less merchandise than they paid for. Proverbs makes it clear that God abhorred this practice and expects His creation to deal fairly and honestly in all areas of life.

BACKGROUND

We are created in God's image. Thus, our character should reflect His character. It should be

obvious to others that we are honest and just in our personal and professional business dealings. There should be no gray areas in which we blur the lines between good and evil, right and wrong, holy and unholy. Although others may not know that we have blurred the lines, God's eyes are always open, and He sees all that we do.

In case we need reminding, Proverbs 11 provides a yardstick by which we can measure our character from God's perspective. It is a call for integrity, backed by the understanding that God hates unjust scales, which often masquerade as favoritism, nepotism, theft, and other unsavory acts that are contrary to God's original purpose for His creation. Answering the call to integrity demands an unswerving commitment to live by the Word of God, despite how old-fashioned, unpopular, or unimaginative we may appear to onlookers.

AT-A-GLANCE

1. Delighting God (Proverbs 11:1)
2. Divergent Paths (vv. 2-8)
3. Community Impact (vv. 9-14)

IN DEPTH

1. Delighting God (Proverbs 11:1)

Children are born with an inherent desire to delight or please their parents. They seek their parents' approval, admiration, and love. Likewise, as spiritual children we should seek ways to discover what delights God. We understand from Scripture that we cannot earn God's favor by good works. However, good works are the means of thanking God for the unearned favor He gives us. Salvation is by grace through faith (Ephesians 2:8). When we seek to please God and demonstrate our thanksgiving to Him, it should not be through external means only. We must place emphasis on the internal means, one of which is integrity.

Verse 11 reveals, for example, that God is delighted when His creation walks the path of integrity. We do so by using just weights in our dealings with our family, friends, and coworkers and with every other person we come in contact with. In our own day, "just weights" translate to honest dealings in our personal and professional lives. Living godly lives in an ungodly world may seem impossible, but that is where the Holy Spirit becomes a vital enabler. John 16:13 declares that the Holy Spirit's job is to lead us into all truth. Christians can measure their spiritual effectiveness and integrity by whether or not they are actually walking in the Spirit morning until night, every day of the year.

Knowledge is power. Knowing that God hates dishonest dealings can inspire us to change our ways. A necessary first step in this direction is to repent of our false ways and forsake those actions or thoughts that are contrary to God's Word. Prayer is also essential, particularly in that it enables us to make good decisions even in "pressure cooker" circumstances. Finally, Bible study helps us to answer the question, "What would Jesus do?" when faced with situations that test our integrity.

2. Divergent Paths (vv. 2-8)

Integrity is often the distinguishing feature between unbelievers and believers, and between spiritual and carnal Christians. Verses 2-8 in Proverbs 11 reveal the very different paths on which the righteous and unrighteous travel. It behooves us to seek the path of integrity, for on it we encounter the purpose, provision, peace, and protection of God. Jesus Christ remains our chief example of how to do this, and the Holy Spirit remains our key inspirer and enabler.

Integrity is the key to God's provision. God rewards those who obey His commands but rebukes and corrects those who don't. In the Old Testament especially, there are many instances of God's provision being either withheld or released, depending on the spiritual fortitude and obedience of the children of God.

Jeremiah 29:11 promises hope and a good future for the believer. This promise is not for those

Choosing the path of integrity.

who will not willingly walk in integrity or take seriously their responsibility as God's creation to live upright before God and man. Other Scriptures also underscore this fact, making it clear that while the path of integrity leads to eternal life in God's presence, the divergent path leads to eternal separation.

3. Community Impact (vv. 9-14)

Living faithfully as God's creation causes people around us to be blessed. Our friends, family, neighbors, and even strangers are positively impacted when we live according to God's Word. On a larger scale, communities and nations are impacted and can be radically changed when one person dares to be different and lives according to integrity rather than by man's standards of excellence.

SEARCH THE SCRIPTURES

1. What delights the Lord (Proverbs 11:1)?
2. What shall guide the upright (v. 3)?
3. Who verbally destroys others (v. 9)?
4. What is the difference between a gossip and a trustworthy person (v. 13)?

DISCUSS THE MEANING

1. Why is integrity as important today as it was when Proverbs 11 was written?
2. If God is a forgiving God, why can't He overlook our character flaws and bless us anyway?

LESSON IN OUR SOCIETY

People are often shocked when someone in good standing in the academic, business, or church arena is discovered to be dishonest or abusive, or worse. The reason is that many times a person's public reputation is perceived to be a mirror image of their integrity. Many unbelievers and unchurched individuals cite hypocrisy as the reason that they refuse to become Christians or align with a local church. How can you use today's lesson to help others understand that God does not condone hypocrisy? What can you do to make sure your actions match your profession?

MAKE IT HAPPEN

This week, record some of the circumstances that tried to block your path to integrity. What made the difference in the outcome?

FOLLOW THE SPIRIT

What God wants me to do:

_____

_____

REMEMBER YOUR THOUGHTS

Special insights I have learned:

_____

_____

MORE LIGHT ON THE TEXT
Proverbs 11:1-14

1 A false balance is abomination to the LORD: but a just weight is his delight.

Proverbs 10-24 contrasts the wisdom of God with the folly of sin. This distinction is seen in Proverbs 11:1, where Solomon uses a marketplace illustration to teach character and integrity. Those who went to the market to buy their goods were offended when the vendors used faulty measures to sell their merchandise.

Solomon acknowledged the seriousness of using defective measures, especially when the vendors knew that the scales were inaccurate and the result was in their favor. Some shop owners used false balances to trick buyers. The Hebrew word for "false" is *mirmah* (**meer-maw'**), which means "deception" or "fraud." The false balance deceived and defrauded unsuspecting customers.

This false balance was an easy way to make a profit. Solomon, however, noted that God had a different view of this moneymaking scheme because false balances were an abomination to Him. The Hebrew word for "abomination" is *tow'ebah* (**to-ay-baw'**), which means "disgusting." The use of deceptive scales was a repulsive business practice in God's eyes.

The honest merchant used a "just weight," rather than deceptive methods, to serve the customer. The Hebrew word for "just" is *shalem* (**shaw-lame'**), which means "complete," "peaceful," or "friendly." The false balance was viewed as an attack upon the unsuspecting buyer, while the honest seller approached his customer in a friendly manner and treated him with kindness. God is pleased when people are dealt with kindly and fairly.

2 When pride cometh, then cometh shame: but with the lowly is wisdom.

The battle to preserve integrity includes the ongoing struggle with self. Solomon was familiar with this because of his own wealth and riches, and he wrestled with issues of pride. The word "pride" in Hebrew is *zadown* (**zaw-done'**), which literally means "arrogance." The conceited ways of the proud person are driven by sinful motivations, and this arrogance results in shame. The word "shame" in Hebrew is *qalown* (**kaw-lone'**), which means "disgrace." Because of their arrogance, the proud end up discrediting themselves.

Solomon continues the series of contrasts, and addresses the opposite of pride. Lowliness is the converse of pride, and the Hebrew word for "lowly" is *tsana'* (**tsaw-nah**), which means to humiliate or humble. The message in this verse is clear: Those who humble themselves before God learn to be wise.

As related to integrity, the lesson in this verse is simple. You cannot be a person of integrity if you are proud because your arrogant spirit will lead you to disgraceful acts. However, those who humble themselves before the Lord discover wisdom. The word "wisdom" in Hebrew is *chokmah* (**khok-maw'**) and can be translated as "wise" or "skillful." Those who are humble in spirit learn to be wise.

In the New Testament, God opposes the proud (James 4:6; 1 Peter 5:5). He resists the proud and gives grace to the humble. God's gracious aid is available to the humble, but the same help and assistance are not available to the self-sufficient.

3 The integrity of the upright shall guide them: but the perverseness of transgressors shall destroy them.

The Hebrew word for "integrity" is *tummah* (**toom-maw'**), which means "complete." Those who walk in integrity are whole persons in that they integrate their faith into every area of life. Some claim to follow God but are not consistent in their walk. In other words, they lack integrity because their walk doesn't match their talk.

Solomon observed that the "upright" (Heb. *yashar*, **yaw-shawr'**, meaning "straight," "correct," or "right") have integrity and that their integrity gave direction to their lives. In addition, integrity is defined as practicing what you tell others to do. It is no wonder that many become cynical when they observe leaders, both spiritual and political, who say one thing and do another. The lack of integrity diminishes the message because the life doesn't complement the words.

How does integrity guide the upright? The Hebrew word for "guide" is *nachah* (**naw-khaw'**) and means to transport. Integrity, which can also be described as spiritual maturity, leads God's people to live consistently. Spiritually mature believers have direction in life, make wise decisions, and use sound judgment.

The contrast continues as Solomon mentions the opposite of righteous living, which is perverseness. The Hebrew word for "perverseness" is *celeph* (**seh'-lef**). It means "crookedness" or "crooked dealing" and describes the distortion of what is right or good. Those who lack integrity are described as transgressors; they break God's laws, and this leads to the distortion of reality. This pattern of distorting reality continues in our day as it did during Solomon's time. And the sad truth is that many who claim to follow Christ lack integrity and engage in perversity.

4 Riches profit not in the day of wrath: but righteousness delivereth from death.

The force of this verse is that character is more important than affluence. In effect, Solomon's words run counter to the philosophy of our day. The Hebrew word for "riches" is *hown* (**hone**), which means "wealth." Solomon realized that the sum of one's possessions means nothing at the Day of Judgment. This is what he called the day of wrath.

What is of value on Judgment Day? The Hebrew word for "righteousness" is *tsedaqah* (**tsed-aw-kaw'**) and is used to refer to what is right. The sum total of one's possessions means nothing when we face God's judgment. The only thing that will matter then is one's standing before God. This is what delivers us from death.

The Hebrew word *maveth* (**maw'-veth**) refers to death and is also used figuratively for pestilence and ruin. When you die, the number of your possessions will mean nothing to God. The only thing that will matter is whether you have character—a character derived from a personal relationship with Christ.

Your relationship with Christ delivers you from spiritual death and ruin. The Hebrew word *natsal* (**naw-tsal'**) is translated "delivereth" and means to snatch away. God is not impressed by what you own.

5 The righteousness of the perfect shall direct his way: but the wicked shall fall by his own wickedness.

Solomon observed that those who followed God would be led in positive directions, while their own devices would destroy those who disobeyed Him. The Hebrew word *tamiym* (**taw-meem'**, meaning "complete," "whole," or "sound") is translated as "perfect." God's people will choose a lifestyle that results in the right choices. They are not flawless or faultless; instead, they seek to preserve their integrity and make sound decisions. God's people are led by a biblical standard of righteousness and choose what is right. Right is defined by God, not determined by the culture or chosen by society. God defines what is right according to Himself, and righteousness is God-centered, not man-centered.

The Bible outlines three major issues related to righteousness. God is righteous and never changes (James 1:17). Man's righteousness is as filthy rags (Isaiah 64:6). God's righteousness is imputed to us through union with Christ (2 Corinthians 5:21).

The Hebrew word for "fall" is *naphal* (**naw-fal**) and can be translated as "lie," "be cast down," or "fail." Whereas the believer will make right choices, the wicked are destroyed by their evil ways. Wickedness is never viewed in Scripture as a healthy standard to live by because it always destroys those who engage in it.

6 The righteousness of the upright shall deliver them: but transgressors shall be taken in their own naughtiness.

We discovered previously that righteousness provides direction for those who choose to live upright. Now we read that along with being a way of life, righteousness delivers the upright. As we saw in verse 3, the term "upright" refers to those who are complete spiritually. This does not mean perfection; it means that those who are upright are spiritually mature.

The Hebrew word used for "deliver" is the same word used in verse 4, where the text says that the righteous are delivered from death. In verse 6, Solomon does not complete his thought about what the righteous are delivered from; however, the rest of the verse sheds some light on this issue.

The way of life the righteous follow delivers them from the things that transgressors don't avoid. The Hebrew word *bagad* (**baw-gad'**) is translated as "transgressors" and can also mean to act covertly. Those who transgress God's laws act treacherously by breaking His commandments, often secretly. They offend God's righteous character and believe that they will get away with their unfaithful acts.

Solomon, on the other hand, declares that these offenders will be snared in their own iniquity. The word "taken" comes from the Hebrew word *lakad* (**law-kad'**) and means to capture or take. Those who transgress God's laws will be ensnared by their own wickedness.

The Hebrew word for "naughtiness" is *havvah* (**hav-vaw'**), which means to covet or desire. Those who break God's laws are following their own unrestrained desires, which capture and ultimately destroy them.

7 When a wicked man dieth, his expectation shall perish: and the hope of the unjust men perisheth.

What do people live for? Some are very selfless by nature and live for others. They dedicate themselves to serving people and find great satisfaction in doing this. Others, as described in this verse, are selfish by nature. They are wicked and self-centered, living for evil purposes.

The Hebrew word *rasha'* (**raw-shaw**) is translated as "wicked" and means to be morally wrong. Those who live immoral lives pursue that which is depraved. The Hebrew word for "expectation" is *tiqvah* (**tik-vaw'**) and refers to that which one is hoping for. The wicked attach themselves to corrupt things, and when they die, the things to which they are committed will also disappear. There is nothing lasting in what they desire.

Not only that, but their hopes and dreams also perish. The Hebrew word for "hope" is *towcheleth* (**to-kheh'-leth**); it can also be translated as "expectation." Because the wicked desire things of an evil nature, their hopes and dreams will not last. According to Solomon, their hopes and dreams will disappear. The Hebrew word for "perisheth" is *'abad* (**aw-bad'**) and suggests vanishing, going astray, or being destroyed.

When the wicked die, God sees to it that their hopes and dreams are destroyed because they are wicked in nature and intent. Only things of eternal significance and purpose will last forever. Unfortunately, those who live wicked lives will not discover this until it is too late. They are too busy pursuing immoral purposes to consider the temporary nature of their evil pursuits.

8 The righteous is delivered out of trouble, and the wicked cometh in his stead.

A predominant theme in Scripture is that God delivers His people. Psalm 34:7 reads, "The angel of the LORD encampeth round about them that fear him, and delivereth them." In addition, Jesus taught His disciples to pray for deliverance. He observed, "And lead us not into temptation, but deliver us from evil" (Matthew 6:13). The Hebrew word for "delivered out" is *chalats* (**khaw-lats'**) and means to remove or draw out. By implication, it also means to deliver or equip to fight. The meaning is clear: God goes before and fights for His people.

The Hebrew word for "trouble" is *tsarah* (**tsaw-raw'**), which means "distress." In this verse, "trouble" refers to situations in which God's people are put in tight spots, face an adversary, or are afflicted. God meets His people at their point of need, equips them to deal with the situation, and rescues them.

But what about the wicked? Where do they turn when they are in a tight spot or encounter difficulty? Solomon said the following: "The wicked cometh in his stead." What does this mean? God rescues the righteous, but the wicked are left to their own devices. God goes before the righteous, but the wicked will be left to sink in their own

demise. God will not deliver them when they fall.

9 An hypocrite with his mouth destroyeth his neighbour: but through knowledge shall the just be delivered.

Integrity is confirmed or destroyed by what we say. The Hebrew word for "hypocrite" is *chaneph* (**khaw-nafe'**), which means to be godless or profane. Solomon noted that integrity is ruined when we tear down our neighbor through our words. How does this happen? The Hebrew word for "destroyeth" is *shachath* (**shaw-khath'**) and means to decay or ruin. The important thing to note here is that your reputation can be ruined by your words. The person with integrity is aware of this. The hypocrite, or one defiled by sin, doesn't care and speaks without reservation.

Solomon continues the discussion regarding integrity and observes that the just are delivered through knowledge. The Hebrew word for "knowledge" is *da'ath* (**dah'-ath**), which means to have knowledge, perception, or skill. The force of this word is not that the just use trickery in their speech; instead, they are careful and skillful to speak that which is appropriate and avoid talk that will harm others.

In addition, it is the skill of the person with integrity that delivers. The Hebrew word for "delivered," used here, is the same as the word in verse 8. In that verse, we read that God goes before His people, fights for them, and delivers them. In verse 9, it is the knowledge of those with integrity that equips them to carefully and skillfully speak well of others.

10 When it goeth well with the righteous, the city rejoiceth: and when the wicked perish, there is shouting.

Everyone can impact the public life of the communities in which they live, and Solomon observes that the city rejoices when things go well for the righteous. The Hebrew word for "rejoiceth" is *'alats* (**aw-lats'**) and means to jump for joy. The community celebrates when people of integrity prosper.

Solomon continues the contrast, and the opposite of integrity is "wicked." He notes that there is "shouting" (Heb. *rinnah*, **rin-naw'**, meaning "a ringing cry") at the fall of the wicked. As it relates to celebration, *rinnah* includes the idea of a shrill shout of gladness. Accordingly, there is intense elation over the demise of the wicked.

11 By the blessing of the upright the city is exalted: but it is overthrown by the mouth of the wicked.

How do the upright exalt the city? The Hebrew word for "exalted" is *ruwm* (**room**) and means to be high or to rise up. One way the city benefits from the righteous is that honest businesspeople employ others and treat them with respect. Another advantage is that they pay their fair share of taxes to improve the infrastructure of their communities. And those who operate their businesses with integrity are generous with their material blessings.

The word "blessing" is *berakah* (**ber-aw-kaw'**), which means "benediction" and, by implication, "prosperity." People with integrity will be liberal with God's blessings and desire to share them with others. This is another way they bless their communities.

The wicked are not a blessing to those around them. The Hebrew word for "overthrown" is *harac* (**haw-ras'**) and means to pull or tear down in pieces. Solomon continues the contrast between integrity and wickedness by observing that the wicked bring reproach upon their communities by how they speak. He says, in essence, that the wicked tear apart the city with their mouths.

The Hebrew word for "mouth" is *peh* (**peh**). Solomon observed the wicked tearing their city apart through the speeches they gave. The wicked preferred to divide their communities with disruptive speeches rather than unite and bless people through their generosity.

12 He that is void of wisdom despiseth his neighbour: but a man of understanding holdeth his peace.

Solomon explains how integrity relates to one's neighbors. As we saw in the last verse, integrity allows us to impact our communities; verse 11 describes this impact on a larger scale. Verse 12 expresses some influence on a smaller level.

Those who lack integrity will relate poorly with their fellow citizens. Here the Hebrew word for "wisdom" is *leb* (**labe**) and literally means "heart." It is also used to refer to feelings, the will, and the intellect. Solomon says that the wicked are people who lack intellectual skill and ability. We know this because he uses the word "void." The Hebrew word for "void" is *chacer* (**khaw-sare'**), which means "without" or "lacking." The wicked cannot effectively relate to their neighbors because they lack wisdom.

In contrast, Solomon describes people with integrity as those who have understanding. The Hebrew word for "understanding" is *tabuwn* (**taw-boon**) and can be translated as "intelligence" or "discretion." The wicked lack discretion, but the righteous, by their integrity, use good judgment in their interactions with their neighbors.

Solomon also observes that the righteous hold their peace. The Hebrew word for "peace" is *charash* (**khaw-rash'**). One observation from this verse is that a person who lacks integrity will not relate well with his neighbors because he may argue over insignificant things. The righteous will choose their battles carefully and will overlook trivial matters.

13 A talebearer revealeth secrets: but he that is of a faithful spirit concealeth the matter.

Matters of integrity influence every aspect of our lives, and this appears to be Solomon's point in this verse. He relates integrity to the matter of what is said in our discussions with others. He defines the difference between how the wicked and the righteous approach this issue.

The wicked, or those who lack integrity, reveal secrets they have heard. Solomon calls them talebearers. The Hebrew word for "talebearer" is *rakiyl* (**raw-keel'**), which refers to one who travels about creating scandals.

However, people with integrity are described as faithful in spirit. The Hebrew word for "faithful" is *'aman* (**aw-man'**) and means to build up or support. Just as the aim of the wicked is to spread scandal, so the goal of those with integrity is to build up and support others.

The righteous build up others by keeping silent about things they have heard. They conceal matters that they believe are not the business of others. The Hebrew word for "concealeth" is *kacah* (**kaw-saw'**). There are times when we should share things with others and times when it is better to keep silent.

When should issues be covered with silence? We should be silent about information given in confidence. We should keep quiet when we are made aware of a special need for prayer. We should not divulge privileged information to be revealed at a later date.

When should we reveal things to others? We should speak up when people are being abused. We should reveal information when others are being defrauded. We should reveal truth when people seek to tear others down by silence or by creating a scandal. These matters, however, should only be shared after receiving counsel and advice from the appropriate authorities.

14 Where no counsel is, the people fall: but in the multitude of counsellors there is safety.

Solomon concludes this discussion of truth and honor by addressing the climate of integrity. Integrity flourishes when people pursue faithfulness to God's Word. However, when integrity is missing among leaders, the people will slip into apathy. When the pursuit of integrity diminishes, the people are left to their own conflicting agendas.

Solomon notes, "Where no counsel is, the people fall." The Hebrew word for "counsel" is *tachbulah* (**takh-boo-law'**) and means "direction" or "guidance." Those who possess integrity will seek to provide the right guidance to those under their care.

However, when leaders lack integrity, they pursue their own agendas and neglect to give proper leadership. Solomon says the result will be that the people will fall. "Fall" is translated from the Hebrew word *naphal* (**naw-fal'**). We read in verse 5 that the wicked fall because of their own wickedness. In this verse, the people fall due to lack of vision or direction.

To avoid this situation, and to give the people a vision for life and ministry, an abundance of counsellors is recommended. The Hebrew word for "counsellors" is *ya'ats* (**yaw-ats'**) and refers to one who gives advice or consults. People of integrity will seek counsel and advice from others,

and this allows them to preserve their integrity in the midst of difficult situations.

Those who lead will benefit from a thorough study of this passage because many churches and organizations struggle with vision. Instead of a vision for the future, many try to maintain the status quo. This is not what Solomon had in mind. Leaders with integrity will pursue God's dreams for the future.

DAILY BIBLE READINGS

M: God's Way Is a Stronghold
Proverbs 10:27-32
T: Wisdom, Not Pride
Proverbs 11:1-5
W: Righteousness, Not Treachery
Proverbs 11:6-10
T: The Importance of Guidance and Counsel
Proverbs 11:11-15
F: Blameless Ways, Not Wickedness
Proverbs 11:16-21
S: Generosity, Not Stinginess
Proverbs 11:22-26
S: Goodness, Not Evil
Proverbs 11:27-31

TEACHING TIPS

May 28
Bible Study Guide 13

1. Words You Should Know

A. Virtuous (Proverbs 31:10) *chayil* (Heb.)—Denotes strength, might, efficiency, and ability.

B. Willingly (v. 13) *chephets* (Heb.)—Something that is a pleasure or is delightful.

C. Strength (v. 25) *'oz* (Heb.)—Might, strength, power, or boldness.

2. Teacher Preparation

A. Read the FOCAL VERSES and BIBLE BACKGROUND for today's lesson.

B. Use a dictionary to study the words "faithfulness" and "diligence." Come prepared to share a personal challenge or triumph.

C. Brainstorm stumbling blocks to faithfulness, and be prepared to address the students' concerns.

D. Proverbs 31, a sensitive text for some modern women, still has value for both men and women when faithfulness is emphasized. Be mindful that not all women are wives or parents.

3. Starting the Lesson

A. Open the lesson with prayer.

B. Ask a volunteer to read the IN FOCUS story, and discuss it in relation to today's theme.

C. Ask the students to share why they believe Proverbs 31 is easy or difficult to incorporate into everyday life.

4. Getting into the Lesson

A. Ask someone to read a definition of "faithfulness," and link it with the lesson.

B. Discuss God's concepts of faithfulness and diligence as they relate to the Christian's use of time, talent, and treasure to honor God while serving others.

C. Discuss the need for balance in the Christian life.

5. Relating the Lesson to Life

A. Discuss the importance of balance within the various roles we live out each day (i.e., as a mother/father, wife/husband, daughter/son, sister/brother, etc.).

B. Allow time for the students to share their challenges, frustrations, or successes in living the balanced life.

C. Use the LESSON IN OUR SOCIETY section to remind the students that Proverbs 31 often seems like an impossible path to follow, but that it's really a picture of the life of a diligent, God-fearing person who puts God first while meeting the needs of others.

6. Arousing Action

A. Encourage the students to reread Proverbs 31 in light of the information gleaned from today's session.

B. Remind the students that God expects them to be faithful and diligent overseers of their time, talent, and treasure.

WORSHIP GUIDE

For the Superintendent or Teacher
Theme: Living Out Wisdom
Theme Song: There is a Balm in Gilead
Scripture: Ephesians 3:18-19
Song: "Deeper, Deeper"
Meditation: I pray that God will pour out His Spirit of wisdom on me so that I may fully comprehend His excellence and understand the depth of His tender mercy. Amen.

MAY 28TH

LIVING OUT WISDOM

Bible Background • PROVERBS 31
Printed Text • PROVERBS 31:8–14, 25–30
Devotional Reading • PROVERBS 4:10–15

LESSON AIM

By the end of the lesson, we will:

UNDERSTAND how all Christians can exhibit faithfulness;

BE PERSUADED that God's guidelines are necessary for a well-lived life; and

CHOOSE to set an example for others by living a balanced life that exudes the wisdom, faithfulness, and integrity of God.

KEEP IN MIND

"Favour is deceitful, and beauty is vain: but a woman that feareth the LORD, she shall be praised" (Proverbs 31:30).

FOCAL VERSES

Proverbs 31:8 Open thy mouth for the dumb in the cause of all such as are appointed to destruction.

9 Open thy mouth, judge righteously, and plead the cause of the poor and needy.

10 Who can find a virtuous woman? for her price is far above rubies.

11 The heart of her husband doth safely trust in her, so that he shall have no need of spoil.

12 She will do him good and not evil all the days of her life.

13 She seeketh wool, and flax, and worketh willingly with her hands.

14 She is like the merchants' ships; she bringeth her food from afar.

31:25 Strength and honour are her clothing; and she shall rejoice in time to come.

26 She openeth her mouth with wisdom; and

LESSON OVERVIEW

LESSON AIM
KEEP IN MIND
FOCAL VERSES
IN FOCUS
THE PEOPLE, PLACES,
AND TIMES
BACKGROUND
AT-A-GLANCE
IN DEPTH
SEARCH THE SCRIPTURES
DISCUSS THE MEANING
LESSON IN OUR SOCIETY
MAKE IT HAPPEN
FOLLOW THE SPIRIT
REMEMBER YOUR THOUGHTS
MORE LIGHT ON THE TEXT
DAILY BIBLE READINGS

in her tongue is the law of kindness.

27 She looketh well to the ways of her household, and eateth not the bread of idleness.

28 Her children arise up, and call her blessed; her husband also, and he praiseth her.

29 Many daughters have done virtuously, but thou excellest them all.

30 Favour is deceitful, and beauty is vain: but a woman that feareth the LORD, she shall be praised.

IN FOCUS

Larry's classroom was empty. He sat crushed beyond belief. Betty, his wife of 25 years, had been diagnosed with terminal cancer. For most of their marriage, he had traveled the country giving motivational lectures. Last night, they had been sitting in hospice sharing and praying when she dropped a bomb on his spirit.

"All your life you've been a male chauvinist. It's the only thing I have regretted in our marriage that I have never spoken about."

Larry was shocked. "What do you mean? Haven't I always treated you with respect?"

"Yes, absolutely. But it's your jokes about women. Think about the advice you gave both our daughters on their wedding days," she prodded.

Larry wrinkled his brow to recall. "I told them I was proud they got men who could take care of them."

"No, Larry," she reminded him, "you said they

needed to stay barefoot and pregnant so they could be all they could be." Larry cringed, and Betty tried to soften the blow by adding, "You're a good man, Larry, and I praise God for you."

Now alone in his office, he reviewed their relationship. Betty had hosted many students for dinner or even overnight. They had both committed their lives to serving the Lord and had kept their lifelong vows. But it was Betty who often was left home alone to care for their four children. He realized that through it all, it had been Betty's faith in God that had seen them through. It hadn't been his dominant personality, but Betty's strong spiritual convictions. Betty had served him because she believed in God's faithfulness.

Larry knew for certain that whatever happened, God would be faithful to her.

Today's lesson in Proverbs exalts the honor and dignity of womanhood. Both Christian men and women should have spiritual confidence that exudes wisdom, faithfulness, and the integrity of God.

THE PEOPLE, PLACES, AND TIMES

King Lemuel. Proverbs 31 contains the only reference to King Lemuel in Scripture; his origins, reign, etc. are unknown. The Hebrew word translated "prophecy" is *massa'* (**mas-saw'**), meaning "burden," "bearing," "tribute," "utterance," or "oracle." It is unclear if *massa'* refers to the "oracle" King Lemuel is about to communicate or if it refers to the location of this king. If the latter is the case, there what follows is from 'Lemuel, king of Massa.'

BACKGROUND

In Proverbs 31, wisdom is exemplified in the life of a God-fearing woman who faithfully makes use of her diverse gifts. Her success is applauded by her family and community. The observant reader will note that her accomplishments stem first from her relationship with God.

The book of Proverbs provides numerous examples of what constitutes a wise or foolish woman or man, but chapter 31 provides perhaps the most complete picture of a virtuous woman. The term "virtuous" encompasses more than sexual fidelity or purity. It actually denotes a person of ability, a faithful, hardworking woman who loves God.

IN DEPTH

1. Wise Words (Proverbs 31:8-9)

Because of their position, kings, presidents, and other government officials have the unique ability to spur positive social reform by wisely using their influence, power, or position for the common good. Thus, King Lemuel was reminded to use his influence to help the poor and needy, people who by virtue of their financial situation had no political clout or "voice."

2. The Diligent Life (vv. 10-14)

Webster's New World Dictionary and Thesaurus defines "diligent" as "persevering and careful in work; hard-working." That definition sums up the virtuous woman extolled in verses 10-31. It also is consistent with the biblical mandate for God's creation to be faithful and hardworking in every arena: home, work, and community. According to Proverbs 12:24 (NIV), "Diligent hands will rule, but laziness ends in slave labor." Meanwhile, Proverbs 22:29 (NIV) notes, "Do you see a man skilled in his work? He will serve before kings; he will not serve before obscure men."

Many women have read these verses and have become discouraged by this seemingly untiring paragon of faith. Men, meanwhile, have often viewed this chapter as being relevant only to women. But when viewed in the light of other Scriptures, these verses are pictures of the God-fearing person who diligently strives to make the most of his or her time, talents, and treasure. Thus, these verses are relevant for both men and women who are seeking practical ways to be diligent on a daily basis. One key term that is often overlooked is "willingly" in verse 13. Translated, it means to take pleasure in or to delight in. Christians who take pleasure in or delight in their tasks will often find that those tasks become easier simply because their attitude is right.

Willingness is only part of the equation. God will honor a person's work, even if they are not initially willing but out of obedience change their minds and become faithful and hardworking. That's the essence of Jesus' parable concerning the obedient son recorded in Matthew 21:28-32.

True diligence, though, is not confined to one's workplace or community. The consistently diligent will also be faithful to their family, displaying the same commitment, respect, and honor to those whom they live with as they do to those without.

3. Honored by All (vv. 25-30)

Living out wisdom daily will result in honor. The virtuous woman garners praise from her family and onlookers because of her successful endeavors. But it's clear that somehow she conveys to others that God is the true driving force in her life and the reason for her success. As God's creation, we must continue to strive to seek God's glory and not our own, even as His blessings bring us local, national, or international honor.

SEARCH THE SCRIPTURES

1. Whom should we speak up for (Proverbs 31:9-10)?
2. What are the "true garments" worn by a diligent person (v. 25)?
3. What is the most praiseworthy aspect of a believer's life (v. 30)?

DISCUSS THE MEANING

1. What is the connection between wisdom and diligence?
2. Discuss the evidence that "sowing" and "reaping" pays off. How does patience play a role in the process?

LESSON IN OUR SOCIETY

The typical Christian wears many hats while fulfilling various roles in the home, workplace, and community. It is often a struggle to effectively juggle these responsibilities with limited time and financial resources. Oftentimes, fatigue or frustration may signal that a person is becoming weary in well-doing (Galatians 6:9) or is doubting God's ability to do the seemingly impossible

(Matthew 19:26). However, over time the wise Christian learns to sacrifice for the greater good of all, to respect God, and to follow His guidance. As John D. Rockefeller aptly noted, "Don't be afraid to give up the good to go for the great."

MAKE IT HAPPEN

Commit to living out wisdom as evidenced by a balanced life that overflows with a willingness to do God's will. Create a list of modern examples of people you know who live out God's wisdom in the ways the passage describes. In this list, include one person you know personally who may be underappreciated, and do something special for that person this week.

FOLLOW THE SPIRIT

What God wants me to do:

_____

_____

REMEMBER YOUR THOUGHTS

Special insights I have learned:

_____

_____

MORE LIGHT ON THE TEXT

Proverbs 31:8-14, 25-30

There seems to be no limit to the attributes and accolades that can be heaped upon the woman of wisdom. Her goodness reaches far beyond herself, since she can be given at least partial credit for her husband's success. As her husband is esteemed and respected, the wise woman's sphere of influence effectively extends to all with whom he interacts.

Throughout this generous extolling of the idyllic, one cannot help but consciously contrast the opposite, the foil, of such diligent goodness. Where wise hands prepare and plan ahead, unwise hands are idle or make trouble. Where a wise heart protects and strengthens her family, an unwise heart sows discord and turbulence and invites disaster. Throughout the discourse, which simply upholds the many facets of virtue, the lack of it is soundly shamed and rebuked.

King Lemuel is identified as the author of chapter 31. Little is known about him (see THE

PEOPLE, PLACES, AND TIMES). His mother is identified as the source of the "prophecy" which follows. Surely one of the inherent qualities in a superb example is a mentoring mother. A wise king like Lemuel would want to record for posterity his most sublime image of the ideal woman, to capture the essence of the one who had mentored him so well. As God teaches us wisdom, He exhorts us to, in turn, teach others; thus, Lemuel's woman par excellence becomes everyone's mentor, both men and women, fulfilling God's teaching example for countless others who would read about, admire, and seek to emulate such noble and godly virtues.

While it may be familiar information to many, some may not be aware that Proverbs 31:10-31 is an acrostic, using consecutively all 22 letters of the Hebrew alphabet. As various writers have put it, these are "the ABCs of wisdom." Some have suggested that the wording of the verses sounds lyrical, which would coincide with something learned during a recent visit to Israel. Some of Israel's ancient harps contained 22 strings—an interesting fact considering that much of Israel's poetry, found in the Psalms, Proverbs, and other poetic books, was created to be sung. With numerous acrostics in the Old Testament (Psalms 111, 112, and 119 are all complete acrostics), one cannot help but connect the 22-stringed harp with the 22-letter Hebrew alphabet and see a beautiful and natural pattern for worship and inspiration. Singing a wise woman's praises is even more notable than writing about them— how much more so singing them "from A to Z" (or, more accurately, from *alef* to *tav*)?

A hymn like this is usually sung to God, but the woman of valor depicted here has characteristics similar to God's. The Lord's works are praiseworthy (Psalm 111:2) and "her own works praise her in the gates" (Proverbs 31:31). Psalm 111:4 says that the Lord is gracious and full of compassion, and she is a woman of compassion (Proverbs 31:26). The Lord gives us food (Psalm 111:5), and she provides food for her household (Proverbs 31:15). The fear of the Lord is the beginning of wisdom (Psalm 111:10), and she fears the Lord (Proverbs 31:30).

8 Open thy mouth for the dumb in the cause of all such as are appointed to destruction. 9 Open thy mouth, judge righteously, and plead the cause of the poor and needy.

The context addresses how a king should and shouldn't act. First, he shouldn't be unwise by chasing after women; and second, he shouldn't use alcohol excessively. Either behavior could open the door to unwise actions or impair his judgment. In contrast to the negative injunctions come the positive, "kingly" actions: Speak up for those without a voice—the powerless, who suffer and perish unseen and unheard. In this case, the king has the power to take a legal stand for those who, metaphorically speaking, don't have any legal legs on which to stand. Elsewhere in the Word, good and wise kings similarly champion the rights of the underprivileged (2 Samuel 14:4-11; 1 Kings 3:16-28; Psalm 45:3-5; 72:4, Isaiah 9:6-7)—"the poor and needy." The word translated as "poor" is *'aniy* (Heb. **aw-nee'**). It means "afflicted," "humble," "lowly," or "weak." The word translated "needy" is *ebyown* (Heb. **eb-yone'**). It means "needing help," "subject to oppression and abuse," or "needing deliverance from trouble." Widows and fatherless children ("orphans") fall into this category and are near to God's heart (Isaiah 10:1-4; Jeremiah 49:11; Malachi 3:5; Mark 12:38-40; Luke 20:45-47; James 1:27).

These opening verses set the stage to carry forward the theme of wisdom (the essence of the entire book of Proverbs). The writer captures a portrait of wisdom embodied in a woman of rare excellence, priceless and beautiful in character like the rarest of jewels. Some debate whether all that the rest of the passage entails could possibly represent an actual woman, in which case it would portray a grand symbol "of all that wisdom is," according to one writer. In the first chapter and in several other places, Proverbs describes wisdom as a woman (1:20; 7:4; 8:1, 11; 9:1, 13), so it would be natural for the writer to end the book with a flourish of the "ideal woman" or "Lady Wisdom." Naturally, as valid and even beautiful as such a perspective is, it isn't the popular interpretation, which of course refers to a flesh-and-blood woman. Along with the first perspective, wisdom itself is as rare and priceless as such a wise, virtuous woman would be, real or imagined.

10 Who can find a virtuous woman? For her price is far above rubies.

This introductory question is rhetorical. The point is that a wife of such noble character is hard to find. Indeed, she is a rare treasure if found (8:11). Noble or "virtuous" in Hebrew is *chayil* (**khah'-yil**) and is a masculine term that refers to strength or valor. Those are heady words when applied to a woman in a sense, a heroic warrior of wisdom, a mighty woman of valor (see also Ruth 3:11; Proverbs 12:4).

The verse is a direct extension of Proverbs 3:15, which also attests to the value of wisdom being "more precious than rubies." Various versions also use "coral" or "pearls." This phrase is repeated again in 8:11, adding, "all the things that may be desired are not to be compared." Using the translation, "Her price is far above rubies" (31:10), Hebrew scholar Christine Roy Yoder offers a unique perspective based on archaeological and documentary evidence of the period. According to Yoder, this wife is not only difficult to find, she is expensive to attain. She has a "purchase price," and it is considerable. Insofar as the woman of Proverbs 31:10-31 is ascribed a "price," it may be argued that the money measured the worth of the woman's dowry, which related to the perceived value of the woman as a wife.

In earlier passages in Proverbs, instruction in wisdom is given to a young man; in the latter verses, one finds the epitome of the ideal wife. The supreme model of wisdom becomes a goal and standard for young women, while young men are trained to cherish "Lady Wisdom." Then as now, both wisdom and a wise wife are beyond price, even above jewels.

11 The heart of her husband doth safely trust in her, so that he shall have no need of spoil. 12 She will do him good and not evil all the days of her life.

The husband of the virtuous woman has "no need of spoil" (Heb. *shalal,* **shaw-lawl'**, meaning "plunder"). That is, he lacks nothing of value. What he gains from his virtuous wife is far more valuable than the spoils of war. The virtuous woman inspires the confidence of her husband

because she is reliable and efficient in the way she conducts her business and domestic affairs (v. 12). In any household, trust in the wife's abilities is crucial.

Elsewhere, Proverbs compares an unreliable person to putting one's weight on a broken bone (25:19); it's both painful and useless. How much more important is the reliability factor if the person upon whom one puts one's weight (trust or confidence) is one's spouse? Confidence or faith is only as good as the object in which it is placed. Faith can be misplaced if the object fails the test; clearly, this is one source of pain the husband of a virtuous woman would never experience. As an aside, this is also one of the glories of having faith in a God who cannot fail (1 Chronicles 28:20; Lamentations 3:22).

13 She seeketh wool, and flax, and worketh willingly with her hands. 14 She is like the merchant' ships; she bringeth her food from afar.

Because the large household pictured in this hymn is wisely managed, it is well respected in the larger community. The same applies to all such households, regardless of size and income. The virtuous woman sees to it that food and clothing are provided. She makes wise choices and is industrious ("worketh willingly with her hands"). Like merchant ships, what she brings to her household is steady and abundant.

Whatever we may say about the symbolism of this passage, few would argue about the timeless values of faithfulness and industriousness. In fact, these are gender-free issues and purely matters of character. Reading Proverbs 31 with the intent to properly apply the Word, one must separate modern cultural clashes (e.g., today's 'gender wars') from the author's original intent and purpose. In this case, acquiring godly virtue fulfills the purpose of the author. Thus, this text is transcultural. These values facilitate mutual trust and respect between husbands and wives. This glorifies God.

If the intent of the writer was for the poem to be sung, hyperbole is a valid poet's tool no different from the trusty metaphor or simile. In either case, poetic license cannot be examined the same as, for example, a doctrinal statement on church or marital policy. The picture is one of a diligent woman providing for her own (in implied contrast to one who isn't diligent). In even the most primitive cultures, however male dominated, women perform many types of work involved with the feeding and care of their families. In the ancient world, working with one's hands was seen as noble; only in today's world is there a presumed superiority of those who work with their minds over those who work with their hands. An even greater reach would be to defend a woman's career outside the home based on the virtuous woman's "profession" or the reference to merchant ships endorsing "business travel," necessitating some extent of traditional role reversal. Such modern enterprises should stand or fall on their own merit, on a case-by-case basis; to secure justification (or condemnation) of any aspect of today's two-income, gender-role controversy from an ancient poetic metaphor is not a responsible dividing of the Word.

Yesteryear's industriousness is today's work ethic, and of all the attributes of the passage, clearly is the most gender neutral. Consider the words of Greg Herrick:

"Work is God's idea and therefore excellent for man. Any attempt to circumvent this process only reveals an inability to perceive the obvious. No price can be paid for the ideal wife who commits herself so wisely and thoroughly to her tasks that she merits public recognition for her abilities."

31:25 Strength and honour are her clothing; and she shall rejoice in time to come.

The work of the virtuous wife is of the highest quality. Her strength (Heb. *'owz*, **oze,** meaning "might") and honor (Heb. *hadar*, Heb. **haw-dawr',** meaning "ornament," "splendor," "honor," or "majesty") arise from her secure economic and financial status. She wears her success well. Thus, she faces the future with confidence ("she shall rejoice in time to come").

Clothing tells something about a person at first glance. The tattered garb of the poor versus the fine garments of the wealthy or of royalty are two ongoing themes in Scripture. Above and beyond physical garments is the symbolic clothing of character (or *lack thereof*, as the case may be), which is also readily evident to others and tells

something about a person. It has been well noted that we cannot "not communicate," and as much as we might try, we can't conceal our character. First Chronicles 16:27 uses some of the very same language in reference to God: "Glory and honor are in his presence; strength and gladness are in his place as do other verses (Job 40:10; Revelation 5:12; 7:12). It seems to be a given that if one is clothed with some of the attributes as God, one has little reason to be overly concerned about what the future holds.

26 She openeth her mouth with wisdom; and in her tongue is the law of kindness.

She speaks wisely and graciously. Her advice is practical and reliable. The words "law of kindness" (*torath hesed*) indicate that she is the source of kind and faithful teaching.

As a good tree produces only good fruit (Luke 6:43), and as from the abundance of the heart the mouth speaks (v. 45), likewise a heart of wisdom, as predictably as an orange tree produces oranges, produces words of wisdom (Proverbs 16:23; James 3:17). Consider the following list of attributes the Proverbs 31 woman possesses, each of which is a chapter title in Elizabeth George's devotional, *Discovering the Treasures of a Godly Woman*: priceless, faithful, good, diligent, enterprising, disciplined, thrifty, energetic, industrious, persistent, kind, farsighted, elegant, helpful, creative, confident, wise, prudent, loving, excellent, reverent, virtuous, and a treasure. If ever such a host of transcultural principles from Scripture were assembled in a single church, it would be a phenomenal place to experience; to ascribe them to one person is to speak in lofty terms indeed. All of the above make up the wardrobe of this rare woman.

27 She looketh well to the ways of her household, and eateth not the bread of idleness.

Unlike other passages in Proverbs filled with head-to-head contrasts, our poem is an outright referral to a solitary negative or unwise action— the infamous sin of idleness or laziness (see also Proverbs 26:14, 15; Ecclesiastes 10:18). Nothing could be further from the heart of sterling character that our noble woman possesses, who, even though she apparently could afford to "take her leisure," did not permit herself the indulgence or temptation.

28 Her children arise up, and call her blessed; her husband also, and he praiseth her. 29 Many daughters have done virtuously, but thou excellest them all.

The husband praises his wife and means it sincerely, he blesses her above all others. Her wisdom inspires these praises. So it is with children, who often seem so slow to learn to express gratitude for all that both parents do for them.

30 Favour is deceitful, and beauty is vain: but a woman that feareth the LORD, she shall be praised.

Even the worst of characters can put on a charming mask, and even the most physically beautiful will experience the ravages of time. At the end of the aging process, what will the once beautiful still claim for beauty if nothing beautiful was allowed to grow and develop within? A good character isn't something one simply dons like a new wardrobe once age has eroded one's physical beauty. That a person would even conceive of acquiring wisdom and character "later" is a sure sign that they understand nothing of its nature, and thus will never have it. Not so for our valorous woman! The passage returns to an earlier verse in Proverbs: "The fear of the LORD is the beginning of wisdom" (9:10). Many rewards await those who fear the Lord: good understanding (Psalm 111:10); blessings from God (Psalm 128:1); length of life (Proverbs 10:27); avoidance of evil (16:6); wealth and honor (22:4); and a treasure of knowledge (Isaiah 33:6).

Bibliography

Herrrick, Greg. "The Teaching of Proverbs on Word." Bible.org.

Yoder, Christine Roy. "The Woman of Substance: a Socioeconomic Reading of Proverbs 31:10-31." Journal of Biblical Literature 122, 3 (Fall 2003): 432-433.

DAILY BIBLE READINGS

M: Advice for Children
Proverbs 4:1-9

T: Keep on the Right Path
Proverbs 4:10-15

W: Wise People Value Wise Conduct
Proverbs 10:18-23

T: Advice from a Mother
Proverbs 31:1-9

F: Portrait of a Capable Wife
Proverbs 31:10-15

S: What an Ideal Wife Is Like
Proverbs 31:16-23

S: A Good Wife and Mother
Proverbs 31:24-31

JUNE 2006
QUARTER AT-A-GLANCE
CALLED TO BE A CHRISTIAN COMMUNITY

In this quarter, we look at letters Paul sent to the infant church at Corinth. Paul wrote 1 and 2 Corinthians to a Christian community plagued with many problems, including struggling to live, unite, and worship together in a morally corrupt society.

UNIT 1. SERVANTS OF GOD

There are four lessons in this unit and they focus on passages from 1 Corinthians. They explore how the Holy Spirit empowers the Christian community to be all that it can be for God.

LESSON 1: June 4
Servants of Unity
1 Corinthians 1:10-17

The church Paul found on his second missionary journey was in trouble. Eighteen months after he left them, the Corinthians fell into divisiveness and disorder. In addition, the surrounding environment was a cesspool of corruption with every conceivable sin, and this spilled over into the church. They needed to answer the question, "What does freedom in Christ really mean?"

LESSON 2: June 11
Servants of Wisdom
1 Corinthians 2:1, 6-16

The apostle Paul wrote to the Corinthians at a time when people were exploring many religions. Seeing the urgency of the situation, Paul sought to bring this immature church back to the fundamentals of the faith.

LESSON 3: June 18
Servants Together
1 Corinthians 3:1-15

Paul noted the spiritual immaturity in the Corinthian church shown by their bickering and jealousy. He used this portion of his letter to emphasize to them three important points: (1) they were workers together under the authority of one Person—Jesus Christ; (2) Jesus is the foundation or cornerstone of the church; and (3) Jesus is the one who paid their sin penalty on the Cross at Calvary.

LESSON 4: June 25
Servants in Ministry
1 Corinthians 4:1-13

Paul, once again, emphasized to the Corinthians that believers are servants of Jesus Christ and stewards of God's mysteries—knowledge of God's offer of salvation through His Son, Jesus Christ. He reemphasized that God is in control of His church, not church leaders.

UNIT 2. CALLED TO OBEDIENCE

There are five lessons in this unit and they also focus on 1 Corinthians. They explore how the Holy Spirit calls on the Christian community to be in relationships, help the weak, and love one another.

LESSON 5: July 2
Called to Relationships
1 Corinthians 7:2-15

Due to the culture's moral depravity, Paul answered the Corinthians' specific questions on human sexuality and marriage. He believed and taught that marriage was the answer to the widespread religious prostitution and sexual immorality that had seeped into the church.

LESSON 6: July 9
Called to Help the Weak
1 Corinthians 8:1-13

In this portion of Paul's letter, he dealt with food sacrificed to idols and gave the Corinthians instructions on Christian freedom. Paul taught that love is more important than knowledge and should govern believers' actions in relation to things that might offend weaker believers.

LESSON 7: July 16
Called to Win the Race
1 Corinthians 9:24-10:13

Paul compares our Christian journey to winning a race. The prize is, however, the privilege of telling others about Christ. Here he taught that all believers are saved by the blood of Jesus and must model their faith and undergo disciplined training for the sake of the Gospel.

LESSON 8: July 23
Called to the Common Good
1 Corinthians 12:1-13

Paul addressed the spiritual gifts that the Holy Spirit gives to every believer and how they are to be used in the body of Christ. He acknowledged to the Corinthians that some people may have only one gift, while others may have more. He emphasized that our spiritual gifts are assigned by the Holy Spirit to build up, serve, strengthen, and unify the Christian community.

LESSON 9: July 30
Called to Love
1 Corinthians 13

After discussing the spiritual gifts that God gives each believer, Paul showed the Corinthians their lack of love in utilizing them. He goes on to discuss the attributes of love. He compares and contrasts the beauty, permanence, and unifying principles of love with that of the other gifts.

UNIT 3. THE SPIRIT OF GIVING

There are four lessons in this unit and they focus on 2 Corinthians. The focus is on giving.

LESSON 10: August 6
Giving Forgiveness
2 Corinthians 2:5-11; 7:2-15

In this lesson, Paul teaches that love and accountability must be held together in the body of Christ. He gave the blueprint for true repentance. He explains how the church should handle discipline and help the wayward believer to repent and keep the church free from sin.

LESSON 11: August 13
Giving Generously
2 Corinthians 8:1-15

In this letter, Paul taught that when believers join with others to do God's will and His work, we promote Christian unity and help build God's kingdom. He recognized that the Corinthians already excelled in enthusiasm, faith, knowledge, and leadership. Now he wanted them to excel in giving.

LESSON 12: August 20
Giving Is a Witness
2 Corinthians 9:3-15

Again Paul addressed a collection for impoverished Christians in Jerusalem. He wanted the Corinthians to know that God would meet their own needs when they generously gave to others who were less fortunate. In return, God will bless bountifully the cheerful and generous giver.

LESSON 13: August 27
The Giving of Sufficient Grace
2 Corinthians 12:1-10

In this lesson, Paul told about his visions and revelations, and then of his own hindrance (thorn) that affected his ministry. It bothered him to the point that he went before God for deliverance and healing. However, God chose not to remove Paul's affliction, but instead demonstrated His power in Paul's weakness.

WE ARE CALLED TO BE A CHRISTIAN COMMUNITY

by Evangeline Carey

What Kind of Christian Are You?

Are you a thoroughfare

Through which beautiful blessings flow?

Can others see our Saviour in you,

No matter where you go?

Or are you a hindrance to the redemptive

Work of our Lord,

A menacing mighty clog,

Who plugs up the healing fountain

Of a Merciful, Loving God?

During the Easter season, we really focus on what Jesus did for all believers on the Cross at Calvary. Before dying, Jesus carried a massive post cross up Golgotha's Hill to pay all believers' sin debt. The fact that He suffered, bled, died, and rose again is the foundation of our Christian faith. But have we really taken time and studied the actual structure of the cross? Vertically, it points upward toward Almighty God. Horizontally, however, it points outward to our fellow man. Symbolically, the cross tells us that, as servants of the Most High God, we are to be in an intimate relationship and fellowship with Him. We are to commune with Him. Also *we are to be witnesses to a lost and dying world by demonstrating togetherness in Christian community*. We are to mentor by dwelling in love and peace with one another.

If we obey Christ's commands and yield to Him as the head of His church, the Christian community would not fall into divisiveness and disorder. God wants us to serve Him by serving each other and those who are in need. We definitely cannot serve God if we are busy devouring one another. We must seek to glorify God by showing the world our best. After all, we are made in His image. To be a Christian is to be Christlike. We need to be disciples of Jesus and make disciples of those around us, teaching by example how to live a life devoted to Jesus our Lord. For us to do this, there must be unity and order in the church! God is calling us to live in Christian community.

In 1 and 2 Corinthians, the apostle Paul shows his concern and care for God's embattled church in Corinth, a church in disorder. We can learn much from these letters about God's mind-set. This struggling new church was plagued by many problems. It was in the midst of a materially prosperous culture that was engulfed in foreign religions and sexual promiscuity. To make matters worse, a spirit of factional strife was so pronounced in the Corinthian church that it was threatening to tear the church apart. The Corinthians were not exhibiting Christian community. They had forgotten that they were working for God. Their actions were not glorifying God. Therefore, Paul wrote to appeal for harmony, to counsel them, and to condemn their division (1 Corinthians 3).

Paul not only addressed the issues of the young Corinthian church, but he offered viable solutions as well. He also told them how to heal their divisions and disorder and how to overcome unwholesome influences through the power of God. In reality, Paul told them how to do the will of God. This was the time for them to stop what they were doing wrong, and listen, learn, and obey the extraordinary God who works through ordinary people.

Paul reminded them that they were workers together under God's own authority and should live and walk in this truth: "For we are labourers togeth-

er with God: ye are God's husbandry, ye are God's building" (1 Corinthians 3:9). The Holy Spirit would give them wisdom and power to walk in God's light, His will, and His way.

In addition, Paul explained the role of church leaders. He communicated that both the leaders and the members of the body must practice what they believed and preached. They must be doers of God's Word, embracing God-ordained self-discipline and being in agreement with no division: "Now I beseech you, brethren, by the name of our Lord Jesus Christ, that ye all speak the same thing, and that there be no divisions among you; but that ye be perfectly joined together in the same mind and in the same judgment" (1 Corinthians 1:10). In other words, they must live united in the same mind (the mind of Christ) and the same purpose (to be a witness for Him).

In addition to all the other problems in the church, some Corinthians had rallied around various church leaders and teachers: Peter, Paul, and Apollos (1 Corinthians 3). This created more divisiveness. To solve this problem, Paul advocated that human leaders not be ranked on the same level with Christ; He is still the head of His church. Only Christ merited their devotion and ours since He was and is the One who died on the Cross and bridged the gulf between sinful man and a holy God. He has a spiritual window to our soul.

In essence, Paul wrote a highly practical letter to the Corinthian church. The church struggled to be a cohesive community in a surrounding corrupt society. In fact, serious sexual sin had crept into the church, and the leaders had not dealt with it properly (1 Corinthians 5). Paul gave insight on how the guilty party must be disciplined: in love, with the aim being to reconcile him to the body and to God. Paul showed by his instructions how we are to solve disciplinary problems in the church. We should glean from Paul's writings that obedience to God's Word counteracts satanic attacks that distort and destroy our Christian witness.

Paul, then, answered many of the questions Corinthians had sent him beforehand on Christian unity (1 Corinthians 7-16), while emphasizing the Gospel-God's Plan of Salvation. He dealt with "marriage, singleness, eating meat offered to idols, clothing worn in worship, the Lord's Supper, spiritual gifts, and the resurrection. All these issues had plagued the church at Corinth and needed answers."

In fact, some in the Corinthian Christian community felt that their freedom in Christ gave them license to hurt their weaker brothers and sisters by eating the meat of animals used in pagan rituals (1 Corinthians 8). Paul wanted to stamp out schisms like this within God's family, which demonstrated their lack of love for one another to a corrupt society. He knew that all believers were new creations and possessed God's Spirit and that therefore there should be cliques and divisions within the body. Therefore, he taught that God's values and principles should always guide believers' actions.

These immature Corinthian Christians also caused disorder by taking the Lord's Supper without first confessing sin (1 Corinthians 11). This caused even more division. Not only was this a grave error, but it was outright disobedience. Coupled with that was the misuse of spiritual gifts, bringing glory to the user and confusion on every hand. Paul explained to the Corinthians that these gifts were given by God for the common good, to edify the church and to glorify God, not the user (1 Corinthians 12). Even the woman's role in the church was a catalyst for contention. Paul's treatise on love in 1 Corinthians 13 certainly address this problem: of faith, hope, and love, the greatest is love (v. 13).

The church's problems were complicated when some members were alienated over whether Jesus Christ indeed rose from the dead (1 Corinthians 15). Paul taught that God's Word is true. When it says, "He arose," it means just that. God is no liar! Paul admonished the Corinthian Christians as well as us to believe and stand on God's Word.

The Corinthian church was not a mature church. When the door is cracked, Satan can come in with devastating effects. This was shown also by the fact that some within the body were even in opposition to Paul and created factions that questioned His apostleship. They promoted propaganda in the church, championing their personal positions. Therefore, Paul even had to defend himself in his letter. He expounded on his record of service to the risen Christ and the suffering that he, too, had encountered on his journey (2 Corinthians).

As we work out our salvation, we should always remember that God holds us personally responsible for our attitudes and actions toward each other, as Paul so vividly illustrated. We are to be committed to and in partnership, not only with Him, but also with our brothers and sisters in Christ. We are called by God to love and care for each other and to give generously to the church and to those in need out of what God has so bountifully given us. We are called to be a Christian community. Let's answer God's call in the affirmative.

Evangeline Carey is a staff writer for UMI.

CORPORATE SPIRITUALITY AND CHRISTIAN COMMUNITY IN PAULINE THEOLOGY

by Rukeia Draw, M.A.C.E.

There's a cluster of values that obscure the communal nature of Christianity. None of these values is good or bad. However, when synergized and in excess, they tend to have harmful effects on community. Let's explore a few concepts that constitute the American psychoculture.

Ethical egoism is an ideology that posits self-actualization as a moral obligation. An example of this is expressed in the sentiment, "I have been looking for a church to call home for years, but have not yet found a place where I am fed and can grow spiritually." This duty-to-self ethic can become so powerful that not working toward one's ideal self is viewed as pathological or sinful.

In the therapeutic motif, the self is improved through contractual relationships (therapy or support groups) and disciplines (like prayer, fasting, meditation, or solitude). Individuals are to attain personal satisfaction, emotional well-being, and peace. Once these are achieved, a person is considered spiritual. In the church, this influence is evident when the Gospel is presented in these terms alone; Jesus becomes the answer to inner peace and happiness.

According to John Lillis (1999), individualism describes how ethical egoism and the therapeutic motif work out in relation to others. The needs and desires of the individual are emphasized. Comments like this one are reflective of individualism's prevalence in the church:

"I would love to participate in ministry, but my family and career already demand too much. On Sundays, I'd like to relax and not be distracted. I'd simply like to focus on receiving what God has in store for me."

The self precedes community. Social relations are voluntary, contractual relationships entered into for self-interest. Community is, therefore, only a means to self-fulfillment.

According to the Whiteheads (1982), most Americans feel more affected by, but less influential in, civic life. The public arena appears unresponsive to individuality, so people retreat to a smaller sphere of control called private life. The individual can still make a difference in this domain. However privatization frustrates spirituality that transcends the individual:

The private person, with their individually chosen set of beliefs, functions as the sole criterion for what is true and applicable. Thus people attempt to find a sense of or sources of identity not in the community, church, or society, but only in the private sphere (Dash 1997).

A friend of mine exemplified this phenomenon when he remarked, "I believe in God, study the Bible, and pray, but I don't go to church and my spiritual life is better than most in the churches I've attended." Here the process of spiritual development is privately understood and experienced.

Called to Christian Community

The "body" metaphor helps recover corporate spiritual formation. The relevant passages in 1 Corinthians read:

"The body is a unit, though it is made up of many parts; and though all its parts are many, they form one body. So it is with Christ. For we were all baptized by one Spirit into one body—whether Jews or Greeks, slave or free—and we were all given the one Spirit to drink. Now you are the body of Christ, and each one of you is a part of it" (1 Corinthians 12:12-13, 27, NIV).

Because Christians "participate" in Christ, they are bound together and form a corporate entity called "the body of Christ." Every person belongs to either the community of the flesh or that of the Spirit (1 Corinthians 5:22; Romans 7:5). Union with these communities is articulated in terms of incorporation, not just identification. To become a follower of Jesus means transferring membership from the first Adamic community to the second. Therefore Christians are a body as a result of divine initiative, not because they congregate.

"Just as each of us has one body with many members, and these members do not all have the same function, so in Christ we who are many form one body, and each member belongs to all the others" (Romans 12:4-5, NIV).

The "body" metaphor in Ephesians reads:

"Instead, speaking the truth in love, we will in all things grow up into him who is the Head, that is, Christ. From him the whole body, joined and held together by every supporting ligament, grows and builds itself up in love, as each part does its work" (Ephesians 4:15-16, NIV).

This passage differs from the other two in that Paul is speaking of the universal church. This chapter also identifies the goal and means of spiritual formation. Together these passages indicate that collective growth is central to Paul's understanding of spirituality. Believers do not exist as such by themselves, nor for their own benefit. Every member is responsible for helping others mature through the diversity of ministries and variety of gifts distributed throughout the community by the Spirit.

Called to Spiritual Maturity

According to Paul, participation in the life of the Spirit through incorporation in Jesus Christ is genuine spirituality. So what makes the spiritually alive, spiritually mature? Let's look at the Corinthian community again. These congregants certainly lacked no gifts or signs of the Spirit, yet Paul refers to them as immature (1 Corinthians 1:7; 3:1). The Corinthian church lost sight of the communal nature of spiritual formation. They were divided by self-seeking and self-indulgent behavior.

The famous "love" chapter (1 Corinthians 13) should also be viewed in relation to community. Love is the bond that holds people together. That's why it's patient, kind, protecting, trusting, hopeful, and persevering. That's also why love isn't envious, boastful, proud, rude, self-seeking, easily angered, or unforgiving (all the things Paul found among the Corinthians). These things destroy community, making it impossible for unity and therefore maturity to exist.

Membership in the Christian community means that building the church, not self-edification, is at the core of spiritual formation. A person matures by finding his or her place in community. Individuals are drawn into the growth of the community, and they mature as the community does. Maturing as a community becomes the goal of spiritual formation and the task of Christian education.

Christian education should help people discover where they fit in the church. This includes helping them understand current needs, how skills employed in other areas of life can be utilized, their shared responsibility to build the church, and aid in stirring up the gifts bestowed upon them by the Spirit.

Bibliography

Dash, Michael I. N., Jonathan Jackson, and Stephen C. Rasor. *Hidden Wholeness: An African American Spirituality for Individuals and Communities. Berea, Ohio: Pilgrim Press, 1997.*

Lillis, John. "Spiritual Formation: The Corporate Dimension of Spirituality." *Lecture, Institute of Theological Studies, Grand Rapids, Mich., 1999.*

Whitehead, Evelyn Eaton, and James D. Whitehead. *Community of Faith: Models and Strategies for Developing Christian Communities. New York: Seabury Press, 1982.*

Rukeia Draw *is an adjunct instructor at Trinity Evangelical Divinity School. She is pursuing a Ph.D. in Educational Studies from Trinity International University in Deerfield, Illinois.*

CHANGE BEGINS AT HOME

by Bianca Elliott

"Comfort others with what has comforted you" is the overarching theme of 1 and 2 Corinthians. Paul writes in these two practical books of the New Testament about real people asking difficult questions. The similarity between the issues Paul deals with compared to the current American culture and the church today is uncanny. As a result, we can learn much from Paul's writings about how to create Christian community.

To say that someone "lived like a Corinthian" was not a compliment in Paul's time. Widespread decadence, pleasing oneself, and selfish living were encouraged, while respect for personhood and family was not valued. Respect for marriage, women, sex inside of marriage, the method of worship, and so much more was either trivialized or marginalized to such an extent that it meant little in one's everyday life. The temple prostitutes—and there were many—were often married women or young women. Corinthians, as a group, were only living for the moment. They habitually listened to all the new beliefs without totally committing to one belief. Located on an isthmus, Corinth had the advantage of hearing many peoples from around the modern world. As a cosmopolitan city, it had the best of many systems. The Corinthians mixed some beliefs that they heard with others until they reached a belief system they could live with in their daily lives. Corinthians had a hedonistic lifestyle and a culture that was known throughout the Roman world for going too far. Into such a culture came the Gospel that Paul preached, lived, and taught.

Scholars are not sure whether Paul made two or three trips to Corinth. They do agree that these two letters (1 and 2 Corinthians) are answers to Corinthian believers who were trying to live out their faith in a challenging world. They wrote to Paul to get clarification on teaching they had heard and guidance on issues not spelled out on his earlier mission trips. Their list of questions is not available but may be construed from the substance and format of Paul's responses to them in 1 and 2 Corinthians. While some of the material may be shocking to discuss and read, Paul demonstrates that there is no division between Christian and public life; there is no such thing as secular and religious. His words to the Corinthians are just as needed today.

Corinthian believers needed desperately to hear about Jesus and see the authentic practice of Christianity. Paul answered difficult questions with grace and truth. He did not concern himself about whether his answers were politically correct. He guided the Corinthians to see through their twisted doctrines to a pure Gospel. Relationships were confused and improper at that time. Paul addressed, without flinching, such topics as incest, marriage, sex within marriage, remarriage, sins of the flesh, and so much more with clear direction.

While he addressed these topics, he strove to not allow the Corinthians to look down on others who were new to the faith. He wanted them to comfort each other with what comforted them in Christ when they became believers. He reminded the Corinthian believers that some of them formerly practiced the sins of which he speaks in these letters. Paul, who had the authority to discipline the believers, gave them hope. He taught them that if they were in Christ, they were new creatures and not bound by sin. Paul wanted these believers to be united in love and not divided in spirit. He taught them how to celebrate the Lord's Supper with a unity and love that became known throughout the world as "the love feast." He stopped people from taking liberties with and hurting other believers, either new (weak) or old (strong). Paul exalted the family and especially marriage. His encouragement provided believers with a future and a hope as well as strength for the present.

Modern cities across America are having difficulties on so many fronts. Notice that I did not say only *urban* cities. Small towns are having troubles that are as complicated and difficult as those of many large cities. Young children commit crimes and are charged as adults. Adults commit crimes against young and old, healthy and sick. Old people sell drugs from their homes or provide resources for others to commit crimes. Churches all across America are dealing with sex scandals and other crimes against their flocks. Hate crimes and other forms of sin are increasing in frequency. The definition of the family is going to be decided by the government soon. Americans have a reputation throughout the world, and it is not a good reputation in many cases. The differences between the cultural climate of Corinth and America are very small.

What can be done? Vote for more school levies for better schools? Encourage the desegregation of schools? Petition local, state, and national government for safer streets and communities? What can be done? Paul tells us in Corinthians. Notice he did not tell his people to legislate morality. He did not have them petition government for changes. It is true to a large extent that morality cannot be legislated. Paul did not, however, leave his people with no plan. He showed them how to effect real change in their communities. He had them start with themselves.

He shares how they need Christ in their everyday lives. They needed to take Jesus to work with them, to the schools with them, and invite Him into their families. Jesus explained that one can't put new wine into old wineskins. Lasting change cannot be accomplished through outward programs. Only with the change of the inner man can true change occur. It cannot be legislated or moralized.

Paul did not change Corinth; God changed *Corinthians*. That is also true today. Where God's Word is preached faithfully and lived devotedly, change occurs. Paul taught the Corinthians their value in Christ. He taught how they must love as Christ loved them. They must have unity and forgiveness along with discipline. They couldn't continue to tolerate sin in their churches and would have to discipline their members. Women would have to be chaste in behavior and spirit. Lawsuits and other specific actions against each other would have to stop because the world was watching them and deciding if Christianity was a viable alternative to their current lifestyles. Paul pressed the Corinthians to walk their talk.

Paul's letter to the Corinthians could have been addressed to a small town or to a major city. The words he penned under the inspiration of the Holy Spirit are yet penetrating and powerful today. They make people uncomfortable. They make people want to make excuses or exceptions. His words also have the power of God in them to change a person into a godly representative of God's love for people. The books of 1 and 2 Corinthians can move a person or a church to be salt and light in their communities. Will some people in the fellowship be uncomfortable? Undoubtedly. But the Word faithfully preached, lived, and taught is transforming and life changing. Do we want to see changes in our communities? Let the changes begin with us.

Bianca Elliott *has a Bachelor of Science degree in Education and a Master of Science degree in Curriculum and Instruction. She is a gifted educator and curriculum specialist.*

BLACK PERSONALITY

DR. MICHAEL JOHNSON
MRS. KAY JOHNSON

by Judith St.Clair Hull, Ph.D.

In the streets of Nairobi, Kenya, 30,000 to 50,000 street children prostitute themselves, collect rubbish, beg, and steal to live. But we know our Heavenly Father cares very much for each one of them. That is why Dr. Michael Johnson and his wife, Mrs. Kay Johnson, left Philadelphia to minister to the physical and spiritual needs of the people of Kenya, East Africa.

Dr. Johnson says, "The challenges are to try to meet the physical and emotional needs of young boys and girls, most of whom have never known hope. As families and communities struggle with the onslaught of AIDS and other deadly illnesses, the children who remain fall between the cracks of the once thriving extended family. Sleeping on the streets, sniffing glue, eating from garbage pails, and bathing in stagnant water from gutters is part of normal life for these children and families. . . . Bringing free medical care to children living on the streets and in the crowded orphanages in Nairobi raises hope within them and helps them to see that they have value before God."

In addition to caring for the children, Dr. Johnson is involved in raising the overall quality of medical care in Kenya through a program called INFA-MED (Institute of Family Medicine), which is a family practice training program for Kenyan physicians. INFA-MED works with government officials, mission organizations, and hospital boards. The life expectancy in Kenya has dropped from the mid-50s to the mid-40s, so bringing healthcare and healthcare awareness are important objectives.

The Johnsons are also feeding young families on the street and providing blankets, beds, and clothes for orphanages. Kay Johnson's special project is also working to provide Christian families for Kenyan orphans by locating adoptive and foster homes. This project includes building schools, clinics, and providing water for the community of families making these children their own. It is important to introduce children to the Saviour's care for them not only for eternity, but for this life also.

Michael was born and raised in Chicago, Illinois, and went to Lawrence University in Appleton, Wisconsin. While he was there, he felt God calling him to do a special work somewhere in the world. Then he went to medical school at the University of Michigan in Ann Arbor, Michigan. At this time, he met and married Kay, a native of Ann Arbor, who was studying accounting at Eastern Michigan University.

The Johnsons moved to Philadelphia where Michael completed his training in surgery. Kay managed the surgical practice and a professional billing service for physicians. However, this was not the desire of God for their lives. God chose to move them along with their four children to Kenya. They have been in ministry in Africa since 1984.

Dr. Johnson could have stayed in the United States and been a successful African American surgeon. He and his family should be admired for what they left behind to follow the will of God. Bringing hope to people with no hope and making the world a better place for them brings immense satisfaction. And to top it all off, they are sharing the wonderful Gospel of Christ.

If you would like to become involved in this ministry, you may e-mail Dr. Michael Johnson at michael.johnson@wgm.org.

TEACHING TIPS

June 4
Bible Study Guide 1

1. Words You Should Know

A. Divisions (1 Corinthians 1:10) *schisma* (Gk.)—A split or gap (schism).

B. Contentions (v. 11) *eris* (Gk.)—Quarrels or wrangling.

C. Name (v. 13) *onoma* (Gk.)—The word or words by which someone or something is called, distinguished, or identified.

2. Teacher Preparation

A. Prayerfully read the BIBLE BACKGROUND and DEVOTIONAL READING.

B. Prayerfully study this entire BIBLE STUDY GUIDE. Highlight parts to emphasize.

C. Think about existing situations in your church that could be resolved by working together in unity and agreement.

3. Starting the Lesson

A. Ask a student to lead the class in prayer, focusing on the LESSON AIM.

B. Ask another student to read the IN FOCUS section.

C. Initiate a preliminary discussion about the destructive effects of quarrels between members or groups within the church.

4. Getting into the Lesson

A. Allow each student to read aloud some portion of THE PEOPLE, PLACES, AND TIMES and the BACKGROUND, KEEP IN MIND, and AT-A-GLANCE sections.

B. Allow each student to read one of the FOCAL VERSES. As each verse is read aloud, discuss and instruct using the portions of IN DEPTH and MORE LIGHT ON THE TEXT that you highlighted during your preparation.

C. Ask the students to respond to the SEARCH THE SCRIPTURES questions.

5. Relating the Lesson to Life

A. Ask the students to respond to the DISCUSS THE MEANING questions.

B. Have someone read LESSON IN OUR SOCIETY.

6. Arousing Action

A. Ask a student to read the KEEP IN MIND verse again, and then ask another student to read the MAKE IT HAPPEN section. Emphasize the need for everyone to be taught correct doctrine and to submit to it.

B. Ask the students to take a few minutes to record their responses in the FOLLOW THE SPIRIT and REMEMBER YOUR THOUGHTS sections.

C. Encourage the students to be prepared for next week's lesson.

D. Close the class with prayer.

WORSHIP GUIDE

For the Superintendent or Teacher
Theme: Servants of Unity
Theme Song: "Onward, Christian Soldiers"
Scripture: John 17:9-23
Song: "Come, Thou Almighty King"
Meditation: Heavenly Father, our Sovereign Lord, give us understanding of Your Word. Fill us with Your Holy Spirit. Conform us to Your image. Let Your peace reign in our hearts. Make us one with You and of one heart and one mind. Bind us together in love. By the authority of Jesus Christ, make it so. Amen.

SERVANTS OF UNITY

Bible Background • 1 CORINTHIANS 1:10–17
Printed Text • 1 CORINTHIANS 1:10–17
Devotional Reading • 1 CORINTHIANS 1:2–9

LESSON AIM

By the end of the lesson, we will:

KNOW that God requires us to be united in Jesus Christ;

BE CONVINCED that unity can be maintained only by submission to the Lordship of Jesus Christ and accurate application of His Word; and

WORK together to glorify Jesus Christ in the things we say and do.

KEEP IN MIND

"Now I beseech you, brethren, by the name of our Lord Jesus Christ, that ye all speak the same thing, and that there be no divisions among you; but that ye be perfectly joined together in the same mind and in the same judgment" (1 Corinthians 1:10).

FOCAL VERSES

1 Corinthians 1:10 Now I beseech you, brethren, by the name of our Lord Jesus Christ, that ye all speak the same thing, and that there be no divisions among you; but that ye be perfectly joined together in the same mind and in the same judgment.

11 For it hath been declared unto me of you, my brethren, by them which are of the house of Chloe, that there are contentions among you.

12 Now this I say, that every one of you saith, I am of Paul; and I of Apollos; and I of Cephas; and I of Christ.

13 Is Christ divided? was Paul crucified for you? or were ye baptized in the name of Paul?

14 I thank God that I baptized none of you, but Crispus and Gaius;

LESSON OVERVIEW

LESSON AIM
KEEP IN MIND
FOCAL VERSES
IN FOCUS
THE PEOPLE, PLACES, AND TIMES
BACKGROUND
AT-A-GLANCE
IN DEPTH
SEARCH THE SCRIPTURES
DISCUSS THE MEANING
LESSON IN OUR SOCIETY
MAKE IT HAPPEN
FOLLOW THE SPIRIT
REMEMBER YOUR THOUGHTS
MORE LIGHT ON THE TEXT
DAILY BIBLE READINGS

15 Lest any should say that I had baptized in mine own name.

16 And I baptized also the household of Stephanas: besides, I know not whether I baptized any other.

17 For Christ sent me not to baptize, but to preach the gospel: not with wisdom of words, lest the cross of Christ should be made of none effect.

IN FOCUS

Albert brought his barber, Duane, to church. Duane was struggling to find a relationship with God. Albert thought that coming to his church could help.

Before the service, Pastor Jackson asked Deacon Sloane to join him at the pulpit. During the previous week's Bible study, Deacon Sloane and the pastor had gotten into a nasty, public argument. "As most of you know," Pastor Jackson began, "Deacon Sloane and I let our emotions get out of hand. We said things that should have been discussed in private."

Albert's stomach churned as he thought of Duane's first impression. *Why did I have to bring Duane to church today?* Albert wondered, sure that airing "dirty laundry" would discourage Duane from coming again.

Pastor Jackson put his arm around Deacon Sloane's shoulders and went on. "We met the next day and resolved our differences. God's grace allowed us to gain a better understanding of one another and fully reconcile. We want to tell you how sorry we are for disrupting the spirit of fellowship. Now we want to pray for forgiveness."

Many members' eyes filled with tears as the pastor and deacon prayed. However, Albert had missed the significance of the moment. Driving home, Duane said, "I can't believe what Pastor Jackson did this morning. I've never known men who had that kind of humility. You better believe it would never happen at the barbershop."

After a while, Duane committed his life to God and made Albert's church his spiritual home.

Paul calls on members of the Corinthian church to resolve their differences and live in unity. When Christians demonstrate unity, it brings glory to God.

THE PEOPLE, PLACES, AND TIMES

Corinth. This is a city and region of ancient Greece occupying most of the Isthmus of Corinth and part of the northeastern Peloponnesus (southern peninsula). The Isthmus of Corinth was a strip of land between central Greece and the Peloponnesus. The city occupied a strategic point for control of trade between these two land masses and the Aegean and Adriatic Seas. During the apostle Paul's lifetime, it became the largest and most flourishing center in southern Greece. Dominating the center of the city was the marketplace.

Corinth served as the capital of the Roman province of Achaia. Here Paul stood before Gallio, governor of Achaia, due to some Jewish accusations (Acts 18:12-13). This probably occurred between A.D. 50 and 52. Paul ministered about one and a half years in the city. Most of the population was mobile producing a mixture of beliefs and conduct. Religious prostitution was practiced in the pagan temples. The depravity of Corinthian morals became a byword in a culture that was already pagan.

BACKGROUND

The purpose of the letter to the Corinthians was to correct errors that were present in the church at Corinth. These errors included division, immorality, abuse of Christian liberties, improper public worship practices, improper regard for the Lord's Supper, misuse of spiritual gifts, and denial of the Resurrection.

Paul's exhortation to correct division in the local church was in response to information he received from the household of Chloe. Chloe was a Christian whose place of residency is not recorded in Scripture. Thus, Chloe could have been a resident of Corinth or the surrounding Achaian province. It is also possible that Chloe was a visitor from Ephesus since Paul was there when he wrote the letter. The mention of the name suggests that this person was known by the believers at Corinth. This household reported that there were quarrels among the believers. The division was the result of people expressing an allegiance to specific servants of God. They claimed that the servant they had an affinity with was the leader of their faction, and, by so doing, they took the body of Christ and carved it up into multiple factions. Although different in appearance, manner, style, and function, all servants of Jesus Christ work for the same Master. None could function for Christ apart from Christ. The Corinthians either forgot or failed to see this.

All believers belong to the body of Christ. A body is a single unit composed of many parts (1 Corinthians 12:12). The eyes provide the body with vision. The ears provide the hearing. The hands provide the ability to serve. The feet provide movement. All parts contribute to the functioning of the one body. In the same manner, the body of Christ has one Head, the Lord Jesus Christ, and as such, has one will, one purpose, and one goal. Since the church represents the body of Christ, it must be unified. Indeed, it must be unified in truth. What is truth? It is found in Jesus Christ who says that He is the way, the truth, and the life (John 14:6). Jesus prayed to the Father that all those who believe in Him would be one, just as He and the Father are one (John 17:21). This oneness is centered in God, His message, and His ministry. The mission of Christ is confirmed by believers whose lives exhibit love and unity with each other and with the Lord (Mark 12:29-31).

AT-A-GLANCE

**1. Servants United Under One Authority
(1 Corinthians 1:10-16)
2. Servants United with One Gospel
(v. 17)**

IN DEPTH

1. Servants United Under One Authority (1 Corinthians 1:10-16)

Paul exhorts the believers based on the authority of Jesus Christ and out of regard for Christ who is Lord. Their love and allegiance to Christ should persuade them to submit in obedience. Paul is speaking under the authority of Jesus Christ to servants who belong to and participate in the household of God (Ephesians 2:19). Believers should all be in agreement with God's word and express it by saying the same thing. There should be no division, or literally, no schism (as in the ripping apart of something, Matthew 9:16). There should be no separate parties, no cliques, and no infighting. There should be no difference of opinion about who Jesus is (John 8:43) or what He commands. Neither should there be any inward feelings of rivalry. Instead believers should be united.

This union is both in mind (intellect and feeling) and judgment (opinion). One mind requires one truth and one way. There must be unity in doctrinal teaching. This requires diligent study of the Word of God so that all correctly interpret the Word of Truth (2 Timothy 2:15). And this requires that all are taught and led by the Holy Spirit, who reveals the truth and will of God.

Thus far, Paul has summarized the nature of the problem and how it should be resolved. Now, in 1 Corinthians 1:12, he reveals their divisive activity. The New Testament church consisted of converted Jews and Gentiles whose differences in culture and religious practice provided fertile ground for contention. Paul was an apostle to the Gentiles and a Roman citizen, so some of these people were more comfortable with him. Peter's demeanor (Galatians 2:11-14) and ministry related primarily to the Jews (2:8; 1 Peter 1:1). Peter's activities seemed to center around Palestine, although he was sent as an apostolic representative from the church in Jerusalem to confirm churches established in other regions.

False Hebrew teachers probably instigated allegiance to Peter and against Paul. They worked against Paul because they thought he was polluting the church with uncircumcised members. Others may have preferred Peter because he was a student of Jesus during His earthly ministry.

Apollos was an Alexandrian Jew. There was a large population of Jews in Alexandria in the first century. Apollos had a thorough knowledge of Old Testament Scripture and was a follower of John the Baptist prior to being taught "the Way" by Aquila and Priscilla in Ephesus. Alexandria, a city in Northern Africa located near the mouth of the Nile River, was respected for its literary culture. Apollos came across as learned and eloquent in his delivery of the Gospel. His delivery style appealed to the educated in Corinth, who were accustomed to philosophical debate and Grecian speech. They were not impressed with Paul's delivery when he spoke. Paul would later find it necessary to defend the words he delivered (1 Corinthians 1:17; 2:1, 13). None of these ministers had any part in the development of factions. Apollos probably was reluctant to return to Corinth as long as the fragmented situation existed (16:12). Paul respected Apollos and his convictions.

Then there were those who seem to have claimed exclusive allegiance to Christ. They erred by claiming a relationship with Christ that others could not obtain. Divisions, schisms, and factions are a work of the old nature, or the flesh and its desire, which fight against the Holy Spirit (Galatians 5:17, 20). Irrespective of nationality, ethnicity, culture, or stature, all true believers partake of the one Holy Spirit who makes known the will and truth of God (1 Corinthians 12:13).

There is only one Son of God, one Saviour, one Lord—and that person is Jesus Christ (Romans 3:30). He died for the sins of the world, and only He provides an acceptable sacrifice to God the Father (3:25). "Neither is there salvation in any other: for there is none other name under heaven given among men, whereby we must be saved" (Acts 4:12). Three rhetorical questions are asked in 1 Corinthians 1:13, and the obvious answer to each one is no. Christ is not divided; there is only one Head, and all the members of the body should be one under Him. Neither Paul, nor Peter, nor Apollos were crucified for humanity. No one is consecrated unto Paul, Peter, or Apollos in baptism. Christians confess the name of Christ (Romans 10:9; Matthew 28:18-20).

Paul was thankful that he gave no cause for anyone to accuse him of making disciples in his own name. Perhaps providentially, he had only baptized a few people. Those he could recall were Crispus, Gaius, and the household of Stephanas. Crispus was the chief ruler of the synagogue in Corinth (Acts 18:8). Gaius was mentioned as a host to Paul, probably in Corinth since the letter to the Romans was written there (Romans 16:23). The household of Stephanas was among the first converts in the province of Achaia and was active in the ministry as well as in reporting to Paul (1 Corinthians 16:15-17). It is probable that Stephanas, along with Fortunatus and Achaicus, brought the letter containing questions from the Corinthians to Paul in Ephesus. Paul affirmed that he had given no cause for anyone to be aligned with him. His message had been and continued to be Christ-centered.

2. Servants United with One Gospel (v. 17)

Paul begins to defend his manner of preaching in 1:17 and continues through chapter 2 before returning to his exhortation on unity in the body of Christ in chapter 3. Paul said that Christ sent him to preach not to baptize. He recounted his calling while traveling on the Damascus Road to support his claim (Acts 9:15, 20, 22, 27, 29; 26:16-18). God did not ordain Paul to recruit followers who would be associated with him through baptism. Perhaps Paul recalled the ministry of John the Baptist and how those John had baptized were called his disciples (John 4:1). It is possible that the apostles left the baptizing to other ministers (Acts 10:48).

Baptism is the sign of the new covenant by which we identify with Christ in His death, burial, and Resurrection. For the believer, baptism is an outward sign of an inward work of the Holy Spirit. Believers are buried with Christ, putting off the sins of the old nature. They are raised with Christ through faith in newness of life (Romans 6:3-4; Colossians 2:11-12). It is the Gospel that is the power of God unto salvation to everyone who believes. Why? Because in it the righteousness of God is revealed (Romans 1:16-17). Through the Gospel, the holiness of God and the sinfulness of man are revealed. Through the Gospel, humanity sees the need for a mediator. Through the Gospel, humanity sees the need for salvation. And through the Gospel, humanity sees that Jesus Christ is their means of redemption. Since Paul was sent by Christ, he was the messenger of Christ. He carried the message given to him by Christ, who is the one authority. Christ testifies of Himself and His message is true. The Father and the Holy Spirit bear witness to the fact that Christ's message is true (John 8:18; 15:26). They all are one in will, purpose, and execution.

Paul's preaching was not with the wisdom of words. His words did not originate from human reasoning, nor were they an aggregate of human wisdom developed over time. Such words are powerless to save. Philosophers have expounded their theories but have not found a solution to the evil in the world. There is no earthly solution to the ills of the world. Only the atoning sacrifice of Jesus Christ will restore humanity to a right relationship with God. This is the hidden wisdom of God. It is hidden in the sense that humans can never discover it on their own. It must be revealed by God. So Paul says that he came not as a philosopher but as a witness to that which has been revealed by God.

SEARCH THE SCRIPTURES

1. What change in attitude and behavior was required of the Corinthians (1 Corinthians 1:10)?

2. How many different factions are identified by Paul? Who were they aligned with (v. 12)?

3. Was Paul against water baptism? Why did he make it an issue (vv. 13-14)?

4. What did Christ require of Paul (v. 17)?

5. Who was the source and the content of Paul's preaching (v. 17)?

DISCUSS THE MEANING

1. Discuss the ramifications of having a favorite church singer, teacher, or preacher.

2. After the passing of the pastor, a church elected a new pastor from among its congregation leaving other candidates and their supporters disappointed. What can be done to maintain unity in this church? Would the departure of some be a reasonable option?

LESSON IN OUR SOCIETY

Jesus told the Pharisees, "Every city or house divided against itself shall not stand" (Matthew 12:25). These words also rang true in the United States back in 1861, the year the Civil War started. The nation was divided over a number of issues. Those in the North fought to preserve the Union and to prevent slavery from spreading into the Western territories. They feared that slavery would threaten free labor. Many Southerners fought to protect and expand slavery because they believed that ending slavery would lead to the destruction of their economy. Even Southerners who did not own slaves considered slavery essential to "the Southern way of life." Much devastation and loss of life could have been avoided had the nation been able to "speak the same thing."

MAKE IT HAPPEN

Commit 1 Corinthians 1:10 to memory. Make it happen by being a good student of the Word of God and a doer of His Word. Submit to the Lordship of Jesus Christ and be filled (controlled) by the Holy Spirit, who empowers believers to avoid a self-centered life.

FOLLOW THE SPIRIT

What God wants me to do:

_____

_____

REMEMBER YOUR THOUGHTS

Special insights I have learned:

_____

_____

MORE LIGHT ON THE TEXT

1 Corinthians 1:10-17

10 Now I beseech you, brethren, by the name of our Lord Jesus Christ, that ye all speak the same thing, and that there be no divisions among you; but that ye be perfectly joined together in the same mind and in the same judgment.

Having concluded the introduction to the letter, Paul came to the main point that he was about to address in the first four chapters of the epistle: an exhortation to the Corinthians to put an end to all squabbles. Verse 10 is an appeal for a common mind and the repudiation of cliques. In this verse, which introduces the body of the letter, Paul calls the Corinthian believers to perfect Christian unity. The word "beseech" (Gk. *parakaleo*, **par-ak-al-eh'-o**) carries with it the connotations of request and exhortation. The basis of Paul's appeal is striking. He does not make his appeal based on his apostolic authority. Instead, first he appealed to them as "brethren," a word that denotes equality. He stood on common ground with those to whom he wrote. Second, he appealed to them on account of the name of the Lord Jesus Christ. The intensity of his feelings was immediately revealed as he solemnly appealed to them in the name of the Lord Jesus.

Paul's appeal was for the Corinthians to do away with all "schisms" (Gk. *schismata*, **skhis'-mah-tah**), a metaphor related to clothing. Thus, Paul was saying that there should be no "ripping apart" in the community. Rather, as one piece of cloth, the people of God should be perfectly united. In turn, such unity was to be evidenced in their confession; they were to speak the same thing. To be united in the same mind is to share the same convictions about God and Jesus Christ. Paul told them to speak the same thing and exhorted them to avoid ministry-based factions.

It is possible to have different views and not be divisive. The reason for the appeal is provided in 1 Corinthians 3:3, where Paul states that if Christians are divided, they are no different from other people. In such a case, it is impossible for them to do the special work to which God has called them. So deep is Paul's concern for the Corinthians that he reiterated his plea for unity three times in this verse: "speak the same thing... [let] there be no divisions among you... [and] be perfectly joined together in the same mind and in the same judgment."

11 For it hath been declared unto me of you, my brethren, by them which are of the house of Chloe, that there are contentions among you.

Verses 11 and 12 show the reason why Paul considered the plea so urgently necessary. Paul had received a report from Chloe's people. The word translated "declare" (Gk. *deloo*, **day-lo'-o**) literally means "make known." The fact that contentions existed among them was something that was made explicitly clear to Paul and was beyond dispute; therefore, he could confidently address the situation. Paul's method was equally instructive. He did not hide the identity of Chloe and just refer to her report as an "anonymous report." The gravity of the divisions is shown in the use of the word "contentions" (Gk. *eris,* **er'-is**). In its original usage, it always referred to disputes that endanger the church. The word points to quarrels and indicates the hot dispute and emotional flame that ignites whenever rivalry becomes intolerable. It is listed as one of the works of the flesh (Galatians 5:20) of which Christians should have no part.

12 Now this I say, that every one of you saith, I am of Paul; and I of Apollos; and I of Cephas; and I of Christ.

Paul became more specific as he wrote about the content of the report that he received. The mistake that the Corinthians were making was to put a human leader in the place of God. What a tragedy—and how true it is even in the twenty-first century. Apparently, members of the Corinthian church were divisively forming allegiances to various leaders within the church. We cannot fully determine the exact nature of the divisions in the church, other than that they were drawn along partisan lines. Each group in the congregation used the name of its particular favored leader—Paul, Peter, Apollos, and even Jesus—as a "war cry." They gave their loyalties to human leaders instead of to Jesus Christ. Somehow, as they magnified the human instruments, they lost sight of the Saviour.

It is a mistake that Christians and others have often made and continue to make. There are still many groups and religious organizations that honor one human being, particularly the founder, as if he or she were a sort of second Christ. But Paul would have none of it. A group in the Corinthian church prided itself on belonging to Christ, probably suggesting that they alone followed Christ properly. However, Paul said many times that Jesus is for everyone. Therefore, no Christians have the right to think that Jesus belongs to their group, rather than to other groups.

13 Is Christ divided? was Paul crucified for you? or were ye baptized in the name of Paul?

Paul asked three rhetorical questions that underline the absurdity of the state of affairs in the Corinthian church that he had just sketched. The answer to each question is an emphatic, "No!"

"Is Christ divided?" Implicit in this question is the notion of the church as the body of Christ, which Paul would later develop in 1 Corinthians 10-12. Christ cannot be divided, for He is one (1 Corinthians 12:12), nor can He be apportioned out so that only one group may claim to follow Him. Rather, all of the Corinthians are supposed to follow Christ.

"Was Paul crucified for you?" Paul was not crucified for them, nor were they baptized into his name. Only to the extent that Paul followed and imitated Christ were the Corinthians to follow and imitate Paul (1 Corinthians 11:1). The point is that the Corinthians were in danger of giving to mere human leaders that ultimate allegiance that belonged to Christ alone as their only Saviour. As Paul puts it in 4:1, the Corinthians should think of him and his fellow apostles simply as servants of Christ to whom the mysteries of God are committed and who are responsible to God.

"Were ye baptized in the name of Paul?" Some Corinthians were probably touting the name of the person who baptized them, suggesting that such persons were either more spiritual or exhibited greater wisdom. Once again, Paul used his own name to show up the error of the Corinthian partisanship. The Greek phrase *en to onoma* (**en to on'-om-ah**) literally "into the name," when used with baptism, implies that the person baptized is the exclusive property of Christ.

14 I thank God that I baptized none of you, but Crispus and Gaius; 15 Lest any should say that I had baptized in mine own name. 16 And I baptized also the household of Stephanas: besides, I know not whether I baptized any other.

Was Paul saying that baptism was unnecessary? Absolutely not. One should by no means interpret or understand these verses to mean that. Paul simply placed the emphasis where it belongs, that is, on the preaching of the Gospel (see v. 17).

Nevertheless, when Paul was with the Corinthians, as far as he could recall he only baptized a few people. He might have considered this to be providential, for if he had indeed baptized many of them, they could potentially have used the fact to support the absurd claims found in verses 12-13. With certainty, Paul can say that he baptized Crispus, the synagogue ruler (Acts 18:8); Gaius, his host (Romans 16:23); and the household of Stephanas (cf. 1 Corinthians 16:15-16).

17 For Christ sent me not to baptize, but to preach the gospel: not with wisdom of words, lest the cross of Christ should be made of none effect.

If baptism is not Paul's primary task, what is? Paul here reiterates his God-given commission. It was "to preach the gospel." However, baptism was by no means insignificant to Paul (Romans 6:3-7), although it remained secondary to the proclamation of the Gospel for which Christ sent Paul. The word "sent" (Gk. *apostello*, **ap-os-tel'-lo**) is the verb form of the noun "apostle," which indicates the special task to which Paul was called as well as the authority that was vested in him by God, who sent him. Paul's authority lies in being Christ's apostle, Christ's "sent one." As for the manner in which his task is to be carried out, it is imperative that this be consistent with the content of his message. The content of his message is the Good News of God's saving work in Christ. As such, Paul's gospel proclamation is to be done not with humanistic rhetorical eloquence or worldly wisdom, which would render the cross of Christ powerless.

For Paul, there can be no room for pyrotechnic displays of rhetorical virtuosity, such as were offered by the traveling sophists whose voices were often heard in the marketplaces of any Mediterranean cities. Such methods of proclamation would only serve to exalt the proclaimer and not the One proclaimed. If Paul had done so, he could have been guilty of promoting the factions spoken of in verses 11-13. On the contrary, Paul promoted true Christian unity through his undiluted proclamation of Christ crucified. The unity of speaking, mind, and judgment that the Corinthian believers are called to have in verse 10 is to have its origin in and be centered on the message of the cross of Christ, which Paul proclaims. In this verse, Paul lays the groundwork for what he will immediately say about his evangelizing (1:18-2:5).

DAILY BIBLE READINGS

M: God Is Lord of All
Romans 10:9-13

T: We Are Reconciled in Christ
Colossians 1:15-20

W: One Body and One Spirit
Ephesians 4:1-6

T: Called Together in Christ
1 Corinthians 1:1-9

F: Be United in Christ
1 Corinthians 1:10-17

S: We Proclaim Christ Crucified to All
1 Corinthians 1:18-25

S: God Brings Us to Christ
1 Corinthians 1:26-31

TEACHING TIPS

June 11
Bible Study Guide 2

1. Words You Should Know

A. Wisdom (1 Corinthians 2:1) *sophia* (Gk.)—Skill, intelligence; insight into the true nature of things; used in reference to God's wisdom and the wisdom that belongs to men.

B. Perfect (v. 6) *teleios* (Gk.)—Fully grown, mature.

2. Teacher Preparation

A. Read the FOCAL VERSES and MORE LIGHT ON THE TEXT for today's lesson.

B. Next read the BIBLE BACKGROUND and DEVOTIONAL READING.

3. Starting the Lesson

A. Ask for a volunteer to lead the class in prayer.

B. Ask if anyone has any questions about last week's lesson and if anyone would like to share their experiences from last week's MAKE IT HAPPEN assignment.

4. Getting into the Lesson

A. Ask the students how they define wisdom. Then ask them if there is more than one type of wisdom and how they think a person gains wisdom.

B. Have one or more students read the FOCAL VERSES aloud.

C. Review THE PEOPLE, PLACES, AND TIMES and BACKGROUND sections with the class.

5. Relating the Lesson to Life

A. Have a student read the LESSON IN OUR SOCIETY section aloud.

B. Ask the students to define wisdom again based on what they have learned from the lesson.

6. Arousing Action

A. Ask for a volunteer to read the MAKE IT HAPPEN section to the class.

B. Ask the students what things they can do to become more spiritually mature and to grow in wisdom.

C. End the class by taking prayer requests and praise reports. Then close by praying that each member of the class might grow closer to the Father and rely on His wisdom rather than that of the world.

D. Close the class with prayer.

WORSHIP GUIDE

For the Superintendent or Teacher
Theme: Servants of Wisdom
Theme Song: "Immortal, Invisible, God Only Wise"
Scripture: Proverbs 2:1-8
Song: "My Hope Is Built on Nothing Less"
Meditation: Thank You, Lord, for Your wisdom and Your Word, which guide us and help us grow closer to You. Father, we pray that our ears would be open to hear what You would speak to us today and that we would follow where You lead us. Amen.

SERVANTS OF WISDOM

Bible Background • 1 CORINTHIANS 2
Printed Text • 1 CORINTHIANS 2:1, 6–16
Devotional Reading • EPHESIANS 1:15–21

LESSON AIM

By the end of the lesson, we will:

UNDERSTAND that God gives wisdom to those who are spiritually mature;

DESIRE to know the Father better; and

COMMIT to seek godly, rather than worldly, wisdom.

KEEP IN MIND

"Which things also we speak, not in the words which man's wisdom teacheth, but which the Holy Ghost teacheth; comparing spiritual things with spiritual" (1 Corinthians 2:13).

FOCAL VERSES

1 Corinthians 2:1 And I, brethren, when I came to you, came not with excellency of speech or of wisdom, declaring unto you the testimony of God.

2:6 Howbeit we speak wisdom among them that are perfect: yet not the wisdom of this world, nor of the princes of this world, that come to nought:

7 But we speak the wisdom of God in a mystery, even the hidden wisdom, which God ordained before the world unto our glory:

8 Which none of the princes of this world knew: for had they known it, they would not have crucified the Lord of glory.

9 But as it is written, Eye hath not seen, nor ear heard, neither have entered into the heart of man, the things which God hath prepared for them that love him.

10 But God hath revealed them unto us by his Spirit: for the Spirit searcheth all things, yea, the deep things of God.

11 For what man knoweth the things of a man,

> ## LESSON OVERVIEW
>
> **LESSON AIM**
> **KEEP IN MIND**
> **FOCAL VERSES**
> **IN FOCUS**
> **THE PEOPLE, PLACES, AND TIMES**
> **BACKGROUND**
> **AT-A-GLANCE**
> **IN DEPTH**
> **SEARCH THE SCRIPTURES**
> **DISCUSS THE MEANING**
> **LESSON IN OUR SOCIETY**
> **MAKE IT HAPPEN**
> **FOLLOW THE SPIRIT**
> **REMEMBER YOUR THOUGHTS**
> **MORE LIGHT ON THE TEXT**
> **DAILY BIBLE READINGS**

save the spirit of man which is in him? even so the things of God knoweth no man, but the Spirit of God.

12 Now we have received, not the spirit of the world, but the spirit which is of God; that we might know the things that are freely given to us of God.

13 Which things also we speak, not in the words which man's wisdom teacheth, but which the Holy Ghost teacheth; comparing spiritual things with spiritual.

14 But the natural man receiveth not the things of the Spirit of God: for they are foolishness unto him: neither can he know them, because they are spiritually discerned.

15 But he that is spiritual judgeth all things, yet he himself is judged of no man.

16 For who hath known the mind of the Lord, that he may instruct him? But we have the mind of Christ.

IN FOCUS

A midnight rain beat against the windows of the storefront church. Faith, a 23-year-old trainee for the 24-hour suicide hotline, sat alone. Her supervisor was in a backroom meeting.

"Bringggg!" The phone startled Faith.

A woman's desperate voice whispered, "Hello, I need prayer."

The phone trembled in Faith's hand. "Hold, please!" She wanted her supervisor.

"Please don't put me on hold. I need to talk!" the woman sniffled.

Faith's worried fingers opened the guidebook.

Help me, Lord, she thought. She asked the first guidebook question. "Are you a Christian having thoughts of suicide?"

She hoped the answer was no, but the woman said, "Yes."

Question two. "How?" Faith asked.

"Huh?" the bewildered woman asked.

"How do you plan to do it?" Faith repeated.

"Cut my wrist maybe?"

Question three: "When?"

"Tonight maybe." It worked. The sniffling stopped.

Question four made Faith nervous. "Do you have everything you need?"

The woman hesitated for a long second. Her voice turned stern. "Are you trying to put ideas in my head?"

Suddenly frantic, the woman began to share her story. She rambled about a failed marriage and children who didn't appreciate her. As she recounted each detail of her 50-year life, she kept repeating the question, "What am I living for?"

All the while, Faith searched the Bible to discern which Scriptures the Holy Spirit wanted her to use. Before Faith could think, she heard herself say, "You are living for God. Do you want God's comfort?"

"The Bible doesn't help."

Faith countered, "You're not spending enough time with God to be spiritually connected. To find God's peace, you cannot reject the message of life." Faith began to pray aloud for the wisdom of the Holy Spirit in the woman's life.

Paul's message to the Corinthians reminds us that the Holy Spirit gives power to our words and uses them to bring glory to Jesus. Do you believe true wisdom can be found only in Jesus?

THE PEOPLE, PLACES, AND TIMES

Corinth. During Paul's day, to "Corinthianize" or "act like a Corinthian" became synonymous with behaving lewdly. Sexual immorality was rampant in the city, as exemplified in the widespread worship of Aphrodite, the Greek goddess of love. Reportedly, 1,000 prostitutes worked in service to Aphrodite in the temple dedicated to her in the city. According to the wisdom of the day, all these things were good. Paul, however, showed the

Corinthian believers that there was another wisdom that they should seek.

BACKGROUND

Paul's first letter to the Corinthians came in response to problems that the church was experiencing. In the first chapter, Paul says he had learned from Chloe's household that there were contentions within the church (v. 11). He urged the church to be unified (v. 10) and to stop quarreling over whose teaching they followed (vv. 12-16). He also stressed the greatness of God's wisdom and how that wisdom is foolishness to the world (vv. 18-31). Paul continues this discussion in chapter 2, explaining to the church just how important God's wisdom is to believers.

AT-A-GLANCE

1. Reliance on Christ (1 Corinthians 2:1)
2. Wisdom through Maturity (2:6-8)
3. Revelation from the Spirit (vv. 9-12)
4. Words from the Spirit (vv. 13-14)
5. Mind of Christ (vv. 15-16)

IN DEPTH

1. Reliance on Christ (1 Corinthians 2:1)

Paul ended the previous chapter by quoting part of Jeremiah 9:24: "Let him who boasts boast in the Lord" (1 Corinthians 1:31, NIV). He begins this chapter by doing just that. In verse 1, he says that when he first came to the people of Corinth preaching the Gospel, he did so without eloquent words or earthly wisdom—things about which many people boast. Paul could easily have said that the success that he had in spreading the Gospel and planting churches was a direct result of his own skill and intellect. Instead, in verse 2, he says he was empowered by Jesus Christ and His resurrection: "For I determined not to know anything among you, save Jesus Christ, and him crucified." Paul cites Christ as the source of his success, boasting in the Lord just as he had reminded the church to do. By doing so, Paul shows that he is living what he preaches. He lays the foundation for the instructions he is about to give by showing that he is and has been practicing all those things that he is directing believers to do.

2. Wisdom through Maturity (2:6-8)

While Paul says he preached to the Corinthians without worldly wisdom, he adds that he did not abandon *all* wisdom. In verse 6, he says there is a wisdom that he and other leaders in the faith share with "perfect" believers. The Greek word *teleios* (**tel-i'-oce**), which is translated as "perfect" in this verse, means "fully grown" or "mature." Paul defines what he means by "mature" later in this letter (3:1-3) and again in his letter to the Hebrews. There he calls his readers immature babies in the faith who can consume only "milk," or the simple, basic principles of Christianity (Hebrews 5:12). The mature, however, live off solid food—that is, the complex, in-depth teachings of the faith. Through frequent consumption of this food and the growth it stimulates, Paul says, mature believers are able to "discern both good and evil" (Hebrews 5:14).

Here in the second chapter of Corinthians, Paul reveals that the mature inherit a wisdom that allows them to practice this discernment. This wisdom, however, cannot be learned or received from this world or its rulers. Instead, it comes from God. The wisdom and rulers of the world, Paul says, are passing away and will soon "come to nought" (v. 6). On the other hand, God's wisdom, which He shares with those who are disciplined in the faith and who long to know Him, existed before this world and was ordained for our glory (v. 7). With this wisdom, then, we can actually enter into the Father's presence.

While this wisdom is empowering to those who know Christ, it is foreign to those who deny Him. Paul says if the "princes of this world" had known this wisdom, they would have known Christ and His glory and would not have crucified Him (v. 8).

3. Revelation from the Spirit (vv. 9-12)

In verse 9, Paul reminds believers that Scripture says that no one has seen, heard, or imagined all that God has prepared for those who love Him. But, as Paul reveals, that "no one" does not include those who love the Lord. Instead, God has revealed His plan to them precisely because they know and love Him. This revelation is given to the mature believer by God's Spirit. Before He returned to the Father, Jesus promised to send the Holy Spirit to His disciples: "But the Comforter, which is the Holy Ghost, whom the Father will send in my name, he shall teach you all things, and bring all things to your remembrance, whatsoever I have said unto you" (John 14:26). Paul shows that the Spirit Jesus promised has come and has revealed the mysteries, or "deep things of God," to those who love Him (v. 10). Paul continues by saying that no one knows a man's intimate thoughts but the spirit that lives within him (v. 11). He adds that no one discerns God's intimate thoughts, except God's own Spirit.

The Spirit that the believer possesses, Paul says, is not the spirit that belongs to the world; rather, it is the Spirit that comes directly from God. Therefore, the same Spirit who knows the private thoughts of God lives in us and knows our private thoughts. Because we, as believers, possess God's Spirit, we are able to know the things that "are freely given to us of God" (v. 12). We are blessed with the opportunity to commune directly with the Father and share His deepest thoughts.

4. Words from the Spirit (vv. 13-14)

We not only have the thoughts of God, but we also have His words as our words. Paul says that we speak those things that are given to us by God through His Spirit in words that are taught to us by the Spirit (v. 13). *The Amplified Bible* translates this as "combining and interpreting spiritual truths with spiritual language [to those who possess the Holy Spirit]" (v. 13). As long as the wisdom that God gives us remains in our thoughts, it is meant for our personal enrichment. But God does not want us to be content with our own growth. Instead, He wants us to share the wisdom that He has given us with others so that they, too, can grow in the faith. Being the loving Father that He is, God freely gives us the words to speak as we share those things that He has given to us. He does not call us to be His mouthpieces and then leave us unequipped; rather, He gives us all that we need to pass on His message. We, in turn, supply our voices for His use.

The spiritual wisdom granted to believers is foreign to the man without the Spirit ("the natural man"). Paul says these things "are foolishness unto him" (v. 14). But not only are these things foolishness to the man without the Spirit, they are impossible for him to attain. The man without the Spirit can attain only worldly wisdom, which, as we learned in verse 6, is fleeting. Spiritual wisdom and spiritual language are available only to believers "because they are spiritually discerned" (v. 14).

5. Mind of Christ (vv. 15-16)

Paul continues by saying that the spiritual man judges and examines all things. Because of the wisdom he attains from God, he is able to weigh all things according to God's standards and judge them appropriately. The spiritual man, however, cannot be similarly judged or appraised by others. Why is this? Paul's answer is that the believer possesses the mind of Christ.

SEARCH THE SCRIPTURES

1. We speak the _____ of God, which was _____ before the world for our glory (1 Corinthians 2:7).

2. What would have happened if the rulers of this world had known God's wisdom (v. 8)?

3. Why have believers received the Spirit of God (v. 12)?

4. Why can't the natural man receive the things of God (v. 14)?

DISCUSS THE MEANING

1. Why do you think spiritual maturity is necessary to attain wisdom?

2. How do you think a person can tell if he or she is spiritually mature? What do you think a believer can do to become spiritually mature?

3. How do you think a believer can tell if he or she is relying on God's wisdom?

LESSON IN OUR SOCIETY

Our society today is not so different from the Corinthian society that Paul addressed in his letter. We, too, have many things that compete for our attention and threaten to draw our eyes away from God. According to the wisdom of this world, we should embrace all these things, even if they draw us away from the Father. But as Paul shows

us, we cannot depend on the world's wisdom because it will quickly disappear. True wisdom, that which comes only from God, is everlasting and unfailing. To attain it, we must place our trust in Him alone.

MAKE IT HAPPEN

Pray that God would help you to grow in spiritual maturity and to rely on His wisdom. This week, pay close attention to situations that require you to use wisdom. Do you make it a point to seek God's wisdom for the situation? Or do you rely on worldly wisdom? Write down how you respond to the situations and note any relevant Scriptures.

FOLLOW THE SPIRIT

What God wants me to do:

_____

_____

REMEMBER YOUR THOUGHTS

Special insights I have learned:

_____

_____

MORE LIGHT ON THE TEXT

1 Corinthians 2:1, 6-16

1 And I, brethren, when I came to you, came not with excellency of speech or of wisdom, declaring unto you the testimony of God.

Paul restates that it was not his own clever preaching or oratorical skill that led the Corinthians to believe in Jesus Christ (cf. 1:17). It was the power of God. Paul alludes to when Paul came to Corinth, the first trip recorded in Acts 18:1-18, when the Corinthians first heard the message and believed. He did not depend on "excellency of speech" (Gk. *huperochen logou,* **hoop-er-okh-ayn log'-oo**), "overpowering oratory," or "wisdom" (Gk. *sophia,* **sof-ee'-ah**), meaning human wisdom or philosophical argument. Instead, he came preaching the "mystery" (Gk. *musterion,* **moos-tay'-ree-on**) of God—the message not fully understood by them before, but now explained by him and illuminated by the Holy Spirit (2:10-14). Although the KJV, RSV, and NIV contain the word "testimony" (Gk. *marturion,* **mar-too'-ree-on**) instead of "mystery," the latter is preferred because of its presence in a combination of early manuscripts. The word "mystery" does not necessarily mean something unknown; it can refer to something that was not as fully understood at one time as it is later (see Daniel 2:18ff.; 4:9; Romans 16:25-26). It also means something whose meaning is hidden from those who have not been initiated but is crystal clear to those who are.

Paul not only affirms that the content of his preaching had been purely and simply the wisdom of God, but also that the manner of his presentation had been entirely consistent with his theme. Paul had come to them without any pretense eloquence or wisdom in declaring the truth about God. By the phrase "with excellency" (Gk. *kath' huperochen,* **kath hoop-er-okh-ayn**), Paul states that he did not depend on superiority of speech. This term is also used in 1 Timothy 2:2, where it refers to rulers in a superior or prominent position.

The word "declare" (Gk. *katangello,* **kat-ang-gel'-lo**), which should be rightly translated as "proclaim," like its synonym "preach" (Gk. *kerusso,* **kay-roos'-so**), is sometimes used (as in 1 Corinthians 9:14) with the word "Gospel" or "Good News" (see the use of *kerusso* with *euangelion* in Matthew 4:23; Mark 1:14; Galatians 2:2).

The contracts Paul made between himself and other preachers is evidenced by his opening word, "I" (Gk. *kago,* **kag-o'**), literally meaning "I for my part." For Paul, the preaching that leads hearers to new or deeper beliefs does not consist of words that draw attention to the preacher's educational attainment or cleverness of voice, but words that point to the presence and activity of God. Good preaching (like Paul's) consists not of words that express what the hearers love to hear, but of words that are spoken so that the hearers may turn to God.

2:6 Howbeit we speak wisdom among them that are perfect: yet not the wisdom of this world, nor of the princes of this world, that come to nought:

Paul outlines the problem that could obscure the Gospel message as he shows why the rulers of the age did not know God's wisdom: It was hidden in a mystery. There are two key words in verse 6: "wisdom" (Gk. *sophia,* **sof-ee'-ah**) and "perfect" (Gk. *teleioi,* **tel'-i-oy**). The word *teleioi* is better translated here as "mature," rather than "perfect," as in the KJV. Although to be perfect is certainly one of its meanings, such a translation is not appropriate here. In the Greek religions the Corinthians knew, maturity could be achieved by one's own efforts; it was a maturity that made no difference in the way people lived in relation to other people. It was a case of spiritual elitism. But the word "mature" here refers to the saved—those enlightened by the Holy Spirit—in contrast to the unsaved.

Lest some Corinthians come to the wrong conclusion that the Gospel is devoid of wisdom, Paul states that it involved a higher wisdom that was discernible by those who were "mature" (*teleioi*). This wisdom, Paul said, did not come from this age of time and space and certainly not from the rulers of this age (those who are of highest importance in the world) because such people crucified the Lord of glory (v. 8). Paul says that these rulers with their wisdom would end up in futility (v. 6). Paul had previously shown human wisdom to be in opposition to the preaching of the Cross. The prideful confidence of the Corinthians in human wisdom is antithetical to the deepest truth of the Gospel. It is important to note that the wisdom of which Paul spoke was not *in addition* to the Gospel. He insists that this special teaching was not the product of the intellectual activity of men; it is the gift of God, and it came into the world with Jesus Christ.

7 But we speak the wisdom of God in a mystery, even the hidden wisdom, which God ordained before the world unto our glory:

Paul now made clear that his presentation of God's eternal plan of salvation (v. 7) was based on the wisdom of God revealed to him and to others, through the Holy Spirit—a wisdom to be understood by those who are God's people. Describing God's wisdom further, Paul stated that it was a wisdom that was contained in a mystery ("God's secret wisdom") not fully revealed, but that God had planned before the beginning of the ages. This redemption plan originated in God's mind.

Speaking as servants of wisdom.

Although it is outlined in the Old Testament, it is not as fully explained and understood there as it is in the New Testament. Moreover, God's plan of redemption will be further revealed in the final glory of believers, when we share with Christ the glory of God (Romans 8:17-18).

8 Which none of the princes of this world knew: for had they known it, they would not have crucified the Lord of glory.

None of the princes—that is, earthly rulers—understood this redemption. The phrase "had they known it," which is in the perfect form of the word "know" (Gk. *ginosko*, **ghin-oce'-ko**—taking the form *egnoken* in this verse), is better translated as "they did not understand," thus conveying the totality of their ignorance of God's wisdom. Had they understood, they would not have crucified "the Lord of glory." Christ's divinity and his humanity are now brought together by the apostle, leading to the conclusion that God the Son, incarnated as man, died on the Cross. By "rulers," Paul meant the leaders of the Sadducees and Pharisees, the teachers of the Law, and Herod Antipas, as well as the Romans represented by Pilate and his soldiers (Acts 4:25-28).

9 But as it is written, Eye hath not seen, nor ear heard, neither have entered into the heart of man, the things which God hath prepared for them that love him.

However, Paul said the "hidden" wisdom that he had been preaching is the wisdom referred to in the Old Testament. It was set forth in the covenant promises that God had prepared and laid up for His people for those who love Him. It is these promises that people like the rulers of this world do not see and have not obeyed. The thought of them has not even entered the mind of man. That God has prepared these things for believers implies that sometime we will know and share in these promised blessings (Romans 8:18-25), which, Paul hastened to say, had been revealed to God's people by the Spirit (v. 10).

The expression, "it is written" (Gk. *gegraptai*, from *grapho*, **graf'-o**) (v. 9), although often used to cite Old Testament Scripture (cf. Matthew 4:4; Mark 11:17; Romans 1:17, et al.), might merely mean to use the language of Scripture or to speak generally from Scripture (cf. John 1:45), without meaning that the passage is formally cited. Paul now returns to the manner of his own preaching (see 1:17). He argued that since salvation is attained, not through human wisdom or might but only through the Cross, he came to Corinth in dependence on the Holy Spirit as he simply preached Christ and the efficacy of His death.

10 But God hath revealed them unto us by his Spirit: for the Spirit searcheth all things, yea, the deep things of God.

Beginning from this verse, Paul stressed the work of the Holy Spirit in revealing the wisdom of God. But, Paul said, God had revealed "to us"—that is, to Paul, to the other apostles, and to their associates—the spiritual wisdom that the unsaved rulers of this world did not understand. The verb "reveal" (Gk. *apokalupto*, **ap-ok-al-oop'-to**) that Paul uses here is usually used in the New Testament to indicate divine revelation of certain supernatural secrets (Matthew 16:17; Luke 10:22) or in an eschatological sense of the revelation connected with certain persons and events (Romans 8:18; 1 Corinthians 3:13). Note also that throughout verses 10-16, Paul speaks mostly in the first person plural, "we" (not "you"), strengthening the interpretation that he is referring primarily to divine revelation given to the apostles. Later, in 1 Corinthians 3:1-3, Paul returns to addressing the Corinthians as "you." But what is true primarily of Paul and the other apostles is true secondarily for all Christians: The Spirit helps them to interpret Scripture. The phrase "by [or through] the Spirit" certainly refers to The Holy Spirit, as is shown by the presence of the definite article "the" (Gk. *tou*, **tu**) since it is impossible through the human spirit to understand the wisdom of God.

The latter part of verse 10 amplifies the first part by showing the extent ("all things") and depth ("the deep things of God") of the Holy Spirit's revelation of God's wisdom and truth. The present tense of the verb "search" (Gk. *eraunao*, **er-yoo-nah'-o**) indicates the continual and effective ministry of the Spirit in His all-pervading, infallible guidance of the writers of Scripture (2 Peter 1:21) and His effective work in the lives of believers (Ephesians 1:17-19; 3:16-19).

11 For what man knoweth the things of a man, save the spirit of man which is in him? even so the things of God knoweth no man, but the Spirit of God.

The connecting particle "for" (Gk. *gar*) points to an illustration that the spiritual wisdom and truths of God can only be understood through the Holy Spirit. The conclusion is that only the Holy Spirit can reveal God's wisdom and truth to man. The concept of the "spirit" in this verse refers to human personality that thinks and acts not a force. The expression "the man's spirit within him," i.e., his human personality being in him, is suggesting that the Holy Spirit is in God. The only analogy made is that as the human spirit knows or understands human wisdom, so the Spirit of God being God "Himself" (Gk. *houtos*, **hoo'-tos**) understands the wisdom of God.

12 Now we have received, not the spirit of the world, but the spirit which is of God; that we might know the things that are freely given to us of God.

Paul states that it is the Spirit of God that they

had received. This is in contrast to some other kind of spirit through which some might try to know God's wisdom and truth, whether by the spirit of the wisdom of this world (1 Corinthians 1:20; 2:6; 3:19) or another kind of spirit (cf. 1 John 4:2-6). The purpose of the Holy Spirit's special work of revelation (v. 10), Paul says, is that "we might know the things that are freely given to us of god" (v. 12).

13 Which things also we speak, not in the words which man's wisdom teacheth, but which the Holy Ghost teacheth; comparing spiritual things with spiritual.

Here Paul reverts to the nature of his own ministry (cf. vv. 4-5). He wanted it known that he and his associates expressed spiritual truths in words taught by the spirit. Again, the contrast is between human wisdom and wisdom from God.

14 But the natural man receiveth not the things of the Spirit of God: for they are foolishness unto him: neither can he know them, because they are spiritually discerned.

Paul will now show that the wisdom revealed in the Gospel is beyond the reach of men not animated by the Spirit. In using the generic term "man" (Gk. *anthropos*, **anth'-ro-pos**), the apostle was speaking of unsaved persons in general, who are governed only by their "human nature" (Gk. *psychikos*, **psoo-khee-kos'**) and do not accept enlightenment and truth from the Spirit of God. The word *psychikos* basically means that which pertains to the soul or life of the natural world, in contrast with the supernatural world and the Spirit. Such a "natural man" (translated "man without the Spirit" in the NIV) considers spiritual truths to be foolish. Paul makes the case even stronger when he says that the man without the Spirit cannot understand because these truths can be discerned and understood only with the guidance of the Spirit. Of the natural man, selfishness is a constant mark.

So, when in 1 Corinthians 2:14 Paul speaks of the "natural man" (man without the Spirit), he is describing a person who lives as if there were nothing beyond physical life and there were no needs other than material needs, whose values are all physical and material. Such a person cannot understand spiritual things. One who thinks that nothing is more important than the satisfaction of sexual urges cannot understand the meaning of chastity, one who ranks the amassing of material things as the supreme end of life cannot understand generosity, and a person who has never thought beyond this world cannot understand the things of God. To him or her, spiritual things seem to be mere foolishness.

No person needs to be like this; but if one stifles the immortal longings that are in one's soul, when the Spirit of God speaks, he or she will not hear. It is easy to become so involved in the world that for all practical purposes, we act as if nothing exists beyond it. We must pray to have the mind of Christ, for only when He dwells within us are we safe from the encroaching invasion of the demands of material things.

The word "discern" (Gk. *anakrino,* **an-ak-ree'-no**) in verse 14, is the same verb translated "judgeth" and "judged" in verse 15. The idea in each case is to make intelligent spiritual decisions. Although the word means examine, here it also includes the decision following the examination (cf. 4:3).

15 But he that is spiritual judgeth all things, yet he himself is judged of no man.

In contrast, the person who is guided by the Spirit draws discerning conclusions about all things, that is, about all kinds of spiritual things. However, such a spiritual man is not subject to spiritual judgments by any man, i.e., by any natural man without the Spirit (v. 14). This is undoubtedly what Paul means in verse 15, for elsewhere he teaches Christians to make judgments concerning the spiritual condition and actions of other Christians (see 1 Corinthians 5:9-12; 12:3; Galatians 1:8).

16 For who hath known the mind of the Lord, that he may instruct him? But we have the mind of Christ.

Paul introduces the phrase "the mind of Christ" to relate it to the Old Testament expression he has just quoted: "the mind of the Lord." This verse implies that we, and all God's people,

can understand spiritual truths and spiritual wisdom in a way similar to the way the Lord knows them. However, the Lord knows these things exhaustively while we know them in part. Verse 16 brings to a climax Paul's argument about his preaching God's "foolishness," the Cross of Christ, without ostentation. Let the philosophers of Greece (cf. Acts 17:18, 32) and the sign-seeking Jews jeer and mock. They cannot really judge the message of Paul, who has the mind of Christ, because they do not have the Spirit of God and cannot judge spiritual truths.

DAILY BIBLE READINGS

M: Faith and Wisdom
James 1:2-8
T: Two Kinds of Wisdom
James 3:13-18
W: A Spirit of Wisdom
Ephesians 1:15-21
T: Warn and Teach Everyone in Wisdom
Colossians 1:24-29
F: Faith Not Based on Human Wisdom
1 Corinthians 2:1-5
S: We Speak God's Wisdom
1 Corinthians 2:6-10
S: Words Not Taught by Human Wisdom
1 Corinthians 2:11-16

TEACHING TIPS

June 18
Bible Study Guide 3

1. Words You Should Know

A. Carnal (1 Corinthians 3:1) *sarkikos* (Gk.)—Pertaining to the flesh; worldly, temporal, or animal; unregenerate.

B. Husbandry (v. 9) *georgion* (Gk.)—A cultivated field, ground, or land.

2. Teacher Preparation

A. Begin preparing the lesson by praying that God will enlighten you with His Word.

B. Read the DEVOTIONAL READING and BIBLE BACKGROUND passages, the LESSON AIM, and FOCAL VERSES to develop a better understanding of today's lesson.

3. Starting the Lesson

A. Open the class with a prayer that includes the LESSON AIM.

B. Introduce the lesson by telling the students that our text is part of a letter that Paul wrote to the Corinthian church. It is called a "pastoral" letter because it was written to resolve doctrinal and practical problems.

C. Have the class imagine that their pastor has written a letter to their congregation. What might the contents be?

4. Getting into the Lesson

A. Ask for a volunteer to read THE PEOPLE, PLACES, AND TIMES to give your students an idea of what the Corinthian church was like at the time of Paul's letter.

B. Ask for a volunteer to re-create the scene of a messenger reading Paul's letter to the church. Have the messenger read the FOCAL VERSES aloud to the "waiting congregation."

C. Afterward ask the class for specifics on why Paul is reprimanding the church. Then ask the messenger how it felt to read the letter, and ask listeners to describe their experiences. Make sure that the students understand that the text points out and discourages dissensions and cliques in the church.

D. Give the students an opportunity to answer the questions in the SEARCH THE SCRIPTURES section.

5. Relating the Lesson to Life

A. Ask the students for clichés to sum up the text. For example, "united we stand, divided we fall," might be one.

B. Have them share stories about how envy, strife, and divisions caused them to fail in an area of their lives or weakened their ability to witness.

C. Ask them to share testimonies about how they overcame a situation by promoting unity or reconciliation.

6. Arousing Action

A. Break the class up into three groups. Have each group come up with real-life scenarios that could cause a rift in the church and identify possible solutions. Allow time for discussion.

B. Remind the students to read the DAILY BIBLE READINGS each day.

C. Close the class with prayer.

SERVANTS TOGETHER

Bible Background • 1 CORINTHIANS 3:1–15
Printed Text • 1 CORINTHIANS 3:1–15
Devotional Reading • MATTHEW 13:3–9

LESSON AIM

By the end of the lesson, we will:

DEFINE carnality and discuss how it paralyzes spiritual growth;

BE HUMBLED in realizing that the overall success of the church is incumbent on its ability to function as a whole; and

COMMIT to work with God in all endeavors.

KEEP IN MIND

"For we are labourers together with God: ye are God's husbandry, ye are God's building" (1 Corinthians 3:9).

FOCAL VERSES

1 Corinthians 3:1 And I, brethren, could not speak unto you as unto spiritual, but as unto carnal, even as unto babes in Christ.

2 I have fed you with milk, and not with meat: for hitherto ye were not able to bear it, neither yet now are ye able.

3 For ye are yet carnal: for whereas there is among you envying, and strife, and divisions, are ye not carnal, and walk as men?

4 For while one saith, I am of Paul; and another, I am of Apollos; are ye not carnal?

5 Who then is Paul, and who is Apollos, but ministers by whom ye believed, even as the Lord gave to every man?

6 I have planted, Apollos watered; but God gave the increase.

7 So then neither is he that planteth any thing, neither he that watereth; but God that giveth the increase.

LESSON OVERVIEW

LESSON AIM
KEEP IN MIND
FOCAL VERSES
IN FOCUS
THE PEOPLE, PLACES, AND TIMES
BACKGROUND
AT-A-GLANCE
IN DEPTH
SEARCH THE SCRIPTURES
DISCUSS THE MEANING
LESSON IN OUR SOCIETY
MAKE IT HAPPEN
FOLLOW THE SPIRIT
REMEMBER YOUR THOUGHTS
MORE LIGHT ON THE TEXT
DAILY BIBLE READINGS

8 Now he that planteth and he that watereth are one: and every man shall receive his own reward according to his own labour.

9 For we are labourers together with God: ye are God's husbandry, ye are God's building.

10 According to the grace of God which is given unto me, as a wise masterbuilder, I have laid the foundation, and another buildeth thereon. But let every man take heed how he buildeth thereupon.

11 For other foundation can no man lay than that is laid, which is Jesus Christ.

12 Now if any man build upon this foundation gold, silver, precious stones, wood, hay, stubble;

13 Every man's work shall be made manifest: for the day shall declare it, because it shall be revealed by fire; and the fire shall try every man's work of what sort it is.

14 If any man's work abide which he hath built thereupon, he shall receive a reward.

15 If any man's work shall be burned, he shall suffer loss: but he himself shall be saved; yet so as by fire.

IN FOCUS

In what seemed like a blink of an eye, Pastor Jackson had served as senior pastor for three years. His congregation of 250 members heaped praise on him for practical counseling, and a fiery preaching style. Unfortunately, however, during these years, the membership did not grow. It seemed that as many new members joined, others left because of problems with the church staff.

The culprits were long-time members, many of whom had belonged to the church for 25 years or more. Cheryl, the pastor's secretary, called off many days and often turned in key work assignments late. Associate Pastor Ken failed to make all of his visitation calls to the sick and shut-in. And Herb, the youth pastor, seemed to have no control over the children's Sunday service.

Pastor Jackson wanted to remain popular and oftentimes covered the botched assignments. As a result, he sacrificed time that should have been spent with family, in sermon preparation, or performing various other pastoral duties.

It all came to a head when his church, along with other local churches, embarked on a missions program. After a month, the local church ministers met with Pastor Jackson to voice their concerns about poor follow-up. The next day he met privately with his staff members behind closed doors.

"Cheryl, Pastor Ken, after much prayer and thought, I am going to have to release you from your church staff duties," said Pastor Jackson.

Pastor Ken spoke first. "We are the roots of this church. If you cut off the roots, the church will wither." Cheryl nodded her head in agreement.

Pastor Jackson looked at them intently before he replied. "Consider this, building a church is much like a tree. In a wholesome tree, the roots and branches must work together for the tree to grow. Your consistent lack of teamwork has paralyzed the spiritual growth of our church and, as a result, many of the church's goals have gone unfulfilled."

The apostle Paul points out that there are no super-stars in God's work, only team members performing their special roles. Are you deeply committed to the work of Christ?

THE PEOPLE, PLACES, AND TIMES

City of Corinth. Corinth was built atop the Acrocorinthus, a rocky hill about 2,000 feet high, making it easy to defend. It was one of ancient Greece's greatest seaports and controlled the trade between northern Greece and the Peloponnesus. It was also the political capital of Greece and was a city of great enterprise, attracting visitors and businessmen from every quarter of the Mediterranean world. Corinth was famous for its production of brass, pottery, and pillared architecture. Its citizens prided themselves on being wise philosophers. The city was also known as a wicked city, overtaken by sexual immorality, which was perpetuated by worshiping the Greek goddess of love, Aphrodite. On his first visit to Corinth, Paul founded the church at Corinth.

BACKGROUND

Most of Paul's background can be found in the book of Acts. His coming to found the church at Corinth is recorded in Acts 18:1-17, while he was on his second missionary journey. Although he left Timothy and Silas, his "armor bearers," in Berea and went to Athens, he called for them as soon as he arrived there. He was so distressed to find Athens overtaken by idolatry that he immediately began preaching against these practices. Many believed Paul's report about Jesus and His Resurrection and were saved, but others mocked him.

Paul left Athens before Timothy and Silas arrived and went to Corinth. Paul met and stayed with a Jewish tentmaker named Aquila and his wife Priscilla. Timothy and Silas soon joined him in Corinth but brought back a disturbing report about the churches in Macedonia. When Paul preached the Gospel to the Jews in Corinth, many opposed him. As a result, Paul directed his ministry to the Gentiles there. Many were converted, including Crispus, the ruler of the synagogue. Paul stayed in Corinth for a year and a half, until Gallio, the proconsul of Achaia, ousted him on account of charges brought against him by the Jews.

Later, while in Ephesus on his third missionary trip, Paul received news from Chloe's household that there was trouble in the Corinthian church (1 Corinthians 1:11). Among the troubles reported were divisions, immorality, litigation in pagan courts, abuse of the Lord's Supper, false teachings about the resurrection, and misinformation about offerings for poverty-stricken believers in Jerusalem. In response to these concerns, Paul wrote a letter to the church. The text for our lesson is a part of that letter in which Paul addresses the first issue—divisions in the church.

IN DEPTH

1. Paul Presents the Problem (1 Corinthians 3:1-3)

Corinth was not a university town like Athens, but it was characterized by traditional Greek culture. The people of Corinth were interested in Greek philosophy and placed a high value on wisdom. Seeking wisdom in itself was not the problem; after all, the Bible says in Proverbs 4:7 (NIV), "Wisdom is supreme; therefore get wisdom. Though it cost all you have, get understanding."

Paul, however, rebuked the Corinthians for being so high and mighty in worldly things and so petty and foolish spiritually. It was not hard to believe that those who ran the political capital of Greece, who oversaw one of the nation's greatest seaports, and produced the best pottery, brass, and pillared architecture could not understand anything more than the "elementary truths" of Christianity. Worldliness (carnality) kept them spiritually stagnant.

Can you imagine how proud the Corinthians must have felt as Paul's letter was being read, teaching them the difference between spiritual and worldly wisdom? They were probably smiling and patting themselves on the back as they accounted themselves as being spiritually wise. But in the first verse of this Scripture passage, Paul let them know that he was not talking about them. He wrote, "And I, brethren, could not speak unto you as unto spiritual, but as unto carnal, even as unto babes in Christ." It must have felt like a sharp blow to the belly to learn that they had not made the spiritual advances that they thought they had made. Even worse was to find that even after a year and a half of being personally taught and mentored by Paul, they were at the same level as when they first believed. Even a 1-year-old baby is developmentally able to handle solid foods and a cup. But Paul wrote that the Corinthians were still on the bottle.

There are some Christians who base their level of spiritual maturity on the number of years that they have attended church. Spiritual maturity is not based on chronological age or anything else in the physical realm. In order to experience true spiritual growth, it is important to spend time with God in prayer and meditation; to study and apply His Word; and to turn away from selfishness, competitiveness, and strife.

2. Paul Challenges the Problem (vv. 4-7)

There are several ways to respond to rebuke, and "shutting down" is one of them. The Corinthians were probably shocked and angry and wanted to withdraw from the place where they were gathered in order to deny what they were hearing. But before they could move, Paul engaged them in a series of questions: "Are ye not carnal, and walk as men? Who then is Paul, and who is Apollos, but ministers (servants)?" (vv. 3, 5).

Paul employed a tactic that Jesus used in the Gospels. When the Pharisees and other religious groups asked Jesus questions in an attempt to discredit Him, Jesus would answer them with a question—not necessarily to get a response from them, but to expose their motives and have them answer their own questions. Paul didn't expect an answer from the Corinthians, but he disregarded himself by giving glory to God to make them consider their ways. He told them that he planted the church in Corinth, that Apollos came behind him and added to what he had already started, and that it was God who, by His Spirit, prodded the Gentiles to conversion. Paul acknowledged that without God, even what they'd experienced would not have occurred.

Carnality runs rampant in today's churches and is evidenced by church splits, church-hopping, and deified pastors and ministers. It is natural that human beings want something tangible to see, touch, and hear. The Bible contains several accounts of people creating tangible things to stand in the place of God. But idolatry is detestable to God, and the truth is that He cannot be mocked or copied. It is irrational to believe that a pastor is a tangible version of God. Yet many congregants believe that their pastors are perfect and do not (or at least should not) make any mistakes. The best qualified and most faithful ministers are those who have a sense of their own insufficiency and give God the glory for their successes.

3. Paul's Prescription for the Problem (vv. 8-15)

Paul knew that the only way the Corinthians were going to be kept from conforming to the ways of the world was for them to be transformed by the renewing of their minds. Thus, he enabled them to renew their minds by teaching them how to think in terms of oneness. In verse 8 he writes, "Now he that planteth and he that watereth are one," and in verse 9 he writes, "For we are labourers together with God." Paul dispels their contentions by saying (to put it in modern terms), "Look, we are all one, employed by one Master, with one goal in mind, and busied in one work." The world operates by a system of competition and selfishness, but God's way of doing things is by unconditional love, unity, and peace.

Being mindful that he was teaching babes, Paul skillfully used metaphors that they could understand to make his point. In verses 6-9, he addressed the agriculturalists by using words like "husbandry," "planting," and "watering." For the architects, in verses 9-12, he used the building terms "masterbuilder" and "foundation." Speaking their language, Paul told them that they did not belong to him or Apollos, but that "ye are God's husbandry, ye are God's building." He let them know that just as they had attended to their work and had enjoyed success, God had attended to and enabled them to achieve that success. Now that he had their attention, he showed them how one with a renewed mind thinks and speaks. In verse 10 he writes, "According to the grace of God which is given unto me, as a wise masterbuilder, I have laid the foundation, and another buildeth thereon. But let every man take heed how he buildeth thereupon." A renewed-minded person gives God the glory for his or her success.

Not only did Paul present and challenge the problem of carnality, but he provided a remedy

for it by teaching them to develop a mind to work, not against each other, but with one another. Paul then presented a warning—he wrote that the only individual concern that they should have is the reward that they would receive for their work. Although they were working together, with like minds, and for one specific purpose, their work and attitudes may have differed. Paul gave six different types of "work" that can be built upon the foundation he had laid: gold, silver, and precious stones, representing precious and durable work that will stand the test of divine judgment; and wood, hay, and stubble, symbolizing a weak, worthless work and lifestyle that will "burn away" on the Day of Judgment.

What a way to build a collective effort—inspire people to work together and hold each person individually accountable for producing excellent work. He further advanced the cause of unity by emphasizing God's mercy in verse 15: "If any man's work shall be burned, he shall suffer loss: but he himself shall be saved; yet so as by fire." In order to work together, we need to be able to separate principles from personalities. Even God separated the people from their actions; He burned their works but spared their lives. Jesus did the same on the Cross when He asked God to "forgive them [His executioners], for they know not what they do." So often, we want to crucify those who fall short, but Paul writes in Galatians 6:1-2 (NIV), "Brothers, if someone is caught in a sin, you who are spiritual should restore him gently. But watch yourself, or you also may be tempted. Carry each other's burdens, and in this way you will fulfill the law of Christ."

SEARCH THE SCRIPTURES

1. What terms did Paul use to describe how he related to the Corinthians (1 Corinthians 3:1)?

2. Why did Paul say he didn't feed them with meat (v. 2)?

3. What evidence did Paul have against the church as proof of carnality (v. 3)?

4. How did the church divide themselves in verse 4?

5. What was Paul's response (v. 5)?

6. Paul emphasized unity in the church, but what did he tell them would be judged individually (v. 8)?

7. Even though one's work will be burned, what will happen to the worker (v. 15)?

DISCUSS THE MEANING

1. In 1 Corinthians 3:1, Paul calls the church "babes in Christ." Relate spiritual advancement to the natural process of child growth and development. Discuss what kinds of things a physically immature child does and relate them to spiritually immature believers. Do the same with physically and spiritually mature persons.

2. What "day" is Paul referring to in verse 13 when he writes, "for the day shall declare it"?

LESSON IN OUR SOCIETY

We are living in a wonderful time in which we are witnessing and participating in the manifestation of the Gospel's power like never before. The Gospel is being preached almost everywhere, and things that are detestable to God are being challenged in courts, schools, churches, and homes nationwide. As we work together in one accord, God's Scripture is being fulfilled. Nevertheless, carnality is a subtle attitude that gnaws at the seams of the work we've produced. What is your view of the many pastors and leaders who are promoted to offices of bishops, elders, and apostles? Is it a sign of spiritual advancement or carnality? What do you think about churches that are changing their names from "Such-and-Such Church" to "Greater Such-and-Such Church of So-and-So?" Is it a sign of spiritual advancement or carnality? Explain your answer.

MAKE IT HAPPEN

Satan loves to show up in meetings. He doesn't just walk in by himself; some people carry him in with their negative, pessimistic, and insubordinate attitudes. Don't let this happen to you. At your next meeting, determine to walk in with God, under the authority of Jesus Christ, and spread the peace and comfort of the Holy Spirit. You can learn to overlook others' nuisances by separating people from their personalities, making a positive impact on them, and changing the outcome of the whole meeting!

FOLLOW THE SPIRIT

What God wants me to do:

_____

_____

REMEMBER YOUR THOUGHTS

Special insights I have learned:

_____

_____

MORE LIGHT ON THE TEXT

1 Corinthians 3:1-15

1 And I, brethren, could not speak unto you as unto spiritual, but as unto carnal, even as unto babes in Christ.

Paul continues to deal with the problem of divisions (vv. 4-5) that plagued the Corinthian church. Here he shows that the problem was due to the Corinthians' spiritual immaturity. They were babies in Christ, who, like children at the breast, had to be fed with milk and not meat. Their immaturity is denoted by the word "babes" (Gk. *nepios*, **nay'-pee-os**), which means infants, as opposed to a mature person, who is described as "spiritual" (Gk. *pneumatikos*, **new-MA-ti-kos**). As infants, they were incapable of judging what is most suitable for themselves. Consequently, they were utterly unqualified to discern between one teacher and another. The distinctions they did make were far from being a proof of mature judgment.

On the contrary, it was proof that they had no right judgment at all. It sprang from their lack of knowledge in spiritual matters. That is, they were not acting like those who were "in the spirit" or "spiritual." Furthermore, Paul describes them as "carnal" (Gk. *sarkinos*, **sar'-kee-nos**). The use of the word "carnal" in conjunction with "babes" or "infants" indicates that Paul was using the word "babes" in a pejorative sense. Their actions showed that they were motivated by the world's thoughts and actions, under the influence of fleshly appetites, coveting and living for the things of this life.

2 I have fed you with milk, and not with meat: for hitherto ye were not able to bear it, neither now are ye able.

In this verse, Paul overturns the Corinthians' high opinion of themselves. In order to show the extent of the immaturity of the Corinthians, Paul says that he has fed them with milk; that is, he has instructed them in only the rudiments or basic truths of Christianity, because they were incapable of comprehending the deeper truths of the Gospel. The apostle thus exposes to them the absurdity of their conduct in pretending to judge between one preacher and another, while they had but a very partial acquaintance with even the first principles of Christianity.

The verse amplifies the reference in verse 1 to infants by explaining that when Paul first came, he fed the Corinthian Christians spiritual milk, i.e., the elementary truths of salvation. He could not feed them with "meat" (Gk. *broma*, **bro'-mah**), that is, "solid food," because as infants in Christ, they could not spiritually digest it. The strong phrase, "neither yet now are ye able" emphasizes their continuing immaturity.

3 For ye are yet carnal: for whereas there is among you envying, and strife, and divisions, are ye not carnal, and walk as men?

Paul continues his description of the Corinthians as being "carnal," using the Greek word *sarkikos* (**sar-kee-kos'**), which means worldly, fleshly, pertaining to the flesh, or controlled by the flesh. To be controlled by the flesh is to have an outlook that is oriented toward self and pursues ones own ends in attempted autonomy from God. They were living in a way that was sub-Christian. The particle "for" (Gk. *gar*, **gar**) prepares Paul's readers for his illustrations of this worldliness: the "jealousy" (Gk. *zelos*, **dzay'-los**) and "strife or "quarreling" (Gk. *eris*, **er'-is**) that plague the Christian community. Paul also mentions their divisions (v. 4).

The question is stated in Greek in such a way that a positive answer is expected. This suggests that the Corinthians, if they are honest with themselves, should admit their failure here. To walk "according to man" (Gk. *kata anthropon*, **kat-ah' anth'-ro-pon**)—that is, "acting like mere men" (NIV)—means to live in the way that only an ordinary sinful person lives: in selfishness, arrogance, and envy. Such a walk indicates conformity to a merely human standard rather than to a godly standard. The word "man" is used here in the negative sense of "fallen humanness." Their immaturity led to contentiousness. The behavior of the Corinthians shows that they were all too worldly, in contradiction to their claim of spirituality. They were continually disputing and contending about whose party was the best, each endeavoring to prove that he and his party were alone in the right. Envying led to strife, which in turn led to divisions. Thus, the apostle asked, "Are ye not carnal, and walk as men?" They acted just like the people of the world who did not have the Spirit of God.

4 For while one saith, I am of Paul; and another, I am of Apollos; are ye not carnal?

Verse 4 brings us back to the actual state of the Corinthian Christians, with their divisive preferences for individual apostles and ministers. Paul's example of himself and Apollos, who shared in the ministry at Corinth (Acts 18:1-28) was used to show the Corinthians that they had a distorted view of the Lord's work. Whenever they thought of God's work in terms of belonging to or following a particular Christian worker, they were simply acting on the worldly level and taking sides just as the world does. The Corinthians were probably captivated by the outward manners of Paul and Apollos, rather than the truth of their teaching. Apollos was more eloquent than Paul. Their preference of one speaker over another based on this proved that they were carnal, led by their senses and mere outward appearances without being under spiritual guidance. There have been thousands of such people in the Christian church up until the present day.

5 Who then is Paul, and who is Apollos, but ministers by whom ye believed, even as the Lord gave to every man?

In using the word "then," Paul shows that he is answering the question, "How should the Corinthians view Paul and Apollos?" Because Paul wants to emphasize that he and Apollos are simply servants, he uses the Greek interrogative *ti* (**tee**), which rightly translated means "what" instead of "who." The question then is, "What then is Paul, and what is Apollos?" The implication is that Paul, Apollos, and whatever other workers there are no more than servants. To some degree, they are expendable. The point is that no Christian worker is ever to be idolized. Indeed, those who are idolized can become instruments for fragmenting the work of God. Believers are to realize that Christian workers are simply God's servants (i.e., agents) through whom people believe in Christ. The word translated as "ministers" (Gk. *diakonoi*, **dee-ak'-on-oy**) can refer to attendants, waiters, or servants. God has not called Paul and Apollos to be masters of the Corinthian Christians, but to serve them and meet their needs.

6 I have planted, Apollos watered; but God gave the increase. 7 So then neither is he that planteth any thing, neither he that watereth; but God that giveth the increase.

Here again we see the self-effacing attitude of Paul. Although Paul was the one who sowed the seed of the Gospel in Achaia, he neither overestimated his own labors nor detracted anything from the real excellence of Apollos as a workman. Instead Paul ascribed all glory to God as the giver of all good. As in the physical, so in the spiritual world, it is by the special blessing of God that the grain that is sown in the ground brings forth thirty, sixty, or a hundredfold. It is neither the sower nor the waterer who produces this strange and inexplicable multiplication; it is God alone. He alone should have all the glory, since the seed is His, the ground is His, the laborers are His, and the produce all comes from Him. Ministers are instruments in God's hand and must depend entirely on His blessing to give the increase to their labors. Without this, they are nothing; with it, their part is to use the gifts and abilities that God has given to do God's will and give Him the glory.

8 Now he that planteth and he that watereth are one: and every man shall receive his own reward according to his own labour.

Paul goes on to make a twofold emphasis. On the one hand, Paul and Apollos, although exercising different roles, are both engaged in the

one mission to which they have been commissioned: to propagate the Gospel. They were both supposed to labor to promote the glory of God in the salvation of the Corinthians. The question then is, "Why should the Corinthians be divided with respect to Paul and Apollos, when these servants are intimately united in spirit and purpose?" Although their functions are different, they are united. On the other hand, each is to be rewarded according to his labor. Each is responsible to God. There is, therefore, no need for competition. It is instructive to note that Paul says that every man shall receive his own reward according to his own labor and not according to their earthly measure of success.

9 For we are labourers together with God: ye are God's husbandry, ye are God's building.

Paul insists once more that he and Apollos are simply fellow workers in God's service. They do nothing of themselves nor in reference to themselves; they labor together in that work that God has given them to do, expect all their success from Him, and refer the whole to His glory. Far from being divided, Paul and Apollos jointly labor, as oxen in the same yoke, to promote the honor of Christ.

Paul employs two images to drive home the point. First he says that they are the "husbandry" (Gk. *georgion*, **gheh-ore'-ghee-on**), better translated as "field." This word signifies an arable field (cf. Proverbs 24:30; 31:16) and is equivalent to the Hebrew word *sadeh* (**saw-deh'**), which signifies a sown field. Therefore, it would be more literal to translate the middle phrase of 1 Corinthians 3:9 as, "You are God's farm." Thus, in speaking of the Corinthians as being God's field and of himself and Apollos and others as God's workers in the field (1 Corinthians 3:6-9), Paul brought to the minds of the Corinthians the farming going on in the plain below the city.

But Paul did not stop there. He introduced another image, describing the Corinthians as God's building. They are not only the field that God cultivates; they are also the house that God builds, and in which He intends to dwell. Generally, the praise for a magnificent building does not go to the quarryman who dug up the

God's servants working together.

stones, nor to the mason who placed them in the wall, nor to the carpenter who squared and jointed it, etc., but to the architect who planned it and under whose direction the whole work was accomplished. Therefore, the Corinthians are not to consider Paul, or Apollos, or Cephas as anything. They are considered only as persons employed by the great Architect to form a building that is to become a dwelling house of God Himself through the Spirit; they work under the direction and the design that is entirely God's own. Moreover, the corporate nuance of the imagery must also be noted. Together, the Corinthians constitute God's building. There is no room for individualism in the body of Christ.

10 According to the grace of God which is given unto me, as a wise masterbuilder, I have laid the foundation, and another buildeth thereon. But let every man take heed how he buildeth thereupon.

As a wise master builder and a man experienced in architecture, Paul had laid the foundation by preaching Christ throughout the Grecian provinces. Those who come after him are to build

according to the plan and grand design of the temple, a design or plan that is from God, making it imperative that all things be done according to the pattern that He has established. One thing that Paul seeks to make clear in this verse is that the building, which is the church, is not the work of any one evangelist, preacher, or apostle, but that of a team. Although God had used him to lay the foundation, Paul acknowledged that others, such as Apollos, also build on this foundation of Christ. Then he gave a warning: Every builder— Paul, Apollos, and anyone else who works for God—must be careful how he builds. The shift in thought is now from the worker to his work.

11 For other foundation can no man lay than that is laid, which is Jesus Christ.

Paul now refers to his own work. The Corinthians had preferences for different leaders. But as Paul had said previously in 1:17 and 2:2, Jesus Himself, rather than His followers, is the one irreplaceable foundation of the church. No church leader should be seen as having more than a strictly subordinate role. Leaders are to be respected but not worshiped. Moreover, although the workers cannot lay a foundation other than Christ, they had better be careful how they build on Him. Any defects in their work will be their own fault, not Christ's.

12 Now if any man build upon this foundation gold, silver, precious stones, wood, hay, stubble;

Nothing could be clearer in this verse than that Paul wanted the preachers and teachers in the church to build a superstructure with the same material as the foundation. So, instead of talking about the details of the building itself, Paul turned his attention to the kind of materials that Christian workers are using: preaching the Cross for the salvation and building up believers (cf. 1:18) and living a Christian life that is commensurate with that preaching (2:2-4).

13 Every man's work shall be made manifest: for the day shall declare it, because it shall be revealed by fire; and the fire shall try every man's work of what sort it is.

Here Paul stresses that those contractors who employ inferior material will have the quality of their work exposed by the fire of God's judgment. Paul's primary meaning is that it shall be made manifest what kind of materials every spiritual builder uses, that is, what kind of doctrines every minister of Christ preaches, whether they are true or false, important or trivial, calculated to produce genuine repentance, faith, and obedience in the hearers or not. As fire tries metals and separates whatever impurities are mixed with them, so shall the strict process of the final judgment try, not only the religion of every Christian, but the work of every public teacher, and manifest whether it came up to the scriptural standard or not. The "day" refers to "the day of the Lord" (1 Thessalonians 5:2-9), the day of the second coming of Christ (cf. 2 Thessalonians 2:2).

14 If any man's work abide which he hath built thereupon, he shall receive a reward.

Perhaps there is an allusion here to the purifying of different sorts of vessels under the law. All articles that could stand the fire were to be purified by the fire (Numbers 31:23). The gold, silver, and precious stones could stand the fire; but the

wood, hay, and stubble must necessarily be consumed. So in that great and terrible Day of the Lord, everything shoddy will be destroyed. But those ministers and Christians whose works stand the test of fire (cf. 1 Peter 1:7) will be rewarded (cf. Matthew 25:14-30; Luke 19:11-27).

15 If any man's work shall be burned, he shall suffer loss: but he himself shall be saved; yet so as by fire.

This is a metaphor, probably based on Amos 4:11 (a brand plucked from the burning). Many good ministers have filled the sanctuary and been applauded by their hearers; yet they have no work of God or revival of true spirituality among their hearers. It is because they have been building with wood, hay, and stubble rather than gold, silver, and precious stones. And when the fiery trial comes, such a person's own soul shall have but a narrow escape from the blaze.

DAILY BIBLE READINGS

M: Spreading God's Word
Matthew 13:3-9
T: Growing Together
Matthew 13:24-30
W: The Need for Teachers
Hebrews 5:7-14
T: Strengthened with Power Through the Spirit
Ephesians 3:14-21
F: Servants Through Whom You Believe
1 Corinthians 3:1-9
S: Building on the Foundation of Christ
1 Corinthians 3:10-15
S: Do Not Boast about Human Leaders
1 Corinthians 3:16-23

TEACHING TIPS

June 25
Bible Study Guide 4

1. Words You Should Know
A. Stewards (1 Corinthians 4:1) *oikonomos* (Gk.)—House manager, overseer, or governor. It figuratively means "preacher of the Gospel."

B. Spectacle (v. 9) *theatron* (Gk.)—To expose as a public show or a gazing stock.

2. Teacher Preparation
A. Prepare for the lesson by praying for wisdom, understanding, and ability to teach passionately.

B. Read the BIBLE BACKGROUND passage, the FOCAL VERSES, and the LESSON AIM to develop a better understanding of the text.

3. Starting the Lesson
A. Open the class with a prayer that includes the LESSON AIM.

B. Review last week's lesson by briefly stating its title and summarizing its points. Present today's lesson as a continuation of Paul's teaching, which was intended to help the Corinthians gain a "right" perspective of ministers.

C. Solicit a volunteer to read the IN FOCUS story. Facilitate discussion about how the story relates to today's lesson.

4. Getting into the Lesson
A. Ask for a volunteer to read THE PEOPLE, PLACES, AND TIMES section.

B. Have the students take turns reading the FOCAL VERSES.

C. Review the SEARCH THE SCRIPTURES questions together.

D. Encourage the students to analyze Paul's personality based on the part of the letter included in the FOCAL VERSES. Do these characteristics add to or take away from his effectiveness as a minister?

5. Relating the Lesson to Life
A. Encourage your students by letting them know that the principles of today's lesson are not only for ministers and those in leadership roles, but are also for them.

B. Ask for a few volunteers to look up Scripture verses that verify they are stewards. Ask for examples of what they are stewards over (i.e., finances, body, family).

C. Using 1 Corinthians 4:10 as a springboard, ask the class for examples of times when they have felt like "fools" for standing on a promise that God made to them. Make sure that they tell how faithfully God honored His Word.

6. Arousing Action
A. Now that your students have read the Scripture that verifies they are stewards, and have identified what they are stewards over, have them write their commitment on an index card to indicate that they accept their assignments.

B. Challenge the students to follow through with the MAKE IT HAPPEN assignment.

C. Remind them to read the DAILY BIBLE READINGS during the week.

D. Close the class with prayer.

WORSHIP GUIDE

For the Superintendent or Teacher
Theme: Servants in Ministry
Theme Song: "I'm Encouraged to Serve the Lord"
Scripture: 1 Corinthians 4:1-13
Song: "What God Has for Me, It Is for Me"
Meditation: Lord, thank You for making us servants of Your ministry. Give us the courage to be the extensions of Your arms, Your heart, and Your love as we serve Your people on earth, as it is in heaven. Amen.

SERVANTS IN MINISTRY

Bible Background • 1 CORINTHIANS 4:1–13
Printed Text • 1 CORINTHIANS 4:1–13
Devotional Reading • MATTHEW 23:8–12

LESSON AIM

By the end of the lesson, we will:

EXPLORE Paul's view of Christian leadership and the responsibilities of steward-ship;

COMPARE and contrast Paul's description of steward-ship with our own circum-stances; and

ACCEPT responsibility for our own ministry as servants and stewards of God.

KEEP IN MIND

"Let a man so account of us, as of the ministers of Christ, and stewards of the mysteries of God" (1 Corinthians 4:1).

FOCAL VERSES

1 Corinthians 4:1 Let a man so account of us, as of the ministers of Christ, and stewards of the mys-teries of God.

2 Moreover it is required in stewards, that a man be found faithful.

3 But with me it is a very small thing that I should be judged of you, or of man's judgment: yea, I judge not mine own self.

4 For I know nothing by myself; yet am I not hereby justified: but he that judgeth me is the Lord.

5 Therefore judge nothing before the time, until the Lord come, who both will bring to light the hidden things of darkness, and will make man-ifest the counsels of the hearts: and then shall every man have praise of God.

6 And these things, brethren, I have in a figure transferred to myself and to Apollos for your sakes;

LESSON OVERVIEW

LESSON AIM
KEEP IN MIND
FOCAL VERSES
IN FOCUS
THE PEOPLE, PLACES, AND TIMES
BACKGROUND
AT-A-GLANCE
IN DEPTH
SEARCH THE SCRIPTURES
DISCUSS THE MEANING
LESSON IN OUR SOCIETY
MAKE IT HAPPEN
FOLLOW THE SPIRIT
REMEMBER YOUR THOUGHTS
MORE LIGHT ON THE TEXT
DAILY BIBLE READINGS

---

that ye might learn in us not to think of men above that which is written, that no one of you be puffed up for one against another.

JUNE 25TH

7 For who maketh thee to differ from another? and what hast thou that thou didst not receive? now if thou didst receive it, why dost thou glory, as if thou hadst not received it?

8 Now ye are full, now ye are rich, ye have reigned as kings without us: and I would to God ye did reign, that we also might reign with you.

9 For I think that God hath set forth us the apostles last, as it were appointed to death: for we are made a spectacle unto the world, and to angels, and to men.

10 We are fools for Christ's sake, but ye are wise in Christ; we are weak, but ye are strong; ye are honourable, but we are despised.

11 Even unto this present hour we both hunger, and thirst, and are naked, and are buffeted, and have no certain dwellingplace;

12 And labour, working with our own hands: being reviled, we bless; being persecuted, we suffer it:

13 Being defamed, we intreat: we are made as the filth of the world, and are the offscouring of all things unto this day.

IN FOCUS

At age 25, Pastor Wright was elected senior pas-tor, but today was his last Sunday at the church. As he preached, a few of the "amens" that followed

411

were thunderous, but some people didn't open their mouths at all.

What had gone wrong? Yes, he had made changes. He replaced the wooden pulpit with a Plexiglas lectern, and he reorganized the Sunday School program. The new music director emphasized modern praise music in place of traditional hymns. Pastor Wright felt those and many other changes in the works were necessary to increase the church's dwindling congregation. Unfortunately, the church congregants were of a different opinion. At the last congregational meeting, one church council member summarized the problem—"Too many changes too fast"—and Pastor Wright was voted out.

That night he sat in his bishop's office, and, with a cracking voice, he told the bishop, "I will never preach again."

"Did God call you to preach?" asked the bishop.

"Yes, He did," replied Pastor Wright.

"Then you must do what God called you to do—don't get derailed."

"What do you mean, bishop?" asked the young pastor.

The bishop took out a worn Bible and opened it to the first page. "At the age of 25, I wrote the names of 40 preachers who graduated with me from seminary school. We were all so young and determined to set the world on fire for the Lord. Sadly, I often have to open this Bible and cross out the name of a fellow seminarian who has left the ministry. Of those original 40, only seven remain. It's a long way to where you're going son, and Satan will chase you every step of the way. You must remember your stewardship is a responsibility not linked to a church, but to Christ."

The apostle Paul insisted that the Corinthians not think of him as leader of factions, but as a servant of Christ. Are your deepest loyalties to Christ and not man?

THE PEOPLE, PLACES, AND TIMES

Spectacle. The Greek word *theatron* (**theh'-at-ron**) means show or gazing stock. Paul used the term as an allusion to the bloody spectacles that took place in Roman amphitheaters. Men were exposed to fighting with wild beasts or to cutting one another to pieces in the arena. If one survived, he was prepared to fight in the next com-

bat. If he survived, his last battle would be against meridian gladiators, whose contentions were said to be merciless and "perfect butchery."

Henry, Matthew. Matthew Henry's Commentary on the Whole Bible. Peabody, Mass.: Hendrickson Publishers, 1991.

BACKGROUND

To purge the Corinthian church of dissensions and cliques, Paul writes to give them a right perspective of what and who ministers are. In chapter 3, he refers to them as "God's building" and "God's husbandry" (field), to help them understand that it is God who has given the outpouring of blessings, not the ministers with whom they've aligned themselves. Not only does Paul de-emphasize the roles of ministers, but he also humbles the church by informing the members that they, too, have roles and responsibilities to enable the church to function. In chapter 4 he writes to abase the prideful church, whose members attributed their wealth, success, and great name to themselves.

AT-A-GLANCE

1. Paul Demands Respect (1 Corinthians 4:1-4)

2. Paul's Warning (vv. 5-6)

3. Paul Points Toward God (vv. 7-13)

IN DEPTH

1. Paul Demands Respect (1 Corinthians 4:1-4)

Although the word "steward" figuratively means "preacher," this lesson is applicable to lay people as well. While many ministers gauge their success by the number of people who request their services, the size of their congregations, and maybe even their salaries, lay Christians sometimes measure their reputation by similar means. They view, as indications of God's approval, the large amount of goods and money they have, their ability to marry and have children, and their social and financial promotions. As soon as challenges present themselves in any of these situations, some believers question God's provision for or approval of them.

Faithful stewards of God's mysteries.

Even though Paul had a large portion of the Corinthian church calling themselves his servants (1 Corinthians 3:4), he scolded them for being overtaken by strife, envy, and divisions. Paul knew that the respect the church had given him was not right; it was either exaggerated or understated. He asked them to consider him a servant of Christ, not a master—steward, not a lord of the mysteries of God (v. 1). Moreover, his office as a minister was not to be undervalued or held as common. Although he was a minister, he still deserved to be respected and honored as one who hears and receives instruction from the Lord.

Paul writes that stewards are required to be faithful, and when they are, respect is due to them. A steward is an overseer or governor. He or she may not necessarily own what they are guarding, but they protect it as if they do. They know that they will have to give an account of their work when the rightful owner returns. It is expected and understood that they will be either faithful and rewarded or wicked and punished.

To illustrate the kingdom of God, Jesus used several parables about stewards (see Luke 16:13) and taught His disciples, as well as the Pharisees and other sects, about their respective positions in the kingdom. His Word still prods and convicts us and assures us of our rightful place as stewards. Not only are we stewards of the Gospel, but God has also made us stewards over our children, marriages, homes, businesses, churches, etc. One day we will be required to give an account for how we've overseen God's entrusted goods.

Therefore, we should seek God's approval rather than men's. Paul says that, as humans, we are so incapable of judging each other that he takes men's opinions of him lightly and that he doesn't even judge himself. He explains that his qualification to judge is so limited that even if he deems himself to be faithful, doing so doesn't clear him of any charges (v. 4). Only God is fully qualified to judge and justify. Humans are so fickle that we can love something or someone one minute and fume with hatred the next. It is a blessing to know that we don't have a heaven or hell to put each other into, lest we condemn ourselves. While it is impossible to seek approval from man and be faithful to God, He assures us that if we seek Him, we will obtain His favor *and* the favor of men (1 Samuel 2:26), and all the things we need will be added unto us (Matthew 6:33).

2. Paul's Warning (vv. 5-6)

Without careful study of the text, it would appear that Paul is doing the very thing he reprimanded the church for—judging others. In verse 5, Paul told them not to *judge* anything before the time—that is, until the Lord comes—but in the preceding chapter, he called them "babes in Christ" and "carnal" and told them that they "walk as mere men."

Moreover, in verse 4 Paul told them that he didn't even judge himself; but in 1 Corinthians 11:31, he writes, "for if we would judge ourselves, we should not be judged." Is Paul contradicting himself? Absolutely not! The English word "judge" means to form a critical opinion about someone. Paul used a Greek word with an equivalent meaning to warn the church against judging and condemning each other. He accurately portrays doing so as useless. But in 1 Corinthians 11:31, the English translation does not change, even though Paul uses a different Greek word. An accurate translation of that verse would read, "For if we [discerned] ourselves, we should not be judged [or condemned]." To "discern" means to show good judgment. Paul showed discernment when he called the church "babes in Christ" and "carnal," since he was using judgment to bring about good. This is evidenced by 1 Corinthians 4:14, where he writes, "I write not these things to shame you, but as my beloved sons I warn you."

The Bible warns that if we judge (condemn), we too shall be condemned. But if we use discernment, we can avoid evil. Verse 6 is an example of Paul's use of discernment. He tells the church that the very things he is telling them, he had applied to his relationship with Apollos so that a division would not occur between the two of them. In giving this example to them, Paul could have used any other minister's name to prove his point, but to avoid further contempt he refused. We, too, should use discernment in our advice and admonitions, but especially in our reproofs. We must not think more highly of ourselves or anyone else than God's Word allows. The Word of God should be our guide when we advise, admonish, or correct others.

3. Paul Points Toward God (vv. 7-13)

According to Paul, the Corinthian ministers were puffed up and arrogant. He rebuked them in verse 7 by asking, "What do you have that you didn't receive?" We can relate to Paul's audience by realizing how hard it can be to stay humble when God, in all of His mercy, grace, and favor, continues to bless and exalt us in spite of ourselves. To further his position against self-conceit, Paul uses irony to bring the Corinthians' attention to their inflated view of themselves relative to Paul. They considered themselves better than Paul because they were rich, lacked nothing, and "reigned as kings" (v. 8). Paul exaggerated their accomplishments and used irony to point out how they had overlooked the Benefactor of their success.

Paul and the other apostles suffered so many hardships that he felt like a man condemned to die in the last fight of a spectacle (see THE PEOPLE, PLACES, AND TIMES) for the entertainment of an audience. The sufferings, deprivations, dangers, and ill treatment they endured were exposed and amplified, but Paul counted it all for the glory of God. The writer of Hebrews says that the world is not worthy of men like Paul and his fellow apostles. Moreover, Paul compares his situations to those of the Corinthians. "We are fools," Paul says, "but you are wise. We are weak, but you are strong. You are honorable, but we are despised" (v. 10, paraphrased). Here Paul points out the difference between reputation and character. The Corinthians had a reputation for being learned teachers, strong and honorable, but their character, the core of their being, was full of envy and conceit. Paul and the other apostles didn't have the fame and fortune, but they had joy, peace, and the power of God.

In spite of the specific sufferings that Paul pointed out in verses 11 and 12—nakedness, homelessness, and starvation—his character was such that he was able to bless those who cursed him and to endure persecutions. We can thank God that we have not had to endure more than grief, lack of resources, trauma, divorces, and such. It can be difficult exercising patience under such circumstances, but with Jesus Christ as our faithful and merciful High Priest who is our atonement, we can hold on to our integrity.

SEARCH THE SCRIPTURES

1. In what two ways did Paul want to be regarded (1 Corinthians 4:1)?

2. It was a requirement that stewards be found _____ (v. 2).

3. "Therefore judge nothing before the time, until the Lord _____" (v. 5).

4. What did Paul say he was for Christ's sake (v. 10)?

5. Paul did not write his letter to the Corinthians to shame the church. Why did he write it (v. 14)?

DISCUSS THE MEANING

1. Give two reasons why Paul warns the church against judging others.

2. What did Paul mean when he said, "God hath set forth us the apostles last, as it were appointed to death: for we are made a spectacle unto the world" (v. 9)?

3. Discuss Paul's use of irony to rebuke the Corinthians (vv. 7-10).

4. What do you think is the significance of Paul's ending this passage by challenging the Corinthians to revere him as a father (v. 14)?

LESSON IN OUR SOCIETY

A string of fragile neighborhoods heralded a local pastor for warding off drug dealers, prostitutes, and addicts from their streets. In just two years, his unorthodox and vigilant practices led to hundreds of crime-related arrests and treatment attempts for perpetrators. Because of this pastor's efforts, the police's presence and security increased in the community and its residents' sense of peace and pride was reinstated. Then one day, the community and its churches were torn apart by the morning news. "Preacher Solicits Prostitute," said the announcer, who then made way for the pastor's picture to be shown on-

screen. Part of the community believed that the pastor had solicited the prostitute for sex and condemned him. The other part of the community believed the pastor's report that he wasn't really soliciting the prostitute, but was testing the police's system to see how readily they would respond. How can we use what Paul has taught us today regarding the pastor in this story?

MAKE IT HAPPEN

Are you a critical person? Do you always have an opinion about someone or something? Do you discredit people before you even get to know them? If so, commit to bringing your judgment under subjection to love today. Every believer has the ability to discern between good and bad through the Holy Spirit. But Satan, our enemy, tries to pervert the ability to discern by making believers condemn and criticize each other and hold each other in contempt. Each day this week, commit to view those with whom you come into contact with tenderness and love.

FOLLOW THE SPIRIT

What God wants me to do:

_____

_____

REMEMBER YOUR THOUGHTS

Special insights I have learned:

_____

_____

MORE LIGHT ON THE TEXT

1 Corinthians 4:1-13

Throughout chapters 1-3, but particularly in the last three verses of chapter 3, Paul is rebutting an exaggerated estimate of himself and of his fellow evangelists. Now he anticipates the questions that were asked in the lesson last week: "How then are we to think of you?" "What exactly is your role in the purpose of God?" The answers are provided in the text that follows.

1 Let a man so account of us, as of the ministers of Christ, and stewards of the mysteries of God.

Having explained what preachers are not, to

show that no man should make himself dependent on them, Paul the apostle declared what preachers *were* to withdraw them from the rash judgments of the members of the church. He did so first by continuing to speak of himself and Apollos ("us," cf. 6:6), then he spoke singly of himself ("me," 5:3).

The word "so" (Gk. *houtos*, **hoo'-tos**), which begins this passage, is to be understood in the sense of "so then." Ministers are to be regarded as Christ's subordinates and as stewards of the mysteries of God. Strictly speaking, the Greek word "minister" (Gk. *huperetes*, **hoop-ay-ret'-ace**) denotes a person who acts under the orders of someone; generally, it refers to a person laboring freely in the service of others. Here it denotes the active and laborious side of the Christian ministry. The word "steward" (Gk. *oikonomos*, **oy-kon-om'-os**) evokes the image of a servant who is in charge— a confidential servant to whom the master entrusts the direction of his house and, in particular, the care of distributing to all the servants their tasks and provisions (Luke 12:42). By extension, the word refers to anyone entrusted with responsibility and therefore accountable to others. Thus, it implies that preachers are custodians and administrators of a truth that is not theirs, but their master's. The trust administered by them is the mysteries of God. The term "mystery" denotes the plan of salvation in general (see 2:7).

2 Moreover it is required in stewards, that a man be found faithful.

Here Paul turns to examine the character of those (including himself) who are handling God's truth: They must first of all show themselves faithful. Paul wanted to clarify the requirements of a servant and a steward. He said that it was required of them to be found trustworthy. This is a requirement, not an option; those who are called must take time to reflect upon the great task that is ahead of them, as well as on the integrity that must characterize their lives as they fulfill the task. Servants and stewards must be trustworthy mainly because what has been entrusted into their hands is greater than anything in this world. Trustworthiness is the benchmark for the evaluation of leaders. The question

is, "Are we worthy of God's trust? Is He able to trust us with His message and His mysteries?"

3 But with me it is a very small thing that I should be judged of you, or of man's judgment: yea, I judge not mine own self. 4 For I know nothing by myself; yet am I not hereby justified: but he that judgeth me is the Lord.

In these verses, the apostle expresses the truth that he is the Lord's servant and steward; therefore, it is to the Lord that he is responsible, and it is the Lord who judges him for the quality of his service. Human judgment has little value. Even self-evaluation is unreliable, Paul says. Christ is the Lord of the conscience and is the only One who can evaluate it properly.

5 Therefore judge nothing before the time, until the Lord come, who both will bring to light the hidden things of darkness, and will make manifest the counsels of the hearts: and then shall every man have praise of God.

In this verse, Paul shows the absurdity of the Corinthians' eagerness to evaluate his work and that of his fellow workers. If Paul exercised such restraint in evaluating his own work, how much more ought the Corinthians to abstain from such rash judgments! The present tense of the word "judge" (Gk. *krino*, **kree'-no**) implies that the Corinthians were already judging. Therefore, Paul told them to wait until the proper time, that is, the time of the Lord's return. Judgment is God's prerogative, and He would surely exercise it. He would bring to light what darkness hides and disclose our inward motives. Those who have been faithful in the service of their Master will receive praise from Him when He returns. Paul was confident. He did not envisage a negative outcome of the forthcoming judgment. He had been faithful.

6 And these things, brethren, I have in a figure transferred to myself and to Apollos for your sakes; that ye might learn in us not to think of men above that which is written, that no one of you be puffed up for one against another.

By addressing the Corinthians as "brethren," Paul puts himself alongside his readers. The word "transfer" (Gk. *metaschematizo*, **metaskh-ay-mat-id'-zo**) means to transform or change the appearance to present a thing or person in a form different from its natural figure; or to transform or alter. In the preceding passage (3:5), Paul presented and applied principles regarding the ministry to the Corinthians as well as to himself and Apollos. He reminded them of these principles because he had observed that certain people in Corinth were puffed up. The phrase "puffed up" (Gk. *phusioo*, **foo-see-o'-o**), meaning to be inflated, describes the bad condition of the Corinthian church. The community was in a terrible malaise. In speaking thus of himself and Apollos, Paul meant to indicate a limit that they should never exceed in estimating preachers that the Lord gave them. All glory is to be refused by a man for the spiritual work of which he is the agent.

7 For who maketh thee to differ from another? and what hast thou that thou didst not receive? now if thou didst receive it, why dost thou glory, as if thou hadst not received it?

In this verse, Paul sarcastically contrasts the Corinthians' perceived and actual spiritual conditions with those of himself and Apollos. On the one hand, the Corinthians were arrogant and claimed to be spiritually rich. On the other hand, Paul and Apollos were weak, despised, and persecuted. Paul did not deny for a moment the reality of their endowment with the grace of God, to which he had already alluded at the beginning of the letter. The problem was that the Corinthians were boasting as if what they had was a result of their human accomplishments rather than gifts from God. "If you received a gift of God," Paul asks, "why do you boast as if you did not?" In God's kingdom, there are no self-made men or women.

8 Now ye are full, now ye are rich, ye have reigned as kings without us: and I would to God ye did reign, that we also might reign with you.

The abrupt questions in verse 7 lead to a sustained contrast between the way the Corinthians see themselves and Paul's own experience of what it means to be an apostle. Paul ridiculed their conceit. The Corinthians see themselves as already blessed with everything God has to give.

They are spiritual millionaires and kings. They have arrived, even without any help from Paul. The Corinthians evidently thought that they had reached full maturity and were ruling and reigning rather than walking humbly with God.

The word "now" (Gk. *ede*, **ay'-day**), literally "already," introduces both the first and second phrases of verse 8 and well expresses the tenor of the whole passage: "Now already!" Paul and the other apostles were still in a world of suffering, but at Corinth the church already lives in full triumph. Their fullness consisted of an imperturbable self-satisfaction. "Riches," no doubt, alludes to the abundance of spiritual gifts that distinguished this church above all others and that Paul himself had recognized at the outset (1:5, 7). The rebuke applies not to the spiritual gifts, but to the feeling of arrogance that accompanied it.

9 For I think that God hath set forth us the apostles last, as it were appointed to death: for we are made a spectacle unto the world, and to angels, and to men.

Paul states that in his opinion he speaks mildly using the expression "For I think" or "it seems to me." The irony is that the Corinthians were trying to "reign," while their spiritual fathers and examples were far from "reigning." Actually, Paul goes on to explain that God had publicly displayed the apostles as humble, despised men who are worthy of death.

The word translated as "set forth" (Gk. *apodeiknumi*, **ap-od-ike'-noo-mee**) or "to exhibit" indicates public exposure to either honor or reproach. The following words, "as it were appointed to death," indicate that reproach is in view. The end of the verse alludes to the gladiators who were presented as a spectacle in the games of the amphitheater and whose blood and last agonies were enjoyed by a great crowd of spectators. By his use of "spectacle" (Gk. *theatron*, **theh'-at-ron**), Paul pictured himself and his fellow workers as condemned to death and led forth by a conqueror. Paul and his fellow workers are also depicted as being despised before the whole "world" (Gk. *kosmos*, **kos'-mos**) and the angelic hosts.

10 We are fools for Christ's sake, but ye are wise in Christ; we are weak, but ye are strong; ye

are honourable, but we are despised.

In a trenchant rebuke of the arrogant form of religion that Christianity was in danger of becoming in Corinth, Paul's words are addressed to the leaders of the Corinthian congregation, and, at the same time, to all its members who share in the pretensions of these conceited party leaders. Paul sets side-by-side once more the perception of the Christian life entertained by his readers and his own experience of apostolic ministry. "We are fools for Christ's sake, but ye are wise in Christ; we are weak, but ye are strong; ye are honourable, but we are despised." Words like "fools," "weak," and "despised" remind us of 1:25, where Paul previously demonstrated that the wisdom of the Cross is foolishness in the eyes of the world, and the power of the Cross is weakness in the eyes of the world. So, although Paul may be a fool, he is a fool for Christ's sake. Though he may be weak, he is weak with Christ.

11 Even unto this present hour we both hunger, and thirst, and are naked, and are buffeted, and have no certain dwellingplace; 12 And labour, working with our own hands: being reviled, we bless; being persecuted, we suffer it: 13 Being defamed, we intreat: we are made as the filth of the world, and are the offscouring of all things unto this day.

In these verses, Paul goes on to describe in detail the hardships that he and his fellow Christian workers have suffered throughout their ministry. Paul is not about to parade his sufferings. His intention is simply to portray the misery of his outward circumstances against the self-sufficiency of the Corinthians. Not only does Paul's experience of apostolic ministry stand in the sharpest contrast to the Corinthians' perception of the Christian life—a perception that is still common today—but there is also a sharp contrast between the treatment that he and the apostles were receiving at the hands of the world and the

response that they made in turn: "being reviled, we bless; being persecuted, we suffer it: Being defamed, we intreat." To sneering, the apostles reply with blessing; to ill-treatment, they reply by exercising self-control and enduring in the absolute sense. By the word "intreat" (Gk. *ane-chomai*, **an-ekh'-om-ahee**), which means to endure or to put up with, Paul shows that he and his fellow workers do not complain. Instead, they responded to slanderers by earnestly appealing that these men turn from wickedness and be converted to Christ.

But by acting this way, what do they get from the world? Paul concludes his list of humiliation and privation by saying that they became the object of its more complete disdain. This is what is expressed in verse 13. Paul and his fellow workers embody the wisdom of the Cross. Had the Corinthians embodied that wisdom, they would have begun to live peaceably among themselves, even though they may have been subject to the

DAILY BIBLE READINGS

M: Good Stewards of God's Grace
1 Peter 4:1-11

T: Jesus Washes Peter's Feet
John 13:2-9

W: Serve One Another
John 13:12-17

T: Become a Servant
Mark 10:41-45

F: Stewards of God's Mysteries
1 Corinthians 4:1-7

S: We Are Fools for Christ
1 Corinthians 4:8-13

S: A Fatherly Admonition on Responsibility
1 Corinthians 4:14-21

TEACHING TIPS

July 2
Bible Study Guide 5

1. Words You Should Know

A. Fornication (1 Corinthians 7:2) *porneia* (Gk.)—Sexual immorality; includes adultery, prostitution, and incest. Figuratively means "idolatry."

B. Benevolence (v. 3) *eunoia* (Gk.)—Something given freely for another's benefit or pleasure; thus, the phrase "due benevolence" figuratively means conjugal duty.

C. Incontinency (v. 5) *akrasia* (Gk.)—Lack of self-control.

2. Teacher Preparation

A. Prepare yourself to teach today's lesson by praying for insight into and understanding of the text, and also by praying for your students since you will be teaching a convicting lesson.

B. Become conversant with the text by reading the BIBLE BACKGROUND, studying the FOCAL VERSES, examining the IN DEPTH section, and considering the LESSON AIM.

C. Bring index cards for each student.

3. Starting the Lesson

A. Open the class with prayer; focus on the LESSON AIM and ask for strength and courage for your students to obey the Word.

B. Tell the students that in today's lesson Paul addresses the church's concerns about sex and relationships. Remind the students that the Corinthians were basically "new converts" and were seeking godly advice about how to conduct themselves. Ask the class how new converts today might be confused about sex, sexual roles, and sexual identities due to influences such as television, music, and radio. Facilitate discussion about where Christians can go for godly advice about sex and relationships.

C. Ask for volunteers to read the FOCAL VERSES.

4. Getting into the Lesson

A. Go through the lesson, soliciting volunteers to read through the IN DEPTH section. Stop from time to time to emphasize points and facilitate discussion about them. Always be ready to help the students apply the points to themselves.

B. Review the DISCUSS THE MEANING section together, and encourage the students to answer the questions.

5. Relating the Lesson to Life

A. Ask the students to share how they can relate to the lesson. Assure them that "There is therefore now no condemnation to them which are in Christ Jesus" (Romans 8:1) so that they will be comfortable sharing how they've overcome divorce or sexual sins.

B. Review the LESSON IN OUR SOCIETY and DISCUSS THE MEANING sections.

6. Arousing Action

A. Challenge your students to fulfill the MAKE IT HAPPEN assignment.

B. Give each student an index card and have him or her write a vow of sexual purity as it relates to singleness or marital vows.

C. Close with prayer, asking God for strength and courage to present our bodies as living sacrifices unto Him.

WORSHIP GUIDE

For the Superintendent or Teacher
Theme: Called to Relationships
Theme Song: "What a Friend We Have in Jesus"
Scripture: 1 Corinthians 7:2-15
Song: "Keep Me Near the Cross"
Meditation: Lord, thank You for being so mindful of us and leaving Your Word with us as a guide to holy living. May what we do be pleasing and acceptable in Your sight. O Lord, You are our strength and redeemer. Amen.

CALLED TO RELATIONSHIPS

Bible Background • 1 CORINTHIANS 7:1–20, 23–40
Printed Text • 1 CORINTHIANS 7:2–15
Devotional Reading • 1 JOHN 4:7–16

LESSON AIM

By the end of the lesson, we will:

KNOW Paul's teachings on marriage and singleness;

EVALUATE our relationships with respect to pleasing God; and

COMMIT to living sexually pure lifestyles, whether married or single.

KEEP IN MIND

"For I would that all men were even as I myself. But every man hath his proper gift of God, one after this manner, and another after that" (1 Corinthians 7:7).

FOCAL VERSES

1 Corinthians 7:2 Nevertheless, to avoid fornication, let every man have his own wife, and let every woman have her own husband.

3 Let the husband render unto the wife due benevolence: and likewise also the wife unto the husband.

4 The wife hath not power of her own body, but the husband: and likewise also the husband hath not power of his own body, but the wife.

5 Defraud ye not one the other, except it be with consent for a time, that ye may give yourselves to fasting and prayer; and come together again, that Satan tempt you not for your incontinency.

6 But I speak this by permission, and not of commandment.

7 For I would that all men were even as I myself. But every man hath his proper gift of God, one after this manner, and another after that.

8 I say therefore to the unmarried and widows,

LESSON OVERVIEW

LESSON AIM
KEEP IN MIND
FOCAL VERSES
IN FOCUS
THE PEOPLE, PLACES, AND TIMES
BACKGROUND
AT-A-GLANCE
IN DEPTH
SEARCH THE SCRIPTURES
DISCUSS THE MEANING
LESSON IN OUR SOCIETY
MAKE IT HAPPEN
FOLLOW THE SPIRIT
REMEMBER YOUR THOUGHTS
MORE LIGHT ON THE TEXT
DAILY BIBLE READINGS

It is good for them if they abide even as I.

9 But if they cannot contain, let them marry: for it is better to marry than to burn.

10 And unto the married I command, yet not I, but the Lord, Let not the wife depart from her husband:

11 But and if she depart, let her remain unmarried, or be reconciled to her husband: and let not the husband put away his wife.

12 But to the rest speak I, not the Lord: If any brother hath a wife that believeth not, and she be pleased to dwell with him, let him not put her away.

13 And the woman which hath an husband that believeth not, and if he be pleased to dwell with her, let her not leave him.

14 For the unbelieving husband is sanctified by the wife, and the unbelieving wife is sanctified by the husband: else were your children unclean; but now are they holy.

15 But if the unbelieving depart, let him depart. A brother or a sister is not under bondage in such cases: but God hath called us to peace.

IN FOCUS

When Duane proposed marriage to his fiancee Dana, there were no hurried words. He methodically chose the words that would convince her to accept his proposal. Marriage to a girl so beautiful seemed the right thing to do. Dana was swept off her feet. She said "yes" immediately. Duane spoke so soft and eloquently that his words carried her beyond the strict rules of her parents home into a world where their undying love would conquer all. Before walking down the aisle, they had set aside two hours for Christian marriage counseling.

Three years, two children, and numerous months without sexual relations, they discovered they had "forgotten" how to be intimate with one another. Dana found herself tired and worn out as she divided her time between her Alzheimer's-stricken mother and increased job responsibilities. Duane, frustrated and hurt, realized that the same smooth talk that sparked their love affair initially had fueled their increasing arguments like a flaming tongue.

In a last desperate attempt to find their lost intimacy, they decided to join the church's marriage encounter group. After a few sessions of deep reflection with other couples, they discovered they were missing a combined spiritual intimacy with God.

One of the couples in the group summed it up for them: "One of the most intimate activities you can share as a couple is prayer. Praying together unites a couple as one voice unto God sharing marriage dreams, distress, and desires. When you talk to God together, sharing your most private thoughts, you develop a spiritual bond that overcomes the constant changes that are bound to occur in life."

In today's lesson, Paul teaches about commitment in marriage and engaging in godly relationships. Are you cultivating your intimate relationships by growing in Christ?

THE PEOPLE, PLACES, AND TIMES

Fornication. See the WORDS YOU SHOULD KNOW section for the definition of fornication. It had been reported to Paul that the Corinthians were fornicating so much that they were doing things that were unheard of among the Gentiles (1 Corinthians 5:1). According to that text, they were practicing incest. Paul preached that they should turn away from such practices and from the people who were indulging in such lewdness. Corinth was so overtaken by sexual sins that the expression "to Corinthianize" meant to engage in prostitution, and Paul called it "the present dis-

tress" (v. 26). The people worshiped Aphrodite, the goddess of love, and in her temple 1,000 female slaves prostituted themselves out to worshipers. An engraved inscription on the soles of the prostitutes' sandals left the words "follow me" in the sand. Because of this grave immorality, Paul encouraged single believers to stay unmarried, and the married to commit to exclusive sexual relationships.

BACKGROUND

Over the last few weeks, we've studied Paul's response to several concerns of and with the Corinthian church. He challenged them to become more spiritually mature and to develop a right perspective on the roles of ministers. Now he was encouraging them to live godly personal lives.

The sexual sins of the world were seeping into the church, and Paul vehemently opposed fornication and incest in chapter 5 and commanded the Corinthians to separate themselves from "worldly" people. He gives a short discourse at the beginning of chapter 6 to give instruction in another area in which the Corinthians needed to conduct themselves differently than the world: legal proceedings. But he quickly returned to preaching against sexual immorality when he received a letter from the Corinthians inquiring about various problems (see 8:1; 12:1). The letter that included questions pertaining to marriage, and Paul's response will be discussed in today's lesson.

AT-A-GLANCE

1. A Dose of Marriage (1 Corinthians 7:2-5)
2. A Shot of Singleness (vv. 6-9)
3. Peace-Proofing Marriages (vv. 10-15)

IN DEPTH

1. A Dose of Marriage (1 Corinthians 7:2-5)

Paul had already warned the Corinthians to avoid fornication, and he provided instructions on how to do so. Paul's prescription for remedying fornication was simple: Get married and confine yourself to that mate (v. 2). How can marriage cure the desire for lawless lust? Well, Paul answers that in verse 3 by saying that when a couple marries, they are to *render to each other due benevolence*. The Greek terms for this expression are very strong and literally mean that the spouses are obligated to fulfill each other sexually. He asserts that the spouses are so bound by this conjugal duty that neither of them has power over their own body. That power has been delivered to the other spouse, and adultery and polygamy (having more than one spouse) are direct breaches of the marital covenant and violations of the partner's rights.

Avoiding fornication is so vital that Paul admonished the Corinthians not to *defraud* or deny each other sexually, except when abstinence is mutually agreed upon for a time of fasting and prayer. Such a period is to be a season of such deep humiliation that even lawful pleasures are to be avoided—but only for a short while, or Satan will use the couple's limited self-control to tempt them to sin against each other and God. Paul warns the couple against exposing themselves to unnecessary danger by attempting to perform what is above their strength. It would be a shame to get caught up in unlawful pleasures while abstaining from lawful ones.

2. A Shot of Singleness (vv. 6-9)

Just as you would find on any prescription bottle, Paul adds a disclaimer to his advice: "I speak this by permission, and not of commandment." Paul knew how literal-minded the Corinthians could be, so he had to tell them that he was speaking from personal preference and that there was no law forbidding singleness—if they did not want to marry, they did not have to. In verse 7, he writes that he wishes all men could be single and celibate. But Paul acknowledges God's divine intervention by saying that God gives to every man his proper gift; to some He gives the gift of marriage, to others the gift of celibacy, and to all the gift of grace to endure whichever state they are in.

Paul made one last attempt to encourage those who were unmarried or widowed by telling them that singleness is good. He gave the advantages and conveniences of singleness later in the chapter, including the ability to worship God without the distractions of a spouse and children and the ability to fast for extended periods of time. Nevertheless, Paul said that in spite of all the inconveniences of marriage, it is better to marry than to burn with impure and lustful desires.

3. Peace-Proofing Marriages (vv. 10-15)

Moses permitted divorce, and the people put away their spouses (see Ezra 3), but here Paul gives a command from the Lord to *believers* that they must not separate and divorce whenever they wanted to, only for reasons that Christ allows (see Matthew 5:32; 19:9; Mark 10:11; Luke 16:18). We know that there are such allowances because verse 11 reads, "But and if she depart." According to Paul, the person who departed must remain unmarried and the person who was deserted must not seek a divorce in hopes of future reconciliation.

Paul also gives advice to couples with only one believing spouse where one becomes a believer after the marriage. He writes that if the unbelieving spouse wants to continue in the marriage, then it shall be so. He informed the Corinthians that becoming a Christian was not a reason to dissolve a marriage. He gives two reasons in our text why a believer should stay with a unbelieving spouse. First, the believing spouse sanctifies the unbeliever. The marriage union itself and the marital conjugal relationship are sanctified to the believer.

Furthermore, Titus 1:15 says, "Unto the pure all things are pure." The believing spouse is in covenant with God, and God is obligated and faithful to fulfill the benefits of the covenant. Therefore, the unbeliever, who is one flesh with the believer, is sanctified for the believing spouse's sake and so are the children. Second, a believing spouse should stay with an unbelieving spouse if he or she is willing to stay with the believer. But if the unbeliever leaves, let him or her do so. A believing man or woman is not bound in such circumstances. God has called Christians to peace (v. 15) and to live peaceably with all men (Romans 12:18).

SEARCH THE SCRIPTURES

1. What does Paul tell the Corinthians to avoid (1 Corinthians 7:2)?

2. When may a married couple abstain from sex (v. 5)?

3. What does Paul suggest to single people who cannot control themselves sexually (v. 9)?

4. If a spouse leaves, what is he or she forbidden to do (v. 11)?

5. What must a believer do when he or she is married to an unbeliever who does not want to end the marriage (vv. 12-13)?

DISCUSS THE MEANING

1. Why does Paul recommend marriage as a safeguard against fornication?

2. In what ways can Satan tempt a married couple when they don't fulfill each other sexually?

3. Discuss the relative advantages of being single and married.

4. How is our society like the Corinthian society?

LESSON IN OUR SOCIETY

In 1999, the Barna Research Group (in Ventura, California) conducted a study that indicated born-again Christians are more likely to go through a marital split than are non-Christians. Among born-again Christians, 27% are currently or have previously been divorced, compared with 24% among adults who are not born again. This research raised questions regarding the effectiveness of churches' ministry to families. While the ultimate responsibility for a marriage belongs to the husband and wife, the high incidence of divorce within the Christian community challenges the idea that churches provide truly practical and life-changing support for marriages.

Paul's advice to the Corinthian church is still solid: Devote yourself to God and stay single, or commit yourself to one spouse. Many churches nationwide are stepping up to the plate to provide practical ministries, counseling, and conferences for married and single persons.

MAKE IT HAPPEN

As this is the beginning of a new month, it would be a great time to renew marital vows and vows of chastity unto God. If you are married, discuss this with your spouse and plan a romantic evening together to recommit yourselves one to another. You may wish to find a set of wedding vows or write your own to recite. If you are single, plan an intimate evening alone with God and commune with him by praying Scriptures, taking communion, listening to worship music, and writing your own vows. You may even desire to buy yourself a chastity ring.

FOLLOW THE SPIRIT

What God wants me to do:

_____

_____

REMEMBER YOUR THOUGHTS

Special insights I have learned:

_____

_____

MORE LIGHT ON THE TEXT

1 Corinthians 7:2-15

2 Nevertheless, to avoid fornication, let every man have his own wife, and let every woman have her own husband.

The word "fornication" (Gk. *porneia*, **por-ni'-ah**) is plural in the Greek, indicating the variety and extent of immorality in Corinth. The city was known for its abundance of opportunities for sexual looseness. Thus, here Paul is addressing a particular situation that cannot be generalized (cf. v. 26, "the present distress" or "the present crisis" [NLT]). In such a context, Paul admonishes: Instead of living in sexual looseness, let each man "have his own wife" and let each woman "have her own husband." Paul is not demanding that everyone get married. His words are addressed to those who do not have the gift of celibacy (cf. v. 7) and are facing various temptations in Corinth. The expressions "every man his own wife" and "every woman her own husband" clearly imply a monogamous life.

3 Let the husband render unto the wife due benevolence: and likewise also the wife unto the husband.

The word "due" or "debt" (Gk. *opheilo*, **of-i'-lo**)

Living in relationship with Jesus.

refers to conjugal rights. It shows the obligation of a husband and wife to each other. They have equal rights as indicated by the word "likewise" (Gk. *homoios,* **hom-oy'-oce**). The verb "render" (Gk. *apodidomi,* **ap-od-eed'-o-mee**) is an imperative, meaning the obligation to give what is due or to fulfill a duty.

4 The wife hath not power of her own body, but the husband: and likewise also the husband hath not power of his own body, but the wife.

The expression "hath not power" (Gk. *exousiazo,* **ex-oo-see-ad'-zo**) denotes the exercise of authority (Gk. *exousia,* **ex-oo-see'-ah**, from the same root as the verb translated as "power"). Husband and wife, by the bonds of marriage, have equal authority over each other for the good of the family.

5 Defraud ye not one the other, except it be with consent for a time, that ye may give yourselves to fasting and prayer; and come together again, that Satan tempt you not for your incontinency.

The word "defraud" or "keep back by fraud" (Gk. *apostereo,* **ap-os-ter-eh'-o**) is an imperative with a negative and refers to a temporary separation by mutual consent. Some Corinthians believed in a spiritual, sexless, ascetic marriage as a solution to the abundance of immorality in their society. Paul the apostle says, "Stop depriving one another." Abstinence in marriage must be: (1) temporary; (2) by mutual consent; and (3) for the purpose of seeking God. (This translates to "fasting and prayer," or "prayer" in some manuscripts. In the early church, fasting and prayer were linked.)

Abstinence within marriage for any other reasons may open the door to temptation by Satan(cf. 2 Corinthians 2:11; 11:3-15). The word "incontinency" (Gk. *akrasia*, **ak-ras-ee'-a**) means the non-mastering of appetite. Here it refers to sexual instincts. Well-intentioned acts of piety carried beyond the limits of natural endurance can open the door for Satan to bring moral or spiritual disaster on those who practice them. Satan uses incontinency by urging people to give the sexual instincts an illicit expression.

6 But I speak this by permission, and not of commandment.

The demonstrative word "this" (Gk. *touto*, **too'-to**) may refer to the statements in verses 2-3, since verses 4-5 express the fact that Paul does not impose marriage on every man and woman (cf. v. 7). Or the word may refer to the statement in verse 5 about temporary abstinence, which is permitted and, indeed, is commanded to be only temporary.

7 For I would that all men were even as I myself. But every man hath his proper gift of God, one after this manner, and another after that.

The expression "as I myself" (Gk. *hos emautou*, **hoce em-ow-too'**) implies that the Corinthian Christians knew that Paul was unmarried (cf. v. 8; 9:5).

The word "gift" (Gk. *charisma*, **khar'-is-mah**) literally refers to a favor or grace received without merit on the part of the recipient. Singleness and marriage are both gifts from God (cf. Matthew 19:12). Everyone must be content with what God gives.

8 I say therefore to the unmarried and widows, It is good for them if they abide even as I.

The word "unmarried" (Gk. *agamos*, **ag'-am-os**) refers to a man or woman without a partner. It does not necessarily refer to those who have never been married. Instead, the word includes singles, widows, widowers, and divorcees (see v. 11 where it is used of divorced women). It is "good" (Gk. *kalos*, **kal-os**) for them to remain as they are (as Paul is—that is, unmarried). Paul probably had in mind the "present crisis" in Corinth (v. 26) and the need for people who were able to serve God without distraction.

9 But if they cannot contain, let them marry: for it is better to marry than to burn.

However, if unmarried men or women do not have self-control or continence (Gk. *egkrateuomai*, **eng-krat-yoo'-om-ahee**; see v. 5; cp. 9:25, where the word is used of an athlete; Acts 24:25; Galatians 5:23; Titus 3:8; 2 Peter 1:6), let them seek marriage (Gk. *gameo*, **gam-eh'-o**.) The word is used in the aorist imperative ingressive, indicating the point of entry into action, not the point of completion.

Common sense (cf. 11:14) teaches that it is better to marry than to pretend to have the gift of celibacy or to be spiritual and "burn." The verb "burn" or "to be inflamed" (Gk. *puroo*, **poo-ro'-o**) here means to be consumed with desires or passions.

10 And unto the married I command, yet not I, but the Lord, Let not the wife depart from her husband:

Those who choose married life are reminded of the command of the Lord Jesus. Paul is not making a distinction between an inspired and an uninspired saying, as though his words were insufficient (see v. 40; 2:16, 4-5; 14:37). He is simply reminding the Corinthians of the words of the Lord that they already know. The Corinthians just need to apply them.

The command from the Lord Jesus says that the wife should not separate from her husband (Matthew 19:3-9; Mark 10:2-12; Luke 16:18). In general, marriage cannot be brought to an end. Exceptions exist as recognized by the Lord

(Matthew 5:31-32). Here Paul is not dealing with these exceptions. He is addressing a particular situation in the church at Corinth—probably the case of a woman seeking to separate from her husband (cf. v. 1; see 11:5-16; 14:34-36).

11 But and if she depart, let her remain unmarried, or be reconciled to her husband: and let not the husband put away his wife.

If separation does take place, the wife has two options: to remain unmarried or to be reconciled (Gk. *katallasso*, **kat-al-las'-so,** literally "return to favor") to her husband. The same applies to the husband seeking separation.

12 But to the rest speak I, not the Lord: If any brother hath a wife that believeth not, and she be pleased to dwell with him, let him not put her away.

The word "rest" or literally "the left behind" (Gk. *loipoy,* **loy-poy'**) refer here to mixed marriages that probably occurred when one party became a Christian during the course of the marriage. They should continue to be married as long as the unbelieving party consents (Gk. *suneudokeo,* **soon-yoo-dok-eh'-o** meaning "to seem good to one and the other") to live with the believer. By saying "I, not the Lord," Paul means that here he is not appealing here to a saying from the Lord Jesus.

13 And the woman which hath an husband that believeth not, and if he be pleased to dwell with her, let her not leave him.

The same instruction is repeated with reference to the woman. The woman should not leave if her unbelieving husband is willing to live with her.

14 For the unbelieving husband is sanctified by the wife, and the unbelieving wife is sanctified by the husband: else were your children unclean; but now are they holy.

The non-Christian partner does not defile the marriage. On the contrary, the Christian sanctifies it. The word "sanctified" (Gk. *hagiazo,* **hag-ee-ad'-zo**) does not refer to salvation here. It simply means that the marriage is special to God because

a Christian is involved. Through marriage a husband and wife become one flesh (Genesis 2:24; cf; 1 Corinthians 6:16). The non-Christian partner benefits from the Christian partner belonging to the community of saints.

Their children are "holy" (Gk. *hagios,* **hag'-ee-os**), meaning that they are under the special protection and covenant oversight of God. Semitic anthropology considers children as one being with their parents.

15 But if the unbelieving depart, let him depart. A brother or a sister is not under bondage in such cases: but God hath called us to peace.

If the unbeliever decides to leave, the believer is no longer "under bondage" or "enslaved" (Gk. *douloo,* **doo-lo'-o**). God has called us (or "you" in some readings) to live in peace. The verb "called" (Gk. *kaleo,* **kal-eh'-o**) is in the perfect tense, denoting that an action has already accomplished results that are still present (continuous).

DAILY BIBLE READINGS

M: God Is Love
1 John 4:7-16
T: Instructions for Husbands and Wives
1 Corinthians 7:1-5
W: Advice to the Unmarried and Widows
1 Corinthians 7:6-11
T: If You Have an Unbelieving Spouse
1 Corinthians 7:12-16
F: Live as God Called You
1 Corinthians 7:17-24
S: Remain as You Are
1 Corinthians 7:25-31
S: Unhindered Devotion to the Lord
1 Corinthians 7:32-40

TEACHING TIPS

July 9
Bible Study Guide 6

1. Words You Should Know

A. Liberty (1 Corinthians 8:9) *exousia* (Gk.)—Privilege or freedom.

B. Weak (v. 9) *astheneo* (Gk.)—To be weak or feeble; to be without strength; powerless.

2. Teacher Preparation

A. Read the LESSON AIM, FOCAL VERSES, and MORE LIGHT ON THE TEXT section for today's lesson.

B. Read 1 Corinthians 10:23-33 to get further insight into how Paul addresses the issue of eating food sacrificed to idols.

3. Starting the Lesson

A. Ask a student to open the class in prayer.

B. Ask if anyone has any questions about last week's lesson and if anyone would like to share their experiences from last week's MAKE IT HAPPEN assignment.

4. Getting into the Lesson

A. Ask for a volunteer to read the LESSON AIM and FOCAL VERSES aloud.

B. Review THE PEOPLE, PLACES, AND TIMES and the BACKGROUND sections with the class.

5. Relating the Lesson to Life

A. Have a student read the LESSON IN OUR SOCIETY section aloud.

B. Ask the students to define the relationship between liberty and responsibility based on today's lesson. Then ask if they have ever chosen not to do something because doing it might have caused a fellow believer to stumble. Ask a few of the students to share their experiences.

6. Arousing Action

A. Ask for a volunteer to read the MAKE IT HAPPEN section to the class.

B. Ask the students for examples of things they can do to make sure that their actions are not causing other believers to stumble.

C. Close the class with prayer.

CALLED TO HELP THE WEAK

Bible Background • 1 CORINTHIANS 8:1–13
Printed Text • 1 CORINTHIANS 8:1–13
Devotional Reading • MARK 9:42–48

LESSON AIM

By the end of the lesson, we will:

UNDERSTAND the responsibility that believers have toward one another;

DESIRE to walk in knowledge and love; and

COMMIT ourselves to living in such a way that we do not cause others to sin.

KEEP IN MIND

"But meat commendeth us not to God: for neither, if we eat, are we the better; neither, if we eat not, are we the worse. But take heed lest by any means this liberty of yours become a stumblingblock to them that are weak" (1 Corinthians 8:8-9).

LESSON OVERVIEW

LESSON AIM
KEEP IN MIND
FOCAL VERSES
IN FOCUS
THE PEOPLE, PLACES, AND TIMES
BACKGROUND
AT-A-GLANCE
IN DEPTH
SEARCH THE SCRIPTURES
DISCUSS THE MEANING
LESSON IN OUR SOCIETY
MAKE IT HAPPEN
FOLLOW THE SPIRIT
REMEMBER YOUR THOUGHTS
MORE LIGHT ON THE TEXT
DAILY BIBLE READINGS

FOCAL VERSES

1 Corinthians 8:1 Now as touching things offered unto idols, we know that we all have knowledge. Knowledge puffeth up, but charity edifieth.

2 And if any man think that he knoweth any thing, he knoweth nothing yet as he ought to know.

3 But if any man love God, the same is known of him.

4 As concerning therefore the eating of those things that are offered in sacrifice unto idols, we know that an idol is nothing in the world, and that there is none other God but one.

5 For though there be that are called gods, whether in heaven or in earth, (as there be gods many, and lords many,)

6 But to us there is but one God, the Father, of whom are all things, and we in him; and one Lord Jesus Christ, by whom are all things, and we by him.

7 Howbeit there is not in every man that knowledge: for some with conscience of the idol unto this hour eat it as a thing offered unto an idol; and their conscience being weak is defiled.

8 But meat commendeth us not to God: for neither, if we eat, are we the better; neither, if we eat not, are we the worse.

9 But take heed lest by any means this liberty of yours become a stumblingblock to them that are weak.

10 For if any man see thee which hast knowledge sit at meat in the idol's temple, shall not the conscience of him which is weak be emboldened to eat those things which are offered to idols;

11 And through thy knowledge shall the weak brother perish, for whom Christ died?

12 But when ye sin so against the brethren, and wound their weak conscience, ye sin against Christ.

13 Wherefore, if meat make my brother to offend, I will eat no flesh while the world standeth, lest I make my brother to offend.

IN FOCUS

The family picnic that Diane organized was under a bright sun with tinges of orange striping a cloudless sky. Running children and people lounging on blankets made everything seem just right until Diane presented a basket of sandwiches to her brother's friend Mike.

Mike smiled and asked, "What kind do you have?"

Diane said, "All we have left is ham on rye and pork roast."

Mike frowned. "Don't you have any beef or tuna?"

Diane replied, "No, sorry, this is all that's left."

"I guess I can't eat then," Mike replied.

Diane knew Mike had recently become a Christian and was concerned that he didn't really understand his new freedom in Christ. Taking a sandwich from the basket, she put it in his hand. "Don't you know that as a Christian you can eat pork if you like?"

Mike pushed the sandwich away and said. "Yes, I know. But I am also free *not* to eat it. The reason I won't eat pork is because I want to set an example for other family members who may consider converting to Christianity." Mike went on. "If I can tell them truthfully that no pork has ever passed my lips, then I can sit at the family dinner table, and tell them about the joy I have found in Jesus Christ."

The apostle Paul tells us that although we have rights, we also have the right not to exercise them for the sake of love. Do you understand your responsibilities to other believers?

THE PEOPLE, PLACES, AND TIMES

Food Offered to Idols. Food used in pagan sacrifices normally consisted of three parts: one small portion used in the sacrifice, a larger portion used by the priests, and the largest part used by the worshiper. The worshiper would use this portion of meat in one of two ways: to serve as the main course of a meal that was eaten at or near the pagan temple or to sell at the local marketplace, where meat was purchased and served as part of a regular meal.

BACKGROUND

Paul wrote 1 Corinthians to address problems that were affecting the Corinthian church. In the first seven chapters of the letter, Paul addresses issues such as sexual immorality, the Corinthians' lack of spiritual maturity, the need to rely on God's wisdom rather than that of the world, and the need for unity within the church.

In this chapter, Paul addresses a question that had been raised by the Corinthian church: Is it a sin for Christians to partake of food that has been sacrificed to idols? The situation posed a very real problem for the Corinthians. Idol worship was very prevalent in their society. Before becoming Christians, many members of the church had worshiped idols and offered food sacrifices. Also, many of their social gatherings had involved pagan rituals, and much of the meat sold in local markets had been used in pagan sacrifices. From Paul's response, it appears that there was conflict within the church about whether members should continue to eat of these offerings or abstain. Paul's letter not only answers the Corinthians' question, but it also teaches them about the importance of love.

AT-A-GLANCE

1. Supremacy of Love
(1 Corinthians 8:1-3)
2. Knowledge of the One True God
(vv. 4-6)
3. Liberty with Responsibility (vv. 7-9)
4. Restraint for Protecting the Weak
(vv. 10-13)

IN DEPTH

1. Supremacy of Love (1 Corinthians 8:1-3)

At the beginning of this chapter, Paul addresses a question that had been posed to him by the Corinthian church: "Now as touching things offered unto idols, we know that we all have knowledge" (v. 1). It appears that the church had been divided over what was required of them in reference to food offered to idols. Paul tells them that there is a proper answer (i.e., "knowledge") to their question. But before answering their question, Paul says that there is something more important than that answer—love: "Knowledge puffs up, but love builds up" (v. 1, NIV). Paul emphasizes that love should be the Corinthian church's primary concern. There may be a "right" answer to their question, but being factually right isn't always the morally right thing in a situation.

Although they have been enlightened through their conversion to Christ, Paul says that their enlightenment should be tempered with love. If believers focus solely on the knowledge that they have gained through their conversion, they risk becoming haughty: "Knowledge puffeth up" (v. 1). But while knowledge alone falsely inflates a believer's ego, love builds a believer up and creates a lasting foundation: "but charity edifieth (v. 1). This love encourages not only the believer who possesses, but it also possesses those around him.

Paul goes on to say that any believer who focuses only on attaining knowledge, actually moves farther away from it (v. 2). It is only by exhibiting love that believers please God: "But if one loves God truly [with affectionate reverence, prompt obedience, and grateful recognition of His blessing], he is known by God [recognized as worthy of His intimacy and love, and he is owned by Him]" (v. 3, The Amplified Bible (TAB)). The word "known" in this verse indicates an intimate relationship between the believer and God. According to *Vincent's Word Studies in the New Testament,* the word "denotes a personal relation between the knower and the known, so that the knowledge of an object implies the influence of that object upon the knower.

2. Knowledge of the One True God (vv. 4-6)

After emphasizing the importance of love, Paul focuses on answering the question. He first confirms the "knowledge" that they already possessed: There is only one true God—the God whom they serve. Idols, he says, are fake, powerless gods and are "nothing in the world" (v. 4). There are many idols or "so-called gods" (v. 5, TAB) that people empower and make lord over their lives. But for Christians, there is only one God and one Lord: "Yet for us there is [only] one God, the Father, Who is the Source of all things and for Whom we [have life], and one Lord, Jesus Christ, through and by Whom are all things and through and by Whom we [ourselves exist]" (v. 6, TAB).

3. Liberty with Responsibility (vv. 7-9)

But while mature believers know that idols are powerless, Paul says, some believers have not attained this knowledge. They still view idols as

real, just as they did before they became Christians, and still view the food sacrificed to idols as having been sacrificed to an actual god (v. 7). Because of their immaturity or weak conscience, they would believe that they were sinning if they were to eat this food. But, as Paul explains, they would be misguided because the food would be just as powerless as the gods to whom it was offered: "Now food [itself] will not cause our acceptance by God nor commend us to Him. Eating [food offered to idols] gives us no advantage; neither do we come short or become any worse if we do not eat [it]" (v. 8, TAB).

One might expect Paul now to chastise weaker believers for not possessing the full knowledge that idols are powerless. But instead, he offers a warning to mature believers: "Only be careful that this power of choice (this permission and liberty to do as you please) which is yours, does not [somehow] become a hindrance (cause of stumbling) to the weak or overscrupulous [giving them an impulse to sin]" (v. 9, TAB).

Paul warns those who possess knowledge in this area not to let the freedom that they gain through this knowledge cause them to become a hindrance for their brothers and sisters who do not possess this knowledge. He emphasizes that with the knowledge gained through Christ comes responsibility as well as liberty. The believer's responsibility, then, is to be concerned not only about his or her own spiritual state, but also about the spiritual well-being of other believers. This is where the love that Paul discusses at the beginning of the chapter comes into play. If believers show genuine love to one another—love that edifies and encourages—they will desire to walk in a way that does not cause their brothers or sisters to falter.

4. Restraint for Protecting the Weak (vv. 10-13)

Paul goes on to give the church a concrete example of how their failure to employ their knowledge responsibly could hurt their weaker brothers and sisters. He says that if a weaker believer sees a mature believer eating food that has been sacrificed to an idol, he might be tempted to violate his own beliefs by eating also. In his letter to the Romans, Paul explains that anything done without faith is sin: "But the man who has doubts (misgivings, an uneasy conscience) about eating, and then eats [perhaps because of you], stands condemned [before God], because he is not true to his convictions and he does not act from faith. For whatever does not originate and proceed from faith is sin [whatever is done without a conviction of its approval by God is sinful]" (Romans 14:23, TAB).

The enlightened believer, then, would have caused the other believer to sin: "And so by your enlightenment (your knowledge of spiritual things), this weak man is ruined (is lost and perishes) the brother for whom Christ (the Messiah) died!" (1 Corinthians 8:11, TAB). Even though the mature believer has the freedom to eat in the temple, he should practice restraint. By causing another believer to go against his conscience, a mature believer would be leading astray someone whom Christ died to save. If Christ died to save someone, shouldn't Christ's followers work to protect that person and draw him closer to the Lord?

In verse 12, Paul reveals another reason for a believer to practice restraint. By leading a brother or sister astray, a believer not only sins against that brother or sister, but also sins against Christ. Our first goal as followers of Christ should be to please Him and the Father. In order to do this, we must demonstrate love to one another. Christ commands us to love our neighbor as we love ourselves (Matthew 22:39). Doing so requires us to be mindful of our brother and to think of his needs in addition to and quite often before our own.

Paul elaborates on this point later in 1 Corinthians 10:23-24 "All things are legitimate [permissible—and we are free to do anything we please], but not all things are helpful (expedient, profitable, and wholesome). All things are legitimate, but not all things are constructive [to character] and edifying [to spiritual life]. Let no one then seek his own good and advantage and profit, but [rather] each one of the other [let him seek the welfare of his neighbor]" (TAB). As believers, then, we should not view our actions as occurring in a vacuum, affecting only ourselves. Instead, before we act, we must consider what effect that action might have on those around us.

Paul emphasizes this point in verse 13: "Therefore, if [my eating a] food is a cause of my brother's falling or of hindering [his spiritual advancement], I will not eat [such] flesh forever, lest I cause my brother to be tripped up and fall and to be offended" (1 Corinthians 8:13, TAB). We must be willing to forego doing some things that may bring us pleasure or satisfaction if those things will cause our brothers or sisters in the faith to stumble. As Paul says later in 1 Corinthians, if one member of the body suffers, then we all suffer (12:26). By placing concern for our brother above concern for ourselves, we truly live out Jesus' command that we love one another.

Paul sums up the issue later in chapter 10: "So then, whether you eat or drink, or whatever you may do, do all for the honor and glory of God" (v. 31, TAB). If we strive to honor God in all that we do, we cannot fail.

Vincent, Marvin R. "Vincent's Word Studies in the New Testament." Precepts For Living™ CD-ROM. Chicago: Urban Ministries, Inc., 2003.

SEARCH THE SCRIPTURES

1. What is the difference between knowledge and love (1 Corinthians 8:1)?

2. What is promised to the person who loves God (v. 3)?

3. Why can Christians be certain that idols are powerless (vv. 4-6)?

4. Christians must be careful that their _____ does not become a _____ for those who are weak (v. 9).

DISCUSS THE MEANING

1. Why do you think Paul began answering the Corinthians' question about eating food offered to idols with a discussion about love?

2. Why do you think Paul addressed his answer to stronger believers and not to weaker ones?

3. How do you think Paul's message applies to believers today?

LESSON IN OUR SOCIETY

In our society, we are often encouraged to think about ourselves first. Many people live by the mantra, "I gotta get mine." But as Paul shows us, as Christians we must be others focused. "Love your neighbor as yourself" is not a suggestion, it is a command. It is a call to concentrate not on ourselves, but rather on those people we are blessed to encounter in our daily lives. This can be difficult, however, in a society in which we are showered with freedoms and encouraged to exercise those freedoms as frequently as possible. But what happens when my rights collide with yours? Paul's response to the Corinthians pushes us to think not about how we can exercise our own rights, but about how we can protect the rights of others. Only by keeping our focus on others can we truly walk in Jesus' footsteps.

MAKE IT HAPPEN

Pray and ask God to open your eyes to areas in your life that you need to change to have a more responsible walk. Keep a journal this week of occasions where you have to alter your behavior or refrain from doing something in order to provide a better witness for those around you. If you don't experience such occasions, ask God to show you if there are things that you should be doing that you are not and to open doors for you to be an agent of His love to His people.

FOLLOW THE SPIRIT

What God wants me to do:

_____

_____

REMEMBER YOUR THOUGHTS

Special insights I have learned:

_____

_____

MORE LIGHT ON THE TEXT

1 Corinthians 8:1-13

1 Now as touching things offered unto idols, we know that we all have knowledge. Knowledge puffeth up, but charity edifieth.

First, we note that the apostle Paul, who was called and anointed by God to preach the Good News of salvation through Jesus Christ, was resolute about walking in his calling. The apostle was adamant about doing the will of God and desired that the Corinthian church, which he helped establish, do so as well. This assembly needed

guidance and strengthening because, in her infancy, she struggled with her environment both within and without. Paul wrote this letter to the Corinthian church, then, while she was in the heat of spiritual warfare and had pressing needs. She was surrounded not only by corruption, but by every conceivable sin, including idol worship. Immorality and spiritual immaturity undermined the church and thus had an impact on her unity.

Even though Paul had left a strong Gospel foundation with this congregation earlier, without his continued presence she floundered. The Corinthian church fell into divisiveness and disorder. These obstacles deterred Christian growth and kept the members from being salt and light in a dying world. Paul understood that this church, as well as all believers, needed a Christlike attitude or outlook when dealing with the vicissitudes of life. Paul appealed for unity and order in this congregation.

The Holy Spirit inspired Paul to teach that unity in the body was and is paramount in being a positive witness for Christ, whose agenda is to build His kingdom. Paul had already addressed this issue earlier in this letter (1:10; 4:21). He emphasized that all the parts of the body make the church whole, including both the strong and weaker saints. The bride of Christ, therefore, cannot afford to disobey God's directives and must operate divine order, not succumb to factions and schism that hinder the spread of the Good News of the Gospel. Paul taught that the church must live with forgiveness, grace, and love. She must epitomize God's standards and mirror His Word to the world she is trying to reach.

Eating meat offered to idols was one of the problems dividing the Corinthian church, and the discerning Paul knew that the abuse of Christian freedom was the culprit. Thus, verse 1 dealt with the believers' freedom in Christ. Paul stressed that exercising our freedom in Christ should not cause us to be abusive. He recognized that the contention between the stronger and weaker believers over the serving of meat sacrificed to idols was symptomatic of a far deeper spiritual problem: the malignant cancers of arrogance, disobedience, selfishness, etc. These detractors eroded the bonds of unity in this

Christian community. There was sin in the camp and sin in God's house, and Satan was behind this negative behavior. Paul knew that this transgression of God's commands had to be eradicated if the Corinthian church was to move forward in their Christian ministry.

The stronger believers forgot that a mature Christian is one who is spiritual, not walking in selfishness, but considerate of others' welfare. Paul believed that a mature Christian is one who sees life God's way and walks in His Word. The Holy Spirit controls the mature Christian's life and produces the fruit of God's Spirit: "love, joy, peace, patience, kindness, goodness, faithfulness, gentleness and self-control" (Galatians 5:22-23, NIV).

Thus Paul saw that the relationships within the Corinthian church must be healed, and the paradigm he set before the assembly called for the mature Christians to take the leadership role. Paul declared in his letter that love could build the bridge to inner healing. To him, love was more important than knowledge.

Paul used the Greek word "knowledge" (*epignosis*, **ep-ig'-no-sis**) to imply full, complete, or real knowledge or understanding. Paul taught that while knowledge may make us believers feel important and more spiritually mature, we are not to use that knowledge to wound a weaker brother, who is also one of God's children. In fact, doing so shows that we do not know what we think we know. Hurting our weaker brother does not build up the church. In fact, it dismantles unity. Therefore, compassionate Paul wanted to help the Corinthians shift their spiritual landscape from self-centeredness to Christ-centeredness. This was foremost since they needed each other to fight the spiritual warfare that threatened their survival.

While these Corinthian believers had some knowledge, they did not have a full knowledge of how God expected them to treat their weaker brother. They were ignorant of the fact that God's righteousness is based on love. Therefore, Paul stressed that: (1) all believers must submit and yield to God's righteousness and (2) it is love that edifies the church.

The words "edifies" and "edification" is from the Greek word *oikodome* (**oy-kod-om-ay'**), which means building up. Because believers are living stones (1 Peter 2:5), we are being built into the church by God's Spirit operating in us. Thus the church should be a great "building," the aggregate of God's saved, justified, and sanctified children. We are joined together by our collective faith in Jesus Christ. We are growing into a holy temple, in union with the Lord Jesus Christ (Ephesians 2:21). The church, therefore, should be guided by God's supporting presence through His Holy Spirit at all times.

2 And if any man think that he knoweth any thing, he knoweth nothing yet as he ought to know.

Paul really drives home his point about unity and order in the church in verse 2. He stresses that love is more important than knowledge because undisciplined knowledge can cause a person to celebrate himself instead of the gifts of others and generate feelings of arrogance and self-importance. Again, these negative attributes are detrimental to the unity of the body of Christ.

The Corinthian church was a part of God's bigger picture of building His kingdom. They were to be God's instruments to win people to Himself by their Christian living and standards. However, with sin in God's house, they were not glorifying God. The surrounding community did not know that they were Christians by their love.

3 But if any man love God, the same is known of him.

Again, Paul speaks of knowledge in the sense of discerning, perceiving, and recognizing based on having a personal relationship with God. Since a weaker brother is also a child of God, Paul wants believers to know that love should definitely keep us all from hurting God's spiritual babies and from hurting each other, period. Therefore, we should promote love and be our best for God's glory. As traveling lights for God, we should allow love to dominate our interactions with others and not arrogance.

4 As concerning therefore the eating of those things that are offered in sacrifice unto idols, we know that an idol is nothing in the world, and that

there is none other God but one. **5 For though there be that are called gods, whether in heaven or in earth, (as there be gods many, and lords many,) 6 But to us there is but one God, the Father, of whom are all things, and we in him; and one Lord Jesus Christ, by whom are all things, and we by him. 7 Howbeit there is not in every man that knowledge: for some with conscience of the idol unto this hour eat it as a thing offered unto an idol; and their conscience being weak is defiled. 8 But meat commendeth us not to God: for neither, if we eat, are we the better; neither, if we eat not, are we the worse. 9 But take heed lest by any means this liberty of yours become a stumblingblock to them that are weak.**

Paul recognized that we are saved by grace through faith (Ephesians 2:8-9), not by keeping the law. Therefore, our salvation freed us from the slavery of sin and imprisonment of the law. In fact, he taught that our spiritual liberty began in its fuller sense after Calvary. It was inaugurated by the Cross, which, Paul declared, freed a believer from all legalism and self-justification (Romans 8:21). Furthermore, Paul recognized that we are justified, or made right with God, by faith in Jesus Christ and His atonement at Calvary (Romans 7:1-6). Still, Paul reminded the Corinthian Christians that believers do not have the freedom to impede a weaker brother's growth in Christ.

Paul affirms that every believer should know that there is only one true God. Here he is speaking specifically to the stronger Corinthian believers who were not bothered by eating meat offered to idols because they knew that idols were phony, had no power, and were not the one true God. Later, Paul hammers home his point that God holds all believers accountable for how we treat each other. Therefore, if the eating of meat offered to idols offended the sensibilities of a weaker brother, the stronger believers were to abstain.

Some of these weaker brothers may have been trying to overcome their dependency on idol worship, and the eating of meat offered to idols hindered them from being an overcomer. Paul knew that these weak Christians, like all believers, "wrestle not against flesh and blood, but against principalities, against powers, against the rulers of the darkness of this world, against spiritual wickedness in high places" (Ephesians 6:12). Thus, eating of meat offered to idols could have been a stronghold of Satan in their life, an opportunity for Satan to get to wreak havoc. It could have been a snare to entrap some weaker brothers.

Paul reiterates the point that the stronger believer should be resolute in helping his brother by refraining. A mature Christian should not want to see his weaker brother stumble or fall. All believers should remember that a heart that belongs to God considers his fellow man.

As a devout teacher, Paul also recognized that the church is composed of many types of people from diverse backgrounds. Yet, now that we are believers, our differences should not divide us. Instead, we should rally around our one commonality: We are all children of God. This truth alone should unite us. Therefore, Paul stressed that we are one in Christ. We are united by the Holy Spirit into one spiritual body—the body of Christ.

Paul preached spiritual wisdom and spoke against spiritual elitism. He articulated that it is love that builds solidarity in the body (the church). He advocated that even though the stronger Christians may have had the right to eat meat that had been offered to idols, because of Christian liberty it was not expedient for them to do so. It's wrong to be so proud of their maturity in Christ that they flaunted it to the detriment of their weaker brothers. Instead, love should guide their behavior—love for God, love for His kingdom, and love for their Christian brothers. Similarly, as believers, we should be compelled by the power of God to help someone else, whom God loves just as much.

10 For if any man see thee which hast knowledge sit at meat in the idol's temple, shall not the conscience of him which is weak be emboldened to eat those things which are offered to idols; 11 And through thy knowledge shall the weak brother perish, for whom Christ died? 12 But when ye sin so against the brethren, and wound their weak conscience, ye sin against Christ. 13 Wherefore, if meat make my brother to offend, I will eat no

flesh while the world standeth, lest I make my brother to offend.

In verses 10-13, Paul further emphasizes God's precepts of Christian conduct or self-discipline in regard to one's weaker brothers in Christ. In his discourse, he looks at the eating of meat offered to idols from the weaker brother's perspective. Paul offers godly wisdom on what can happen to the weaker brother when he feels violated by an insensitive Christian who is motivated by knowledge and not by love. Again, Paul's letter is a tutorial not only to the Corinthian church, but to all believers. He emphasizes that our freedom in Christ does not give us carte blanche to do anything and everything we please just because we are no longer under the curse of the law. Even though our salvation is not gained by good deeds or keeping legalistic rules, but is the free gift of God, Paul saw that God still commands us to maintain self-discipline in our Christian freedom. We still must obey His rules of conduct.

Thus Paul advocates that our Christian freedom is tied to our Christian responsibility. We have a responsibility to our weaker brother in Christ to facilitate his growth in Christ, not nullify or damage it. Paul taught that "God has combined the members of the body and has given greater honor to the parts that lacked it, so that there should be no division in the body, but that its parts should have equal concern for each other" (1 Corinthians 12:24-25, NIV). Then, in 13:4 (NIV), Paul says, "Love is patient, love is kind. It does not envy, it does not boast, it is not proud." Of course, real love for others produces empathy and sympathy that lead to tangible action in meeting their needs.

Through Paul's letter to the Corinthian church, Christians should recognize that God is calling every believer to live on a higher plane. Paul warned that if we cause our weaker brother to stumble by eating meat or doing anything that hurts our brother's walk with God, we have offended God as well. If we hurt one of God's children, we hurt God the Father, who will chastise us for our disobedience.

Paul knew that when God engages the human spirit through salvation, we are indeed concerned about our fellow man. He knew that when we are truly transformed by being filled with God's Spirit, love dominates our interactions with others. Therefore, true wisdom is knowing that we need God to order our steps. We need God to direct and guide us over the treacherous terrain of life so that we will not hinder our brother. We need the whole church, the united church, to fight the spiritual warfare that challenges us on every hand. God has the final word when it comes to righteousness, and we must all obey His edicts. We must submit to His will.

Finally, Paul wanted us to remember that love and righteousness are God's ways! A stronger believer may sometimes have to give up his rights to encourage, help, or protect his weaker brother. A mature Christian does this out of love, recognizing that he still hasn't given up as much as Jesus did. *He still hasn't given up all.* Christ gave His life so that we could be saved. There is no doubt that the enemy (Satan) had come into the Corinthian church like a flood. Paul wanted this quarreling congregation to yield to God so that His Spirit could lift up a standard against Satan (Isaiah 59:19).

DAILY BIBLE READINGS

M: Called to Life and Light
John 1:1-5
T: Do Not Tempt Others
Mark 9:42-48
W: Love Your Neighbor as Yourself
Mark 12:28-34
T: Do Not Make Another Stumble
Romans 14:13-19
F: We Have One God, One Lord
1 Corinthians 8:1-6
S: Do Not Create a Stumbling Block
1 Corinthians 8:7-13
S: Do All to God's Glory
1 Corinthians 10:23-11:1

TEACHING TIPS

July 16
Bible Study Guide 7

1. Words You Should Know

A. Striveth for the mastery (1 Corinthians 9:25) *agonizomai* (Gk.)—To struggle; literally, to compete for a prize; generally, to endeavor to accomplish something.

B. Temperate (v. 25) *egkrateuomai* (Gk.)—To exercise self-restraint (in diet and chastity).

C. Corruptible (v. 25) *phthartos* (Gk.)—Subject to decay; perishable.

D. Castaway (v. 27) *adokimos* (Gk.)—Disqualified; not approved, that is, rejected; worthless (literally or morally).

2. Teacher Preparation

A. Prayerfully read the FOCAL VERSES and the DEVOTIONAL READING.

B. Prayerfully study the entire BIBLE STUDY GUIDE 7. Highlight parts to emphasize.

C. Ask if anyone would like to share their experiences from last week's MAKE IT HAPPEN assignment.

D. Be prepared to discuss the false sense of security that pervades the Christian community.

3. Starting the Lesson

A. Assign a student to lead the class in prayer, focusing on the LESSON AIM.

B. Ask a student to read the IN FOCUS section.

C. Initiate a preliminary discussion about the demands of physical conditioning.

4. Getting into the Lesson

A. Allow each student to read some portion of THE PEOPLE, PLACES, AND TIMES, BACKGROUND, KEEP IN MIND, and AT-A-GLANCE sections.

B. Allow each student to read one of the FOCAL VERSES, and as each one is read, discuss and instruct using the portions of IN DEPTH and MORE LIGHT ON THE TEXT sections.

C. Ask the students to respond to the SEARCH THE SCRIPTURES questions.

5. Relating the Lesson to Life

A. Ask the students to respond to the DISCUSS THE MEANING questions.

B. Have someone read the LESSON IN OUR SOCIETY section and initiate comparisons.

6. Arousing Action

A. Read the MAKE IT HAPPEN section. Invite the students to share how God honored their self-sacrifice for the cause of Christ.

B. Ask the students to take a few minutes and record their responses to the FOLLOW THE SPIRIT and REMEMBER YOUR THOUGHTS sections.

C. Encourage the students to be prepared for next week's lesson.

D. Close the class with prayer.

WORSHIP GUIDE

For the Superintendent or Teacher
Theme: Called to Win the Race
Theme Song: "Higher Ground"
Scripture: Hebrews 12
Song: "Stand By Me"
Meditation: Dear Lord God, though we shun discomfort, we ask that You reinforce our will to be dedicated to every detail that is expected of us and is necessary. Stir our hearts, kindle our spirits, open our eyes, and deliver us from the evil one. Amen.

CALLED TO WIN THE RACE

Bible Background • 1 CORINTHIANS 9:24–10:13
Printed Text • 1 CORINTHIANS 9:24–10:13
Devotional Reading • HEBREWS 12:1–12

LESSON AIM

By the end of the lesson, we will:

KNOW that God has given us a race to win;

BE CONVINCED that the race of life can only be won with chastity, diligent effort, self-control, and confidence in God; and

BE FULLY COMMITTED to complete our assigned course.

KEEP IN MIND

"Know ye not that they which run in a race run all, but one receiveth the prize? So run, that ye may obtain" (1 Corinthians 9:24).

FOCAL VERSES

1 Corinthians 9:24 Know ye not that they which run in a race run all, but one receiveth the prize? So run, that ye may obtain.

25 And every man that striveth for the mastery is temperate in all things. Now they do it to obtain a corruptible crown; but we an incorruptible.

26 I therefore so run, not as uncertainly; so fight I, not as one that beateth the air:

27 But I keep under my body, and bring it into subjection: lest that by any means, when I have preached to others, I myself should be a castaway.

10:1 Moreover, brethren, I would not that ye should be ignorant, how that all our fathers were under the cloud, and all passed through the sea;

2 And were all baptized unto Moses in the cloud and in the sea;

3 And did all eat the same spiritual meat;

LESSON OVERVIEW

LESSON AIM
KEEP IN MIND
FOCAL VERSES
IN FOCUS
THE PEOPLE, PLACES, AND TIMES
BACKGROUND
AT-A-GLANCE
IN DEPTH
SEARCH THE SCRIPTURES
DISCUSS THE MEANING
LESSON IN OUR SOCIETY
MAKE IT HAPPEN
FOLLOW THE SPIRIT
REMEMBER YOUR THOUGHTS
MORE LIGHT ON THE TEXT
DAILY BIBLE READINGS

---

4 And did all drink the same spiritual drink: for they drank of that spiritual Rock that followed them: and that Rock was Christ.

5 But with many of them God was not well pleased: for they were overthrown in the wilderness.

6 Now these things were our examples, to the intent we should not lust after evil things, as they also lusted.

7 Neither be ye idolaters, as were some of them; as it is written, The people sat down to eat and drink, and rose up to play.

JULY 16TH

8 Neither let us commit fornication, as some of them committed, and fell in one day three and twenty thousand.

9 Neither let us tempt Christ, as some of them also tempted, and were destroyed of serpents.

10 Neither murmur ye, as some of them also murmured, and were destroyed of the destroyer.

11 Now all these things happened unto them for ensamples: and they are written for our admonition, upon whom the ends of the world are come.

12 Wherefore let him that thinketh he standeth take heed lest he fall.

13 There hath no temptation taken you but such as is common to man: but God is faithful, who will not suffer you to be tempted above that ye are able; but will with the temptation also make a way to escape, that ye may be able to bear it.

IN FOCUS

Race to God

Can you hear God softly speaking?
Gentle breezes—
Whispering

Win the crown
Victory—To those who run to Me

Can you hear our Lord?
Clouds of witnesses beside you
Listen—Sin-heavy flesh
Fights to finish
Trampled demons cry out—

Gospel Spirits whistle
Salvation's Prize
Awaits

Do you hear His promise?
Righteousness will anoint your stride
Those called to Him—

Listen
You will hear our Lord calling
Come to Me—

Love runs strong
Faith stays the course
Patience sets the pace

Can you hear God softly speaking?
Gentle breezes
Whispering

Victory
Victory
Everlasting Victory

Paul teaches that the Christian community is called by God to win the final prize. Do you know that God has given us a race to win?

THE PEOPLE, PLACES, AND TIMES

Athletic Games. Games were very important in the Greek culture. In fact, the Greeks were known for their athletic games. People from all parts of Greece attended the Olympian, Isthmian, Nemean, and Pythian games. The Olympian games were the most prestigious. They occurred every four years in honor of the Greek god, Zeus. The Isthmian games were held in Corinth (on Isthmus, see BIBLE STUDY GUIDE 1) in a grove sacred to the Greek god, Poseidon, in the second and fourth years of the Olympiad. The Nemean games took place in the valley of Nemea, at the end of each first and third years of an Olympiad, in honor of Zeus. The Pythian games were next to the Olympian games in importance, taking place in the third year of the Olympiad, below Delphi in central Greece. The prize for the winners was a wreath of leaves, but it was a great honor to win.

BACKGROUND

In chapter 8, the apostle Paul warns the Corinthian believers to "take heed lest by any means this liberty of yours (in Christ) become a stumblingblock to them that are weak (v. 9)." In chapter 9, Paul continues by presenting himself as an example of a person who denies himself of wages, comforts (such as a wife), and dignity (though free, he conducts himself as a slave) in order to achieve the goal of winning people for Christ.

AT-A-GLANCE

1. Run to Win (1 Corinthians 9:24-27)
2. Run with Knowledge (10:1-12)
3. Run with Confidence (v. 13)

IN DEPTH

1. Run to Win (1 Corinthians 9:24-27)

Paul proceeds with a cultural example of self-denial and determination in the lesson today. He relates to activities that the Gentiles in Corinth are quite familiar with. Knowing Corinth to be a commercial and cultural center of Greece and host to the Isthmian athletic games, the apostle Paul employs the example of a champion athlete as a model of the discipline and determination required to win an athletic event.

In any race, there can be only one winner

Starting the race and not finishing it is not good enough. Even completing the race does not entitle the competitor to a crown. The person who exerts himself or herself and finishes first according to the rules gets the crown. A strict regimen of practice, conditioning, diet, and training puts the competitor in a position to win. This regimen proceeds regardless of environment or how one feels on a given day. Self-serving activities cannot be satisfied—they must be denied.

Athletic training is a classic example of self-discipline in order to achieve a goal. In the Christian race, all participants who complete their course receive their crown (2 Timothy 4:8; Revelation 3:11); nevertheless, Paul urges the Christian to run like the victor in the games. Put forth the same effort, training, and dedication that the one champion of the games puts forth in your own Christian service. Run as if it is a "win or lose" situation with no in-between. Do the best that you can do. Every Christian has their own individual race to win. (There will be different degrees of reward based on works of faith (cf. 2 Corinthians 5:10; Romans 14:12; 1 Corinthians 3:14).)

Paul says that he beats his own body into subjection. He makes his body cooperate (leads it like a slave in submission) with requirements for success. The "flesh" often represents the fallen or sinful nature in humankind (Romans 8:13). Any thought or desire contrary to the direction and work of the Holy Spirit must be beaten into submission or eliminated. The body is the temple of the Holy Spirit. It should be the dwelling place of God. The servant cannot allow contamination of the body with profane or immoral deeds. Engaged in warfare, the embattled saint is able to say by the Holy Spirit, "Thanks be unto God who gives me the victory!" Complete submission, self-denial, and effort are required so that, after preaching and ministering to others, the servant is not disapproved (or in athletic terms disqualified). The lazy and self-gratifying person will not have an assurance of reward.

2. Run with Knowledge (10:1-12)

The example of the Israelites' exodus from Egypt and the failure of many to reach the Promised Land is a solemn warning to followers of Jesus Christ. In spite of all that God had provided on their behalf, and in spite of all the miraculous works (even in Egypt) that they witnessed for themselves, most of them failed to complete the course.

All the Israelites left Egypt. All were led under the guidance of a pillar of cloud by day and a pillar of fire to give them light by night. This symbolized divine presence and security because God led the way both day and night. All miraculously passed through the parting waters of the Red Sea on dry ground. All were shepherded and instructed by Moses throughout their journey. Passing through the Red Sea, while guided by the cloud under the authority of Moses, associated them with Moses in the same manner that water baptism associates and places Christians under the authority of Christ. All ate the food, including the manna from heaven that God miraculously provided. There was no natural food, adequate for so many people, available to them in the desert. Thus some scholars estimate that there were over two million people. Thus "spiritual meat" or spiritual food was provided by a special intervention of God.

All drank the water (provided by a special intervention of God—spiritual drink) miraculously provided from the Rock. The Israelites were constantly supplied with water miraculously, and the Source of that spiritual water was Jesus Christ. Jewish tradition states that the Rock literally moved with the Israelites as they journeyed. Some see in Psalm 105:4 the possibility that the waters from the Rock followed them like a river gushing forth. The probable meaning of verse 4 is that Christ (the spiritual Rock) followed them. It was He who supplied their wants. The manna and the water were spiritual in their origin. The Rock was spiritual in its essence. "Rock" is figurative language in the same sense as Christ is the "Vine." Here, and in verse 9, is an affirmation for the pre-incarnated Christ in Old Testament times.

The next characteristic of the Israelites to be avoided is idolatry (Exodus 32:6). The Israelites used a golden calf as an object of worship to represent the one true God and they proclaimed a feast. Some of the Corinthians made a similar mistake by participating in feasts in the temple of the gods. Neither thought that they did anything wrong. God prohibits His people from worshiping any representation of Himself. God's people must worship God alone (Exodus 20:5).

Historically, there has always been an association between idolatry and fornication among pagan nations. Many pagan religions used prostitutes as a way of relating to their gods. One of the first examples given in the Bible occurred in Moab (Numbers 25:1-9). This practice was also prevalent in Corinth. Fornication is another example of gross self-indulgence that we must avoid. God considers it spiritual fornication or adultery when those who are His abandon Him for another object of adoration.

There are two possible incidents that Paul could be referring to here—when the Israelites committed fornication and idolatry in Moab or when they "rose up to play" after sacrificing to the golden calf (Exodus 32:6). The difficulty with the Moab incident is that 24,000 people are recorded as slain. The author in Numbers or Paul could have been speaking in round numbers, but it is more probable that Paul is still speaking of the golden calf incident at Mount Sinai. The expression "rose up to play" allows for more than just dancing and can include revelry, drunkenness, and immoral activities as was common in pagan worship. The Living Bible (TLB) clearly states what happened, "So they were up early the next morning and began offering burnt offerings and peace offerings to the calf idol; afterwards they sat down to feast and drink at a wild party, followed by sexual immorality" (Exodus 32:6). In this case, the number of those killed is recorded in Exodus 32:35.

People tempt God when they put His wisdom, His power, or His integrity to the test. This is forbidden (Matthew 4:7). This passage equates Christ with God. He is the authority to whom people of God answer. The Israelites tried God with impatience and contempt. They spoke against the direction and will of God and questioned His ability to sustain them (Numbers 21:4-9). God killed many of them with venomous snakes that had a fiery lethal bite.

The term "murmur" means to complain against God with a rebellious heart. The Israelites did so out of discontent with God. They murmured against the judgment and punishment of God, and they murmured against the leaders that He chose, directed, and supported (Numbers 16:41-50; compare 14:2). A plague destroyed 14,700 people. The agent used was an angel (destroyer—Exodus 12:23; 2 Samuel 24:16). Again as stated in verse 6, these events are historical pictures used to admonish the people of God against committing these sins and receiving punishment from God.

When the Israelites crossed the Red Sea and saw the Egyptian army destroyed, they probably thought that their distress had ended. Many of them were lured into a false sense of security. They misused their freedom from slavery and became overconfident. It is not enough to just start out, nor is it enough to be the recipient of divine favors. Their privileges did not save them from death in the wilderness.

Many church attendees have a false sense of security. Their assurance is not anchored in submission to Christ but rather in the participation of religious activities. To the church, Paul writes, "Let him who thinks himself secure, to take heed to what happen to the chosen people in the wilderness; otherwise, the same will happen to you" (10:12, paraphrased). Self-denial and effort are required. Believers must persevere in holiness to the end. The Christian must press toward the mark for the prize of the high calling of God in Christ Jesus.

3. Run with Confidence (v. 13)

The word "temptation" can also be translated as a "test" or "trial" for the purpose of proving one's character. It is a trial for those who are obedient to God and place their confidence in Him. A trial is an opportunity for growth and maturity. It is a temptation to those who disobey God and lose faith in Him (James 1:2-4, 12-15). Humans are only subject to temptations that are "common to man." To endure God will not allow anything to happen that the child of God cannot bear. The integrity of God is at stake. He is faithful and trustworthy. The only security the people of God have rests in this fact. If God is the author of the trial, "with the trial," He provides or designs a way of escape (out of the trial). If the enemy brings temptation (solicits or attempts to seduce into sin), God "makes" a way of escape. The committed, diligent servants can run to win with the confidence that God will preserve them.

SEARCH THE SCRIPTURES

1. Name three characteristics that Paul says the successful runner must have (1 Corinthians 9:25).

2. What does Paul do to avoid disqualification (vv. 26-27)?

3. Who were the people referred to as "our fathers" and where did this period in history take place (vv. 10:1, 5)?

4. What did "our fathers" fail to do (v. 5)?

5. What were the five examples of failures (vv. 6-10)?

DISCUSS THE MEANING

1. What makes the champion athlete a good example for Christian service?

2. Which verse sums up the lesson learned from the performance of "our fathers"?

3. What is the difference between a temptation and a trial?

4. Complete the following statement, "A false sense of security leads to _____."

LESSON IN OUR SOCIETY

Here are a few comments from a career website for athletes: "People in this career consider achievement important. They like to see the results of their work and to use their strongest abilities. They like to get a feeling of accomplishment from their work. They consider support from their employer important." Try to identify parallels to those in Christian service.

MAKE IT HAPPEN

Make a commitment to practice these conditioning activities: studying, praying, obedience, self-denial, time allocation, effort, and endurance. Be prepared to report on your progress and the results.

FOLLOW THE SPIRIT

What God wants me to do:

_____

_____

REMEMBER YOUR THOUGHTS

Special insights I have learned:

_____

_____

MORE LIGHT ON THE TEXT

1 Corinthians 9:24-10:13

24 Know ye not that they which run in a race run all, but one receiveth the prize? So run, that ye may obtain.

In previous verses, Paul exhorted believers to give up their "rights," to think first of others, and to focus on bringing others to Christ. He challenged Christians to deny themselves as they anticipated future reward. In 1 Corinthians 9:24-10:13, Paul continued that theme by comparing the Christian life to a race and by contrasting this race to the ancient Isthmian games. In those ancient games, only one received the prize, even though all ran. In the Christian race, if all run, all will receive the prize: "So run, that ye may obtain."

The Hebrew word *trecho* (**trekh'-o**), translated as "run," expresses the decisiveness of the act of running. The same Hebrew word is used in Matthew 28:8 to describe the actions of the women when they joyfully ran to tell the disciples that they had seen the risen Lord! In Matthew 28:8, the women were focused on telling the disciples what they had seen. In this passage, Christians are told to run the race with their eyes focused on the reward to be obtained by faithful believers.

25 And every man that striveth for the mastery is temperate in all things. Now they do it to obtain a corruptible crown; but we an incorruptible.

To get into the games and emerge as victors, athletes had to be of a respectable family. (The family of God certainly qualifies as a respectable family!) These athletes had to be "temperate in all things" (practicing self-control). Typically, for 10 months prior to the games, dedicated athletes denied themselves ordinary pleasures in order to prepare and be in top condition for the competition. They observed a strict regimen, ate food they might have disliked, abstained from delicacies, and faithfully exercised whether it was hot or cold outside! During the contest, athletes set aside everything and put forth their greatest effort in order to win the prize. They endured much, even though they were uncertain of victory.

One lesson that we can learn from this verse is that believers who faithfully run the race are assured victory. Believers are to put out the same amount of effort to gain the reward of God's kingdom that an athlete expends to win a mere wreath. The redeemed are to willingly practice self-control and focus on bringing others to Christ because they are running toward an eternal prize.

The crowns won by the victors in the various ancient games were corruptible, being made of the wild olive, parsley, or pine branches. They began to disintegrate as soon as they were cut from the trees or pulled out of the ground. In contrast, the Christian's crown, a heavenly inheritance, is incorruptible. It does not relate to worldly honor but to honor that comes from God.

26 I therefore so run, not as uncertainly; so fight I, not as one that beateth the air:

The word *adeelos* (**ad-ay'-loce**), translated as "uncertainly," has other meanings, as well. First, it denotes ignorance. Paul did not run like one ignorant of what he was doing. He knew the laws of the course and the way to the end. He knew the reward had eternal significance. His eyes were fixed on a definite goal (2 Timothy 1:12). In this race, all who ran as they ought to would receive the prize. Second, it communicates that he knew that the eyes of all the spectators were fixed on the runners. The world waited for him to fall, the church watched with anxiety, and God, who saw every step, was willing and able to strengthen him, encourage him, and to lift him up.

27 But I keep under my body, and bring it into subjection: lest that by any means, when I have preached to others, I myself should be a castaway.

In this passage and in the previous ones, Paul the apostle spoke of three competitions from the Isthmian games: (1) Running (1 Corinthians 9:24, 26); (2) Wrestling (1 Corinthians 9:25: "Every man that striveth," or "he who wrestleth" and (3) Boxing (1 Corinthians 9:26-27). In all cases, the athlete had to work hard to keep his body in subjection. The word "rejected" or "reprobate," translated here as "a castaway," is a metaphor taken from the testing of metals and the disposing of those that are false.

Athletes were supposed to keep to a strict diet and observe the laws of racing. The announcer prevented people of bad character from being included in the Olympic games. As each participant was brought before him, he would ask, "Who can accuse this man?" In verse 27, Paul indicated the possibility that he (the announcer and the preacher) could become a castaway (rejected by the great Judge) even though other portions of Scripture described the redeemed as having a secure position, saved by grace, under the blood of Christ, and bought with a price! First Corinthians 9:27 should serve as a warning to those unrepentant Christians who trample on the gift that God has given them by living a lukewarm life of willful disobedience even though they are given clear directives in Scripture.

Paul considered his old nature to be an enemy that must be mortified by self-denial, abstinence, and labor. His body was to be his slave instead of him being the slave of his body. Paul stated that a person must strive lawfully. He indicated that it is possible to lose the crown if a Christian does not fight the good fight or finish the course. This means that believers who become lazy are vulnerable to Satan's attacks and are, therefore, at risk of losing their reward (see Romans 7:14-25).

Self-control requires us to say "no" to behaviors condemned by Scripture and "yes" to righteous behaviors. Say "no" to situations or friends that will lead you away from Christ and "yes" to positive relationships and regular time spent with God in prayer and meditation.

Are you a self-controlled person who has committed yourself to learning godly attitudes that do not come naturally? Have you changed your focus from natural appetites to God's purposes? In what areas do you need to grow? Find a friend to serve as an accountability and prayer partner so that you can keep your eyes focused on the prize.

10:1 Moreover, brethren, I would not that ye should be ignorant, how that all our fathers were under the cloud, and all passed through the sea;

Paul had previously used his own example to show the importance of careful watchfulness and effort. Here he used history. By saying, "I would not that ye should be ignorant," Paul did not refer to ignorance of the facts, but of the meaning of the facts. The Corinthians had mistakenly taken their salvation for granted since they had taken part in the ordinances of the Gospel, such as baptism and the Lord's Supper. Because of this, they felt free to trample on their salvation by participating in idolatrous feasts! Paul reminded them that the ancient Israelites has been given a privileged position, yet they were still subject to judgment due to their disobedience.

Exodus tells how God gave the Israelites a dynamic leader (Moses) and used great miracles to deliver them from slavery in Egypt (Exodus 1-12). God's very presence, represented by a miraculous cloud, guided them through the wilderness and toward the Promised Land! During the day, the cloud shaded them from the scorching rays of the sun and sprinkled them with moisture to refresh them and their livestock (Exodus 13:21). At night, the cloud provided continued guidance and light. God brought them all safely through the waters of the Red Sea on dry ground (Exodus 14). He provided them with food (manna). In spite of all the miracles, though, many Israelites turned away even though all of them experienced the miracles of God's protection and guidance. They thought that, as "God's people," they were assured the Promised Land. In reality, their disobedience disqualified them from entering the Promised Land. Their privileged position did not spare them from judgment.

The Jews' ancestors were a perfect Old Testament example that contradicted the false idea that a saved person could live a faithless life without being judged. The Israelites had been delivered from Egyptian oppression, but they were still captive to the lust and unbelief in their hearts. Similarly Christians today have the wonderful heritage of God's faithfulness as well as a lengthy history of human sinfulness. We are admonished to learn from the past instead of repeating the same mistakes.

2 And were all baptized unto Moses in the cloud and in the sea;

The Israelites were baptized into the covenant mediated by Moses. Because of this, they were under obligation to act according to that Mosaic covenant. In comparison, Christians who have received Christian baptism are described in Scripture as being baptized *into* Christ, being obligated to keep the requirements of the Gospel covenant.

3 And did all eat the same spiritual meat; 4 And did all drink the same spiritual drink: for they drank of that spiritual Rock that followed them: and that Rock was Christ.

The manna was called spiritual because it was provided supernaturally by God, and because it was a type of Christ Jesus (John 6:31; 10:33, 48). (Note that Jesus calls Himself the Bread of Life in John 6:48.) God also provided the spiritual drink as Moses struck the rock (Exodus 17:1-7; Numbers 20:2-13). Paul indicated that Christ was the Rock who had actually accompanied and sustained the Israelites during their journey. The Old Testament often refers to God as a "rock" (Genesis 49:24; Deuteronomy 32:4; 2 Samuel 22:32). The term "rock" is also used to refer to Jesus in the New Testament. The Greek word used for "rock" in either case refers to a massive boulder, not a pebble.

5 But with many of them God was not well pleased: for they were overthrown in the wilderness.

Of the Israelites who were led out of Egypt by Moses, all but Caleb and Joshua died due to their disobedience and unbelief (Numbers 26:64-65; comp. Jude 5). This was in spite of the fact that they were all under the cloud, were passed through the sea, and were baptized into Moses. They all ate the same spiritual meat and drank the same spiritual drink and were made partakers of the spiritual Rock, Christ.

6 Now these things were our examples, to the intent we should not lust after evil things, as they also lusted. 7 Neither be ye idolaters, as were some of them; as it is written, The people sat down to eat and drink, and rose up to play.

It appears that the Corinthians lusted after the sinful practices that took place during the idol feasts and therefore frequented them. The judgments that God inflicted on the Israelites are presented as examples of what happens to Christians who walk in sin. The examples of sin were specific: idolatry, sexual immorality, testing the Lord, and complaining. The consequences were death. The Corinthians' sin was similar in nature as that of the rebellious Israelites who were punished. If God did not spare the rebellious Israelites, there was no possibility that the rebellious Corinthians would be spared.

Romans 1:22-25 describes "idolatry" as the sin of the mind against God. An "idolater" is a slave to the warped ideas that his idols represent. In Exodus 32, the people were condemned for worshiping an idol and for indulging in "pagan revelry." "Revelry" referred to singing, shouting, and dancing that promoted sexual immorality. They dishonored God when they said they were really worshiping God by participating in idol festivals. God does not overlook sin, and neither should his followers.

8 Neither let us commit fornication, as some of them committed, and fell in one day three and twenty thousand.

Fornication was actually a consecrated part of idol worship. The Israelites participated in sexual immorality as a part of their worship of Baal. This was the reason that 23,000 of them died in one day!

God has many laws about sexual sin because it is powerful and destructive in the church and in individual relationships (Colossians 3:5-8). This is why the Bible sets forth strong rules. The intimacy of sex is reserved only for marriage. Sexual sin brings confusion and will tear down the respect and trust so necessary for enduring marriages and well-adjusted children.

Many things can become "idols" to Christians. It is so easy to allow things like money, fame, work, things, or pleasure to become gods. As we focus more of our time, attention, and thoughts on these things, they can become objects of worship above the One True God, the Creator of the Universe! He alone is worthy of worship! We must work to give Him the central place in our lives.

9 Neither let us tempt Christ, as some of them also tempted, and were destroyed of serpents.

Christians "tempt Christ" by disbelieving the goodness and providence of God and by arrogantly telling Him how He should do things. While in the wilderness, the people complained (Numbers 21:5; cf. Exodus 16:31-32; Hebrews 3-4): "And the people spake against God, and against Moses, Wherefore have ye brought us up out of Egypt to die in the wilderness? for there is no bread, neither is there any water; and our soul loatheth this light bread." They tested God to see how much they could get away with, and He sent poisonous snakes among them to punish them for their complaining attitudes.

10 Neither murmur ye, as some of them also murmured, and were destroyed of the destroyer.

In this case, the Corinthian Christians were complaining how Paul was stopping them from participating in the idolatrous feasts. The phrase "destroyed of the destroyer" (v. 10) is significant. The Jews thought that God used destroying angels to punish those ancient rebellious Israelites. God viewed it seriously when Christians grumbled against Him or His leaders because those leaders were applying God's Word.

It's easy to complain about what we don't have, instead of focusing on what we do have. God had done a lot for the Israelites; He had set them free, had done miracles for them, and had given them a new land. However, instead of being thankful, they focused on what God wasn't doing for them. They could only think of the delicious Egyptian food that they had left behind (Numbers 11:5). Time had caused the torturous conditions that they had been delivered from to fade in intensity. Are we guilty of doing the same thing? Are we grateful for God's great provision or do we focus on what we would like to have? If so, we need to change our focus or we may miss God's blessing!

11 Now all these things happened unto them for ensamples: and they are written for our admonition, upon whom the ends of the world are come.

In Romans 15:4(NIV), we see this same concept, "For everything that was written in the past was written to teach us." In 1 Corinthians 11:30, Paul indicated that the Corinthian Christians were facing an unusual amount of sickness and death because of their sinful actions. One should not come to the conclusion, though, that all sickness and death is a result of personal sin. Our bodies are temporary housings available only to us while we reside on this earth. In the future, we will gain new bodies! At the same time, though, it is true that some sickness is a result of sin.

The Israelites received punishment when they disobeyed. In the same way, Christians who sin without repentance or desire to change and without concern for God's laws, will also receive judgment.

12 Wherefore let him that thinketh he standeth take heed lest he fall.

The Corinthians were proud of their declaration, "an idol is nothing in the world." They were right in a sense that there is only One True God but they were wrong in opening themselves and other, weaker, brothers, up to temptation. Their arrogance put them at risk of falling away. Paul was telling them the same thing that he had told the Romans, "Be not highminded, but fear" (Romans 11:20). Paul warned that if the Israelites fell into idolatry, so could some in the Corinthian church. No human being is ever beyond temptation while they live on this earth! Believers were cautioned to keep their guard up or they might fall. Paul was challenging the Corinthians to walk humbly before God and to stay clear of even the appearance of evil! They were urged to place their confidence in God instead of their own personal effort.

It is important that we listen to this warning, for not even the most godly person can stand unless he or she depends on God's strength and walks in faithful obedience. Failing to do so leads to a coldness of heart and understanding. Our own recent history is full of tragic examples of moral and ethical failures among Christians who grew lax.

13 There hath no temptation taken you but such as is common to man: but God is faithful, who will not suffer you to be tempted above that ye are able; but will with the temptation also make a way to escape, that ye may be able to bear it.

While the previous verse was a warning, verse 13 is a welcome encouragement. We should be glad that Paul reminds us that temptations are common to man and are to be expected. We are not expected, though, to go through the temptation alone. With any temptation, God makes a way out. He is willing and able to deliver us if we will trust Him as our Source and our Strength. God is faithful to those whom He has called to be His children. When Satan tries to block our way, God makes a way, around or through the wall (2 Thessalonians 3:3)! The trial will never be above the strength that God gives to bear it. But the key is that we must rely on Him as our strength!

Paul gives strong encouragement about temptation to those of us who live in a sin-depraved culture. He tells us: "You aren't the only one who has wrong desires and temptations at times. Others have resisted temptation and you can too. God has promised to help you resist in His Strength. Stay away from even the appearance of evil. Be aware of people and situations that create trouble for you. Run from anything you know is wrong" (2 Timothy 2:22, paraphrased).

DAILY BIBLE READINGS

M: Run the Race with Perseverance
Hebrews 12:1-12
T: Keep Alert and Always Persevere
Ephesians 6:10-20
W: Be Doers, Not Just Hearers
James 1:19-27
T: Press on Toward the Goal
Philippians 3:12-16
F: Run for the Gospel's Sake
1 Corinthians 9:22-27
S: Do Not Follow Our Ancestors
1 Corinthians 10:1-7
S: God Will Help You Endure Testing
1 Corinthians 10:8-13

TEACHING TIPS

July 23
Bible Study Guide 8

1. Words You Should Know
A. Diversities (1 Corinthians 12:4) *diairesis* (Gk.)—A distinction or variety.

B. Gifts (v. 4) *charisma* (Gk.)—A divine gratuity; a spiritual endowment, that is, a spiritual qualification or miraculous faculty.

C. Administrations (v. 5) *diakonia* (Gk.)—Attendance as a servant; services of a Christian.

D. Operations (v. 6) *energema* (Gk.)—An effect or result.

E. Baptized (v. 13) *baptizo* (Gk.)—To make clean; to wash.

2. Teacher Preparation
A. Prayerfully read the FOCAL VERSES and DEVOTIONAL READING.

B. Prayerfully study the entire BIBLE STUDY GUIDE. Highlight parts to emphasize.

C. Be prepared to discuss the challenge offered in the MAKE IT HAPPEN section.

D. Look for situations in your church that may indicate that believers are neglecting supernatural gifts. Be familiar with other spiritual gifts listed in BIBLE BACKGROUND.

3. Starting the Lesson
A. Assign a student to lead the class in prayer, focusing on the LESSON AIM.

B. Ask a student to read the IN FOCUS section.

C. Poll the students' awareness of their spiritual gift(s) and service that utilize their spiritual gift(s).

4. Getting into the Lesson
A. Allow each student to read some portion of THE PEOPLE, PLACES, AND TIMES, BACKGROUND, KEEP IN MIND, and AT-A-GLANCE sections.

B. Allow each student to read one of the FOCAL VERSES. As each one is read, discuss and instruct using the portions of IN DEPTH and MORE LIGHT ON THE TEXT sections that you highlighted in your preparation.

C. Ask the students to respond to the SEARCH THE SCRIPTURES questions.

5. Relating the Lesson to Life
A. Ask the students to respond to the DISCUSS THE MEANING questions.

B. Have someone read LESSON IN OUR SOCIETY and respond to it.

6. Arousing Action
A. Ask a student to read aloud the KEEP IN MIND verse again and then the MAKE IT HAPPEN section. Be sure to emphasize their obligation to Christ and others.

B. Ask the students to take a few minutes to record their responses to the FOLLOW THE SPIRIT and REMEMBER YOUR THOUGHTS sections.

C. Encourage the students to be prepared for next week's lesson.

D. Close the class with prayer.

CALLED TO THE COMMON GOOD

Bible Background • 1 CORINTHIANS 12:1–13
Printed Text • 1 CORINTHIANS 12:1–13
Devotional Reading • 1 CORINTHIANS 12:27–31

LESSON AIM

By the end of the lesson, we will:

KNOW that all believers receive spiritual gifts for the benefit of all members of Christ;

BE CONVINCED that all believers have an obligation to use their spiritual gift(s) as the Holy Spirit directs; and

BE MOTIVATED to constantly petition Jesus Christ to fill us with the Holy Spirit for every good work.

KEEP IN MIND

"But the manifestation of the Spirit is given to every man to profit withal" (1 Corinthians 12:7).

LESSON OVERVIEW

LESSON AIM
KEEP IN MIND
FOCAL VERSES
IN FOCUS
THE PEOPLE, PLACES, AND TIMES
BACKGROUND
AT-A-GLANCE
IN DEPTH
SEARCH THE SCRIPTURES
DISCUSS THE MEANING
LESSON IN OUR SOCIETY
MAKE IT HAPPEN
FOLLOW THE SPIRIT
REMEMBER YOUR THOUGHTS
MORE LIGHT ON THE TEXT
DAILY BIBLE READINGS

FOCAL VERSES

1 Corinthians 12:1 1 Now concerning spiritual gifts, brethren, I would not have you ignorant.

2 Ye know that ye were Gentiles, carried away unto these dumb idols, even as ye were led.

3 Wherefore I give you to understand, that no man speaking by the Spirit of God calleth Jesus accursed: and that no man can say that Jesus is the Lord, but by the Holy Ghost.

4 Now there are diversities of gifts, but the same Spirit.

5 And there are differences of administrations, but the same Lord.

6 And there are diversities of operations, but it is the same God which worketh all in all.

7 But the manifestation of the Spirit is given to every man to profit withal.

8 For to one is given by the Spirit the word of wisdom; to another the word of knowledge by the same Spirit;

9 To another faith by the same Spirit; to another the gifts of healing by the same Spirit;

10 To another the working of miracles; to another prophecy; to another discerning of spirits; to another divers kinds of tongues; to another the interpretation of tongues:

11 But all these worketh that one and the selfsame Spirit, dividing to every man severally as he will.

12 For as the body is one, and hath many members, and all the members of that one body, being many, are one body: so also is Christ.

JULY 23RD

13 For by one Spirit are we all baptized into one body, whether we be Jews or Gentiles, whether we be bond or free; and have been all made to drink into one Spirit.

IN FOCUS

As a young boy, I used to sit in my grandma Mary's Alabama kitchen and listen to her hum gospel music as she baked. Smelling the yeast in the rising breads and the cinnamon and butter in the pies, I would be filled with a warm feeling of peace, contentment, and love. It was the love she poured into every dessert that made them famous.

What my grandmother did with her cakes was also legendary. Whenever there was a death in the congregation or someone was going through a tough time, Grandma Mary would be Johnny-on-the-spot with one of her famous chocolate, coconut, or golden brown pound cakes. Grandma Mary remembered who liked which cake, and she would match the cake to the person and the occasion.

Grandma Mary, as far as I know, had one gift, the gift of making cakes. She used that gift beautifully as a tangible sign of her love, concern, support, and encouragement. In fact, whenever I think about the biblical phrase, "the ministry of encouragement," I think of Grandma Mary and her cakes.

Grandma Mary's great gift was not simply making desserts, but it was knowing that she, as a Christian, had an obligation and opportunity to use whatever gift God had given her for the good of others.

The apostle Paul teaches all believers have spiritual gifts that can benefit the body of Christ. Do you recognize the spiritual gifts that you have to edify the church?

THE PEOPLE, PLACES, AND TIMES

The Corinthians. During this time, the Corinthians had begun to misuse their spiritual gifts. Some of them were envious of others and often pitted their spiritual gifts against one another in an attempt to prove who was the more spiritual or gifted church member. Some were puffed up as they put on a public display. Some made false proclamations. Others caused confusion in the worship services. Their practices were self-serving. As a result, the most needful (best) gifts were not utilized and the people suffered.

BACKGROUND

The sole purpose of the Holy Spirit empowering Christians is to glorify Jesus Christ. Jesus told His disciples, "But, you will receive power when the Holy Spirit comes on you; and you will be my witnesses" (Acts 1:8, NIV). Ancient prophets also predicted the outpouring of spiritual gifts on all flesh (Joel 2:28-29). This prophecy was first fulfilled on the Day of Pentecost after the ascension to heaven of Jesus Christ. Spiritual gifts are distributed to all classes of people. These gifts enable believers to be instruments of the Holy

Spirit. Some are greater in usefulness, but none should be despised. The proper motive for desiring and using gifts is love (a way of excellence).

AT-A-GLANCE

1. The Holy Spirit Glorifies Jesus Christ (1 Corinthians 12:1-3)
2. The Holy Spirit Distributes Gifts to Serve the Body of Christ (vv. 4-11)
3. The Holy Spirit Unifies Believers in the Body of Christ (vv. 12-13)

IN DEPTH

1. The Holy Spirit Glorifies Jesus Christ (1 Corinthians 12:1-3)

Paul proceeds to correct ministry and worship practices in the Corinthian church. Concerning spiritual "gifts" or "matters," by context, the church should not be ignorant due to a lack of information or understanding. So it is the intent of Paul to teach them.

The Corinthians were Greeks, and as such, Gentiles who worshiped false gods prior to their conversion to Christ. Their past practices were governed by fallen spirits that they did not understand. They could not resist the influences of idolatry. This is in contrast to the leading of the Holy Spirit, which is not forced upon the individual and leads to good practices.

The believer needs a criterion for recognizing the works of the Holy Spirit. There must be a distinction made between what a person can say, what an evil spirit can say, and what the Holy Spirit can say. A person can say anything of his own volition. No person speaking under the influence of the Holy Spirit can say that Jesus is accursed (that is, anathema, which means justly condemned to death). The Holy Spirit does not speak anything that takes away from the Person of Jesus Christ. The word "Lord" here, is the common word used to represent the word "Yahweh" in the Old Testament. The work of the Holy Spirit is to glorify Jesus. To truly believe and confess from the heart that Jesus is God manifested in the flesh requires the illumination of the Holy Spirit (Matthew 16:17; 1 John 4:2-3, 15). This confession and submission are confirmed by the conduct of the person (1 John 4:12, 16).

2. The Holy Spirit Distributes Gifts to Serve the Body of Christ (vv. 4-11)

The apostle next talks about the relationship between the spiritual manifestations and each member of the Godhead. These are not three different classes but rather three different aspects with relation to the Person of the Godhead. Viewed in relation to the Holy Spirit, they are "gifts." Viewed in relation to Jesus Christ (Lord), they are ministries or services. Viewed in relation to the Father, they are effects (operations) wrought by His power.

There are diversities (distinctions or a variety) of spiritual gifts (an endowment of a miraculous faculty, that is, a supernatural capability freely given by the Holy Spirit; "grace-gift"), but they all proceed from one and the same Holy Spirit. There are differences of ministrations (ministries or services) but the one and same Lord. All the different ministries or services are for the one Lord and under His authority. There are diversities of effects, but the same Father, who exalted the Lord Jesus Christ and sent the Holy Spirit.

The Holy Spirit alone is the source, but the manifestation of His gifts is available to all members of the body of Christ. The indwelling Holy Spirit will exhibit one aspect of His works in one person and another aspect of His works in a different person. The purpose is for everyone's profit or benefit (edification). Believers are equipped with spiritual gifts for the work of the ministry (Ephesians 4:12). The idea is that all members will contribute to one another by bearing the ministry together. This interdependence is by design, since no one person is empowered to minister to every need. People give natural gifts to benefit the recipient, but spiritual gifts are given so that the recipient can benefit other people. Using a spiritual gift for self-exaltation, self-satisfaction, or self-profit is an abuse of God's grace.

Neglecting your grace-gift causes other members to suffer (1 Timothy 4:14). Sadly many believers are ignorant of their grace-gift and their obligation to fellow believers. Pastors (or church leaders) are not the only people with the responsibility to minister to others. In the parable of the talents (Matthew 25:14-30), two men with different abilities received the same reward for their faithfulness in using what they had while the third was condemned for neglecting his responsibility. The story illustrates the gravity of wasted opportunity. The diversity of spiritual gifts is illustrated; though this is not a comprehensive list since other Scripture verses provide additional types of spiritual gifts (see 1 Corinthians 12:28; Romans 12:6; Ephesians 4:11; 1 Peter 4:10).

The first gift mentioned in this passage is "a word of wisdom." It is wisdom communicated or spoken. Since wisdom is the ability to understand God's will (which is always best), as it applies to situations in life, this gift enables the believer to speak to the specific circumstance of another believer. The gift of "a word of wisdom" applies God's truth in a way that brings the believer in line with the will and purpose of God. It is the practical application of God's Word to the problem at hand. This wisdom may defy conventional wisdom or it may venture into "uncharted waters." This wisdom is revealed by God and is unknown without divine illumination. This gift may have been manifested in the disciples' decision to appoint seven deacons (Acts 6:1-6).

The gift of "a word of knowledge" is closely related to the gift of wisdom. It is the general application of knowledge from Scripture communicated or spoken with authority. Some see in this gift the ability to understand and speak God's truth with insight that can only be provided by God. Paul often prayed for believers to be filled with wisdom and knowledge (Ephesians 1:17-23; Colossians 1:9-10). Jesus said that the Spirit of God would testify of Him, teach all things, and guide into all truth (John 15:26; 14:26; 16:13). These illuminations enable the believers to know the hope of their calling, the riches of their inheritance, and the exceeding greatness of God's power toward them. Given this knowledge, the believer walks in a manner worthy of the Lord, pleasing Him in all respects, and bearing fruit in every good work.

The spiritual gift of faith is distinct from saving faith, which is common to all believers. The gift of faith enables the believer to do extraordinary things by the power of God. Gifts of healing(s) are plural. The supernatural gift of healing not only reverses the condition (cures), but also draws attention to the divine power that performs it, so as to prompt those who witness it to glorify God (Luke 5:17; 6:19; 8:46-47).

The working(s) of miracles or, literally, the effects of miraculous powers, are deeds of mighty power that go beyond what is humanly possible. Such was the case when Paul, filled with the Holy Spirit, pronounced blindness on Elymas, a magician who attempted to turn a man that sought to hear the Word of God from the faith (Acts 13:11).

The gift of prophecy enables the believer to speak words to others that are inspired by the Holy Spirit. Generally, the purpose is to exhort, edify, and comfort (1 Corinthians 14:3). Foretelling of future events is sometimes inspired (Acts 11:28). This gift also convicts and brings to repentance by exposing the hidden thoughts of the heart (1 Corinthians 14:24-25). The illuminations associated with this gift discloses hidden conditions and circumstances. In some cases, part of the knowledge revealed to the "gifted one" may already be known to the recipient to serve as an affirmation of further instruction.

The gift of "discerning of spirits" enables believers "to separate thoroughly" or "to distinguish" between the inspiration and works of the Holy Spirit and other spirits (human or demonic). There is a spirit of deception that believers must guard against (1 John 4:1) and prophetic utterances must be tested as well (1 Thessalonians 5:20-21).

The gift of (divers) kinds of tongues enables the believer to speak a language previously unknown and unlearned. The Holy Spirit "gives utterance," that is, reveals the words to speak on a given occasion. A good description of this manifestation is given in the second chapter of Acts. This gift can be used for prayer, praise, and thanksgiving (1 Corinthians 14:14-17). It can be used to prophesy if interpretation of the language is provided (1 Corinthians 14:13). Without interpretation, it does not exhort, edify, convict, or comfort others, and therefore, is inappropriate in a public assembly of worship. In the absence of interpretation, believers speak only to God and edify only themselves (1 Corinthians 14:1, 4). This is only suitable for private devotion (v. 28).

All the different spiritual gifts originate from the same Holy Spirit. What was performed by God the Father in verse 6 is now also attributed to God the Holy Spirit. They are one in essence and work together. The Holy Spirit also distributes these gifts to every believer as He sees fit, that is, as He wills.

3. The Holy Spirit Unifies Believers in the Body of Christ (vv. 12-13)

The apostle has taught in the previous verses that there are many different gifts and functions and that specific gift(s) are distributed to each believer. He now illustrates how all believers and their functions contribute to a single unit using the human body as a model.

The human body is a single unit composed of many functional parts. Some parts are seen and some parts are hidden. By God's design, each part knows its function or responsibility. Each part does the function assigned to it and does not seek to do a function assigned to a different part. All parts are mutually dependent on the other parts and cannot function alone. All the parts of the body have a common object. That object is to sustain the life and function of the body. All parts of the body are controlled by a brain and nervous system. The parts of the body respond immediately to the commands issued by the central nervous system and keep the central nervous system informed of any conditions encountered. When any part suffers or malfunctions, the entire body is affected and is sympathetic—"so also is Christ," or the body of Christ, that is, the church. All believers (members), under the control of Jesus Christ, carry out His commands. His commands are conveyed by the Holy Spirit. The Holy Spirit is one with the Father and the Son. As the Holy Spirit fills (controls) the believer, the believer is empowered to accomplish the assignment given.

The unity of the one body of Christ exists because it is formed by one Holy Spirit. People are made members of the body by the baptism of the Holy Spirit. This is not a reference to water baptism, which is a public acknowledgment or sign. The Scriptures make a distinction between water baptism and Spirit baptism (Matthew 3:11; John 1:33). The Scriptures speak of the Holy Spirit as poured out, whether in regeneration, sanctification, inspiring or empowering, and those He is poured out upon are said to be baptized. Previous differences between the members do not matter. Regardless of national origin, social status, economic status, or gender, all who are baptized by the Holy Spirit are unified in the body of Christ. The Holy Spirit is able to transform diverse lives into one common life centered in the body of Christ. Jesus invited those who are thirsty to come unto Him and drink (John 7:37). He spoke of the Holy Spirit. All who come to Jesus for salvation drink of one Holy Spirit and He indwells them. Living by the Holy Spirit fulfills the purposes of God (Romans 8:14).

SEARCH THE SCRIPTURES

1. What does the word "accursed" mean (1 Corinthians 12:3)?

2. What is meant by the expression "spiritual gifts" (v. 4)?

3. What spiritual gifts does the apostle list? Are all listed (vv. 8-10)?

4. What is the purpose of spiritual gifts (v. 7)?

5. Who determines which gifts are needed for the benefit of all (v. 11)?

DISCUSS THE MEANING

1. How do believers determine their calling and function? Consider 1 Thessalonians 5:16-22; Acts 2:17; 6:3; 2 Thessalonians 3:5; 1 Timothy 1:18-19; 4:14-15; 2 Timothy 1:3-7; Romans 8:5, 28; 12:1-2.

2. Do you see ministries in your church that lack resources? What causes the church to be short of needed help?

3. What does the parable of the talents (Matthew 25:14-30) teach about responsibility?

LESSON IN OUR SOCIETY

There was a church that lacked teachers for the children and youth age Sunday School classes. Certain factors contributed to this problem. One factor is that Sunday School requires attendance two hours before the morning service. Another factor is that adults prefer to teach adults rather than children. Could a third factor be that some are neglecting their spiritual gift and calling?

MAKE IT HAPPEN

Submit to the Lordship of Jesus Christ and seek to be constantly filled (controlled) by the Holy Spirit. Someone accurately said, "we leak," so we must be filled repeatedly as we execute God's work. Do not determine what you can do based on your own assessment of your capabilities. Identify your gift(s) and calling(s). Only God can enlighten you to what He will do by the Holy Spirit in your life, but God will also confirm your gift(s) and calling(s) to others with spiritual discernment.

FOLLOW THE SPIRIT

What God wants me to do:

_____

_____

REMEMBER YOUR THOUGHTS

Special insights I have learned:

_____

_____

MORE LIGHT ON THE TEXT

1 Corinthians 12:1-13

1 Now concerning spiritual gifts, brethren, I would not have you ignorant.

To be "ignorant" (Gk. *agnoeo,* **ag-no-eh'-o**) means not only a lack of knowledge, but also a lack of understanding that leads to err or even sin through mistake. In this instance, to be ignorant is to be wrong. Often we sin because we do not know or understand correctly. Concerning spiritual matters, this can have grave consequences for the body of Christ. Much of disunity, bigotry, and other errors in the body of Christ are committed by well-meaning, devoted Christians who are either ignorant of the truth or wrong about the truth, concerning spiritual or other things of God. This is especially true concerning "spiritual gifts" (Gk. *pneumatikos,* **pnyoo-mat-ik-os**).

2 Ye know that ye were Gentiles, carried away unto these dumb idols, even as ye were led.

Paul was not impressed by their enthusiastic worship and religious frenzy. Idol worshipers (which many of them were) could boast of the same religious excitement. Spirited worship services are not necessarily evidence of the Holy Spirit. There are many kinds of spirits (pagan/idols). The Holy Spirit is the Spirit of Christ. Only one's attitude toward Christ and consideration for those in the body can distinguish which spirit you worship. Some who worship are gifted in music, others with enticing speech, many with elegant liturgical dance, and still others lively praise while paying little attention to the doctrines being taught—whether they are of Christ or not.

3 Wherefore I give you to understand, that no man speaking by the Spirit of God calleth Jesus accursed: and that no man can say that Jesus is the Lord, but by the Holy Ghost.

Under persecution or distress or religious frenzy, believers were often forced or led to curse the name of Jesus. "Accursed be Jesus" could not come from the lips of one under the influence of the Holy Spirit (the Spirit of Christ). Similarly Jesus is "Lord" (Gk. *kurios,* **koo'-ree-os**) was the battle cry of Christians. *Kurios* was the same title the Romans demanded of all those who came under their power to ascribe to Caesar when saying "Caesar is Lord!" *Kurios* was also the title given to Yahweh God by Jews, God-fearers, and Christians alike. To say "Jesus is Lord" was to commit to ultimate loyalty to Jesus. Thus those who would not be ignorant or wrong about the Holy Spirit must examine their confession of faith.

4 Now there are diversities of gifts, but the same Spirit.

There are "diversities" (Gk. *diairesis,* **dee-ah'-ee-res-is**) of allocations of gifts but they are derived from the same Holy Spirit. Paul wants to make it plain that there can be unity in diversity. It is the Spirit's function to connect, not divide. These gifts are given not for individual glory but to glorify or edify the body of Christ as a whole. If one does not want to be ignorant or go wrong, one must understand the underlying unity of the

operations of the Holy Spirit, remembering that these people once worshiped many gods according to their function (i.e., war gods, fertility gods, gods of the harvest). The Greek city-states were divided by various gods, such as Athena and Sparta. This was not so with the Spirit of Christ. With the Holy Spirit there is unity in diversity.

5 And there are differences of administrations, but the same Lord.

There are a variety or "differences (Gk. *diairesis,* **dee-ah'-ee-res-is**) of adminstrations" (Gk. *diakonia,* **dee-ak-on-ee'-ah**) rendered at the command of the same "Lord" (Gk. *kurios,* **koo'-ree-os**). As each has a different gift given by the same Spirit, each renders a different service command by the same Lord and Master. Once again, Paul emphasizes unity in diversity because the church was in danger of being fractured by the very instruments of God that should have brought them together. Monotheism (belief in one God) was relatively new outside of the Jewish faith in this region of the world. Thus among the Corinthians, who were largely not former Jews, but instead former pagans who worshiped many gods, it was necessary to emphasize oneness of the Lord and operations of the Holy Spirit.

6 And there are diversities of operations, but it is the same God which worketh all in all.

There is a *diairesis* (**dee-ah'-ee-res-is**) of "operations" (Gk. *energema,* **en-erg'-ay-mah**) of energy, efficacy, actions, or activities, but it is the same God that is active in all that happens. The Corinthians were divided by those who brought them to Christ and baptized them (1 Corinthians 3:5-9). Paul faults their immaturity in the faith. Using the metaphor of building a house, he shows how God is the general contractor, and he, Apollos, Cephas (Peter), and others who brought them the Gospel and nurtured them were mere subcontractors in building the temple of God (1 Corinthians 3:10-23).

The same principle is at work in Paul's rhetorical argument that all *gifts* are mere tools put into their hands by God to build up the body of Christ. Each member is a part of God's construction crew.

7 But the manifestation of the Spirit is given to every man to profit withal.

The spiritual gifts are given by the Spirit. Gifts are to be used in service of the Lord; with power and efficacy made possible by God, they are the manifestation of the Spirit in Christian community for the good of all. It is not a benefit to the individual but the whole community. It is a benefit to the individual insofar as it enhances one's value to the community. However, the manifestation of the Spirit is given to each expressly for the benefit of the whole community. The body of Christ is Paul's metaphor for the functioning Christian community.

8 For to one is given by the Spirit the word of wisdom; to another the word of knowledge by the same Spirit;

Paul begins to list the toolbox of gifts given by the Spirit to be used to build the temple of God, which is the body of Christ. He painstakingly emphasizes to these babies in Christ (who were given over the pride of flesh) that the spiritual unity is the foundation for these diverse spiritual tools that have been given as gifts.

The first gifts are the tools for the teaching ministry of the church. The word or utterance of "knowledge" (Gk. *gnosis*, **gno'-sis**) is to know what to do in any given situation, and "wisdom" (Gk. *sophia*, **sof-ee'-ah**) is the knowledge of the best things to do that are according to God's will. They both come from the same Spirit and are used to build up the church with knowledge of what Jesus Christ would do in a given situation (John 14:26), and the wisdom to understand the will of God for mission in the world (Acts 2:17-18, 32-33). This is the wisdom and knowledge that did not come from academic achievement alone, but from communion with God and the study of His Word.

9 To another faith by the same Spirit; to another the gifts of healing by the same Spirit;

Paul names faith as a gift and tool. Everyone has a measure of faith, especially those who claim personal salvation, which comes by faith. Paul has in mind here an all encompassing trust in God that can speak to mountains (Matthews 17:20-21), cause blind persons to see (Matthew 9:29), and

lame persons to walk (Mark 2:4-5). It was the faith of former slaves in America that built institutions of higher learning and great churches while bearing the burden of racism and slavery. This kind of faith is a gift and a mighty tool.

The gift of faith and the gift of healing are closely associated through the Gospels. The gift of healing, along with faith and prayer, are important tools in the building of Christian fellowship because they demonstrate the unity of the mind, body, and spirit. Even more than that, the laying on of hands, the anointment with oil, and mutual prayer builds intimacy as it brings healing both individually and communally.

10 To another the working of miracles; to another prophecy; to another discerning of spirits; to another divers kinds of tongues; to another the interpretation of tongues:

The Greek word for "miracles" is *dunamis*, (**doo'-nam-is**), or power. Miracles were a demonstration of power as evidenced by the Messianic age. When John sent his disciple to inquire whether Jesus was the Messiah or not, Jews responded with a recitation of His demonstrations of power as evidence (Matthew 11:2-5).

The gift of prophecy is the ability to make plain the will of God for our lives and communities. The prophet through the Spirit knows the mind of God and speaks it into the lives of God's people. The Spirit works either to rebuke those persons or institutions who are not in the will of God by foretelling the dire consequences of their actions, or by advising persons or institutions who seek God's guidance to live according to His will.

The discerning of spirits is the ability to distinguish whether one is speaking or rather preaching (prophesying) or whether one's performance of miracles is by the Holy Spirit or some other spirit. It is necessary to understand the source of a demonstration or power to know its intent.

Diverse kinds of "tongues" (Gk. *glossa*, **glocesah'**) were not exactly the same as the Pentecost experience (Acts 2:4) where the Spirit enabled them to speak known foreign languages. In Corinth they spoke unlearned languages that no one understood, except perhaps (not necessarily) the one speaking or someone who had the gift of interpreting unknown tongues.

11 But all these worketh that one and the self-same Spirit, dividing to every man severally as he will.

Again Paul reminds us that all the diversity of *gifts* has one source: the Spirit of God, who chooses who gets what gift. Therefore, no one has reason to boast. More importantly one does not choose a gift; the Spirit chooses the person for the gift. The same Spirit that gives the gift, gives according to the will of God.

12 For as the body is one, and hath many members, and all the members of that one body, being many, are one body: so also is Christ.

The metaphor of the body is extended to reinforce the point that there can be diversity in unity. The body of Christ is the assembly of believers in Christ, which comprises His bodily presence on Earth. Believers become His hands, feet, eyes, toes, head, arms, and so on. But each individual makes up one body.

13 For by one Spirit are we all baptized into one body, whether we be Jews or Gentiles, whether we be bond or free; and have been all made to drink into one Spirit.

The centerpiece of Paul's metaphor of the body of Christ is spiritual baptism. The Spirit connects us to each other, to God, and to creation. The Spirit obliterates distinctions in race and status for the sake of the mission of reconciliation to God. However, diversity remains and individuality remains as a part of the integrated whole. The gifts of the Spirit equip the body that will carry on Jesus Christ's mission on Earth.

DAILY BIBLE READINGS

M: Strive to Excel in Spiritual Gifts
1 Corinthians 14:6-12

T: Be Rich in Good Works
1 Timothy 6:13-19

W: Varieties of Gifts
1 Corinthians 12:1-6

T: All Gifts Activated by the Spirit
1 Corinthians 12:7-11

F: The Body Consists of Many Members
1 Corinthians 12:12-20

S: If One Member Suffers, All Suffer
1 Corinthians 12:21-26

S: Strive for the Greater Gifts
1 Corinthians 12:27-31

TEACHING TIPS

July 30
Bible Study Guide 9

1. Words You Should Know

A. Charity (1 Corinthians 13:1) *agape* (Gk.)—To love in a moral or social sense; love unconditionally.

B. Mysteries (v. 2) *musterion* (Gk.)—Secret or imposed silence.

C. Abideth (v. 13) *meno* (Gk.)—To stay (in a given place, state, relation, or expectancy).

2. Teacher Preparation

A. Prayerfully read the FOCAL VERSES and the DEVOTIONAL READING.

B. Prayerfully study the entire BIBLE STUDY GUIDE. Highlight parts to emphasize.

C. Be prepared to discuss the MAKE IT HAPPEN section.

D. Be prepared to differentiate between "agape" love, brotherly love, and romantic love. Discuss the benefits of each.

3. Starting the Lesson

A. Assign a student to lead the class in prayer, focusing on the LESSON AIM.

B. Ask a student to read the IN FOCUS section.

C. Initiate a discussion on how the word "love" is used in society today.

4. Getting into the Lesson

A. Allow each student to read some portion of THE PEOPLE, PLACES, AND TIMES, BACKGROUND, KEEP IN MIND, and AT-A-GLANCE sections.

B. Allow each student to read one of the FOCAL VERSES. As each one is read, discuss and instruct using the portions of IN DEPTH and MORE LIGHT ON THE TEXT section that you highlighted during your preparation.

C. Ask the students to respond to the SEARCH THE SCRIPTURES questions.

5. Relating the Lesson to Life

A. Ask the students to respond to the DISCUSS THE MEANING questions.

B. Have someone read the LESSON IN OUR SOCIETY section.

6. Arousing Action

A. Request a student to read the KEEP IN MIND verse again and then the MAKE IT HAPPEN section. Be sure to emphasize their obligation to Christ and others.

B. Ask the students to take a few minutes to record their responses in the FOLLOW THE SPIRIT and REMEMBER YOUR THOUGHTS sections.

C. Encourage the students to be prepared for next week's lesson.

D. Close the class with prayer.

WORSHIP GUIDE

For the Superintendent or Teacher
Theme: Called to Love
Theme Song: "Love Lifted Me"
Scripture: John 13:34-35
Song: "Lord, I Want to Be a Christian"
Meditation: Heavenly Father, fill us with Your Spirit of love. Make us steadfast in our commitment to love unconditionally. Provide strength in our areas of weakness and vulnerability. Amen.

CALLED TO LOVE

Bible Background • 1 CORINTHIANS 13
Printed Text • 1 CORINTHIANS 13
Devotional Reading • JOHN 3:16–21

LESSON AIM

By the end of the lesson, we will:

KNOW that acceptable Christian service is motivated by love;

BE CONVINCED that all believers are required to love unconditionally; and

BE MOTIVATED to serve others with the love provided by the Holy Spirit.

KEEP IN MIND

"And now abideth faith, hope, charity, these three; but the greatest of these is charity" (1 Corinthians 13:13).

FOCAL VERSES

1 Corinthians 13:1 Though I speak with the tongues of men and of angels, and have not charity, I am become as sounding brass, or a tinkling cymbal.

2 And though I have the gift of prophecy, and understand all mysteries, and all knowledge; and though I have all faith, so that I could remove mountains, and have not charity, I am nothing.

3 And though I bestow all my goods to feed the poor, and though I give my body to be burned, and have not charity, it profiteth me nothing.

4 Charity suffereth long, and is kind; charity envieth not; charity vaunteth not itself, is not puffed up,

5 Doth not behave itself unseemly, seeketh not her own, is not easily provoked, thinketh no evil;

6 Rejoiceth not in iniquity, but rejoiceth in the truth;

7 Beareth all things, believeth all things, hopeth all things, endureth all things.

LESSON OVERVIEW

LESSON AIM
KEEP IN MIND
FOCAL VERSES
IN FOCUS
THE PEOPLE, PLACES,
AND TIMES
BACKGROUND
AT-A-GLANCE
IN DEPTH
SEARCH THE SCRIPTURES
DISCUSS THE MEANING
LESSON IN OUR SOCIETY
MAKE IT HAPPEN
FOLLOW THE SPIRIT
REMEMBER YOUR THOUGHTS
MORE LIGHT ON THE TEXT
DAILY BIBLE READINGS

8 Charity never faileth: but whether there be prophecies, they shall fail; whether there be tongues, they shall cease; whether there be knowledge, it shall vanish away.

9 For we know in part, and we prophesy in part.

10 But when that which is perfect is come, then that which is in part shall be done away.

11 When I was a child, I spake as a child, I understood as a child, I thought as a child: but when I became a man, I put away childish things.

12 For now we see through a glass, darkly; but then face to face: now I know in part; but then shall I know even as also I am known.

13 And now abideth faith, hope, charity, these three; but the greatest of these is charity.

IN FOCUS

Aisha sat up in her hospital bed, alone. She cried, then coughed a vicious hacking cough until a bloody fluid came up. Catching it in her Kleenex, she tossed it in the trash can. Earlier that day, doctors drained her lungs and collected a pint of fluid. It didn't do much good. Neither radiation nor chemotherapy could help her. Aisha's immune system was failing. The AIDS virus had taken its toll. Intravenous drug use had brought her to this end. In these last days, she renewed her love of Christ. Nevertheless, she

JU
30

couldn't accept the truth that Christ loved her.

She believed that God would never forgive her for giving her child away nine years ago.

The chaplain discussed how God's love had never forsaken her. "So when you last saw your child, was she in a good home?"

Aisha talked though a muffled cough, "Yes, a beautiful Christian home."

"Can't you see that God used your child to bless that family?"

"But now it hurts so bad...."

"Aisha, you have to look beyond your hurt and focus on the loving act you did for your child. You didn't choose to end the precious child's life; you chose to give life. That unconditional act of love is an attribute of Our Lord and Saviour."

In morally corrupt Corinth, Paul taught that love was the greatest of all human qualities. Do you realize agape love is the only spiritual gift that keeps on giving, long after other gifts cease?

THE PEOPLE, PLACES, AND TIMES

Charity. The Greek term for "charity" is not appropriate for the context in 1 Corinthians 13. It is a word that has no pagan origin because it is not a pagan concept. Its use was rare in classic Greek literature. The word "charity" connotes the idea of love based on respect or that which is costly or dear. It evolved into a word that expressed the feeling arising from being cognizant of a condition of need or suffering. This common meaning is insufficient for the Greek term for "love," used in chapter 13. The proper meaning denotes a self-giving and unselfish personal commitment regardless of a gratifying response from the recipient. It seeks a person's highest good. It is not a natural inclination. It is an act of the will and an inclination of the heart.

God manifests this type of love (John 4:11). It is His very essence (1 John 4:8, 16). This type of love originates from Him and not from people (Romans 5:5). People love God as an act of the will. By doing this, people satisfy the greatest commandment (Mark 12:29-30). People's love for God is proved by obedience (John 14:15). People fulfill the second greatest commandment by loving other people (Mark 12:31). This is the only type of love that loves enemies. Love is the evi-

dence for discipleship (John 13:34-35), sonship (1 John 4:7), and new life (3:14). Love displays God in the life of the believer (3:16-18; 4:16).

BACKGROUND

In chapter 13, the apostle Paul paints a portrait of godly love. He does so in a very methodical way. He takes the behavior of the Corinthians apart piece-by-piece and demonstrates how each piece, or characteristic, exhibited by them is absent of love. These attributes include the inappropriate use of gifts, impatience, rudeness, enviousness, arrogance, pride, repulsiveness, selfishness, resentfulness, suspicion, and indifference. Acts of service must be motivated by love. Believers are encouraged to seek the most useful gifts and the apostle shows them an excellent way to do it.

AT-A-GLANCE

1. Love Utilizes Spiritual Gifts Effectively
(1 Corinthians 13:1-2)
2. Love Makes Benevolence Profitable
(v. 3)
3. Love Manifests Essential
Characteristics (vv. 4-7)
4. Love Abides Forever (vv. 8-13)

IN DEPTH

1. Love Utilizes Spiritual Gifts Effectively (1 Corinthians 13:1-2)

The apostle Paul continues to discuss spiritual matters or gifts in chapter 13.

The gift of tongues is mentioned first since it was so prominent in the Corinthian church. The gift of tongues is the supernatural ability to speak an unlearned language for a duration as long as the Holy Spirit provides the words. Paul says that a believer endowed with this gift, even to the extent of speaking in an angelic or heavenly language (to the highest conceivable extent), without love (that originates from God), is nothing. The example given is a piece of clanging brass metal that makes a meaningless and perhaps an annoying sound. The other example given is the sound of a cymbal, which is the simplest of instrumental sounds. The Corinthians spoke out loudly in discord at the same time, with multiple incoherent sounds resulting in mass confusion (1 Corinthians 14:23, 27). This situation resembled the noise of pagan rituals. The absence of love reduces the effort to nil.

The person displaying the highest level of prophetic knowledge of revealed mysteries (hidden truth of God that can only be known by revelation) or the highest level of (the gift of) knowledge, without love, is of no value. There is normally a distinction between these two gifts, so it is assumed here (compare 1 Corinthians 13:8). Prophecy is the gift of revelation or illumination by which God gives special communication to people. The gift of knowledge provides divine insight and understanding into God's Word (truth already revealed) and the general application of truth. The prophet utilizes the former while the teacher benefits from the latter (compare 1 Corinthians 14:6). Perhaps Paul had Jesus' words in mind (Matthew 21:21) when he says that a person lacking love with faith great enough to remove mountains is nothing (worthless). Spiritual gifts do not attest to character.

2. Love Makes Benevolence Profitable (v. 3)

Taking his discourse to the next level, the apostle discusses the emptiness of benevolent acts without love. A person not motivated by love gives away all possessions but it counts for nothing with God. Martyrs die for others in vain in the absence of love. Though they die in the most painful way imaginable, it counts for nothing. Think of the countless people who seek to relieve their conscience or buy their way into heaven with charitable acts and those motivated by a desire for notoriety. Giving penance is a simple but ineffective act. Consider the terrorist martyrs, prominent in the world today, driven by duty yet expecting an eternal reward. They inflate their condemnation. An outward act is not a substitute for an essential inward condition.

3. Love Manifests Essential Characteristics (vv. 4-7)

Love is described and its characteristics are in sharp contrast to the behavior exhibited by the Corinthians. Love is patient ("suffereth long") and is not quick to assert its rights or react to injury. Love is kind in the sense that the person shows himself useful in a compassionate way. Love is not quick to resent mistreatment but instead is inclined to do good. Love does not heat up or kindle inappropriate feelings toward another. These inappropriate feelings include envy, jealousy, hatred, strife, and so on. Love does not seek to get all the credit and all the applause ("vaunteth not itself"). Love does not put others down by building oneself up. It does not inflate its true credentials. Love does not view others as insignificant. The puffed up person is boastful and seeks the praise of others. Love does nothing that results in shame. It is not unbecoming in appearance.

Love does not seek itself; instead, it is self-sacrificing. It is not easily exasperated to hostility ("provoked") by personal attacks. Love does not take inventory (reckon or take account) of evil deeds suffered and, as a result, avoid provocation. Instead love is forgiving. Love is not happy about any unrighteous act or situation. Love is not comfortable with sin. It takes no pleasure in the advances or triumphs of evil.

Alternatively, love rejoices in truth, that is, activity that conforms to God's truth. It identifies with it, is sympathetic toward it, and supports it. Love patiently endures (bears) all things, that is, annoying and troubling situations. Love believes, or gives credit, or gives the benefit of the doubt to others. It is not unduly suspicious. Love hopes for the best in people with pleasurable anticipation. Love does not abandon support even when challenged. It perseveres in adverse conditions ("endureth") such as suffering and persecution.

4. Love Abides Forever (vv. 8-13)

Love never fails, that is, comes to an end (by context). It endures forever. It has everlasting necessity. How can it cease when the eternal God is love? This fact elevates it above ministry gifts. Ministry gifts are beneficial for the present age to convert, correct, edify, exhort, and comfort, but these gifts will not be necessary once this age is ushered into eternity. In the eternal age, prophecies are not necessary to reveal aspects of redemption because redemption is already accomplished. Prophecies will be abolished (made entirely nonexistent). The gift of tongues is not needed in the perfect state as a form of prophecy or devotion. A perfect way of communication between all will prevail. Knowledge will be complete, so the gift of knowledge (insight) becomes obsolete. Here are additional reasons why the spiritual gifts of prophecy and knowledge eventually become obsolete. They are partial and limited in the revelation of information. They give bits and pieces but not the whole picture. They are suited to imperfect people and an imperfect existence. What are but glimpses of God now will be superseded by full revelation in the presence of God.

The apostle clarifies the distinction between the present condition and the future glory by using two illustrations. First he contrasts childhood with maturity. The current state of the church is likened to the immaturity of a child exhibited in the way a child talks, thinks or feels, and ponders. The way a child talks, feels, or reasons is simple but adequate and normal for a child. As an example, the child can grasp legitimate aspects of an animal but not completely like a veterinarian can. However, when the child matures and becomes an adult, he discards the immature ways. The mature adult's conversations, observations, and conclusions are more complete, or perfect.

The second illustration contrasts seeing an obscure reflection of an object with seeing the object directly and clearly. Ancient mirrors were made of polished metal so the reflected image was obscure. Believers see things now indirectly as through a mirror or symbolically in dreams, visions, and parables. In other words, they see by comparison. They are constrained by descriptive language, limited experience, partial knowledge, and insufficient understanding. What has not been clearly seen cannot adequately be put into words.

God made such a comparison when He compared the revelations received by Moses to those of other prophets (Numbers 12:8). Moses saw things plainly while others saw representations in dreams and visions. Yet even the things Moses wrote in the Law were an enigma compared to the Gospel, and the Gospel is not as enlightening as presence in glory will be. Believers see God veiled in Scripture, but one day will see Him directly face-to-face (2 Corinthians 3:18). They see now imperfectly, but then perfectly or completely even as God sees them now.

Spiritual gifts have temporary usefulness and existence, but faith, hope, and love remains ("abideth") forever. As previously mentioned, love is understood as having eternal duration, but faith and hope requires some clarification. Other Scriptures, such as Hebrews 11:1 and Romans 8:24-25, speak of faith and hope coming to fruition when that which is anticipated is received. Therefore, for faith and hope to abide, they must take on a new dimension when full redemption is realized in heaven.

There will always be faith and confidence in God, and apparently, there will always be more from Him to anticipate. However, love is the greater of the three. In what way is it greater? If the term "greatest," in 1 Corinthians 13:13, is compared with its use in 1 Corinthians 12:31 and 1 Corinthians 14:5, the meaning suggested is that it is the most useful to the body of Christ. Faith and hope primarily benefits the individual (self) while love benefits others.

SEARCH THE SCRIPTURES

1. Which spiritual gifts are used to explain the necessity of love (1 Corinthians 13:1-2)?

2. Can the ultimate sacrifice be made without love (v. 3)?

3. In what way does love "believe all things" (v. 7)?

4. What two examples are used to compare the capability of the church in the present age to its future existence (vv. 11-12)?

5. What abides forever (v. 13)?

DISCUSS THE MEANING

1. Distinguish between charity and the love described in 1 Corinthians 13.

2. Explain whether love makes spiritual gifts unnecessary.

3. What are some essential characteristics of love?

4. Is the love described in 1 Corinthians 13 humanly possible?

5. With respect to God, what is meant by the words faith, hope, and love?

LESSON IN OUR SOCIETY

Erskine College Netnews reported on some comments made by Mark Mathanabe on a recent visit to the college. Mark Mathanabe is a native of South Africa. He has written about his life experiences, and on the subjects of apartheid, education, and race relations. At Erskine College, he told of a South African woman whose son was murdered. The authorities captured the murderers and asked the woman how she wanted the murderers punished. She told them that her only interest in finding the murderers was to know who she had to forgive.

MAKE IT HAPPEN

It has been said that only what you do for Christ will last. First Corinthians 13 teaches that only what you do with the love of God will count. Faith without works is dead, and works without love is dead. People are pleased by desirable acts, but God is pleased only by acts of faith and love. Love does whatever is best for another person. Please God and benefit others with a conduct ruled by love.

FOLLOW THE SPIRIT

What God wants me to do:

_____

_____

REMEMBER YOUR THOUGHTS

Special insights I have learned:

_____

_____

MORE LIGHT ON THE TEXT

1 Corinthians 13

"Charity" (Gk. *agape*, **ag-ah'-pay**) is the lifeblood of the body of Christ. It builds up the body of Christ by providing each member the life forces that animate the individual spiritual gifts as instruments of God rather than the inanimate tools of persons. Spiritual gifts without love is like a fish out of water, a bee without honey, or an automobile without wheels.

1 Though I speak with the tongues of men and of angels, and have not charity, I am become as sounding brass, or a tinkling cymbal.

The word "charity" means love, brotherly love affection, goodwill, or benevolence. Agape love means the decentering of the ego. The person is no longer the center of his or her universe or ultimate concern. "The other" is now in the center Love is a radical reordering of priorities and ultimate values. God is love (1 John 4:8). God gave His only Son (John 3:16) to save us. Without love, everything we do is for our own self-glorification and benefit. With love, what we do is for God and others. Love is not a feeling; it is what we do for others without regard for self. It is partaking in the very nature of God.

Spirit-inspired speech spoken in ecstasy, in different languages, in brilliant rhetoric of humans, or in superhuman entities, means nothing if it is not of God. Any intention whose source is not the God of love is in vain. If the Spirit of God animates the body, it is love that holds it together. Tongues without love are only so much noise.

2 And though I have the gift of prophecy, and understand all mysteries, and all knowledge; and though I have all faith, so that I could remove mountains, and have not charity, I am nothing.

The gift of prophecy or preaching is mere entertainment or scolding and of no effect if the speaker is not motivated by love. The gift of intellectual accomplishment without love leads to contempt and snobbery. The gift of great faith that achieves or sacrifices much leads to false pride. Without love, none of these gifts edifies the body of Christ or pleases God.

3 And though I bestow all my goods to feed the poor, and though I give my body to be burned, and have not charity, it profiteth me nothing.

Benevolence and even self-sacrifice done with ill intention or with the wrong spirit might as well not be done at all. To give out of obligation, self-promotion, or even contempt is worse than not giving at all. It does not build up the body of Christ. Likewise, to seek persecution or make sacrifice for selfish intentions may very well hurt one's cause more than it helps.

Paul has made it clear that agape love is more important than spiritual gifts. In this passage, he explains exactly what is *agape*. Love is that which

The greatest gift is love.

connects us to God and to one another. Like the blood that circulates through the veins of the body carrying oxygen and nutrient from cell to cell, so love also brings us into a life-giving relationship to God and one another.

4 Charity suffereth long, and is kind; charity envieth not; charity vaunteth not itself, is not puffed up,

Love "suffereth long" (Gk. *makrothumeo*, **mak-roth-oo-meh'-o**), or endures, patiently the errors, weaknesses, and even meanness of people. Love makes us slow to anger and to repay hurt for hurt. It will suffer many things for the sake of the relationship. Love is kind (Gk. *chresteuomai*, **khraste-yoo'-om-ahee**); it shows kindness whenever possible. Love does not "envieth" (Gk. *zeloo*, **dzay-lo'-**

o). It does not earnestly covet another's good fortune. Love does not get angry because someone else is doing well. Love does not "vaunteth" (Gk. *perpereuomai*, **per-per-yoo'-om-ahee**), or brag, about oneself. It is not boastful or stuck up. Love does not have a swelled head and is not "puffed up" (Gk. *phusioo*, **foo-see-o'-o**), snobbish, or arrogant. A person in love esteems others higher than themselves.

5 Doth not behave itself unseemly, seeketh not her own, is not easily provoked, thinketh no evil;

Love is never rude. Love is full of grace and charm. It does not go around hurting others' feelings. It always uses tact and politeness whenever possible. Love never demands its rights, but seeks its responsibilities toward others. It is not self-centered or self-assertive. Love does not fly off the handle. It does not lose its temper. It is not easily exasperated at people. Love does not keep the books on the wrong done to it. Love does not keep score in order to repay wrong for wrong. It forgets the evil that people do to it. It does not carry a grudge.

6 Rejoiceth not in iniquity, but rejoiceth in the truth;

Love does not like to hear about the moral failures of others. It does not get pleasure out of the misfortune of others who are victims or perpetrators of evil. There is a sick joy from witnessing or hearing gossip about the misdeeds of others. We often judge our own righteousness and well-being as measured by the failings of others. However, love is happy to hear the truth (or what is right) no matter how painful. Love rejoices when what is true, correct, and righteous wins the day regardless of how that may impact it directly.

7 Beareth all things, believeth all things, hopeth all things, endureth all things.

If God is love and if God created all things good, then love also is the progenitor of all things good. Love is our participation in God's nature. Thus love is the only foundation for Christian community and relationships. Love, like God, is eternal. Love "beareth"(Gk. *stego*, **steg'-o**) the errors and faults of others. Love does not expose one's weakness because it does not rejoice in the misfortune of others. Yet it does not excuse sin or wrongdoing because it equally rejoices in truth. Instead as Christ bore our sin on the Cross, we take on the weakness and faults of others as though they were our own.

Love believes the best, trusts in the object of its love, has confidence in him or her, and gives credit to the object of love that may not be self-evident except through the eyes of love. Love can bear all things because it believes all things with the special insight into that which only a loving relationship can bring. Love "hopeth" (Gk. *elpizo*, **el-pid'-zo**) with joy, full confidence in eager expectation the salvation of the Lord to come. Love bears all things because it believes with only the insight of God the maker, thus it can wait for

the true nature of people to reveal itself. Love trusts in the eventual reconciliation with God. Love "endureth" (Gk. *hupomeno*, **hoop-om-en'-o**) and continues to be present; it does not perish or depart in spite of errors, faults, or wrongs done.

8 Charity never faileth: but whether there be prophecies, they shall fail; whether there be tongues, they shall cease; whether there be knowledge, it shall vanish away.

Love is eternal; it never comes to an end. It is absolutely permanent. Whereas all the gifts in which the Corinthians pride themselves are transitory at best, love is transcendent. While the gifts may stand alone individually, love is—exists only in and for—relationship. Yet it is more than the sum of its parts; like life itself, it is always renewed, even in the age to come.

The gifts, on the other hand, have no such guarantee. They were given by the Spirit as instruments to be used in this age. Paul anticipates that these gifts will no longer be needed when the next age occurs, marked by the return of Christ and fulfillment of the reign of God. They will pass away with the old age. Love, on the other hand, is essential not instrumental; it will never pass away. In contrast, when all prophecy has been fulfilled, tongues will no longer be necessary as a language; signs, missions, and knowledge will vanish because there will be no more mysteries.

9 For we know in part, and we prophesy in part.

Love, like God, is complete. On the other hand, we are imperfect creatures who can only apprehend reality—both material and spiritual—in an incomplete manner. Therefore, we can only preach or prophesy in an imperfect and partial way. For Paul, the kingdom of God was near, but not yet. It was not fully revealed in this age, so our knowledge and prophecy of it could only be partial.

10 But when that which is perfect is come, then that which is in part shall be done away.

The "perfect" (Gk. *teleios*, **tel'-i-os**) maturity or completeness will come with the end of this present, imperfect age and the beginning of the new perfect age—namely the "eschaton." Paul describes the times in which the Corinthians lived as transitory at best. Thus they should not make gods or idols out of the gifts they esteem so highly because their gifts are both imperfect and temporary.

11 When I was a child, I spake as a child, I understood as a child, I thought as a child: but when I became a man, I put away childish things.

Paul uses the metaphor of the maturing spiritual human being who grows from childhood to adulthood. The spiritual gifts become mere toys or childish things. Paul, who had called the Corinthians "babes in Christ," chided them once again to grow up and put away their toys (1 Corinthians 3:1).

12 For now we see through a glass, darkly; but then face to face: now I know in part; but then shall I know even as also I am known.

Mirrors were a primary industry in the city of Corinth. Mirrors made in Corinth were made of finely polished silver and bronze. The image was often concaved and distorted much like the amusement park house of mirrors. Thus we see only dimly through the distorted reflections of our own limited apprehensions. However, when Jesus returns and God makes His dwelling place among His people, we will see face-to-face (Revelation 21:22-23).

When we look through a mirror, we see only a reflection of ourselves and have only a knowledge that is filtered through our senses. However, when we come face-to-face with another, we see clearly, but are also seen. We not only come to know, but are also known by another.

13 And now abideth faith, hope, charity, these three; but the greatest of these is charity.

After everything that has been said, we come to the conclusion of the matter. Spirit gifts are transient, given to a particular community, for a particular purpose, and for the particular time. It is childish to esteem them too highly. However, by faith we are saved according the grace of God. In hope, we wait upon the return of Jesus and the coming of the reign of God. All this is due to

God's love for us. These are what remain when one matures in Christ.

However, when Jesus returns, the reign of God is fulfilled. We have no need of hope. When we stand face-to-face with God and clearly see all that there is to see, then we have no need of faith. Yet we will continue to love and be loved by God. Love never ends; it is eternal.

Love has revealed itself completely in the revelation of Jesus Christ in His life, death, and Resurrection. Thus we can love the Holy One. Jesus says, "This is my commandment, That ye love one another, as I have loved you. Greater love hath no man than this, that a man lay down his life for his friends" (John 15:12-13). Love is the greatest.

DAILY BIBLE READINGS

M: God So Loved the World
John 3:16-21

T: God's Love in Christ Jesus
Romans 8:31-39

W: Love One Another
John 13:31-35

T: Loving One Another Fulfills the Law
Romans 13:8-14

F: Let Us Love
1 John 3:11-18

S: Love Defined
1 Corinthians 13:1-7

S: The Greatest Gift Is Love
1 Corinthians 13:8-13

TEACHING TIPS

August 6
Bible Study Guide 10

1. Words You Should Know

A. Grief (2 Corinthians 2:5) *lupeo* (Gk.)—To cause pain or sorrow. Paul uses the word to refer to the sense of pain or hurt that happens when individuals act harshly toward each other.

B. Forgive (v. 7) *charizomai* (Gk.)—To deal with someone graciously.

C. Repentance (vv. 9-10) *metanoia* (Gk.)—To change one's mind; to turn away from sin.

2. Teacher Preparation

A. Begin by praying and asking God to help you forgive others as He has forgiven you.

B. Read the DEVOTIONAL READING and FOCAL VERSES.

C. Read the LESSON AIM and study the IN DEPTH and MORE LIGHT ON THE TEXT sections.

D. Materials needed: Bibles, paper, and pens.

3. Starting the Lesson

A. Open the class with prayer, asking God to help the class learn how to forgive others as He has forgiven them.

B. Review the LESSON AIM with the class.

C. Give each student a pen and piece of paper. Ask them to write down one offense that God has forgiven them for on the top of the paper. On the bottom, have them write the name of someone that they have not forgiven.

D. Have your students read the FOCAL VERS-ES aloud.

4. Getting into the Lesson

A. Have a student read the BACKGROUND and THE PEOPLE, PLACES, AND TIMES sections and discuss them with the class.

B. Review the WORDS YOU SHOULD KNOW section.

C. Have a volunteer read the AT-A-GLANCE outline. Discuss the IN DEPTH section with your class.

D. Review the SEARCH THE SCRIPTURES sec-tion and have the students search out the answers

5. Relating the Lesson to Life

A. Review the DISCUSS THE MEANING sec-tion with the class.

B. Ask two or three students to share an experi-ence when a person offended them. How did they react? How would God want them to respond?

6. Arousing Action

A. Have the students read aloud the LESSON AIM.

B. Remind the students that God wants us to forgive one another and reconcile our differences Likewise, Jesus reconciles us with God by forgiving our sins when we repent (2 Corinthians 5:18-21).

C. Challenge the students to write a prayer below the name of the person whom they have not forgiven, asking God to help them to forgive this person.

D. Close the class with prayer, thanking God for His forgiveness and for assisting us in forgiving others.

WORSHIP GUIDE

For the Superintendent or Teacher
Theme: Giving Forgiveness
Theme Song: "Amazing Grace"
Scripture: 2 Corinthians 5:18-21
Song: "If I Have Wounded Any Soul Today"
Meditation: Father, I thank You for being my Redeemer. I am grateful that You sent Your Son to Earth to shed His blood for the forgiveness of my sins. Help me to love and forgive others. Amen.

GIVING FORGIVENESS

Bible Background • 2 CORINTHIANS 2:5–11; 7:2–15
Printed Text • 2 CORINTHIANS 2:5–11; 7:2–15
Devotional Reading • MATTHEW 18:21–35

LESSON AIM

By the end of the lesson, we will:

UNDERSTAND why God wants us to offer forgiveness and reconciliation;

FEEL the joy in being forgiven by God; and

BE ENCOURAGED to forgive and be reconciled with others.

KEEP IN MIND

"For godly sorrow worketh repentance to salvation not to be repented of: but the sorrow of the world worketh death" (2 Corinthians 7:10).

FOCAL VERSES

2 Corinthians 2:5 But if any have caused grief, he hath not grieved me, but in part: that I may not overcharge you all.

6 Sufficient to such a man is this punishment, which was inflicted of many.

7 So that contrariwise ye ought rather to forgive him, and comfort him, lest perhaps such a one should be swallowed up with overmuch sorrow.

8 Wherefore I beseech you that ye would confirm your love toward him.

9 For to this end also did I write, that I might know the proof of you, whether ye be obedient in all things.

10 To whom ye forgive any thing, I forgive also: for if I forgave any thing, to whom I forgave it, for your sakes forgave I it in the person of Christ;

11 Lest Satan should get an advantage of us: for we are not ignorant of his devices.

LESSON OVERVIEW

LESSON AIM
KEEP IN MIND
FOCAL VERSES
IN FOCUS
THE PEOPLE, PLACES, AND TIMES
BACKGROUND
AT-A-GLANCE
IN DEPTH
SEARCH THE SCRIPTURES
DISCUSS THE MEANING
LESSON IN OUR SOCIETY
MAKE IT HAPPEN
FOLLOW THE SPIRIT
REMEMBER YOUR THOUGHTS
MORE LIGHT ON THE TEXT
DAILY BIBLE READINGS

7:2 Receive us; we have wronged no man, we have corrupted no man, we have defrauded no man.

3 I speak not this to condemn you: for I have said before, that ye are in our hearts to die and live with you.

4 Great is my boldness of speech toward you, great is my glorying of you: I am filled with comfort, I am exceeding joyful in all our tribulation.

5 For, when we were come into Macedonia, our flesh had no rest, but we were troubled on every side; without were fightings, within were fears.

6 Nevertheless God, that comforteth those that are cast down, comforted us by the coming of Titus;

7 And not by his coming only, but by the consolation wherewith he was comforted in you, when he told us your earnest desire, your mourning, your fervent mind toward me; so that I rejoiced the more.

8 For though I made you sorry with a letter, I do not repent, though I did repent: for I perceive that the same epistle hath made you sorry, though it were but for a season.

9 Now I rejoice, not that ye were made sorry, but that ye sorrowed to repentance: for ye were made sorry after a godly manner, that ye might receive damage by us in nothing.

10 For godly sorrow worketh repentance to salvation not to be repented of: but the sorrow of the world worketh death.

AUG
6TH

11 For behold this selfsame thing, that ye sorrowed after a godly sort, what carefulness it wrought in you, yea, what clearing of yourselves, yea, what indignation, yea, what fear, yea, what vehement desire, yea, what zeal, yea, what revenge! In all things ye have approved yourselves to be clear in this matter.

12 Wherefore, though I wrote unto you, I did it not for his cause that had done the wrong, nor for his cause that suffered wrong, but that our care for you in the sight of God might appear unto you.

13 Therefore we were comforted in your comfort: yea, and exceedingly the more joyed we for the joy of Titus, because his spirit was refreshed by you all.

14 For if I have boasted any thing to him of you, I am not ashamed; but as we spake all things to you in truth, even so our boasting, which I made before Titus, is found a truth.

15 And his inward affection is more abundant toward you, whilst he remembereth the obedience of you all, how with fear and trembling ye received him.

IN FOCUS

Hal sat at the kitchen table watching his wife cooking. Bouncing his 3-year-old in his arms, he whistled a tune. His love for his wife seemed to be pouring out of him. He looked out into the springtime yard and vividly recalled the tension with his wife a few years before.

An avid golfer, Hal practiced hard for several weeks to win the club championship. Dressing for the final round of the golfing tournament, his wife asked, "Hal, are you going to church this morning?"

"No, I can't. I made the finals," he said smiling.

She went silent. "But Hal, you can be out of church in plenty of time to golf."

He grinned and winked. "Practice. Practice. You can never have too much."

His wife's eyes looked hurt.

Gathering his golf clubs, Hal ignored her disappointment. Walking out he said, "Nothing will get me into church today."

Hours later on the first tee, Hal realized that church was a big event for her because it was her first Mother's Day. They had waited 7 years for their first child.

At church, mothers would be honored and given flowers. Too focused on the tournament, he wouldn't be there.

Her anger greeted him at the door when he came home with flowers for her and his trophy. Angrily she tore up the flowers saying, "This is the way you crushed my heart."

He tried to apologize realizing there never would be another *first* Mother's Day.

"I can't change what I did. But I promise I'll never be that insensitive again."

They talked, embraced, and shed tears together. She gave the gift of forgiveness. He never put golf over her wishes again. Now they were blessed with feelings of joy for each other.

Restoration in our human relationships gives us a finite taste of the joy God experiences when we admit our sin and repent. Do you know God loves to forgive?

THE PEOPLE, PLACES, AND TIMES

Titus. He was a Greek convert and trusted companion of Paul. He accompanied Paul and Barnabas to Jerusalem during the time of the Gentile controversy (Galatians 2:1). He possessed great administrative skills. He had a great fondness for the Corinthians. Paul enlisted his help to be a mediator between himself and the Corinthians. Titus carried letters from Paul to the Corinthians. He was also commissioned by Paul to organize the collection for the poor from the Corinthians. Later in his ministry, Titus became the overseer of the churches in Crete (Titus 1:5). Paul wrote a letter advising Titus in his responsibility of supervising the churches on the island of Crete.

The Corinthian church. The apostle Paul reached Corinth from Athens about A.D. 49 or 50 and stayed there for 18 months during his second missionary journey (Acts 18:1-8). There he established a Christian community. Paul returned to Corinth twice (2 Corinthians 13:1). The Corinthian church was plagued with problems including division, immorality, and idolatry. Consequently, Paul wrote at least three letters to the Corinthians. One of them is now lost. The first letter, 1 Corinthians, dealt with moral issues in the church, and answered questions about sex and marriage. After the letter was received, the Corinthians accepted Paul's call for commitment to Christ. However, false teachers denied his authority and slandered his name. This led to Paul's "painful visit" (2:1; 12:14, 21; 13:1-2).

BACKGROUND

In 2 Corinthians, Paul defends his ministry and message. Paul had been verbally attacked by a spokesman of the anti-Pauline clique (2:5-8, 10; 7:12) during a brief and painful visit to Corinth. No one came to his defense so he left angry and disappointed. Titus was sent to Corinth with the "severe letter" (lost) calling for the punishment of the wrongdoer (2:3, 4, 6, 9; 7:8, 12). Sometime later he traveled to Troas to preach. After not being able to locate Titus, he changed his travel plans and went to Macedonia. Paul was anxious to know the response of the Corinthians to his letter. In Macedonia, Titus reported that the majority of Christians had reaffirmed their allegiance to Paul and disciplined the man who attacked him. They had repented and wanted to be reconciled with Paul. After being informed about new problems at Corinth, Paul wrote 2 Corinthians.

In this lesson, Paul urged the Christian community to offer forgiveness and reconciliation to the one who had offended him and them.

AT-A-GLANCE

1. Paul Encourages Forgiveness
(2 Corinthians 2:5-11)
2. Paul's Appeal for Love (7:2-4)
3. Paul's Comfort During Time of Trials
(vv. 5-7)
4. Paul's Joy in Their Repentance
(vv. 8-12)
5. Paul's Confidence (vv. 13-15)

IN DEPTH

1. Paul Encourages Forgiveness (2 Corinthians 2:5-11)

Paul acknowledged the man who verbally attacked him and caused grief to himself as well as the whole community of believers. He used the word "grief" to express the sense of pain or hurt that was inflicted because of the man's harsh actions. One person's actions can affect a whole community. We are all of one body of believers and "whether one member suffer, all the members suffer with it" (1 Corinthians 12:26).

The Corinthian church disciplined the man. The "Lord disciplines those he loves" (Hebrews 12:6, NIV). When a person sins, God corrects them in love so it can lead to repentance. Titus reported that the man had repented so Paul encouraged the believers to forgive him and offer comfort. In forgiving a person, we reflect the character of God. "Be kind and compassionate to one another, forgiving each other, just as in Christ God forgave you" (Ephesians 4:32, NIV). God forgives us, so we should forgive others. Moreover, the person should be encouraged and restored into the community.

Paul knew forgiveness and reconciliation were essential in resolving the church conflict. Excommunicating a person from the Christian community due to harsh discipline could lead to Satan gaining leverage in their lives. Satan seeks to steal, to kill, and to destroy. Therefore, the discipline given was sufficient.

Paul forgave the man as Christ commanded. The Corinthian church was encouraged to imitate Paul's behavior. He knew that the church needed to heal and move beyond the present conflict.

God wants Christians to be ambassadors of peace who bring reconciliation between Himself and the world. "All this is from God, who reconciled us to himself through Christ and gave us the ministry of reconciliation" (2 Corinthians 5:18, NIV).

2. Paul's Appeal for Love (7:2-4)

Paul had a great affection for the people of Corinth. They were a people very near and dear to his heart. He had labored faithfully among them sharing the Good News and establishing the church. The present conflict had caused many to grow discontented with Paul.

He reminded the Corinthians that he had not harmed anyone, preached or taught false doctrines, nor deceived anyone. Paul defended his reputation and ministry while appealing for them to receive him once again in love. Paul did not judge the Corinthians but wanted to be reconciled with them. He wanted unity in the church and among the believers.

The community was being encouraged to be reconciled with the man who had caused them grief, and Paul wanted the same affection to be extended him. However, he had committed no evil. Paul's affection for the Corinthian Christians was so great that he would be willing to identify with them that in life or death. God loved us so much that He sent Jesus into the world to live among us and die for us. Through His death, we were reconciled unto God (Romans 5:10). Paul wanted them to know that it was his affection for them that caused him to speak so freely and boast about them. Even though Paul and the Corinthians had experienced sorrow, he was overflowing with joy in the midst of it.

3. Paul's Comfort During Time of Trials (vv. 5-7)

The apostle Paul was in Troas sharing the Good News, but was troubled when he could not locate Titus. Paul was supposed to meet Titus there to receive his report on the response of the Corinthians to his letter. Titus had delivered the harsh letter to the Corinthians. Paul was so distraught; he shortened his stay in Troas and went to Macedonia (2:12-13).

Upon reaching Macedonia, Paul was greatly distressed. He faced continual opposition from his enemies and feared that the fellowship of the believers would be corrupted. However, the apostle was not without comfort. God sent him comfort through the coming of Titus. Paul was comforted by the Comforter (1:3). Titus relayed the positive response of the Corinthians to his letter. They were sorrowful, repentant, and desirous of reconciliation with Paul. He rejoiced. Their positive response provided relief to Titus as well. If one sinner repents, we ought to rejoice (see Luke 15:7).

4. Paul's Joy in Their Repentance (vv. 8-12)

Paul was sorry that he had grieved them with the letter. However, he did not regret sending it. The letter caused them grief for a season. However, it produced the fruit of repentance. Their obedience and godly conduct in repenting caused Paul to rejoice. Now he wanted them to rejoice and accept the offender back into the fellowship of believers because of his godly response to them.

For Paul, all sorrow is not bad. "For godly sorrow worketh repentance to salvation not to be repented of" (v. 10). That is, a person who feels pain because he or she has offended God and/or another person can repent and be forgiven. King David committed adultery and murder. When confronted with his sin, he confessed, repented and sought forgiveness (2 Samuel 12:13; Psalm 51). As Christians, we must be willing to offer forgiveness even as God forgives us. Repentance can lead to a restoration of relationships between God and people. Paul wanted to be reconciled with the Corinthian church.

True repentance does not have to be regretted, but worldly sorrow does. "The sorrow of the world worketh death" (v. 10). Sorrow that does not lead to repentance can only lead to death. Many people express sorrow for what they have done. Often they are trying to escape or minimize the effects of their sins. Judas, the disciple who betrayed Jesus, felt sorry for his actions but committed suicide (Matthew 27:4-5). He did not seek God's forgiveness. His sorrow brought about death. Sin produces not only a physical death but an eternal one as well. "For the wages of sin is death; but the gift of God is eternal life through Jesus Christ our Lord" (Romans 6:23).

The apostle Paul praised the Corinthians for repenting, turning from their sin, and living transformed lives. The conflict had been resolved and reconciliation with God had taken place. God wants us to live in harmony with Him and others. Therefore, we should make every effort to make amends when we have offended someone. God sent His Son, who, through His sacrifice, redeemed us and forgave our sins (Ephesians 1:6-7). This was all so we could be reconciled unto God.

Paul's motive in writing the letter was not to let the conflict remain unresolved (v. 12). We have to be aware of Satan's devices (2:11) and take appropriate action to resolve discord in our churches, communities, and families. God commands that we love and forgive one another. These two commands embody the character of God. As God's ambassadors, we should imitate Him.

5. Paul's Confidence (vv. 13-15)

The Corinthians refreshed Titus's spirit. His love for them grew deeper because of their obedience in repenting. Their reception of him and desire to repent and be reconciled caused Paul comfort and joy. He had confidence that once the letter was received, they would acknowledge their sins and repent. Paul was confident the Corinthians had a relationship with Christ, so they would respond to the words of correction.

SEARCH THE SCRIPTURES

1. "So that contrariwise ye ought rather to _____ him, and _____ him, lest perhaps such a one should be swallowed up with overmuch sorrow" (2 Corinthians 2:7).

2. Who did Paul warn the Corinthians not to allow to get the advantage over them (v. 11)?

3. "Nevertheless God, that _____ those that are cast down, _____ us by the coming of Titus" (7:6).

4. To what does godly sorrow lead (v. 10)?

DISCUSS THE MEANING

Mr. and Mrs. Williams had collected money from their church to purchase a wedding anniversary gift for the pastor. Their son Malik, who is the church organist, stole the money and bought drugs. How should Malik's parents handle this problem? How should the church respond?

LESSON IN OUR SOCIETY

We should not scorn a person because of their sin. Jesus wants us to exhibit His love in action by accepting them into the fellowship of believers. Through God's love, they can receive forgiveness. Their reconciliation with God can lead to transformed lives. Across the nation, many people are incarcerated. Society, communities, families, and churches have ostracized them. Once prisoners are released, they need to rebuild their lives. Churches can serve as a vital link for ex-offenders.

MAKE IT HAPPEN

During the week, take the time to pray for the people you have not forgiven. Ask God to forgive you for not forgiving them. Seek God's direction for steps to take so reconciliation can occur in some of these relationships. Follow God's instructions.

FOLLOW THE SPIRIT

What God wants me to do:

_____

_____

REMEMBER YOUR THOUGHTS

Special insights I have learned:

_____

_____

MORE LIGHT ON THE TEXT

2 Corinthians 2:5-11; 7:2-15

5 But if any have caused grief, he hath not grieved me, but in part: that I may not overcharge you all. 6 Sufficient to such a man is this punishment, which was inflicted of many.

The word for "grief" in Greek is *lupeo* (**loo-PEH-o**), which means distress. The Greek word for "overcharge" is *epibareo* (**ep-ee-bar-EH-o**), which means "to be severe toward someone." Paul explains that despite the offense that was done in the church, he is not overly distressed by what is going on. Paul is also careful not to blame the Corinthians too much for what has happened. The Greek word for "sufficient" is *hikanos* (**hik-an-OS**), which can be translated as "competent" or "fit." Paul said that the way that the offender was punished was sufficient for the offense that he did.

7 So that contrariwise ye ought rather to forgive him, and comfort him, lest perhaps such a one should be swallowed up with overmuch sorrow. 8 Wherefore I beseech you that ye would confirm your love toward him.

Paul encouraged the Corinthians to forgive

and comfort the man who committed the offense. The Greek word for "forgive" is *charizomai* (**khar-ID-zom-ahee**), which means to pardon or to rescue. The word for "comfort" in Greek is *parakaleo* (**par-ak-al-EH-o**), which means to call near. Not only was Paul asking the Corinthians to forgive the offender, but he was asking the church to welcome him back openly. Paul was concerned about the well-being of the offender. He was concerned about the offender being "swallowed up" with sorrow. The Greek word for "swallowed up" is *katapino* (**kat-ap-EE-no**), which actually means drown. Paul did not want the offender to deal with depression over his offense. Paul wanted the man who committed the sin to understand the love of the church.

9 For to this end also did I write, that I might know the proof of you, whether ye be obedient in all things.

Paul is explaining why he is writing this letter in the first place. He wanted to know if the Corinthians would listen to him. The Greek word for "proof" is *dokime* (**dok-ee-MAY**), which means to test. The word for "obedient" in Greek is *hupekoos* (**hoop-AY-koos**), which means submissive. Despite the problems in the Corinthian church and the disobedience of the people, Paul wanted to test the Corinthians to see if they would listen and submit to his authority.

10 To whom ye forgive any thing, I forgive also: for if I forgave any thing, to whom I forgave it, for your sakes forgave I it in the person of Christ; 11 Lest Satan should get an advantage of us: for we are not ignorant of his devices.

Paul continues to emphasize the importance of forgiveness. He repeats the word "forgive" five times just in this verse. Paul was saying that he would forgive whomever the Corinthians would forgive. Paul was clearly taking the initiative in this matter of forgiveness. Paul again showed his concern for the well-being of his people. Paul said that it is important to forgive so that Satan will not get an advantage of the Corinthians as well as Paul himself. The Greek word for the phrase "get an advantage" is *pleonekteo* (**pleh-on-cek-TEH-o**), which means to make a gain. Paul knew that unre-

solved conflict could be used by Satan to get leverage in and bring dissection to the Corinthian church.

7:2 Receive us; we have wronged no man, we have corrupted no man, we have defrauded no man.

The Corinthians had rejected Paul and others who taught the Gospel. They had started listening to more charismatic preachers who were teaching false doctrine. Paul was imploring the Corinthians to receive the truth of the Gospel. The word for "wronged" in Greek is *adikeo* (**ad-ee-KEH-o**), which is also translated "unjust." The Greek word for "corrupted" is *phtheiro* (**FTHI-ro**), which means to ruin. The word "defrauded" in Greek is *pleonekteo* (**pleh-on-ek-THE-o**). This is the same Greek word that was used earlier in 2 Corinthians 2:11 for the phrase "gain an advantage." Paul was giving the Corinthians reasons to trust him. No one had been treated unjustly, no one had been ruined, and no one had been taken advantage of as a result of Paul's ministry.

3 I speak not this to condemn you: for I have said before, that ye are in our hearts to die and live with you. 4 Great is my boldness of speech toward you, great is my glorying of you: I am filled with comfort, I am exceeding joyful in all our tribulation.

Paul continues to express his love for the Corinthians. He explained that he was not trying to condemn or embarrass them. Paul also said that the Corinthians were always in his heart and that he lived and died together with them. The Greek word for "great" is *polus* (**pol-OOS**), which means abundant. Paul said that he was abundantly proud of the Corinthians, and he bragged about them often. In fact, the word for "glorying" in Greek is *kauchesis* (**KOW-khay-sis**), which means boasting. Despite the troubles going on in the Corinthian church, Paul said that he was not only worry-free, but joyful. The scandal of the Corinthian church had not changed Paul's love for the Corinthian church.

5 For, when we were come into Macedonia, our flesh had no rest, but we were troubled on every

side; without were fightings, within were fears. 6 Nevertheless God, that comforteth those that are cast down, comforted us by the coming of Titus;

Paul went to Macedonia to try to find Titus; however, he never found him. In addition, conflict was taking place all around Paul. The word for "fightings" in Greek is *mache* (**MAKH-ay**), which means battle. Outside of Paul, battles were taking place, while Paul was feeling fearful inside. However, the coming of Titus brought comfort to Paul. In this verse, Paul says that God comforts those who are "cast down." The Greek word for the phrase "cast down" is *tapeinos* (**tap-I-NOS**), which means lowly. Seeing Titus again reenergized Paul.

7 And not by his coming only, but by the consolation wherewith he was comforted in you, when he told us your earnest desire, your mourning, your fervent mind toward me; so that I rejoiced the more.

The word for "consolation" is the same word used for "comfort" used many times in this text. The Greek word is *paraklesis* (**par-AK-lay-sis**), which can mean consolation, comfort, or exhortation. Paul was not only comforted by the coming of Titus, but he was also consoled by what he said about the Corinthians. Titus told Paul about what had happened in Corinth as well as how the Corinthians had reacted to the scandal. The Greek word for the phrase "fervent mind" is *zelos* (**DZAY-los**), which is also translated as "zeal." Paul took note of the intense desire, mourning, and zeal of the Corinthians, which made him rejoice.

8 For though I made you sorry with a letter, I do not repent, though I did repent: for I perceive that the same epistle hath made you sorry, though it were but for a season.

The Greek word for the phrase "made you sorry" is *lupeo* (**loo-PEH-o**), which is also translated as "grieved" in this text (see above in 2 Corinthians 2:5). The word for repent in Greek is *metamelomai* (**met-am-EL-lom-ahee**), which means "regret." Earlier, Paul expressed regret for writing such a severe letter and for grieving the Corinthians. However, he takes back that regret. He sees that the epistle that he originally regret-

ted writing actually brought on the Corinthians the sorrow that they needed to have, no matter how long the sorrow was.

9 Now I rejoice, not that ye were made sorry, but that ye sorrowed to repentance: for ye were made sorry after a godly manner, that ye might receive damage by us in nothing.

Paul's emotions about writing the sorrowful letter completely changed from repentance to rejoicing. The word "sorrowed" in this verse comes from *lupeo*, the same Greek word used for "made you sorry" in the previous verse. In both cases, *lupeo* is translated as "grieved." Paul says that the Corinthians were made to grieve for godly reasons. The phrase "receive damage" comes from the Greek word *zemioo* (**dzay-mee-O-o**), which means to suffer loss. Paul says that godly sorrow has prevented the Corinthians from suffering loss in the future.

10 For godly sorrow worketh repentance to salvation not to be repented of: but the sorrow of the world worketh death.

Paul distinguishes the difference between godly sorrow and the sorrow of the world. Godly sorrow leads to salvation. The Greek word for "salvation" is *soteria* (**so-tay-REE-ah**), which means rescue or safety. Godly sorrow can actually be used by God to rescue the sorrowful person through repentance. Therefore, there is no reason to repent for godly sorrow. However, the "sorrow of the world" does not involve repentance at all. Often the sorrow only comes from getting caught in sin. Paul says that this "sorrow" only leads to death. This "death" is more likely a spiritual death rather than a physical one.

11 For behold this selfsame thing, that ye sorrowed after a godly sort, what carefulness it wrought in you, yea, what clearing of yourselves, yea, what indignation, yea, what fear, yea, what vehement desire, yea, what zeal, yea, what revenge! In all things ye have approved yourselves to be clear in this matter.

Paul continues to talk about the benefits of godly sorrow for the Corinthians. The Greek word for "carefulness" is *spoude* (**spoo-DAY**), which means diligence. The word for the phrase "clearing of yourselves" is *apologia* (**ap-ol-og-EE-ah**), which is translated "defense of self." Godly sorrow brought about diligence in the Corinthians. It allowed them to clear their names, and it brought desire, fear, and even vindication to the Corinthians. Because of this, the Corinthians purified themselves of responsibility in this matter.

12 Wherefore, though I wrote unto you, I did it not for his cause that had done the wrong, nor for his cause that suffered wrong, but that our care for you in the sight of God might appear unto you. 13 Therefore we were comforted in your comfort: yea, and exceedingly the more joyed we for the joy of Titus, because his spirit was refreshed by you all.

Paul continues to put things in perspective. He says that he did not write the severe letter on behalf of the offending member of the church. Paul also says that he did not write the letter on behalf of those who were done wrong. He says that he wrote it so that the Corinthians would know how much Paul cares about them. The Greek word for "appear" is *phaneroo* (**fan-er-O-o**), which means to manifest. Paul wanted to manifest his care for the Corinthians by teaching them about godly sorrow. Paul cared so much that he, along with Timothy, was comforted by the godly sorrow of the Corinthians. Paul was also overjoyed because of the joy Titus had when he finally saw Paul again. Of course, Titus had joy from the reaction of the Corinthians to their sin. The Greek word for "refreshed" is *anapauo* (**an-ap-OW-o**), which means at ease. Titus was put at ease by the repentance of the Corinthians.

14 For if I have boasted any thing to him of you, I am not ashamed; but as we spake all things to you in truth, even so our boasting, which I made before Titus, is found a truth.

Titus could be at ease with the Corinthians because Paul boasted about them often. The word for "boasted" in Greek is *kauchaomai* (**kow-KHAH-om-ahee**), which means gloried. Paul was not ashamed to boast about the Corinthians, and he did not have to exaggerate. He spoke the truth to the Corinthians, and when he boasted, he told the truth about them. This once again showed how much he cared about them.

15 And his inward affection is more abundant toward you, whilst he remembereth the obedience of you all, how with fear and trembling ye received him.

The Greek word for the phrase "inward affection" is *splagchnon* (**SPLANGKH-non**), which is also translated as "tender mercy." Titus remembered the obedience of the Corinthians, and he developed mercy for them. Titus also remembered how the Corinthians received him with godly fear and trembling. The word for "trembling" in Greek is *tromos* (**TROM-os**), which literally means quaking with fear. Titus realized that the Corinthians' fear of God had led to their receiving of Titus, as well as their godly sorrow that led to repentance in the scandal in the Corinthian church.

DAILY BIBLE READINGS

M: Forgive Others Their Trespasses
Matthew 6:9-15
T: Jesus Teaches About Forgiveness
Matthew 18:21-35
W: Forgive, So God May Forgive You
Mark 11:20-25
T: You Also Must Forgive
Colossians 3:12-17
F: Forgive and Console Your Offender
2 Corinthians 2:5-11
S: Paul's Pride in the Corinthians
2 Corinthians 7:2-7
S: Paul's Joy at the Corinthians' Repentance
2 Corinthians 7:8-16

TEACHING TIPS

August 13
Bible Study Guide 11

1. Words You Should Know

A. Grace (2 Corinthians 8:1, 6-7, 9) *charis* (Gk.)—An act that bestows pleasure, delight, or causes favorable regard, and the spiritual state of those who have experienced its exercise (deeds of grace).

B. Poor (v. 9) *ptocheuo* (Gk.)—To be destitute.

C. Rich (v. 9) *plouteo* (Gk.)—The spiritual enrichment of believers through Jesus' poverty.

2. Teacher Preparation

A. Review last week's FOCAL VERSES and THE PEOPLE, PLACES, AND TIMES section.

B. Study the FOCAL VERSES and KEEP IN MIND verses for this lesson.

C. Study the LESSON AIM and WORDS YOU SHOULD KNOW. Be prepared to share with your class the meaning of Christ's act of sacrifice on our behalf.

D. Examine the MORE LIGHT ON THE TEXT section.

3. Starting the Lesson

A. Open with prayer.

B. Let the students share how the application of last week's lesson on giving forgiveness impacted their lives.

C. Have the students read aloud this week's LESSON AIM and FOCAL VERSES.

D. Read the IN FOCUS story and discuss its meaning.

4. Getting into the Lesson

A. Focus on the love and generosity of Jesus Christ, who gave His life on our behalf.

B. Review the BACKGROUND and THE PEOPLE, PLACES, AND TIMES sections.

C. Ask a student to read the AT-A-GLANCE outline. Choose another student to read the Scripture text as outlined and discuss the IN DEPTH section with the class.

D. Discuss the answers to the SEARCH THE SCRIPTURES questions with the class.

5. Relating the Lesson to Life

A. Go over the DISCUSS THE MEANING section with the class.

B. Share with the class an opportunity you had to give to another person in need. Allow the students to share their experiences in giving to others.

6. Arousing Action

Close this session with prayer, thanking Jesus for giving His life for the atonement of our sins. Pray that His love will motivate us to give to others so that their needs will be met.

WORSHIP GUIDE

For the Superintendent or Teacher
Theme: Giving Generously
Theme Song: "Give of Your Best to the Master"
Scripture: 1 Timothy 6:17-19
Song: "You Can't Beat God's Giving"
Meditation: Dear God, thank You for giving us Your Son, Jesus Christ, who gave up His throne and came into the world on our behalf. His gift to us could never be repaid. But help us to give back to Him our talents, time, and money.
Amen.

GIVING GENEROUSLY

Bible Background • 2 CORINTHIANS 8:1–15
Printed Text • 2 CORINTHIANS 8:1–15
Devotional Reading • LUKE 20:45–21:4

LESSON AIM

By the end of the lesson, we will:

UNDERSTAND that we are saved by God's grace manifested through His Son Jesus Christ, who died for our sins;

EXPRESS our gratitude to God for His wonderful gift; and

COMMIT to give our all to Him in response to all He has done for us.

KEEP IN MIND

"For ye know the grace of our Lord Jesus Christ, that, though he was rich, yet for your sakes he became poor, that ye through his poverty might be rich" (2 Corinthians 8:9).

FOCAL VERSES

2 Corinthians 8:1 Moreover, brethren, we do you to wit of the grace of God bestowed on the churches of Macedonia;

2 How that in a great trial of affliction the abundance of their joy and their deep poverty abounded unto the riches of their liberality.

3 For to their power, I bear record, yea, and beyond their power they were willing of themselves;

4 Praying us with much entreaty that we would receive the gift, and take upon us the fellowship of the ministering to the saints.

5 And this they did, not as we hoped, but first gave their own selves to the Lord, and unto us by the will of God.

6 Insomuch that we desired Titus, that as he

LESSON OVERVIEW

LESSON AIM
KEEP IN MIND
FOCAL VERSES
IN FOCUS
THE PEOPLE, PLACES, AND TIMES
BACKGROUND
AT-A-GLANCE
IN DEPTH
SEARCH THE SCRIPTURES
DISCUSS THE MEANING
LESSON IN OUR SOCIETY
MAKE IT HAPPEN
FOLLOW THE SPIRIT
REMEMBER YOUR THOUGHTS
MORE LIGHT ON THE TEXT
DAILY BIBLE READINGS

had begun, so he would also finish in you the same grace also.

7 Therefore, as ye abound in every thing, in faith, and utterance, and knowledge, and in all diligence, and in your love to us, see that ye abound in this grace also.

8 I speak not by commandment, but by occasion of the forwardness of others, and to prove the sincerity of your love.

9 For ye know the grace of our Lord Jesus Christ, that, though he was rich, yet for your sakes he became poor, that ye through his poverty might be rich.

10 And herein I give my advice: for this is expedient for you, who have begun before, not only to do, but also to be forward a year ago.

11 Now therefore perform the doing of it; that as there was a readiness to will, so there may be a performance also out of that which ye have.

12 For if there be first a willing mind, it is accepted according to that a man hath, and not according to that he hath not.

13 For I mean not that other men be eased, and ye burdened:

14 But by an equality, that now at this time your abundance may be a supply for their want, that their abundance also may be a supply for your want: that there may be equality:

15 As it is written, He that had gathered much had nothing over; and he that had gathered little had no lack.

IN FOCUS

In September 2003, a small church took up its entire Sunday offering, $622.45, and sent it to a mega-church as a contribution toward its $55 million building project.

The pastor of the 20-member church said it was to teach his congregation a biblical lesson that those with little to give should still be generous.

"I was trying to convince them that size doesn't matter," he said. "I was hoping it would have a good effect on our congregation."

The larger church was in its first phase of expansion and could have easily overlooked the gift. Several months went by, and the little church didn't get a thank-you note or acknowledgment from the big church.

Then in January 2004, the mega-church's video crew visited the 20-member church to interview the members and ask them why they sent the money.

The pastor told them, "We were in awe of your great work for the body of Christ."

The next Sunday the mega-church took up an offering for the 20-member church and presented the small congregation with a check for $28,157.29.

The pastor of the small church tried to return the money saying it would dilute his message of giving. Then he added, "I can't imagine why such a large church that is trying to raise money would give away $28,000."

After more prodding, they graciously accepted. The small church donated $3,000 of the money to mission work, and then spent the rest making upgrades to the church building and parking lot.

Writing from Macedonia, Paul encouraged the Corinthian believers to give generously and to unite with other churches in fellowship. Do you believe God gives so we can give to others?

THE PEOPLE, PLACES, AND TIMES

The Jerusalem church. Jerusalem is considered the political and religious capital for the Jewish people. During the Day of Pentecost, the disciple Peter preached and 3,000 people were saved. Day by day the Lord increased the number of believers. The believers in Jerusalem developed into the first church (Acts 2).

After Paul's conversion, he visited Jerusalem on many occasions. At one time, he met with the leaders of the Jerusalem Council to get their approval of his preaching to the Gentiles (Galatians 2). Barnabas and Titus were also present during this visit. The leaders gave their approval and requested that Paul remember the poor. The Jerusalem church was suffering from a serious food shortage due to a drought in Palestine (Acts 11:28-30). Many of the other Gentile churches were financially stable and prospering. During Paul's missionary journeys, he took collections for the poor in Jerusalem.

BACKGROUND

Paul, who had written this letter from Macedonia, was appealing to the Corinthians to participate in the collection for the poor in Jerusalem. This letter tried to build on the success of his harsh letter (lost). It led to forgiveness and reconciliation among the believers in Corinth. He was building upon the foundation that they had realigned themselves with him and obeyed his commands (2 Corinthians 2:9). Since they had been obedient to his directions before, Paul wanted the Corinthians to continue in their allegiance to him. His goal was their full participation in the collection for the saints in Jerusalem.

AT-A-GLANCE

1. Give Like the Macedonians
(2 Corinthians 8:1-5)
2. Give as You Promised (vv. 6-8)
3. Give in Response to God's Grace (v. 9)
4. Give According to Your Ability
(vv. 10-15)

IN DEPTH

1. Give Like the Macedonians (2 Corinthians 8:1-5)

Paul wanted to call attention to the grace of God given to the Macedonian churches. He acquainted the Corinthians with the gifts of God given through them. The Macedonians were Christians who gave toward the collection for the poor in Jerusalem. They were in the midst of affliction and poverty, but joyfully responded because of the sense of favor God had bestowed upon them. The Macedonians gave sacrificially on behalf of other saints in need. They wanted to assist other believers and show their commitment as followers of Christ.

When we think about the gift that God gave to the world through Jesus Christ, we should be motivated to respond. We should show our appreciation for the sacrifice He made. The Macedonians not only were appreciative, but also proved it by their actions. "As we have therefore opportunity, let us do good unto all men, especially unto them who are of the household of faith" (Galatians 6:10). Paul was challenging the Corinthians to emulate the Macedonians.

2. Give as You Promised (vv. 6-8)

Titus, who was Paul's representative, had previously encouraged the Corinthians to give toward the collection for the poor. But in light of their recent conflict with Paul, they had lost their zeal for collections (7:2-15). When affliction abounds in our lives, we should still be committed to God and ministering to others. The Macedonians were rejoicing in the midst of their troubles. Paul was encouraging the Corinthians to do the same. He told Titus to complete the gathering of collections from the Macedonians. Paul wanted them to prove their allegiance to him and their love for others.

The Corinthian believers excelled in everything. They had strong faith, good preaching, much knowledge, much enthusiasm, and much love. Paul appealed to them to have the same passion and commitment for the collections. For him, the offering is a remembering (Galatians 2:10), collection of money (1 Corinthians 16:1-2), a ministry (Romans 15:25), and a gift (2 Corinthians 8:6).

He was not commanding them to give, but urging them to prove that their love was sincere. Love manifests itself in action. "Little children, let us love, not in word or speech, but in truth and action" (1 John 3:18, NRSV). Our actions reveal

our hearts. Paul wanted the Corinthians to reveal where their devotion and affection was focused.

3. Give in Response to God's Grace (v. 9)

The grace of our Lord Jesus Christ is the greatest example for all believers to follow. "Who, being in the form of God, thought it not robbery to be equal with God: But made himself of no reputation, and took upon him the form of a servant, and was made in the likeness of men" (Philippians 2:6-7). Jesus gave up His position and became a human. He was born in poor circumstances, lived a poor life, and died in poverty—all so that He may bestow His favor upon us. "In whom we have redemption through his blood, the forgiveness of sins, according to the richness of his grace" (Ephesians 1:7).

4. Give According to Your Ability (vv. 10-15)

Paul urged the Corinthians to complete the collections for the poor that they had planned a year earlier (2 Corinthians 9:2). The gifts offered should be in proportion to what they are able to give. God does not want us to be burdened by giving that which we cannot sacrifice. Whatever we give, do it willingly. "Every man according as he purposeth in his heart, so let him give; not grudgingly, or of necessity: for God loveth a cheerful giver" (2 Corinthians 9:7).

When you have given to others, when you are in need, they will help you. Paul could be reflecting on the charity of the early Jerusalem church. There was a voluntary sharing among believers in Jerusalem (Acts 4:32-37). Everyone shared possessions equally so no one lacked anything. Believers should willingly share with others. The collection symbolizes for Paul a unified people of God whom there is no Jew or Gentile (Galatians 3:28). We are of one body in Christ. The "material blessings" are shared by the Gentile believers in appreciation of "spiritual blessings" that the Jewish believers have shared with them (Romans 15:27).

SEARCH THE SCRIPTURES

1. What was bestowed upon the churches of Macedonia (2 Corinthians 8:10)?

2. "Praying us with much intreaty that we would receive the _____, and take upon us the

fellowship of the ministering to the saints" (8:4).

3. "For ye know the _____ of our Lord Jesus Christ, that though he was _____, yet for your sakes he became _____, that ye through his poverty might be _____" (v. 9).

DISCUSS THE MEANING

Reverend Wilson's church is a small, urban congregation. He announces during Sunday's worship service that the school a block away is in great need. The school district cut their budget so most of the students do not have textbooks or writing materials. How should the congregation respond?

LESSON IN OUR SOCIETY

In today's society, some people give out of a sense of obligation. Their motivation is to strictly adhere to the law as commanded in the Word and by the pastor. However, God wants us to give liberally, not under compulsion, but as an acknowledgment of His love and favor.

Others give out of selfish reasons. They give just to get something in return. However, our focus in giving to others is remembering all God has given to us through His Son, Jesus Christ. Jesus gave His life for us so we should give generously to others.

Giving is not limited to financial gifts. We can also share our time and talents. We can volunteer at homeless shelters, schools, hospitals, and prisons. Every day we have opportunities to give to others. We should give, within our ability, as the occasion allows.

MAKE IT HAPPEN

After praying in the morning, ask the Holy Spirit to reveal to you someone who is in need. Seek wisdom in how to meet their need. As God leads you, obey His instructions.

FOLLOW THE SPIRIT

What God wants me to do:

_____

_____

REMEMBER YOUR THOUGHTS

Special insights I have learned:

_____

_____

MORE LIGHT ON THE TEXT
2 Corinthians 8:1-15

This passage is about the generous and gracious act of our Lord Jesus Christ when He gave His life for our sins on the Cross. In the previous chapter, Paul praised the Corinthians for sacrificing their feelings in order to forgive a Corinthian who made an offense in the church. In this text, Paul talks about the sacrifices that Jesus made for the Corinthians, as well as for us. Paul encourages the Corinthians to continue to give unselfishly for the benefit of the church. Paul also wants to make sure the Corinthians have the proper attitude as they give to the ministry. Please feel free to use the *Precepts For Living*™ CD-ROM included in the lesson commentary to gain additional information on this lesson.

1 Moreover, brethren, we do you to wit of the grace of God bestowed on the churches of Macedonia;

The Greek word for "to wit" is *gnorizo* (**gno-RID-zo**), which means to make known. The word for "grace" in Greek is *charis* (**KHAR-ece**), which is also translated as "gift." Paul wanted to make known God's gift of grace delivered to the churches of Macedonia.

2 How that in a great trial of affliction the abundance of their joy and their deep poverty abounded unto the riches of their liberality.

Paul says that the trials the Corinthians had gone through have become a benefit to them. The Greek word for the phrase "trial of affliction" is *dokime thlipsis* (**dok-ee-MAY THLIP-sis**), which means test of tribulation. Despite their tribulations, the Corinthians had maintained their joy. The Greek word for "liberality" is *haplotes* (**hap-LOT-ace**), which is also translated as "sincerity" or "generosity." Although the Corinthians had dealt with deep poverty, they had been rich in generosity.

3 For to their power, I bear record, yea, and beyond their power they were willing of themselves;

The generous giving of Jesus: our Lord and Saviour.

The Greek word for "power" is *dunamis* (**DOO-nam-is**), which means ability. The word for "bear record" in Greek is *martureo* (**mar-too-REH-o**), which means to testify. The phrase "willing of themselves" comes from the Greek word *authairetos* (**ow-THAH-ee-ret-os**), which means self-chosen or voluntary. Paul complemented the Corinthians on their willingness to serve. He testified that the Corinthians gave above and beyond what they had financially.

4 Praying us with much entreaty that we would receive the gift, and take upon us the fellowship of the ministering to the saints. 5 And this they did, not as we hoped, but first gave their own selves to the Lord, and unto us by the will of God.

The Greek word for "praying" in this verse is *deomai* (**DEH-om-ahee**), which means urgently pleading. *Paraklesis* (**par-AK-lay-sis**) is the Greek word for "entreaty," which is also translated as "exhortation." The Corinthians almost begged Paul to receive the gift that they were giving. The

Corinthians also wanted Paul to accept the fellowship of ministering to the saints. The Greek words for "fellowship" and "ministering" are *koinonia* (**koy-nohn-EE-ah**) and *diakonia* (**dee-ak-on-EE-ah**), respectively. *Koinonia* means community, communion, or joint participation, and *diakonia* means serving. The Corinthians not only wanted to continue communicating with Paul, but they also wanted to continue servicing Paul in any way possible.

In this verse, Paul continues to emphasize how the Corinthians have gone above and beyond expectations. The phrase "not as we hoped" actually means beyond our hopes. The Corinthians gave themselves to God first, and then they gave their money to Paul. They even gave their money "by the will of God." The Greek word for "will" is *thelema* (**THEL-ay-mah**), which means pleasure. The Corinthians pleased God with their giving.

6 Insomuch that we desired Titus, that as he had begun, so he would also finish in you the same grace also.

Titus encouraged the Corinthian church to give in the first place. Paul hoped that Titus could encourage them to keep giving. The Greek word for "desired" is *parakaleo* (**par-ak-al-EH-o**), which means to encourage or exhort. The word for "finish" in Greek is *epiteleo* (**ep-ee-tel-EH-o**), which is also translated as "to fulfill completely." Paul was urging Titus to encourage the Corinthians to fully complete their giving.

7 Therefore, as ye abound in every thing, in faith, and utterance, and knowledge, and in all diligence, and in your love to us, see that ye abound in this grace also.

The Greek word for "abound" is *perisseuo* (**per-is-SYOO-o**), which means excel. The word for "utterance" in Greek is *logos* (**LOG-os**), which is translated as "word." *Spoude* (**spoo-DAY**) is the Greek word for "diligence"; it means earnestness. Paul says that the Corinthians have excelled in their faith, their speech, their knowledge of the Word, their earnestness, and their love for Paul and Titus. However, Paul wanted to make sure that they excelled at the grace of their giving as well.

8 I speak not by commandment, but by occasion of the forwardness of others, and to prove the sincerity of your love. 9 For ye know the grace of our Lord Jesus Christ, that, though he was rich, yet for your sakes he became poor, that ye through his poverty might be rich.

The Greek word for "commandment" is *epitage* (**ep-ee-tag-AY**), which means decree. The word for "forwardness" is *spoude* (**spoo-DAY**), which is the same word used for "diligence" in the previous verse. Paul was not making a decree that the Corinthians must give more, but he wanted the Corinthians to have the chance to prove the sincerity of their love.

Paul also reminded the Corinthians of the unselfishness of Christ in order to encourage the Corinthians to remain unselfish as well. Paul says the Corinthians "know the grace of our Lord Jesus Christ." The Greek word for "know" is *ginosko* (**ghin-OCE-ko**), which means to be sure of something. The word for "grace" in Greek is *charis* (**KHAR-ece**), which can be translated as "favor." Christ did the ultimate favor for the Corinthians, and all of us, by leaving His throne in heaven as King of kings and coming down to earth in the form of a child. Despite His eternal royalty, Christ came to earth as a baby born in a manger, who grew up having to work as a carpenter. Ultimately, Christ made the ultimate sacrifice by allowing Himself to be crucified on the Cross, to accomplish salvation for all who are in Him. Christ's poverty made us rich in grace and mercy.

10 And herein I give my advice: for this is expedient for you, who have begun before, not only to do, but also to be forward a year ago. 11 Now therefore perform the doing of it; that as there was a readiness to will, so there may be a performance also out of that which ye have.

Paul gives the Corinthians his advice on what to do with their giving. The word for "advice" in Greek is *gnome* (**GNO-may**), which means counsel or judgment. The word "expedient" comes from the Greek word *sumphero* (**soom-FER-o**), which means profitable. The word for "be forward" in Greek is *thelo* (**THEL-o**), which means determined or willed. Paul wants them not only to continue to give, but he also wants the Corinthians to continue to be determined, just as they were a year ago. The Greek word for "perform" is *epiteleo* (**ep-ee-tel-EH-o**), which means to finish. Paul challenged the Corinthians to finish their giving. He said that just as there was a readiness and determination to give before (the word for "will" is the same word used for "be forward" in the previous verse), the Corinthians should be determined to finish their giving according to what they have to give.

12 For if there be first a willing mind, it is accepted according to that a man hath, and not according to that he hath not.

Paul reminds the Corinthians that they can only give what they have. He emphasizes the importance of the right attitude in giving. The Greek word for "willing mind" is similar to the word for "readiness" in verse 11. *Prothumia* (**proth-oo-MEE-ah**) is the Greek word used in this verse, and it can be translated as "forwardness of mind" or "readiness of mind." There is a definite theme of willingness to give within this text. The word for "accepted" in Greek is *euprosdektos* (**yoo-PROS-dek-tos**), which means well-received. Paul suggested that the proper attitude in giving is more important than the amount being given. He says that the gift is well-received according to what the Corinthians are able to give and not according to what they cannot give.

13 For I mean not that other men be eased, and ye burdened: 14 But by an equality, that now at this time your abundance may be a supply for their want, that their abundance also may be a supply for your want: that there may be equality:

Paul does not want to put the entire burden on the Corinthians to do all of the giving to the ministry. He also doesn't want the Corinthians to give so much that they suffer from not having enough for themselves. Paul knows that others need to give as well, but he believed there should be equality in giving. The word for equality in Greek is *isotes* (**ee-SOT-ace**), which means "equity." The Greek word for "want" is *husterema* (**hoos-TER-ay-mah**), which means lack. Paul says that the Corinthians should be able to meet the lack of others now, so that in the future, if the Corinthians are ever in lack, others can be a help

to them. Since Christians shared supplies in times of need, this is entirely possible.

15 As it is written, He that had gathered much had nothing over; and he that had gathered little had no lack.

Paul quotes Exodus 16:18 in this verse. The word for the phrase "had nothing over" in Greek is *pleonazo* (**pleh-on-AD-zo**), which means did not abound. The Greek word for "no lack" is *elattoneo* (**el-at-ton-EH-o**), which is also translated as "fall short." Since everyone was working together and all that was gathered was put together, those who gathered a lot did not have too much, and those who could only gather a little did not fall short in supplies. This principle only worked if the children of God remained unselfish. The unselfishness of others is what helped the Christian church to maintain the support it needed. Paul encouraged the Corinthians to not only continue giving, but to give with the right attitude and perspective.

DAILY BIBLE READINGS

M: The Widow's Offering
Luke 20:45-21:4

T: Chosen to Serve the Poor
Acts 6:1-6

W: Generosity, a Gift from God
Romans 12:3-8

T: The Collection for the Saints
1 Corinthians 15:58-16:4

F: Generosity, a Fruit of the Spirit
Galatians 5:16-26

S: Excel in Generosity
2 Corinthians 8:1-7

S: Rules for Giving
2 Corinthians 8:8-15

TEACHING TIPS

August 20
Bible Study Guide 12

1. Words You Should Know

A. Confident (2 Corinthians 9:4) *hupostasis* (Gk.)—A setting under (support), that is, essence or assurance.

B. Bounty (v. 5) *eulogia* (Gk.)—A matter of blessing, but by extension a benefit or largess (generosity).

C. Purposeth (v. 7) *proaireomai* (Gk.)—To choose for oneself before another thing (prefer), that is, by implication to propose (intend).

D. Cheerful (v. 7) *hilaros* (Gk.)—Hilarious, that is, prompt or willing.

2. Teacher Preparation

A. Prayerfully read the FOCAL VERSES and DEVOTIONAL READING.

B. Prayerfully study the entire BIBLE STUDY GUIDE. Highlight parts to emphasize.

C. Be prepared to discuss the MAKE IT HAPPEN section.

D. Think about existing needs in the body of Christ that you can share with the students.

3. Starting the Lesson

A. Assign a student to lead the class in prayer, focusing on the LESSON AIM.

B. Ask a student to read the IN FOCUS section.

C. Initiate a preliminary discussion about the meaning of missions.

4. Getting into the Lesson

A. Allow each student to read some portion of THE PEOPLE, PLACES, AND TIMES, BACKGROUND, KEEP IN MIND, and AT-A-GLANCE sections.

B. Allow each student to read one of the FOCAL VERSES. As each one is read, discuss and instruct using the portions of IN DEPTH and MORE LIGHT ON THE TEXT sections that you highlighted in your preparation.

C. Ask the students to respond to the SEARCH THE SCRIPTURES questions.

5. Relating the Lesson to Life

A. Facilitate the discussion of the DISCUSS THE MEANING questions with the students.

B. Have someone read LESSON IN OUR SOCIETY.

6. Arousing Action

A. Ask a student to read the KEEP IN MIND verse again and then the MAKE IT HAPPEN section. Talk about opportunities to spread God's provisions.

B. Ask the students to take a few minutes and respond to the FOLLOW THE SPIRIT and REMEMBER YOUR THOUGHTS sections.

C. Encourage the students to be prepared for next week's lesson.

D. Close the class in prayer.

WORSHIP GUIDE

For the Superintendent or Teacher
Theme: Giving Is a Witness
Theme Song: "I Surrender All"
Scripture: Psalm 112
Song: "Jesus Paid It All"
Meditation: We thank You, God, for Your grace and Your love. You are our bountiful supplier of all good things. Praise be to You for Your unspeakable gift. Praise be to You for Jesus Christ our Saviour. He must increase as we decrease. Let us crucify self-will and selfish attitudes so that You may come forth and bless our brothers and sisters in Christ. Amen.

AUG 20TH

481

GIVING IS A WITNESS

Bible Background • 2 CORINTHIANS 9:1–15
Printed Text • 2 CORINTHIANS 9:3–15
Devotional Reading • PSALM 37:16–24

LESSON AIM

By the end of the lesson, we will:

KNOW that God freely gives to those that freely give;

BE CONVINCED that the Christian heart finds fulfillment in bountiful giving; and

BE COMMITTED to take advantage of the opportunity to bless others by giving.

KEEP IN MIND

"And God is able to make all grace abound toward you; that ye, always having all sufficiency in all things, may abound to every good work" (2 Corinthians 9:8).

FOCAL VERSES

2 Corinthians 9:3 Yet have I sent the brethren, lest our boasting of you should be in vain in this behalf; that, as I said, ye may be ready:

4 Lest haply if they of Macedonia come with me, and find you unprepared, we (that we say not, ye) should be ashamed in this same confident boasting.

5 Therefore I thought it necessary to exhort the brethren, that they would go before unto you, and make up beforehand your bounty, whereof ye had notice before, that the same might be ready, as a matter of bounty, and not as of covetousness.

6 But this I say, He which soweth sparingly shall reap also sparingly; and he which soweth bountifully shall reap also bountifully.

7 Every man according as he purposeth in his heart, so let him give; not grudgingly, or of necessity: for God loveth a cheerful giver.

8 And God is able to make all grace abound toward you; that ye, always having all sufficiency in all things, may abound to every good work:

LESSON OVERVIEW

LESSON AIM
KEEP IN MIND
FOCAL VERSES
IN FOCUS
THE PEOPLE, PLACES,
AND TIMES
BACKGROUND
AT-A-GLANCE
IN DEPTH
SEARCH THE SCRIPTURES
DISCUSS THE MEANING
LESSON IN OUR SOCIETY
MAKE IT HAPPEN
FOLLOW THE SPIRIT
REMEMBER YOUR THOUGHTS
MORE LIGHT ON THE TEXT
DAILY BIBLE READINGS

9 (As it is written, He hath dispersed abroad; he hath given to the poor: his righteousness remaineth for ever.

10 Now he that ministereth seed to the sower both minister bread for your food, and multiply your seed sown, and increase the fruits of your righteousness;)

11 Being enriched in every thing to all bountifulness, which causeth through us thanksgiving to God.

12 For the administration of this service not only supplieth the want of the saints, but is abundant also by many thanksgivings unto God;

13 Whiles by the experiment of this ministration they glorify God for your professed subjection unto the gospel of Christ, and for your liberal distribution unto them, and unto all men;

14 And by their prayer for you, which long after you for the exceeding grace of God in you.

15 Thanks be unto God for his unspeakable gift.

IN FOCUS

After drying her hands on a towel, Nate's 90-year-old mother tossed it onto the counter. Nate watched his mother in wonder. His life had changed so much. His wife had died recently and now his mother was living in his home. She was thinner than he liked, but her face still glowed when she smiled. Sipping breakfast coffee, he couldn't take his eyes off her. She turned and stared at him with a childlike smile.

"What's wrong? Why are you staring at me like that?"

Nate blinked backed into reality. "I was remembering how you raised the seven of us cooking breakfast and dinner every day, then washing the dishes and cleaning our rooms."

"We wanted for nothing; our home was a palace."

"Son, you're only 60." She chuckled. "And your memory is worse than mine. We lived in the poorest country town in Alabama. Are you forgetting how many times we ate chicken and more chicken?"

"Funny, Mom, that's just what I was thinking about—your fried chicken and how all of us sat at the table eating, but you sat on that old wooden stool because there was no room for you."

"That's God's truth," she interrupted.

"Mom, I remember you sitting on that stool eating the neck and back. You never ate a leg, wing, thigh, or breast. But you raised the chicken, killed it, plucked it, cleaned it, and fried it."

"I liked gnawing on them necks."

"Yeah, I know that's what you always said, but later I realized you really wanted us to have the best part of the chicken. Even though you deserved better, you chose lesser for our sake and you never complained."

Paul assured the Corinthians that God was able to meet their needs. Do you realize that a Christian heart finds fulfillment in bountiful giving?

THE PEOPLE, PLACES, AND TIMES

Macedonia. Macedonians were believers in the churches in the Roman province of Macedonia. During the time that the apostle Paul ministered, Macedonia included the northern part of Greece and portions of Bulgaria, Yugoslavia, and Albania. These churches were located in the cities of Berea, Philippi, and Thessalonica, which was the capital city. Other cities in this province that Paul visited were Neapolis, Amphipolis, and Apollonia. Macedonia bordered the southern Roman province of Achaia. Paul was led to preach in Macedonia by a vision from God (Acts 16:9). Two visits by Paul to Macedonia are recorded in Acts 16:10-17:15 and Acts 20:1-6. A possible third visit is alluded to in Philippians 2:24 and 1 Timothy 1:3.

Achaia. This was a Roman province in southern Greece where Corinth was located.

BACKGROUND

Paul spent 18 months with the Corinthians, so he had firsthand knowledge of their eagerness to assist others in need. This specific need was for the believers in Jerusalem. He was impressed to the extent that he boasted about it when he was with the Macedonian churches. The Macedonians were encouraged to do the same, even to the point of completion. In fact, they earnestly pleaded with Paul to allow them to show grace and to fellowship with the believers in Jerusalem (2 Corinthians 8:4). They viewed giving as a privilege, not an obligation. This was an opportunity for them to be like their Heavenly Father, who gives good gifts to His children. It was still fresh in Paul's mind even while he was writing to the Corinthians. Paul gloried in the grace of God manifested in the lives of people.

Christian giving is an outflow of the grace of God bestowed on the giver. The Corinthians had started their collections a year prior, but now needed to complete it. Paul was sending Titus and two companions to help the Corinthians complete what they had started. In 2 Corinthians 8:23, Paul describes Titus as, "my partner and fellowhelper concerning you (the Corinthians)." One of Titus's companions was a man well-known in the churches and appointed by the churches to travel with the collections. His service served as a precaution against any accusations of misuse of church funds. Accountability must be maintained not only before God, but before people as well (8:21). The other man sent had been proven worthy on many occasions and was particularly motivated to complete this task because of his confidence in the response of the Corinthians.

AT-A-GLANCE

1. Preparation for Giving
(2 Corinthians 9:3-5)
2. Principles for Giving (vv. 6-7)
3. Provisions for Giving (vv. 8-10)
4. Praise to God for Giving (vv. 11-15)

IN DEPTH

1. Preparation for Giving (2 Corinthians 9:3-5)

Preparation should always be made for giving. That which a person purposes in his heart to give must be earned or acquired. This may require pursuit of new enterprises or sources of income specifically for a special purpose. Then it must be set aside; otherwise, it may be spent on something else. The primary concern of Paul is that the Corinthians be prepared when he comes for the collections. His planned trip would be his third visit to the church at Corinth (2 Corinthians 12:14). He is confident of their readiness to give but he wants to assist them in accomplishing what they desire to do. What they may lack in organizational and administrative skills should not put the help of the needy in jeopardy. It is like someone saying, "I want to help, but I need you to show me how."

To set the expectation that assistance will be provided, and then come up empty when the assistance is required is quite an embarrassment. This expectation was based on substantial and concrete confidence (firm support that leads to an assurance) in the Corinthians. To make matters worse, some Macedonians may accompany him with their collection from the churches and find that those who got a head start on collections and spurred them on somehow failed to deliver.

Paul encourages Titus and two unnamed "brethren" to go ahead of him to Corinth to "organize beforehand" or to prepare in advance the beneficial blessing (rendered bounty). Paul was convinced that this was a necessary precaution. Any amount was not sufficient to address the need. The collection must meet the needs of those in Jerusalem.

The magnitude of the word "bounty" used by Paul is more appreciated when compared with its use in passages such as Genesis 33:11 and Joshua 15:19 (also Judges 1:15). Jacob presented his brother Esau with 220 goats, 200 ewes, 20 rams, 30 camels and their colts, 40 cows, 10 bulls, and 30 donkeys. He persuaded his brother to take the gift because God was gracious to him and he had plenty. Giving should be a blessing both to the one who gives and the one who receives. When giving is done begrudgingly, it is equated to an act of covetousness (reluctantly given hindered by greed). Gaining reward should not be the motive for giving; otherwise, it becomes covetousness (selfish desire for gain). God desires a generous, eager, cheerful (hilarious) heart.

2. Principles for Giving (vv. 6-7)

It is a simple earthly agricultural principle that few seeds planted yield few results and many seeds planted yield much results—everything else being equal. The seed must be sown in fertile ground in order to be fruitful and multiply. It must be sown where God wants to bless.

A seed sown is released, but contrary to appearances, is not lost. It is freed to produce and multiply. The depravity in humans (flesh) blinds them to this truth. Flesh will persistently attempt to rise up and control the heart. The Word of Truth must prevail and faith in God must be exercised. There is a waiting period before the return is realized; nevertheless, believers are encouraged not be weary in well doing for in due time they shall reap if they do not faint (Galatians 6:9). This being the case, the believer takes advantage of every opportunity to bless. Even those without can find some means to give (Matthew 10:42; 25:36).

"One man gives freely, yet gains even more; another withholds unduly, but comes to poverty" (Proverbs 11:24, NIV). Jesus spoke of the quality of giving as opposed to the quantity of giving. The woman that gave all that she had, though small, gave more (she sowed bountifully) than those who had given much in quantity out of their abundance (Mark 12:44). The word "bountifully" in verse 6 has the same meaning as "bounty" in verse 5. The person who sows a blessing will reap a blessing from God because that person gives to God so that God can bless another. The person lends to God and God is faithful to restore that lent with proportionate magnitude (Proverbs 19:17).

The source of the gift is not the bank account but the heart. In the heart, people decide what to give. The type of heart a person has will make a different gift. Things that influence the heart will also play a part. There is individual freedom in giving. It is not forced but voluntary. The word "purpose," as used here, is to make a preferable choice by oneself (Exodus 25:2). Giving that produces blessings must flow freely out of the heart without regret. The heart should not be made sorrowful at the thought of releasing the gift. The cheerful giver looks forward to an opportunity to participate in the things that God is doing. This person is said to have a generous eye (Proverbs 22:9). This person is alert and prepared with an earnest desire to participate in the blessings of God. The giver finds real pleasure in giving. It is an exhilarating experience. This heart is open to the illumination of the Holy Spirit. The Holy Spirit bestows gifts of giving (Romans 12:8).

3. Provisions for Giving (vv. 8-10)

The grace of God enables believers to give (1 Chronicles 29:14). It was God's grace that enabled the Macedonian churches to give out of their poverty (2 Corinthians 8:1).

God enabled them to do what they could not do by themselves. The power of God operates in giving. His power is made perfect (accomplished) in weakness (12:9). If He could do it for the Macedonians, He can certainly do it for those in Corinth! Though it is possible for God to rain manna from heaven, He provides material needs to people through people. God's provisions are without bounds. He provides the liberated giver with all that is required to abound to the needs of others whenever it is needed. God provides all grace for all sufficiency in all things for every inherently good (beneficial results) work. Contrary to conventional thinking, as the believer participates in what God is doing, and gives out, rather than suffering loss, the believer's resources are replenished constantly for every good work. It is accomplished by Christ Jesus (Philippians 4:19).

The quotation from verse 9 is from the Greek Old Testament version of Psalm 112:9. This psalm speaks of the righteous person who trusts and fears the Lord. This person obeys the commandments of the Lord (Deuteronomy 15:10). This person gives freely (scatters with an open hand) and is gracious and compassionate and blesses others. Wealth and riches are in this person's house and there is no fear of bad news. The heart

of this person is upheld as this person steadfastly trusts the Lord. The teaching by Paul is a continuation of what God required in the Law, the psalms, and the prophets. But believers are also encouraged by the grace provided in Jesus Christ (Matthew 10:8). The transforming power of Jesus Christ turns even a thief into a benevolent giver (Ephesians 4:28).

God supplies the seed; provides the ground, nutrients, and water for the seed to grow; and brings forth fruit from the seed, which brings forth more seed and produces food (Isaiah 55:10). All things are of God and from God (2 Corinthians 5:18). The potential result of that sown is much greater than that sown. Jesus took what little bit the boy gave and fed thousands! The Corinthians can joy in the fact that whatever they give will be transformed by God into even greater blessings for all involved.

4. Praise to God for Giving (vv. 11-15)

Giving is an enriching experience for the giver and the receiver, promoting cause for both to lavish God with thanksgiving. Those who love them and fellowship with them offer thanksgiving as well. So there is a double benefit. People are blessed, and they, in turn, bless God, who richly gives us all things to enjoy. By glorifying God, they fulfill the purpose for which they were created.

The faith and obedience (to the confession of Christ) of the Corinthians are demonstrated by the outflow of their generosity to those in need. This confirms or proves that their faith is not dead, but is alive and working (James 2:17). Given that the recipients were believers in Jerusalem (that is, Jews), the assistance from Gentiles proves all the more the transforming power of God. This act of love begets love from those who are blessed. They minister to the needs of the body of Christ making the body all the more healthy and functioning. Communion is demonstrated in a practical way. God is even more glorified.

Not only do those that receive glorify God, but they bless those who gave by laboring for them in prayer to God.

In the process of writing about the blessings of giving, Paul is overwhelmed by the thought of the gift of all gifts. Thanks be unto God for the gift of

His Son. It is a gift beyond words (indescribable) and beyond explanation; yet, it is a gift that can be received by all. The Son is a gift that was sown by the Father and resulted in the salvation and blessings of many (John 12:24). He did not spare His own Son, but delivered Him up for us all. Believers are challenged by the love of God to also love another (1 John 4:11).

SEARCH THE SCRIPTURES

1. Paul expected to be accompanied by representatives from what churches (2 Corinthians 9:4)?

2. What type of giver does God love (v. 7)?

3. What is it about giving that goes against conventional wisdom (v. 8)?

4. How would you give witness to those in need (v. 13)?

5. Aside from the material benefit, what other benefit do those in need realize from the giving of believers (vv. 12-15)?

DISCUSS THE MEANING

1. How can a believer be encouraged to give bountifully without being compelled to give?

2. What type of giving provides the greatest witness to the body of Christ?

3. What makes the gift of God's Son indescribable?

4. Why don't more believers desire the spiritual gift of giving?

LESSON IN OUR SOCIETY

There are three general areas in the life of every believer where God has sown seeds of grace. God has given every believer talents, time, and resources (materials). They are the reservoirs from which servants of God pull in order to distribute God's gifts to those in need. Opportunities are present in the home, the local church, and the community. More opportunities are available in local missions, shelters, hospitals, and nursing homes. Still more opportunities are available in other parts of the world. Through local church organizations, the message of Christ reaches into other regions of the world by the establishment and maintenance of churches, schools, orphanages, and medical facilities.

MAKE IT HAPPEN

God makes all gifts abound to you so that you may abound to every good work. You are responsible for what God gives you. You can invest it in things that don't last or you can invest it in things that have eternal reward. You have the opportunity to be an emissary for God and experience the exhilaration of giving.

Seek the heart of God for guidance in where to give and what to give. God will reveal Himself to the sincere heart and provide whatever is required to accomplish His purpose.

FOLLOW THE SPIRIT

What God wants me to do:

_____

_____

REMEMBER YOUR THOUGHTS

Special insights I have learned:

_____

_____

MORE LIGHT ON THE TEXT

2 Corinthians 9:3-15

Although our study passage begins in chapter 9 of 2 Corinthians, Paul mentioned sending members of the Macedonian congregation with his fellow missionary Titus to visit the Corinthian church in chapter 8. Since he referred to Achaia and Macedonia (2 Corinthians 8:19), which were large regions rather than specific cities, he may have meant representatives from more than one church.

In the verses that precede those we are studying today, Paul told the Corinthian church that he had boasted to the Macedonian Christians about how they were ready several months earlier to give help to the Jerusalem church.

Christians in Jerusalem had become persecuted and needy (Acts 8:1; 12:1-2; 24:17). Paul's concern was to ensure that the financial aid Corinth had promised was collected and ready. In Paul's effort to collect money to help the church in Jerusalem, we see several lessons about how generously God blesses us when we are willing to be a blessing to others.

3 Yet have I sent the brethren, lest our boasting of you should be in vain in this behalf; that, as I said, ye may be ready:

Paul had told the church in Macedonia that the church in Achaia was ready to help the needy Jerusalem Christians a year ago when they had first learned of their need. To make sure his confidence in them did not prove to be empty bragging, he told Titus and another respected Christian (2 Corinthians 8:18-19) to go on ahead and make sure their offering was ready.

Notice Paul does not say "my boast" but rather "our boast." Apparently Titus was remaining in Macedonia where Paul had sent him that the Corinthian church stated they would give to financially to help the Jerusalem Christians. Paul does not want his boasting to "be in vain." The NIV uses "prove hollow" here. The Greek word Paul used is *kenothe* from *kenoo* (**ken-o'-o**) meaning to be empty. Paul does not want his expression of confidence to be just empty or hollow words with no action to fill them with meaning. "In this behalf" means in this matter.

4 Lest haply if they of Macedonia come with me, and find you unprepared, we (that we say not, ye) should be ashamed in this same confident boasting.

If Paul and representatives from the Macedonian churches had come to Corinth to pick up the Corinthian's offering and no collection was ready, he would have appeared to be a blowhard and they would have looked like big talkers who made promises that they did not keep. Where the text says "we should be ashamed" Paul uses the Greek word *kataisxuno* (**kat-ahee-skhoo'-no**) meaning to be disgraced or humiliated by someone or something. If, after Paul and his party arrived, the church leaders at Corinth had to go around to their members on the spur of the moment and rustle up the offering, they would have certainly been humiliated. The NIV translation ends the verse: "we not to say anything about you would be ashamed at having been so confident."

5 Therefore I thought it necessary to exhort the brethren, that they would go before unto you, and make up beforehand your bounty, whereof ye had notice before, that the same might be ready, as a matter of bounty, and not as of covetousness.

When Paul says he thought it "necessary," the Greek word he used was *anagkaios* (**an-ang-kah'-yos**) meaning physically necessary. Paul understood that in human nature our tendency is often to put things off, to procrastinate. So Paul felt it necessary to press Titus to handle without delaying what might be an unpleasant task.

Paul says he "urged" Titus and the man (or men) with him to go ahead of him and the others. When Paul's party arrived later, they picked up the Corinthians' offering, carried it on, and presented it to the Jerusalem church (2 Corinthians 8:19).

The Greek word translated as "urged" is *parakaleo* (**par-ak-al-eh'-o**). It can mean to gently comfort, to call alongside or encourage, or to sternly exhort, warn, or beg. Likely Titus and the others did not look forward to confronting the Corinthian Christians about their need to get their offering ready, so Paul pressed them to go and do it.

Paul wanted their offering ready when he and the other delegates got there, not scrounged together at the last minute. "Make up beforehand" translates the Greek word *prokatartisosin* (**prok-at-ar-tid'-zo-sin**). This word combines the Greek preposition *pro*, meaning before and the verb *katartizo* (**kat-ar-tid'-zo**), meaning to prepare or repair. *Katartizo* is the word used to describe James and John cleaning and repairing their nets for their next day of fishing (Mark 1:19).

Paul wanted the Corinthian Christians to feel that their giving was a blessing to other Christians in need. He did not want them feeling that it was merely the fulfillment of a promise to Paul, nor that he coveted a big offering and had pressured it out of them in order to have an impressive gift to present in Jerusalem.

6 But this I say, He which soweth sparingly shall reap also sparingly; and he which soweth bountifully shall reap also bountifully.

What Paul says here fits with what he wrote to the churches in Galatia, "whatsoever a man soweth that shall he also reap" (Galatians 6:7). If you skimp on seed, expect a skimpy crop. Plant plenty of seed and expect a big crop. In other words, do not be stingy.

We must remember that as a devout Pharisee, Paul's mind was soaked with the Old Testament. What he says here is likely Proverbs 11:24 put in his own words. The NIV translates it: "one man gives freely, yet gains even more; another withholds unduly, but comes to poverty." Here was Paul's first big lesson about Christian giving: it should express an attitude of generosity, not stinginess.

7 Every man according as he purposeth in his heart, so let him give; not grudgingly, or of necessity: for God loveth a cheerful giver.

Paul emphasizes here that each Christian must decide for himself or herself how much to give. The Greek word for "he purposeth" is the verb *proeretai* (**pro-EAR-ee-tay**), which means to decide on something beforehand. It is in the past tense. Paul was telling them that whatever any of you decided to give last year now is the time to give it.

"Not grudgingly" in Greek was *me ek lupe* (**may ek loo'-pay**) meaning not out of sorrow. Paul was telling them not to feel bad about giving. He says neither should their giving be determined "of necessity" (Gk. *ex anagkeis,* **ex an-ang-kays**). He was emphasizing that the person's motive for giving should not be determined by other people's giving or expectations. The lesson for us today is that we should give generously from what we have to give. But at the same time God wants us to be honorable people and pay our debts.

When Paul wrote "God loveth a cheerful giver," the Greek word he chose for "cheerful" is *hilaron* (**hil-ar-on'**). Our modern word "hilarious," meaning boisterously merry, is derived from it.

The Greek language has several words for different kinds of love. Paul uses here its strongest word *agapao* (**ag-ap-ah'-o**), which is not sentimental, romantic, family, or affectionate love, but pure, deep, unconditional love.

8 And God is able to make all grace abound toward you; that ye, always having all sufficiency in all things, may abound to every good work:

In verse 8, Paul gives his second major lesson

about Christian giving. God will provide the means to give generously. When Paul says God "is able," he used the Greek verb *dunateo* (**doo-nat-eh'-o**). *Dunateo* is related to our modern word "dynamite." God has power far beyond our ability to understand. He has the power to provide for our needs as well as those of others.

The word "grace" here comes from the Greek word *charin* (**khar'-in**) and refers to the "exceptional effects of divine grace, above and beyond those usually experienced by Christians. After affirming God's great power, Paul states that God can "make all grace abound toward you." "Make abound" in Greek is from *perisseuo* (**per-is-syoo'-o**), meaning to cause to be present in abundance or to make someone rich.

Then he says "always having all sufficiency in all things." What a great promise! God has the power to give you power to help those in need always, every time having all sufficiency, giving you the power to act, and in all things, in every situation.

The purpose of God's grace is that His people "may abound to every good work." This is not a promise that any individual Christian can meet all the needs of another person or group. In English "you" and "your" are used whether referring to one person or a group of people, but the Greek language had separate words for you singular and you plural. This is important here because when God promises to make "all grace abound toward you," the "you" is the Greek plural *humas* (**hoo-mas'**), not the singular for "you," *se* (**seh**).

Each Christian has an individual responsibility to offer loving ministry in human needs, but meeting needs is the task of the whole church, not just one person. Some can do a lot (Romans 12:8), others only a little. However, as Paul wrote in 1 Corinthians 12:7, "But the manifestation of the Spirit is given to every man to profit withal," or as NIV renders those last three words for the common good.

9 (As it is written, He hath dispersed abroad; he hath given to the poor: his righteousness remaineth for ever. 10 Now he that ministereth seed to the sower both minister bread for your food, and multiply your seed sown, and increase the fruits of your righteousness;)

"As it is written" in the New Testament is almost always a tip-off that something from the Old Testament is being quoted. In these two verses, Paul first quotes Psalm 112:9, and then he uses the last line from Isaiah 55:10. Psalm 112 describes how the man who trusts God and cares for needs he sees in the world about him will be blessed. In the phrase, "he hath dispersed abroad," Paul uses the Greek word *skorpizo* (**skor-pid'-zo**), which means to scatter something in all directions. One ancient writer used the word of a farmer scattering fertilizer over his fields. The writer of Psalm 112 was saying that the person who trusts God will use his money to help in a lot of different ways.

Then he says "he hath given to the poor." Here for "poor" Paul uses the Greek word *penes* (**pen'-ace**), which is the opposite of the Greek word for wealthy (*plousios*). Often this word is paired in the Bible with *ptochos* (**pto-khos'**), the Greek word for poor. When used together, they indicate people who are penniless and helpless.

"His righteousness remaineth forever" refers not just to a person's standing with God or behavior that pleases God. Rather the Greek word translated as "remaineth" is in the present tense, which describes action that is habitual, something a person does over and over. A third major lesson for our giving is that God wants our generosity to be a holy habit. His generous provision for our needs as Christians is to be the model we follow as we relate to others in need.

In verse 10, Paul adapts the last line of Isaiah 55:10 to tell how God helps us be generous. Isaiah said that God sends rain and snow onto the earth so plants can sprout and grow. Isaiah said God does that so farmers will have seed to plant that in turn will produce grain for bread to eat. Taking Isaiah's basic thought that God gives seed to sow and bread to eat, Paul adds that He will supply more than enough to meet a Christian's needs, and even multiply it so we can be generous.

Notice Paul wrote God will "multiply your seed," not "seeds." The collection from the Corinthian church was the seed, not each believer's individual gift. That is confirmed by Paul's use again of the Greek plural form of "your," *humon* (**hoo-mone'**).

If everyone gave what they were able to, when it was all added up God would cause it to "increase." In 2 Corinthians 8:12 (NIV), commenting on collecting this same offering, Paul wrote, "For if the willingness is there, the gift is acceptable according to what one has, not according to what he does not have."

The Greek word given as "increase" is *auxano* (**owx-an'-o**) meaning to cause growth. Verse 10 assures Christians that God will "minister bread for your food, and multiply your seed...and increase the fruits of your righteousness." All these promises are given as certainties, not possibilities.

11 Being enriched in every thing to all bountifulness, which causeth through us thanksgiving to God.

Verse 11 follows up by assuring us that the result will be "being enriched...to all bountifulness." This phrase is not promising that any Christian who is generous will get rich; rather it is saying that God will make us rich enough to be generous.

"Bountifulness" here comes from the Greek word *haplotes* (**hap-lot'-ace**). The word has two meanings. Sometimes it is used to mean simplicity or sincerity. In other settings it means generosity. Scholars in the Greek language debate over which meaning Paul intended here; both fit. If a Christian is single-minded in his faith or generous because of his gratitude for God's grace, then every part of that person's life is going to be made richer. Paul may have used the word with both meanings in mind. Whichever Paul meant, he was sure the result would be gratitude to God for His blessing through His church.

12 For the administration of this service not only supplieth the want of the saints, but is abundant also by many thanksgivings unto God;

"Administration" here refers to practical, often physical, work. Paul uses the word *diakonia* (**dee-ak-on-ee'-ah**). This word is related to the word "deacon." However, this action refers to practical ministry anyone can perform. Then Paul mentions "this service." The Greek word he used was *leitourgia* (**li-toorg-ee'-ah**), which meant an official act of worship. Paul's point is that when

Christians give practical help to others in need, in this case, financial aid, it is as much an act of worship as anything they might do in a formal worship service. Such ministry not only meets a practical need, but also brings about many instances of thanksgiving to God because of the faithfulness of His church.

13 Whiles by the experiment of this ministration they glorify God for your professed subjection unto the gospel of Christ, and for your liberal distribution unto them, and unto all men;

"Experiment" sounds like something we would do on a trial basis, but the word Paul used here is *dokime* (**dok-ee-may'**), which means the character or the proof of something. The NIV states it as, "this service that you perform." This approved service might be even better. Paul says their giving brings honor to God because of their visible commitment to the Good News of God's love in Christ. The little phrase "and unto all men" reminds us of the importance of our witness our concerned giving can be to the world about us, lost in its unbelief.

14 And by their prayer for you, which long after you for the exceeding grace of God in you.

Paul tells them that long after the financial help they send is used up, God will be praised. His grace will continue to show by their prayers of the Jerusalem church for the Greek Christians. The Greeks were likely people they would never meet, except for the men who brought the gift from the Gentile churches in Greece to Jerusalem. But together, the financial help from Gentiles and the prayers of Christians from a mostly Jewish background would combine to affirm the grace of God that unifies His church.

15 Thanks be unto God for his unspeakable gift.

As Paul thinks of the accumulated gift of the Gentile churches in northern and southern Greece, he finds it impossible to put into words God's incredible gift of forgiveness and new, eternal life through Christ. When he calls God's gift indescribable, he uses the word *anekdiegetos* (**an-ek-dee-ay'-gay-tos**). It meant beyond the human ability to appreciate or grasp, and was the opposite of to tell in detail. Paul had written earlier in 1 Corinthians 2:9: "However, as it is written: 'No eye has seen no ear has heard, no mind has conceived what God has prepared for those who love him.'" It is beyond our human capacity to grasp God's capacity to forgive, to love, and to unite all kinds of people. And as we will see next week, what lies ahead is even more indescribably wonderful.

DAILY BIBLE READINGS

M: Every Giving Act Is from Above
James 1:12-17
T: Give and You Shall Receive
Luke 6:32-38
W: Do Your Giving Quietly
Matthew 6:1-6
T: Pleased to Share Their Resources
Romans 15:25-29
F: Arrangements for the Jerusalem Collection
2 Corinthians 9:1-5
S: A Cheerful Giver
2 Corinthians 9:6-10
S: Generosity Glorifies God
2 Corinthians 9:11-15

TEACHING TIPS

August 27
Bible Study Guide 13

1. Words You Should Know

A. Expedient (2 Corinthians 12:1) *sumphero* (Gk.)—To bear together (contribute); advantageous.

B. Glory (vv. 5-6, 9) *kauchaomai* (Gk.)—To vaunt (in a good or bad sense).

C. Infirmities (vv. 5, 9-10) *astheneia* (Gk.)—Feebleness of the mind or body; malady; frailty.

D. Sufficient (v. 9) *arkeo* (Gk.)—To ward off, that is by implication to avail.

2. Teacher Preparation

A. Prayerfully read the FOCAL VERSES and DEVOTIONAL READING.

B. Prayerfully study the entire BIBLE STUDY GUIDE. Highlight parts to emphasize.

C. Be prepared to discuss the MAKE IT HAPPEN section.

D. Be prepared to talk about the natural tendency of people to exalt themselves and the role society plays in motivating that behavior. Who wants to be considered weak?

3. Starting the Lesson

A. Assign a student to lead the class in prayer, focusing on the LESSON AIM.

B. Ask a student to read the IN FOCUS section.

C. Initiate a preliminary discussion about healthy or unhealthy self-confidence.

4. Getting into the Lesson

A. Allow each student to read some portion of THE PEOPLE, PLACES, AND TIMES, BACKGROUND, KEEP IN MIND, and AT-A-GLANCE sections.

B. Allow each student to read one of the FOCAL VERSES. As each one is read, discuss and instruct using the portions of IN DEPTH and MORE LIGHT ON THE TEXT sections that you highlighted in your preparation.

C. Ask the students to respond to the SEARCH THE SCRIPTURES questions.

5. Relating the Lesson to Life

A. Facilitate a discussion of the DISCUSS THE MEANING questions with the students.

B. Have someone read LESSON IN OUR SOCIETY.

C. Our society rewards competitiveness. Ask your students how they can reconcile societal norms with God's available grace.

6. Arousing Action

A. Request a student to read the KEEP IN MIND verse again and then the MAKE IT HAPPEN section. Invite a student to share an experience that God obviously orchestrated.

B. Ask the students to take a few minutes and respond to the FOLLOW THE SPIRIT and REMEMBER YOUR THOUGHTS sections.

C. Encourage the students to be prepared for next week's lesson.

D. Close the class in prayer.

WORSHIP GUIDE

For the Superintendent or Teacher
Theme: The Giving of Sufficient Grace
Theme Song: "Amazing Grace"
Scripture: 2 Corinthians 4:5-11
Song: "God Will Take Care of You"
Meditation: Our Father in heaven, hallowed be Thy name. Let Your kingdom come. Let Your will be done in our lives, as it is in heaven. As we submit to You, remove fear and doubt. Where we are weak, make us strong. We know that Your grace is sufficient, and we thank You for it. Amen.

AUG 27TH

THE GIVING OF SUFFICIENT GRACE

Bible Background • 2 CORINTHIANS 12:1–10
Printed Text • 2 CORINTHIANS 12:1–10
Devotional Reading • JAMES 4:1–10

LESSON AIM

By the end of the lesson, we will:

KNOW that God's grace favors, protects, and empowers and that without Him they can do nothing of eternal significance;

BE CONVINCED that God does everything for our good; and

BE COMMITTED to glorify God in all circumstances that the grace of God provides.

KEEP IN MIND

"And he said unto me, My grace is sufficient for thee: for my strength is made perfect in weakness. Most gladly therefore will I rather glory in my infirmities, that the power of Christ may rest upon me" (2 Corinthians 12:9).

FOCAL VERSES

2 Corinthians 12:1 It is not expedient for me doubtless to glory. I will come to visions and revelations of the Lord.

2 I knew a man in Christ above fourteen years ago, (whether in the body, I cannot tell; or whether out of the body, I cannot tell: God knoweth;) such an one caught up to the third heaven.

3 And I knew such a man, (whether in the body, or out of the body, I cannot tell: God knoweth;)

4 How that he was caught up into paradise, and heard unspeakable words, which it is not law-

ful for a man to utter.

5 Of such an one will I glory: yet of myself I will not glory, but in mine infirmities.

6 For though I would desire to glory, I shall not be a fool; for I will say the truth: but now I forbear, lest any man should think of me above that which he seeth me to be, or that he heareth of me.

7 And lest I should be exalted above measure through the abundance of the revelations, there was given to me a thorn in the flesh, the messenger of Satan to buffet me, lest I should be exalted above measure.

8 For this thing I besought the Lord thrice, that it might depart from me.

9 And he said unto me, My grace is sufficient for thee: for my strength is made perfect in weakness. Most gladly therefore will I rather glory in my infirmities, that the power of Christ may rest upon me.

10 Therefore I take pleasure in infirmities, in reproaches, in necessities, in persecutions, in distresses for Christ's sake: for when I am weak, then am I strong.

IN FOCUS

In the middle of a snowstorm, Margie's car began to fishtail on an ice patch. She crossed in the opposite lane and when she applied her

LESSON OVERVIEW

LESSON AIM
KEEP IN MIND
FOCAL VERSES
IN FOCUS
THE PEOPLE, PLACES, AND TIMES
BACKGROUND
AT-A-GLANCE
IN DEPTH
SEARCH THE SCRIPTURES
DISCUSS THE MEANING
LESSON IN OUR SOCIETY
MAKE IT HAPPEN
FOLLOW THE SPIRIT
REMEMBER YOUR THOUGHTS
MORE LIGHT ON THE TEXT
DAILY BIBLE READINGS

brakes, the car skidded 15 feet and fell 100 yards down the side of the hill, hit a drainage ditch, and rolled over. It was a one-vehicle accident. She was only driving 30 mph when she tried to navigate a left bend in the road. The impact of the crash alone should have killed her. Margie got out of the car in the middle of the blizzard. Her face was smeared in blood, she had a loose tooth, and her upper lip was sliced open. She spat out blood and staggered to her feet, happy to be alive.

Margie awoke in the quiet sunlight showering her bed, but the nightmare was true. Only one detail was missing—both of Margie's hands had been amputated. For months she had to go through the trials of fighting depression, losing her hands, and accepting God's will to live that way.

Margie shared her testimony of God's love and grace following her tragic accident to encourage others to trust in God. Margie praised God because as a gifted artist, she still did all her artwork using a paintbrush between her teeth.

Her pastor would often remark, "Her faith in God should be an inspiration to all of us! If she could make it, so can you by trusting in God's love. Her faith in God and His grace enabled her to learn to live one day at a time and accept her disability as God's will to use her in this special way."

Although God didn't remove Paul's physical affliction, he demonstrated his power in Paul. Are you convinced that God can use everything for our good?

THE PEOPLE, PLACES, AND TIMES

Vision. A vision is a presentation to the mind of a person while awake. They are used by God to reveal His Word or will to His servants. Visions are also used to warn and to encourage. The Bible gives examples of God speaking to His prophets and apostles through visions.

Six of Paul's visions are recorded in the book of Acts. He alludes to others in his letters to the churches. At the time of Paul's conversion, in a vision he saw a man named Ananias come and lay hands on him for the restoration of his sight (Acts 9:12). After Paul's conversion, he returned to Jerusalem and saw a vision of the Lord warning him to flee while praying in the temple (22:17). When Paul was on his second missionary journey

in Troas, God gave him a vision of a man calling him to Macedonia (16:9). In Corinth, after the rejection of the Gospel by some of the Jews, the Lord appeared to Paul in a vision and told him not to be afraid but to continue speaking because He had many people to save in Corinth (18:9).

After Paul's third missionary journey while on trial before the Council in Jerusalem, he saw a vision of the Lord telling him to take courage because he will be a witness in Rome also (23:11). When Paul was on a ship headed for Rome, he saw a vision of an angel telling him not to be afraid when the storm wrecks the ship because he must appear before Caesar (27:24). At the end of Paul's first missionary journey, because of a revelation, Paul went to speak before the church at Jerusalem (Galatians 2:2; Acts 15:4).

BACKGROUND

The apostolic authority of God given to Paul was challenged by some who had listened to the false teachers. There were those who viewed Paul as a weak minister. They judged him strictly by what they saw during his last visit. His humility was misinterpreted as weakness (10:1). This being the case, Paul feels compelled to boast, but the difference is he boasts in the Lord. He boasts about the awesome power of God and he boasts about how weak he is in comparison to God. Paul says, "If I must boast, I will boast of the things that show my weakness" (11:30, NIV). Talking about his infirmity required him to talk about the reason for the infirmity. The reason for his infirmity was related to visions and revelations that he had received from the Lord. The fact that the visions and revelations were from the Lord is a very important distinction.

AT-A-GLANCE

1. The Privilege of Grace
(2 Corinthians 12:1-4)
2. The Humility of Grace (vv. 5-8)
3. The All-Sufficient Power of Grace
(vv. 9-10)

IN DEPTH

1. The Privilege of Grace (2 Corinthians 12:1-4)

Paul did not want to lose any souls to false teaching. His deep concern for their salvation forced him to reveal one of his most intimate experiences with God. The claims of the false teachers paled in comparison.

The humility of Paul continues to be displayed in the way he shares his experience (12:2). Instead of saying, "I," he speaks in the third person as if he is speaking of someone else. He does not return to the first person until he speaks of his infirmity. He also shares that he remained silent about this for 14 years. During all this time, he did not allow pride to speak out.

The experience of Paul consisted of him being caught up to the third heaven. He is not sure if this "rapture" was of his entire body or just his spirit. Whether in the body or out of the body, Paul was alert and conscious to what was happening around him. Paul seems to have a concept of the universe consisting of three layers, though the last layer transcends the physical world as is known by human beings. The first heaven is the sky around the earth. The second heaven is where the stars, plants, and galaxies exist. The third heaven is a spiritual place where God dwells. The Old Testament makes a distinction between "heaven" and "the heaven of heavens" (Deuteronomy 10:14; 1 Kings 8:27; Nehemiah 9:6; Psalms 68:33). Paul went to the dwelling place of God.

Bible scholars have questioned whether verse 3 is repetitive of the experience previously spoken of in verse 2, or whether it is a second experience. "Paradise" (literally a park or more specifically a place like Eden or a place of future happiness) seems to describe the third heaven more precisely. The word "paradise" appears two other times in the New Testament. Jesus speaks of the penitent thief on the cross as being with Him in paradise (Luke 23:43). In Revelation 2:7, those who overcome will eat of the tree of life in the midst of the paradise of God. These speak of a heavenly paradise. This heavenly paradise is a restoration of the paradise lost in the Garden of Eden (Revelations 22:1-5). This is the place where

those who are dead in Christ now go (Philippians 1:23). It appears that Paul is giving additional information about the one experience and not describing a second experience. He went as far as the third heaven into the place of paradise in the third heaven. He was given the unique privilege to enter into glorious heaven. What all he saw is not recorded (and yet to be revealed) but he heard "unspeakable" words (inexpressible utterances). The words spoken could not be translated into human and the words spoken were not lawful for humans to speak. This experience certainly had a great affect on Paul and his ministry.

2. The Humility of Grace (vv. 5-8)

Paul could legitimately glory in the experience but not in self because it was wholly of God. There is nothing in this experience he could claim credit for. All aspects of it are beyond human capabilities. He knew that nothing good dwells in his flesh (Romans 7:18). God was gracious to him. God had blessed him with this special spiritual experience. What he could do as a result of his experience is glorify God now more than ever before. What he could not do is deflect glory from God to himself. That would be foolish. The servant of God brings people to God, that is, exalts God, not himself.

Verse 7 confirms that the man Paul speaks of in verse one is himself. It also reveals that the reason Paul shared the experience was to show the reason for his weakness. A "thorn of the flesh" (literally, "stake for the flesh") was given to him to keep him from glorying (lift up self exceedingly) as a result of this experience. This testifies to the magnitude of his experience. It was so great that God found it necessary to counteract it. God wanted to keep Paul humble. God allowed it but it was caused by a messenger of Satan, that is, a demonic spirit. This was not a single attack; it was a recurring attack. He describes it as buffeting or being hit sharply and swiftly.

There has been much discussion over what this "thorn of the flesh" is. Some believe it to be severe headaches. Some believe it refers to Paul's adversaries who were constantly persecuting his ministry and those converts he shepherded. Some believe he had an eye disease and referenced such Scriptures as Galatians 4:15; 6:11. Some believe that he had a type of malaria fever that is reoccurring and when it attacks, it totally incapacitates the victim leaving them weak and shaking with a severe headache that feels like a hot bar thrusting through the forehead. Since Paul does not identify the condition, people can only speculate. This could be a blessing in disguise in that any believer that God allows the enemy to attack in a variety of ways can identify with Paul's ambiguous "thorn in the flesh."

Paul "besought" (called on) his Lord three times to relieve him of these attacks. He probably did it on three separate occasions when the attacks occurred. This is reminiscent of Jesus' experience in the Garden of Gethsemane. Jesus also prayed in agony three times for the removal of the cup from Him (Matthew 26:44).

The prayers of God's people never go unheard. God encourages His people to persevere in prayer in order to prove their faith and sincerity (Luke 11:9). In all situations, children of God should always pray and not give up (Luke 18:1; 1 Thessalonians 5:17). God may not give what his child asks for but He always answers with good things (Matthew 7:11).

3. The All-Sufficient Power of Grace (vv. 9-10)

The Lord answers Paul in the Greek perfect tense "He has said to me." This means that what the Lord said to Paul on that one occasion continues in the present with the same force. His Word stands unshakable and it cannot be denied or inhibited. God effectively said, "My grace is sufficient for you, Paul, and it continues to be sufficient for you. Every time the enemy raises his ugly head, my grace will prevail." The word "sufficient" here means to raise a barrier ward off or avail. Though the enemy attacks, his attacks are restrained by God Almighty. God draws a line, that is to say, He establishes a bulwark that the enemy cannot cross or penetrate (Job 1:12). The "stake for the flesh" remained, but the grace of God remained also and it avails much.

God's grace is more than enough for whatever He allows. "God is faithful, who will not suffer you to be tempted above that ye are able; but will with the temptation also make a way to escape, that ye may be able to bear it" (1 Corinthians 10:13). This is faith in action, a determined conviction that God is doing what is best.

Paul does not resign himself to what must be. He enthusiastically embraces it. Given a choice between the removal of the weakness and having the power of Christ rest upon him, Paul gladly chooses the latter. The abiding presence of God grants His people favor, protection, and power. Jesus said that He sends the Holy Spirit to abide with His people. He comes alongside to assist, and He comes with power. This is the defining moment of Paul's ministry and the impact of his ministry speaks for itself. God's grace is sufficient and His power accomplishes its purpose in human weakness. Flesh must decrease in order for God to increase. The greater the human inability, the greater is the magnification of God.

If suffering must come for the sake of Jesus Christ, then it is necessary in the eternal scheme of things. Believers can take pleasure in whatever God deems necessary. Jesus declared blessings on those that suffer for His sake (Matthew 5:11). They rejoice in the hope of the glory of God. Not only that, but they rejoice in tribulations also, knowing that tribulations worketh patience (perseverance), and patience, experience (proven character), and experience, hope (Romans 5:3-4). Paul spoke from his own experience (2 Corinthians 6:4-10; 11:23-28). Jesus said that in this life His servants have tribulations but be of good cheer because He overcomes all these things (John 16:33).

The servant of God testifies that when affliction comes (in every way or from every side) he is not crushed (hemmed in or restrained). When he doesn't understand, he does not despair; when persecution comes, he is not forsaken. Though he may be struck down, he is not destroyed; he is suffering in the body so that the life of Jesus can be put on display (2 Corinthians 4:8-10). Therefore Paul took pleasure in (approved) infirmities (weaknesses), in reproaches (insults), in necessities, in persecutions, in distresses (difficulties) that were for Christ's sake because these situations presented opportunities for Christ to exhibit His power in deliverance. When adversity attacks the believer, the grace of God much more abounds. "Nay, in all these things we are more than conquerors through Him that loves us" (Romans 8:37).

SEARCH THE SCRIPTURES

1. Did Paul consider it profitable to boast (2 Corinthians 12:1)?

2. What unique experience did Paul have and when did it occur (vv. 2-4)?

3. What could Paul boast about (v. 5)?

4. As a result of Paul's experience, what was given to him and why was it given (v. 7)?

5. What solution did God provide to Paul's prayer request (v. 9)?

DISCUSS THE MEANING

1. How does the expression, "to whom much is given, shall much be required," apply to Paul and to other believers?

2. Can believers promote their accomplishments without robbing God?

3. How does the believer distinguish between a "thorn in the flesh" and a trial or a temptation or an illness?

4. Explain whether God really deserves all the credit all the time.

5. How is silence from God still an answer from God?

LESSON IN OUR SOCIETY

God gives humanly impossible assignments to His servants. He places His people in unnerving situations. He allows indefensible attacks to come upon those He loves. Often people will turn to Jesus when they have nowhere else to turn. A song by Andre Crouch contained the words, "if we never had a problem, we wouldn't know God can solve them. We wouldn't know what faith could do." It is said that experience is the best teacher, but in some situations, it is the only teacher. God knows that His love must be experienced in life impacting situations in order for His children to really love and appreciate Him.

MAKE IT HAPPEN

Allow God to "raise the bar" in your life to a point that is humanly unattainable. God has to show you what He wants to accomplish in your

life. God is waiting on you. He has gifts reserved for you. You must approach Him to receive them. Invite God to put Himself on display in your life. When He pours out His grace, and puts His power to work in your life, it becomes evident to others. Then you will enthusiastically and sincerely testify about what could have only been done by the Lord.

FOLLOW THE SPIRIT

What God wants me to do:

_____

_____

REMEMBER YOUR THOUGHTS

Special insights I have learned:

_____

_____

MORE LIGHT ON THE TEXT
2 Corinthians 12:1-10

In the final verses of 2 Corinthians 11, Paul (vv. 23-33) cataloged a long list of threatening experiences, which he has feared or gone through during his missionary journeys. He told of beatings and being jailed. He mentioned "perils by mine own countrymen" and "perils in the sea," including three shipwrecks, not knowing that the worst of both was still ahead. If Paul had been allowed to know what was ahead, that knowledge might well have overwhelmed his ability to live for Christ from day to day. And the same would be true for most of us. In this passage, we will see that God's alternative for Paul was to give him grace sufficient to live for Him each day in spite of whatever problems came his way.

1 It is not expedient for me doubtless to glory. I will come to visions and revelations of the Lord.

This has been a difficult verse for translators to render. A difference in one letter changes the tone of the entire verse. The earliest manuscripts of 2 Corinthians begin the verse with the Greek word *dei* (**dee**) meaning to be necessary for a moral or emotional reason. Later manuscripts drop the final "I" creating the Greek word *de* (**deh**) indicating a contrast without difference, thus the word can be translated as one of several conjunctions: and, now, then, or rather. The KJV translators used the later text and translated *de* as "doubtless."

Modern translations with access to the earliest biblical texts word the verse "I must go on boasting" (NIV), or "this boasting is foolish, but let me go on" (NLT). Paul does not want to boast about his spiritual experiences, but deems it necessary to respond to the unsettling effect these "false apostles" are causing. So Paul says, "I will tell you about what Christ has revealed to me." "Of the Lord" can be interpreted two ways—as something Paul experienced about Christ or as something Christ revealed to Paul. The difference in interpretation depends on where you place the emphasis. Many, if not most, scholars think the emphasis was on Christ revealing, rather than Paul experiencing, the revelation.

2 I knew a man in Christ above fourteen years ago, (whether in the body, I cannot tell; or whether out of the body, I cannot tell: God knoweth;) such an one caught up to the third heaven.

When a person first comes to this verse, the natural tendency is to assume that Paul is describing what happened to someone he knew 14 years ago. But as you read the following verses, it becomes obvious that Paul is describing his own experience. Speaking of himself in the third person is Paul's way of taking the focus off himself. This verse shows how Paul puts minimal emphasis on spectacular spiritual experience. Rather than telling about some amazing vision or startling revelation, which he had last night, last week, or the last time he was in the temple in Jerusalem, he searches back through his life 14 years. He said this happened to "a man in Christ." No name, no place, no special position, and no qualifications are given, rather this happened to a person who could have been any Christian.

The addition of the phrase "whether in the body" indicates that he had gone into some kind of a trance. What he saw and heard may have been a vision in his mind or the actual transport of his physical being to a place where he could see and hear. When Paul adds, "I do not know," it was in the Greek present tense capturing the sense after

14 years I still do not know. The common belief in Paul's time was that heaven consisted of multiple levels. F. F. Bruce says that the most common belief was that it had seven levels. The non-biblical books of Enoch refer to 10 levels. In the New Testament, Ephesians 4:10 states, "He ascended up far above all heavens, that he might fill all things," referring to Christ. The third heaven may have been the top level in Paul's mind or as far as a living person was allowed to ascend. The Bible does not say.

"Caught up" was not a gentle term. The Greek word here, *harpazo* (**har-pad'-zo**), means to be snatched. The natural use of the word shows that Paul is not describing something he set out to do voluntarily. Instead it describes action inaugurated by Christ in which he chose Paul and grabbed, or snatched, him up to heaven to experience a revelation.

3 And I knew such a man, (whether in the body, or out of the body, I cannot tell: God knoweth;) 4 How that he was caught up into paradise, and heard unspeakable words, which it is not lawful for a man to utter.

Only as we come to verses 3 and 4 do we begin to sense how completely Paul refuses to hold his own spiritual experiences up for admiration by others. In verse 3, he repeats almost word for word what he had written in verse two, again referring to himself indirectly as "a man." So Paul is not focusing on the male sex. He is simply saying I know a person, a Christian man, to whom this happened. If Paul had wanted to put the emphasis on his masculinity, he would have used the Greek word *aner* (**an'-ayr**), which means male.

In verse 4 Paul says that he was snatched up into paradise. The Greek word *paradeisos* (**par-ad'-i-sos**) is a Persian word that originally meant a landscaped park. It was the word used in the Greek translation of the Old Testament for the Garden of Eden. While in Babylonian exile, Jews adopted the word and used it as their word for the place where the righteous dead went after death to await Judgment Day. This is the same word Luke used in Luke 23:43 for the place where Jesus told the repentant thief on the cross that they would be together later that day after they died. John used this word in Revelation 2:7

to refer to where the Tree of Life was located and where faithful believers would go after death. Most likely this was the garden that he had in mind in Revelation 22 where he described the garden in front of God's throne.

In John's vision in Revelation 4:1, he was told to enter heaven through an open door that he saw. He describes in vivid detail what he saw. In contrast to that, Paul refuses to give any clues about what he saw or heard during the revelation. Instead he says that he heard "unspeakable words, which it is not lawful for a man to utter." The NIV says he heard "inexpressible things, things that man is not permitted to tell." The Greek word Paul uses that is translated "unspeakable" and "inexpressible" (NIV) is *arrhetos* (**ar'-hray-tos**). These words refer to things that were not possible nor permissable, which, perhaps, explains why the KJV renders the word as "unspeakable" and the NIV as "inexpressible." Words "not lawful for a man to utter" is probably closer to what Paul is emphasizing than "inexpressible things" in the NIV.

5 Of such an one will I glory: yet of myself I will not glory, but in mine infirmities.

Bible scholars picture Paul from two sides in this verse, almost as two different people, which was how Paul presented himself. C. K. Barrett calls the first side, "Paul the apocalyptist." Apocalyptist is a scholarly term for a person who focuses on the end of time, the Day of Judgment, and heaven. The other side of Paul he calls "Paul the man and apostle." Paul's emphasis here is that privately he stood in awe and amazement at the exalted spiritual event he had experienced when he was transported into heaven. However, he is not using that spiritual occurrence to garner followers by boasting about it publicly.

What he is willing to share and delight in telling is of God's involvement with his "infirmities." This was the rendering of the Greek *astheneia* (**as-then'-i-ah**) meaning weaknesses, as the NIV and the NLT translate it. The word was also used for sicknesses or diseases. Paul repeatedly affirms that the value and strength of his faith in God was seen in the difference it made in dealing with his weaknesses.

6 For though I would desire to glory, I shall not be a fool; for I will say the truth: but now I forbear, lest any man should think of me above that which he seeth me to be, or that he heareth of me.

Many scholars believe that the "false apostles" that Paul mentioned in the previous chapter (11:13) belittled him to the Corinthians for failure to trumpet his personal spiritual experiences as they almost certainly did. Paul responds here by saying that if he allowed himself to publicly delight in his heavenly revelation it would not be the trivial talk of a fool, but rather, the truth. The word "fool" here comes from the Greek *aphron* (**af'-rone**), which referred to a person who could but did not think, not a person who was unable to think clearly due to limited intelligence. Sin often results from the actions people take because they fail to stop to think through what the right choice would be in that situation or at that moment. Dr. Scott Peck, in his bestselling book *The Road Less Traveled*, contends that the initial cause of much sin is laziness. Jeremiah 6:16 (NIV): "This is what the Lord says: 'Stand at the crossroads and look; ask for the ancient paths, ask where the good way is, and walk in it, and you will find rest for your souls.'"

Paul refuses to parade the extraordinary spiritual events he experienced in order to build up his standing as a spiritual leader. He said, "I forbear." Rather he declares the desire to be judged on how well his life matched up with his words. He asserts that he wants all evaluation of him to be based on what people saw him do or heard him say.

7 And lest I should be exalted above measure through the abundance of the revelations, there was given to me a thorn in the flesh, the messenger of Satan to buffet me, lest I should be exalted above measure.

After Paul's heavenly vision, God foresaw the possibility that because of it Paul would be tempted to see himself as having risen above the spiritual frailties that often trip up Christians. The words "exalt myself" come from a word meaning to rise above, *huperairomai* (**hoop-er-ah'-ee-rom-ahee**). The word describes God's concern that Paul may think because of his heavenly revelation that he has risen above other people. To counteract this potential temptation, God gave Paul some kind of distracting problem, a "thorn in the flesh," which Satan could use to disable or hamper him. Although the word "thorn" comes from the Greek word *skolops* (**skol'-ops**), that is, sometimes used for a splinter of wood, its basic meaning is a sharply pointed piece of wood, a stake. That was clearly Paul's use of the word here. The thorn, whatever it was, was disabling, more than simply annoying. What that "thorn" was has sprouted as many theories as there are Bible scholars. Those theories fall into two groups, a physical thorn or a spiritual one.

Those who believe Paul's "thorn" was physical have guessed that it was bad eyesight, recurrent bouts of malaria, migraine headaches, epilepsy, or a speech impediment. Tertullian, an African church Father, who lived from A.D. 160 to 225 thought Paul's problem was recurrent earaches. One pastor suggested in a sermon that Paul's "thorn" may have been a nagging wife. For spiritual thorns, Bible scholars have guessed it was depression, doubt, lust, or despair over his inability to persuade his Jewish brethren to accept Jesus as their Messiah, or perhaps frustration at dealing with unfaithful, deceitful, or troublesome church members (1 Timothy 1:19-20; 2 Timothy 2:17-18; 4:14). Several commentators have considered it was a speech impediment that could have caused a recurring lack of self-confidence in Paul as he preached and taught. That would explain Paul's comment earlier in 10:1, 10 that some Corinthians said he was unimpressive in person, but just the opposite when he wrote to them.

Paul says God sent it "to buffet me." "Buffet" can sound mild. However, the Greek word that Paul used, *kolaphizo* (**kol-af-id'-zo**), meant to strike a person with the fist, to slug a person, an action that is hardly mild. The tense of the verb also suggests that the "thorn" was something Paul had to deal with repeatedly. Whatever the nature of the thorn, it was something Satan could use to sidetrack Paul's faith. As such, it repeatedly reminded Paul of his human frailty and his need to draw close to God for spiritual strength in order to resist the temptation the thorn presented (Hebrews 10:22; James 4:7-8). We must take note

that Paul said these moments of forceful temptation were the result of a weakness that God sent to promote his growth in grace and more effective service.

8 For this thing I besought the Lord thrice, that it might depart from me.

As Jesus prayed three times in the Garden of Gethsemane that the hour of His crucifixion might pass (Mark 14:32-42), and perhaps following His example, Paul asked God three times for His thorn to be removed. "Besought" comes from the Greek word *parakaleo* (**par-ak-al-eh'-o**), meaning to plead or beg. Paul begged for God to take away the "thorn."

9 And he said unto me, My grace is sufficient for thee: for my strength is made perfect in weakness. Most gladly therefore will I rather glory in my infirmities, that the power of Christ may rest upon me.

When the KJV says that God "said unto me," we cannot tell when reading in our English Bibles that Paul uses the Greek perfect tense. Perfect tense referred to something that took place in the past but has continuing effects in the present. By using perfect tense, Paul is emphasizing the continuing importance of what Christ said to him. Thus Paul is suggesting: I continue to remember what the Lord said whenever this temptation confronts me. The word Paul uses for "is sufficient" is *arkeo* (**ar-keh'-o**) meaning is enough or is adequate. God was telling Paul, "My help is all you need." Then He explains, "My strength is made perfect in weakness." The word "perfect" means complete, just as a new car with a full tank of gas is perfect. Whether it is a Volkswagen or a Mercedes, it will take you wherever you want or need to go.

God's power finds fulfillment in our lives when we are willing to admit our weaknesses and rely on his unearned generosity toward us. Accepting our immaturity, inexperience, ignorance, or susceptibility to sin is the first step toward a life we can be proud of. So Paul says he was as happy as it was possible for him to be as indicated by "most gladly," which in Greek is *hedeos* (**hay-deh'-oce**). Paul says he will take pride in and accept his "infirmities" ("weaknesses" in NIV), *astheneia* (**as-then'-i-ah**) in Greek (see explanation in verse 5). By doing so, the power of the Resurrected Christ could dwell on him. The Greek word Paul used was *episkenoo* (**ep-ee-skay-no'-o**), which meant to take up residence or to move into a new dwelling. Paul is agreeing with Jesus' first Beatitude, "Blessed are the poor in spirit: for theirs is the kingdom of heaven" (Matthew 5:3). Letting God into our lives begins with admitting there is an emptiness that only He can fill.

10 Therefore I take pleasure in infirmities, in reproaches, in necessities, in persecutions, in distresses for Christ's sake: for when I am weak, then am I strong.

Although verse 10 begins with Paul saying that he takes pleasure in a variety of situations most of us would find unpleasant, the word Paul uses does not mean that he necessarily enjoys them. While the word *eudokeo* (**yoo-dok-eh'-o**) can mean to take delight in something and enjoy it, the word can also mean to consent or approve of something. While we may not like a situation, God can use it to show His love, to strengthen us spiritually, and to reveal Himself. God did that through all of these situations in Paul's life. God used sickness when Paul arrived in the territory of Galatia (Galatians 4:13). Surviving near-death from a storm at sea allowed the opportunity to declare God's providential care (Acts 27:10).

When Paul was falsely charged with defiling the temple by bringing in a Gentile, the necessity of appealing to Caesar gave him the opportunity to preach the Gospel to governors and kings. Being beaten and jailed at Philippi was a problem that led to the conversion of the jailer and his whole family (Acts 16:19-33). Persecution forced Paul out of Pisidian, Antioch and onto Iconium, Lystra, and Derbe, where they were pursued, eventually stoned, and left for dead. However, Paul and Barnabas were able by God's power to make new converts for Christ and establish more churches in all those towns (Acts 13:49-51; 14:21-25).

Without a doubt, Paul had great physical endurance, otherwise he would not have been able to survive the repeated physical abuse and the extensive and often difficult travel into dangerous regions. What Paul tells us he learned is that God's grace will see us through if we trust in His sufficiency rather than our own. And so he says in Romans 5:2-5 (NIV), "We rejoice in the hope of the glory of God. Not only so, but we also rejoice in our sufferings, because we know that suffering produces perseverance; perseverance, character; and character, hope because God has poured out his love into our hearts by the Holy Spirit, whom he has given us." Hebrews 5:8 tells us concerning Jesus, "Although he was a son, he learned obedience from what he suffered." Paul, following His example, learned that we can trust God to see us through trying, often unfair, times. If we are willing to be honest and accept our inability to satisfy our own deepest needs, our Heavenly Father will graciously and generously fill them.

DAILY BIBLE READINGS

M: Grace Abounds All the More
Romans 5:12-21

T: Grace for the Humble
James 4:1-10

W: The God of Grace Will Restore
1 Peter 5:5-10

T: Paul Receives God's Grace
1 Corinthians 15:3-10

F: Paul Experiences Many Difficulties
2 Corinthians 11:23-29

S: Paul's Deep Spiritual Experience
2 Corinthians 12:1-7

S: God's Grace Is Sufficient
2 Corinthians 12:7-13

TOPICAL INDEX

TOPICAL INDEX/continued.

221, 251, 277, 315, 326, 328, 334, 336, 337, 341, 343, 354, 362, 414, 429, 433, 462, 465-469, 472, 474, 477, 485

Judgment, 63, 68-69, 83, 131-132, 135-136, 143, 149, 193, 207, 211, 215, 252, 267, 284, 304, 309, 311, 336, 338, 341, 360, 363, 369

Labour, 197, 202-204, 207, 213, 229, 322-323, 325, 327-329, 401, 407, 411, 418, 453, 501

Liberty, 141, 143, 158, 163-164, 202-203, 329, 427-429, 430, 434, 438, 453

Majesty, 31, 43, 153, 164-165, 249, 252, 259, 261-262, 265, 269- 270, 274, 287, 291-293, 304, 307, 312, 371

Mercy, v, 19, 27, 45, 53, 57, 122, 123, 125, 128-129, 148-151, 154-156, 168-175, 206-208, 211, 215, 263, 273, 282, 286-287, 290-292, 316, 340, 343, 345, 365, 404, 414, 472, 479

Peace, viii, 4, 9, 32, 81, 85, 250-251, 272, 297, 307, 317, 322, 323-329, 332-337, 340, 343, 345-346, 351, 356, 358, 363

Perfect, 29, 31, 35, 54, 112, 250, 278, 282, 284-285, 290, 296, 300, 329, 343, 350-351, 356, 361, 388, 391-392, 394, 396-397, 404, 412, 426, 443, 456, 459, 462-463, 485, 492, 495, 499

Poor, 8, 9, 16, 22, 29, 31, 34, 264, 329, 366-367, 369, 371, 402, 453, 456, 460, 466, 473-476, 479-480, 482, 488, 489, 500

Rebuke, 122, 206-209, 212, 214, 233, 235, 238, 242, 248, 269, 270, 276, 403, 415, 417, 418, 453

Repentance, 14, 17, 94, 115, 119, 179, 211, 225, 231, 290, 317, 374, 409, 445, 450, 464-468, 471-472

Rich, 22, 26, 145, 148, 154-155, 170, 239, 300, 309, 411, 414, 417, 454, 473, 474, 477, 479, 488-489

Seducers, 232-233, 237

Sepulchre, 313-314, 320

Shun, 224-225, 229

Sober, 187, 189, 191, 194, 200, 231, 239, 241, 242, 245-246, 328

Sorrows, 124, 140, 147-148, 153-155 292, 334, 342

Strength, v, 27, 28, 30, 33, 40, 110, 122, 128, 136, 138-140, 144-146, 148-149, 152, 154-155, 159, 168–174, 176, 192, 216, 218–220, 224, 251, 260–262, 266, 268 272, 291, 292, 298, 303, 318, 354-355, 365-366, 370, 371, 381, 419, 422, 427, 445, 455, 492, 498-499

Upright, 238, 250, 252, 296, 300, 302, 316, 355-356, 359, 360- 361, 363, 427

Vanity, 122, 252, 322-328, 330, 333

Vex, 79-80, 84

Virtuous, 365-366, 367-371

Vow, 105-106, 108-111

Weak, vi, 38, 112, 120, 154, 188, 227, 247, 256, 266, 309, 369, 373, 381, 404, 411, 414, 417, 418, 427-430, 431, 434, 438, 491-493, 495, 500

Woman, v, 2, 9, 29-30, 56-57, 61, 81, 86-87, 96-97, 102-103, 107, 109, 111-112, 129-130, 139-140, 153, 190-191, 198, 226, 244, 257-258, 263, 268, 303-304, 308-309, 341, 343, 366—371, 372, 377, 392-393, 420, 422-423, 425-426, 460, 484